# Children Learn to Communicate

# Children Learn to Communicate

Language Arts Through Creative Problem-Solving

Written and Primarily Illustrated by
Sara W. Lundsteen
University of California, Irvine

Prentice-Hall, Inc., Englewood Cliffs, New Jersey

*Library of Congress Cataloging in Publication Data*

LUNDSTEEN, SARA W
Children learn to communicate.

Includes bibliographies and index.
1. Language arts. I. Title.
LB1575.8.L79 372.6 75-19324
ISBN 0-13-131888-8

*To Alex B. Lundsteen, to the memory of David H. Russell, and to students who have read this book in its beginning stages and given invaluable criticisms and reactions*



Printed in the United States of Amerca

10 9 8 7 6 5 4 3 2 1

Prentice-Hall International, Inc., London
Prentice-Hall of Australia, Pty. Ltd., Sydney
Prentice-Hall of Canada, Ltd., Toronto
Prentice-Hall of India Private Limited, New Delhi
Prentice-Hall of Japan, Inc., Tokyo
Prentice-Hall of Southeast Asia (Pte.) Ltd., Singapore

# Contents

Preface, ix

Prologue
Where Are We and Where Are We Going?, 2

What Is Problematic? (Mass Media, Oversimplicity, and Passivity), 4
What Productive Alternatives Might Be Used in the Classroom?
(Language and Creative Problem-Solving), 15

**PART 1**
**DEVELOPMENTAL BASES, 31**

Chapter 1
A Base in the Development of Language & Thought, 32

Piaget's Stage III: Concrete Operations
(The Elementary-School Years), 34
How Can Teachers Assist General Learning and Communication
in the Stage of Concrete Operations?, 42
How Does Developmental Information Help the Teacher of
Culturally Different Children?, 50
Summary and Conclusions, 63
Additional Activities for Children, 65

Chapter 2
A Base in Listening, 73

Why Put Listening First?, 75
What Is the Relationship of Listening to Thinking?, 78
How Does Listening Relate to the Other Language Arts?, 80
Summary and Conclusions, 97
Additional Activities for Children, 99

## PART 2
## USES OF LANGUAGE, 109

### Chapter 3
### Using Oral Language to Express & Expound, 110

Why Bother with Oral Interaction in the Language Arts Curriculum?, 112
What Is the Teacher's Responsibility?, 113
How Does a Child Use the Aim of Language Called "Self-Expression"?, 116
What Are Some Dimensions for the Oral Language Curriculum?, 120
How Does a Child Use the Aim of Language Called Exposition?, 130
Summary and Conclusions, 138
Additional Activities for Self-Expression, 139

### Chapter 4
### Discussion Roles & Goals
### How Can Teachers Help Children Learn Discussion Skills, 146

What Are Some Roles?, 148
How Can the Teacher Evaluate?, 154
Practical Considerations, 156
How Does the Teacher Guide Discussion?, 157
What Specific Topics or Content Can a Teacher Find to Motivate Discussion?, 166
The Creative-Problem-Solving Discussion (CPS), 169
Summary and Conclusion, 175
Activities, 175

### Chapter 5
### Children's Literature
### Using Language to Make It Memorable, 180

What Is Children's Literature and How Can Teachers Guide Responses?, 181
How Does a Communication Triangle Help to Distinguish Literature?, 192
The Mirrored World, 193
The Author, 200
The Audience, 202
The Work, 204
Organization of Literature, 205
Language of Literature, 209
A Few Selected Discussion Questions on the Organization and Language of a Work, 214
Bibliotherapy for Children, 216
Summary and Conclusions, 219
Additional Activities, 220

## PART 3
## INTO PRINT, 227

### Chapter 6
### Developing into Composition, 228

What Are Some Reasons that Writing Development in School Seems Difficult?, 230
The First Step in the Developmental Teaching of Writing, 233
What Features of Language Are Noticeable in the Developing Child from Grade to Grade?, 235
Some General Developmental Activities, 248
How Do You Motivate Children to Write?, 252
Summary, 260
Activities for Beginning Writing, 260
Activities for Motivation, 266

### Chapter 7
### How to Teach Composition, 273

Why Is Providing for Composition so Essential?, 274
What Are Some Types of Composition in the School?, 279
What Are Some Major Areas of a Teaching-Learning Strategy for Written Composition?, 284
A Sample Schedule and Environment for a Writing Day, 302
Summary and Conclusions, 305
Activities for Self-Expressive, Imaginative, Fantastic Writing, 308

### Chapter 8
### Spelling: Contemporary Developments & Controversy What's Happened to Spelling?, 323

What Is Spelling?, 324
What Is the Nature of the Modern Spelling Program?, 327
How Are Children Instructed?, 334
Summary and Conclusions, 349
Activities, 351

### Chapter 9
### New Approaches to Handwriting, Punctuation, & Other Conventions of Written Composition, 357

How Is Handwriting Related to Problem Solving?, 358
Some Advice, 361
Punctuation and Mechanics of Written Composition, 363
Summary and Conclusions, 374
Additional Activities for Expository Writing, 375

Chapter 10
Grammar & Usage
Contemporary Developments & Controversy, 379

What Is Grammar? (Three Kinds), 380
Grouping Language Concepts, 391
Summary and Conclusions, 394
Activities on Grammar and Usage, 396

Chapter 11
Evaluation & Accountability in Language Arts Instruction, 404

Why Assess?, 405
What Are Needs and Problems in Assessing Written Composition? (The More Negative Side), 407
Assessing Some Specific Language Arts Areas (Composition, Listening, Literature, and Problem Solving), 411
Conclusions on Accountability and Evaluation in the Language Arts, 450
An Activity for the Reader of this Chapter, 452

Epilogue, 456

Index, 458

# Preface

This book, a basic text for language arts methods, tells how to help children learn to communicate. I believe that the most productive ways draw upon creative problem-solving as a key motivation to mastery of language. The language arts program needs to be basically a program in thinking. Ideally, this development of thought processes (and related products from the arts and uses of language) *is* the school program.

Behind the skills of communication lie the skills of thinking. Behind the meaningful use of thinking skills lies the *organizing* process, creative problem-solving.

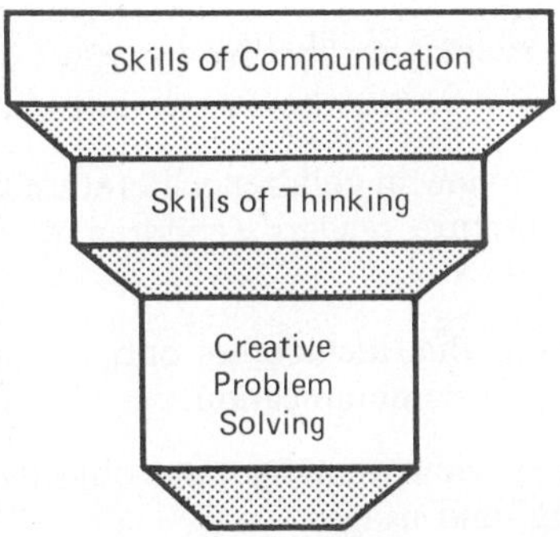


Why adopt this approach? When teachers and children work at mastering communication skills through solving problems creatively, they are economically and meaningfully using almost all their thinking skills. Children then need little drill-type practice in basic mental processes, attentiveness, fact recall, or skills of associative, inferential, creative, and critical thinking. These basic processes are usually integrated in creative problem-solving. Such a focused approach tends to avoid the encyclopedia-type fragmentation typical of language arts textbooks. Problem-solving concepts fit naturally with the challenge of learning the language arts. If there is dissatisfaction with the present curriculum, a focus on problem solving is worth a try. Much of this book suggests how.

The need for structures. Teachers cannot approach everything in the language arts field through creative problem-solving. There is a need for other frameworks. It is unwise to toss into a student's lap unstructured information about the disciplines of English. Students react to this as if their instructors had taken a watch apart and flung the pieces at them, saying, "Here's all you need to make a watch." By failing to present structure, instructors confess that they do not know what to do with all the material they have compiled about language.

Maybe language arts texts have to be fragmented and encyclopedic—English is relatively unstructured when compared with some scientific disciplines. But a text can furnish some organization of information if it (1) treats learning areas as challenges to be solved by teachers and children; (2) furnishes teaching approaches; and (3) gives frameworks with illustrative activity and suggested assessment wherever possible.[1] The following are some areas explored in this way.

- Development of language and thought (organized around information from linguistics and cognitive psychology).
- Proficient listening and objectives to promote it.
- Thinking and problem-solving strategies.
- Aims of discourse (or uses of language).
- Teaching-learning strategy for discussion and questioning.
- Structure and point of view in children's literature as an aid in developing responsive and mature readers (children who read well *and* are also well read).
- Curriculum dimensions that include not only the personal but also the interpersonal aspects of communication.
- Instructional points of view, strategy, and objectives for composition, spelling, handwriting, and usage.

It is impractical—even undesirable—to present one overall theory to account for language-arts instruction; several carefully chosen frameworks may help to organize new and old knowledge. In this way instructors can avoid the voluminous lists of isolated language skills and concepts that plague current material. (See the Prologue of this book for an overview of the above structures, especially creative problem-solving.)

Sources of ideas. This text's basic point of view about creative problem-solving (and the structures for the language arts) is synthesized from many sources. Ideas are referenced and credited when they can be separated and presented within reasonable limits for the flow of communication. Some substantiation is needed so that readers can retrace a position and form one of their own. This book combines some scientific

[1] See also the companion (student) guide to this book, *Ideas into Practice*.

detail, direct informal communication, currently popular ideas, and forward-looking hunches about language arts instruction. The aim is to build some bridges between information from several disciplines and the needs of the language arts teacher. These disciplines include the following: psychology of learning, social psychology, cultural anthropology, linguistics, rhetoric, semantics, communication science, and especially child growth and development.

Given the present state of research knowledge about how to develop children's communication, it appears almost impossible to say that experimentation substantiates this practice or that one. Little instructional method is backed up conclusively at this point in time. The purpose here is not to give one right answer and defend it, but to stimulate thoughtful application and rethinking.

## SOME OTHER SPECIAL EMPHASES OF THIS BOOK

**Uses of language.** One of the organizing elements of this book is the idea of *uses of language* (or aims of discourse), taken from the field of rhetoric. These uses are self-expression; exposition (including informative, exploratory, and scientific language); literature; and persuasion. The discourse of the book itself is generally exploratory, but may be provoking, as in the Prologue. Sometimes it has elements of the literary. The point is that all these uses have a place in a balanced instructional program. And a place is especially needed for the neglected aim of self-expression.

**Listening.** Listening may be thought of as a set of subskills prerequisite to creative problem-solving. This text gives careful attention to its interrelationships. You will find objectives, evaluation, current materials, and roles of various people in the school program, lessons, and units in the companion guide to this text, *Ideas into Practice.*

**Discussion strategy.** Another subject developed extensively in this text is the role of discussion strategy, which includes question asking. The child's development in any area of language arts may first begin with discussion. Strategy includes an examination of roles that facilitate and roles that block, as well as patterns in questioning, pacing, discussion topics, specifics of organization in the classroom, and evaluation.

## THE SCOPE OF THE BOOK AND SPECIAL FEATURES

**Scope.** I have organized this book on the basis of what topics appear to be most important to communicate about at this time. I believe that essential elements of the language arts program have received appropriate treatment (including some elements that have not previously been given much recognition). Coverage of the decoding and recoding of sounds and letters, and other mechanics of reading is left to other books. But implications for and applications to reading are many.

The book is divided into three parts. Part 1 emphasizes developmental bases of language and thought and listening; Part 2 centers on oral language and the uses of language, including literature for children; Part 3 deals with children's imaginative composition and modern perspectives on subskills of writing—including punctuation, spelling, handwriting, grammar, and usage. This third part concludes with a substantial chapter on assessment and accountability.

**Features.** Many features of this book were specially designed to assist the reader. Each chapter begins with an overview, which briefly describes what the chapter can do for the reader. Frequent headings and marginal topics act as organizers and summarizers. The reader in a hurry can simply skim through a chapter, noting the ideas in the margins. The reader wanting details and examples can explore the paragraphs. Skimming a chapter is recommended before careful reading. Most chapters can be read on several levels: superficially, for activities and practical applications; in depth, for the basic points of view; and probingly, with a careful follow-up on the footnotes and references.

For the purpose of stimulating "learn-as-you-do" behavior, activities are given to illustrate important concepts. (Sections entitled Think About It, designed to provoke discussion, and Look at It, designed to stimulate observation, are in the instructor's manual.) A section at the end of each chapter called If You Want to Learn More (containing references) helps the student find and read original or related sources if he is curious or if she wants to go into further depth. Finally, "stopping places" within the chapter (for those who want only to read small amounts at one sitting) are indicated by spacing and the following signal:

---

**Audience.** The intended audience for this book is a broad one. The book constructs a meaningful triangle between roles of teachers, roles of pupils, and a body of knowledge about the language arts. The material speaks to the prospective teacher and the teacher already in the classroom, to the undergraduate and the graduate student in colleges and universities. It is designed for any who are interested in language arts in the elementary-school and in the middle-school years.

Those who do not actually intend to teach language arts in the classroom may also be interested. These people may be consultants, principals, librarians, and those in related content areas who realize the importance of thinking skills in children's communication. In fact, the audience is anyone who wants to listen with more understanding to children and who has concern for what becomes of them through their language and thought. But the main intent is to consider the reader as potentially (if not currently) a teacher-artist-professional, rather than as a teacher-technician or lower. This book assumes that the first kind of teacher needs to know the *why* as well as the how.

Humanistic approach. The content of this book (although in touch with modern psychological and technological know-how) stresses a humanistic, joyful approach to the language arts. Gleeful, enthusiastic inquiry and the excitement of pleasurable emotional response are the essence of a successful classroom.

By the term *humanistic* I mean a deep caring for students as persons. Above all, the effective curriculum appears to be one where there are feelings for creative, self-initiated problem-solving. Humanistic emotional overtones characterize the optimal teaching approach with lasting impact—whether the use of language under study is the most simple recording of self-expression during free verbal play or the most intricately organized and thoughtfully complex use of exposition, literature, or persuasion. Against this humanistic background, this book develops thematically both cognitive and affective ideas and their applications for creative problem-solving. In this vein the following might be a motto—

Be enthusiastic; be humanistic; be prepared.

---

## ESPECIALLY TO THE STUDENT READING THIS TEXT

*The limits of my language mean the limits of my world.*
Ludwig Wittgenstein [2]

If Wittgenstein meant that we can know only what we can put into words, then you may think he's wrong. We experience a thousand times more than what we can ever put into language. It is depressing to think of the sometimes meager tool of language as the limits of our world. You may feel that your world explands far beyond the realms to which mere language can take you.

But if Wittgenstein meant that language gives us new present and vicarious experiences (e.g., through poetry, novels, humor, lectures, lyrics, and conversation), if he meant that experiences are limited by the grip we have on the symbolic handle of language, then you may think he's right. On continuing this book, consider the implications of Wittgenstein's quotation. Consider this idea as a teaching problem awaiting some of your creative solutions.[3]

[2] *Tractatus Logico-Philosophicus* (Atlantic Heights, N.J.: Humanities Press, 1922).

[3] I would be pleased to receive any comments, criticisms, and suggestions that you think may help me in preparing future editions. Thank you. Have a productive teaching experience.

# Acknowledgments

I am indebted to the hundreds of students, teachers, professors, consultants, administrators, and youngsters who have shared their ideas about the communicating child. The *we* used at times in the text refers to these people and especially to past research participants in Santa Barbara County, California. The Charles F. Kettering Foundation, The University of Texas at Austin, and the University of California at Santa Barbara and at Irvine have assisted me in the study of the happy complexities of children—their language and thought.

I find it a paradox to be unable, in a book about language, to find words that can reach the depth of my gratitude to the many who have given moments of their lives to help me and this project to grow. I particularly want to thank Mary Wilcox, Stanford Research Institute, who read and commented on almost every word, and reviewers Constance McCullough, California State University at San Francisco; Helen Lodge, California State University at San Fernando Valley; E. Jane Porter, University of Delaware; Bernice E. Cullinan, New York University; Sarah Moskovitz, California State University at San Fernando Valley; and Mary Cover Jones, University of California, Berkeley (in chronological order of involvement). Students aiding me considerably during this project are Jennifer Acosta, Sharon Jennings, and Debbie Zippin.

Without the many broadening teaching opportunities afforded by Kenneth P. Bailey, Director of the Office of Education, University of California, Irvine, this book would have lacked much. I also wish to thank Glen C. Hoskins, Southern Methodist University, who first helped me to realize—"I can think!"; Pearl Wallace Chappell, who helped me realize the excitement of the spoken language; my parents, who encouraged my writing and creating "practically from birth"; and Helen Rayne, who early stimulated me to draw pictures (culminating in the illustrations in this volume). Special thanks to Editor Joan Brooks Lee and her crew in Redwood City, California, who helped to shape this book. The activities, publications, and people associated with the National Council of Teachers of English have been a continual source of inspiration.

But the largest year after year after year contribution to this book in the way of empathy, support, and prodding is gratefully acknowledged to Alex Lundsteen.

# Children Learn to Communicate

# Prologue

## Where Are We & Where Are We Going?

What can this prologue do for you? It gives background framing some of the existing problems. It suggests that current methods of instruction are badly in need of changes. In order to help effect some of these changes, I propose and illustrate a creative problem-solving approach while giving reasons for such a strategy. The ideas invite reaction from inquiring, skeptical, and original minds.[1]

[1] Probably some of the ideas in this Prologue are already familiar to you. Fine. Part of a textbook's job is to reinforce attitudes, anticipations, and awareness already developed.

If the purpose of this book is to show ways to move from an undesirable classroom situation to a desirable one, the first task must be to define *language arts*. Briefly, the term embraces the varied uses to which the native verbal symbols may be put. It includes both intake and output during listening, reading, speaking, and writing; not only development of skills, but also the enjoyment of literature and the chance to satisfy any curiosity about the nature of language, its uses and misuses.

**Language arts defined**

Ideally, teachers help develop language in the school by an interrelated program designed to encourage various uses. The emphasis is on thinking skills, because the curriculum for language learning is a program in thinking, designed to help children with something to say, say it better; and to help them have something better to say because they listen, read, and think well. To regard language arts only as channels for communication is to oversimplify. It is when we view language as a tool for thinking that exciting implications for teaching open up. The rest of this book develops this broad concept of language arts instruction.

## WHAT IS PROBLEMATIC? (MASS MEDIA, OVERSIMPLICITY, AND PASSIVITY)

**Present system and barriers to change**

The next step in this Prologue is to examine the "undesirable classroom situation," some of its problems, and reasons for them. Apparently the present educational system fails to guide young people to do their best thinking, communicating, and problem solving. If any children do clear, insightful, and creative thinking during school time, it is mainly in the classrooms of the most gifted teachers. After 12 years of schooling in communication skills, many children appear to have little to show for it (Flannagan, 1971). Why? Past and present barriers to progress stem from misunderstanding of diverse cultures, from the family, from the peer group, from within the individual, and from educational procedures. Some barriers grow out of simplistic thinking, mass media, and the undue suppression of the child's autonomy. Look closely at these; part of being successful in new language teaching strategies is being aware of past mistakes.

### How Do Simple Solutions Hinder?

**Simplistic thinking**

Do we tend to fixate on solutions that are too simple? Pick up any newspaper and you can see human beings young and old falling into this trap: armed with only a small bit of knowledge about a problem or about how to solve it, they believe that solutions are simple. People tend to reduce problems to a false simplicity by ignoring complicating factors. But in human affairs these "easy ways" create larger problems. The headlines, "Busses Bombed," and "Protester Arrested for Attempted Murder," tell us of the "simple" solution, violence, where skillful words might have been helpful. In such cases there has been a bankruptcy of ideas and of communication. The use of simple solutions of violence produces problems worse than the original ones. Too often lives resemble a bird's-eye view of ski tracks—people careening from one problem to another through time. Some problems are solved satisfactorily but most are worried about, postponed, or handled so that worse ones plague the future. Simple solutions may cause us to pay a high price later.

For these reasons, today's thoughtful educators are looking for more than mere simplistic, how-to-do-it, cookbook-type solutions. They know that the challenges facing today's schools are too complex to be solved by simple revision of administrative procedures (such as class scheduling for team teaching), or by more efficient, accountable ways to do what is useless in the classroom. They look for instructional ideas that are practical, feasible, and (if possible) grounded in basic and in applied research. They also look for ideas that avoid the empty promise of instant results. They search for ideas of intelligent men and women, ideas designed to be discussed and used by other intelligent men and women.

A YOUNG CHILD WATCHES TV

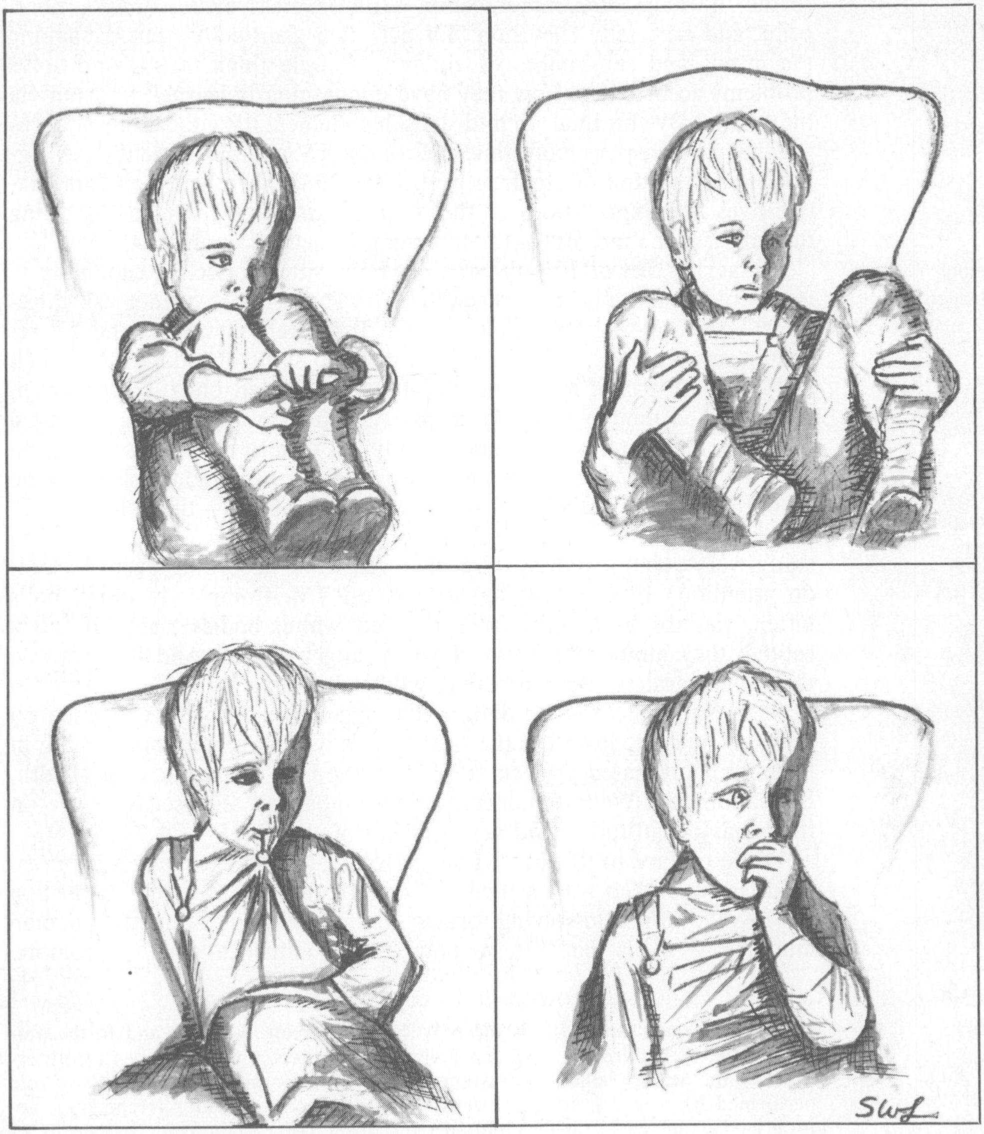

What is its impact on him? What can a language arts teacher do?

## What Is The Impact of Mass Media?

The molding power of TV

Another factor that sometimes encourages simplistic thinking and adds to the blockage of communication skills is mass media—radio, films, print, and especially television. TV acts as a giant cookie-cutter shaping the minds and self-images of children. People think, react, and solve problems according to how they have unconsciously learned to listen via the media. By the time a child ends his elementary education, chances are that he has spent more time before the TV set than in school. A significant proportion of children born after 1945 have had their imaginative lives and expectations of the world *created* by TV (the first thing turned on in the morning—the last thing turned off at night).

Interpersonal communication and TV

Is a steady diet of TV (the nation's baby-sitter) affecting capability in interactive communication of children? "They simply cannot ask questions!" deplores one first-grade teacher. It is likely that, since the TV set cannot answer back, children fail to develop skills of inquiry. Although children may parrot letters of the alphabet learned on a TV program, they may be unable to apply them. As Hayakawa has said, having a puppy is (from an interpersonal standpoint) more important to a child than having a TV set. From age three to eighteen, children spend some 22,000 hours in passive contemplation of the screen—time stolen from the time needed to learn to relate to others (Hayakawa, 1966). In one study, very young children were observed while absorbing (with locked-on attention) rapidly varying horrors on TV. Completely quiet, nails bitten, thumbs in mouth; faces drained white, bodies rigid—if interrupted, they jumped or broke down in angry crying. And if led away, they disintegrated into combative, wildly thrashing beings.[2]

In addition, there is the danger that aggressive behavior witnessed on TV may be contagious. At the time of this writing reports are coming in from 23 coordinated projects funded by the U.S. Department of Health, Education, and Welfare, concerning the impact of televised violence on the behavior, attitudes, and development of children.[3]

In the preface to this book I suggested that the language arts program needs to be unified with a focus on creative problem-solving. A portion of creative problem-solving draws upon skills of thoughtful human interaction—skills that TV, so powerful an influence, fails to promote.

[2] Of course, mass media is not the only factor affecting the back and forth communication of children. Studies by Bellack and others (1965) imply that unfortunately the act of "soliciting" responses from children is not traditionally a role performed by teachers. But such teaching functions as soliciting, responding appropriately, and encouraging children's responses (of certain kinds by means of certain questions) can be learned.

[3] T. Berry Brazelton, M.D., testimony to the Federal Communication Commission, October 1971. See, for example, the reports on violence published by Michigan State University (1971), and Liebert, Neal, & Davidson (1973).

I would also caution that the constant motion inherent in TV programming leaves the child no time to savor details, no time to puzzle, "Is it for real?" How can a child learn to sustain thought and imagery with this kind of visual perception? Of course, TV has given children a visual sophistication denied their parents and grandparents (Burrows, 1974). But how can the child process so much information so fast and without too much glibness, empty verbalization, and confusion? What, in general, is TV's message to youth, as compared with those from other institutions?

**Institutional messages compared with TV's message**

Ideally, the message from Education is "Be thoughtful, be well-informed"; Religion's message, "Be spiritual"; Industry's message, "Work hard, improve your skills, save your money and invest it wisely"; and Government's message, "Be a good citizen, strive for a better community and nation." And TV's message? Advertising may be unique in having no intent to improve the listener. Instead, commercials encourage impulsive and thoughtless buying. The message of advertising says nothing about the hard work, the long apprenticeship in a trade or profession, the years of study, the patient postponement of gratification, and the sense of responsibility that one needs in order to secure the jobs that pay for the beautiful way of life depicted in the commercials. There is cause for alarm when advertisers consider youth to be living, talking records of what is told them every day (Packard, 1957). Given that the message we receive from TV rarely is designed to improve us, is it too much to ask that at least the message from advertising not mislead us? Adlai Stevenson (1960) estimated that we spend almost as much on advertising, per person, in order to increase the private desires, as we do on education. (He also made the comment that with the supermarket as the temple and the singing commercial as the litany,[4] we cut a ridiculous picture before the rest of the world.) TV's message is apparently designed to create passivity, disintegration, and impulsive buying instead of encouraging creative interaction and communication necessary to human problem-solving.

[4] Stevenson used the term *litany* here in an ironic way to refer to a form of liturgical prayer or responsive reading.

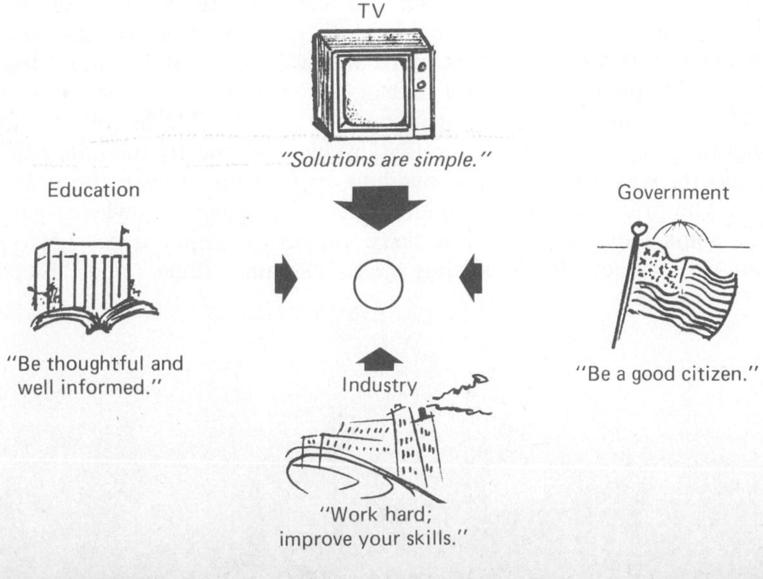

**A closer look at TV messages**

Along this line, let's look in more detail at TV's message in the programs that are financed by sponsors' advertising. In these programs, social problems are rarely complicated. "Bad guys" can never be reasoned with; just shoot it out with them. There is a simple, instant solution to every problem. For example, relieve acid indigestion with brand XXXX; overcome unpopularity by using brand XXXX hair color; banish feelings of insecurity by buying brand XXXX car.

Not only does TV's implied message of simple solutions disturb us, but also its omission of any message about the realities of seeking productive and lasting answers. One opinion is that the militancy of young people anxious for social change may be accounted for by their loss of faith in the slow process of democratic decision-making—*because these processes rarely appear on TV*. The arduous, day-to-day debates, fact-finding, inquiry, and researching by which social decisions are made in democratic bodies from the town council to the United States Congress are not usually what top-rated, moneymaking shows are made of.

There are many speculations and probably no complete villains in this story. We may simply be victims of unforeseen consequences of this technological revolution. The difficulty may not be commercial TV itself, but the presence of biased messages almost to the exclusion of other possible ones. The misfortune may be that Education does not understand TV's molding of student perceptions or how to exploit the effects of TV that could be helpful to learning.

**The need for the school to meet this challenge**

The problems stemming from media's blocking the development of communication skills are passed on to teachers in the language arts classroom. What kinds of TV programs are beneficial to children and at what developmental stage should use of such programs start? How can teachers capitalize on this broadener of experience that takes us around the world and into outer space? How can they guide children in unscrambling but relating the real and the imagined? If educators put their minds to this challenge, they can do something. Mass media has already been used for the public information, such as in the people-to-people crusade culminating in the TV anticigarette commercials. We can hope that media will increasingly be used to "comfort the afflicted and afflict the comfortable." Since TV is proving to be more powerful and pervasive than print, children and teachers need to think of themselves as using it rather than being used by it. By now we have heard this expression many times, but it is still well said: "If we aren't trying to solve the problem we are a part of it."

The following are examples of positive uses of TV in schools. One program prepared children for that problem of the frightening visit to the doctor with suggestions about how to face up to even the possible pain. The pride with which children display language knowledge gained from some shows designed especially for them is impressive. "This program is for me!" is the feeling (e.g., "Sesame Street" and "Electric

Company"). Some children hear and assimilate useful levels of communication not heard on the playground or at home. Not all programs need to be learning or problem-solving experiences; not all need to be watered-down emotional experiences felt to be "appropriate for small children." A balanced and healthful diet is the aim. Role playing (portioned out to groups so that they can replay problems after TV viewing) or guessing games encourage personal interaction. With choices from cartridge television, teachers can match programs to needs. For instance, for a needed "quiet time," a soothing storyteller might be appropriate. Children need some serene TV materials so that they can look for significant details and images. Exposure to children's books of high quality can be and has been done on TV. For data needed in inquiry, a cartridge on the hunting habits of lions from the show "Animal Kingdom" might be just what the class needs. The active involvement of adults in helping children make the choice of what to watch, and then their participation in a follow-up with interpersonal activity and assessment could counteract the passivity problem. When viewing is related to creative problem-solving, it can become a valuable experience.[5]

### What Part Does Lack of Guidance for Child Autonomy Play in the Problematic Situation?

More opportunity for self-direction needed

There is another factor, besides simplistic thinking and mass media, that adds to the problematic situation facing language arts instructors. This factor is the lack of chances that some children get to promote autonomy of thought. By the term *autonomy* I mean ability to respond and react independently. Autonomy implies self-governing behavior without outside control. Some children are taught to be neurotic rather than autonomous. The conflict is this: although parents and teachers may want children to be meek and obedient in the family and in the classroom, they want them to be strong and competitive when they are grown. Parents and teachers do most of the thinking for children, protecting them and ordering them around. At home, children are told, "Act this way," "Now you eat," "This is what you must wear," "Go to sleep," "Wake up." If children protest, they may be punished or ignored. The overmanipulated child learns to be dependent upon a parental wish before he acts. He develops little skill in making autonomous decisions.

In some classrooms, teachers are as guilty as the above-mentioned parents. Children are made to submit, year after year, to a teacher whose view of education may be one of "filling up a container with facts" that are easy to grade. The child is told, "This is when and how you

[5] See chapters on listening, for further suggestions; see the companion guide, *Ideas into Practice,* for more ways TV can be used as an effective tool.

speak," "This is when you listen," "This is what you think." Some teachers subject children to great periods of waiting and boredom throughout which they are expected to remain polite and docile. The schoolchild who protests this wasted slice of life becomes a troublemaker in the eyes of the teacher. Picturesquely speaking, children are the largest minority in the world. The adult with authority seldom tries to understand the child by saying, "I listen to you," "I try to arrange your school world to help you to think and to express yourself on your own." It may sometimes be the janitor who actually sets up the communication/thinking structure of the classroom, if he prevails in his idea that the desks be arranged in neat rows all facing forward for easy cleaning. In this case each child communicates with the back of another child's head.

**Antagonistic defense and uninvolvement**

When children have little or no autonomy, their behaviors may take the form of antagonistic defense and uninvolvement. Some children, reacting against restrictions, become so rebellious against training felt to be unfair that they develop a disrespect for all authority. Subjected to a paralyzing level of control, they may "crawl up the walls," screaming for freedom (Binstock, 1972). They may then find a simple solution—violence. And teachers wonder, "Why aren't the kids scared like they used to be?" In this context, Glasser (1969) suggests that in the best schools 50 percent of the children are not involved. The children see no challenging problems in school. They have no rewarding role. In the worst schools the uninvolvement figure is speculated to be closer to 90 percent. Children long for genuine internal choice—not choice forced on them by guilt feelings toward authority (Binstock, 1972).[6]

### What Happens in the Typical Language Arts Classroom?

**A picture of an undesirable school program**

The greater problem, however, cannot be attributed totally to mass media's provocation of simplistic thinking, or to failure to promote child autonomy. Part of the problem lies within the language arts classroom. Is it a national disaster area? Irrelevant, yet common activities in the English curriculum crowd out use of communication and problem-solving skills desperately needed for enhancement of language/thought processes.

For example, children may spend their time reading tiny bits of prose; they may rarely experience large, important units of discourse from the wealth of award-winning books for children. In general they may be engaged in "busy-work" designed to make sure they do the assignment. The answering of questions designed to elicit low levels of factual thought is as deadening as the mechanical writing of compositions to match titles irrelevant to the child's life. Besides writing assign-

[6] For activities designed to develop child autonomy, see especially Chapter 4, on discussion. All the chapters describe activity designed to promote self-direction.

ments that no one ever reads or cares about, children may spend large amounts of time changing from one handwriting form to another, parroting "may" instead of "can," and perfecting elaborate systems of headings. All this is done with a dull, sodden tone of feeling that implies that the language arts are motor skills rather than cognitive and affective activities.[7]

The state of problem solving in the classroom

If problem-solving skills developed as a matter of course, without guidance, it would not be so unfortunate that such trivial activities tend to crowd out the productive use of higher mental processes. But such unassisted development does not appear to be the case according to certain studies (Lundsteen, 1970; Wilcox, 1972). In the Lundsteen studies, if a child could not respond either orally or in writing to a question designed to provoke a step in the problem-solving process a zero score was given on the question. For example, the child might be unable to do one of the following: (1) classify a problem as to type in order to see the larger picture; (2) classify and label facts; (3) produce an idea on how to find information he did not have (search strategy); (4) accept the idea that there even could be missing information; (5) produce several alternative ideas for solving a problem (hypothesis); (6) support an idea with reasons; and (7) put himself in the place of someone else (empathy). There were many zero scores across all ability and socioeconomic levels of a sample of 900 fifth-grade children. Quality of response (when made) was frequently low. (Scores showed problems in listening to material and in abstracting information in the first place.) Even most adults fail to make maximum use of problem-solving skills. Complex as this educational challenge may be, we can still take it on. How can it be done?

Three rules that children can use autonomously

Wilcox (1972), for example, made progress toward this goal with three simple rules. She found that results were significantly different if she guided small groups of inner-city children so that they did the following: (1) made sure that everyone had a *turn to discuss* a story problem, (2) produced many *different ideas,* and (3) gave *reasons* for their ideas. In groups led by children who had received guidance there was more participation than in teacher-led groups and in groups led by unguided pupils. Moreover, in the groups led by guided pupils, the phases of problem solving used multiplied.[8]

[7] The term *cognitive* refers to obtaining knowledge. It includes judging and reasoning. *Affective* is related to feeling, emotion, mood, or temperament. *Motor* refers to muscular movement. The expression *motor learning* is sometimes used to contrast with learning in which the task is to understand certain ideas or relations (i.e., a more cognitive activity). Although these domains of behavior are separated for analytical purposes, there is much overlapping.

[8] For more how-to-do-it, there is a classroom scene later in this chapter and an extended treatment of procedures in Chapter 4, on discussion; Chapter 5, on children's literature; and Chapters 6 and 7, on composition.

Failure of fact giving as a teaching method

Finally, although creative problem-solving may flourish in some classrooms, more generally teachers fail to promote it because of the common practice of teaching by merely telling. For example, "Now children, in this year's curriculum there are 12 steps and 9 qualities in problem solving; memorize them for the test Friday, and we have fulfilled the central purpose of American education." This sort of indoctrination ensures the child's early obsolescence instead of his continuous renewal.

Fact giving (while expediting the collection of test scores) is prone to failure in promoting genuine communication and "learning how to learn" for two basic reasons:

1. Fact giving places too much emphasis on (for example) the teacher, author, linguist, professor, and scientist as the authority. The result is that children may exclude their own processing of happenings. Children then operate at too high a level of abstraction, and react as if the expert's words were based on a special kind of knowledge unknowable to people in general.
2. The giving of facts assumes that young children think in the manner of miniature adults and can readily absorb (or accommodate) abstract evidence into their knowledge systems.

But, according to the work of Jean Piaget and others,[9] children need to move through stages of thinking, responding initially on a level of specific concrete operations before taking on the more generalized, abstract levels of thought. Piaget's research does not mean that children cannot produce generalizations; it does suggest that the best quality of children's abstractions fails to come from just telling them facts. Children may be bombarded with an explosion of facts about the English language: e.g., facts about hundreds of punctuations rules, format requirements, and phonic generalizations and exceptions; facts about devices of simile, metaphor, and personification; the fact that *he doesn't* is considered good standard usage and *he don't* is poor; the historical fact of a word's origin, that cuneiform was an ancient writing system, that different words may be from different parent languages.

Such facts may be appropriate to the classroom if an individual child has the problem of what to do with leisure time, or if they trigger meaningful language production for the child. In that case, the teacher should be able to direct the information gathering of the child who is curious.

Of course, there is still a time when deductive teaching is more appropriate than inquiry methods; for instance, "Since you ask me, the

[9] See Chapter 1, on language and thought development, for further treatment and references.

label people use for this is *hexagon*." There are times when a teacher needs to be direct with children: "I am looking for one right answer to this question." But the occasions when such a method is best are far fewer than actual practice. Giving a child today's facts (which may be tomorrow's errors) does not necessarily turn a child into a powerful communicator. We do not teach children in order to create small, living libraries on a subject, but we teach so that children may embody the process of knowledge getting.

### Do We Know How to Think?

**Adults as models**

There is one more question: Do we know how to think? Some of us have a tendency to display terms from logic in order to avoid thinking (especially notable during an election year). We may use rationalizations to avoid having to face facts. We may believe we are so superior that there is no room for improvement in our thinking/communicating skills. Conversely, we may believe we could not improve our skill anyway; thinking is inaccessible. We may decide that if we keep busy, we will not have time to think. We may march blindly through the muddled streets of our lives shouting "Up with this," "Down with that," following the crowd. We may hire an expert to think for us. Or, we just may not think about thinking, taking it for granted.

This inability of so many to think and solve their own problems creatively has enabled the few to direct the minds of the many. We are allowing mass media experts, advertisers, anyone who comes along, to do our thinking for us. It is unfortunate that this happens, especially when it happens to our children. It is crucial, therefore, that teachers act as models of problem solving. They can do this by being actively curious, open to new experiences and to the brainstorming of ideas. They can look for and point out the assumptions behind a given statement; they can listen critically and creatively; and they can demonstrate the testing of alternatives. They can even change their opinions.[10] An appropriate place to start is during instruction in the language arts.

### Why Is Language Arts at the Center of Education?

**One subject—communication**

Why place all this responsibility at the door of the language arts teacher? Communication skills are not subjects separated from the rest of education. A current trend of thought is that the division of learning into mathematics, science, social studies, and English is a huge mistake. People express themselves in their native languages about subjects while employing many levels of thinking. From this point of view, com-

[10] There is more about the teacher as a motivating model in Chapter 6, on composition.

munication skills are basic to other aspects of learning. There is only one subject—communication, which includes not only listening, speaking, reading, and writing but also experiencing oneself as a thoughtful human being. Since the language arts are a part of the whole school program, their imprisonment in a 40-minute class period is a huge mistake. Over half the teaching time in the elementary school is related to some aspect of English (NCTE, 1968). Whether the data deal with botany, geography, or literary hopes and dreams, the crucial understandings children need for problem solving relate to how experience is abstracted, symbolized, coded, comprehended, and communicated. From this perspective, science and social studies are subcategories containing either content or special ways of processing information. Failures in any of the content areas (e.g., mathematical story problems) can be traced to a failure to understand and to communicate with skill. That is why the language arts classroom bears the burden of criticism and takes up the challenge; it is the hub of the educational wheel.

**Call for action**

The purpose of this Prologue is broader than just the pouring forth of a great lament. Increased knowledge can be turned into new teaching approaches and materials designed to help us survive on this planet—with even a degree of human dignity, joy, and grace.[11] Fortunately, children are basically interested in communicating, in problem solving, and in using their language to relate to other people. This curiosity makes a call to action easier. Children, moreover, are becoming more and more sensitive to larger problems of humanity at younger and younger ages. This is not to say that after the school unit on ecology, they never pick flowers or make litter. But this increased sensitivity of the young creates a challenge for us in planning the language arts curriculum. Once pupils have dealt successfully with their own particular difficulties and with problems of literary characters that they relate to closely, they can begin to feel involvement in broader issues affecting a larger portion of mankind. It is time to stop running away from problems (as Linus advocates in the cartoon at the beginning of the chapter). It is time to communicate thoughtfully in an attempt to find creative solutions.

---

**Conclusions**

In conclusion, there appears to be a problematic situation that an educator can define and attack. The foregoing section of this Prologue has developed an image of the present undesirable situation, though the general problem is more complex than treatment in these pages permits. In essence, there are barriers to effective communication that educators

[11] A popular speculation is that we have 30 years to find ways to continue our existence on this earth.

need to consider. But there are also general courses of action that can push away the barriers.

- If we avoid leaping to simple solutions, we can think creatively toward better ones in the long run.
- If we work to guide children's experiencing of media such as TV, we can avoid passivity or violent reactions and reap benefits in the broadening of their experience.
- If we guide children to be autonomous, they can take responsibility for their own actions with less hostility.
- If we avoid trivial activity unrelated to children's creative and autonomous language production and lessen the use of limiting teaching methods such fact giving, we can turn our attention to crucial skills of learning how to learn, through creative problem-solving.
- If we look to ourselves as examples of problem solving and communicating, children benefit.

Such teaching in the language arts classroom can have great impact, because communication is at the center of education.

## WHAT PRODUCTIVE ALTERNATIVES MIGHT BE USED IN THE CLASSROOM? (LANGUAGE AND CREATIVE PROBLEM-SOLVING)

Now it is time to see what a successful classroom might be like. To illustrate, there is first a brief kaleidoscopic view and then dialogue from a classroom discussion. The focus is on creative solving of problems representing "opportunities in work clothes." Children are meeting challenges with confidence in their growing communication skills and in a spirit of joyful adventure.

### What Are Some Details of Successful Programs?

**A kaleidoscopic view**

Look into a language arts classroom and watch one small group solving a problem with the help of dramatic improvisation or role-playing. The characters have supposedly broken a school microscope and are planning what they will do about it. However, the role-play is not just for its own sake or for mere exercise. Instead, it represents a way to find out more about the children's own thinking.[12] Another small group

[12] See Chapter 3 on oral language for development of role-play and pantomime, and Chapter 5 on literary discourse. There are units and series of lessons in the companion guide, *Ideas into Practice*.

is involved in a literary problem—creating a poem about toys for choral reading to a younger grade.

> "I think the problem is that we need a refrain to repeat . . . to tie at least some of our ideas together."
>
> "I'm open to that. Who's got some lines we can try?"

While another group is inquiring through puppetry, yet another is solving a problem with pantomime, with nonverbal communication. Here the focus is on how to comfort a friend who has lost a pet. Meanwhile, another group is depicting parts of a problem using a picture or photographic essay about pollution in their playground and the parks. The definition of this problem might take the form of a wastebasket collage, a barrel with pictures and objects such as candy wrappers, paper napkins, and empty plastic juice bottles glued to it. Since this product will be shared with other classes, a subgroup is writing invitations for seeing the display in a genuine audience situation.

> "Look, instead of just diving in and writing the invitation, why don't we *think* about it first. Is it going to be for our own grade or for the kindergarten? There'd be a difference in the kind of words and writing we'd use."
>
> "Where are some of the last invitations a committee wrote? Maybe we could get ideas from them."
>
> "Or, we could interview someone in the class that the invitation is for. We can find out what they'd like to get. We need a plan."

On another day a class may deal collectively with a creative problem by writing some dialogue or a class play. Ideas for it may have been collected in a problem box located at the back of the room. Some of the ideas in the box may reflect an attitude of respect for other life styles and for language/culture differences in the classroom. To this end children may have collected stories from Black, Chicano, Filipino, and Chinese classmates. Concurrently, children in another group are exchanging poetry they wrote about expressed feelings—"Times I Felt Lonely." Meanwhile, over in the listening center one group may be formulating a listing of "don't miss" TV programs from a collection they recently evaluated for themselves and for others in the school.

Finally, some children are evaluating their own progress on language problems using record sheets showing tasks completed. A sample:

> "I have listened to myself in my group's discussion and found these things. I made five suggestions. Two were used. I got someone else to give an idea. I helped soothe over a fight. I have read and given my opinion on five books on our discussion topic. I would like to find out something now about another country."

One assessment group might be constructively evaluating the progress of peers:

> "I really thought that part was funny! Why don't you make your character talk some more like that."
>
> "If you would explain why he kept quiet about it being stolen, it might help me understand your story."
>
> "Why don't you write some more about what the dog and his friends did to the mean lady? That was the best part of all!"

## What Is the Focus of the Successful Classroom?

Building on individual challenges

By examining the details in the classroom described, we can see that each child is getting a progressively clearer hold on a problem that has some meaning and value to him and toward which she can feel a sense of progress. All the activities described are based on needs and problems of both the individual child and the group. Unless the language arts program is built on the problems of individual children, we will find ourselves going nowhere. We build the appropriate school housing, construct advanced programs with our new knowledge, master appropriate teaching strategies, purchase beautifully illustrated materials, and then when the bell rings—the wrong children walk through the door! The core of the successful classroom is the individual child motivated by personally felt challenges. Of course, not everything in a successful classroom can be tucked under the umbrella of creative problem-solving, but more such activities are definitely needed.

Individuals as a main program resource

The language arts program is a program in thinking; therefore, one major resource lies in the mind of each teacher and in the mind of each child in the class. The ideal program will grow out of their processes and their products—their own oral and written composition, and high quality works of literature written for children. As one teacher said, "It lies between your ears, an inside job." You and your children are the program and are responsible to one another. Consequently, the job of any text, consultant, or college instructor is to help learners release this latent richness. The emphasis is on stimulating active output and joyous use of language. Consequently readers of this book are free to incorporate their own ideas into the suggestions given and to adapt them to capabilities, interests, and special classroom needs.

## How Does a Teacher Conduct a Discussion so Children Can Solve Problems Creatively?

Shift from a kaleidoscopic view and examine a more-detailed illustration, a stenographic report. The dialogue to follow was excerpted from an actual videotape recording of a discussion in a sixth-grade class. The teacher of this class had previously spent much time helping the children learn how to do more than leap from an ill-defined problem to a surface solution.

**Discussion of literature to stimulate processes**

The teacher's overall design included the following: (1) a plan for discussion, including types of questions designed to bring out certain problem-solving behaviors; (2) stimulus situations, frequently from award-winning literature for children, to get learning started; and (3) audio and video recorders to catch class discussion for later analysis. In this particular instance, *Crow Boy* by Taro Yashima had been chosen. The story begins:

> On the first day of our village school in Japan there was a boy missing. He was found hidden away in the dark space underneath the schoolhouse. . . .

The boy is a strange, shy, silent child. He is ignored or derided by his classmates, who name him Chibi, meaning "tiny boy."

The teacher, Mr. Warren, pauses at selected points in the story to conduct a discussion about Chibi's problem.

MR. WARREN: From what we've read so far, what would you people say about the boy they called Chibi? Let the thoughts race from your mind. Record a key word or so in your notebook to help you recall your thoughts, if you need to. Taking turns, present your ideas as rapidly as you can.

This first question serves to bring out facts and conditions about the problem. During the flow of answers, the teacher can evaluate subskills of listening and verbal fluency. Mr. Warren continues.

MR. WARREN: Remember in this discussion time, I'm not looking for any one right answer. We're interested in recording and examining any ideas you might have. What would you say about Chibi? Joe?

CHILD: He knows where the wild grapes grow and can make interesting drawings.

CHILD: He knows and can make every call the crows make. [This child already knew how the story ended, but still participated actively in the process.]

CHILD: Well, I would agree with what Joe said; but because he can't get along with his friends, I think that he tries to keep away and wants to do it himself . . . by himself.

CHILD: That's right, and the people don't really appreciate him; it makes him feel kinda bad.

CHILD: Chibi seems like he's lonely and if people got to know him, they could like him better, because he has those talents of studying insects and everything.

CHILD: What do you mean, "everything"?

CHILD: Like we said, he knows where wild grapes and potatoes grow and he can make interesting drawings.

**Free and autonomous generation of facts and conditions**

During this exchange, Mr. Warren wrote key words from each response on the board. He allowed many children to respond to the same stimulus question. Some children tended to model after other children's responses. Other children familiar with the task moved the discussion along to facts that defined the problem situation for themselves. Some children supported, and some asked for clarification. In this class, children soon learned that all answers were respected by their teacher as being offered toward thoughtful discussion.

Setting the task

When the situation called for one right answer, the teacher was direct with the children and informed them of the task. When the situation was open (as in the present discussion) they understood that, too. The next teaching step would be to help the children make generalizations by grouping some of the facts and conditions on the board. Concluding that the children showed readiness, Mr. Warren felt it was time to change focus, to lift to a question designed to stimulate direct defining of the main character's problem. This is a step in the classic approach frequently sought too soon.

Defining the problem

MR. WARREN: To summarize, some of you have suggested that you felt Chibi has some kind of a problem. What would you say it was?

CHILD: Making friends.

CHILD: A homeless child.

CHILD: Did you say homeless?

CHILD: I mean. Well, now I'm not so sure—I need to think.

CHILD: He lacks companionship; well, that would be like Kim just said, "making friends," wouldn't it? [Mr. Warren recorded the two contributions and drew a line connecting them.]

CHILD: I think it might be his environment at home and he should change that if he can. Fred brought out the point that if he had brothers or sisters it would help him. Maybe so. But I don't think so. Maybe he does have brothers and sisters and they beat him down and say that they're better than him and maybe they get more rice than he does at dinner and first use of the shower. Well, maybe there wasn't a shower, but stuff like that.

MR. WARREN: Before we make more hypotheses and evaluate them, I believe some more people have things to say about the problem. [Mr. Warren intended to control the *process,* not the content, and refocused on the problem.]

CHILD: Well, now I disagree with myself when I said his main problem is . . . I now disagree with saying that he was a lonely child because I think that could be a subproblem; it could be a smaller problem related to a bigger problem, like Jay said, lacking companionship.

Looking for reasons

MR. WARREN: Why do you think he was a lonely child?

CHILD: Well, he never had anyone to talk to. Well, maybe he had someone to talk to, but he didn't really have someone to maybe tell his problems to.

CHILD: Well. I think making new friends, the reason he can't make new friends is because he's shy. And I think that would be one of his subproblems.

MR. WARREN: If you think we've gotten out a fairly clear idea of the problem, let's go back to what Carlos started to do. How do you think Chibi might go about solving this problem—lacking companionship? Let your hypotheses flow freely. Hold off criticizing and weighing alternatives until we've gotten most of them out.

Generating hypotheses and weighing alternatives

CHILD: I think it could solve his . . . I think if maybe a new person that came into the school . . . He could make friends with him or her. That's my hypothesis.

CHILD: Well, he could get up enough courage to join in some different games or activities of the other children.

CHILD: Show them how he feels; show the kids how he feels. And then he could get them to make friends.

CHILD: Well, maybe they would become interested in what Chibi liked.

CHILD: I think that the teacher might be hindering him by putting almost all of his work up and everything, and praising him so high, because people might begin not to like him . . . even more . . . because they think he's the teacher's pet; they'd think he's not really that good; he's just a big show-off.

CHILD: Back to Lois's idea of them becoming interested, well, I think, maybe out on the playground Chibi could tell some guy that he might want for a friend, "Let's see who can catch the biggest lizard," or something, and the guy he wanted for a friend wouldn't have as much practice as Chibi would, and Chibi would get the bigger one. And so Chibi could offer to tell him the rules he's found for catching lizards. And while he's doing this, he could make friends.

CHILD: If he was interested in bugs, he could show the drawings of their anatomy and other people would get interested in this illustrating how they were built and try to follow in his footsteps.

MR. WARREN: Have you ever tried this way . . . that is, getting others to share your interests so you could make friends? How could you try this?

Some other considerations about problem solving

Again, Mr. Warren was controlling the *process,* not the specific content. In designing his questions to elicit *transfer* of ideas,[13] he tried to help the children see applications. Although the children were careful to gather facts and conditions before attempting hypotheses and decisions, the instructor helped children realize that prolonged postponement (unless the issue was earthshaking) had its reasonable limits. The discussion group also considered whether or not the problem was something they (or a book character) could act on now, as opposed to just worrying about it. By the end of a discussion, most of the children could identify with the problem in some way. It was helpful to them to feel that personal problems are not unique and that most people have the same sort of problems at some time in their lives. Children were learning to be persistent (to "stick to it"), to feel free to be original and open-minded, to empathize ("get into another's skin"), to think of the *whys,* and to communicate.

This excerpt has given some idea of how children can gain problem-solving concepts through discussion of selections from children's literature. Of course, Mr. Warren did not follow every story or episode from children's literature with this kind of discussion. Sometimes the children responded through art or drama, or just by silent appreciation.

Agreed, creative problem-solving in the classroom is easier said than done. Guilding this kind of discussion is especially challenging for those who have never been taught in this way before. Mr. Warren, for example, felt unable to trust his students this much at first. He kept fishing for answers and cutting the children off. Acquiring the necessary strategies (and especially learning to keep quiet himself) required time, required seeing others do it, being dissatisfied with himself, and then trying again and again. Finally, these additions to his teaching repertoire called for outside encouragement, support, and the thrill of seeing change in his children.[14]

## How Is Creative Problem-Solving Defined?

It is time to pull together ideas and state more precisely what is meant

[13] Generally, *transfer* refers to change in a person's ability to perform a future act (or thought) as a consequence of having performed another related to it. For example, it is easier to learn Italian if one has studied French and Spanish. *Transfer* implies the use of recalled information or procedures in a new context. There is, as one teacher put it, a *transferring in* from a store of earlier knowledge and skills and a *transferring out* when skills and ideas are applied to a separate experience, either past or future. This separate experience may be at about the same level of complexity, or it may be more complicated.

[14] For more on problem solving, see the other chapters. But especially see Chapter 4 on discussion, Chapter 11, on evaluation and accountability. Also see Chapter 5, on the bibliotherapeutic approach using children's literature, and the companion guide, *Ideas into Practice.*

by creative problem-solving. Definition can fill a sentence, a paragraph, a chapter, or a book. Briefly, here are a few paragraphs.

**Definition in a sentence**

As used in this book, creative problem-solving refers to the process of selecting alternatives that lead toward a goal the child desires and result in a pattern that is new, at least to the child.

**Creative component**

As applied to thought processes, the terms *creative* and *problem solving* represent certain similarities and differences. The contrast between the two lies in the greater part played in creative thinking by the following aspects: novel insights; illumination (ah-ha!); lucid expression; the insinuation of less-conscious fringe thoughts; emotion; and fantasy—which is playlike, free-rising, fanciful, and dreamlike.

**Procedural component**

Problem solving (in contrast to pure creative fantasy) depends on careful, conscious preparation, organization, direction, and verification. It is more factual and goal oriented. For example, the teacher (Mr. Warren) usually asked questions designed to elicit thinking about missing data, procedural steps, multiple alternatives, and consequences. Problem solving economically and meaningfully brings into play almost all cognitive skills that children need to attain. Actually the two processes (the playfully creative and the goal oriented) can occur closely together. The ability at will to make creative thinking coordinate with more logical reasoning may make the difference between lunacy and creativity.

**Opportunity for attacking unknowns**

The creative dimension in problem solving is related to the number of knowns and unknowns in the situation. Getzels (1964) recommends that school problems be full of unknowns, both as to the problem and as to the solution, at least for the pupil and sometimes even for the teacher. The problem then requires various amounts of innovation before it can be solved. Too often both pupil and teacher know what the problem is and what the one right answer is, and all that takes place in the classroom is an exercise in rote drill. Take this example. After pupils listen to an unfinished story episode about a boy and his transfer to a new school, they could either be told that the boy's problem was integration into a new peer group, or they could infer for *themselves* what his problem was (a much more creative experience). Next, the one right solution could be told to them, or the solution could be left as a challenging unknown. If the teacher avoids giving the answer, then individual children can think creatively toward a solution (if they have interest in the problem in the first place).

**Divergent and convergent thinking**

Before we move on, the concepts *divergent thinking* and *convergent thinking* need explanation. (See Guilford, 1964.) Convergent thinking is usually restricted to the production of one right answer, with little or no peripheral thought. In a sequence of divergent thinking, children are free to generate their own factual material. This divergent response is usually provoked by a problem for which there is little information given. (For example, Mr. Warren's children, who did not know the ending to the story, generated some of their own ideas for solution.) Children in this more open situation may then take a new direction in their thinking, or gain a new perspective. Of course, if a problem is too unfamiliar, a child may be blocked rather than challenged to divergent thought. If complete unfamiliarity is the case, the problem is simply irrelevant. But complete familiarity with all aspects of a problem produces habitual, rote, or mere practice behavior. In essence, creative problems present opportunities for growth and learning.

**Four parts of problem solving**

To sum up this brief exploration, problem solving in its most creative sense accepts the challenge of unknowns. The problem-solving procedure generally moves through four broad areas.

1. Clarifying the problem by recalling information, by making new connections, and by categorizing—with flexibility.
2. Generating hypotheses fluently.
3. Consciously planning procedure with elaboration and with openness.
4. Organizing evaluation with suspended judgment.

These four general areas (with their many possible steps and strategies) constitute creative problem-solving. To be a creative problem-solver can be an act of joy, a measure of growth, and a way of becoming a person with feelings of self-worth. We all have creative problem-solving abilities that make it possible to live with more enchantment and zest.

**Creative problem-solving for very young children**

Kindergarten—primary-grade children and problem solving. Are ideas about promoting children's communication/thinking skills only applicable to older children? Not at all; the earliest school experience is the place for teachers to begin. For example kindergarten teachers can ask divergent *how, why,* and *if* kinds of questions, instead of convergent *yes* and *no* questions. Here are some examples: "How do you know the mother was angry (or happy)?" instead of, "Is the mother often angry?" "Why do you think this is called a *lipstick* instead of a *nose stick?*" "Why do you think it is called a *handbag* instead of a *foot bag?*" Contrast, as used in the foregoing examples, clarifies the context, which is helpful to young children. One preschool child, illustrating the *if* question himself, said, "If my eyes are so little, how come it looks so big?" Other examples of questions are "What would happen if . . . ?" or "If the box were not filled with marbles, would it make a sound?" (Blank, 1972).

Similarly, a group of first-grade children, who had been curious about what was in essence the operating of gravity, had been guided in some study about it by their teacher. One day a small "thinking group" took its usual place on the rug in the corner of the room and was presented with this task. "Suppose gravity were doubled?" suggested their teacher. "What then?" She left them (as usual) with the tape recorder to discuss a problem. Small voices began to share ideas:

"That's a tough one."

"Yeah."

"Say, if gravity were doubled, then the rain would come down twice as fast. Wouldn't it?"

"Yeah."

"If the rain came down twice as fast, then we would sink down twice as fast into the mud. Wouldn't we?"

"Yeah."

"If we sink down twice as fast into the mud, then we might as well build our houses underground. Right?"

And thus the conversation in the thinking group continued.[15] Make no mistake; creative problem-solving belongs just as much in the beginning of education as throughout the remainder.[16]

---

**Conclusion**

This Prologue has implied that fact giving, a standard method of teaching language arts, has provided little or no motivation for learning. An understanding of social context touched on in this introduction makes imperative a help-the-child-to-think approach. The exploration of this approach is the purpose of this book. The chapters detail some possible routes to a more successful classroom where language is learned with enthusiasm and with humanism.

Part 1 starts with some of the fascinating understandings derived from studying the development of language and thought in the child. Chapter 1 explores what this knowledge means for the modern classroom teacher. In this part and throughout the remainder of the book you will find this theme developed: *Approach the teaching of language arts through creative problem-solving because it is a central motivating process.* As mentioned in the Preface, behind the skills of communication lie the skills of thinking, and behind the meaningful use of thinking skills lies the organizing process of creative problem-solving.[17]

[15] Class of Mrs. Polly deGraaf, Goleta, California.

[16] Many annotated storybooks for very young children that teachers can use for promoting problem solving are listed in the companion guide, *Ideas into Practice.*

[17] This prologue has dealt with where we are and where we might go. If there is curiosity about "where we think we have been" by the time the book is completed, the reader is invited to skip ahead to the Epilogue found at the end of the book.

## If You Want to Learn More

BECKER, G. J. *Television and the Classroom Reading Program (If You Can't Beat 'em, Join 'em).* Newark, Del.: International Reading Association, 1973.

A practical little bulletin for the classroom teacher.

BELLACK, A. A., ET AL. *The Language of the Classroom.* U.S. Office of Education (USOE) Cooperative Research Project No. 1497. New York: Columbia University, Teachers College, Institute of Psychological Research, 1965.

One of the most comprehensive studies of classroom verbal behavior, makes use of a category system.

BINSTOCK, J. Motherhood: An Occupation Facing Decline. *The Futurist: Journal of the World Future Society,* 1972, *6* (June), 99-102.

Suggests that one factor in the lack of provision for autonomy of the child is the current struggle to hold onto motherhood, by an occupational group fighting for survival in a context of increasing technological obsolescence.

BLANK, M. Analysis of Cognitive Abilities in the Preschool Age. Paper presented at the meeting of the American Psychological Association, Honolulu, 1972.

BURROWS, A. T. Media and Reading. Paper presented at the International Reading Association Annual Convention, New Orleans, May 1974.

CHOATE, R. Television's Children: Television Fare, Alias TV Dinners. *Learning: the Magazine for Creative Teaching,* 1974, *2,* 39.

This author, chairman of the Council on Children, Media, and Merchandising (1346 Connecticut Ave. NW, Washington, D.C.) presents a helpful column in each issue.

COVINGTON, M. V., CRUTCHFIELD, R. S., DAVIES, L., and OLTON, R. M. *The Productive Thinking Program: A Course in Learning to Think.* Columbus, Ohio: Charles E. Merrill, 1972.

Contains 15 lessons on creative problem-solving, plus response booklets, and teacher's guide and chart. Mainly mystery story content for grades 4-6.

FLANNAGAN, J. The Psychologist's Role in Youth's Quest for Fulfillment. *Educational Psychologist,* 1971, *8* (February), 1-2.

Provides survey data on effectiveness of school programs.

GELLER, R. Commercial TV as a Classroom Tool. *K–Eight: Instructional Management and Leadership,* 1973 (January–February), 89-91.

Describes a program for capitalizing on children's viewing habits.

GETZELS, J. W. Creative Thinking, Problem Solving and Instruction. In E. R. Hilgard (Ed.), *Theories of Learning and Instruction.* The 63rd Yearbook of the National Society for the Study of Education (NSSE), Chicago: University of Chicago Press, 1964. Pp. 240-67.

Forms part of the base for the present position on creative problem-solving.

GLASSER, W. *Schools Without Failure.* New York: Harper & Row, 1969.

Presents the undesirable aspects of the school's impact on children, and offers some solutions.

GUILFORD, J. P. Creative Thinking and Problem Solving. *Education Digest,* 1964, *29,* 29-31.

Forms part of the base for the present position on creative problem-solving.

GUSZAK, F. L. Teachers' Questions and Levels of Reading Comprehension. In T. C. Barrett (Ed.), *Perspective in Reading No. 8: The Evaluation of Children's Reading Achievement.* Newark, Del.: International Reading Association, 1967. Pp. 97-109.

Examines the impact of questioning levels on reading and indicates needs regarding questioning.

HAYAKAWA, S. I. On Communication with Children. *ETC: A Review of General Semantics,* 1966, *23,* 174-203.

Spoken from the general semanticist's point of view, this highly readable article explores impacts on children from early communication roles.

HAYAKAWA, S. I. Semantics and Sexuality. *ETC: A Review of General Semantics,* 1968, *25* (June), 135-53.

An indictment of television's impact on the child.

ILLICH, I. The Alternative to Schooling. *Saturday Review,* June 19, 1971, 44-48, 59-60.

A provocative article developing a point of view on "disestablishing" schools or "deschooling" culture as solutions.

KAISER ALUMINUM & CHEMICAL CORPORATION. Telecommunications: One World-Mind. *The Markets of Change Series,* No. 6, Kaiser News. Oakland, Calif.: Author, 1971.

A highly pictorial essay suggesting that if there is any direction to evolution at all, it appears to be to create more channels for communication, e.g., the new universal languages, extrasensory perception, electronic villages.

LIEBERT, R. M., NEAL, J. M., and DAVIDSON, E. S. *Early Window: Effects of TV on Children and Youth.* New York: Pergamon, 1973.

Explores the question, "What are and will be the effects of continuous exposure to TV?" This material is based largely on recent National Institute of Mental Health (NIMH) studies.

LITTNER, N. A Psychiatrist Looks at Television and Violence. *Television Quarterly,* 1969, *8,* 3-19.

This article is based on a lecture at the Northwestern University Television Symposium. Available from Television Information Office, 745 Fifth Avenue, New York, N.Y. (No. SB52).

LUNDSTEEN, S. W. Language Arts in the Elementary School. In W. B. Michael (Ed.), *Teaching for Creative Behavior.* Bloomington, Ind.: Indiana University Press, 1968. Pp. 131-61.

Emphasizes how curriculum planning and instructional procedures in a variety of the arts of language can facilitate creative problem-solving.

LUNDSTEEN, S. W. Promoting Growth in Problem Solving in an Integrated Program of Language Skills for the Fifth Grade. Paper presented before the International Reading Association, Anaheim, Calif., 1970. (ERIC Document Reproduction Service No. 045 304)

Reports research designed to examine the dimensions of children's problem-solving skills.

LUNDSTEEN, S. W. On Persuasive Language, in preparation.

MICHIGAN STATE UNIVERSITY. Project VIM (Violence in the Media). Seven reports available as of July, 1971. East Lansing, Mich.: MSU, College of Communication Arts, Department of Communication.

An example of the research projects investigating the impact of television for the National Institute of Mental Health, U.S. Department of Health, Education, and Welfare (HEW).

MINTON, J. H. The Impact of "Sesame Street" on Reading Readiness of Kindergarten Children. Unpublished doctoral dissertation, Fordham University, 1972.

Investigates the effects of the first season of Sesame Street as measured by the Metropolitan Readiness Test (MRT) with its subtests of Word Meaning, Listening, Matching, Alphabet, Numbers, and Copying.

NATIONAL COUNCIL OF TEACHERS OF ENGLISH (NCTE). The Workload of the Elementary School Teacher: A Statement of Policy of the NCTE. *Elementary English,* 1968, *45,* 224-27.

NATIONAL EDUCATION ASSOCIATION (NEA), Educational Policies Commission. *The Central Purpose of American Education.* Washington, D.C.: Author, 1961.

Develops and explores the concept that the central purpose of teaching is to help children to think.

NOSSOFF, B. C. Is Sesame Street a Dead End? *Early Years,* 1971 (Spring), 56-59.

Offers six major points of criticism: (1) need for preschool learners to have firsthand experience for learning abstractions; (2) absurdities and inaccuracies (even for the purpose of humor) confusing to learners this young; (3) teaching of problem solving, personal interaction, and avoidance of one correct answer as opposed to neglect of the child's own creative resources; (4) overuse of repetition and possible danger to learning habit patterns; (5) neglect of areas of aesthetics, auditory perception (sounds of the real world), eye movement patterns, or motor patterns (development through more active physical participation); (6) pictures (close-ups) more recognizable and with clearer narration for better representing the real and avoiding confusion.

PACKARD, V. O. *The Hidden Persuaders.* New York: David McKay, 1957.

A pioneer exposes the impact of television advertising.

PARSON, D. W., and LINKUGEL, W. A. (Eds.). *Television and the New Persuasion.* Proceedings of the University of Kansas Symposium on Public Communication, 1970.

PAUL, N. L. Invisible Factors in a Child's Reaction to Television. *Childhood Education,* 1971, *47,* 303-6.

Parents have a strong effect on their children's relationship to violence. To cite TV violence as the cause of a child's violent behavior can contribute to unwarranted neglect of more probable and painful causes. Parents need to provide empathy and reality input to counter the fantasy of programs.

ROSNOW, R. L. Poultry and Prejudice. *Psychology Today,* 1972, *5* (March), 53-56.

Individual childhood prejudices, cited as beginning at age four or earlier, have a way of enduring a lifetime, no matter how irrational they come to seem. Trivial experience may enlarge into blind intolerance, with its emblems of unflattering ethnic stereotypes. The article describes four stages in the progressive development of intolerant concepts. Since prejudiced attitudes harden with age, the best time to attack them is in early childhood.

RUSSELL, D. H. *Children's Thinking.* Boston: Ginn, 1956.

A classic treatment of the topic, scholarly, yet filled with ideas for application. This work forms the base for part of the present point of view on the child's language, thought, and instruction.

SHAFTEL, F. R., and SHAFTEL, G. *Values in Action: Role-Playing Problem Situations for the Intermediate Grades.* New York: Holt, Rinehart and Winston, 1970.

The package contains filmstrips, records, and teacher's guide.

SIEBERT, W. F. *Instructional Television: The Best of ERIC.* Lafayette, Ind.: Purdue University, Measurement and Research Center, April 1972.

This publication represents a collection of the best of the ERIC documents concerning instructional television, categorized as follows: Newest, General, Bibliographies, Literature Guides and Overviews, National Issues, and Project Reports.

STEVENSON, A. E. National Purposes. *Life,* May 30, 1960, 87-102.

A brilliant essay (still timely) written prior to the Kennedy–Nixon presidential campaign. An excellent example of persuasive and exploratory rhetoric as well.

TOBIN, R. L. The Power of the Press—and of Television. *Saturday Review,* June 14, 1969, 47-48.

An editorial on the use of television for the benefit of the public.

WILCOX, M. A. Comparison of Elementary School Children's Interaction in Teacher-Led and Student-Led Small Groups. Unpublished doctoral dissertation, Stanford University, 1972.

A study designed to investigate child autonomy in group discussion (grades 5–6). The investigator predicted and confirmed that children in groups led by a trained student leader responded with proportionately more task-related acts than did children in groups led by a teacher.

# Developmental Bases Part 1

Chapter 1

# A Base in the Development of Language & Thought

*"I'm barefoot all over."*

*"The baby looks just like you, only newer."*

*"Look at that upholstered worm!"* (a caterpillar)

These are examples of young children's basic creative thinking in the development of their language. What happens to this development and its natural creativity as the child moves on through the elementary school? How can teachers understand, assist, and avoid blocking a child's natural development of language and thought? How can we help children grow to be the communicating individuals that they would like to be? This chapter tries to answer such questions.

Look back a moment. The Prologue to this book suggested that in order to best help children, teachers need to base their language arts program on creative problem-solving. Then they will be able to integrate the separate language skills in their program, while stimulating the children's interest and increasing motivation. But before we try to use teaching suggestions that pave the way for creative problem-solving, it is well to explore how language and thought develop in children. Such knowledge improves a teacher's decisions about the language arts program.

A basic framework from Piaget

The basic framework of this chapter has been built around stages of child development proposed by the famed developmental psychologist, Jean Piaget. On this skeleton are hung some outstanding features of thought and language development, broken down into *sound, vocabulary,* and *sentence.* The framework also serves to organize implications for adult assistance. See the following figure.

PIAGET'S MAJOR STAGES OF INTELLECTUAL DEVELOPMENT

| | | | |
|---|---|---|---|
| Early childhood | Stage I | (From birth onward) Sensorimotor | → |
| | Stage II | (About age two onward) Preoperational | → |
| Later childhood | Stage III | (About age six onward) Concrete Operations | → |
| | Stage IV | (About age eleven onward) Formal Operations | → |

In general, this chapter gives you background on what we know about the development of the child as a thoughtful language user and thinker, and as a social being. There is a body of knowledge emerging. It is to the teacher's advantage to be aware of it in order to assist children in the most productive, well-rationalized, and humanistic way.

Children first come to know their world of objects. This base then enables them to know a more symbolic world. In time they come to know a world with rules and generalizations that they understand first only concretely—then more abstractly. Specifically, this chapter answers questions about Piaget's third growth stage, that of *concrete operations.*[1]

[1] See Lundsteen (in press, a) for a treatment of the other stages and some other views.

Stages of concrete and formal operations

First, a *brief* explanation: Piaget believes that before reaching the age of about eleven, children see events from their own concrete viewpoints. They are unable to justify events through abstract logic. That is, between the ages of six and eleven the child may perform problem-solving actions accurately. But he/she does this only when using *concrete* materials (blocks, clay, actual objects).

For example, a child knows that when he is pulled in a wagon, other children see the ball in his hand as a moving object, even though *he* sees he is holding it *still.* The experience is a concrete expression of relativity.

However, in the concrete stage children cannot explain problem-solving actions by using abstract logic; neither can they simply perform these actions in their minds. For example, they cannot abstractly relate the measurements of observers who are accelerated relative to each other and thus are no longer in an inertial system; nor can they grasp $E = mc^2$.

Thus, in the school program *concrete materials* are vital to the child for development of concepts, rules, and generalizations. The child's study of history, for instance, requires concrete materials such as pictorial time-lines with pictures of buildings, dress, and customs of the period in order to make past events something pupils can grasp. Then they can relate in terms of space, picture, and physical sequence, instead of the abstractions of centuries, even of decades. Abstract reason does not become possible until children are able to detach themselves from their own viewpoints and the concrete reality of the moment. When this detachment happens, they reach the fourth stage, *formal operations.*

Questions this chapter is designed to answer

This chapter dealing with the concrete operations stage investigates specific questions such as these:

- What is sentence maturity and what is concept maturity in later childhood?
- What does helpful adult–child dialogue include? And how might a classroom be arranged to promote this exchange?
- What does information from developmental and social dimensions imply for those working with children who are culturally different? And what are the priorities?

## PIAGET'S STAGE III: CONCRETE OPERATIONS (THE ELEMENTARY-SCHOOL YEARS)

*Operations* defined

The Piagetian term *concrete operations* appears in much educational literature. What does it mean? Examine first the portion of the term called *operations.* It refers to mental actions organized into a system (or into rules). That is, the child performs actions that he can reverse in order to perform them in opposite directions (e.g., adding, subtracting). (However, the operations of this stage are still connected to concrete objects and to things that the child can perceive and manipulate.)

Examples of operations include the process of learning to classify (joining objects in a class, e.g. *all red boats here*). Another instance is learning to rearrange earlier classes on the basis of new information (ordering: *These rocks will scratch those rocks*). An additional example is constructing new classes (*These rocks are a mixture*).

An operation is not isolated but is linked to some other operation, as part of a total structure. For example, a logical class, *tree,* does not exist in isolation, but exists in the total structure of classification itself.[2]

A child can pour the same amount of water from one container to a taller (but skinnier) one many, many times; he can do and do and do and still remain mystified, "I just don't understand where the extra water came from!" To understand the relatedness of the two dimensions (height and width) constitutes an example of an operation.

Concrete defined

The other key word in the title of this stage is *concrete.* What does that mean? It describes ideas gained through sensory impressions or refers to individual facts sensed at a particular moment. (*Here is a tall stick; here is a short stick*). It does not refer to inclusive abstract considerations of relationships and classifications (*This object is both dark and tall and can belong to two classes*). Although children at this stage take the *past* into account, they still accomplish new learning through concrete experience of the here-and-now. With the help of actual objects to manipulate, children can use logical thought (such as in counting, addition, multiplication, and measurement of space, time, equality, and inequality). These operations, however, are rarely verbally expressed hypotheses (characteristic of the fourth Piagetian stage). But the operations do contain the elementary logic of mathematics, geometry, and physics.

New intellectual feats

At this stage of concrete operations children can now perform many feats that they could not earlier. They can now pay attention to more than one event or attribute at the same time. Examples are that they can attend simultaneously to subclasses (e.g., to all grandchildren, who

[2] For example, *tree* is found in one of two major, contrasted groups—plant and animal kingdoms. Whereas plants are delimited by the ability to manufacture food, animals are delimited by the eating of plants or other plant-eating animals to satisfy their need for nourishment. Plant cells have a cellulose wall, and animals cells have a membrane wall. Because animals have a nervous system (absent in plants), they have a greater ability to respond to stimuli. And while animals generally locomote, plants generally do not have this ability. Just as animals are classified according to natural evolutionary relationships, so are plants—with the range from algae through the most advanced flowering plants.

are also white, and who are city dwellers). Given an overall collection of black and white wooden beads, children can respond correctly to the question: "Are there more wooden beads that white wooden ones?" They can think of white *and* wooden at the same time. They can grasp an overall inclusive concept (e.g., wooden beads).

Toward the end of this period, the child has a fairly successful understanding of the conservational principles. For example, a ball of clay does not become more or less when pulled out or squeezed flat (conservation of substance).[3] This conceptual intelligence enables the elementary-school child to learn rules verbally laid down from the outside. (Preschool children have trouble when they must apply general rules to particular situations, as in certain games. Older brothers and sisters may accuse the younger ones of cheating in games when in fact they are having conceptual difficulties. The older children forget how difficult such thinking was when they were younger.)[4] *If children in this concrete operations stage are having trouble in their learning, it is well for the teacher to look to the rules they think they are using.* They may be using a rule that the teacher is not aware of (e.g., *Capital letters are never words,* or, *are always words.*)

For further clarification of the concrete operations stage examine Piaget's example of *seriation of sticks.* After having grouped a number of sticks into (1) two parts (large–small), (2) then three parts (large–medium–small), and (3) used trial and error to create a series, finally, at the stage of concrete operations, the child discovers a method. (4) He chooses the tallest of all the sticks, and puts it on the table. Next he selects the largest of all the remaining sticks, and places it beside the first stick. He repeats the operation until he has put all the sticks on the table. Thus he has constructed a progressive series, a perfect series without any trial and error. Moreover, this reconstruction assumes a relation that could be *reversible.* That is, one stick is both smaller than the ones before it and larger than the ones after it (Piaget, 1969).

**Comparison of concrete and sensorimotor stage intelligence**

So how does intelligence at this stage compare with intelligence at earlier stages? Go back to the diagram of Piagetian stages—you will see that the very first stage is called *sensorimotor.* It differs from the concrete operation stage in this way: *Sensorimotor intelligence refers to the knowing of real objects on a level of practical satisfaction perceived simply through the five senses and coordinated with observable physical movements.* ("If I pull on that blanket I can get that toy nearer to me.") The *conceptual* intelligence characteristic of the concrete operations stage is capable of an entire rebuilding of structures of thought. These

[3] Conservation refers to sameness across change in appearance or shape.

[4] Elkind (1973) suggests that the preschool child appears to have one rule for games: "I win—you lose."

distinctions are indicated by stages in the construction of operations—as in the example of seriation of sticks just concluded.

It is now also apparent that, with development, more-elementary structures (such as *big–little*) become incorporated into higher level structures (such as *big–medium–small*). These in turn become parts of structures at an even higher level (such as *bigger than this but smaller than that* in the case of true seriation). According to Piaget these structures do not replace but are integrated into one another. Later we will see how important this development is to classroom learning.

### What Are Some Features of the Development of Sound Production and Intake?

**Sound production**

Moving from Piaget's emphasis on development of thought, let's take a close look at some features of language (sound, vocabulary, and sentence) and their significance within this stage. Later I will try to relate them to the thought stage.

Most children have control of sounds that characterize their dialect by the time they enter school. Their sound system is approximately the same as the *model* or person(s) with whom they have lived. Of course, learning is not complete at this stage and individual children vary greatly in their mastery of the sound system. Even adults do not always correctly discriminate between separate sounds when they have no basis or context for what to expect. ("Did he say *god* or *guard? Mary* or *merry?*") Mistakes in speech or articulation (stemming from need for further development) do not appear to retard school achievement in reading and spelling. But the gross inability to tell the difference between speech sounds may be a hindrance.

What sounds might a teacher expect a child to be able to produce in a fairly adult manner by the age of six or seven? By age six the only distinctive speech sounds *not* produced by at least 90 percent of the pupils in one sample were /s/, /sh/ (as in *mission*), /z/ /zh/ (as in vision), /th/ (as in *either*), /ch/ (as in *church*), and /hw/ (as in *why*). A child's sound substitutions such as *wady* for *lady,* and *tat* for *cat* may not mean inability to make the correct sounds, but may mean failure to note the difference in sounds another person makes—failure to listen (Templin, 1957).

### What Are Some Developmental Features of Vocabulary?

The educated adult acquires most of his vocabulary during the school years, although a lot of vocabulary learning goes on before school. In other words, the vocabulary of the child entering elementary school is incompletely developed. The concept "map" that follows is one a teacher might hold in mind during instruction, and particularly during a discussion. It shows the anatomy and depth of the meanings a vocabulary word might have; in this case the word is *apple.*

ON VOCABULARY DEVELOPMENT

"I know lots of big words, 'infuriating,' 'obstinate,' 'vandalism,' 'incorrigible.' . . ."

*Building Concepts.* (From *Handbook for Teaching the Language Arts,* by Constance McCullough, reprinted with permission from Intext Educational Publishers, New York. Copyright © 1969. Marginal material has been added.)

## A MAP OF A CONCEPT AND ITS RELATIONS

Concept-building is essential to meaningful communication. We are too often in a hurry to explain a term and go on to something we think more important. Actually, time spent in concept-building is productive of many meaningful relationships. Below are some of the possibilities in the word *apple*. What is an *apple?*

SENSORY IMPRESSIONS:

*The first attributes a child will learn—concrete*

Behaviors: reddens, softens, drips, drops

Qualities:

- Number: per tree, per acre, per season, per pound
- Amount: per pound, per recipe
- Texture: of skin, of flesh, of seed
- Flavor: of varieties
- Moisture: under varying conditions; in varieties; at stages of development
- Solidity: effect of touch, of dropping
- Size: to hold in one hand
- Shape: general; details
- Color: of varieties; at stages of development
- Sweetness: taste; after-taste
- Acidity: degree of
- Odor: of varieties; at stages of development
- Sound: in eating; in dropping

*The second attributes a child will learn—functional*

Uses:

- Food: in sauce, pie, and the like
- Housing: by insects
- Jelling: by man
- Decoration: by man
- Hunting: by robin looking for worm in apple
- Entertainment: bobbing for apples on Halloween
- History of human uses: evidence in early art
- Geography of human uses: cultivation and harvesting

COGNITIVE RELATIONSHIPS:

*The third learning achievement of the child—abstract*

Whole-part: tree-apple; apple-skin

Cause-effect: pollination-fruit

Sequence: seed-tree-blossom-fruit

Comparison-contrast: apple, pear

Subordination-coordination (awareness of hierarchies and parallelisms); appleness, kinds of apples; apples which ripen at same time

COGNITIVE PRODUCTS:

*Abstract*

Theories: An apple a day keeps the doctor away.

Laws and principles: Sweetness is affected by rainfall.

Generalization: Apples are fruit, a form of food.

Summarization: Apples grown in the West are Gravensteins, and so on.

Definition: An apple is a tart, juicy fruit.

Classification: Apples, oranges, and bananas are fruit.

Procedure: Apples are grown, picked, sorted, boxed, and shipped.

PRACTICAL EXTENSION OF COGNITIVE OBSERVATIONS:

Example: the Gravenstein

Elaboration: description of various kinds of apples

Application: irrigation based upon principle that rainfall affects sweetness

AFFECTIVE RELATIONSHIPS. How we feel about apples. *Connotations*

LINGUISTIC RELATIONSHIPS: We depend heavily on these in our teaching because they provide quick answers, but they are once removed from reality and less useful than the preceding relationships. Some are:

Pronunciation: [ap′ l]

Derivation: original form or meaning of word; changes in form or meaning of word, historically or regionally or in slang

Derivatives: plural—apples; compound—applesauce

Synonyms (word meaning the same or about the same)

Antonyms (word meaning the opposite)

Homonyms (word the same in sound)

Heteronyms (word the same in form but different in meaning)

Multiple meanings: apple as tree, fruit, design, color

Uses of word: as noun, as adjective

Application of word: an apple; an apple orchard; apple-green dress

How large a vocabulary does the average child have—in terms of the ability to recognize and produce words—at varying grade levels? It is probably safe to assume that children enter first grade with a typical vocabulary of 2000–3000 words, leave that grade with approximately 3000 (little gain!), and add 1000 words a year as they continue through school. There is usually some specialization in vocabulary (e.g., scientific, literary) developing in later years. While the child is growing in terms of his grasp of a wider *range* of words, he is also growing in the *depth* and accuracy of his speaking vocabulary. Probably her listening or understanding vocabulary continues to outnumber her spoken one. Even adults have a larger vocabulary of words they recognize than of words they speak.

### What Are Some Developmental Features of Sentence Production?

**Growth of sentence length and other features of language effectiveness**

Most teachers want an idea of what length of sentence a child might typically produce at various ages. At age six, the average spoken sentence is about six or seven words long. In the period from kindergarten to the twelfth grade there is a gradual and progressive increase in the skill of the typical child according to the following criteria: (1) length of communication unit (or sentence); (2) grammatical maturity (or complexity); and (3) semantic (meaning), rhetorical (aim), and stylistic differences.

For example, a six-year-old might bemoan: "It was a dead fish and the teacher won't let me bring it to school and the poor thing's stream got stinky."

A university student (with similar content) might bewail in a news editorial: "Perhaps any curriculum that deals with relevant matters such as ecology and refuses to worship the 'sacred' boundaries of conventional academia will be less than enthusiastically embraced by the school's power-brokers." [5]

**Indices of sentence maturity**

What are some ways of looking at maturity and immaturity in sentence construction? One index is the stringing together of main clauses with one *and* after another, as in the child's sentence on the dead fish. *Maturity is not represented so much by long sentences, but by how they are made long.*

Children throughout grades one to six are most likely to use a sentence pattern consisting simply of subject, verb, and outer complement or direct object, such as, *He hit him.* Incidence and flexible use of movable parts of sentences and subordination increase with grade level. An example is *The surfer started home and he was chilled to the bone,*

[5] Analysis of sentences does not touch many of the subtle differences in language. See the section on the language of literature, e.g., sounds, figurative language, symbolism, and style, in Chapter 5.

superseded in writing by *Chilled to the bone, the surfer started home,* or *The surfer, chilled to the bone, started home.* (There are large individual differences especially between extremes of high- and low-performance children.) The average main clause produced by older children has more subordinate clauses of greater length attached to it. That is, mature language may show the use of transformations that recast the ideas of more than one simple sentence into a single clause.

As an example, take the following simple sentences:

> The sheriff captured the convict.
> The convict *escaped* from prison.
> The sheriff was *triumphant.*

Combining the three, using noun modifiers (such as adjectives and *-ed* participles), gives this sentence:

> The *triumphant* sheriff captured the *escaped* convict.

In sum, although the typical child in the fourth grade may produce almost all the grammatical structures taught in school, he does not use as many, at the same time, inside of one another, as do children in more advanced grades; for example, *The girl who was wearing the boots* is later compressed to *The girl wearing boots* (O'Donnell, Griffin, & Norris, 1967). All languages appear to have rules for rewriting sentences (or for transformations). Skill in this rewriting indicates maturity, according to some points of view.[6]

**Development of meaning**

More significant than surface grammatical development, however, is the development of the child's grasp of meanings. Growth is not just the addition of vocabulary and selection of more sophisticated sentence patterns. Important growth is seen in the understanding of *relationships* among words and phrases and how these relate to greater meaning contexts within the sentence, the paragraph, and the total experience.

During the elementary-school years, as children continue to develop, they comprehend the multiple meanings of words and use more abstract concepts (Lundsteen, 1974). They develop different categories of meaning, such as, object–nonobject, animate–inanimate, human–nonhuman, male–female. The game of 20 questions (in which the players attempt to narrow the definition of meaning under consideration) relates to a child's performance with different categories. (See Activity 2.12, p. 101.)

[6] See Cooper (1973) for an outline for constructing exercises for sentence-combining problems. Some award winning writers, notably Hemingway, have used short, staccato sentences for effect.

### How Can Teachers Assist Development of Grammatical Sentence Maturity?

*To force growth in compactness and complexity—or not to force*

A current idea growing out of work on the social uses of language is that classroom teachers need to emphasize not so much what language is as *what it is for.* In light of this emphasis, what about assistance of sentence maturity in the elementary school? It may be that forcing growth in sentence compactness and complexity in the elementary school is a poor idea for the following reasons: (1) Such a practice may make the child overly self-conscious about his language. (2) Sometimes a very simple style of expressing an idea in a simple declarative sentence (with no embedding) is most appropriate and effective, depending on the thought.[7]

*Focus on the uses of language*

Rather than forcing children to speak or write in certain grammatical forms for practice exercises, school time is probably better directed to the developmental task of encouraging appropriate speech and writing in communication situations. In this case the focus is on the aims of discourse or uses of language—(1) self-expression with increasing use of socialized expression, abstracting, defining; (2) information giving in exposition;[8] (3) "life-lifting" literature or poetry making; and (4) directing–persuading.

Some class time may well be spent on deciding when *restricted* language is appropriate (e.g., when many meanings are shared by a closely associated speaker and listener), and when an *elaborated* code is appropriate (e.g., when pronouns need to be returned to noun status for clarity, when missing parts of sentences need to be restored to avoid ambiguity, and when precision in verbs and concreteness of detail belong). In perparation for writing (and for living in the "now"), these actual language *uses* add up to time better spent than do sentence–pattern practices. Let pupils listen to fine language with various purposes; let them produce, then listen again. (See Chapter 10, on grammar, for sentence construction activity; Chapter 5, on literature; and Chapter 6, on development of composition.)

---

## HOW CAN TEACHERS ASSIST GENERAL LEARNING AND COMMUNICATION IN THE STAGE OF CONCRETE OPERATIONS?

This section on teacher assistance deals with the following questions:

[7] E.g., "In the beginning was the Word, and the Word was with God, and the Word was God. . . . In Him was life and the life was the light of men. . . ." (John 1:1–9, AV).

[8] Here *exposition* refers to cognitive or scientific language, use leading to hypothesizing and solving in the manner sought by Piaget.

- How much abstractness in teaching is appropriate in the elementary-school classroom?
- How can teachers diagnose and teach children's concepts?
- What does helpful adult–child dialogue include?
- What does developmental information imply for those working with children who are culturally different?

How much abstractness in teaching? The key instructional idea derived from Piaget's work is the realization that abstract teacher-talk may be premature or "empty" for a child in this stage. The teacher may feel (based on his own "formal–operational stage") that it is reasonable and easy to be abstract. But such abstract verbalization usually results in noncommunication. While a teacher may overestimate a child's stage of development (talking right over his head), the teacher might also *under-estimate* the child's developmental stage. Then the teacher fails to stimulate and to stretch what the child might do. These potentialities might be found both within a stage and in getting ready for the next stage.

How can teachers diagnose children's concepts? The teacher needs to have some idea of his children's thought boundaries. The diagnosis of children's concepts has been approached in several ways. One approach is to study the words a child uses to identify concepts; for example, the teacher might have a child tell or make up a story about a word, such as *job* or *sky* or *cooperation.* Another way is to have the child provide a word, such as *fruit* or *evergreen,* that would include instances (e.g., *fruit* subsumes *apple* and *banana; evergreen* includes *pine, juniper*). Or the child can tell why some examples are *positive* instances of the concept the teacher has in mind, or *negative* (not instances of the concept—a truck is not a car.) Yet another way is to have children sort objects (e.g., geometric figures of varying sizes and shapes) by responding to aspects such as size or form of a concept (say, circularity) and by disregarding other aspects (e.g., color or borders).

In other words, teachers check to see if children grasp attributes the concept must have (their nature and number). Teachers see if children can discriminate attributes that are close, but are wrong or irrelevant (e.g., a stool does have legs, but it is missing a back that a *chair* must have). (Grasp of concepts becomes more difficult as the information load gets bigger and as the load is carried by negative (*no, don't, wrong*) instances rather than by positive ones. More and more educators realize that language performance problems (including reading) are closely related to the creative process of concept development problems. More effort and materials will be directed toward this kind of diagnosis. (See "A Map of a Concept and Its Relations," p. 39.)

Ingredients for dialoging as assisting concept development

What does helpful adult–child dialogue include? One way to assist concept development and to guard against teacher-talk that is too abstract is through *dialoging*. The availability of adults to dialogue with the child is an important aspect of language acquisition. The fact that "only" children acquire language faster than those with siblings (who acquire it faster than do twins), seems to speak for the advisibility of as much adult–child dialoging as possible. Helpful dialoging between the elementary–school child in the stage of concrete operations and his teacher probably includes the following terms and other ingredients:

- Because ▪ Why ▪ On the one hand . . . on the other hand
- Although ▪ Given that ▪ Statements reflecting logic (e.g., This is true, therefore . . .)
- Plenty of concrete items, pictures for manipulation, and events that the child has experienced

Questioning

Skillful questioning, as part of the dialogue and well matched to the child's learning stage and style of thinking, is often helpful. When Piaget became interested in what lay behind a child's answers (especially incorrect or immature answers given during intelligence testing) he attempted to clarify the reasons for the child's responses by skillfully questioning and interviewing children in an open-ended manner. One implication from this breakthrough in research is that the art of questioning and diagnosis constitutes a large part of productive teaching (although this "spin-off" for teachers was not necessarily what the philosopher researcher Piaget originally had in mind).

Emphatically, the teacher's questions during dialogue can bring about a deliberate stimulation of concept learning. A fatal teaching error is throwing answers (like stones) at people who have not asked questions. In order to implement productive dialogue, the teacher may divide the class into small discussion groups, sometimes bringing additional people into the classroom (such as high-school students, college people, community aides) to stimulate talk in small groups so that the situation is not always the teacher with 27-plus children.[9] The diagram on the next page suggests how such a classroom might look in action.

The principal instructor or teacher moves from center to center (which he has set up bit by bit during the school year). Aides or pupil leaders in this opened-up classroom are present. Children with a richer language repertoire can learn to help the less-fluent children in such a classroom environment.

Once the teacher has carefully analyzed the concepts needed for each child in a chosen area, he can orchestrate, making a match between the

[9] For more information see Chapter 4; also Strasser (1973).

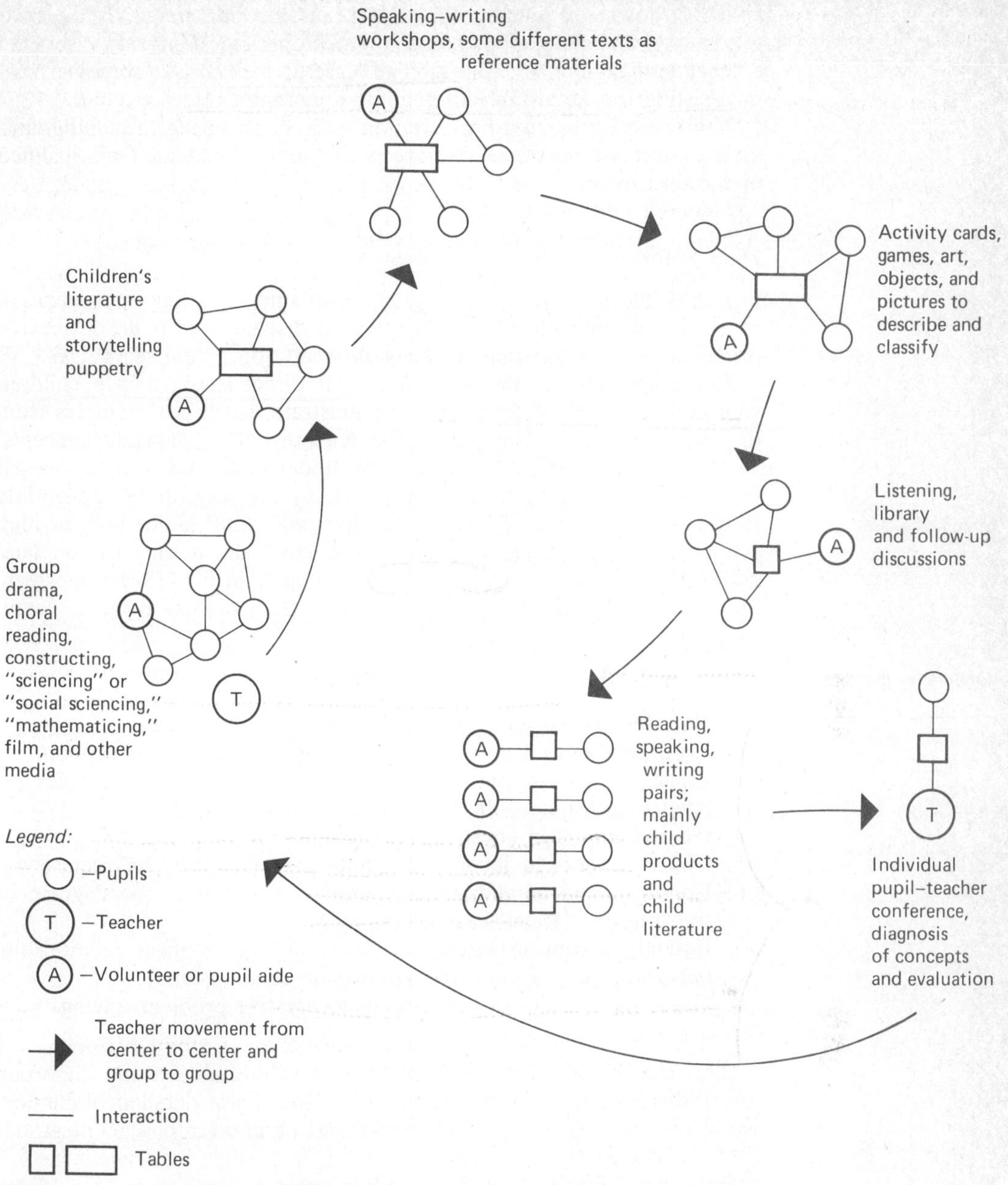


**A CLASSROOM ARRANGEMENT DESIGNED TO PROMOTE DIALOGUE**

**If language use and dialogue are keys to language growth, how is the classroom stage set for them to occur?**

child's structure of thought, the concrete instructional materials the child needs to manipulate, and dialogue (including question asking by the teacher and children). This kind of careful matching becomes crucial in assisting the culturally different or apparently retarded child.[10]

The preceding section has given an indirect approach to helping children to attain concepts. There are other, more direct methods justified in certain cases.

## What Is Direct Teaching for Concept Attainment?

Is it possible to have children grasp with understanding and retention something as difficult as, say, persuasive discourse with its devices of propaganda? Is it possible to *evaluate* such conceptual learnings?

A teacher can use the following eight direct steps to help children gain understanding of concepts.[11] To illustrate, I will use examples from the persuasive use of language—the teaching of propaganda concepts. These are difficult but important to understand and defend oneself from. The teaching of these concepts is, by the way, quite appropriate to the elementary-school level. If teachers wait until junior high or high school or college to explore this use of language, it may be too late; children are exposed to propaganda quite early in life. (See Lundsteen, in press, c.) I will first outline the steps, then discuss them in detail.

**Outline for the teaching of concepts**

### *Steps for Instruction in Concept Attainment*

1. Note the crucial attributes of the concept under study.
2. Note nonessential attributes that might lead to misconception.
3. Construct and administer teaching examples and nonexamples related to attributes—both crucial and nonessential.
4. Guide learners in constructing examples of their own.
5. Guide learners in labeling attributes and concepts by themselves.
6. Construct and administer new examples to test learners' grasp of the concept. (Reteach, if necessary.)
7. Extend concept to larger context (e.g., cause–effect relationship, subordinate, superordinate, coordinate relationships).
8. Guide the transfer of the concept to creative problem-solving.

This instructional process is useful in teaching almost any important and difficult concept in the curriculum. Now for a detailed discussion, using the study of propaganda tricks and other examples to illustrate:

[10] For some materials designed for such a classroom arrangement, see Moffett (1973). See other chapters in this text and *Ideas into Practice.*

[11] This section on concept development is based on Markle & Tiemann (1970).

**Step 1. Crucial attributes.** Decide on the crucial attributes of the concept under study. A crucial attribute would be a property that every example of the concept would have. If you removed this property, the example becomes a nonexample.

For instance, "persuasive intent in the interests of the sender" is crucial to all propaganda. And "the existence of words with provocative, emotional connotations" is essential to the Name Calling or Glad Words–Bad Words method of propaganda. For the Bandwagon device some inference must be possible that since others are doing something you should, too. For the Testimonial device, a crucial element is a personage helping or testifying to the goodness of some product or idea. Thus, the instructor's first step is to think of the attributes shared by all members of the subclass of propaganda selected.

Take a simpler concept to develop, the eye. You can think of *pupils* as crucial attributes of *eyes*.

**Step 2. Nonessential attributes.** The next step is to think of the nonessential or irrelevant attributes of the concept that might lead children to make errors—to (1) overgeneralize by including nonexamples as members of the class and to (2) undergeneralize by failing to recognize some true examples as members. Nonessentials are usually attributes related to time, place, media, and person. For instance, the nonessential facts that chairs have rockers, arms, and various sizes and shapes of backs, and are made of different materials do not destroy their "chairness" (as long as the crucial attributes are there: four legs, a back, and a single-person seat). Similarly, you can think of false eyelashes as nonessential attributes of eyes. The good looks of the propagandist are irrelevant.

**Step 3. Teaching examples and nonexamples related to attributes.** Get plenty of teaching examples and nonexamples (or positive instances and negative instances). A maximum set of *nonexamples* has enough to *exclude* each crucial attribute of the concept. And a minimum set of *examples* has enough to vary each nonessential or irrelevant attribute that you think might cause the child the most confusion or misconception.

Suppose, for instance, you were teaching the Bandwagon propaganda trick. Some examples would vary the vocabulary: "everyone is," or "everybody has," "others do," "all buy," "every child in the block thinks," and so on. Other examples could vary the content related to the real world. Others could vary the author or message sender. Still others could vary the audience. The message itself might vary in media (comics, TV, phone, film, color magazine, pamphlet); in mode (narrative, series of classifications, criticism, description); or as to whether or not it was found in poetry, drama, or song. (Similarly, you could think of various shapes of eyes as positive and kinds of false lashes as negative instances.)

**Step 4. Learners construct examples themselves.** Have the children think up examples and nonexamples. The instructor gives pupils feedback about their accuracy regarding the crucial attributes.

**Step 5. Labeling attributes and the concept.** When the children seem to know the concept, ask them to think of names or labels for its attributes. Then ask them to generalize these common elements and devise a label for the concept itself. Then you could tell them some names that other people have used in the past (e.g., "bandwagon").

**Step 6. Testing examples.** Use *new* examples to test whether or not children can generalize to new instances of the concept. Thus you evaluate the children's attainment of the concept after instruction. Again identify the variation of the nonessential or irrelevant attribute in each example of the concept. Also identify the crucial attributes that have been excluded or are lacking in each nonexample. If the test examples are constructed with care and the responses are analyzed with equal care, the instructor should be able to put his finger on troubles in the child's concept attainment.

**Step 7. Relating the concept to a larger context.** Think about relationships involving the concept, such as cause and effect. For a propaganda device being studied, children might note examples of use of the device that might serve the general welfare or be in their own best interests or "good" (e.g., fire prevention slogans and other such persuasion). Then they might note examples in which the cause–effect relationship is most probably neutral to their own best interest, or "harmless." Finally they might note examples in which the cause–effect relationship might be against their own best interests, cause harm, mentally or physically, be misleading, or add up to a lie causing mistrust—events which they would label as "bad." After having derived a standard, pupils can then judge other propaganda examples according to it. (As still another example, children might think of cause–effect relationships among eyes, crying, and other factors.)

**Step 8. Using the Concept in Creative Problem-Solving.** The final step in using attained concepts is getting the children to generalize to problem-solving situations in their lives, to extend and use these concepts. The teacher needs to continually encourage this transfer.[12]

Think now in terms of the brief, capsulized version below, right.

[12] For example, see if once the child has learned the Bandwagon technique he can tell his "friend" he has spotted the technique and resisted an "everybody's-doing-it" invitation to ride his motorcycle in an unauthorized place.

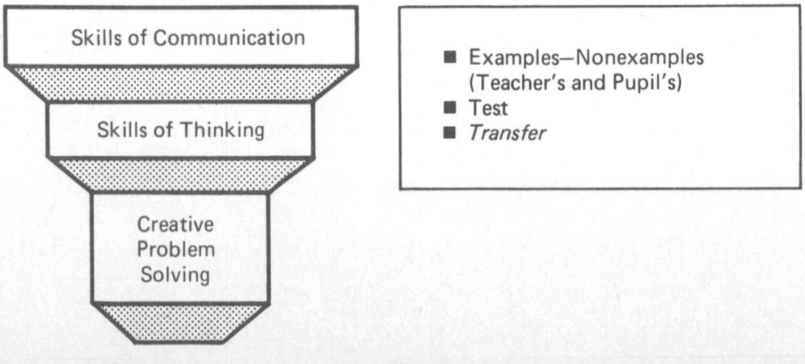

## What Is a Formal Concept?

According to Markle and Tiemann (1970), a concept is a class with members or examples. The members vary sufficiently to permit us to speak of generalizing to a *new* example. The new example is not an "identical twin," which one could not tell apart from the first example. Take the case of a punctuation mark. It is an identical twin (or identity) because it does not vary. But the *concept* for an exclamation point, an exclamatory statement, is a concept. The punctuation mark is not. Discriminating identical twins is a matter of attending, discrimination, and rote memory, not formal concept attainment. Another way of defining a concept is that it is a class having members that *share* some crucial attributes. Knowing *all* these shared crucial attributes makes it possible for a child to generalize to new examples and attain a formal concept.

Definition of a formal concept

**Errors in concept learning (inductive logic).** Markle and Tiemann (1970) discuss three errors in concept learning: (1) overgeneralization, (2) undergeneralization, and (3) misconception. These errors may be recognized by certain *symptoms,* which follow.

1. The symptom for *overgeneralization* is that the child accepts nonexamples. He may produce or select a clear instance of the Bandwagon trick as a Testimonial device. He may say a pickup truck is a car, or a stool is a chair (missing the crucial attribute of a back) or a knot on a tree trunk is an eye. He may say that *desert* and *dessert* are homonyms; that a rectangle is a square. Reteaching (or the cure) involves more or better (or "close-in") examples for which he can discriminate crucial and nonessential attributes.
2. The symptom for *undergeneralization* is that the child rejects true examples. He may not recognize an instance of Bandwagon persuasion because an admired friend said it. He may reject an example of an antique car as being a car. He may reject glasses as being a "pair," or a crab's extended eye as an eye. The cure is more "far-out" examples.
3. The symptoms for *misconception* are the same as (1) and (2) above, in varying combinations. A misconception is cured by combining both treatments.

The following is a suggested and related classroom activity:[13]

[13] Activities are numbered consecutively throughout each chapter, for easier reference.

**1.1. Conceptualize, Name, and Judge a Propaganda Trick.** Present to the pupils many pictured examples from magazines and oral (taped) examples from TV or radio. Use the eight concept development steps. You might select, develop, and note differences between the Glad Words, Bandwagon (everybody-else-is-doing-it), and Testimonial (using a person as supposed authority) tricks. (See Lundsteen, in press, c.)

## HOW DOES DEVELOPMENTAL INFORMATION HELP THE TEACHER OF CULTURALLY DIFFERENT CHILDREN?

**Dialect, cultural variation, and acceleration of stages**

What does developmental information (including knowledge of concept attainment strategy) tell those who work with children who speak a different dialect, or who have a different cultural background, or who appear to be retarded from effects of poverty? Of course, from the standpoint of what the human brain is capable of learning and the use we make of it, we are all "culturally deprived." Remember that the culturally *different* environment is not *deprived* of stimulation and contains many rich communication themes that go unused in the schools. However, effects of social class (including the factors of childrearing practices, health, and motivation) may be cumulative. For example, fifth-grade children appear to show greater differences between social classes in performance of school language tasks than first-grade children do.[14]

But how does Piaget's work relate to instructors coping with cultural variation? Teachers of young children who take the Piagetian scheme into account attempt to get the right toy, material, or experience to the right child at the right level of abstraction. This idea could apply to later childhood. But a person versed in the philosophy of Piaget might argue against the notion that early academic, intellectual instruction for economically impoverished preschoolers can help them "match" their peers from more affluent homes and can remedy what appears to be later retardation of thought processes valued in school. A Piagetian might say that this instructional idea has little plausibility since the pre-

[14] An example of a school language task is skilled subordination of sentences, e.g., *The sharp-toothed cat bit me* or *The cat with sharp teeth* versus *The cat bit me and the cat had sharp teeth.* For evidence see the Loban study (1963).

ON THE PROPAGANDA DEVICE OF TESTIMONIAL

schooler has a *qualitatively different* mode of thought from the older child. Here is an area of debate. Piaget himself has no interest in acceleration or assistance of the emergence of his stages.

But some children vary from the standard to the extent that their personal happiness and success are jeopardized. In their case perhaps a judicious inclusion of the principles of concept attainment will be useful in their education. Other useful principles include emphasis on the role of language, continuity in development, influence of school environment, and instruction in information-gathering strategies.

At this point I must differ somewhat with Piagetian theory. Certain *basic* thought processes of children change relatively little from age to age and from culture to culture. For the most part the symbols of children's interpretations of the world are usually adapted to their day-by-day social structures or to the environment with which they are familiar. In fact, all basic thought processes appear even in the very young child. These processes may be called perceptual and associative thinking, concept formation, creative thinking, critical thinking, and problem solving (Russell, 1956). But the child's *materials* of thinking, his experiences, and images may be severely limited. With respect to this sort of limitation an intervention program can diagnose it and do something about it through a match of child, basic thought process (such as creative problem-solving), strategies, experiences, and material.

More advice comes from linguists. Labov (1967) has described eight problem areas for teachers trying to cope with teaching culturally different children. Where to start? What to attend to first? In answer to such questions (and with some adaptation) here is his list of priorities:

**Labov's rank-order of language areas needing teacher attention with respect to the linguistically different child**

*Problem Areas for the Child Who Is Linguistically Different, in Order of Priority*

1. Understanding the teacher's spoken English. (A child with this problem solved—"The teacher speaks so I can understand.")
2. Reading (and that means with comprehension).
3. Communicating with the teacher in spoken English.
4. Communicating in writing.
5. Writing in standard English grammar.
6. Spelling correctly.
7. Using standard English grammar in speaking.
8. Speaking with a prestige pattern of pronunciation (and avoiding stigmatized forms, e.g., *ain't*).

Should a teacher have much difficulty himself understanding a child's oral language, he needs to attend first to this area.[15]

[15] Note that a problem *not* given any priority is "getting a child through" his language arts textbook with its vague goals, which was probably written for polite society and not for a racial mix.

Teacher evaluation of children's language variation via audiotape

A big part of the problem is teacher preconception and attitude. In one study, a sample of teachers were set to the task of evaluating language of children they did not know (via audiotape recordings). Results suggested that teachers are quick to stereotype when cued by certain stigmatized language forms (e.g., I *ain't got* or *He come yesterday*). In response to such forms the teachers in this study labeled the speakers as "less competent," "less eager," or "lazy." These teacher behaviors (observed at the University of Texas Center for Communication Research) suggest the importance of the social dimensions of language development. This is the next area to explore under teaching implications from developmental knowledge.

### What Are Classroom Effects from Social Dimensions of Language?

Language self-picture and self-fulfilling prophecies

From the time that the child in the preoperational stage first begins egocentrically to carry on conversations with himself and about himself (monologing), he probably begins to reinforce a socialized self-picture by means of speech feedback. Through the child's language this self-picture becomes progressively stronger. In other words, when children hear themselves talking, they suggest things to themselves that they eventually come to believe rather firmly. (See Heisey, 1969.) (Recall the cartoon earlier in this chapter under the topic of vocabulary development.) One child may convince himself that he is a lucky one in a world that is a lot of fun, because he has listened to himself (and to adults) talking that way. Another child hears himself saying that he can do nothing right (probably having heard it first from adults), that he is always making mistakes, that people have it in for him, that he can never succeed, and that he is stupid. Finally he becomes thoroughly convinced in his pessimism. We can speculate that these self-pictures have been auditorily self-reinforced in the monologue stage. The self-views are now likely to be carried on and reinforced during the inner-speech stage accompanying concrete operations.

Confusion of hypothesis with reality

This speculation has foundation in what Piagetian stages mean for personality development. Such consideration illustrates the broad implications for cognitive development growing out of Piaget's work. From the stage findings there is evidence that children in the concrete operations stage still confuse hypothesis with reality (Elkind, 1973). That is, they make guesses about the world and then make any data that come along fit their hypothesis. The *child's idea* (that he has "set out" or externalized) becomes more real than any evidence that accumulates after it. A child tends to believe his own idea once he has created it and put it outside of himself (e.g., he is stupid, or ugly, or good in geography, or the neighbor is a spy, or someone is his enemy, or the pencil he took could not possibly have belonged to anyone else). The child truly believes it and holds it as truth against all evidence to the contrary.

This behavior may occur especially during the elementary-school years.[16] Teachers tend to forget the tremendous impact that their most casual derogatory words can have in fostering poor self-images, and they sometimes fail to understand why their words of honest praise are so strenuously rejected (when in fact they are going against a child's carefully nourished, though unfavorable, self-portrait).

Cognitive conceit

An interesting (and for some teachers infuriating) dimension of this self-picturing comes to many children during the concrete operations stage. This is the child's experience of feeling he has "put himself up" by putting someone else *down*. At about the age of seven or eight some children (who previously felt that adults were all-perfect and all-knowing) catch an adult making a mistake, being wrong. The child then pounces on this event and feels somehow superior or brighter than the "stupid" adult. He finds that he is not only able to put the big man or woman down, but to put himself up. Then the child may feel that he is on top and knows a great deal more. He had suddenly inflated his own poor little self-picture and is somehow brighter or smarter than the adult.

This aspect, labeled *cognitive conceit* (Elkind, 1973), is noticed by teachers in some of the stories that children dictate or write, and the jokes and stories that they like. (For example, the storybook character, Winnie the Pooh, is thinly disguised as the bungling adult, whereas Christopher Robin, the child, is the smart one, the hero.)

Putting adults down is part of the pleasure children get out of a unit on advertising propaganda, when they get to exaggerate and garble adult commercials. In the elementary school this display of cognitive conceit usually is partially hidden in the safety of the group or in disguised animal characters in their stories.[17] Understanding this sort of behavior as a developmental phenomenon gives teachers in later grades the ability to overlook or to accept with grace, patience, and a sense of humor some otherwise insulting language.

Impact of language on the schoolchild's satisfactory coping with developmental tasks

Further related to self-picturing and fulfilling through language is the idea that a child in the stage of concrete operations begins to meet certain developmental tasks. What are these tasks and how are they related to language? For one, the child begins to face the developmental task (or crisis) of internalizing the attitude of "industry in school"; or he slips into attitudes of "inferiority in school" (Erikson, 1950).[18] The

[16] Perhaps this phenomenon is not limited to childhood but persists in certain governmental instances.

[17] The phenomenon of cognitive conceit does not necessarily end in the elementary-school classroom.

[18] Note the strong self-picture of the child who responds "I don't believe that any teacher ever got in the way of my learning" to a query about teaching behaviors that helped and hindered. Generally, however, children tend to think they are "dogs" and need to have their self-pictures regarding language built up.

child begins to put his hope in his "tools" (language and academic skills). The middle-class child in particular learns to enhance his self-picture by applying himself to the mastery of these communication skills. Thus he attains status among his "tool" partners or peers.

At the same time he is encountering another significant social and developmental task: learning to give as much love as he receives. This forming of friendships with peers begins to hinge on informal, adaptive communication skills. The preadolescent child becomes newly capable of seeing himself through the eyes of others as an aid to correcting wishful, fantastic ideas about himself, and as a substitute for his new resistance to apparently arbitrary adult standards and values (Havighurst, 1972; Sullivan, 1953). In other words, this impact of language on self-perception through developmental tasks becomes closely related to a child's continued *survival* as a worthwhile person. When a child's language is "messed up," his social survival is at stake.

**Impact on language of various social "registers"**

Recent light shed on the social dimensions of children's language development comes from linguists' investigations of social "registers." These are used in "greasing the wheels" of communication by talking in differing ways. That is, the speaker switches language styles to match the interactions in many differing cultures and contexts. How do these registers operate in school? For one thing, children (and adults) use language to exclude certain people and to include others, as in peer-group jargon that subtly gets across the meaning, "He is one of us; he speaks the same language."

Research is uncovering various registers of language in the school. Even first-grade children know that the register *I ain't got* is a forbidden one for school (even infants may be observed to go from the register of babbling to the register of no babbling when a stranger walks in). Minority children (and boys) are likely to have trouble with politeness registers, the lack of which can get them thrown out of the classroom when they are unable to disagree in a way personally acceptable to the teacher. For example, the unskilled child may say, *You're all wet,* or *That's a lie,* rather than, *That's interesting, but let me suggest we consider an alternative point of view.* Though sometimes it takes all a child's linguistic energies to make a flat statement (Loban, 1963), some minority children prefer to expend their considerable linguistic energy in "rapping" with and "topping" their peers (e.g., *Your apartment is so skinny that the cockroaches have to walk single file.*)[19]

Other characteristics of minority group registers include the greater fluidity of interaction, with the speaker taking cues from the audience's

[19] See the children's book *Street Smart* (New York: McGraw-Hill, 1972), with photographs and text by Bob Adelman. In it Black children are enjoying themselves by trading insults back and forth. Also see *On & Off the Street* (New York: Viking, 1973), B. & S. Adelman.

reactions (e.g., *right on*). In contrast, the reaction from middle-class audiences is much more passive. At the far extreme is a native American Indian child believing that during communication it is grossly impolite to look one another in the eye.

Even teachers employ various language registers in the classroom with their "spelling register" differing from their "reading instruction register." For example, the spelling register tends to show extremely careful articulation (*Children, the spelling word is "desks." There are seven desks. . . .*) When the lesson is over, the children may hear this: *Chuldren, spellin's over; move your des into a circle for readin.* Teachers may also show "kindergarten" or "very-young-children" registers, "mathematics-instruction" registers, and "guest-in-the-room" registers. It is interesting and insight producing to hunt for these. (See DeStefano, 1972.)

Beyond the stage of concrete operations, there is, according to Piaget, one more stage, formal operations. Ultimately, instruction that strives to stimulate the growth of achievement is aimed at helping children to reach the mental modes of operating in this formal stage. However, since adolescence is not within the scope of this book, the formal stage is omitted in this discussion. (See Lundsteen, in press, a).

## What Are Six Areas that Demand Special Attention?

The next section discusses six areas in which the child's special developmental patterns affect methods of teaching. These areas are labeled in the following way: (1) gradualness of growth; (2) modes of thought; (3) cognitive motivation; (4) listening (including questioning and an interpersonal, humanistic view of teaching); (5) readiness; and (6) beginning reading.

Appreciating the slow process of intellectual development

### Taking into account the gradualness of growth.

Understanding comes s-l-o-w-l-y for children. Just as it may take an adult a long time to arrive at a logical conclusion about economic policy or the underlying nature of apparent social ills, a child's knowing of his world builds gradually, layer upon layer. Each vital step in the intellectual structure lays the foundation for those to follow. Teachers become patient when they realize that time is needed for children to grasp such abstract learnings as multiple classification concepts, time concepts, rules and codes of ethics, reading *well,* and being *well read.* We do not grow frogs more quickly by cutting off the tails of tadpoles. To use another analogy, attempts to grow a reader quickly with the supposed fast-growth fertilizer of more and more phonics instruction in beginning reading contributes more harm than good to long-term development. Do such ideas about the need for gradualness keep a child on one level and hold him back? No. Piaget's work suggests to teachers that helping a child to gain a solid foundation, to master a level, is the best preparation for moving a child forward securely.

Ways children "know"

The child's modes of thought. Studying the developmental work on intelligence by Piaget and others helps educators to understand an idea closely related to "gradualness of growth." The thinking of the child is not just miniature adult thinking in a lesser quantity; it is qualitatively different. Children base their early perceptions on their subjective, egocentric view of their surroundings. Gradually, they separate their ideas from the here-and-now and engage in more and more abstract thought. Modes of thought change both during childhood and between childhood and adulthood. Children may need to handle "knowing" first by actions (or in a muscular manipulative way) with real objects before they can handle knowing through pictures, and finally handle knowing through symbols (such as abstract talk and print). Just as the tadpole differs from the frog and the caterpillar from the butterfly, the child's ways of knowing differ from the adult's ways of knowing. Realizing this should help educators to resist presenting a child with watered-down adult language during which the following may occur: a concept is merely told, a label simply given, an artificial demonstration (erroneously called "an experiment") set up and then accompanied by a desperate fishing for certain words and "right" answers.[20]

There are other examples. Knowing about ways children "know" prepares a teacher when material with simile and metaphor confronts them. For example, to the line "My love is like a red, red rose" the child may respond concretely (or take it literally), saying, "It means she pricks you?" Or the teacher might say, "Let's suppose that ice is hot." "But ice is cold!" protests the concrete-minded child who has difficulty in reasoning from contrary propositions.

Elkind (1973) gives the example of the young child who asked his teacher, "What is the opposite of time?" Rather than launching into an abstract theory, the teacher wisely turned the question back to the child to probe the structure of his thought: "What do you think, or what do you mean?" It seemed that the family at home had been unusually pressed and had had few moments for the child. In this case the opposite of *time* was *no time*.

Piaget's scheme not only as a description but as a framework for evaluation of curriculum materials

Piaget's work helps teachers to be alert to a child's questions as reflecting the kind of structure he or she is imposing on material at that time. When teachers understand the children's structure and their ways of thinking, it makes it easier for them to offer instruction in a way

[20] See Lundsteen (in press, b) for a comparison of language acquisition and beginning reading instruction.

that makes the most sense to the individual child from his or her point of view. Thus Piaget's scheme provides not only a description but an analytical tool for deciding whether or not material matches the child's stage of development and the way of knowing.

As a negative example, there are some language arts textbooks for elementary-school children that contain a great deal of unproductive "cerebrating" and symbol using with respect to language. Such texts require an inordinate amount of term learning and language analyzing rather than getting children actively into language production. Thinking about child thought developmentally prevents such error.

Alternatively, assume that educators accept Piaget's theory that children get knowledge through interaction with things and with the relations existing among them. Then a large part of the preschool and elementary-school day would be given for free choice of activity with educational equipment in a carefully prepared environment in order to stimulate use of both language and thought. In this view, children's dictation, oral and written composition and their special literature, linked with threads of creative problem-solving, are the important elements of the language arts program. Textbooks serve as reference materials.

**Cognitive motivation from equilibrium seeking.** Following closely upon the first two ideas (gradualness of growth and the child's modes of thought) comes the Piagetian concept of cognitive motivation. Instead of merely "being told" abstract facts, children need to be caught up in an active search for solutions that they feel impelled to investigate themselves (creative problem-solving). Otherwise, learning may be superficial. The dissonance of an inadequate grammar (or reading ability) for communicative effectiveness (or some other unexplained event in the environment) may be all that children need to motivate them to higher levels of attainment. They are impelled to regain their own balance or *equilibrium*. In other words children actively seeking stimulation get their reward when they restore their sense of balance by using their concepts and structures of concepts to analyze and categorize problems creatively.

**Intrinsic, cognitive self-motivation**

According to Piaget, for example, children at the age of about five or six show a spontaneous, intrinsic interest in learning about numbers. They do this because quantitative thinking is an ability that emerges and begins to mature at about this time. Children count passing headlights, buttons, steps—they look for all sorts of number experiences. Perhaps this is partly why they like old tales with numbers, such as *The Three Bears,* which contains gradations of hardness, size, heat, and softness. Children actively seek out the stimuli that will help them to build the intellectual abilities they are developing at that time. Of course this intrinsic interest rises and wanes. It can be squelched and may wither and die. When a skill is no longer a felt challenge or a problem, when they have mastered it, children play with it. Then they tire of it in its present form, wanting to go on to something more challenging (Elkind, 1973).

Teacher as listener

**Listening.** "Listening" ideas deal both with (1) the teacher listening to the child and (2) the child, in turn, listening to others.

Teachers who listen for the evidence of stages can sharpen their diagnosis of a child's language and level of concept attainment. A teacher can better understand children's words in light of the experiences that have led them to a certain stage in a certain area of learning. The teacher listens not only to the sound, vocabulary, and syntax of the child but to what *meaning* he/she is trying to convey. When the teacher listens, the child finds new pleasures in language. This is especially true in the case of children from homes where people do not listen to them. Being listened to means that what they say is important to someone. Therefore *they* are important to someone.

When the teacher listens, the effect can be far-reaching beyond mere diagnostic usefulness. Being listened to not only upgrades children in their own eyes, but also tends to cause them to upgrade their spoken utterances. When their speaking takes on new significance, so will their listening. They will be more likely to think what the other person has to say is important; they will then be willing to listen—even to a teacher's directions. And, when the child begins to listen to the adult, then the adult can become a useful language model.

How to converse with children

To move to a more interpersonal dimension of teacher listening, one question to ask is: "How does an adult converse with children?" This way: avoid starting with some of the trite, blanket remarks and questions that adults usually make to children. You might start with questions about the child's favorite holiday. "What is it all about for you?" "Can you tell me more about it?" "How is it different from your birthday?" "Why is that?" In other words, use questions that stimulate the child to elaborate his experience and that are open-ended. Avoid focusing on right or wrong answers because the child will then be more concerned with *them* than with communicating. While you respectfully accept all answers and comments, avoid judging children's responses by adult standards. Try to understand the role of the child and do as much analysis and individualizing as you would with an adult. Show interest in children as people because they are much like adults in their feelings. Children will know that you like and respect them, even if they have a different (not deficient) way of knowing. This difference is not something to be eradicated but to be understood and appreciated. (For more on the process of role-taking and listening, see Chapters 2 and 11.)

Piagetian interpersonal view of teaching

What can the teacher, as a person, get out of Piagetian theory? From this view, teaching is an interpersonal process, a part of human living, growing, thinking, and communicating. The process is not represented by the teacher doing all the talking, filling up the child, who is doing all the listening. It is a relation of give-and-take between teacher and pupil, both of whom are interested in the teaching–learning process and in thinking about challenges. Without this interpersonal ingredient, it matters little what else the school has, how modern the facilities, how new the materials, how behavioral the objectives. The teacher is a person and the child is a person.

Part of the personal growth and change for a teacher comes from the interaction with children as he comes to know the pain, joy, failure, success, and values that his children wonder about. In this process the teacher is still actively discovering himself and his world—just as the child is doing. That is, the same developmental philosophy applies to the teacher; Piaget teaches him about himself. This Piagetian way of thinking about children is reflected in each of the teacher's acts. He continually recalls that children are to be respected, to be understood, to be learned from. It is not so much what teachers do *to* children as what they *are* to children. *Teach humanistically* is the message.

Child as listener

Piaget's message for the *child listener* is to guard against egocentric thought while trying to understand explanations, insofar as the child's developmental stage allows this. Awareness that first interpretations of what is being said may not be what the speaker has in mind keeps the listener open to alternative interpretations and away from jumping to conclusions. This ability typically is relatively undeveloped in young children. Absence of this awareness has been noted even in situations with high attention and response pull, where a child is trying to teach a new game to another child (Dittman, 1972). Young children tend to talk *at* another rather than *with* another. (This "shoe" may fit some adults.)

Adult assistance

The implication for adult assistance is that a teacher who explains well is likely to anticipate what the child's various interpretations might be. While judging from the child's background, such a teacher might say, "You may be thinking I mean this, but if you notice this you can see I mean. . . ." When this kind of behavior is modeled, the child may imitate it and become a less egocentric listener himself.

At the same time that these awarenesses of interactive listening are being encouraged, the teacher can see to it that there is *interesting* listening material. Children will listen attentively to a fast-moving story, such as Skorpen's *We Were Tired of Living in a House*.[21] This is a repetitive type of story (encouraging children's language-prediction abilities) about a family of children who decide to run away to find a new place to live. Since each place they find turns out to be not quite the same as

[21] Skorpen, *We Were Tired of Living in a House* (New York: Coward-McCann, 1969). Primary level.

home, they keep moving. Eventually they return to the best place—home.[22]

Teachers can apply listening "attention stretchers" of accompanying enactive movement, picturing, and egocentric purpose-setting. For example, one teacher found a way to stretch the attentive listening of young children to stories (joyfully and enthusiastically) beyond belief. The teacher allowed the children to place themselves before a long strip of butcher paper spread on the floor, and to (enactively) paint their impressions of the tales.

Another teacher found the addition of setting an egocentric purpose helpful, such as in the following example. The teacher was about to read a story, R. Lawson's *Rabbit Hill,* judged to be challenging listening material for young children. She told them that the author would like to know if this story was suited to each of them. If so, or if no, they would each have a chance to tell the author about it through the teacher. Later each child was allowed to dictate his reaction, which was forwarded to the author. The listening attention span amazed the teacher. The idea is to promote the child's listening by relating the task to his developmental stage and to his ways of knowing.

**General readiness concepts in teaching**

Readiness. The teacher's awareness of Piaget's stages is related to the "readiness" concept prominent in educational methodology. To Piaget, readiness is not just a matter of simply sitting there and letting the world's verbal ocean imprint itself on you with truth. Piaget does not believe that the acquisition of thought structures, such as conservation, come with straight maturation. But he feels that the child must go out, interact aggressively, and eventually assimilate and accommodate insights himself. Obviously, use of stages as readiness criteria for teaching certain concepts does not mean you can not learn mathematics if you are not good at skipping rope. But it may refer to the idea that reading is easier if visual and auditory motor skills are normally developed.

The behaviorist accusation, however, that passive acceptance of stages may mean hiding in safety or being lazy is worth considering. A behaviorist would say that you do not have to sit around and wring your hands because the child is not "ready." If it is important, you find the critical stimuli designed to produce the appropriate response, and the problem is solved. The idea is to build up intellectual development by breaking down a task into a hierarchy of smaller and smaller elements. Then you teach them, building up to a complex skill. (See Gagné, 1970.)

[22] See Chapter 5, on children's literature, for other read-aloud ideas for older children; also, *Ideas into Practice.* See Huck & Kuhn (1968) for books of appropriate age level and other book selection aids. Another excellent source is Root's *Adventuring with Books* (1973), which contains 2400 annotated titles, from prekindergarten to grade eight level.

A policy to use when in doubt as to whether or not a child is ready to learn is to try teaching and find out—as the teacher in the earlier example did with the Newbery Medal–winning *Rabbit Hill* as first-grade listening material. Any other policy may mean, "I teach when it is easy for *me* to teach it, or when somebody else has really already taught the child someplace else." In other words, the idea is to keep these stages related to readiness concepts in mind, but not to use them as excuses for no action or to say "It's all up to the child and his biological mechanisms." Taking the initiative is especially warranted in the case of children against whom a different culture (or a higher social-status group) has already discriminated. (The teacher's commitment to responsibility here includes taking care not to destroy children's images of a home language that they have heard and revered.) [23]

**Readiness and development of moral values**

Consider another aspect of the Piagetian implications for readiness. Readiness and then development take place when discrepancies arise between the child's current stage and his/her perception of reality. Take stages of moral development. A child may have been operating in a premoral or obedience-and-punishment orientation with egocentric deference to superior power, or at the conventional role-conformity level of the good-boy stereotype. If this child moves to a peer group in an elementary-school class run as a participatory democracy with purposes of rules explained, then he experiences discrepancy with his earlier view of social and moral values. When the child tests and tries to make sense out of these higher-order values, readiness occurs and development takes place.

It is necessary developmentally, however, for the child to have assimilated his earlier moral system before he is ready to go beyond it and to question it. According to Piaget, only by applying a given level of reasoning across a wide variety of experiences does the child begin to see its limitations. Only when children see its limitations and the things that a certain level of reasoning cannot explain, will they ever go on to reject it and adopt a more advanced way of thinking (See Gilligan, 1974.)

---

Reading. Besides these general ideas of readiness, developmental linguistic research has something to say about reading readiness, reading, and the material that accompanies this school instructional area.

[23] See *Ideas into Practice* for further discussion of the readiness concept and teaching strategy. (See Maccoby & Zillner, 1971.)

Reading as requiring concrete operational thought

From a Piagetian standpoint many young children will naturally have trouble with learning to read because a high level of concrete operational thought is needed for the logical, conceptual aspects. These necessary mental processes include seriation, classification, and conservation (hinging on transformation). An earlier example of these processes dealt with the child thinking a clay ball had changed, becoming more or less, just because its form was changed. Similarly, in reading, children must meet transformations such as a capital *D,* a lower-case *d,* a cursive *d.* If the child had trouble grasping the idea that a bead could be white and wooden at the same time, he may have trouble understanding that the letter *t* in *to* is the same letter *t* as in *the.* He may still be having trouble distinguishing the part from the whole, e.g., reading *to* for *toward.* It is the conceptual difficulties that make the push for earlier and earlier reading questionable. Reading is a complex process from the child's point of view. Adults forget how complex it was to learn. It has elements of logic, and general rules for using syntax, context, and for getting meaning by prediction and hypotheses testing that need to be applied to particular situations. The process may seem like a simple association task to an uninformed adult—matching sounds to letters. But until children have "constructed" this whole reading area, speeded it up to avoid memory overload, and put it outside of themselves, it remains highly complex—simple to adults, complex to a child.

Linguistically appropriate material

In teaching beginning reading (and also in later grades) teachers need to diagnose when the difficulty lies in the child and when the difficulty lies in inappropriate teaching material. First, it is an important day when children realize that reading is a freezing of the oral symbol system and that their task is to process and get *meaning* from large chunks of these frozen paper scratches. Children have an innate sense of what should be "right" or typical in English language. When they meet a strange event in reading such as (1) word order reversed from that of their usual language, or (2) imagery to which they have not been introduced, children who read for meaning become puzzled, regress, and try again. Take this word-order example from a child's reader, which is an un-English sentence representing a "reading trap": Tom swung his bat. Over the fence went the ball. Children may read the sentence in this way: *Tom swung his bat over the fence,* then realize that it does not make good sense and try again. (This attitude—to try again if it doesn't make sense—needs to be a crucial portion of beginning reading programs.)

Child's overgeneralization of his language knowledge to atypical book language as indicating positive growth

The problem is not usually simply that a child fails to know what a period means among those frozen paper scratches. It more probably reflects positively on his strength of knowing what should be "right" in his English language and the typical word order. Children will tend to overgeneralize what they know about typical examples of language concepts and exclude less-typical examples from their classifications, even on into the elementary-school years. "Hey, this error may well be developmental, or a result of a sentence that is not typical in English," is a more positive teacher approach to diagnosis of children's miscues while reading. Overgeneralizing errors can be evidence of acquired English patterns and represent positive learning in the right direction rather than being abhorred.

Communicatively appropriate material

Another problem growing out of the inappropriateness of beginning reading material occurs when there is a load of imagery in book language.[24] Book material for instruction needs to move from what the child knows to what he is less familiar with. Such a perspective has little room for the *Mat is a fat rat and he sat on a thin tin pin* sort of language instead of an author's meaningful natural communication. In any case, awareness of reading traps in material and the illumination received from developmental linguistic study create greater patience and understanding in teachers, who then demand appropriate material, a positive attitude toward seeking meaning, and a tolerance of oral reading error (or miscue) that indicates children's willingness to risk, and to predict while using their language backgrounds (Burke, 1975; Goodman, 1975; Lundsteen, in press, b; Smith, 1973).[25] To be right a lot of the time, you need to be willing to risk being wrong some of the time.

Learning to read can develop in a natural progression. It begins with listening, moves on to speaking, then to the written representation of the child's own dictated, home-rooted language, and finally it culminates in the wide reading from the vast treasury of material written by other authors. In this way children come to know the wholeness of language as a changing, growing extension of their humanness.

## SUMMARY AND CONCLUSIONS

As teachers examine the writings on the development of language and thought, they may feel resentment that there are more questions than answers—and that the answers are far from definite. "Wouldn't it be nice if we could have total agreement and be done with it!" But that is one "stage" unlikely to occur as the inquiring minds of investigators strike out in new directions. They do not necessarily repudiate everything done earlier, but they combine, supplement, and transform. At present, investigators who are linguists seem to agree on these points:

### *Areas About Which Most Linguists Presently Agree*

Current agreements among most linguists

1. In general, children have a solid underlying competence in their language by age six. (They have language; it is the teacher's job to help

[24] An example likely to be misread is the sentence, *Round is a kitten,* in which *as* will usually be substituted for *is,* i.e., *Round as a kitten. A kitten is round* would be a more typical construction (Shuy, 1973).

[25] Unfortunately, space constraints in this book allow only a scratching of the surface of developmental implications for reading instruction.

them use it.) However, not all children have learned their basic language structures *equally well.* There is wide individual variation, which some linguists ignore.

2. The language acquisition process is not haphazard with enormous variation from child to child. Instead, there is a natural ordering of phonological distinctions made and of various sequential child grammars acquired. A well-ordered, structural grammar could be written for children at almost any age—and most adults would flunk a test on it (Shuy, 1973).[26]
3. Children tend to hypercorrect, to overgeneralize their language principles (*I cutted my finger*)—even during elementary-school years. Such developmental errors represent a high, creative level of cognitive functioning (Shuy, 1973).
4. Each dialect is more or less equally complex (overall) for the language it represents. Since there is a "humanness" of all languages, it is not a social question to the linguistic scientist. In other words, there are no inferior, second-class languages or dialects (Owens, 1973). (The concept of language *difference* is replacing the concept of language *deficiency.* For example, Black English is not a deficient system. There is a magnificent language variability in our pluralistic society.)
5. Oral talk and written language differ. But an oral language base is a crucial "first freezing" of the verbal symbol system before a child is optimally introduced to reading which is the "second freezing" of our symbol system (Shuy, 1973).
6. The public language changes over the centuries, and over the years of our life spans.

**Conclusion about common ground in language and thought development**

Is there any consensus about the common ground between the development of language and the development of thought? It seems that the outstanding common clue lies in the child's ability to (1) find the stable or the predictable as distinguished from the changing and the irrelevant; (2) string together causes, effects, and relationships; (3) plan or decide (through a sense of the future) and make inferences (through a sense of the past). Within the child there is a *common process of hypothesis testing for both language and thought* (John & Moskovitz,

[26] Although language is learned in sequences, there are wide individual differences in time—a normal range of variation. That means a child who fails to produce a two-word sentence until he is twenty-four months old is no more likely to be retarded than the twelve-month-old conversationalist is likely to be a prodigy.

ON THE UNDERLYING EXPERTISE OF CHILDREN

1970). And hypothesis testing is a part of the total *creative-problem-solving process.* It is this common process that educators can make it their business to promote, thus giving assistance to language and to thought at the same time.

### What Conclusions Can We Make About Development of Creative Problem-Solving?

**Conclusions about development of creative problem-solving**

It is not possible to detail typical milestones throughout the range of child development for creative problem-solving. But even at the beginning of children's long push toward knowledge, they have some competence in comprehending, imaginative kinds of thinking, and hypothesis making. Such behavior is cued in words such as *because, although, however,* and expressions such as *This is true, therefore* and *If this were true, then this.* Children are testing such ideas long before the ages suggested for Piaget's stages of concrete and formal operations. This kind of hypothetical thinking may begin quite early, especially in regard to behavior with people—social behavior. Problem-solving development related to human relations or "people problems" may have a different developmental schedule than does Piaget's logical–mathematical problem solving.

It may be more crucial to assist and cultivate the early development of "people-problem solving." Verbal instruction can channel the direction of problem-solving activity (e.g., help the learner to formulate his goal, select hypotheses, uncover principles, and make plans). To be effective general problem solvers, children must somehow acquire masses of structurally organized knowledge that they can use in new, complex situations. Solutions come to a prepared mind. Teachers coming to the classroom well prepared in the developmental bases of the language arts program can be more helpful in the promotion of children's language and thought.

## ADDITIONAL ACTIVITIES FOR CHILDREN

**Dictation from junior authors**

1.2. Dictation from Junior Authors. Take down children's words and phrases and share them. Examples: "Crunchy, crunchy celery," said Dennis. "Now I take a white bead; now I take a red bead; now I take a white bead; now I take a blue bead," said Nancy. This recording reinforces their language mastery, acknowledges their accomplishment, and builds readiness for concepts of reading and writing.

1.3 Through the Looking Glass. Hang a drop sheet of heavy, clear plastic. With an overhead projector, put a child's drawing (and captions or a brief story he or she has dictated or written) on the wall. Let the child walk behind the drop sheet (or "looking glass") into his or her own picture and tell or read and comment on the story.

1.4. Art and Language. Try combining young children's art and language products for display. Have a child make a foldout storybook, with story and pictures on alternating pages. Or children could make cutout self-portraits of themselves holding a sign. On the sign they could write a story about themselves. Children can make animals out of yarn pasted on paper and write a free-verse poem about the animal.

1.5. Problem Compo. Invite children to name as many ways as possible to make friends. Pick one way and develop it into an oral story; then dictate, tape, or write it. (See *Ideas into Practice.*)

1.6. Thinkbox Hideaway. Cover the inside of a large packing box with colorful terry cloth. Let the class decorate the outside. Invite a child to crawl in through a small, low opening in order to think, read, dictate into a portable tape recorder, or write. Interview the child afterward.

1.7. Polly Parrot. In order to expand children's language options so that they can switch to another dialect when they wish, the following activity is suggested. Let the children listen to and enjoy the following poem about a parrot (especially relevant when social studies is touching on the Hawaiian Islands). Let children prepare verses for choral reading. Then show them a puppet of Polly Parrot. (It can be made out of a bright green sock with paint or felt or paper claws, beak, eyes and a few bright feathers.)

Tell the children that Polly got tired of being fussed at for repeating things she should not. She decided that she is going to say things in a certain way and then ask humans to repeat after *her,* precisely as she said it, and be very particular about it. Then have children practice portions of Polly's poem that illustrate certain language features that would expand the children's dialect to include other options.[27]

[27] Activity based on research by Strickland et al. (1973).

*The Talkative Parrot*

I'm glad I was born a parrot,
  Called Polly just for short,
And that I live where southern breeze
  Blows gently like it ought.

And that outside my window,
  The garden, sea, and palms
Are joined beyond the mountain tops
  Where sun sinks bright and calm,

And that folks dress in gay muu-muus
  With flowers in their hair
And fragrant leis around their necks
  With laughter in the air.

I'm glad that when the family dines
  They eat out where I am
And give me bites of what they have
  Though it is Luau ham.

Now when their friends come in to dine,
  They let me share their feast.
I tell them everything I know.
  Sometimes I am a beast.

At least that's what my family says
  When company has gone.
They should not say words I repeat,
  Especially, if wrong.

For example, the first line of the poem affords practice on use of the linking verb, as does the first line in the last verse. The last line in the second verse and the first line in the last verse afford practice in pronouncing verb endings. The first line in the third verse, the third line in the fourth verse, the first line in the fifth verse, and the third line in the last verse afford practice in pronouncing the ending of plural words.

The teacher can use other material from time to time, such as the lines from the story *The Three Pigs* ("He huffed and he puffed") or the lines from the story, *Three Billy Goats Gruff*. The following lines would give practice on use of linking verbs.

Who's that tramping over my bridge?
Who's that tramping over my bridge?
It's the Little Billy Goat Gruff.
I'm coming to gobble you up.

Take care not to use such activities in a way that limits language that comes from the children; such repetitive practice is intended as a very small part of the child's total language program. Include other activity such as free discussion with open-ended questions (e.g., "I wonder if . . ." "What did you feel . . ." "What did you think . . ."); dramatic play; and children's storytelling. (For example, expand the poem or other material to other times and places adding new events and characters. Suppose, for example, that Polly is mistakenly taken to the dentist's office to have a tooth filled, shows up at school for lunch, or flies to the topmost shelf of a supermarket).

1.8. Concept Development Story Collections.[28] Round cutout circles of tag board (held together with rings or yarn) contain children's stories and pictures illustrating their ideas of a concept. These are shared so that a child's concept is added to by others. Here's an example:

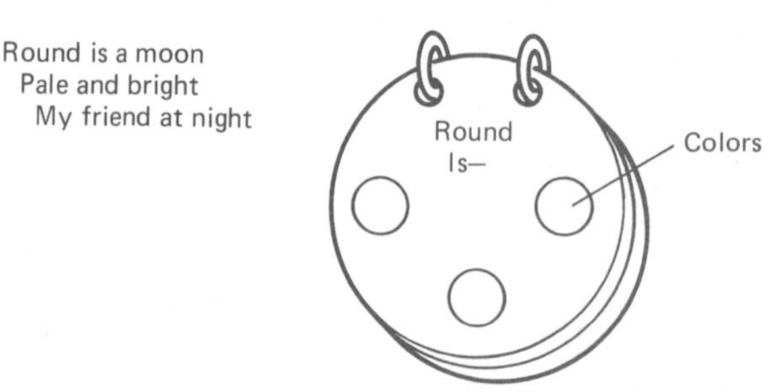


[28] There are more developmental activities in the companion guide, *Ideas into Practice,* and in chapters to follow.

## If You Want to Learn More

BROWN, R. *A First Language: The Early Stages.* Cambridge, Mass.: Harvard University Press, 1973.

BURKE, C. In W. D. Page (Ed.), *Observing the Reading Process: Insights and Interpretations.* Urbana, Ill.: NCTE/National Conference on Research in English (NCRE)/ERIC, 1975.

CAZDEN, C. B. *Child Language and Education.* New York: Holt, Rinehart and Winston, 1972.

CHOMSKY, C. S. *The Acquisition of Syntax in Children from 5 to 10.* Cambridge, Mass.: M.I.T. Press, 1969.

Studies the presence, or absence, of four syntactic structures in the language of children from five to ten years of age. Examples of the structures tested are (1) *John is easy to see,* in which the difficulty is presumed to be the subject of the sentence and the subject of *see;* (2) *John promised Bill to go,* in which the problem is the subject of *go;* (3) *John asked Bill what to do,* in which the problem is the subject of *do;* and (4) *He knew that John was going to win the race,* in which the problem is the referrent of *he.* Structure 3 is still imperfectly learned by some child even at age ten, and structure 4 is acquired fairly uniformly at about age six (p. 121).

CHUKOVSKY, K. I. *From Two to Five.* Berkeley: University of California Press, 1963.

COOPER, C. R. An Outline for Writing Sentence-Combining Problems. *English Journal,* 1973, *62* (1), 96-102.

DESTEFANO, J. S. Register: Social Variation in Language Use. *The Elementary School Journal,* 1972, *72* (4), 189-94.

DITTMAN, A. T. Developmental Factors in Conversational Behavior. *The Journal of Communication,* 1972, *22,* 404-23.

DUCKWORTH, E. Piaget Takes a Teacher's Look with Eleanor Duckworth. *Learning: The Magazine for Creative Teaching,* 1973, *2* (2), 22-27.

Focuses on the problems and needs of the elementary-school teacher. The book reviews in this issue include three on books about Piaget. These are of particular interest to classroom teachers. Highly recommended.

ELKIND, D. Quantity Conceptions in Junior and Senior High School Students. *Child Development,* 1961, *32,* 551-60.

ELKIND, D. *Piaget in Childhood Education.* Listener In-Service Cassette Library. Hollywood, Calif.: Listener Corporation, 1973.

ERIKSON, E. H. *Childhood and Society.* New York: Norton, 1950.

FLAVEL, J. H. *The Developmental Psychology of Jean Piaget.* New York: Van Nostrand Reinhold, 1963.

GAGNÉ, R. M. *The Conditions of Learning.* New York: Holt, 1970.

GILLIGAN, C. Fostering Moral Development in Children. *EDC News,* 1974 (4), 7-10. (Educational Development Center, Newton, Mass., 02160.)

Gives observations relating Piagetian developmental theory to Kohlberg's theory of moral development with his three levels and six stages. The hierarchy of stages moves from concrete to abstract, from narrow egotistic centering to universal awareness. The most readable and applicable article I have seen to date, with implications for language use in the classroom.

GOODMAN, Y. In W. D. Page (Ed.), *Observing the Reading Process: Insights and Interpretations.* Urbana, Ill.: NCTE/NCRE/ERIC, 1975.

HAVIGHURST, R. J. *Developmental Tasks & Education.* (3rd ed.) New York: David McKay, 1972.

HEISEY, M. J. An Investigation of Self-Perceptions of Oral Communication Skills Among Fifth-Grade School Children. *Dissertation Abstracts,* 1969, *29,* 4326A.

Students who had a high estimate of their own ability to communicate orally with others tended to be rated higher in adjustment by teachers than students with low estimates of their oral communication skill.

HODGES, R. E. Language Development in the School Years. In A. H. Marckwardt (Ed.), *Linguistics in School Programs.* 69th Yearbook of the National Society for the Study of Education (NSSE), Part II. Chicago: University of Chicago Press, 1970. Pp. 215-28.

Gives an excellent, concise, linguistically oriented review of available research.

HUCK, C. S., and KUHN, D. Y. *Children's Literature in the Elementary School.* New York: Holt, Rinehart and Winston, 1968.

JOHN, V. P., and MOSKOVITZ, S. Language Acquisition and Development in Early Childhood. In A. H. Marckwardt (Ed.), *Linguistics in School Programs.* The 69th Yearbook of the NSSE, Part II. Chicago: University of Chicago Press, 1970.

KNUDSON, R. L. The Effects of Pupil-Prepared Videotaped Dramas Upon the Language Development of Selected Rural Children. *Research in the Teaching of English,* 1971, *5* (1), 60.

Found significant growth in four language characteristics and gains in IQ scores.

LABOV, W. Some Sources of Reading Problems form Negro Speakers of Non-Standard English. In A. Frazier (Ed.), *New Directions in Elementary English.* Urbana, Ill.: NCTE, 1967. Pp. 140-67. (Reprinted in J. C. Baratz and R. W. Shuy, *Teaching Black Children to Read.* Washington, D.C.: Center for Applied Linguistics, 1969. Pp. 29-67.)

LABOV, W. The Logic of Nonstandard English. In J. E. Alatis (Ed.), *Monograph Series on Language and Linguistics: Report of the Twentieth Annual Round Table Meeting on Linguistics and Language Studies.* Washington, D.C.: Georgetown University Press, 1970. Pp. 1-43.

LOBAN, W. *The Language of Elementary School Children.* Urbana, Ill.: NCTE, 1963.

This first part of a longitudinal study (carried out through high school) collected and analyzed language used by over 300 children, following them from kindergarten to grade six.

LUNDSTEEN, S. W. Levels of Meaning in Reading. *The Reading Teacher,* 1974, *28,* 268-72.

LUNDSTEEN, S. W. *On Development of Language and Thought,* in press. (a).

LUNDSTEEN, S. W. On Developmental Relations Between Language, Learning, and Reading, *Elementary School Journal,* in press. (b).

LUNDSTEEN, S. W. *On Persuasive Use of Language,* in preparation. (c).

MACCOBY, E. E., and ZILLNER, M. *Experiments in Primary Education: Aspects of Project Follow-Through.* New York: Harcourt Brace Jovanovich, 1971.

MARKLE, S. M., and TIEMANN, P. W. *Really Understanding Concepts.* (3rd ed.) Champaign, Ill.: Stipes, 1970.

MELLON, J. C. *Transformational Sentence Combining: A Method for Enhancing the Development of Syntactic Fluency in English Composition.* Urbana, Ill.: NCTE, 1969.

This study has been replicated by Frank O'Hare, of Florida State University, who worked with seventh- and eighth-grade students. Results suggest 2–4 years growth for sentence combining in 1 year's time.

MENYUK, P. *Sentences Children Use.* Cambridge, Mass.: M.I.T. Press, 1969.

MOFFETT, J. *Interaction, Language Arts and Reading Program, K–12.* Boston: Houghton Mifflin, 1973.

O'DONNELL, R. C., GRIFFIN, W. J., and NORRIS, R. C. *Syntax of Kindergarten and Elementary School Children: A Transformational Analysis.* NCTE Research Report No. 8. Urbana, Ill.: NCTE, 1967.

O'HARE, F. *Sentence Combining: Improving Student Writing Without Formal Grammar Instruction.* Urbana, Ill.: NCTE, 1973.

PAGE, W. D. (Ed.) *Help for the Reading Teacher: New Directions in Research.* Urbana, Ill.: NCTE/NCRE/ERIC, 1975.

PIAGET, J. *Judgment and Reasoning in the Child.* New York: Harcourt, 1928.

Suggests that even when children use conjunctions grammatically, their logic is far from clear; e.g., *The man fell from his bicycle because he broke his arm* (from a seven-year-old); *I walked for 1 more hour even though I like walking* (from a six-year-old).

PIAGET, J. *The Theory of Stages in Cognitive Development.* An address presented at the CTB/McGraw-Hill Invitational Conference on Ordinal Scales of Cognitive Development, Monterey, Calif., February 1969.

A clear exposition by Piaget himself.

ROOT, S. L. *Adventuring With Books.* Urbana, Ill.: NCTE, 1973.

RUSSELL, D. H. *Children's Thinking.* Boston: Ginn, 1956.

A classic.

SHUY, R. What Teachers Should Know About the Language of Children. Paper presented at the Fifth Annual National Conference on the Language Arts in the Elementary School, Chicago, 1973.

SINCLAIR-DE-ZWART, H. Developmental Psycholinguistics. In D. Elkind and J. H. Flavel (Eds.), *Studies in Cognitive Development: Essays in Honor of Jean Piaget.* New York: Oxford University Press, 1969.

Found that (1) children able to conserve used comparative language (*The boy has more than the girl*) while children without conservation used absolute terms instead (*The boy has a lot; the girl has a little*); (2) the conservation of discrete units (marbles) was acquired before that of continuous quantities (plasticine); (3) verbal training leads children without conservation to direct their attention to pertinent aspects of the problem (covariance of the attributes), but does *not* necessarily bring about the ability to conserve; and (4) language is not the source of logic, but is structured by logic. A Piagetian theorist studies language as part of the total cognitive activity of the child, not as isolated language.

SMITH, F. Twelve Easy Ways to Make Learning to Read Difficult. In F. Smith (Ed.), *Psycholinguistics and Reading.* New York: Holt, Rinehart and Winston, 1973.

STRASSER, B. B. Teach for Inquiry: Any Day, Any Level, Any Subject. *Instructor,* 1973, *82* (7), 86.

STRICKLAND, D. S. A Program for Linguistically Different Black Childern. *Research in the Teaching of English,* 1973, *7* (1), 79-86.

Suggests a special literature program in the kindergarten emphasizing related oral language activities to bring about more ease in using standard English, not as a substitute for but as a supplement to the child's own dialect. Also see the article by B. E. Cullinan, A. M. Jaggar, and D. Strickland, Language Expansion for Black Children in the Primary Grades: A Research Report, in *Young Children.* Washington, D.C.: National Association for Education of Young Children, in press.

SULLIVAN, H. S. *The Interpersonal Theory of Psychiatry.* New York: Norton, 1953.

TEMPLIN, M. C. *Certain Language Skills in Children: Their Development and Interrelationships.* Minneapolis: University of Minnesota Press, 1957.

THOMAS, O. Language, Confidence, Respect, and Survival. Paper delivered at the annual convention of the California Association of Teachers of English, San Diego, February 1973.

WINKELJOHANN, R. SR. Jean's Influence on Dick and Jane. *Elementary English,* 1974, *51,* 870-73; 877.

Presents some Piagetian concepts and their relationship to teaching reading. Outlines Jean Piaget's four stages of development and mentions recent related research projects.

# Chapter 2 A Base in Listening

This chapter tells why the teaching of listening skills is one of the most important things you'll ever do in the classroom. It shows how listening forms a base for speaking, writing, and reading. It shows in detail how listening is related to these other communication skills. One topic suggests some self-analysis. Specifically, the chapter deals with the question, "Does instruction in listening improve reading?" It offers suggestions, games, and activities for helping the child who is linguistically and culturally different.

### Listening as hard work

The Peanuts cartoon refers to some of the problems mentioned in the Prologue. It also foreshadows some of the difficulties of listening effectively. In defense of Charlie Brown in the comic strip, it is extremely difficult to really listen all the time. The sustained act of listening can be an exhausting, demanding business. The brain waves, heartbeat, and temperature of the active listener accelerate. Fatigue sets in after a time even under the best conditions. Sometimes not listening is a necessary protection from an incessant, relentless avalanche of useless information. (If we reacted to every input, they would need to lock us up.)

It is no wonder that children listen as if our message goes in one ear and out the same ear. "Tuning out" for a child is often a perfectly legitimate reaction. But we teachers can usually make listening worth the hard work when we tie it, meaningfully, to a creative challenge for the child

As a teacher of listening, what will be *your* creative challenge?

### Objectives

- Getting children to listen to you? (Or getting yourself to listen to them?)
- Getting your directions followed? (Or helping children get a "direction" to follow themselves?)
- Knowing what the child's role is in listening? (Or knowing your role as a listener?)
- Conducting one listening activity? (Or being in command of a whole framework where isolated activity becomes meaningful?)
- Having children use reading to improve listening? (Or using improved listening to promote reading comprehension?)

## WHY PUT LISTENING FIRST?

Listening has been called the primary language skill. Why? One reason is that listening is the first language skill to appear. Chronologically speaking, children listen before they speak, speak before they read, and read before they write. As more evidence of listening's primacy, studies of physical disabilities (such as hearing disorders and brain damage) have pointed to an interdependence among these language skills, with listening in the forefront (Brown, 1954).

**Listening passed over**

Oral language has long been considered as the base for the other language arts, even for proficiency in spelling. However, surveys show that the importance of oral language is not generally reflected in language arts materials for children or for teachers. (One survey showed that less than 1 percent of the content of texts for children is devoted to lessons on listening—Brown, 1967.) A short section on training for reading readiness, devoted to discrimination between similar sounds, is often the extent of guidance in many textbooks.

Prospective teachers are usually told, somewhere along the line, that "the development of language skills proceeds from listening to speaking, to reading, and to writing—in that order." But then the teacher in the classroom finds only instructional materials that seem to forget all about listening and speaking. This neglect is unwise, not only because listening is the first skill to appear, but also because it may provide the key to unlocking progress in any other area related to language. These related areas include science, history, mathematics—the whole of education.

### How Much Time Is Spent in Listening and in Its Instruction?

Historically, the importance of listening was first demonstrated through studies of the amount of time spent listening both in and out of school. (It might be said that we listen a book a day; speak a book a week; read a book a month; and write a book a year.) To see for yourself the amount of time you spend listening as opposed to speaking, reading, and writing, versus the amount of direct instruction received in each of these areas, ask yourself the following questions:

1. How much time do you spend, on a typical day, writing, reading, speaking, and listening?

The Language Mobile

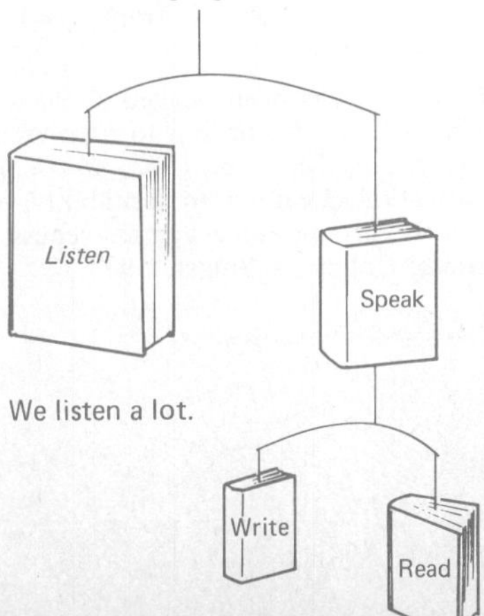


We listen a lot.

**Comparatively speaking, how much do you listen?**

2. How much direct, systematic instruction have you ever had in writing, reading, speaking, and listening?

Much listening—little instruction

When these questions are asked of groups, the usual conclusion is that the amount of time spent in listening is impressive; the amount of time spent in its instruction is not.[1] But the amount of time spent is only one reason for emphasizing listening here, and perhaps one of the least important.

### Noise Pollution: A Danger

Effects of noise pollution

The growing menace of noise pollution is another reason to bring listening to the forefront today. Noise pollution, doubling every 10 years, affects willingness and ability to listen attentively. Not all sound enters the body through the outer ear; the inner ear can receive sound energy by way of bone and tissue conduction. Penetrating the skull, the torso, and the groin, intense sound waves cause far more than the sensation of hearing. To almost every nerve center and organ of the body goes the sound signal transmitted by the brain. Sound can influence the entire physiological, emotional, and psychological response system of the organism.

Implications for the classroom

What effects might the level of noise have on the learning process in the classroom? Disruptive noises influence both the effectiveness and the dignity of teaching. For example, children in the Dalton School of New York calmed considerably with change from the typical noise-box classrooms to new sound-treated ones. Some of the tension leading up to ghetto-school riots may be attributed to interrupted sleep at home due to the high noise level of the inner city. Having no lids and always vulnerable, the ears (similar to the heart) might be said to work 24 hours a day.

Noise and deafness

Noise can also cause deafness. Most people are already a little deaf—pneumatic drills and fire sirens have seen to that. Prolonged exposure to a noise level above 85 decibels (lower than heavy city traffic) can eventually result in loss of hearing for sounds in the range most crucial for understanding human speech.[2] People are beginning to take Thomas

[1] Surveys report more than half the school day is spent by pupils in listening activity (as high as 90% for the academic day of a college student). Children may hear at least 20 times as many oral contributions from classmates as they themselves give. One of the pioneer studies found that the child's chance of getting to speak (instead of listening to the teacher) is about 60 to 1 (Corey, 1940). See Lundsteen (1971) for further references on this topic.

[2] Amplified music, widely listened to by the young, has been pegged at 90 to 105 decibels, with peaks at 130, a dangerously high level. According to a news interview with Dr. David C. Glass (*National Enquirer*, June 18, 1972, *46* (42), 3) exposure to noise lowers tolerance for frustration. Leading to irritability, noise can lower task performance, constrict blood vessels, produce aggressiveness, violent outbursts—even cause murder. (See Glass, Cohen, & Singer, 1973.)

Edison's suggestion seriously—as urban noise continues to grow, the man of the future might be born deaf.

Educators need to be aware that noise can do a great deal of damage. But perhaps people with limited foresight would like to delay until the blood runs out of the ears.

*Educational action*

In short, the impact of noise pollution on education deserves attention. Here is an area needing further research. Results can be disseminated among school people, and through them to children. Educators can accomplish this task in much the same way that curriculum specialists are now working with content on ecology and drugs (Brown, 1970).

Along this line, school people can attend to the safety of the classroom listening center. If a child using earphones increases the volume too much while manipulating the controls, he runs the risk of irreparable hearing loss through damage to the delicate inner ear. Probably it is inadvisable to allow children to touch the volume control for earphone equipment (Bryant, 1970). School administrators and instructors need to be *as aware of the listening environment* as they have been in the past of temperature, light, and ventilation.

## Is There a Need for Systematic Instruction?

*Growth of listening skill not automatic*

An appropriate listening environment free from noise pollution is necessary but not sufficient to ensure skillful listening. The stage has been set for the assertion that growth in both general and critical listening skills is not automatic. If it were, there might be less harm from unconscious assimilations from mass media. Intelligence and age fail to account totally for growth in listening skills. However, education helps (see Duker, 1969; Russell, 1964).

*Resistant prejudice from uncritical listening*

Wait—too late? When it comes to giving instruction in critical listening, if we wait, it may be too late. One early study of children as young as the third-grade level showed how misconceptions gathered from mass-media stereotypes of people of other nationalities appeared to be permanent. In spite of vivid instruction (films, personal contact, discussions), these children still considered Chinese people to be either evil spies or laundry operators. (Klee, 1949).[3] If half of all the mental growth a child will ever achieve typically is completed by the age of about four, it seems unwise to delay instruction in critical listening until college. And on a pragmatic level—being able to separate facts from sales pitch while listening to a commercial can save the child money otherwise unrecoverable.

[3] See also Rosnow (1972) on prejudicial attitudes in children as young as four years old.

To refer to the cartoon at the beginning of this chapter, the aim is to help teachers find the reasons why some children fail to listen. And when children do listen, informed teachers can help them bring considerable skill to bear on that process.

## WHAT IS THE RELATIONSHIP OF LISTENING TO THINKING?

**The role of listening in problem solving**

Suppose you agree that the language arts program is actually a program in thinking. Next, see if you will agree that listening skills are crucial supporting tools for such a program. Agreed, not all problems are solved by using effective listening. But it is doubtful that many are solved without it. In that case, how is listening related to problem solving?

Listening represents a crucial link in the chain of subskills. How can the teacher help children to gain insight into attitudes that hinder them if they are unable to control their conscious listening? For instance, how can students (even college students) learn how to learn about people when their attitudes block their reception?

**Two-way responsibility**

The following anecdote illustrates what active listening is and how it can pay off: A small group of college students conducted a listening experiment in the class of a professor of anthropology who was far from skilled in lecturing. This scholarly speaker rarely lifted his eyes from his lecture notes while speaking in a monotone barely audible beyond the first row. As their experiment, the students decided to see what would happen if they demonstrated keen interest in the lecture by paying attention to every word, reacting with obvious elation, and asking questions before, after, and even during the lecture.

The results of this experiment were astounding. The professor began to look up from his notes, even tried a bit of witticism (with most gratifying results), added new material in light of reaction, and (while still unlikely to ever win the university's Best Teaching Award) was a changed communicator by the quarter's end. As for the students, although they might have felt a little "phony" at first, they became thoroughly caught up in the interaction. They learned more than the outcome of testing a hypothesis: two decided to major in anthropology. All learned the power of active listening. The lesson for the prospective teacher? Listening is not merely a passive absorbing. Taking on a large share of the communication burden is a facet of listening that teachers need to encourage in their children and practice themselves.

**Productive use of leftover thinking space**

Active listening reduces not only to listener attention and body cues shown to the speaker, but also to productive use of the time between the reception of a speaker's message and his/her next words. The amount of this leftover thinking space during communication varies, but generally people can count upon a large amount. What do people do with this leftover time for thought? Do they do any of the following?

- Focus thought by having a conscious purpose for listening?
- Impose organization where needed on scattered, confused communication?
- Frame questions that are on target?
- Try to anticipate the speaker's point?
- Call up attitudes of openness toward the speaker's ideas and employ suspended judgment?
- Summarize?
- Search to clear up hidden meanings?

Or, hindering communication, do they

- Concentrate on faking attention while daydreaming, planning privately, or pursuing their own parallel argument?
- Fail to screen out irrelevant details and distractions?
- Dismiss the material as too boring or difficult? (Is everything interesting from at least some point of view?)
- Wonder why someone else does not take care of distractions in the environment, such as a too-hot classroom?

Use the "pie" diagram for recording self observations. Think of the circle as representing leftover thinking space after you've cut out a wedge for the space taken up by simply hearing. Suppose only one-tenth of the total thinking space is taken up by hearing, leaving nine-tenths of the thinking space open until the next message comes. The speed of thought can far outstrip the speed of speech. Think about what you do to enhance attention and concentration (or hinder it). Add to the circle other intellectual activities that took place during the leftover thinking space. Or check off those items already represented on the circle, if they occurred. More specifically, an individual chart might have phrases entered on it to represent thoughts occurring during

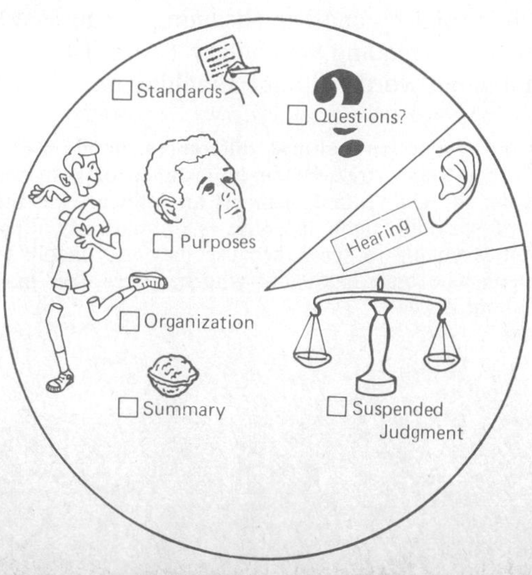


THINKING SPACE
**Only a small fraction of thinking space is used for hearing. What do you do with your left-over thinking space? (Can you add to this chart?)**

the message, such as these: "I have so much to do . . . ," "Will I get into trouble for . . . ?" "That was fun last night . . . !" and so on.

Teachers can use such diagrams to help children assume responsibility for the control of their own attention. Much can be done by simply bringing the idea to the level of consciousness, talking with the children about it, recording it on charts such as the "pie" chart, and providing practice. Guiding the direction of our own thought is one of our finest gifts. Such activity is another illustration of the intertwining of communication and thinking.

## HOW DOES LISTENING RELATE TO THE OTHER LANGUAGE ARTS?

Listening compared with the other language arts

Productive use of leftover thinking space is common to all the language arts skills. Besides the role of two-way responsibility and its relation to thinking, listening plays specific interactive roles with speaking, writing, and reading. Sometimes there is a danger that the language arts become fragmented when instructors fail to integrate them. On the other hand, a neglected skill such as listening needs to be analyzed carefully. Just as *cold* may be better understood by defining *hot,* listening may be better understood and interrelated if compared and contrasted with speaking, writing, and reading.

### How Is Listening Like Speaking?

Listening compared to speaking

Listening is like speaking because both (1) have a common code, (2) draw on the same background, and (3) have (in many cases) a common vocabulary. Both listening and speaking use a code of sound instead of print, and speech used resembles speech consistently heard. It follows that the words in a child's speaking vocabulary are also part of his listening vocabulary. However, a child may be able to use a difficult word in speech or in writing, understand it while listening and reading, but not know it in isolation. An example is the word *confiscate,* used in the classroom context of removing forbidden objects such as gum, candy, and knives. Although a child might meaningfully listen to it and speak it, he might not be able to read it or to write it. Thus, words a child knows well enough to understand when used by another (listening vocabulary) may not be in his speaking or in his reading vocabulary (even if he has so-called skill in simply sounding out words without attaching meaning).[4]

[4] Cazden (1966) gives a relevant review on cultural differences in children's language. Piaget and scores of others have stressed the importance of response to the listening environment during the child's first years as an influence on the child's speech. The dependence of speaking upon listening is dramatically illustrated by the example of deaf-mutes unable to speak because they are unable to hear. Without reeducation, a person who once heard but who becomes deaf may lose his ability to speak within about 5 years.

The following diagram illustrates the four overlapping vocabularies, the usual direction of development (depicted by arrows), and the relative size and overlapping of the listening vocabulary. What does this interrelationship mean for teachers? It means that teachers need to concentrate on listening and speaking vocabularies before expecting competence and performance in written vocabulary. It means that teachers read challenging stories each day to children and otherwise provide a captivating, rich, and varied listening diet. It means that teachers encourage children to demand meaning for words they encounter, to become word-meaning conscious. That is, once children capture a new meaning in their listening vocabularies, teachers help them to use it in their speaking, reading, and writing vocabularies. (See Chapter 5 for story suggestions, and Activity 2.9 for a word game.)

Diagram of four overlapping vocabularies

Various distortions occur during the listening–speaking situation. Messages sent and messages received are sometimes very different. Four chief distortions might be labeled (1) attitude cutoff, (2) motive attributing, (3) organizational mix-up, and (4) self-preoccupation.

Four kinds of distortions

1. *Attitude cutoff* blocks the reception of information at the spoken source because expectation acts on selection. For example, if a student has a strong negative reaction every time he hears the word *test,* he might not hear the rest of this message: "The test of any man lies in action." [5]
2. *Motive attributing* is illustrated by the person who says of a speaker, "He is just selling me a public relations line for the establishment," and by the child who thinks, "Teachers just like to talk; they don't really expect me to listen the first time because they are going to repeat directions ten times anyway."
3. *Organizational mix-up* happens while one is trying to put someone else's message together—"Did he say 'turn left, then right, then right, then left,' or . . . ?" or "Did he say 'tired' or 'tried'?"

[5] Pindar (522?-443 BC.).

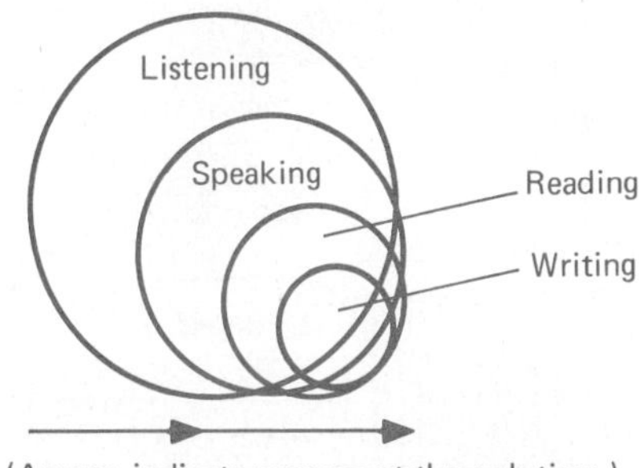


FOUR OVERLAPPING VOCABULARIES
Are all vocabularies basically dependent on listening?

4. *Self-preoccupation* causes distortion because the "listener" is busy formulating his reply and never hears the message: "I'll get him for that; as soon as he stops talking, I'll make a crack about how short he is, then. . . ."[6]

Throughout all this cognitive (mental) and affective (feeling) activity, irrational and unconscious attitudes are being reinforced, or weakened and changed. Attitudes (which may not be the same as those held by the speaker) are determining the meaning in the mind of the listener. There is a long, tortuous trail between speaking and listening in the communication act. The listener "creates" the language of the speaker. Thus, although ideally the message is the same for the speaker and for the listener, it is usually possible to find contrasts.

Two activities for refining the interrelationship between listening and speaking are Message Checkout, and Mirroring.

[6] Preoccupation with one's own message is a frequent distortion for young listeners. Hanging on to their own thoughts during communication takes a great deal of their attention and energy. Some teachers help out by suggesting that young listeners make small, quick pictures to help cue their ideas when their turn to speak arrives. That way they can get back to listening. Older children may jot down "shorthand" notes to help them hold on to ideas and return to the line of communication.

ON DISTORTION DURING MESSAGE TRANSMISSION

Wizard of Id by permission of John Hart and Field Enterprises Inc.

Activities that interrelate speaking and listening

2.1. Message Checkout. (For preschool through junior high.) The rule for this activity is that the listening person repeats, restates, or summarizes the message sent him and secures the sender's agreement as to accuracy before he goes on, in turn, to send his message. Participants take turns going through this process, using questions such as these:

"Is this what I hear you saying?"
"Do you mean this?"
"Do you feel this way?"

In this kind of interpersonal speech, fidelity is the goal to the extent that the message sent is the message received. This kind of activity encourages the suspension of judgment and the prevention of misinterpretations and premature, unchanging conclusions. This checking out, this being able to restate to the other's satisfaction, is probably one of the most important teacher and pupil behaviors in the oral language program. Questions a sender might use to check on his receiver's impressions are illustrated by the following:

"Now I've just said something. What does it means to you?"
"How do you know?"
"Why?"

This technique has helped move labor management negotiations through bottlenecks. It has worked between parents, between parent and child, teacher and child, and child and child. Next time you face a problem with people (and before communication slows down to the "I don't even want to talk to you about it" stage) try saying something like this: "To be certain we understand one another—see if this is what you meant to express. . . ."

A related technique is the use of a low-frequency word, a wrong answer, or a bit of illogical reasoning to provoke feedback and questioning.[7] With large groups, members may be given colored "feed back cards" to hold up. For example, green might represent "Okay, I agree, I understand." Black might mean "Not okay, unclear, I disagree." And red might represent "Stop. I must speak."

In general, teachers can praise children for giving and for seeking feedback in order to reinforce this behavior. Speech that fails to seek and receive without fidelity may resolve into ritual. To overstate for emphasis, *speech does not exist without a listener.*

2.2. Mirroring. (For preschool through junior-high levels.) A pair of children face one another. Then one of them says something, such as,

"Am I glad it's Friday!"
"I really want to apologize to you."
"I want you to be my friend."

[7] For example, "All Indians walk single file—at least the one I saw did."

The other child tries to mirror the verbal and *nonverbal* message (facial expression, gestures) as closely as he can. The sender says, "Yes, that's it," when the child who is playing the role of the mirror succeeds. Then the partners change roles.

### How Is Listening Like Writing?

In the communication diagram (toward the end of this chapter), listening is represented as most distant from and thus least like writing, which transmits to the sense of sight. Speaking and writing have some common elements, as skills of *transmission;* listening and reading are skills of *reception*. Moreover, from the standpoint of sound, grammar, tonal patterns, and vocabulary, people rarely talk in the same way they write. (As a brief example, they say *winshiel* but write *windshield.*)

Comparisons: internal listening and writing, common background

However, there are some associations between listening and writing, such as (1) the internal listening that accompanies writing, and (2) the common background including vocabulary (already mentioned). While composing ideas in written form, children speak and listen internally as they record; for example, "Let's see, I'm going to write about a dog that ate a mean man . . . no, let's make it a woman. . . ." [8] Since listening acts as a beginning and continuing foundation for writing, the improvement of listening is likely to affect composition. However, progress may not be immediately apparent because of the complexity of the process, the slow pace of such growth, and the imprecision in measurement of language arts skills.

Sensory images

Another influence of listening on writing relates to the careful discrimination, observation, and translation into sensory images of sound that a writer may use. The use of vivid auditory imagery to help the reader experience a setting is one of the tools of writing discussed in Part 3, on composition. For example, a writer may help to set a mood by noting the plaintive throb of a cricket, the incessant tick of a clock.

Relationships from studies of deaf children

Finally, evidence of dependence upon listening comes from studies of deaf children, who lag considerably behind children with normal hearing in writing skill (Cooper, 1965). Compositions written by deaf children show less unity in style, less variety, and less use of probability; they resemble compositions of normal children about three years younger.[9] Thus writing is both directly and indirectly dependent upon listening.

[8] Inner speech also happens during speaking and reading. Auditory word impressions traveling at high speeds are largely unconscious (Brown, 1954). The term *auditory* refers to the sense by which one hears, or to the hearing process.

[9] Normal children use more compound and complex sentences with a larger number of verbs in clauses. The deaf show practically no increase in clause use with age (Heider & Heider, 1940; Cooper, 1965). To be deaf, to be doomed to the lonely, limited world of solitary, soundless confinement may be more emotionally disabling than blindness (Ratcliff, 1971).

What does this interrelationship between listening and writing mean for classroom activity? First, children need freedom to talk aloud and listen to themselves while they write. They need a chance to get oral feedback on their ideas before they write, during, and after. (See Part 3 for detailed classroom procedures.)

Classroom implications

The following classroom activities show the relationship between listening and writing. They can be adapted to almost any grade level, especially if people are available to write for children (take their dictation), or give help.

Activities that interrelate listening and writing

2.3. Last Day to Hear. Children pretend that it is the last day they will be able to listen to any sound. They are to observe as vividly as they can and record impressions to preserve them. It may help to block out their other senses, for example by having them close their eyes and asking other students to lead them on a "blind-walk" while listening. Examples of an author's auditory observations, such as Mark Twain's "A deep peal of thunder went rolling and tumbling down the heavens and lost itself in sullen rumblings in the distance," may stimulate some children. (You might anticipate children's literal-minded questions, such as, "How can thunder roll by?") Older children can be given a bare-bones statement about sound, such as, "Thunder sounded," and be asked to elaborate it. Then they can compare their efforts with the author's original, as just another person's way of expressing images of sound.

2.4. Sound-Based Compositions. Once children have collected written observations on sounds, they can select and arrange language in a time sequence that builds to a climax. A beginning might be, "At first the noise was faint and far away." Or children might write about what they heard today that made them laugh, or what they like best to hear and listen to. They could write about who they would most want to hear (or communicate with) and what might be said if they could listen via Telestar to anyone in the world. Or they could compose, pretending, "I am a fire siren," (or foghorn, jackhammer, wind chime in a garden, creaking stair step, whining door, an electric guitar, or buzzing fly). Help children move from general ideas about sound images to vivid, specific details in their compositional writing.[10]

---

[10] Children may draw inspiration from a poem such as J. Pope's "Noise." It begins, "I like noise./The whoop of a boy, the thud of a hoof,/the rattle of rain on a galvanized roof, . . ." (In, for example, *Robert's English Series,* 4th grade (New York: Harcourt, 1966), p. 10.)

## How Is Listening Like Reading?

Dependence of reading on listening

Reading may depend so completely upon a listening base that it appears to be a special extension. What child does not read a selection better after hearing and talking about it? A filmstrip or movie about *Tom Sawyer* presented before reading may help a child through Mark Twain's complex prose to the delightful rewards waiting there. Since reading is normally superimposed on a foundation of listening, the ability to listen seems to set limits on ability to read. Show me a child in need of remedial reading and I will show you a child in need of remedial *listening*.

Specific links

There are many specific links between reading and listening, such as (1) the act of receiving, (2) analogous features, (3) vocabulary, and (4) common skills of thinking and understanding.

1. Whether a speaker says, "See that bomb," or a writer sends a note to that effect, a *receiver* in both cases gets material to decode into meaning.
2. Initially, the process of learning to read may include finding analogies among features of listening and reading. For example, a beginner may translate and superimpose the symbol read upon the one to which he has listened. It seems that no one ever reads totally by vision alone (Edfeldt, 1960). Even proficient readers regress and sound out words when they are difficult or unfamiliar, *if the words are important* to meaning. Also, children need to translate the printed, left-to-right spatial relation of reading into the first-to-last relation of spoken sounds. Once the child has adequate reading skill, the two receptive processes (reading and listening) should be mutually supportive. The understanding of features in one can enhance development in the other. For example, a drop in pitch and a definite pause in oral language can be associated with the punctuation mark of a period in written language.[11] However, sounds are more abstract than visual symbols that can be pointed to, even felt, and they are short-lived.

Classroom implications of links between reading and listening vocabularies

3. A previous section mentioned the common and differing aspects of vocabulary among the language arts. The only time a child meets the phrases "If I were" and "I presume" may be in "book language." Chances are that he will translate these phrases into his own language when he reads them, be able to leap over them, or find them a meaningless stumbling block. In other words, a child needs to experience language as a listener and as a speaker before he com-

[11] There is some evidence that instruction has the effect of transferring knowledge gained from listening skill to reading. See studies by Dumbie (1968), Hill (1968) and Maden (1968). See also Chapter 9, on punctuation and handwriting, and Chapter 10 on grammar.

prehends as a reader. As the saying goes, first he needs to "get it in the ear." The implications of this relationship for the classroom are that size of *listening* vocabulary may indicate possibility of improvement in reading; size of visual vocabulary may represent one test of reading achievement.

4. Common skills of thinking and understanding are found in reading and in listening. Both listening and reading make use of many of the same feelings, background experiences, concepts, and thought strategies. Processes that go beyond the mere physical acts of seeing and hearing are similar. A book that gives a child a problem of understanding when he reads it probably gives him the same problem of comprehension when he listens to it.

**Common thinking skills**

But, of course, the physical way sounds are received and translated into meaning through *listening* differs from the reception of print in *reading*. Learning to be efficient while taking in a spoken message might include the following behaviors: practice in concentrating and attending to auditory stimuli, dealing with noises that mask (or cover up) a message, dealing with listener fatigue, and being more conscious about calling up past auditory background in order to aid in *recoding* sound to language and in anticipating the spoken message.[12] Only when listeners are able to perceive accurately what is said, are they free to move to the crucial matter of what is meant.

**Physical differences and accuracy of reception through listening**

Does instruction in listening improve reading? There are ample studies designed to illustrate that listening skills can be improved with direct instruction. There is also some evidence that instruction in listening may bring improvement in reading skill, especially at first-grade level.[13] The following factors may be involved: improved attitudes of receiving, grasping the analogous features more securely, raising common skills of vocabulary, general improvement in memory and in thinking skills, and

[12] *Encoding* refers to the process of transforming a message *sent* into signals or symbols, usually by an oral or written symbol system, but also by gestures. Encoding may include *recoding* or transformation, into several encodings, such as when an individual writes out a telegram, which is then transformed by another into electric signals. *Decoding* refers to the process in which the person receiving transforms stimulating signals into messages that he comprehends.

[13] Trebilcock (1970) reports one of the more recent studies of improved listening through lessons at the kindergarten level. Duker (1968) reports 12 studies, covering almost all grade and IQ levels, that imply listening instruction enhanced reading performance. Five studies, however (one with retarded children, one of doubtful design), implied that listening instruction failed to improve reading skills. A project in Alameda County, Calif. concerns children with listening (auditory perceptual) problems who are reading below grade level (Witkin, 1972). Also see Devine (1967, 1968) and Duker (1969).

increased auditory perception, discrimination,[14] and blending. Whether reading improvement comes from these or from some other factors is at present unclear. Reading is an extension and continuation of a listening and speaking program that begins with language acquisition long before a child starts school. And this integrated program needs to continue at all places in the curriculum.

---

**Linguistically different children and reading**

How can the teacher help the culturally different child to read? Teachers of pupils who are linguistically different need to know about each child's auditory discrimination in order to individualize instruction. Omissions, additions, distortions, and substitutions in the sounds of what we call standard (or national network) English may be associated with difficulties in auditory discrimination, or they may relate to the child's own dialect and nonstandard usage (or to both). For example, when a child says, *Ee 'it me,* for *He hit me,* is it dialect, discrimination, or hearing that prompts the omissions? [15] In an article "Black Children and Reading," Johnson and Simons (1972) suggest that when a child reads *kill* for *killed* or *pass* for *passed,* he may or may not know that the past tense has been signaled. The teacher must determine if the child needs to learn that *ed* is a marker for past tense. But if listening and reading comprehension are not impaired, beginners will generally feel more security and comfort if they can impose their own sound system on the standard English spelling in school reading materials. Essentially, the child translates or recodes standard English into his own dialect and a teacher needs to respect his reading of *He going* for *He is going* as long as there is comprehension.

**Teacher responsibility**

Typically, a teacher who is not from the same background as the dialect user has more trouble than the child in understanding during attempted communication. Thus teachers as well as children need educated ears for recoding language variations of the message. This means

[14] The term, *auditory discrimination* usually refers to ability to notice separate, minute sounds in spoken words. For example, a third-grade child reads the word *must* as *mus.* The teacher says, "You mean *must,* don't you?" and the child replies, "Sure, *mus,* that's what I said." (Of course such cases do not necessarily prove lack of competence. The child may understand the difference, but be unwilling or unable to perform.) Nonetheless, poor discrimination, poor pronunciation, and poor reading tend to go together. There appears to be little relationship, however, between auditory discrimination and scores on most intelligence tests. (See Witkin, 1969.)

[15] Or, *Joe is no here,* for *Joe is not* [*or isn't*] *here*—difficulty with negatives because of dialect? Or, *She a baby,* for *She is* [*or she's*] *a baby*—difficulty with present tense of verbs or with hearing? Also see Goodman (1967) and Johnson & Simons (1972). See especially Johnson (1973).

that the teacher needs to know the standard dialect, probable changes in the child's dialect and points of conflict or confusion. Of course, educators are learning to accept deviations, rather than to curb and suppress them. They are helping children to appreciate variations in community and in regional accents in the school group. The child can expand his language not by rejecting his own culture but by seeing it in a broader setting and as part of a legitimate minority culture. If teachers listen carefully and objectively to language that is different, they will not only find areas for helpful practice but also beauty, spice, system, and a base for communication. Nonetheless, a child's skillful auditory discrimination, a factor in his successful communication, is the teacher's responsibility. (See Imhoof, 1971.)

**Sources of help for the linguistically different child**

Teachers who accept the idea that listening skill, both their own and that of the linguistically different child, plays a role in learning to read have another problem. Where do they turn for help? How does the teacher specifically instruct the speaker of Spanish, Chinese, Tagalog, and so on? Two examples of sources that have been and probably will continue to be useful for some time are the section on nonstandard dialects [16] in McCullough's *Handbook for Teaching the Language Arts* (1969), and *Let's Communicate, A Guide for Teachers with Foreign Speaking Students,* by J. A. Gerwick (1970).

McCullough points out that the speaker of a dialect is often shocked when he sees so many different endings for words that he or she pronounces much alike. For example, if final consonants sounds /t/, /d/, /r/, and /l/ are weak or missing, then *fat, fad, far,* and *fall* are all pronounced (with only slight variations) as *fa.* Black, Chinese, and Japanese children who are exposed mainly to nonstandard English dialects may need listening and speaking activities that attend to both word meaning and to the sounds of consonants as they are pronounced in the middle of words (such as /r/ in *carry,* /l/ in *always*) and in final positions (as in *about, did, black, his, far, during*). Informal observation of words and sounds that are *consistently* troublesome to a child during reading instruction can provide teachers with possible cues for individual practice needs.

Besides sound variations, there are also points of difficulty growing out of sentence structure in typical nonstandard dialects. McCullough (1969) deals with these grammatical difficulties. She gives the corresponding basic, standard English type of sentence, and a question a teacher can ask in order to stimulate an acceptable response patterned

[16] Based on the work of Labov (1967). There are certain substitution rules for sounds in black dialect. For example, if a word ends in two consonant sounds and the last is /b/, /d/, /k/, /p/, or /t/, then the last consonant is reduced or omitted, e.g., *test* becomes *tes, desk* becomes *des, lift* becomes *lif,* and *killed* becomes *kill* (Johnson & Simons, 1972). Grammatical system is found in omission of *is, am,* and *are,* in the present progressive tense (e.g., *He looking at me.*).

after a standard practice model. For example, if the point of difficulty is the habitual present tense, and the nonstandard example is *You don't be here Saturdays,* a stimulus question designed to elicit appropriate practice might be, *I'll see you at school Saturday,* and the patterned practice response might be, *You're not here on Saturdays!* The subject of the practice sentences can be varied (e.g., *I'm, he's, we're*) for related, analogous practice. McCullough gives exercises for Black, Chicano, and Chinese dialects.[17]

I would suggest, however, that such practice receive minimum emphasis. Instead, a rich, active, and creative program based on children's own dictated (when necessary) composition and their literature (as described elsewhere in this book) gives more meaningful practice. At the same time, such a program with more natural, creative opportunities develops long-term goals, such as positive attitudes in children.

The second source, the Gerwick (1970) guide, gives different help. For the teacher faced with a single student who understands no English, the guide presents an entire 18-week unit of instructional lessons. Among the guide's many features are a short list of universally used word signs (e.g., for "me" point to yourself, and so on), a review of methods for teaching English as a second language (including equipment and motivational approaches), categorized foreign language phrases (Cantonese and Mandarin Chinese, French, German, Italian, Japanese, Portuguese, Spanish, and Tagalog), and advice on the training and selection of tutors. Some generally helpful guidelines include these:

- Establish communication at once in welcome.
- Make sure that beginning instruction is bilingual, even if the teacher knows only a few words of the child's language.
- Above all, smile.
- Do not abandon the child to his own devices.
- Send the child with a guide on errands (physical and social response to language).
- Use praise for tasks of ascending difficulty in which you know the child can succeed, e.g., just copying a simple picture at first.
- Recognize conflicts in cultural values and explain or reflect them carefully, respectfully, and seriously.

[17] Also see *Framework in Reading* (1973), especially under "Reading Instruction in Specific Language Communities," pp. 19-26.

What are some cultural differences that may affect both listening and reading? Some current ideas on this subject follow. For example, in certain cultures a male would not be expected to listen to (and might even resent) female commands and directions. This attitude may be brought to school. Or, it might be natural for the male learner to be severely embarrassed by being singled out for achievement and praise. He might not want to listen to it, or to anything else the complimenting teacher said. A child from a Black culture might not be used to carrying on a discussion with an adult as if he were almost an equal. Moreover, a Black child from an extended family consisting of mother, grandmother, aunts, and cousins may have difficulty in identifying with the nuclear white family found in the stories he listens to in school and encounters in reading material.

**Impact of cultural values on listening and reading**

How do you get children who are culturally different to listen? Try "understanding" as a part of teaching. For example, the teacher who knows that dancing and participating in musical activity are emphasized in a culture might put rhythmic activity to use in auditory and in reading practice. Or, the understanding teacher who has learned cultural differences in nonverbal behavior, such as body movements, eye movements, and postures that communicate meaning might find ways to use these, or at least not let them block communication between instructors and learners (Johnson & Simons, 1972; see also Horn, 1971; Imhoof, 1971; Malmstrom & Ashley, 1963; Past & Gilson, 1970).[18]

**Group context and individual motivation**

Group context and individual motivation also effect the learning of linguistically different children. Given an appropriate start, the young child in a class of relatively standard English speakers, if socialized, will learn rapidly. He will lose most traces of dialect in social situations requiring conformity. The child whose dialect is reinforced by a substantial peer group in school will not be quick to pick up standard English. Surrounded by peers sharing the same minority dialect, some children generally fail to hear the target language. Thus, much depends on the child's motivation and selective listening. An unwilling child can resist any approach to teaching; he can turn on a mental filter so that he is surrounded by language noise he never hears. In any case, the teacher's task is to help the child listen to the patterns of the target language, and to take all these factors into account.

Whether the problem is one of dialect variance, cultural variance, lack of auditory discrimination, or all three, simple games of auditory discrimination (such as the following) are useful tools for a teacher to have in the repertoire for improving reading subskills.

---

[18] Most chapters in this book include sections relevant to the child who is linguistically different.

Games for auditory discrimination

lollipop:
Larry Lori Lou

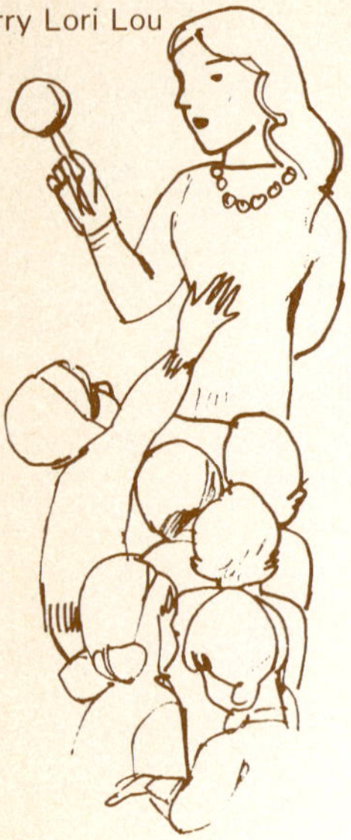

**2.5. Name Game.** (For preschool through primary grades.) Auditory discrimination activities for beginners and linguistically different children frequently include guided inductive approaches where the teacher begins to develop the concept of *sounding alike*. Calling attention to lips and sounds, the teacher repeats the names of children in the class, such as *Mary, Michael,* and *Martha*. Next the teacher contrasts them with a name such as *Jerry,* and later with a closer example, such as *Nancy*. Then the teacher asks the children to produce their own examples of names or words that begin with the same sound as *Mary,* and those that do not. Once auditory discrimination develops to some extent, the teacher can combine the sound with the written letter. If the child actually forms or writes the letter, it may help him or her in attaining and reinforcing the concept, *sound alike—look alike*. Some teachers make a game of letting children get their coats (or other dismissal activities) on the basis of the sounds in their names. "If your name begins like *lollipop,* you may go."

**2.6. Object Sorting by Sound.** (For preschool through primary grades.) Have children sort unlabeled objects or pictures into categories of names that start with the same sound. The child can then name other objects that would belong in the group. The objects (such as button, box, ball, marble, money, mirror, pencil, pen, pin, etc.) are named aloud first.

As a variation for added interest, the objects could be hidden in a grab bag. The child draws out an item, says its name, and gets to "keep" it, if he or she can say another word that begins or ends with the same sound.[19]

Cautions

It is advisable that the words and sounds be in the child's listening and speaking vocabulary, that they be interesting to the child, frequently used, and fairly consistent in the match between letter and sound.[20] In order to avoid boredom, frustration, and waste of time, activity needs to be provided on the basis of individual diagnosis and need rather than as rote exercises going on and on as ends in themselves. Teacher X's class, where all children at one time are chanting together words that begin with the same sound (as in *monkey, mouse, moon, money, mother)* every year in the third week of school, probably fails as a place where individual needs are met.

19 Other activities are found at the end of this chapter and in the next chapter.

20 An example of an interesting word stimulating reading is the case of a severely retarded student asked to tell his favorite word. It happened to be *motor*. After sounding, tracing, saying, and writing this word, the student was asked, "Suppose you were going to make a manual for someone like me who knew nothing of motors. What would be the first thing you'd say?" The student responded, "Lift the hood." This oral expression became not only the first page of his own "book," but also the beginning of extensive progress in reading—all from a powerful, interesting word. (Adapted from Veatch, 1971.)

Teachers need to maintain a proper perspective about activity designed to develop auditory discrimination. Most of the time readers have so much meaning, context, and grammatical content helping them that they are relatively independent of letter–sound information. "A little dab will do you," is an expression that usually fits the amount of practice in auditory discrimination (or *phonics*) that a child needs for reading. Such auditory practice is more useful to the child for spelling than for reading.

A balanced point of view

Although children do memorize a number of words for an important sight-reading vocabulary, they cannot memorize all the printed words of the language. Along with other word attack skills, at some point in the primary grades children profit from having skill in sight-sound relationships, even a knowledge of *phonemes* (the smallest unit of sound in a particular language that can change the meaning of a word if exchanged for a different sound, such as *man* versus *can*). Auditory discrimination (phonic skills) can aid children to figure out unfamiliar words when they have to resort to it. Older children with severe reading disabilities are usually missing the skill to discriminate some of the patterns of sound. If children are severely lacking in this perceptual experience, they are likely to have trouble reading.

---

Meaningfulness and a broad background of listening uppermost

Meaningfulness (related to a broad listening background) as the major aid to reading. In the last analysis, sounds heard are not the significant part of language; meanings are. This generalization applies to reading. Mechanics of word recognition and pronunciation are not the significant part of reading; getting meaning is. Simply to "bark" at letter signs with certain sounds is neither reading nor speaking; this barking may represent going from a sound code to a print code (recoding), but not comprehension. For instance, when a child barks out the sounds, "If . . . you . . . look . . . under . . . this . . . sign . . . you . . . will . . . find . . . a $5 . . . bill . . . and . . . you . . . keep . . . it . . . ," and then, uninformed, wanders away none the wiser or richer, he has failed to read, according to the present definition. Listening *comprehension* is probably more helpful than specific auditory discriminations for isolated sounds. Thus, long periods of auditory discrimination practice with drill materials (including mechanical aids such as earphones) are not nearly as effective as face-to-face communication between teacher and child (Bryant, 1970). This person-to-person interaction calls into play empathy, projective interpretation, and reactive abilities in listening. (See Activities 2.1 and 2.2.)

For example, a child might be heard to say something like this:

> "I thought you said 'junk' instead of 'jump,' and that's why I read it that way. I wasn't trying to be smart with you. Do you understand?"

Or a child might respond in words like these:

> "I liked listening to that story! Let's all try reading it along with you this time, like we did before."
>
> "Let me make up a story something like it. You write it and I'll read it! Suppose it wasn't a *friendly* monster. Suppose it was a *mean, menacing* monster."

And the teacher might respond:

> "Let me write that for all of us to read. I'll draw a line under the words describing the monster. . . . Now, we have read it what other kinds of monster could it have been? Okay, *crawling* you say, and *creeping,* you say, and *crouching;* let me get that written in the space below, too."

**Grammatical content helpful to reading**

With this kind of listening activity children are realizing the function of grammatical slots in a sentence. Then when they meet an unfamiliar word in reading they will have some idea of its use. For example, if the child meets the unfamiliar word *speckled* in a sentence he is reading, *It was a speckled bird,* he has two ways to attack his problem. He can first read the sentence over, using the larger sentence sense he has gotten from listening activity. In this case he knows he needs a "describing word" (or adjective). Next he can use his knowledge of phonics, of sound–letter correspondences (in this case for the blend / *sp* / at the beginning) to unlock the printed symbols.

**Emotional motivation for reading habits**

Using emotional stimulation to motivate a child to read. You, yourself, may have been inspired to read after having listened to an impelling movie or TV version of a novel. You may have developed a passion for reading the work of a certain poet after having heard a sensitive oral rendition. In like vein, many a child has tackled E. B. White's *Stuart Little* after having heard an expressive oral reading of his *Charlotte's Web*.

Try recordings if you do not yet consider yourself sufficiently skilled in dramatic oral presentation to thrill, delight, and motivate your young listeners. For example, at the primary level Bill Martin has made read-along cassette recordings of the 30 books in the Instant Reader Program.[21] This series capitalizes on rhythmic grammatical patterns, and on

[21] Available from Holt, Rinehart and Winston, New York.

structure that helps children predict much of the language in their beginning reading. Dependable literary structures include the repetitive, the interlocking, and the cumulative. For example:

> Brown bear, brown bear, what do you see?
> I see a redbird looking at me.
> Redbird, redbird what do you see? [And so on.]

Children can later substitute other nouns and verbs, thus composing and reading their own (but patterned) stories. For children of all ages, NCTE has published an annotated list of recordings (1971). Among selections available are the excellent oral renditions of Boris Karloff (e.g.. *The Little Match Girl* and *Other Anderson Fairy Tales*)[22] and the vivid artistry of Julie Harris (*Stuart Little.*) [23] However, *you,* the teacher, right there, alive and reacting, will do more to bring about the children's productive listening.

In sum, reading comprehension depends on the child's general understanding of how oral language functions. Classroom opportunities to raise the level of this language need to be more than mere auditory or phonic skill building activities. Sharing ideas while thinking about and valuing real books brings about a more positive long-term attitude. If the child acquires skill in recognizing a few letter-sound combinations, words, or other sequence of trivia at the cost of the pleasure and meaning of reading, the price is too high. At any level children need to recognize the outcome of their efforts to master language as worthy of their time and effort, as important to them and for them.

**Implications for the classroom**

Reading and listening: some suggestions. The preceding section has shown many associations between listening and reading, an area of great interest to educators. What the interrelationship means for classroom activity in general falls into five broad areas: (1) readiness for school learning, (2) relaxed social situation, (3) units of comprehension, (4) common or analogous signals, (5) critical thinking and emotional aspects.

1. *Readiness.* The teacher needs to be aware of the child's general readiness to learn during both listening and reading instruction. Readiness is based on the following criteria:

   - Experience with English language.
   - Speaking and listening vocabulary equal to the task.
   - Evidence of interest in or positive feelings for language activity.
   - Ability to remember and follow short sequences.

[22] Caedmon Records, Inc., 505 8th Ave., New York, N.Y. 10018.

[23] Pathways of Sound, Inc., 102 Mt. Auburn St., Cambridge, Mass.

Some children come to school with listening abilities well developed. Some are more ready for listening instruction than for reading instruction. Some need practice in simple listening activities, such as whether or not two sounds are the same or different, near or far, high or low, loud or soft, fast or slow. To illustrate more specifically, some teachers upon filling boxes with rattling objects (such as peas, beads, shells, tacks, and paper clips) invite children in pairs to play discrimination games.[24]

2. *Relaxed social situation.* Both listening and reading flourish in a relaxed social situation where the ideas and language in the spoken and written material are at least partly familiar to the child. To illustrate, some teachers provide familiar hats and costumes for a play corner. Then they record the children's conversations via tape and play them back, transcribing them for reading material.

Three in a tub

One enterprising teacher created an enticingly relaxed social situation for reading by painting an old cast-iron bathtub orange, throwing in some cushions, and declaring it a reading center. The rules were: three in the tub, keep reading, no splashing. There was no moment, from the opening of the school building to its close, that the tub was not filled with readers.

3. *Units of comprehension.* For both listening and reading, the sound or even the word is not the unit of language comprehension, although sounds and words do affect meaning of phrases, sentences, paragraphs, and larger units of discourse. (Example of a word affecting meaning: *I can't take my eyes off of you,* versus *I can't take my spies off of you.*) The unit of comprehension, however. is more likely to be the phrase, the sentence, the paragraph, and the whole unit of discourse, in context.[25] (Here is an example of need to know the larger context: *We are in support of striking Afghan hemp workers.* Does the message mean "hitting" or does it mean "Afghans who refuse to work"?) An instructor who grasps the principle of large units of meaning connected with grammatical and literary patterns is careful to provide classroom activity related to complete language products. These include original stories, dramatizations, children's literature (to tempt, inform, and delight), and other relevant and exciting products of child language used as the central material. The understanding teacher uses these sources rather than a steady diet of isolated, drill-type exercises.

4. *Common signals.* Both listening and reading use signals, such as

[24] For additional readiness activities, see Russell & Russell (1959); the next chapters, and the early listening lessons in the companion guide, *Ideas into Practice.*

[25] See McCullough (1968, pp. 98-114) for detailed examples of varied relationships of ideas.

pauses and intonation for oral language and their more or less corresponding punctuation marks for written language. Here is a classic example of the use of pause corresponding to punctuation and related changes in reading: "What's that in the road [,] a͡head?" [26]

5. *Critical thinking and emotional aspects.* Listening and reading may take place in either individual or in social situations, with sometimes varying effects. Research shows that the analytical and the critical thinking processes may function better when one is reading as an individual. For example, children would be more cautious while reading a propagandistic selection by themselves in a quiet room than they would be if the same message were delivered orally to them in a group (Carver, 1935; De Lile, 1968). In contrast, appreciative, emotional, and creative reactions may flourish under the stimulus of the lively group situation. For instance, listeners get more enjoyment and sensitive interpretation from the choral reading of the poem "John Brown's Body" in an enthusiastic group than they would in isolation. Because of a group member's greater susceptibility, however, it is well for teachers to put special learning emphasis on critical thinking during the listening situation. It is also important to remember that powerful motivation for reading takes place during vivid, intimate, and sensitive oral presentation to the group. (Relevant to critical listening, see the activity on propaganda on concept attainment at the end of Chapter 1.)

## SUMMARY AND CONCLUSIONS

In this chapter listening has been related to speaking, to writing, and to reading. A diagram of these interrelationships is presented here. *Listening* is placed in the upper-left hand corner of the diagram in order to

Summary diagram of interrelationships

[26] See Chapter 9, on punctuation, for activities involving such correspondences. Sometimes, however, the written punctuation corresponds inadequately to the oral signals of pause and intonation.

*Listening Compared to the Other Language Arts*

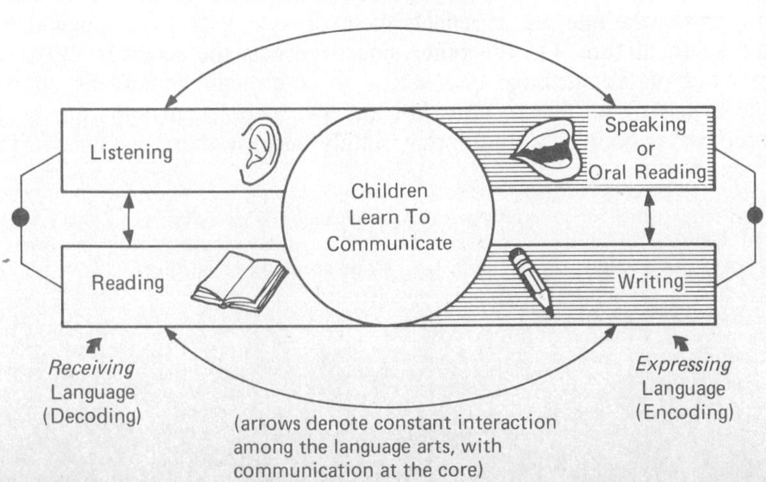


Language operates in pairs, in constant interaction, with listening foremost. Note that the child is the central focus, the child especially as creative problem solver. Language activities are student produced or received. Some of the communication is nonverbal, of course.

represent a beginning position. (Listening vocabularies are normally learned first). Since it is not the intention to show listening (or any language art) in a watertight compartment by itself, arrows denote interaction with the other language arts. Furthermore, notice the discrimination of the language pair for *receiving* messages (by placing them together on the left) and the language pair for *expressing* (by placing them on the right in the striped area).[27]

**A classroom illustration for the summary diagram**

For the sake of illustration, take a child named Ted who is moving through the parts of this diagram. Ted *listens* to his name being called for a game, or he *reads* it on the class chart that lists the taking of turns. In both cases he *receives* a message. This type of act is represented by the left-hand side of the diagram. If (in response) Ted then moves over to the game center of the classroom, observers are reasonably sure of his reception of the message. And if he receives no remonstrance that he has done the wrong thing, he himself has increased assurance of his reception. He has used adequately the receiving side of the diagram.

On the right-hand side of the model, however, Ted might be *speaking* the name of a game player (calling it out), or *writing* the name for the chart. In both cases he is *expressing* a message. If the appropriate child responds, an observer may be reasonably sure that Ted has adequately used the expressive side of the communication diagram. But if Ted (as receiver or expresser) had never heard and comprehended the sound symbols that represent the name in the first place (listening background), it is doubtful that any kind of communication would take place.

This listening primacy and the pairings and interrelationships are all that this simple diagram attempts to represent. To repeat, the essence is the duality of communication and the constant interaction within it, with listening as the starting point of skill. A balanced program based on this diagram slights none of these mutually reinforcing arts of language.

---

**The interactiveness of listening**

Of all the language arts, listening is both the commonest and the most mysterious. In a way, interactive listening is like a two-sided mirror. On the one side it reflects the expresser, with psychological state and secret nature. On the other side it reflects the receiver. What one gets out of the message one listens to is directly dependent on what one brings to it. The response of any two people participating in oral discourse is bound to be different simply because there are no two indi-

[27] Another word for *receiving with comprehension* is *decoding* (i.e., while reading and listening). Another word commonly used synonomously with the term *expressing* (or *sending*) is *encoding* (i.e., while speaking or writing).

viduals in the world who are completely identical. To reduce instruction in listening to an identical, drill-type dose is to deny its two-sidedness.

I am often asked the question, "How can I get my children to listen to me?" My first thought is to serve as a model with attentive, sensitive, empathetic listening. My next thought is to have material and purposes worth listening to and for. And my next thought is not to expect attentive, demanding listening every moment, to vary the listening environment with chances to speak, read, and write. And finally, I suggest interrelating these arts with a challenging problem to be solved creatively.

Space constraints make it possible for me to say only a small fraction of what I'd like to about teaching listening in the classroom. I refer you to the references, to the companion guide, *Ideas into Practice,* and to the sections on evaluating listening in Chapter 11, for further ideas, e.g., a "Checklist of Listening Roadblocks" for children to use, and activity related to problem solving at the end. In *Ideas* see how to construct a large instructional unit.

## ADDITIONAL ACTIVITIES FOR CHILDREN

2.7. Bounce It. (For preschool through primary grades.) The purpose of the following activity is to help a child who still needs to use gross motor behavior to discriminate nonverbal sound. Have children note the number of times a ball bounces. Bounces can then be symbolized with dashes drawn on a flat surface, or by blocks placed on the ground. To tie in mathematics, children can add together two or three bounces in a sequence to get a total. Or there can be fast bounces and slowly spaced bounces to discriminate. Words or jingles can accompany the fast or slow pattern.

Different things can be bounced, and children can discriminate the loudest and the softest bouncing sound. Various surfaces can be tried, from a drum to a cushion. If a marble is bounced on a xylophone, children can make discriminations between higher and lower tones. Bounces can represent the number of syllables in children's first names and/or last names. If a child thinks she hears her name represented in the bouncing, she can stand and repeat the same pattern by clapping. Pupils can record their own successes with an eye to moving on to more complex, abstract activity.

2.8. I-Am-Going-To. (For preschool through intermediate grades.) The following is a possible activity for developing auditory sequencing. This game, played preferably in small groups, starts when a leader says, "I am going to school (or any familiar place) and I am taking my. . . ." Then each pupil in the group adds an item (e.g., lunch, book, sweater, pencil). All the preceding items must be repeated in sequence before another item is added. Picture cues (or even small objects to hold and to cover up) can aid the child's memory in early stages of sequencing.

You can form ties with social studies by adding the name of a geographical location (Mexico, Japan) plus the words "and I am going to see" (touch, taste, smell, or feel) instead of the words "I am taking." If you use a literary setting children can go on to sequence events in a story, unscramble scrambled events, or (given a clear-cut sequence of events) predict what might happen next. If a sequence of events is unclear, older children can criticize the sequence and suggest ways to clarify it. This kind of activity moves beyond the simple physical act of hearing and discriminating sequence and into numerous other steps including comprehending and intellectualizing.

Record keeping for each pupil aids in determining whether or not the child needs more simple sequencing with accompanying physical movement, sequencing of greater complexity, or no activity of this sort at all.

2.9. The New-Word Bird. (For preschool through junior high.) On a bulletin board (or a portion of one), display an intriguing bird, such as the hooting owl from Tom Sawyer's graveyard scene. Call him the New-Word Bird. To interrelate listening, speaking, reading, and writing, encourage younger children to dictate new words, with as much context as possible, and older children to write them (and their context), spelling the words phonetically. New words can then be added to the New-Word Bird bulletin board. During this inquiry, the teacher can find and elicit examples to help children attain the following concepts and generalizations:

- One word may have many meanings.
- Different words may mean almost the same thing.
- Words may be made of distinct parts.
- Two words may be put together.
- Some words are more colorful or expressive than others.
- Some have been borrowed from other languages.
- People develop words and change their meaning unconsciously or to meet needs.
- Some words may become worn out.

Older children can work with partners. They can (1) look a new word up in the dictionary, (2) write a meaning, (3) learn the pronunciation, (4) use the new word in a sentence or write an advertisement using it, and (5) try to use the word at least three times that week in their speaking and writing. At the end of the week the partners can check one another to see if they can spell each new word, orally give its meaning, pronounce it correctly, and use it in longer discourse.[28]

For example, one child who had found the word *sputter,* constructed this advertisement:

[28] See Brewer (1966) for how an inner-city school principal encouraged vocabulary development with the game of "capping," i.e., trying to find an unusual and vivid word to express a thought (in standard English) more aptly than the speaker just before you. The game turned to advantage the institution of trying to outdo the previous speaker when exchanging friendly insults.

"Come to our service station: We repair knocks, grinds, gasps, coughs, and sputters."

2.10. Comic Strip. (For preschool through junior high.) This activity can interrelate all the language arts but depends on a listening base for producing ideas as to what the characters might say. Invite the children to draw a comic-strip-type sequence of illustrations. After inviting them to discuss or act out a story, have them draw "balloons" to the mouths of each character and dictate or write what each is saying. Then the children could place a narrative under each picture series. Finally the comic strips can be exchanged, read, and shared with other classes.

2.11. Two-Sided Mirror Game. (For preschool through intermediate grades.) Two children sit facing each other, heads sticking over the top of a two-sided (pretend) mirror. In boxes attached to each side of the mirror are placed instructions or directions for the other to listen to, write, read, and actually follow. After listening and writing, children can get immediate feedback on accuracy by having their partners show them the original directions card from the "other side of the mirror." For example, there can be routine directions to follow, such as: "Get chalk and eraser." "Get up; bend down; touch your toes; sit down." "Sing a line from a song." "Do a dance step." But directions can also suggest imaginative pantomimes based on intriguing books for children: "Be a happy ant, tired shoes, a dragon who knows children love him, a stately tree, an adventurous bicycle zooming through fall leaves, or an independent cat." The core of the game is accurate listening to clear speaking.[29]

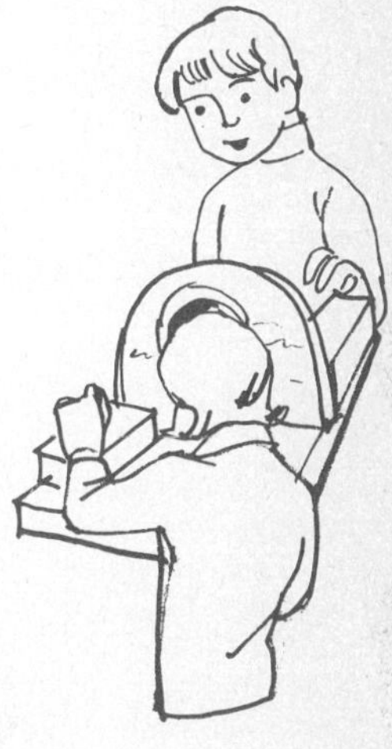

2.12. Twenty Questions. (For intermediate through junior-high school grades.) The classic game of 20 questions gives practice in well thought-out, interactive listening and develops comprehension skills just as important to high-level reading. Some teachers interrelate social studies, science, and literature content by selecting the target item from geographical place names (country, city, continent), biological classes (reptile, bird, mammal) and literary facts (authors, titles, or main characters). To introduce the game, to motivate, to minimize children's hesitancy in question asking (for fear of asking poor questions that hold back a team), and to build class spirit, the whole group can be pitted as a team against the teacher. There can be situations where the teacher does not know the target item and models abstract, categorizing types of questions. Or the teacher can be the one who selects the target item and praises productive questions offered by the children.

**Procedures**

In essence, players are told that the leader is thinking of an object (with appropriate limitations, e.g., animal kingdom, book character). As the players ask questions to narrow the field of possibilities, the leader answers each question with "Yes," "No," "Partly," "Sometimes," or "Not in the usual sense of the word." Players must try to restate their question, if it

[29] For material to stimulate these pantomimes see Karla Kuskin's sprightly new book of poems (funny and wise), *Any Me I Want to Be* (New York: Harper & Row, 1972).

cannot be so answered. The players try to name the object within a set number of questions (e.g., 20) or within a time limit. It is well if wide reading in the area selected precedes this game.

Guided, inductive learning

For some teachers and groups the best way to proceed is with an inductive, inquiring approach to the game. With no previous instruction to the class, the teacher can simply tell them that he is thinking of an object and will give them 20 questions to find out what it is. He might introduce the lesson with some comments to the effect that questioning skills are important and that the class is going to play a game that will help them develop this skill. The teacher then records on the board the topic of each question and his yes or no response (e.g., "Can you eat it?" "No").

After the game has been played through once, the children are then ready to evaluate their questions. The teacher might ask which were the most helpful questions, the ones that helped them get to their goal faster, the ones that decided a lot, that got them on the right track.

> What questions did you *not* really need? What was your reason for asking that question? What did you have in mind? Would you ask it again? Would there be some way to ask this question so that you would get a more useful answer? How? Is the question useful in light of the earlier questions on the board and their answers?

Emphasis is on the effectiveness of the question, not on the person.

Then the class plays the game again with fewer questions and with a pause after each question in order to let the children decide if they want the teacher to answer the question (using up their allotment) or not—and why not. From time to time the children pause to review what they know thus far by looking at the questions and responses on the board. The teacher uses flexibility in cutting off the number of questions allotted in order to make the task more challenging, or he adds more in order to make success possible. For homework, children can prepare and bring to class just six questions they would ask in order to try to guess an object that the teacher is thinking of (say, a person in their room). The idea is to develop a safe, flexible, no-lose situation in which children learn to profit from error as they play a game with joy and enthusiasm.

Sample questions

Here are some classic limiting, categorizing questions:

> Is it bigger than a bread box? Is it animal? Vegetable? Mineral? Consumable? Is there one in this room? Do we own one? Have we seen it in the last year? Is it in the Eastern hemisphere?

Productive questions are ones that deal with place, use, and size; that categorize, generalize, and give certain kinds of information; that restrict; and that build on the knowledge gained from earlier questions and clues.

Once the teacher introduces the game and various question strategies, the children can play the game in concurrently running small groups. They can compete with the clock and may be given more or less than the usual number of questions. The teacher can limit the area of the target item to make the game easier at first.

Over time, you can see the skill in listening and the economy and planning involved in question asking grow and transfer. For groups unable to respond to inner, intrinsic motivation, the teacher can use extrinsic rewards for winners (such as extra minutes of play) and gradually phase them out as higher levels of motivation develop.

The teacher could also use parts of the problem-solving process as target items, such as: "What is the problem?" (e.g., how to get over being afraid) or "What is the decision?" (e.g., to go out to sea alone in a boat or not), "What is the missing information?" (e.g., the island is inhabited by cannibals), or "What is the author's solution?" (e.g., to lose fear by doing the thing feared)[30] or "What is the criteria?" (e.g., the word must have a doubled letter in it, or the target is always both large and dark). Such listening activity represents a high level of convergent thinking, and a base for productive, divergent thinking.

2.13. Reflecting on a Poem. (For preschool through junior high.) There is nothing like poetry full of sound images to interrelate listening and all of the other language arts. Try using some poetry just for sheer enjoyment with no attempt to encourage responses. Then try some and attempt to promote thinking aloud afterward. The following is an example.

*Water Magic*

A rainbow comes, a rainbow goes
In rhythm with the sprinkling hose.
It arches over the green lawn
In colors seen at early dawn.

And then it disappears; but where?
How does it hide itself in air?
How does it reappear again,
Forming itself from hose or rain?

Sara Brandon Rickey © 1968 (First two of three stanzas)

Children might express feelings about the rhythmic, lyrical quality and recall similar experiences. In order to reconstruct the experience, children can look into a "sheet" of water droplets that is illuminated by strong, white light from behind their backs.[31] (Use a little device for giving a mist spray to plants.) As children examine their wonderings about cause-effect relationships between spray, light, and color, they might plan procedures for finding information, or write their own impressions. (Interrelating language arts and science)

[30] Example based on Armstrong Sperry's Newbery Medal–winning book, *Call It Courage.* (New York: Macmillan, 1940). Other problem-oriented plots with which the children are familiar can be used in this way. For more information on questions see Chapter 4, on discussion.

[31] Children may recall seeing one, sometimes two rainbows, the inner one brighter, narrowed, and with the colors reversed (i.e., red on the outside, violet on the inside edge for the smaller rainbow).

An excellent source of poems using sound images themselves is the series called *Aware,* the poetry booklet "Sound," published by Random House, School Division (New York, 1971). It contains J. Pope's poem "Noise," haiku poems on sound, a poem you can hear as if it were a wave (by a seven-year-old), and many others that make listening well worth the time spent.

BREWER, J. M. Ghetto Children Know What They're Talking About. *New York Times Magazine,* December 25, 1966, 32-35.

BROWN, D. P. Auding as the Primary Language Ability. Unpublished doctoral dissertation, Stanford University, 1954.

BROWN, K. L. Speech and Listening in Language Arts Textbooks. *Elementary English,* 1967, *44,* 336-41 (Part I), 461-465 (Part II). (ERIC Document Reproduction Service No. ED 031 480)

BROWN, R. A. *The Tyranny of Noise.* New York: St. Martin's Press, 1970.

BRYANT, J. E. Listening Centers: A Sound Investment in Education? *Journal of Learning Disabilities,* 1970, *3,* 156-59.

CARVER, M. E. Listening Versus Reading. In H. Cantril and G. W. Allport (Eds.), *The Psychology of Radio.* New York: Harper, 1935. Pp. 159-80.

CAZDEN, C. B. Subcultural Differences in Child Language: An Interdisciplinary Review. *Merrill-Palmer Quarterly of Behavior and Development,* 1966, *12,* 185-219.

COHEN, S. A., and COOPER, T. Seven Fallacies: Reading Retardation and the Urban Disadvantaged Beginning Reader. *The Reading Teacher,* 1972, *26* (1, October), 38-45.

After examining fallacies (from their point of view and backed with some research) the authors conclude that high quality of teaching is what makes a difference in helping beginning readers. Examples of fallacies were "Urban Black children tend to be less verbal than middle-class children," and "If we improve oral language patterns of disadvantaged children, we will be able to teach them to read better."

COOPER, R. L. The Ability of Deaf and Hearing Children to Apply Morphological Rules. Unpublished doctoral dissertation, Columbia University, 1965.

The average scores of nineteen-year-old deaf children were below the average scores of ten-year-olds who could hear, for example, in applying suffixes (boy-ish).

COREY, S. M. The Teachers Out-Talk the Pupils. *School Review,* 1940, *48,* 745-52.

DELILE, In S. Duker (Ed.), *Listening Bibliography.* (2nd ed.) Metuchen, N.J.: Scarecrow Press, 1968.

DEVINE, T. G. Listening. *Review of Educational Research,* 1967, *37,* 153-58.

Reviews research on teaching listening, factors affecting it, reading and listening, tests of listening.

DEVINE, T. G. Reading and Listening: New Research Findings. *Elementary English,* 1968, *45,* 346-48.

Reexamines the belief that instruction in listening (or reading) affects pupil competence in reading (or listening).

Duker, S. *Listening Bibliography.* (2nd ed.) Metuchen, N. J.: Scarecrow Press, 1968.

Represents an updating of the 1964 annotated bibliography in which 1332 references were listed. Over 100 studies in this listing relate listening to reading.

Duker, S. Listening. In R. L. Ebel (Ed.), *Encyclopedia of Educational Research.* (4th ed.) New York: Macmillan, 1969.

Dumbie, In S. Duker (Ed.), *Listening Bibliography.* (2nd ed.) Metuchen, N.J.: Scarecrow Press, 1968.

Edfeldt, A. W. *Silent Speech and Silent Reading.* Chicago: University of Chicago Press, 1960.

Fasold, R. W. Tense and the Form *Be* in Black English. *Language,* 1969, *45,* 763-76.

*Framework in Reading.* Sacramento, Calif.: State Department of Education, 1973.

Gerwick, J. A. *Let's Communicate: A Guide for Teachers with Foreign Speaking Students.* Napa, Calif.: Office of Napa County Superintendent of Schools, 1970.

Glass, D. C., Cohen, S., and Singer, J. E. Urban Din Fogs the Brain. *Psychology Today,* 1973, *6* (12), 94-97.

Goodman, K. S. Dialect Barriers to Reading Comprehension. In E. L. Evertts (Ed.), *Dimensions of Dialect.* Urbana, Ill.: NCTE, 1967.

Heider, F. K., and Heider, G. M. A Comparison of Sentence Structure of Deaf and Hearing Children. *Psychological Monographs,* 1940, *52,* 42-103.

Hill, In S. Duker (Ed.), *Listening Bibliography.* (2nd ed.) Metuchen, N.J.: Scarecrow Press, 1968.

Horn, T. D. (Ed.) *Research Bases for Oral Language Instruction.* A Research Bulletin Prepared by a Committee of the National Conference on Research in English (NCRE). Urbana, Ill.: NCTE, 1971.

Contains articles on the nature of nonstandard dialect divergence; when to begin instruction; listening and the linguistically different learner.

Imhoof, M. I. (Ed.) *Social and Educational Insights into Teaching Standard English to Speakers of Other Dialects.* Bloomington: University of Indiana, School of Education, 1971.

Contains sections on Black–White speech differences; Puerto Ricans; the question of Black children learning standard English; and a highly recommended section on preparing language arts teachers for working in ghetto schools in order to accomplish dialect extension. Suggests a program for 60 days to be spent in a ghetto district learning (1) Black English (not necessarily for the teacher's own communication); (2) family and community structures (what the ghetto family unit is like and who has high authority in the community); (3) the effects of poverty as it affects expectations, aspiration, and performance; (4) peer relations, learning styles, and the high priority children in the street place on their oral language. States that there is a need for teachers who are resourceful, and magnetic (i.e., have strength, energy, self-confidence, bearing, color or a sense of the dramatic, and a feeling for language and rhetoric); who also have self-knowledge of their potential as teachers (e.g., know if they are miscast); and who reflect nonpossessive love.

As Iris Origo says in the book, *Images and Shadows, "figures that stand out are the people to whom I have been bound by affection . . . it is only through them that I have learned anything about life at all . . . my past life passes through the filter, not of my mind, but of my affections."* It is the loving teacher who is needed and who makes a lasting impact.

JOHNSON, K. R. A Comparison of Black-Dialect-Speaking Children and Standard-English-Speaking Children and Their Ability to Hear Final Consonant Stops. Paper presented at the annual convention of the International Reading Association, Denver, May 1973.

Found that Black-dialect-speaking children failed to hear certain final consonant stops. Suggests that teachers take extra steps to help these children (1) realize their linguistic system does not include these sounds in pronunciation; (2) listen to these sounds; (3) discriminate between the standard and Black dialect sound patterns (i.e., between *chest* and *ches, called* and *call;* and (4) reproduce the standard English pronunciation of words ending in final consonant stops. Standard-English-speaking white children do not need such practice because they have these skills by the time they reach the third grade.

JOHNSON, K. R., and SIMONS, H. D. Black Children and Reading. *Phi Delta Kappan,* 1972, *53* (January), 288-90.

KLEE, L. E. Larger Horizons for the Child: A Fourth Grade Experiment. *Social Education,* 1949 (February), 69-71.

LABOV, W. Some Sources of Reading Problems for Negro Speakers of Non-Standard English. In A. Frazier (Ed.), *New Directions in Elementary English.* Urbana, Ill.: NCTE, 1967

LUNDSTEEN, S. W. *Listening: Its Impact on Reading and the Other Language Arts.* NCTE/ERIC Studies in the Teaching of English. Urbana, Ill.: NCTE, 1971. (Order No. 50517.)

LUNDSTEEN, S. W. *Ideas into Practice.* Englewood Cliffs, N. J.: Prentice-Hall, in press.

See lesson series on listening and how to create a unit of instruction.

LUNDSTEEN, S. W. On Listening, in press.

MADER, In S. Duker (Ed.), *Listening Bibliography.* (2nd ed.) Metuchen, N.J.: Scarecrow Press, 1968.

MALMSTROM, J., and ASHLEY, A. *Dialects: USA.* Urbana, Ill.: NCTE, 1963.

Contains chapters on dialect differences and their causes, linguistic geography of the United States, influence of foreign language settlements, and dialect in literature.

MCCULLOUGH, C. M. *Preparation of Textbooks in the Mother Tongue.* Newark, Del.: International Reading Association, 1968.

McCullough, C. M. *Handbook for Teaching the Language Arts.* New York: Intext, 1969.

Sections on nonstandard dialect in Chapter 1, and also Chapter 3 on speaking and listening, are particularly relevant.

National Council of Teachers of English. *An Annotated List of Recordings in the Language Arts.* Urbana, Ill.: Author. (List supplemented, 1971.)

Past, R., and Gilson, J. W. Listening and Response Theory: Implications for Linguistically Different Learners. *Elementary English,* 1970, *47* (December), 1060-66.

Ratcliff, J. D. I Am Joe's Ear. *Reader's Digest,* 1971 (October) 131-34.

Rosnow, R. Poultry and Prejudice. *Psychology Today,* 1972, *5* (10), 53-56.

Russell, D. H. A Conspectus of Recent Research on Listening Abilities. *Elementary English,* 1964, *41,* 262-67.

Russell, D. H., and Russell, E. F. *Listening Aids Through the Grades.* New York: Teachers College, Columbia University, Bureau of Publications, 1959.

A collection of activities divided into primary and intermediate levels.

Trebilcock, E. L. Can Auding by Kindergarten Children Be Improved in a Normal Classroom Situation Through Direct Teaching of this Skill? *Dissertation Abstracts,* 1970, *31,* 687A.

Veatch, J. *Individualized Reading.* Listener In-Service Casette Library. Hollywood, Calif.: Listener Corporation, 1970.

Witkin, B. R. Auditory Perception—Implications for Language Development. *Journal of Research and Development in Education,* 1969, *3,* 53-68.

Other articles in this issue also deal with listening and thinking.

Witkin, B. R. *Reading Improvement Through Auditory Perceptual Training.* USOE Title III Project No. 0471. Hayward, Calif.: Continuation Proposal, Alameda County School Department, 1972.

Wolfram, W. Black–White Speech Differences Revisited. In M. I. Imhoof (Ed.), *Social and Educational Insights into Teaching Standard English to Speakers of Other Dialects,* Bloomington: University of Indiana, School of Education, 1971.

# Chapter 3 Using Oral Language to Express & Expound

*If there is a "new English," it is to be found by reexamining and reinterpreting the child's experiences in language rather than by introducing new content.*

Albert H. Marckwardt

With this chapter begins the investigation of *speaking*—on the other side of the oral communication mirror from listening. The chapter explains why it is important for the teacher to pay serious attention to the individual child's self-expression as he uses his language to talk, and subsequently to write (Marckwardt, 1967). I will explore the uses of language (aims of discourse), particularly as they apply to oral language. Although spoken language is stressed, much of the material also applies to the child's writing activity. Many illustrative activities are suggested for classroom trial.

**A definition of discourse.** The term *discourse* is used to include more than talk or conversation. It includes public speaking, writing, and more formal endeavors, such as scientific reports and plays. It includes all four aims of language use: *self-expression, exposition, literature,* and *persuasion.* Of course, when people talk and write, their language easily moves from one aim to another. Sometimes it is hard to categorize and distinguish language in this way. But for the purpose of study and emphasis and in order to ensure a balanced school program, it is well to make these distinctions.

**Discourse defined**

Brief definitions of the four uses of language follow:

**Brief definitions of the aims of discourse**

1. *Self-expression* (with fluency, awareness, and sensitivity sought). In this use of speech the person is mainly talking to and for himself. He is not motivated to communicate with another person. He is not transacting any business, giving information, or trying to move another to action. (*Ouch!*!#!#!, I hit my thumb!*)

2. *Exposition* (with objectivity, factuality, and careful judgment). This aim of speech includes argumentative discussion, informative show and tell, the analytical processes in roleplay, and informational uses of language in content areas (such as science and social studies.) Exposition is language used to get things done. It fits into the daily activity and business of participants. (*What time is it?, The way you get to the post office is to go three blocks to the next stoplight, turn left. . . .*)

3. *Literature.* Literature grows out of a person's contemplation of life in the role of spectator. It is a sharing of experience. Careful attention is given to the form, arrangement, or organization, and to the language of a product that is pleasing to the creator. The creators of literature seek audiences with which to share their contemplations. This sharing may come about as the child responds to an author's position by using puppetry, dramatic improvisation, storytelling, and discussion. The child progresses on a continuum toward literature by giving his self-expression more and more of a satisfying shape and more and more of a performance when displaying his product. Beyond oral language, this aim includes the child's poetry, and other imaginative writing that seeks an audience.

4. *Persuasion* is the use of language to influence. In persuasion attention is given to the attributes of the *receiver* that best enable the *sender* of the message to move the receiver to action or belief. Ideas for classroom activity are drawn from the fields of rhetoric, general semantics, and propaganda analysis.

What are the uses of language?

These aims of discourse might be pictured as liquids poured carefully into a glass to form layers. The quick stir of the reality of discourse in action quickly mixes them.

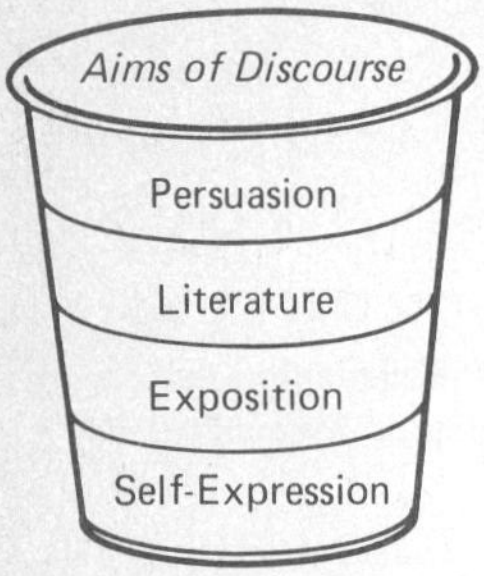


If a teacher knows how to help children master these uses of language, he can equip them with the means not only for survival, but also for comfort, and pleasure.

## WHY BOTHER WITH ORAL INTERACTION IN THE LANGUAGE ARTS CURRICULUM?

*"Give me some specific reasons why I should plan for children's spoken language in my classroom?"*

**Speaking: another crucial basis for reading and writing**

One reason for taking time to develop an oral language program is that (after listening) speaking is prerequisite to both reading and writing. To put it strongly, the basic vocabulary that a child understands and speaks is his only vocabulary; there is no other base on which to build comprehension skills in reading and skills of expression in writing.[1] One term suggested for oral skill (including listening as well as speaking) is *oracy,* as a parallel and prerequisite to *literacy* (Wilkinson, 1970). Children who have little or no oracy may learn to read, but it is not likely.

After children can produce sentence sounds with their tongues, they can use printed symbols as triggers to meaningful reading. They can talk their way into reading. In this sense, reading instruction can begin if children have the sound patterns of their language ringing in their ears and shaped on their lips. A reminder for the teacher: elementary-school children are not likely to read with understanding language that is much more mature, involved, or atypical than what they use in speaking.

Moreover, oral language is basic to writing, both draw on past experience of organizing speech in appropriate sequences, choosing words properly, and using language patterns. If a child's written composition is poor, the teacher probably needs to help him work on his oral language. Usually a child will not write better than he talks. Whether the aim is effective reading or effective writing, the factor of spoken language skills sets the child's ceiling of performance.

**Social and personal importance**

There is another reason, personal and social, why teachers need to provide for oral language instruction. To be spontaneous and fluent in the use of language gives comfort to the child, and to be awkward with speech means social distress. Speaking difficulty leads to self-consciousness, and ultimately to lack of confidence in self-worth. Eventually the

[1] This statement is a generalization. The deaf and dumb do manage to communicate without oral language, but with great difficulty.

linguistically inept child shrinks from contact with others or becomes an aggressive bully who relies on his physical prowess to enhance his self-picture. Since inadequate speech may be a factor in a warped social adjustment, the teacher's first job is to help the child who has this problem feel welcome, accepted, and at home. Then the teacher can set about getting the child involved with climbing the first rung of his ladder of language progress.[2]

**Speaking: a way of relating self to the world**

Without speech, a child is hard put to relate most of his world. Of course, there are other ways a society explains itself—music, art, pantomime, ritual, religion, literature, cooking, mathematics, tattooing, and kinesics or body language. A teacher might use some of these nonverbal means of communication in the classroom program for the child with severe communications problems. But it would be going too far to say that spoken words are not important.

Without spoken words there are thousands of things that children could not relish. For example, the concept of an eagerly anticipated future event such as a birthday party exists mainly in words. Children need language to help them formulate the rules of their games; for example, the language contrasts of *ball* and of *strike* in baseball. Speech helps give a child organized patterns, which permit him to remember what he experiences, and these are some of the reasons why oral *interaction* deserves a prominent place in the classroom. Oral expressiveness in the classroom is important both personally and socially.

## WHAT IS THE TEACHER'S RESPONSIBILITY?

**The need for the teacher's educated influence**

The responsibility for providing appropriate instruction and plenty of chances to practice and enjoy oral language is the teacher's. If the classroom teacher fails to provide meaningful occasions for speech, then sequential language skills fail to appear or develop poorly. If children find little satisfaction (or much negative reinforcement from overcorrective teaching), they may turn away from language and deny themselves further development. For some children, silence becomes protection from criticism. Some teachers try to be more correct than the language itself. These preservers of the "good" English condemn expressions firmly established in the speech of the nation's elite (Fries, 1940). They do this in spite of the fact that some linguists suggest that there can be no basis of appropriateness except common usage itself and that this usage is continually and gradually changing.

[2] Consider the case of one preschool child from a home where demands were made on him to speak two languages and where parents and relatives appeared unsatisfied with his performance in either language. He would open his mouth to speak when in a confrontation with other children but nothing would come out. It was then that he would bite, hard, drawing blood on occasion, and earning a formidable reputation.

**The error of the silent classroom**

Another problem is the supposed virtue of the silent classroom. Unfortunately the guiding words in some schools have been "shut up." Talking has been considered bad behavior. Some teachers (prompted by tradition, administration, or other factors) appear to consider their job to be the silencer and subduer of small children. ("Don't talk! We're learning language.") In such classrooms, while children are taught to listen passively, to mimic, and to answer factual questions, they are seldom given the opportunity for self-expression. Unfortunately oral expression may be becoming more limited instead of less as modern classrooms become more and more mechanized and individualized. It is a courageous act of faith for a small child to address an adult he does not know. To do this across the silence of 35 other children magnifies the ordeal. Add to that the fear of rejection of what he offers and the formidable picture is complete.

What goes on in the silent classroom? Talk about the "real" world. Is there intellectually honest academic and scientific discipline and method? Is talk harnessed for learning purposes? Is there talk about relevant feelings, hopes, interests, doubts, fears, and challenges? Are there chances to develop the full range of oral capabilities? Usually the silent class is a world all its own, where children are cheated of their "first mighty step." If attention is given to children's speech in such classrooms it may be directed to the mechanics of posture, articulation, and "bad habits." The need is for teachers to be more interested in *what* children say than how they say it.[3]

Maintaining silence, then, is not an appropriate role for the teacher. —The first duty of the teacher is to free the child to communicate. Until children talk freely, the teacher can diagnose nothing of their language attainment and can know nothing of where to help them help themselves. Since the entire curriculum is a language program, the teacher's job is *to make talking in school "legal," with an educational payoff*. And since oral language is the child's greatest show, it is the school's responsibility to allow the show to go on.

**Teacher–pupil responsibility: three levels of strategy**

In order to provide such a payoff, the oral language program needs an appropriate functioning of teacher and pupil responsibility. There are times when the teacher needs to *structure* highly the oral language situation. (For instance, "When I give you an example, such as 'this boy is smiling,' you tell me whether it is a description, or an opinion, and why.") There are times when the teacher more appropriately *negotiates* with the children. ("Which procedure would you rather follow? Should

3 The story goes that when the centipede was asked how he could walk with so many legs, he suddenly became conscious of moving his hundred legs in rhythmic unison as an intricate process. As a result, he could no longer walk. Something of the same misfortune happens when teachers try to make children conscious of all the separate workings of their bodies when they talk.

the whole group play the simulation game together first; should a small group do it and then teach it to other groups; or do you have another idea for the procedure?") There are times when the teacher needs to allow the children to *construct their own* oral language activity. ("What would you like to talk about today?") The process will depend upon the purpose of the lesson.

Of course, it is important that there be a match between the teacher's strategy and the one the children are using. For example, if the teacher intends to give the children autonomy in their oral activity, and the children act as if the situation were highly directed by the teacher (or the other way around), there is an unfortunate mismatch in responsibility and class time is spent unproductively. Responsibility includes arriving at a mutual understanding of the teaching strategy for oral language development.

In conclusion, then, speech is an important vehicle that the child uses to get what he needs for physical and mental survival. It is the child's main tool for establishing and maintaining human contact, and for exploring and finding a place in his emotional environment. Such considerations put into perspective the activities in the chapters to follow that suggest uses of speech in the classroom. Children will become aware of their speech, not out of embarrassment, but because of curiosity, and the problems it gets them into and helps them to solve. They will make efforts to change their speech, not out of obedience to directions from educational administration or society, but out of their own desire to make it a more effective and useful communication tool.

"But Miss Gromeo, we were only engaging in self-expression."

## HOW DOES A CHILD USE THE AIM OF LANGUAGE CALLED "SELF-EXPRESSION"?

### What Is Self-Expression?

It is not easy to find examples of continuous discourse that are pure self-expression. The language that the children were using in the cartoon might be classed as self-expression. Another example, though certainly bordering on the literary, is the following prayer of an unknown soldier which was found on a scrap of paper.

> Stay with me, God. The night is dark,
> the night is cold: my little spark of courage dies.
> The night is long;
> Be with me, God, and make me strong.[4]

**Egocentric self-expression in children**

In language behavior many complex aims dissolve into one another, especially as the child grows older. As children develop, they are typically motivated more and more by the desire to communicate and less and less by the sheer involvement or delight in their words. But *young* children's speech will tend to be self-expressive because of their egocentrism. Egocentrism in children simply means that they find it difficult to escape from their own points of view, to take account of their listener's, or to suppose that things could be different from the way that they see them. This *egocentric* behavior in the child is not intentional, immoral, or uncaring—qualities the word commonly carries when applied to adults. In self-expression the stress is on the importance of children's speech to themselves, not to their listeners. The focus is on themselves as they tell how they feel and what they have, are, or are about to do. Early phases in a child's speaking may resemble poetry, with its aims to express feeling, and "to celebrate, to mourn, or to pay homage." A young child's use of language may tend to do this sort of thing rather than to make reference to interactive participation, to instruction, or to aim to convince someone (Britton, 1970).

**Classroom importance of self-expressive discourse**

Self-expressive discourse is important in classrooms, even though it is a private matter, whose symbols, unfinished sentences, vague references, disjointed organization, and peculiar logic are difficult to follow. Let self-expression flourish rather than squelching it. More complex or advanced uses of language (such as exposition and literature) need to be led up to gradually by the teacher, so that the child's identity is not lost along the way. Moreover, a teacher will simply not have much success in helping

[4] From *Poems from the Desert,* by members of the British Eighth Army. The scrap of paper was found in a trench in Tunisia during the battle of El Aghelila. (Reprinted in *Bartlett's Familiar Quotations,* 14th ed. Boston: Little, Brown, 1968.)

pupils develop skills in the other aims of oral discourse (not to mention the other language arts) until children are successful in spontaneous, unrehearsed, and sincere self-expression. They will remain unskilled in complex forms of communication until they show fluency, awareness, and sensitivity in talking—actually to themselves. The inconspicuous self in language use furnishes point of view and coherence needed to vitalize impersonal or expository kinds of writing.

**Self-expression: necessary starting point, continuing thread**

What does the teacher need to know about self-expression? The teacher needs to understand the nature of the self-expressive use of language. No teacher can afford to ignore all that has gone on previously in the development of a child; school learning must build upon the learning of infancy and subsequent stages. The child's use of language as self-expression provides a necessary starting point in school because it is language that is close to the child's self. The teacher needs to know that his pupils' language will largely be self-expressive, that from the standpoint of "celebration" of feelings, much of the schoolchild's oral and written language will be closer to poetry than to prose. In fact, some educators find primary-school children capable of being more responsive to poetry than their teachers had thought possible (Britton, 1970).

The teacher needs to know that a child requires *time* to learn how to respond in order to produce language for uses other than self-expression, such as for literary speech (formal poetry or descriptive narration in the sense of a finished product) or for informative speech (report or exposition). The uses the child puts his language to in school need to be ones that help him to make sense of his world. A meaningful starting point and a crucial continuing thread in this interactive constellation of uses is *self-expression.*

**Use of language as self-expression dissolving into other uses**

How does change from childlike uses of language such as self-expression to other aims of language take place? Changes from self-expression to exposition come about when the child's language must be used to get something done involving other people. Change from self-expression to literature occurs when the child becomes a spectator who wants to share his language by giving it a more artistically satisfying construction and performance. Both these changes move the child's language in the direction of becoming less private and more public. The following transcript of a child approached by an aide gives examples of such changes in use.

CHILD: [to no one in particular] Zoo, zoo, zoo. I went to the zoo. [self-expression]

AIDE: [approaching and taking out paper pad and pencil] What you're saying sounds almost like a song. May I take it down?

CHILD: [nods] Zoo, zoo. I went to the zoo. Bird, bird. I saw a big bird. [moving toward the literary kind of language use with dramatic voice and motions accompanying] It made a blue umbrella with its tail . . . Do you like that? What was the bird called? [moving more toward exposition and transactional use of language]

AIDE: Yes, I like it; but don't interrupt yourself. Tell me more. The bird is called a peacock.

CHILD: Tail, tail, I saw a big tail. It belonged to an . . . alligator! [more dramatic voice use and accompanying motions]

### How Does the Teacher Encourage Fluency, Sensitivity, and Awareness in Self-Expression?

The teacher who is aware of the importance of oral language is unlikely to shout, "Hooray, there are at least eight quiet children in this class, three who don't talk at all!" Examine the following case, sketched briefly, of a teacher who was concerned about a child who seemed loath to talk to anyone about anything. Although there are many alternatives, the major strategy here was to involve the child in autonomous, creative problem-solving.

**A case study employing a creative problem-solving approach**

The teacher had surmised that the child had brought his shyness and vocal reticence with him from home. The teacher had already tried general methods of drawing the child into informal play and work activities with other children, but he had had little or no success. In desperation he even considered a behavioristic approach of "shaping" the child through food reward, but he rejected such an idea in favor of providing more opportunities for verbal fluency. When even that didn't work, he decided to try motivating the child through an intrinsic, creative approach to problem solving.

The first step was a private conference with the child in which the teacher expressed what he saw, his concern, and asked the child if *he* felt any concern. The teacher explained that he felt unable to help the child with language if he could not get him to express himself more. He suggested that what he felt needed to be done was for the child to take hold of a corner of the problem, that the child's lack of communication was not just the teacher's problem, but it was also the child's problem. He wanted the child to think with him about what to do next. In calling upon the child's autonomy, he was not saying, "It is all up to you," but "Let's work on this problem together." Having a heart-to-heart talk or "leveling" with a child, giving him a chance to feel that he is going to be helped to attack his own problem as he sees it himself, does not always work—but this time it did.

The teacher had noticed that the child's face lit up a bit when the automatic slide-tape machine was operating. The teacher and child worked out the idea that the child could go into another room by himself, taking the machine with him, and talk to himself about the slides. What he said

the child is moved from the more egocentric end of self-expression to the more social, interpersonal end of this dimension. (Some thought processes provoked could be recalling, sequencing, inferring, and evaluating.)

**Dialects**

3.5. How Many Ways Can You Say It? (Dialect). (For intermediate through junior high.) This activity begins to introduce children to the concept of dialect. There are various legitimate and viable linguistic systems; one of them has been labeled *Black dialect*. There are others. Although teachers accept any dialect with which a child enters school, optimally the class also offers a standard classroom dialect appropriate for wide communication. In a game-like, let's-learn-together spirit, the teacher can offer this sentence on the board: *Every day the child be walking this way*." Children can suggest how the sentence might be varied, such as *Every day the child walks this way*. This would represent a more standard English syntax. A child with a German dialect might say, *The child will every day this way walk*. In this case, the main verb comes at the end of the sentence.

Children can also operate with the sound-structure, at the phonological level, for example dropping the *th* and substituting the sound for *d* in the word *this*. Or they might substitute the *sh* sound for the *ch* in chair or *ee* for the *i* in *bit*. One class in Hawaii collected on a recording the voices of children around the world reciting the same English sentences. These Hawaiian children even learned to reproduce sentences in many different dialects at will. The repertoire of possibilities for pronunciation and syntax gained should be useful to these children as communication beyond immediate locales becomes more and more a reality and a necessity—as children become brother and sister to all. (Thought processes stimulated: analyzing, translating. Notable movement toward interpersonal end of the dimension is possible.)

Also, there are many ways a sentence can be transformed in standard English dialect. A mastery of the craft of transformation is part of the know-how of the accomplished communicator. (See Chapter 10, on grammar; see also Folkways and McGraw-Hill in references for recordings to use in regard to dialect.) For other activities illustrating the interpersonal end of this dimension, see the Mirroring part of Activity 3.10, and the self-expression activities at the end of this chapter. Also see Activity 2.1, Message Checkout.

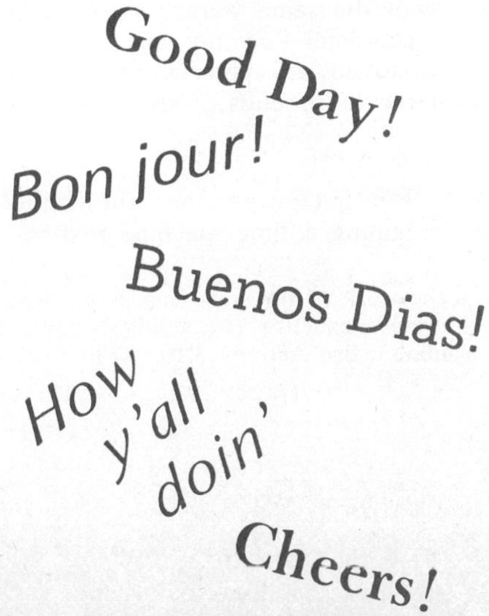

As mentioned in earlier chapters, the regional or social dialect brought to class by a pupil can sometimes affect school learning adversely. And pupils who already speak what could be called a prestigious dialect may find "school language" dull or antisceptic. Some teachers, unknowledgable about dialects differing from their own, need to comprehend the effects of differences on the language uses of their children. An interpersonal dimension with as much interchange, awareness, sensitivity, and respect as possible is a necessary ingredient for activity aimed at examination of dialect.

### 3. The Concrete—Abstract Dimension

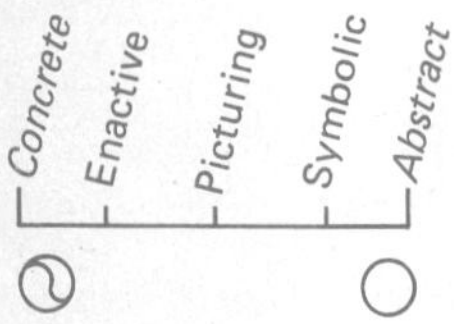


This dimension provides the child with the opportunity to move from concrete objects and events in the real world to symbols that are further and further removed from specifics. For example, when a certain child said *Geography is polar bears at the top and penquins at the bottom,* he was being somewhat concrete. When he said *Geography is study about the earth and its life,* he was being more abstract. You will probably recall this dimension as related to Piaget's progression of stages of intellectual growth, discussed in Chapter 1. An additional aspect of this dimension is the movement from practicality and reality to the theoretical and imaginative use of words. The child moves from action and picture to symbolizing.[11] In the activities to follow, Ball-Roll-Say is fairly concrete, whereas Time-Machine Sound Finder and What-Would-Happen-Ifs belong at the more abstract and imaginative end of the continuum.

3.6. Ball-Roll-Say. (Preschool through primary grades.) Sitting in one of a series of small circles on the floor, a child rolls a ball across the circle toward another child. (You have only one ball? Well, use wads of paper with rubber bands around them.) Keep the groups to no more than about six children. Upon receiving the ball the child gives his name. Then the child quickly rolls the ball to a child who has not had a turn or to the child on her left, and so on around the circle. For variation, the children might also give their addresses or birthdays, a word that rhymes with a stimulus word or that begins with the same sound, a line of a poem or song, a favorite book title or character—or any kind of self-expression. (Some thought processes encouraged are perceiving, recalling, and associating. Stimulates language at the lower ends of the first, second, and fourth dimensions.)

3.7. Time-Machine Sound Finder. (For preschool through intermediate grades.) Try constructing or imagining a time machine that takes you forward or

[11] Those familiar with the work of the American psychologist Bruner will recognize his "ways of knowing"—enactive (by action), ikonic (by picturing), and symbolic (by using symbols). See Activity 3.10, Word-Tells.

backward in time. Go back to the time of cavemen, imagining and producing the kinds of sounds, grunts, growls, whines, and so on that they may have created in attempts to communicate about hunger, self-defense, and so on. Move the time machine forward to outer space talk, to machine talk. (Some thought processes stimulated are creative associating, synthesizing, predicting. Moves children toward the higher end of all six dimensions.)

3.8. What-Would Happen-Ifs. (Preschool through junior high.) The idea of this activity is to encourage children to self-express (as freely and fluently as possible) some immediate or remote consequences of changes in the world. Some of the suggestions work better against a science or social studies background. Here are some examples. What would happen if—

1. There were no more trees.
2. This school found a way to raise intelligence scores of its students at least 60 points.
3. Gravity were doubled.
4. All people lost the ability to speak.
5. Animals all suddenly got the ability to talk.
6. No one had to work for a living any more.
7. All decisions about television programming were turned over to children.
8. All boys were suddenly changed into girls and girls were changed into boys.
9. Any book character you wished could come and be in your classroom and be your friend.
10. All children could change any one physical characteristic they wished for a penny (or for a strand of hair, or a kiss; e.g., they could have different color eyes, different shaped nose, no freckles, long hair, or be taller, shorter.
11. Dreams were for sale for a penny (or for a strand of hair, or a kiss). (What would you buy?)
12. Bottles started talking to you. What would they say?
13. You had not just a twin, but maybe there were even more *just like you.*
14. The skies turned bright green.
15. You hurt someone's feelings and you wanted to make it up to them.
16. You were a snowflake. Where would you like to fall?
17. You were a caterpillar. Where would you like to crawl?
18. Historically, you were the only one in a party, westward bound and heading for a mission, who could read, write, and record what others coming after you would need.
19. You were a realtor and were trying to sell the state of California or any other state. (Note the positive and negative sales aspects.)
20. You were a Japanese child for a year and a Japanese child were you. (Any nationality currently being studied in the Social Studies could be substituted.)
21. The more you chewed something the bigger it got.
22. You could travel in a bubble.

Part of the fun is in allowing the pupils to dream up the change. What-Would-Happen-Ifs make a productive stimulus for *written expression,* too. (Thought processes stimulated are shifts of perception, associational fluency, analyzing, inferring, inventing new and unexpected relations. Moves children toward the abstract end of the third dimension.)

### 4. Small-Larger Parts of Language Organization

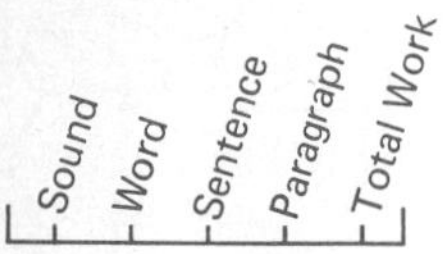


This dimension brings to a level of consciousness movement from smaller parts of language such as sound, vocabulary, and sentence to larger and larger organizational entities such as paragraph, conversation, discussion, story, and novel.

The bringing of this dimension to the teacher's attention does *not* imply an instructional sequence which limits the child to moving rigidly from word to sentence to paragraph to longer pieces. This word/sentence/paragraph fallacy can destroy the use of language as a means of expression and thought. The fallacy does not match children's ability to handle their language. But children will tend to express themselves in smaller pieces of discourse before (for example) planning an opening sentence, paragraph, and chapter to fit a certain kind of novel. Some of the following activities can be useful in those specific cases where there is justification for emphasizing sound or word.

3.9. Mystery of the Missing Sound. (For preschool through intermediate grades.) Suggest that children self-express by making up mysteries about a sound disappearing—such as the sound beginning the words *milk, mother,* and *mule.* Since the sound is missing, people have to go around saying words without that auditory symbol. Pretend that people knew the sound had disappeared when they tried to speak and their talk came out minus that missing sound. Here is an example of one of the make-believe people speaking.

"Suddenly __argerie couldn't re__e__ber her __ultiplication tables, or whether it was __onday or Tuesday. The __onkey in the zoo was gone as were all of the __otors out of the cars, the __ops from the broo__ closets and the __ushroo__s fro__ the __ushroo__ soup."

Besides supplying the missing sounds so that these items can magically reappear in the story (which might be accompanied by chalkboard sketches, flannel board figures,[12] or children's drawings) pupils can also pick other sounds to be missing, such as the first sound of the words *bottle, baby,* and *bib.*[13] (Thought processes used might be perceiving, discriminating, associating, and reorganizing sounds. Stimulates movement at the lower end of the fourth dimension, smaller–larger parts of language, i.e., letter sounds.)

[12] You can make a flannel board from a piece of cardboard covered with flannel or felt. The figures to be placed on the board will stay put if you attach a small piece of sandpaper to the back.

[13] For other examples see *World of Language, Book 1* (Chicago: Follet, 1970), pp. T158-161.

3.10. Word-Tells and Mirroring. (Preschool through primary grades.) Drawing upon the developmental concept of the *picturing* way of knowing, the teacher or children might sketch or show various animal pictures that suggest certain *descriptive* words, such as the following:

rejecting, mischievous, attentive, thirsty, belligerent, warning, romping, dignified, innocent, loving, unhappy, greedy, pensive, worried, terrified, dejected, sly, gleeful, fleeing.

Using the concept of the *action* way of knowing, have several children in small groups (1) pose for, act out, or pretend these expressions; (2) talk about the word; and (3) give hunches about facts and conditions that might have led to the dramatization. Then children could self-express other, similar personal feelings and instances (transfer).

The same procedures may be used with animal *action* words, such as these:

nosed, scratched, stretched, leaped, pawed, chased, scampered, retreated, fled, charged, nested.

Again children can act out or pantomime in small groups. This activity might lead to several others, which follow.

For example, *Mirroring* can be fun. One child pretends to be a mirror for another child while facing him. He might try to copy the animal movements mentioned in the activity above. The child who is being "mirrored" gives feedback, saying for example, "Yes, that's it," when he feels that the child acting as the mirror has succeeded. Then the partners exchange roles. (This activity moves the child toward the interpersonal end of the second dimension.)

Going back to the theme of animal action words, children might next construct oral dialogues between animals. Also the pupils can create pictures designed to illustrate and stimulate activity with other action or description words.

This activity in turn might lead to the making of charts for appropriate names and musical selections to go with the mood and action of these animals. Besides animals, the class can carry out similar descriptive activities with the words *water* or *wind,* or others.

Getting children to express action words involves encouraging them to—

1. Notice actions taking place around them (e.g., a leaf trembling as it tries to balance in the air, the light glinting and shifting on a jet airliner as it soars by).
2. Select a word that seems to best describe the action.
3. Mimic the action.
4. Record the word in a list and use it as often as possible, say, at least three times that day.

In order to explore children's vocabularies, ask questions such as this: "Does anyone know what word is used to describe this?" (Dimension of smaller–larger parts of language.) For *evaluation,* the teacher can tape small-group activity for later playback. The instructor, noting increase in fluency and in variety of sentence patterns and words used, can make notes for parent and pupil conferences.

(Thought processes stimulated by these activities are perceiving, associating, discriminating, analyzing, inferring, classifying, extrapolating, personifying, translating from nonverbal to verbal, transferring from outer world to self and back, making increasing extended and discriminating choices among words, evaluating—almost all thought processes possible.)

### 5. The Unfinished—Finished Product Dimension

This next dimension moves from little or no organized product (which is typical of self-expression) to a highly organized product, or one of great structural beauty. From the standpoint of expository language, the panel, the symposium, and discourse guided by parliamentary procedure exemplify the organized end of this dimension. Oral ballads passed on from generation to generation may exemplify structural beauty in a relatively finished product from the standpoint of literary oral language.

There is some connection between the concept of this dimension and the description of levels of children's concepts presented by Vygotsky (1962). For example, the lower end of this dimension (unfinished product) might be likened to the *unorganized heaps* into which a child places blocks. The child goes on to arrange his product next as a *loose family* with changing, varying attributes, and finally as *true concepts* based on single, definitive attributes. In reference to a language product, style and logic within this dimension move from the casual and unconscious to a tightly monitored control. Another part of this dimension is a movement away from much ambiguity in the message toward less ambiguity depending upon the child's aim. This increase in clarity is especially true with respect to expository language.

The following activities illustrate how a teacher can introduce children to this dimension of moving toward a finished product.[14]

3.11. Something-out-of-Almost-Nothings. (For preschool through intermediate grades.) Have children draw three random, ambiguous lines or squiggles on a sheet of paper (or give them a set). The idea is to then exchange and unify the lines in order to complete a drawing. Then children can tell what is happening in their depiction, possibly in what sequence, and how any depicted situation might end.

[14] Activity 3.3 (Graph-sems) and Activity 3.8 (What-Would-Happen-Ifs) help children to play with a finished product. Also see discussion and activities in Chapter 5, on literature, and Chapters 6 and 7, on composition.

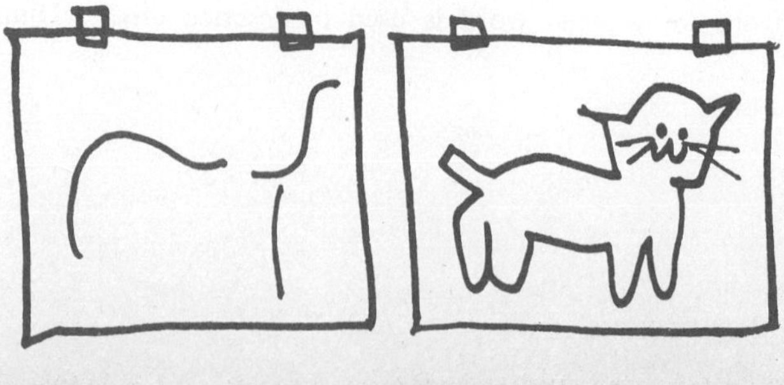

Another approach is to give each child (or small group) a picture that is covered up so that there is only a small peephole. The child reconstructs the rest of the picture by drawing according to the limited clue or view. Then the child can remove the cover and talk about what happened—the contrasts in the complete depictions, the similarities, and so on.

The goal is fluency and free, open self-expression—combining art and language. For evaluating the part of this activity that involves speaking (which might be taped), the teacher of older children might use standards for the group's uniqueness of response, sensitivity to detail, and ability to make inferences from specifics.

Finally, bits of tape of the various children's recorded talk can be cut apart and leader tape attached to the ends. The child can give the product along with the drawings to parents and to others as oral (but preserved) gifts. This activity illustrates the child's movement in the fifth dimension from an unfinished disorganized product to a finished one. It also moves children from a concrete level to a more abstract picturing or symbolizing for the third dimension. (Some thought processes activated are perceiving, analyzing, associating imaginatively, inferring a form from minimal cues or a whole from a part, extrapolating.)

**Sense of syntax**

3.12. Outer-Space Dictionary. (For preschool through intermediate grades.) Here is another activity suggested for sentence sense and fluency. Have children pretend that people have come from outer space where they have mastered our dictionary and know our words and their meanings but have no sense at all about how to arrange the words in the right order in standard English sentences. Let children construct sentences and then scramble up the words and present them to partners for unscrambling. Example: "Erasers I to am you give going some and pencils." (Thought processes involved are perceiving, analyzing, sequencing. This activity is especially notable for movement on the unfinished–finished product dimension.)

## 6. The Aims of Discourse Dimension

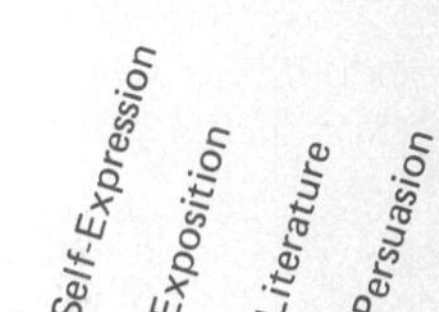

*Uses of Language*

All the previous dimensions of the oral language curriculum feed into a description of the various uses of discourse. Sometimes one of the ends of these dimensions is particularly characteristic of a certain aim. The major aims were categorized earlier in this chapter as the following: (1) *self-expression* (which has been a major topic in this chapter); (2) *exposition,* which is oriented more to fact and communication in active participation with others; (3) *literature,* for which the person first draws back as a spectator and then wishes to share his product with others (elaborated in Chapter 5); and (4) *persuasion,* which deliberately manipulates any aim of the communication process in the effort to get the audience to do what the sender wants. (See Lundsteen, in press.)

## HOW DOES A CHILD USE THE AIM OF LANGUAGE CALLED EXPOSITION?

### What Is Exposition?

In children's expository use of language there are several features. In contrast with self-expression, the emphasis is on instruction, on reality, on communicating, on transacting "business" with the message receiver. It may be language used to "get something done." It shares known facts and conditions. It is public and seeks a wide audience. In the classroom children give descriptions, explanations, instructions (*Here is how to set up an aquarium*). They dictate titles, letters, and observations. They make plans, formulate standards, solve problems and hold discussions. Major types of exposition are *exploratory* (which asks), *informative* (which answers), and *scientific* (which tests and rejects).

The following show and tell activity demonstrates the informative use of expository language in the classroom, where the child has facts and conditions that he wants to communicate about.

3.13. Show and Tell (or Bring and Brag) and the Unity of English. (For preschool through intermediate grades.) This activity can easily degenerate into a ritual during which the teacher with a let's-get-it-over-with attitude catches up on some clerical work. The children march to the front of the room where they monologue, mainly ignored by the other children as well as by the teacher. Members of the audience may tolerate them only awaiting their turn to get to stride to the front and continue the ritual. Some teachers see the only advantage in show and tell as this: A child gets to tell once and for all what he might otherwise whisper to 40 different children all day long. Some, labeled the tea-for-two type of teacher, form duets with children. But then the teacher asks all the questions, makes all the remarks, and gets all the language experience.

Handled with a little more thoughtfulness and planning, this sharing (or oral reporting activity) can provide valuable opportunities. There can be chances for expository discourse, interpersonal communication, and even creative problem-solving.

"This morning I have brought my *Father* to share," she said.

*Advantages.* There are several other advantages inherent in the show and tell activity.[15] Sharing can bridge the gap between school and home. In developmental terms, and from the standpoint of the speech–thought dimension, show and tell rises above prattling monologue because the child's audience is unfamiliar with the object he or she has to display. The new photo, the beloved turtle, the familiar book (or whatever was brought) is a focus to which the child can direct his attention. While the object is looked at and manipulated, it gives some organization to the child's exposition.

Out of this behavior comes the following: continuity and elaboration; the past, (e.g., stories about how he got it, what he does with it); information and operation; explanation; possibly evaluation; and expression of his feelings. Moreover, as children turn the object in their hands, they are prompted to give the whats and the wheres, i.e., description, classification, exposition of characteristics, and anecdotes that narrate a bit of autobiography. Organization also occurs when children, aware of their audience, may find they need to structure by mentioning some things first so that later events make sense.

*Teacher's role.* In light of securing these many advantages, the teacher's role is varied. His first concern may be with a shy beginner who may "show" the thing brought to share only to the teacher at first. Then when the child progresses with a few words just to the teacher, the teacher (in turn) can encourage him to repeat to a larger group or to the class. During show and tell, there is opportunity for the teacher to model attentive listening and interactive questioning behavior, and to encourage the children to imitate his model. The teacher can help children and their audiences to formulate questions. Questions help children to extend their topics.

Besides encouraging awareness of audience response, the teacher can also be alert for opportunity to develop vocabulary. The teacher does this by helping the child do such things as attach labels and note multiple meanings and needs for qualifying. Rather than playing nervous hostess or filling out office forms, the teacher can be alert to arouse curiosity and to point out interesting sounds, intonations and stress patterns, elaborations, effective sentences, contrasts, similarities, if–then deductions, subjective feelings, wonderings, future predictions, alternatives, and clues suggesting challenging problems for solving.

A caution, however. Excessive concentration on trying to change the young child's language usage at this point is probably unsound. The idea is to *extend* utterances. But the teacher can use this period to many other advantages. He can encourage children to add to their own picture dictionaries, word boxes, or books. He can stimulate curiosity about words and their precision. Also, teacher and children might be alert to movement from concrete to abstract thought, and the need to reverse the move, i.e., from abstract to concrete for clarification.

**Unity**

The teacher can be alert for interrelationships of aims of discourse and the language arts during this period. If a child has treated a topic or content

[15] One University of California student offered this comment about this activity: "I was happy to see a section on show and tell. I hope that many teachers-to-be read it because I remember how many of my teachers made a waste of this useful activity."

in expository or factual discourse, the teacher might be alert to contrast with a poetic or dramatic treatment of the same thing. For example, if a child tells about a new swing, the teacher may recall Stevenson's poem "The Swing" or Mary Ann Hoberman's "Hello and Good-by." [16] Or with certain memorable portions of language ringing in the children's ears, the teacher may wish to record or write for all to see and read. Thus, *in this activity we can see in operation the integration of listening, speaking, reading, writing, and literature.*

*Procedures.* A bit on concrete procedures: One teacher taped a bright, yellow paper "spotlight" to the classroom floor (or why not get a real spotlight for experiment). With the group seated around, "show-and-tellers" could take turns being in the "spotlight" answering questions. Many small groups with spotlights could be participating simultaneously around the room. To stimulate showing and telling, teachers can select themes such as these: asking all to bring something they have made or grown themselves, something with a history or anecdote, something they feel strongly about, something funny, dolls or animal toys for a character sketch, something they can make work or move, something blue and made of paper (double classification), something tiny and made of wood, and so on.

One first-grade class told about favorite clothes (or food, or toys) and why they liked them. Prepared for the topic the day before, they were helped to stay on the subject, helped to tell why (supporting opinion with a simple sentence), and helped to summarize with the aid of teacher questions that drew out responses. They told what they did and what they learned, while the teacher asked questions to help them generalize that not everyone liked the same things or the same colors, for the same reasons (individuality concept). Sessions continued over several short periods, with the teacher emphasizing the fun of talking.

*Evaluation.* Children can help to formulate standards for these sessions and apply the standards toward the end as well as before and during show and tell. Older children, especially as their show and tell moves into more-formalized "reporting," can formulate and apply standards such as the following five:

*Our Standard for Reporting*

1. Think before you talk.
   Why do I want to say anything?
   What do I want to say about it?
2. Consider the audience.
   What do I know about my audience, their feelings?
   What do they already know about my topic?
3. Test run your talk.
   Can I get someone to listen beforehand?
   What questions do they raise that I've overlooked?

[16] The Hoberman poem begins—"Hello and good-by/ Hello and good-by/ When I'm in a swing/ Swinging low and then high/ Good-by to the ground/ Hello to the sky." (Boston: Little, Brown, 1959). Reprinted by permission of Russell & Volkening, Inc., as agents for the author. Copyright © 1959 by Mary Ann Hoberman.

4. Make it two-way.
   Did I encourage my audience to offer their own thoughts and feelings with my questions to them?
   Did I ask them what they knew about it? What they noticed about it? How they felt about it? What they would do with it?
5. Is there any way my talk can be followed up?
   Does my audience know how to find out more? What to do with what I talked about? When and how could we go into this further?

The show and tell activity can continue throughout the school years with increasing sophistication. (The range of thought processes is unlimited.)

---

## Dramatic Play, Pantomime, and Creative Dramatics

Probably the best single set of related activities to develop not only self-expression but almost any use of language is dramatic play, pantomime, and creative dramatics. All of the curriculum dimensions presented in this chapter are possible in this activity.

### Explanations

*Dramatic play* is the make-believe activity of young children that is spontaneous, boasts no plot, needs no audience, has no set sequence. As children assume the role for the moment of the person, animal, or thing, they may shift instantaneously according to impulse. For example, as simply as with easels marking off a corner of the classroom, breakfast utensils, a grown person's jacket, a briefcase, and "car keys," young children can play getting off to work. **Definitions**

*Pantomime* is an expression of doing, feeling, and reacting without words through bodily action. As an art form, it requires great concentrated effort and is not perfected at the elementary-school level. Children, however, do pantomime spontaneously, becoming increasing adept at telling a simple story by this means. Pantomime may start with a simple prop and one action and develop into whole scenes. It may start with one child and end up with the whole group interacting. Pantomime is an important part of creative dramatics.

*Creative dramatics* is a group experience in which children enact events based on children's literature or their own lives by taking the roles of the characters. The events form a plot that builds toward a climax. But it is improvised without script, without memorized lines, and is not played the same way twice. In fact, the absence of any prewriting, memorizing, and formal audience is an important and deliberate distinction, to be desired at the elementary-school level.

Educational values

Why is this sort of activity considered important? Key words are these: stretched imagination, sharpened observation, and heightened comprehension. It is here that children not only gain prowess in self-expression, but learn about themselves and their society, establishing their value structures. It is here that they move in the personal–interpersonal dimension, acquire the pleasures of entrance into a social world, and gain skills of mind-meeting interaction. It is here that they practice conversation to an extent that would be grueling if it were not voluntary. It is here that children can identify with and enjoy a wide range of character projections. They can change places with adults.

Children build constructive imagination as they use a variety of effects for making characters real. Such activity tends to make a child a more poised, self-reliant, self-confident, and flexible person. An example is a shy child who gets out of himself when taking the role of a character he admires.[17] This flexibility in identifying with characters becomes an aid to *reading comprehension.*

Creative dramatics also encourages the child's leadership and organizational abilities. From a cognitive standpoint, it increases abilities to listen for sequence, to observe, to think logically, interpretively, and to solve problems. (See Heathcote, 1970.) Dramatic activity provides an outlet for a child's abundant energy, and for thoughts and feelings. Such activity also promotes variation in voice quality and pitch, and promotes accurate enunciation and pronunciation. It develops ability to criticize constructively, i.e., to accept as well as to give evaluation on the group's performance. It increases enjoyment of literature and promotes new interest in books and book characters.

Types of material

There are many *types of material* that lend themselves to creative dramatics. Types of dramatic activity include the reenactment of *everyday* events. For example, a child is invited to pantomime that his brother has just hit him in the eye, or to come up and be angry about something, or to hang out clothes on a windy day, or to make a phone call and then to make an angry phone call (adding emotion or humorous elaboration to action), to be a big daddy walking around the room and then to turn into a mouse scampering for food, or to be a child who realizes that he is lost.

Another type of activity includes enactment of simple poems or nursery rhymes. The material for creative dramatics might be taken from stories, events in social studies or science, and problem situations close to the child. It might come from original stories that the children have created for this purpose, perhaps from titles picked out of a hat. Here are some suggestions. For the book, *Where the Wild Things Are,* children can name themselves (if they were a wild thing), create a costume, and decide what they would do. Young children also enjoy acting

[17] For example, a child improvising a scene from Ed Clayton's *Martin Luther King: The Peaceful Warrior* (Englewood Cliffs, N.J.: Prentice-Hall, 1968).

parts from *Winnie the Pooh*.[18] Have the classroom become the world of the character in the story that you read.

Older children (age ten through junior-high-school age) might enact scenes from books such as Wojciechowska's *Don't Play Dead Unless You Have To* and *A Single Light;* or Bonham's *Viva Chicano*.[19] Annotations for these books are found in Root (1973).

### Procedures

How can teachers guide such activity? What are the *steps,* basic principles, and teacher and pupil roles?

Classroom procedures

The first role of the teacher is to provide the time and the place—but no formal audience. In the classroom's dramatic play the author, players, and audience are one. In the case of the dramatist's stage play these roles are separated into three distinct ones.

Familiarization with the material

1. In order to stimulate creative dramatics the teacher could start by reading or telling an interesting story so that the children become familiar with it.

Planning the action

2. Next, the teacher or aide can help the children plan the story line, choose who will take what role in the episode, and select what action has to happen. (There is no script writing.)

Pantomiming

3. The activity can begin with a pantomining of the story, i.e., acting it without words. This initial procedure has advantages because no one needs to worry about remembering words and the task can be broken down into parts that are easier to handle. After 3 or 4 minutes of pantomining, the players can stop and decide if they put in all the action that they feel they need. (See Activity 7.1 Pantomime Time.)

   Pantomime is nearly always useful for getting dramatic play moving. You might also have a pretend tug-of-war for groups of children who follow and play to the pantomime of a leader. This leader may suddenly drop the tugging motion and the pretense at resistance and start circling her hand as if turning a jump rope. The other tug-of-war group follows suit with one of the children at the end running around and starting to jump. Then the leader may shift to a new pantomime and so on. Other loosening-up activities in which all can participate at one time are these: wrapping a present; being different animals walking around; being trees in the wind; being rain (with some tired people being puddles).

[18] A. A. Milne, *Winnie the Pooh* (New York: Dell, 1970).

[19] *Don't Play Dead Unless You Have To* (New York: Harper, 1970); *A Single Light* (New York: Harper, 1968); *Viva Chicano* (New York: Dutton, 1970).

Putting action and words together

4. Next, the children add words to supplement the pantomiming. It is easier for the children to find words after they have acted the story line physically. The focus now is on what the characters might both do and say. At this point children can discuss in order to elaborate upon the story and create consistent characters. ("Make a picture in your mind." "Think the thoughts of your character.") Or they may concentrate on creating characters who change as they become confronted by situations that alter them as a result of dealing with problems and challenges that face them. Have children play the episode for about 5 to 10 minutes.

   The idea is to work on one small unit of the story at a time. Going on to the next and then to the next episode can eventually result in stringing together a whole series. Eventually, the group gets through the entire story. The idea is not to get the story presented correctly down to the smallest detail, but to focus on spontaneity, imagination, exploration, and even improvisation by adding new bits of action, new characters, new times and places beyond the original material.

Discussing during the process

5. Constantly change and improve the dramatization by discussing it after the children play each scene.

Varying the players

6. Change the cast after each repetition. Cast-changing again illustrates that developmental process, spontaneity, and exploration are the basics.

Total group involvement

   If possible, try to get everyone in the room involved at once. For example, count off by fives so that there are many small groups participating at the same time.

Total group discussion

7. After the 5 to 10 minutes of enactment, call the whole class together for discussion, final evaluation, and sharing. Expect first attempts to be rough and unpolished. A process is foremost, not a finished product. It is important to keep the activity fluid rather than try to tie everything up neatly.

Evaluation

Ask the children what they thought were the best ideas used to make the characters seem real (i.e., what specific attributes and effects). Again, there is no one right way. This end discussion is not of course, the only evaluative session At each stage in the process, children need to talk about their planning and their intent. Keep these planning and evaluation sessions brief, letting the time spent on them depend on age and the attention span of the children. Some other points that might come up in the evaluative discussions are the following:

- What makes the scene interesting?
- How might we improve the way we played it?

- Did we stay in character? How did the character develop or change?
- Did we interact?
- Did we keep the story moving?
- How did we use the space we had?
- Did you like the way it ended?
- Did we all work together?
- How could we improve our voices?
- Did we spend enough time in planning?
- What were our successes?
- What would you like to do next time?

Another alternative to use with older children is to stop a story at a crucial point and then have the class divide into groups in order to develop and act out different conclusions. Then, at the end of the enactments, bring the whole group together to share the children's different conclusions before reading and discussing the author's conclusions.

In brief, the process of creative dramatics boils down to getting familiar with the material, pantomiming it, acting it, and talking about it. Keeping in mind the following series of continuums can be helpful in planning and evaluating procedure and sequence throughout a child's entire schooling.

#### PERSON

Individual child⟶pair⟶group⟶whole class

#### MOTOR–VERBAL

Movement-in-space⟶free play⟶pantomime⟶verbal improvisation (with selection of dialogue and action)

#### STRUCTURE

Relatively unpatterned spontaneity⟶planned performance for others (unscripted)⟶children's scripts⟶interpretation of scripts created by adults.

**Extension**

In order to further stimulate children's creative thinking, Stewig (1973) suggests "extending" dramatic play based on children's stories.

It might be extended backward in time, forward in time, or it might be broadened in the middle. For example, suppose children were going to play out *Cinderella.* After talking about what they might do and doing it following the story, they might come together again. This time they could extend back in time: How did Cinderella's mean stepmother get that way? Or they might extend forward in time after Cinderella and the prince were happily married. Was it "ever after"? Maybe Cinderella meets the "stepmother problem" all over again in her mother-in-law, the queen. Or the children might extend in the middle of the story with greater specificity or the addition of new characters. Maybe Cinderella finds a brother who gives her some advice about this prince. Or another character manages to give her some dancing lessons. (Some might object to this procedure as destroying the structure of the tale.) In other words, through extending, children can help "flat" characters to become "round" and in the process develop their own creative thinking by redoing, reshaping, and transforming a simple tale.

## SUMMARY AND CONCLUSIONS

The section on creative dramatics concludes and highlights the sampling designed especially to promote fluency, sensitivity, and effectiveness in self-expressive discourse. Self-expression has been emphasized as a necessary starting point, a thread whose freshness and vitality need to be kept alive and integrated into creative problem-solving and communication. To promote such a goal, six developmental curriculum dimensions become a part of the language arts program: (1) speech to thought-before-speech; (2) personal to interpersonal; (3) abstract to concrete; (4) smaller to larger language parts; (5) unfinished to finished product; and (6) simple aims of discourse to more complex ones. The aim of exposition was touched on and illustrated with Activity 3.13, Show and Tell.

What happens when teachers are aware of the teaching strategies for the various uses of language (expression, exposition, literature, persuasion) and these dimensions? They are better able to set a more realistic and inclusive pattern of evaluation for children themselves and for the programs that they use and design for the children. Teachers with this kind of knowledge know what they have to offer—and when not to offer it.[20] The language arts program needs to give attention to all these dimensions and aims. Such structure helps teachers and children get more out of the language arts activities that they do use. With such an emphasis teachers pay attention to the individual child, his

[20] Karl Dykema of Youngstown College raised the question as to why teachers should know so much about language, and answered: so they'll know when not to meddle.

self-expression and exposition in talk and in writing, and his affective response to literature. They pay less attention to preordained, traditional, and even new but limiting sequences of speaking, reading, and writing activities. They promote in their classrooms confidence instead of distrust, sympathy instead of skepticism, and warmth instead of wariness.

A reexamination of the quotation at the beginning of this chapter is appropriate in this light. "If there is a 'new English,' it is to be found by reexamining and reinterpreting the child's experiences in language rather than by introducing new content." What this quotation implies is that even a child's language consists of discourse, cast according to aim, occasion, audience, motivation, topic, available knowledge, and values. It is toward competence in *uses* of discourse (rather than language as a mere sentence system) that teachers need to direct their programs.

## ADDITIONAL ACTIVITIES FOR SELF-EXPRESSION

**About the activities**

The following activities further illustrate the first aim of discourse, self-expression. Most of the activities in this chapter can be adapted upward or downward as to grade level. Self-expressive activity acts as both a foundation and a transition. Many of the activities are just as appropriate for written as for oral expression. Almost every activity in this and in the following chapters lends itself to integration of listening, speaking, observing, reading, spelling, writing, use of the dictionary, appreciation of literature, movement, music, and thinking. At the end of each activity are reminders of the relationship between the language activity and some of the underlying thought processes from the first dimension, speech–thought, as well as the other dimensions. Integration handled as alertly as possible leads to the unity of English.

3.14. Constructing a Word Building. (Preschool through junior high.) Games such as the following may help build vocabulary power. Invite children to construct word buildings in small groups by speaking, dictating, or writing words. The idea is to try to get the tallest building (possibly within a time limit). Each block (or pictured block) represents a floor of the building, and each floor represents a word about sound (or touch, smell, or sight). An example of a sound building is the following: blabbermouth, hullabaloo, melodious, monotonous, rhythm, snuffle, sonic boom, soothing, sputter, stereophonic, supersonic, tom-tom, whisper. How high will the building be before it topples? A tape recorder can catch these words for preservation and later collection on a reference chart.

Besides words for the five senses, words can be collected referring to other topics, such as, words for dimension (naming as a function of size), e.g., little words that can grow to giants (baby elephant), and words about weight. The class can also collect funny words, words for living places, for communication, for uses, to show growth, change, even words or labels for themselves. (Thought processes stimulated include recalling, associating, and concept formation using positive instances all symbolizing sound.)

Related activities would be to ask, for example, "What is quiet?" Possible children's answers: "Butter is quiet." "Sand blowing is quiet." Try, "What is love?" Possible suggestions: "Love is a hard thing to give away. It usually comes back to you." "A mother cat licking her kitten is love." "Love is touching." "Love is noticing what would please someone." (This activity may move children on the inner-speech–thought end of the first dimension; there may be some upward movement in building a finished product; relatively minimal parts of language organization, since the unit is the single word.)

3.15. Word Liberties for Laughter. The classroom where children feel at home with smiles and relaxed laughter is probably a place where fluency, awareness, and sensitivity of self-expression are well developed. Let there be appropriate times and places to be silly.

One bit of popular word fun is to play with word endings. Standard English has certain inflections used in certain set ways; but since there are few words that will not undergo some change at some time in the history of man, why not start now? Thus, in the spirit of Harry Behn's verse about "Circleses"—running in part, "The things to draw with compasses/Are rows of Humptydumpasses"—children might play with expressing (with or without rhyme) concoctions such as the following:

*Ariums*

The things to put in aquariums
Are fish and sand and snail-ariums
And maybe a castle-arium—
But never a hungry cat-arium.

*Onics*

The thing to do with a tonic
Is to make sure its not supersonic,
Or even stereophonic,
Or your pains may become chronic
Or your plague may become bubonic.
Just pour it down the drainonic.

Similar nonsensical word-plays may be made with: *-asms, -ishes, -isms, -icals, -ics, -ables, -gles, -izers,* and other typical word endings with amusing sound. (This activity applies particularly to the lower end, of the first dimension.)

Crazy characters, outrageous animals, puns (*I have an ice cub in my drink and a tub of toothpaste*), silly stories (*My Atomic Trashcan*), lim-

A FANTASTIC ANIMAL: THE BIBBIDI-BOBBIDI-BOO. The creature illustrated on the following page inspired a child to write the following script: "One day a Bibbidi-Bobbidi-Boo woke up angy and hungry. 'I'm going to eat me some glass—or a child,' he rumbled. . . ."

ericks, utterly senseless exaggerated surprises, and ridiculous recipes (*Linda's Luscious Lizard Leggs*)—are all good "warmer-uppers" for oral expression.

3.16. Fun with Exaggeration. (For preschool through junior high.) Some further ideas: children can talk about what crazy thing could hatch out of an egg, what it looks like, does, and how it interacts. The tale could start as a straight story that forgot to stay life-sized and became exaggerated. Stories from Dr. Seuss such as *Horton Hatches the Egg, If I Ran a Zoo, Thudwich, the Big Hearted Moose, Yertle the Turtle,* and material from the pen of Edward Lear (the father of English nonsense) are highly likely to get laughter and expression started. Children can tell the funniest thing that happened that day or week.[21] (Some may be moved to make up two-line rhymes, i.e., move toward the finished-product dimension.)

Language-arts interrelationships quickly become apparent. These ideas usually go easily from speech into writing. For literary delight in words try Kipling's *The Elephant Child.* A tie-in with the language of music might be from some of the songs that use made-up words, such as these from Disney motion pictures—"Zip-a-dee-doo-dah," and the magic-making song, "Bibbidi-bobbidi-boo," from *Cinderella,* or "Super-cali-fragi-listic-expi-ali-docious," from *Mary Poppins. Let language be a thing of joy.*

In evaluating this activity, consider fluency and uniqueness of response. But probably the ultimate criterion of the worth of this activity is the presence or absence of laughter, especially on the part of those children who do not usually laugh and speak in class. (Some thought processes stimulated could be perception, associative fluency, memory, divergent production, cognition of auditory symbolic units, and transformations.)

By all means combine various kinds of art activity with these ideas.

3.17. Pantomiming a Poem. The following poem is provocative of pantomiming action—a necessary ingredient and sometimes a prerequisite for creative dramatics. Children can hang a sheet on a clothes line in the classroom and place strong lights and an electric fan behind it in order to create moving shadows. Children can enact the shadows in the following poem by holding leaves to drop, branches to wave, flapping their arms (or "wings"), and by sporting tails and pointed ears of squirrels. Children can pretend to be the shadows that invited the child to run out and join in the rhythmic movement.

Musical recordings such as "The Birds" or "The Aquarium" from Saint Saens' *Carnival of the Animals* can further enhance the celebration of feelings expressed by this poet as interpreted by children. During the planning, execution, and follow-up discussion, it is likely that the teacher can promote high levels of sensitivity, awareness, fluency, and effectiveness in children's self-expression and transaction. (See Activity 7.3 with shadows.)

[21] The guide accompanying this text, *Ideas into Practice,* contains a series of lessons sequenced into a unit on humor as part of creative and critical listening to the speaker's purpose.

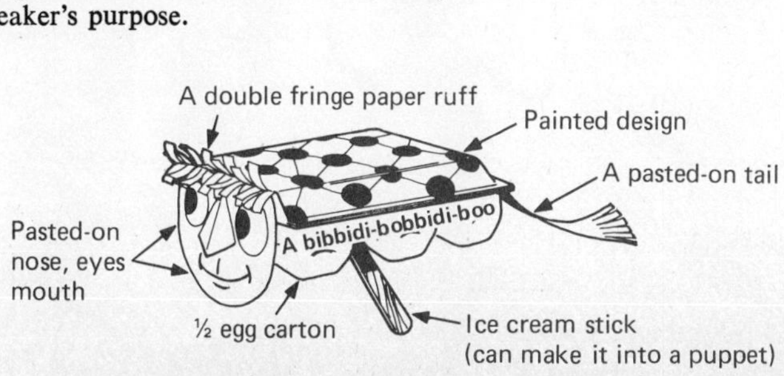

*Shadows on a Clothes Line*

Dancing shadows on a swinging sheet
And on the green grass beneath my feet,
Stray leaves hastening to join the chase,
Cast their shadows in the self-same place.

Squirrel climbing on a branch above,
Throws his shadow to his waiting love,
Birds in flight with a quick watchful eye,
Trail their shadowings in passing by.

I, to enter in this merry game,
Ran outside again where I became
Dancing shadow on a swinging sheet
And on the green grass beneath my feet.

## If You Want to Learn More

BREWTON, J. E., and BREWTON, S. W. *Index to Children's Poetry.* New York: H. W. Wilson, 1942. (First supplement, 1957; second supplement, 1965.)

Gives topic, title, first line, and author. Allows the teacher to locate virtually any poem published.

BRITTON, J. *Language and Learning.* Coral Gables, Fla.: University of Miami Press, 1970.

Develops the idea of language uses or aims of discourse through the roles of *participant* and *spectator.* Action, transaction, and decision in interaction with others are the keynotes of the participant role. The keynote of the spectator, or more literary role in language use is a freedom from the participant's responsibilities of the moment. Then evaluation becomes broader, feelings and ideas are savored and arranged formally into contemplated forms for expression after assimilation. Make-believe play, daydreaming aloud, chatting about experiences in a way designed to entertain, gossip, traveler's tales, and other storytelling, fiction, novels, drama, and poetry represent uses of language in the spectator role. Spectator language invites others to share in the process by which the sender pays homage to, celebrates, or gloats over his past experience.

BURROWS, A. T. *Involving the Child in Language Arts.* Listener In-Service Cassette Library, Album 3. Hollywood, Calif.: Listener Corporation, 1970.

Excellent and immediately applicable to the classroom.

CARLSON, R. K. *Speaking Aids Through the Grades.* New York: Columbia University Press, Teachers College, 1973.

A helpful resource guide. Also see Carlson's *Acting Aids Through the Grades* and *Acting Aids for Adolescents* (in press) under the same publisher.

CHAMBER, D. W. *Storytelling and Creative Drama.* (From the series entitled Literature for Children, Pose Lamb, Consulting Editor). Dubuque, Iowa: Brown, 1970.

Identifies readiness activities leading into drama; describes procedures in planning the first session; describes in detail an actual instance of work with an old folktale by a fourth-grade class.

CURRELL, D. *Puppetry for School Children.* Newton Center, Mass.: Branford, 1971.

Even goes into writing scripts and building theatres for glove, sock, rod, and shadow puppets and marionettes. (For grades 1-6)

DUKE, C. R. Space and Body-English: Keys to Speech Evaluation. *Classroom Practices in the Teaching of English, 1972-1973.* Urbana, Ill.: NCTE, 1973.

Provides suggestions for teaching pupils to consider the movement of speakers as well as their words. Certain guidelines concerning personal spatial territory, speech, and distance.

DUPREE, D. Inside Berkeley High. *The Wall Street Journal* (Pacific Coast Edition), May 5, 1971, p. 1.

Article describes a reporter who insinuated himself in an avant-garde high school. The writer concludes that need for instruction in self-direction will be an important condition in the future.

EASTMAN, M. H. *Index to Fairy Tales, Myths, and Legends.* Boston, Mass.: Faxton, 1926.

Has two supplements (1937 and 1952). A convenient reference tool for locating almost any example of this type of literature.

EVERTTS, E. L. (Ed.). *Dimensions of Dialect.* Urbana, Ill.: NCTE, 1967.

Contains useful articles, such as Raven McDavid's "A Checklist of Significant Features for Discriminating Social Dialects."

FRAZIER, A. Developing a Vocabulary of the Senses. *Elementary English,* 1970, *47,* 176-84.

Lists words collected for the sense of sound, sight, touch, taste, and smell.

FRIES, C. C. *American English Grammar.* New York: Appleton, 1940.

HEATHCOTE, D. How Does Drama Serve Thinking, Talking, and Writing? *Elementary English,* 1970, *47,* 1077.

HOPPER, R. W. Expanding the Notion of Competence: Implications for Elementary Speech Programs. *Speech Teacher,* 1971, *20,* 29-35.

Expands narrow notions of communication competence. Suggests that emphasis be placed by investigators not on how much grammar a young child knows, but on the ways he can put to *use* what he knows in a functional, appropriate manner.

LUNDSTEEN, S. W. *On Persuasion,* in preparation.

MARCKWARDT, A. H. The Dartmouth Seminar. *NASSP* [*National Association of Secondary School Principals*] *Bulletin,* 1967, 50 (April), 104-10.

Briefly describes a conference of historic importance to the teaching of the language arts with respect to children's use of language.

OPIE, I., and OPIE, P. *Lore and Language of School Children.* London: Oxford University Press, 1959.

Describes an area of the language arts that is a part of most children long before they enter any school. Termed *oral literature,* it is a tradition of children between two and fourteen years of age. It is a part of children when away from the watchful eyes of adults, a large part of their private reality. Carried on outside of the home without supervision, this self-expression-become-oral-literature is a system of communication influenced only occasionally by such outside adult media as TV. This oral literature appears to change little from generation to generation. Oral literature of children is often passed on within the very hour that it is learned, in contrast with nursery rhymes. (Nursery rhymes are learned in early childhood and not usually passed on until one has children of one's own.)

In guiding children's relations, this lore covers an awkward meeting, helps with an embarrassing silence, or hides a strong emotion. To children, still having difficulty in expressing themselves, their rhymes and oral tradition help them to communicate with more ease and security. This oral lore also helps them to maintain their private community. It can function as a retort and help through a troubled moment: "Sticks and stones will break my bones, but names will never hurt me!"

PRENTICE, N. M., and FATHMAN, R. E. Joking Riddles: A Developmental Index of Children's Humor. *Proceedings of the 80th Annual Convention of the American Psychological Association,* 1972.

ROOT, S. L. (Ed.) *Adventuring with Books.* Urbana, Ill.: NCTE, 1973.

SIKS, G. B. *Children's Literature for Dramatization: An Anthology.* New York: Harper & Row, 1964.

The plots of the stories have been tightened and descriptive material has been eliminated. Especially dramatic incidents have been excerpted from longer stories.

STEWIG, J. Instructional Strategies: The Owl, the Pussy-cat, and Oral Language. *Elementary English,* 1973, *50* (2), 325-30.

Discusses how elementary-school children's oral language skills are developed, practiced, and stimulated by discussing illustrations from children's literature. With recommendations shading into expository discourse, Stewig pinpoints three oral language skills: describing, comparing, and valuing. For example, he gives a list of materials consisting of many editions of three works: A poem, "The Owl and the Pussy Cat"; a fable, "The Hare and the Tortoise"; and a folktale, "The Three Billy Goats Gruff." The pictures for one of these works may be put up in the room for a few days so that children can observe them. Then an oral discussion session can center on describing one illustration, using questions such as these:

> What do you see in the picture? What colors has the artist used? Where is this happening? How can you tell? What things did they take along? Is the boat like any you've seen? How is it different?

Another session can center on comparing two of the illustrations. And a third can center on reasons for preferring or valuing one of the illustrations above the others.

VYGOTSKY, L. *Thought and Language.* Cambridge, Mass.: M.I.T. Press, 1962.

WILKINSON, A. The Concept of Oracy. *English Journal,* 1970, *59* (January), 71-77.

# Chapter 4 Discussion Roles & Goals

## How Can Teachers Help Children Learn Discussion Skills

The first section of this chapter deals with many problems that occur during class discussion. It suggests how to work with monopolizers, nontalkers, and children who adopt other roles that block communication and cripple discussion. It gives suggestions for the teacher who is concerned about disorder in small-group discussion (or at any time). How to evaluate discussion, what the dos and don'ts of questioning are, how to pace questions and plan or "map" a question series—all these topics are discussed. The chapter concludes with some specific topics or content ideas to get discussion started and with various types of discussions related to creative problem-solving and how to use them.

Discussion is built upon the foundation of self-expression. It fits mainly into the portion of exposition called *exploratory discourse*. A discussion is an experience in group thinking in which, ideally, everyone contributes and each member learns from the others.

In the past, language arts programs were concerned almost solely with learning to read and to write. Since oral language and the instruments that display and record it are just as important, it is crucial to teach some of the skills that promote productive discussion. Discussion can be a key learning, motivating, and thinking activity in any curriculum area. Even children in the early grades need to understand the functions of group discussion—what it is and what it is not.

**Usefulness of discussion**

Discussion is not only academically educational, but also useful in handling a host of problems, including those of behavior from the shy to the aggressive type. Discussion is an integral part of any learning because it gives children the opportunity to ask questions, answer, voice opinions, and clarify their thinking; it can motivate them to find out more.[1] Discussion is a subject of significance to teachers at any level, and to anyone who has or will ever function in a group. It provides a bridge between the child and fellow human beings. It helps to develop identity in relation to other people. One objective for the teacher is to help children, through discussion, to articulate and illuminate their points of view on issues important to them so that there is little or no misunderstanding. In reverse, the objective is that children will come to receive the views of others so that there is little or no misunderstanding there either.

There are several components of discussion to consider. One of the most important is that of the roles that people play during it.

[1] Testimonial from a university student: "When I was in school we seldom had discussions. On the rare occasions when we had a semblance of one, it was no fun for anyone but the teacher and the one or two 'talkers' in the class. I don't think any of my teachers ever realized how discussion operates. As it is, only toward the end of college am I finally forced to speak enough so that I'm gaining some sort of confidence while doing it. I can see how important more help, earlier, would have been. I want to make discussion a more valuable experience for my children than it has been for me."

"So-o-o we lost the contest—we had some good discussions!"

## WHAT ARE SOME ROLES?

What are some of the social, interpersonal roles that participants play during a discussion? Try to think of roles you have noticed yourself. (Take a pause for remembering.)

After a classroom discussion, the teacher can ask the children to tell the behaviors that the different participants showed. Then the children can try to group these behaviors and give them labels, such as, "all those that initiate," "all those that clarify." The following is a partial list of roles that other students and teachers have spotted. (Four especially valuable roles for children have been starred in the list.) You have probably thought of others, or of different terms you would prefer.

*Some Roles Taken During Discussion*

| | | |
|---|---|---|
| Initiator * | Expert | Goal definer |
| Fact giver | Problem typer | Definer |
| Facilitator or encourager | Labeler | Dissenter, devil's advocate, or stimulator |
| Harmonizer | Questioner | Noncontributor |
| Relator or associator | Monopolizer | Clarifier or qualifier * |
| Appreciator | Fact or missing data seeker | Evaluator * or observer |
| Listener | Comparer | Example giver |
| Compromiser or error admitter | Hypothesizer | Spokesman |
| | Physical condition arranger | Summarizer * |

Some roles are excellent helps to communication; some tend to cripple it. These roles might be categorized as showing task functions, maintenance functions, and hindrances.

### What Roles Block Communication?

Assessment as a first step

The teacher can anticipate problems that may arise in organizing instruction and in using discussion by looking at, and trying to uncover the reasons for, the roles that block communication. At least five roles emerge that may halt communication: (1) the monopolizer or chronic interrupter, (2) the nonparticipant, (3) the off-the-tracker, (4) the scapegoat, and (5) the shocker.

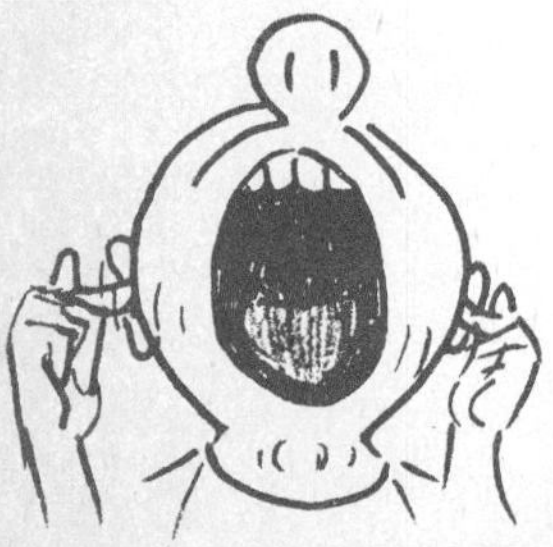

The monopolizer. A monopolizer is one who jumps right into the middle of others' sentences with both feet—if anyone gets a chance to present even a sentence when "monop" is around. He appears to sit in one place with his mouth open wagging, his eyes shut, and his fingers in his ears, while the other members of the group begin thinking . . . one would rather not guess.

What to do? An aggressive monopolizer might try the role of the *recorder,* who gets to summarize the proceedings of the discussion periodically, and who also gets to report the group findings to an outside group—a delayed but definite hearing. Once a monopolizing child sees himself as others see him, as precipitating a group problem, as hindering effectiveness, he tends to change his egocentric disregard and to try other roles.

What to do

The simply talkative student who enjoys impressing a large class may feel different in a small-sized, intimate group involved in enhancing cooperative skills. The excessively verbal child can learn to channel his valuable fluency so that it makes a greater impact. Also, the teacher can guide the child to sharpen his skills in listening for interpersonal insights that are more valuable than his pouring forth on every point. During a discussion the teacher might ask the aggressive child questions such as these from time to time:

Intimate grouping and skillful questioning

> "What do you think was helpful (or interesting) about (so and so's) idea?"
>
> "Ask her a question to see what she means."
>
> "How could our words show that we respect other speakers, even if we don't agree with them?"

Along with the teacher giving the monopolizer suggestions for alternative actions, the group will usually handle the consistently impulsive, overanxious interrupter or chronic arguer, in the nonpunitive restraining yet pleasantly helpful way that the teacher models. Role-play may also help. The basic idea is that the teacher values the talkative child's contribution, but wants to include others.

Group control, modeling, role playing

Furthermore, helping the child pinpoint his interruptive behavior, its base level (usual level of frequency), and guiding him to chart his daily progress in restraining himself, will bring behavior to a tolerable level quickly—if the child himself sees the behavior as something he wants to do something about. Then he might say: "Week before last I interrupted 50 times, last week only 30, and this week, I'm down to 10." In the main it is his problem, his responsibility, his progress, and his success.

Pinpointing and charting

Frequently the aggressive, monopolizing child especially needs help with courtesy. The teacher might say, "What words can we use when we have interrupted?" "How could we say that in a more kindly way?" "Say it differently so that you leave out people's names." It takes more linguistic energy to be polite, to say, "Excuse me, yesterday I read in [gives reference] that the fact was this instead. . . . I wonder what reference you used," instead of, "That's a lie!" or "You're wrong!"

Learning to be courteous

**Learning to disagree and to value differences**

Learning to disagree with courtesy and respect is particularly difficult for this type of child. The teacher might say to such a child, "You don't have to agree completely. Just listen to see if there isn't a bit of the other person's idea you might want to explore or to borrow." Then have him and his group play this game for a while: they must find something in the last speaker's message that they can agree with or at least find interesting, or worth exploring before they can state their own disagreement.

People often mentally leap to their disagreements and tenaciously cling to them before seeing what the areas of agreement are. A major task of the teacher is helping children (especially this kind of child) to learn that differences are valuable, that unanimous views may be dangerous, and that one can still value a person even when strongly disagreeing with his ideas. The teacher can help make it easier for the child to accept views that are well supported by pointing out that such open-minded behavior is a mark of maturity in a discussion (Burrows, 1970; Stanford & Stanford, 1969).[2]

**Assessment**

The nonparticipant. What about the timid nonparticipant? Again, perhaps the first step is to try to find the reasons. Does the child's behavior stem from timid patterns brought from home? Fear of exposure? A preference for daydreaming?

**What to do**

As for what to do, after leveling with him and helping him to take some responsibility for the problem, the teacher can guide him to pinpoint for himself his nonparticipating behavior and chart his own progress. Help him to participate by preparing him beforehand for the discussion. Perhaps the teacher needs to reverse the usual procedure of always asking the question first and then mentioning a pupil's name. Forewarned of expected response the timid child has some extra time to think. Give him plenty of time, extending and rephrasing the question if necessary. Try him in small groups with others who do or who will agree to play *supportive,* respectful roles. A group (or a teacher) who does not treat individuals with basic respect blocks communication.

If asked, the timid child may say that another child said what he was going to contribute. In this case, the teacher can ask him to explain why he agrees with the other child's comment. The reason for agreement may even turn out to be different, and a contribution of new information.

**Motivation and supportive social climate**

Even the slowest and most inarticulate child can learn to discuss, unless he has no motivation or the topic is over his head. Actually, the first objective is to get nonparticipating children to like or want to communicate, to feel that it is not only their right, but their duty to

[2] Also see Activity 2.1, Message Checkout, in which a message has to be restated to the satisfaction of the last speaker before a new message may be spoken by the next.

have defensible opinions. Of course, a facilitating social climate is important for this objective and a teacher who can weld the class into a constructive unit with basic group solidarity has most of the battle won.

The problem of the nonparticipant may be deeply rooted in feelings of social and performance inferiority. If some children always know less about all group discussion tasks and topics, then they come to have such a low opinion of their skills and potential success that they will not participate. The teacher can coach these students to the point of genuine competence in a given area (animal care, a foreign culture, operating a machine) and then place them in an expert role. The idea would be to let this role of expert rotate so that all get a chance to play it at some time and to assert themselves.

Procedures

There are several procedural things (Burrows, 1970) that the teacher could do (and teach children to do) when shy children withdraw and aggressive children take over. The discussion leader could ask the group to say nothing at all for a minute or so while they take time to just think. They might think about what the most important thing the group could accomplish in the next few minutes would be. With older children the leader could ask everyone to write down a brief note of his thoughts during this time. The leader could then call on children who have not contributed earlier. "Can you help us?" With their notes at hand, they may be able to get over their fear or hesitancy.

Another way to reduce take-over by monopolizers, but still allay their fear that they will not get a chance, is to follow this procedure. The leader says, "The next 5 minutes are for those who haven't had a chance yet. Those of you who want to speak, I'll write your initials here on the board so you'll get a turn later." As the withdrawn children are then encouraged to contribute, the aggressive children, reassured that they will get a chance to speak, can listen more attentively to what the others have to say.

Acting as summarizer

A final procedure designed to draw in the nonparticipant is to ask for a summary of the discussion several times. "Bob, will you tell what we've said so far?" "Beth, will you state what we think we know, our agreement?" Such contributions will help the group to become clear on what has been accomplished, and what may lie ahead. Some children make few contributions, but when they do, they are valuable. (See also Olsen, 1966.)

**The off-the-tracker.** What about the child who always appears to be getting off the track during a discussion? Much depends on the type of discussion and on its goal. Repetition, irrelevancies, and comments on points and questions made much earlier are an unavoidable part of most normal discussions. Oral speech and its ideas do not come in a linear way with parade-like precision. Severe control blocks creativity and spontaneity.

What to do

However, if some off-the-tracker consistently creates an outstanding problem, provide the kind of discussion in which wild brainstorming is appropriate, as well as the type of discussion in which a sharply delineated task creates discipline. The teacher can ask questions and make statements such as these:

> "Does this help us with our task?"
>
> "What has this idea to do with the earlier one?"
>
> "We may have missed a useful lead; tell the idea you gave earlier again."

Let the child also chart his own progress. He can tell better than anyone whether or not he was trying to stay on target.

Reasons for irrelevant statements

There are several reasons why children may make an apparently irrelevant statement. Their private planning or debating may have been triggered by a few words that have caused them to leave the stream of discourse. Also, there is little that is more distressing than having a good idea to present and being afraid of forgetting what it is before there is a chance to give it. The effort to hang on to an idea can occupy children so much that they lose the trend of the discussion, and may fail to realize that they agree with what someone else has just said.

Note taking and picture cuing

A piece of paper and pencil handy for quick jotting or for drawing picture cues can help the child get back to the main trend of the discussion. The note taking (for older children) or picture cuing (for younger ones) may help the chronic interrupter and the timid child, too.

What to do

The scapegoat. What about the scapegoat or the child the others ridicule? Again, the teacher can model a demonstration of support, valuation of and right of every contribution, especially minority opinion, to be heard. Clever facilitators can find something of value to the group in almost anyone's comment. They can model the desire to see a situation corrected rather than an offender punished. They can help the group take care of problems when they present themselves, in order to clear the air and maintain a healthy emotional climate so that grudges do not build. Role-play using fictitious names and masks also helps.

What to do

The shocker. What about the intentional shocker? The obvious response is not to be shocked, if this is the child's purpose. Nonreinforcement usually extinguishes behavior while you are searching for and developing more desirable behaviors for the child to engage in. Ignore it (taking others into your confidence if necessary). If "shocker" fails to provoke that deliciously horrified reaction, he'll forget it.

## What to Do About Disorder?

What do you do about disorder? Some teachers fear to have several discussion groups going on simultaneously because there might be some loss of classroom control. When and if general disruption and disorder do occur, let natural consequences of *postponement* for disruption and disorder operate. For example, you might say,

**Postponement**

> "The noise level from discussion is this classroom is too high. Since you cannot lower it, for the sake of the class next to us we will have to postpone our discussion until they have gone to recess or until you think you can discuss more quietly."

Your group will help in establishing and maintaining limits for the behavior of its members if this responsibility extends reliably and reasonably to all areas of classroom experience. However, this group valuing of constructive behavior is not a trick pulled out of the bag to meet some crisis, or to be played with superficially. It evolves with struggle and testing through problem situations met and overcome. Each success sows the seeds of the next success.

The teacher trusts, gives freedom for action; the children dare to try—success—they dare to try again. Progress takes two factors (1) the confidence that any errors will not be fatal, and (2) the confidence to let children make some bad choices (for they learn from those, too) as they help to make and review the rules.

**The class vs. the teacher**

Sometimes a classroom suffers from the "versus" disease—the children versus the teacher. The teacher asks the question,

"Who knows more, you or I?"

- I with my experience and training?
- You with your feelings and knowledge of where you are and your understanding of your friends?
- All of us together?

If the belief is "all of us together," this interactive rapport shows clearly in the observed classroom discussions.

**Duties before rights**

The gradual and painstaking development of an autonomous, responsible, and cooperative room climate is essential if chaos is to be avoided, but another factor is this: the acceptance, by all concerned, not only of rights but also of responsibilities. We hear a lot about rights. But we cannot have rights until we can or will fulfill duties. This is a natural consequence that can operate instructively in the classroom.

For example, the person who drives a car could not have the rights of a driver (to go where he wishes in that car) without fulfilling the duties of a driver (to drive on the correct side of the road, to respect the rights of other drivers, to keep adequate gas in the car). So it is with children—they cannot have the right to engage in small-group discussion if they cannot fulfill the duties of students involved in discussion. It is the old principle that you get out of something what you put into it. The teacher's idea in the classroom, however, is not *denial* of rights, but *postponement for another trial,* when the class is ready to fulfill its duties related to productive discussion.

Rewards for the teacher

The patience needed for trial and retrial is worth it. There is nothing like a vital exchange of constructive and appropriate leadership roles in a group to enhance the growth of thought and speech. It is here that children shape fuller statements as they build on what others say. These thinking–expressing groups serve as much (if not more) to develop total language progress as do reading groups.

Teacher as process guider

In these discussion groups, teachers participate mainly as *guiders* of process—*not* as content givers. In fact, if the teacher is really skillful at development, eventually he eliminates the need for teacher guidance in the discussion.[3] If a teacher needs compulsively to be needed and to play the role of dominator, then this open-ended, developmental activity is not for him.

Next, turn to some other questions that teachers raise in regard to conducting discussion in the classroom.

## HOW CAN THE TEACHER EVALUATE?

Some teachers do not want to spend any time on discussion because they think that there is no way to evaluate it. This section deals with the many modes of evaluating discussion. Assessment procedures are important from the beginning to the end. In the beginning the teacher may need a rough estimate of the levels of fluency in the class in order to plan for the most productive composition of small groups.

Initial fluency check

A way to find out about fluency is to ask children to check one of these two statements as more nearly describing them.

I talk a lot.
I never talk.

[3] There are, of course, times when the teacher functions as disseminator of information and "chief operator" in the classroom.

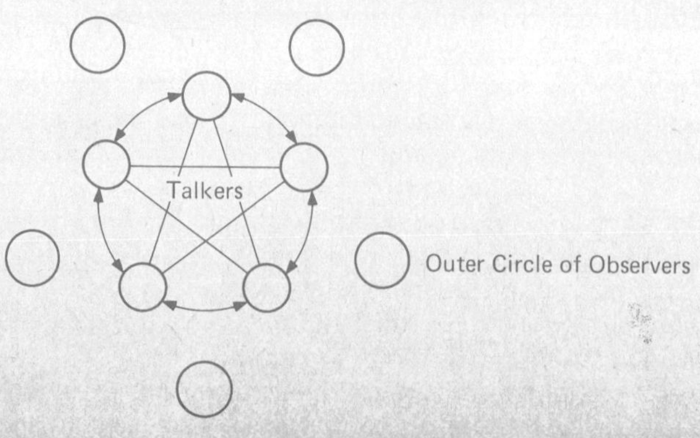

Then, conduct a brief discussion using almost any one of the seven types described later in this chapter. But place the talkers in the middle in a circle to discuss and the nontalkers around them in an outside circle to participate as silent but involved (and later, as reporting) observers. Then have the two groups switch places and have the nontalkers in the center do the talking while the talkers sit in the outside circle as involved but silent observers. This kind of activity is sometimes stimulating for the child who otherwise participates very little.

## Evaluating Through Children As Observers

Goldfish game

The inner circle–outer circle procedure is sometimes referred to as the *fishbowl* game and is useful when children are at the stage of developing evaluative skills as observers. Their evaluation may be a simple keeping track of who says what to whom. Or it may be a more elaborate look at who initiates, who agrees, who makes positive or negative contributions, who makes obstructive ones, and other dimensions such as (1) clear–confused, (2) related–unrelated, (3) trust–distrust, and (4) helping and concern–unconcern.

What observers do

Observers keep track of participation, the processes, the roles used, the interactions, the types of discussion, group–member relations, leader–member relations, or whatever the group decides it wants to include on its checklist. For example, maybe the group decides to work on supported opinions or vividly expressed feelings. An observer (who takes no part in the discussion) keeps count of these, or some other specific behavior that the group has chosen to pinpoint. These behaviors can even be charted week by week. Children need to understand that an observer's report does not tear down personalities, but points out behaviors that helped or hindered the discussion, or other skills or parts of the process under focus.

Some components of evaluation

Children as observers can evaluate two basic components: ideas, and processes. As process improves, ideas become of more concern. In all the discussion-type activities suggested in this chapter, evaluation is probably best accomplished by having pupils take an active part in developing their own standards, applying them, and then discussing the application. They can then revise their standards if need be. Children can turn these standards into personal rating scales. Thus a third component in evaluation is child involvement and autonomy. Children can tape, transcribe, and (using abbreviations for the scale items) code their discussions themselves.

Teacher questions

To ready the children for these evaluative responsibilities, the teacher might frequently ask questions such as the following: "Which statement is more useful?" "How can we find out?" "What ideas were brought out today that you had not thought of before?" "How far did we get by working together?" "How do we still need to improve?" "What objectives do we need to set for ourselves in order to make our discussion better?" [4]

### Individual Evaluation

By the pupil

Regarding self-evaluation, pupils can make entries in their own personal discussion logs. Included might be a personal chart indicating each skill, role, or type of discussion as it is practiced. General goals, such as fairness, open-mindedness in maintenance functions can be inferred from specific behaviors and words caught by the tape recorder, such as, "You haven't had a turn. Go ahead." "Tell us more why you think so."

Need for successes

Do not expect every group discussion to be successful every time, no more than you would expect any other learning situation to be successful every time. Not all learning outcomes are best accomplished by discussion, important as it is. But a guiding idea for the teacher is that groups need to achieve numerous small successes before undertaking complex tasks.

## PRACTICAL CONSIDERATIONS

### Physical Room Setup for Discussion

Some might be discouraged from organizing small-group discussion because they feel they have an inappropriate physical room arrangement. But if determined teachers in classrooms with 48 seats (screwed inexorably to the floor) can block them into eight groups (with vacant seats providing some insulation) and find success at the high-school level, those of us with fewer (and smaller) pupils ought to be able to organize small-group settings in our classrooms. During brief discussions, two to a seat is not too uncomfortable; extra stools help.

Even if your furniture is readily movable, try sitting on small rugs, cushions, or wrapping paper on the floor. Getting 48 children into and out of groups does require some of the following provisions: preplanning, prearranged signals, and a breaking down of the task into small practice parts concerning the *with whom,* the *where,* and the *what then.* The rewards in the growth of oral communication—the base of learning—are great enough so that it is well worth the trouble.

[4] Research shows that children usually have a limited opportunity to raise questions themselves in school (Gall, 1970). This fact makes it difficult to get much information about evaluating pupil's questions or teaching them skills of question asking.

The companion guide to this book, *Ideas into Practice,* includes lessons with questions that children can be helped to use themselves. In this same guide there are sections devoted to evaluation that are appropriate here, too.

### Group Size and Composition

The size of the discussion group depends on the following: the type of discussion, the shyness factor, the number and kinds of skills inherent in the members and needed for success, the use of uneven numbers to discourage ganging up, the leadership skill in allowing a hearing for the minority viewpoint, and so on. You simply have to experiment. Try groups of five as a "first shot in the dark." You can try total group discussion, then follow-up with small-group work, making sure to include any nonparticipants.

Group variety and permanence

What about group composition? A balanced group seems to be best—heterogeneous, not too many of one type of child. As a rule place not more than four shy children in a group of ten students. Once groups are formed, teachers have to make the decision of whether to keep the membership the same or to switch pupils around. Again, the suggestion is to experiment. However, if groups are to become a keeping place for values, a place where there is mutual trust and respect, they need some continuity and tradition.

### How Often and How Much Time?

If group effects are to be cumulative, discussion must occur regularly. Children cannot learn to discuss without discussing. If the skills of this week are to progress from those of the last, practice must be continued.

How much time per discussion? A general rule is to stop while the participants are still interested. Closure is of secondary importance, if the goal is improved process. Five minutes the first time? Ten? Twenty? Allow too little time rather than too much. Let the children conclude the formal class discussion with questions and issues still churning in their minds. Let the discussion spill over into the playground and lunchroom. Exploratory discourse uncovers and discovers rather than covers.

## HOW DOES THE TEACHER GUIDE DISCUSSION?

### Guiding by Questioning

Each teacher needs to ask himself the purpose of his questions, as they are one of the basic language units underlying discussion and most of classroom instruction. This section deals with the teacher's habits and ways of reacting to pupil responses; with various purposes of discussion and how questions are phrased to match them; and with the pacing or sequencing of questions.

What are habits to be avoided? According to some encouraging studies, teachers do not have as many bothersome teaching habits during ques-

tioning as they used to (Gall, 1970). The following are some of the undesirable behaviors:

1. Repetition of questions and of pupil answers so that accurate, first-time listening on the part of the pupils becomes nonessential. (Generally it is better practice to have a *pupil* who was listening repeat if necessary. Let pupils have the "set" to try to get the message the first time.)
2. Consistent answering of one's own questions. (Why not simply "tell," if it is important that children know the teacher's thinking?)
3. Interruption of a child's responses. (Interruption, besides showing lack of respect for the child as an individual, can cause the discussion to stray from the line of communication.)

Next, examine some positive aspects of dealing with the children's answers to the teacher's questions.

How do teachers react to pupil's responses? Teachers play several roles during the questioning process when they react relevantly to their children's responses. Among these roles are the following: recording, reinforcing, clarifying, and challenging or lifting.

*Teachers' Reactions to Children's Responses to Questions*

1. *Function as a nondirective recorder.* Teachers can do this by writing the response for all participants to see, suspending judgment, simply absorbing the literal message. The teacher's mind can be busily at work analyzing what is happening and planning ahead. But he does not respond overtly, and children *expect no response,* realizing that they are to act autonomously. Possibly the teacher is replanning the development of the content of the discussion in light of pupil response. (The three reactions that follow are directive.)

2. *Accept with positive reinforcement.* Especially in the beginning, children may need a lot of praise and warm verbalization of teacher approval to reassure them that they are on the right track and are behaving successfully. Later, when process skills are well mastered, natural consequences of productivity, self-satisfaction, and peer-group response can act as the major reinforcers rather than authority-figure approval.
3. *Seek to clarify answers.* The instructor may need to have the child rephrase, elaborate, and support his response. The teacher may "extend" with that student or with others. The teacher may need to refocus for the student who is wandering helplessly in a verbal

maze or apparently straying from the communication line. He may need to help the child backtrack to an earlier, easier level.

4. *Challenge the answer*. The instructor may disagree, correct, disapprove, even modify as he challenges the answer. He may even act to lift the respondent and others to higher, more complex, more abstract levels of thought. In that case he may not reject the answer, but may hitchhike on it in order to ease the next responses upward to a more sophisticated level.

Of course, the pupil response may trigger some managerial role of the teacher not exactly relevant to the line of communication (e.g., "Go put your gum in the wastebasket").

You might use the four reactions just given along with the sample questions to follow as a checklist for your own behavior regarding questions during discussion time. Tape-record yourself and play the recording back, hunting for these strategies. Generally, if the teacher sits with the children as part of a discussion group, the members immediately begin to defer appeals to the teacher's authority. When a child seeks an answer from the teacher, the teacher can either pass the question to another child, or, upon answering it, open up another question.

### Purposes Behind the Teacher's Questions

The behavior that teachers show in reacting to children's responses is in large part a result of the questions they ask the pupils in the first place. A question is phrased in a particular way to produce a desired change of behavior in the pupil, for instance, to get the pupil *ready* (or to motivate), to *reinforce* his learning, to help him *transfer* an idea, and to get a factual response or an inference, application, or principle. Questions are not ends in themselves. And what you ask is what you get.

A list of objectives and questions designed to implement them is helpful during expositional discourse. The sample objectives and questions fall into four categories that match useful discussion roles designed to carry the process along: (1) Initiating or focusing, (2) clarifying or extending, (3) lifting and evaluating, and (4) summarizing. The categories are in the order in which they might occur during a discussion. Although a brief example of a classroom setting is given, for the most part the questions are pulled out of realistic context for display purposes.

### *What Are Some Sample Objectives and Questions?*

Classroom setting. The class is studying the difference between facts, inferences, and opinions. Two children have just role-played an incident in which one child has taken and broken another's toy airplane.

| OBJECTIVE | QUESTION |
|---|---|
| 1. *Initiating and Focusing Questions* | |
| To focus on facts and conditions | What actually happened?<br>What did you notice? |
| 2. *Clarifying and Extending Questions* | |
| To get children to clarify and to interpret | Can you tell more? Was it this way?<br>What do you mean?<br>Can you give an example?<br>What are some reasons for your choice?<br>How do you define this key word you used?<br>Does this make our decision clearer? |
| To extend inquiry | What else would you like to know about the airplane?<br>What is similar about this incident and the last one? |
| To predict | What would be some consequences if he goes on in this way?<br>What will it mean for tomorrow, next month, year? Where does it lead?<br>What will be the probable result?<br>If one child changed his whining behavior to a "let's compromise" type of behavior, what do you think would happen?<br>What do you think will happen next? |
| To determine concepts as to what is or is not a class member | How would you group those three comments? As facts, inferences, or opinions? |
| To stimulate search strategy | How would you go about finding out if he could get another airplane like it? |
| To bring out opinion, attitude, feeling, and *valuing* | What do you think about what the younger boy did?<br>If it is good for one of them, will it be bad for the other? How important is that?<br>Which of the ideas for solving the boys' problems seems to hold less promise now? |

| | |
|---|---|
| | If that idea is acted on, will one of the boys be hurt? |
| | What could be the best thing that could happen? The worst? |
| | Would the boys' lives be better if your idea carries? |
| | What would you do? What do you feel should be done? |
| 3. *Lifting and Evaluating Questions* | |
| To elicit evidence | What makes you sure it's true? |
| To seek unique responses | How could he make him an airplane he might like even better? How could you change its material, size, color; can you brainstorm other ways? |
| To seek multiple alternatives | Can you try thinking about the airplane another way? What else could he do to make it up to him? What ways might be open to him now? What other ways have you considered? |
| To promote organization | What plan could he make? What steps could he take? What needs to come first?" |
| To relate and to transfer | What goes along with this plan? Could you ever use a plan like that someplace else? |
| To evaluate | What standard could you apply to that solution? |
| | Think about all the ideas we have brought out and what you inferred and said you thought would be most valuable; what would you finally conclude? |
| 4. *Summarizing Questions* | |
| | What big ideas can you see coming out of all this? |
| | Suppose you wanted to tell a friend who had been absent the highlights of our role playing the broken airplane story and our discussion, what might you say? |
| | What have we decided so far? |
| | Who will state our agreements? |
| | What did you learn? |

The trouble with these relatively isolated examples is that they give you little sense of progression. They fail to show how the teacher would adapt his questions in light of pupil responses. However, it is helpful to see such groupings while learning to analyze questioning techniques. (Do *you* agree? Is this clear? What is your feeling?)

Focusing, extending, and lifting

What is pacing? Progression in light of students' responses is known as pacing. Questions, such as those listed previously, are balanced between guidance functions of focusing, extending, and lifting—all according to students' needs emerging during the discussion.[5]

The well-paced discussion avoids the pitfalls of "rushing by" the subject or of becoming so complex that almost all students (except the most brilliant) become lost—that is, fail to process the data and fail to progress through the desired mental operations. The teacher needs the following kinds of questions for pacing, whether he carries out the pacing function himself or rotates it among the children:

1. Questions that *focus* (What did you see in the film about their clothing?)
2. Questions that *extend* with respect to both the type of question itself and the number of children sampled to respond to it (Can more of you recall or remember?)
3. Questions that *lift* or assist progression to higher and higher levels of thought (How would you group these facts about this country? Now, how would you label these groups of facts? Is there some idea that connects them all? Some principle? What would happen if? What ideas might account for ________? What would it take for ________ to be true?)

Questions that leap over levels of thought and demand generalizations and abstracting too soon cause the discussion to flounder back to lower concrete, confused, or trivial levels. Much in pacing success depends on the teacher's careful premapping of the terrain of the discussion area. Much depends on the teacher's on-the-spot, sensitive decision making. Such decisions grow out of a teacher's extremely careful listening to the responses that he elicits from his children.

What are some other sources of questions? The teacher can find additional questions in many of the references at the end of this chapter (e.g., Bartolome, 1969; Guszak, 1967; Shaftel & Shaftel, 1970). The *Taxonomy of Educational Objectives* edited by B. S. Bloom (1956) gives examples of questions directed to different levels of thinking. These

[5] In the Prologue to this book, Mr. Warren's class discussion of the book *Crow Boy* also illustrates pacing. See the cognitive map by Taba (1964) later in this chapter, p. 165.

levels are as follows: (1) knowledge, (2) comprehension, (3) analysis, (4) application, (5) synthesis, and (6) evaluation. Another way of looking at questions related to these levels is to describe them as using simple memory or convergent, divergent, or judgmental thinking (Cunningham, 1971, pp. 81–131).

### Need for Higher-Level Questions

Surveys show that teachers' questions tend to overemphasize factual knowledge (Gall, 1970). A child can learn on this level just as well by using programmed instruction, teacher aides, and pupil tutors. He does not need a highly educated teacher by his side for this kind of learning. The teacher can better use his time for more complex, open-ended, unconstrained sequences. He can guide children's higher levels of thought. If a teacher can be replaced by a machine—then he should be. But when it comes to the high-level processes of discussion explained in this chapter, no machine can act as a teacher replacement. Keep in mind—what you ask is what you get.

### Process Maps

The sets of functions (such as focusing, extending, and lifting; and readiness, reinforcement, and transfer) might be called process maps for a discussion. The teacher may also keep in mind maps of skill or content areas. Such maps serve as important focusing components for discussion. They keep the discussion from rambling pointlessly over a broad area. For example, in a second-grade *social studies* unit on rules, "Learning How to Act," a discussion of rules might range over the following areas: maintaining order in home and school; health and safety; government resolution of conflicts and its effort to make interaction easier among people; process of value seeking; and concept seeking for the idea of social control (e.g., "Look at this picture—would you ride your bike here?").[6]

The possibilities of which areas to treat are vast. A teacher needs a map, and he needs to decide what part of that map he is going to use at a certain time. To illustrate, a map of a tentative hierarchy of listening skills that one teacher had in the back of his mind during discussion follows. The circles represent prerequisites that the teacher wanted to be certain were operating before he began the discussion. I give a sample pupil response below the teacher's questions. The idea for content of the discussion is based on an example in the SRA (Science Research Associates) filmstrip-tape series, *Basic Teaching Skills.* The children

[6] *The Social Sciences, Concepts and Values,* Unit 2 (New York: Harcourt, 1970). (Text for second-grade pupils.)

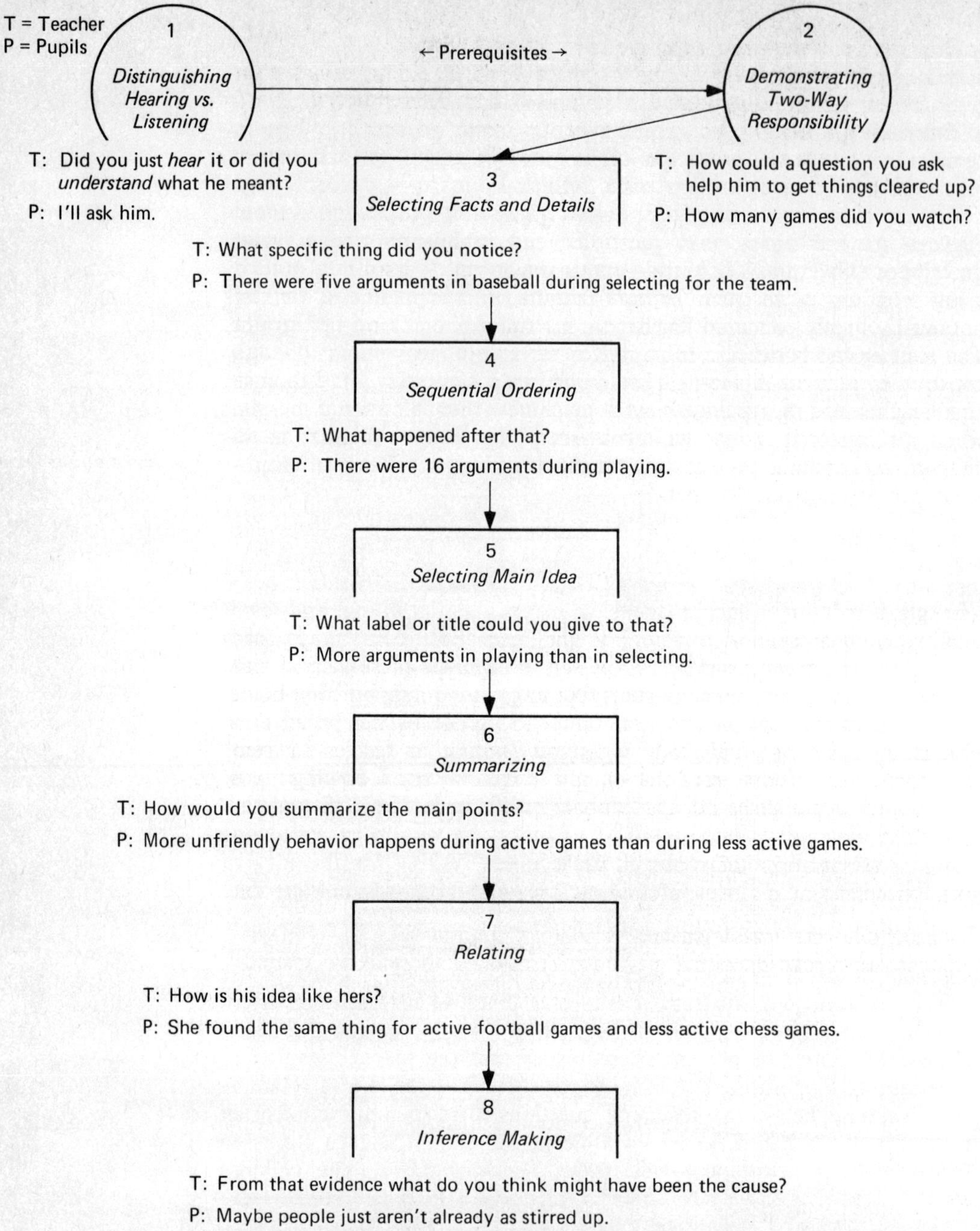


**A MAP OF SKILLS FOR A TENTATIVE LEARNING HIERARCHY OF GENERAL LISTENING OBJECTIVES**

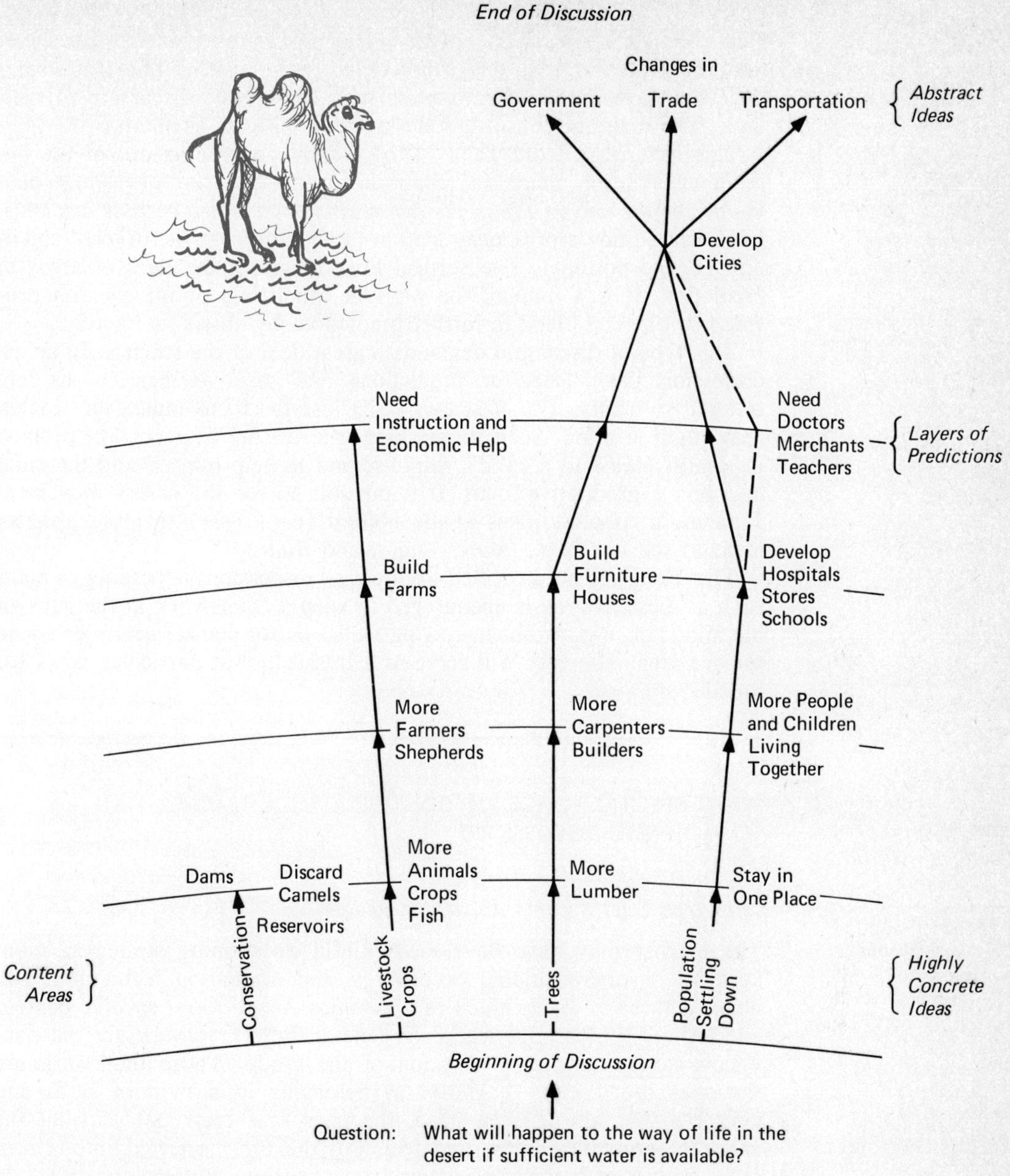


**COGNITIVE MAP OF CONTENT IN THIRD-GRADE DISCUSSION**

**After H. Taba, S. Levine, and F. E. Freeman, *Thinking in Elementary School Children*. USOE Cooperative Research Project No. 1574, 1964. San Francisco State College, p. 131.**

observed and tabulated unfriendly acts during various activities–baseball, football, chess, and studying. The blocks represent six listening–thinking skills (in addition to the circled prerequisites) that the teacher hoped to have the children operate with during this discussion of their data. The diagram constitutes the map, or process skeleton.[7]

This next map, from Taba (1964), shows a fanning out of the hypotheses children made in response to the question of *what would happen to the way of life in the desert if enough water became available.* Each curved line represents a leap in prediction from the original condition (at the bottom). The vertical lines represent the lines or areas of prediction. It is a map of the ways in which bits of information provided by one child lead to further predictions by others interacting.

This type of discussion demands a great deal of the teacher. In actual discussion these leaps of predictions and their verification are not ordered so neatly. The class can easily lose the focus unless the teacher has a map in mind. Such a map helps the teacher to recognize promising leads related to a child's response and to help himself and the child maintain a productive focus. It is possible to see the class's movement from more concrete ideas at the bottom (e.g., *trees*) to more abstract ideas at the top (e.g., *houses, build,* and *trade*).

The teacher is not expected to direct all discussions according to maps such as these. But he is encouraged to keep a framework in the back of his mind for, e.g., problem-solving skills, or for some science or social science area. The map will serve as a useful tool at particular times for specific purposes.

## WHAT SPECIFIC TOPICS OR CONTENT CAN A TEACHER FIND TO MOTIVATE DISCUSSION?

*"How can I get a group discussion going?"*

Class needs and interests

The teacher may have developed skillful questioning strategies, management or organizational procedures, and evaluation techniques. But none of these is worth much in a vacuum. What about specific content and topics? Which ones work? In general those that work are the ones uncovered by careful observation of the group. Those that work are the ones the teacher diagnoses as belonging in a map of skills and concepts that his children need, the ones that grow out of what the children think they know and feel. Put the topic selected into a sentence with a verb implying action—an assertion or question: What do

[7] Map from the first unit of listening lessons in the companion guide, *Ideas into Practice.*

we need to learn about drugs?, What does a president do?, What good are rules?, What is a law and why was it made?, What are customs and why do you follow them?, What is a group? (Do the members have the same goal? Do they depend on each other? Is this a group? Why or why not? When does concern with groups go too far and the individual lose out?).

A topic for discussion needs to be able to accommodate honest differences of opinion, rights and wrongs, and relative merits of causes or solutions (Which of two field trips?). No matter what the topic, however, the quality of opinion depends on the amount and accuracy of the information held by those discussing. Children cannot very well discuss the relative merits of a television show that only one child in the group has actually seen. Open for alternatives

Help children to become notetakers and collectors of information. One mark of a successful speaker and discusser is his awareness of the potential value of almost all experience as material for discourse. If the child continually collects an ample store, he will be more convinced that he has something worthwhile to say.

Specific suggestions

- Children might pretend that their home was burning, and they could carry only three things away with them (or one thing). They could be asked what they would choose and why. They could talk about the things in detail, and then be asked if any members of the group had things in common, and why, or why not.
- Topics stemming from problems and challenges both personal and academic may be collected in a "problem box" and brought up for discussion weekly. Ask pupils to contribute an item a week to the box.[8]
- Or, have each pupil construct as many as five topics he would like to hear discussed and possibly also as many as five he would actually like to work on. A class committee can tabulate these topics and build a program from the list. Or, more indirectly, the teacher might determine possible topics by means of an anonymous opinion poll.
- For upper-grade children try a bull session on the topic "What's Right with the World?"—the bright side of civilization. It could be a discussion growing out of content from social studies, the history of language, science, and personal observation. Discuss humanity's successes; the fantastic achievements of human beings who found themselves alone in a vast universe and set about to make something useful out of an impossibly fearsome and threatening environment.

[8] See such a sample lesson in the companion guide to this book, *Ideas into Practice.*

Which of their achievements is most important and why?
  Pooling efforts to build shelters.
  Raising food.
  Transporting themselves:
    Tunneling through mountains.
    Descending beneath the sea.
    Venturing into the air and into outer space.
  Discovering that gentleness can be more practical than brute force (think of the large percentage of time people are kindly and decent when they could be vile and spiteful).
  Developing ability to appreciate, to discover and to create beauty and humor.

Gradually broaden the base of the content of the discussion as children widen and deepen interests and increase in skill. (See also Shaftel & Shaftel, 1970; also topics for discussion and writing in other chapters of this book.)

**Ponderables or stretchers**

- As a stretcher for discussion, try topics growing out of questions that people living shallowly do not ask, let alone try to answer. That is, try topics such as these:

  What do you want to do with your life? What should we become in the short stretch between birth and death? What do you want to be known for? Is life worth living? What is courage? Children need a chance to talk about important, serious topics as opposed to a constant dose of trivial ones. Kierkegaard, the philosopher, wrote that there are too many people who reach their conclusions about life, if they think at all about it, in the manner of schoolboys who cheat their teacher (and themselves) by copying the answer out of a book without ever having worked out the sum for themselves. Why not have the courage to bring dimensions of depth and of passionate seriousness about the meaning of existence, right into the classroom discussion? Do not be frightened of what the pupils may bring up. It is not the teacher's function to have all the answers to life; it is his function to prompt the exploration and to demonstrate learning how to learn.

**Moderate to music**

- Finally, musical selections in varying orchestral moods are often good activators for discussion; for example, the finale from *Symphony no. 2 in D-major, op. 43,* or *Finlandia* (both by Sibelius) or the *New World Symphony,* or the overture to *Lawrence of Arabia.*[9] Parts of these might create an appropriate listening mood preparatory to the discussion suggested earlier on the "bright side of the world—human-

[9] Overture to *Lawrence of Arabia,* composed by Maurice Jarre (London Philharmonic Orchestra, Colpix Records CP514).

ity's successes." Other musical possibilities for this particular activity are two songs from *The Man of La Mancha,* "I, Don Quixote," and "The Impossible Dream."

**Relation to reading and writing**

How does a wise selection of content for discussion create unity in the program? The last chapter (on self-expression and exposition) pointed out many relationships among subject areas, in the language arts program, but there are others. One of these is between discussion and reading. Discussion is related to reading in this way: children do not need to depend solely on direct experience for their discussion content, but can read for topic ideas and for supporting material. Hopefully, however, children will not feel impelled to go to an encyclopedia and then regurgitate a pale, confused, and poorly digested imitation of the original writing. This misfortune is unlikely if they are secure and value their own autonomy and experience. The reading–discussion relationship links up with writing to form a chain: discussion stimulates reading; reading uncovers ideas for discussion, which in turn can stimulate writing. And the discussion on the environment becomes an editorial for the school or class paper, which prompts reading of a related article in a magazine.

The teacher can prompt *content* relationships through discussion. Using content from other elementary-school subjects as the major source of discussion material saves time, too. For economy of time and for unity, find problems for discussion in math, social studies, science, literature, music, and language history or language science.

## THE CREATIVE-PROBLEM-SOLVING DISCUSSION (CPS)

The creative-problem-solving discussion might be thought of as the "grandaddy" of all the other types of discussion (i.e., tutorial, bull session, brainstorming, task, inquiry, and Socratic). Many of the characteristics of these other types are found in (or are supportive of) problem-solving discussions. A creative-problem-solving discussion probably uses the greatest number of skills and the highest degree of creativity. This is mainly because of the type of problem it demands.

What type of problem allows for creativity? In the Prologue to this book the specification was made that (within reason) the more unknowns in the problem, the greater the chance for creativity. The problem must have no clear-cut right or wrong answer. This openness of inquiry is a difficult concept for those who have grown up learning that there is a right way to behave, speak, and do things. Spokesmen for the social sciences and the humanities say that right and wrong are relative to the values and characteristics of different cultures. These spokesmen say that there are more than two sides to an issue; each person is entitled to an opinion, which will be influenced by various past experiences. This point of view gives backing to the creative type of discussion in this section.

In any case, the creative-problem-solving type of discussion needs no one best solution. The *process* is what is important. There may be a range of more plausible, more satisfactory, more workable solutions from various points of view. But not one right answer. The common compulsion for closure is referred to as *lysophobia,* meaning that everything must be terminated favorably, everything must be tied up in a neat little package. The view from general semantics is that regarding human language and experience there *is no last word on a subject*. We need to remind ourselves that we can never know all about everything. We can only abstract a limited amount. To say that a group *must* come to a consensus is in this sense invalid. Instead, human situations continue "etc., etc., and etc.," with unceasing learning in store for participants.

**Humanistic quality**

Apparently then, there is a more *humanistic* quality to this type of discussion problem. There is a taking into account of feelings of sympathy and empathy, not just internal and external logic and validity. (How did you feel about this problem? Could you see it from his point of view? Did your feelings change? How would you feel if *you'd* lost your pet?) At the same time the leader is encouraged to use his sense of humor whenever possible, to use the light touch, to avoid the grim, demanding, one-upmanship way of delivery characteristic of some probing or Socratic discussions. Also in this vein, the leader is encouraged to use a permissive, allowing silence in order to give the participants time to become aware of the nonverbal aspects of what is going on in and around the participants.

**Four major areas**

As mentioned earlier, the emphasis in a problem-solving discussion is on process, not product. Thus the problems for the discussion need to be *complex* enough to make worthwhile the use of at least four areas of problem solving and (hopefully) nine steps and nine qualities within them. The four areas (described in the Prologue) are the following:

1. Planned procedure
2. Problem area
3. Hypotheses
4. Planned evaluation

What are some steps? Suggested steps include discrimination of the following:

1. Facts and conditions
2. Definition of key terms in the problem
3. Subproblems
4. Missing data
5. Search strategy

6. Main problem
7. Type of problem
8. Hypotheses
9. Planned evaluation of hypothesis selected for first trial

A planned progression is implied in the listing of steps. But certainly some circling back, almost simultaneous attention, and leaping ahead goes on. This ordering is suggested as a logical instructional sequence. Surprised to find the *main problem* halfway down the list? Usually the step *not* to begin with is a definitive statement of the main problem. That would be too much of a conceptual leap for children. Placing it first can bring empty verbalization and overgeneralization. If a more inductive approach to stating the problem is used, the children are not overwhelmed by the abstractness of the statement.

What are some qualities of such a discussion? There are nine characteristic qualities of a creative-problem-solving discussion to be kept in mind while guiding the discussion, and later, evaluating it.

*Some Qualities in Problem Solving*

1. Comprehension (literal) of meaning
2. Relevance
3. Elaboration
4. Originality or uniqueness
5. Alternatives (multiple)
6. Empathy
7. Casual thinking
8. Testability of hypotheses (Could they be tested?)
9. Evaluative thinking

How can this type of discussion be diagrammed? The following diagram indicates the many interactive roles that the participants play (graduated circles). They play these roles as the one assuming the leadership function (L) helps to guide the thinking process. This process is based on the problem-solving steps and enhancing qualities just listed. The leader may be the teacher or a prepared pupil. The process of discussing a

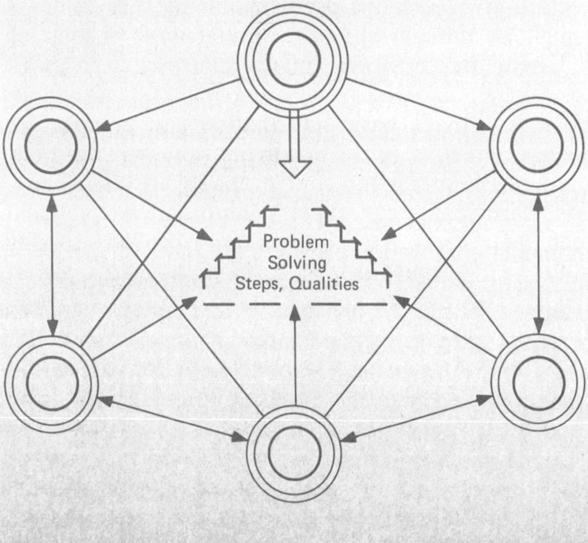


CREATIVE-PROBLEM-SOLVING DISCUSSION

challenge can provoke many pleasant feelings. The "staircase" suggests the presence of a certain number of sequential steps and accompanying qualities. Spaces are left open in the problem area to show that it is open-ended.

**What are some classroom examples?** Groups of children may meet for the purpose of engaging in creative problem-solving for several reasons. Examples of practical topics are the following: How to improve the housing for the rats and mice kept as pets; how to help band members make up their work when they are excused from their regular classes; how to improve behavior among the children riding the bus; how to establish workable standards for care of the classroom; and how to increase the respect for the belongings of others when you share the same desk.

I mentioned a creative-problem-solving session with a simple structure for children in the Prologue (Wilcox, 1972). Children trained for leadership followed three rules: all (1) take turns, (2) give many ideas, and (3) give reasons. The problems for the group to discuss came from the Shaftel & Shaftel (1970) materials concerning what a child will do about a problem. The children are to try to state many hypotheses and then to select the best in light of the story facts and the group's combined value standards.

For example: would the girl scout who is up for election, and likely to win, admit that she had mistakenly accused and slandered her competitor? Would the older brother let his younger brother go into the place where the dangerous motorcycle was kept, in order to keep his younger brother from tattling? Would the group destroy the microscope, or admit that they unintentionally had broken it during unauthorized after-school use?

The children are engaged in projected "What would you do—what does your group agree should be done?" situations. Much excellent children's literature, of course, abounds with dilemma situations just waiting for children to discuss them. (See the discussion of the book *Crow Boy* in the Prologue.)

**What are similarities and contrasts with other discussion types?** At the beginning of this description of creative-problem-solving discussion, I said such discussion might be thought of as the "grandaddy" of most of the discussion types. There are, however, many contrasts as well as similarities.

*Tutorial* discussions may provide basic information and practice for skills that are used later in creative problem-solving, although tutorials differ vastly in the amount of interaction and probably in complexity. During the *bull session,* participants can express important feelings and values, which they can later carry over into creative-problem-solving discussions. The uninhibited making of hypotheses in *brainstorming* represents a portion of the creative-problem-solving process. These two processes differ in that brainstorming does not include an evaluation step. In the *task group,* the development of procedure is clearly related to creative problem-solving. But the task-group problem may be one with a right answer, and the group may be on a schedule. The task group may employ few of the kinds of steps and leadership roles found in creative problem-solving. The problem is narrowed to a "we-gotta-finish-a-product" orientation. (See Activity 4.3, p. 177.)

Closed *inquiry–training* discussions differ from creative-problem-solving ones on at least two counts. These are (1) the direction of thinking (convergent–divergent) and (2) the formulation of questions by the leaders. For example:

1. In creative problem-solving, pupils do not need to converge toward one correct response. Participants value multiple alternatives. There is no attempt to tie the discussion up into a neat, closed package. In closed inquiry there is one right answer and the teacher usually "fishes" for it.

2. In a creative-problem-solving type of discussion, questioning is not designed for yes–no answers from an all-knowing source; questions are more open-ended. They are designed to provoke certain steps in the process and in divergent thought. In closed inquiry the yes–no response serves as a responsive environment for learning. (Child: "Is it made of wood?" Teacher [acting as responsive environment]: "No."

Finally, the creative-problem-solving discussion differs from the *Socratic* one especially in process. Problem solving is, of course, concerned with the steps and procedures in solving. The Socratic leader is trying to stir people from their complacency by provoking them to explore the sides of an issue, and by probing critically in the manner of the devil's advocate. The leader in the creative-problem-solving discussion avoids challenges and criticism. Criticism even implied merely by a probing question can be taken personally and blight a child's desire to learn. Criticism may promote a defensiveness that blocks communication. The creative-problem-solving leader treads more carefully.

Like the brainstorming session, creative problem-solving suspends evaluation of contributions, at least until the planned evaluation step. Or final judgment may be suspended until a task-oriented group takes over. Then the newly formed task group can follow-up and carry out a likely hypothesis and its plan, for subsequent evaluation. (The plan itself would have been processed and formulated during the earlier discussion.) Of course, there is some evaluative decision-making inherent in the fact that problem solving progresses from step to step. (See the activities at the end of this chapter for more on some of these discussion types.)

But, although there are differences between creative-problem-solving discussion and other types, the many modes can feed into and complement problem solving in a productive way. An example showing most of the types of discussion groups in action follows.

The broken tree: classroom example of group type relationships

*Broken Tree Day* A small bull session took place before class started in the morning. Some of the children had noticed that over the weekend a little tree in the playground had been ruthlessly hacked in two. Since the children appeared interested and concerned, the teacher let them draw a picture of it on the board and then took the class out to the playground, where they formed a circle on the grass around the broken tree. After children had expressed their feelings over the death of the tree (with some moments of silent thought), they proceeded to brainstorm about what they might do. Occasionally a child would lapse into the Socratic role and ask why someone would do such a thing. The group then progressed into a creative-problem-solving session to plan and to elaborate on the favorite hypothesis, or remedy, which was (by group consensus) that they would collect money and buy another tree.

The children pursued some of the problem-solving steps, e.g., what they still needed to find out, what steps they would take, how they would know if they got a good tree, and so on. By the end of the school day, the children had formed task groups concerned with who would do what. Thus they began to carry out plans generated in that creative-problem-solving session around the tree. Some of the tasks that the children carried out were the following: They made and decorated cans for each room in the school in order to collect money for replacing the dead tree. One group designed and constructed written invitations to others to come watch the new tree planting. Later the children wrote creative stories about the event, which they read to one another and to other classes.[10]

[10] The teacher commented on this happening that it was one of the best discussions to date. She hadn't dreamed that the children would come up with such good ideas. She had not even thought that the discussion experience would develop such an ecological attitude in her class. The author is indebted to Mrs. Mary Cummings, third-grade teacher, San Clemente, Calif. for furnishing the material on which this example is based.

In sum, if a group has a genuine and challenging problem, they will face and overcome disruptive elements of confusion, ambiguity, misunderstanding, and frustration. Students work together better if they can explain how they feel, even if they are very upset. An important element of the creative-problem-solving discussion is helping children to be aware of this group process as they work together over time.

## SUMMARY AND CONCLUSION

This chapter was designed to clarify role behaviors, evaluation, questioning, and content structure for discussions. It treated troublesome as well as productive roles, classroom procedures and attitudes, functions of observers and purposes behind carefully designed questions and their pacing, other practical considerations, and types of discussions such as creative problem-solving. After the introduction of the concept of maps (or the hierarchical structuring for a series of questions), the chapter concluded with suggestions for generating topics and content for discussion and specific examples.

The next chapter

While this chapter and the preceding one have dealt with two girders for the child's bridge to society (self-expression and exposition), the next girder, literature, is designed to make language beautiful. John Burroughs (1837–1921) called literature an "investment of genius paying dividends to all subsequent times . . . news that stays news." [11] Yet many children are cheated of this use of language because *their* teachers were cheated. In partial remedy, the next chapter shows the teacher some whys and hows about literature in the classroom.

## ACTIVITIES

4.1. Bull Session. What is the nature and use of the type of discussion called bull (or buzz) session? It is a casual, free, and uninhibited rap session on any topic of great interest to the group. Once the group starts, teacher involvement is negligible. A purpose and value in this kind of group is to have small, realistic audiences for children's attempts at self-expression, exposition, and interaction. It gives them a chance to share themselves with others.

This type of group can serve many purposes. The session may simply represent an exchange of ignorances, prejudices, and aimless random talk. Or it may serve useful social and release purposes. Although a bull session can be just a means to get to know another, to get to know feelings and experiences, it can also be an important step in the preparation for other, more complex types of discussion. For example, it may be an important first step in the developing of brainstorming techniques.

[11] *Bartlett's Familiar Quotations,* 14th ed.

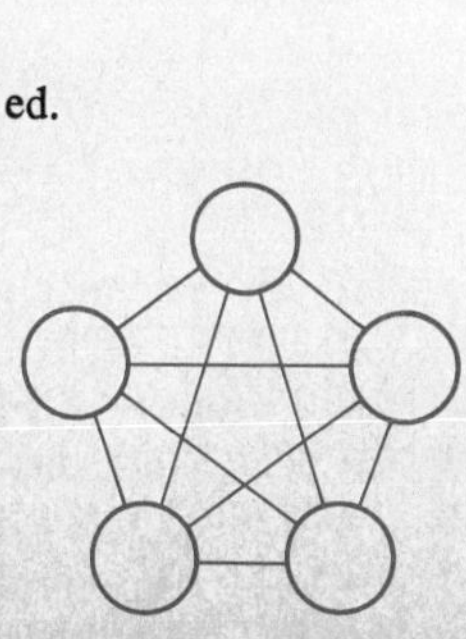

The session may be a time when a teacher can observe and learn much about the children's thought processes, needs, and interests. For example, a teacher might learn that one pupil needs more background in an area, that another has trouble with some listening skills, and that another shows skill in synthesizing ideas. And the session may be a chance for the teacher to share himself just as a human being.

In the diagram, the lines represent interactive communication, each participant interacting with every other one. Note a teacher or leader is not necessarily present.

Classroom topics

The following are some possible topics for bull sessions: Times We Want to Remember—Times We Want to Forget; We Wish Friends Wouldn't—We Wish Friends Would; Who Am I?; What is Power and How Do You Get It?; How I Feel About This School; What Is the Best Program on TV and Why; Motorcycles; Masks, False Faces, and Makeup; Signs and Symbols; How Do Teenagers [or any other older group] Spend Their Time?; If You Could Be Anywhere Else but Here, Where Would You Choose and Why; Plants Without Leaves; Living Under the Seas; Spiders; and Money. (Also see topics listed in Activity 3.8, and topics given in Chapters 6 and 7.)

The bull session might also furnish a small audience for the reading of poetry, songs, exchange of jump-rope rhymes, or jokes.

4.2. Brainstorming. Brainstorming is free and uninhibited like a bull session, but it is organized around the hypothesis-making part of creative problem-solving. Here the fluency, confidence, and respect for others' feelings can carry over to other discussion types.

Brainstorming is set apart by certain rules, as follows:

Rules

1. The group needs to be made up of enough people in order to get a group of heterogeneous skills. The range of skills needs to be relevant to the problem area. Some arbitrarily set the number of participants in the group at around 12. In other words, the groups needs to be *just* large enough in order to contain people with the kinds of competencies needed.
2. Wild ideas are welcomed; none are excluded.
3. Quantity is sought, stressed, and desired. The group works *quickly*.
4. Group members seek to combine ideas, to hitchhike on others' ideas, and to improve them.
5. Adverse judgment of ideas is held off until later, until all ideas have been entered and reviewed. There is no attempt during the process to sort out the good solutions from the bad ones.

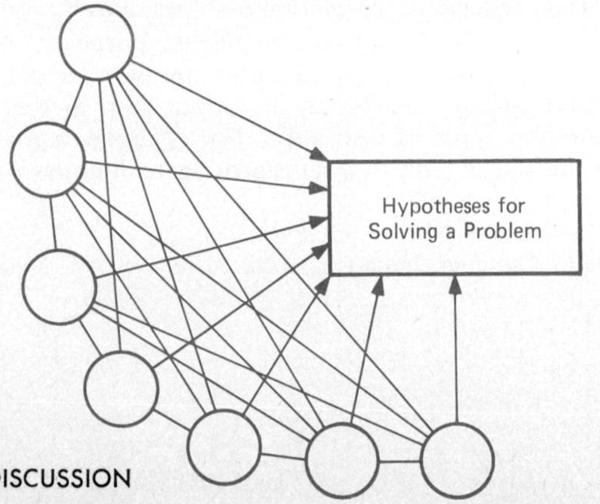

The diagram shows not only the free-flowing interaction, but also the major centering on the generation of hypotheses. Participants are probably best seated so that they can see one another; perhaps a chalkboard is in view, for a quick recording of the ideas. They might be around a table. Some people need a table in front of them during close interaction so that they will not feel quite so exposed. Note that the teacher is not necessarily present. He may act as a recorder, having already prepared the group with the rules for this session. He may need to step in to see that the rules are followed.

Some interesting brainstorming discussions might begin from statements like these: "We've got all this leftover velvet material—what could we do with it?" "We can't go to the zoo today—what could we do instead?" "We're shipwrecked—here's a box of objects [Egg-slicer, girdle, etc.] washed up on the beach. What might we use them for?"

4.3. Task-Group Discussion. The task group usually has a clearly defined and understood job to do. The child will be thinking to himself, "What we decide will affect me because I am going to have to do something if we decide to do this instead of that." Although the structure varies, the components are usually the following:

1. A clearly defined and understood task.
2. Clearly defined individual assignments.
3. Necessary resources or books, known about and available.
4. A schedule and a close supervision of progress within a limited amount of time.
5. A final reporting to a larger group on the product.

Since each group member has his own assignment, coordination and interactive communication may occur mainly at the beginning planning session and at the end of the work period.

The diagram represents the major focus on a task. It shows some interaction, and the teacher present in the room, but generally apart from the work and the interaction.

Classroom examples

The following are typical of task groups found in the school: Social studies projects in which committees focus on the making of murals, plays, scripts, dioramas, and so on. A group might have the task of building a tent, planning a meal, eating it, and cleaning up.

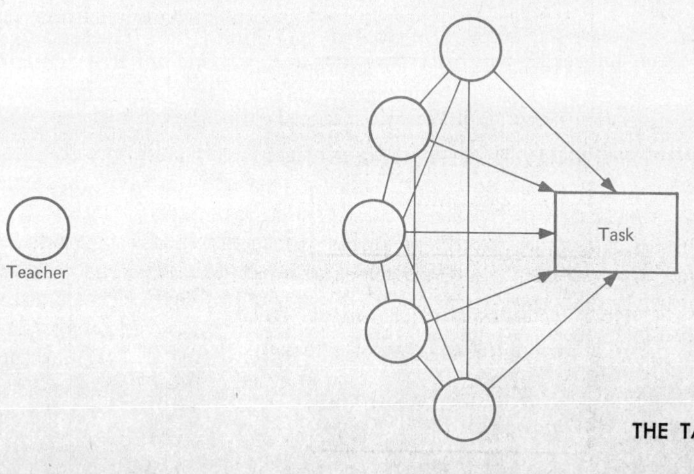

## If You Want To Learn More

BARTOLOME, P. I. Teachers' Objectives and Questions in Primary Reading. *The Reading Teacher,* 1969, *23,* (1), 27-33.

BIDDLE, B. J. Teacher Roles. In R. L. Ebel (Ed.), *Encyclopedia of Educational Research.* London: Macmillan, 1969.

BLOOM, B. S. *Taxonomy of Educational Objectives.* New York: David McKay, 1956.

BURROWS, A. T. *Involving the Child in Language Arts.* Listener In-Service Cassette Library, Album 3. Hollywood, Calif.: Listener Corporation, 1970.

CUNNINGHAM, R. T. Developing Question-Asking Skills. In J. E. Weigand (Ed.), *Developing Teacher Competencies.* Englewood Cliffs, N.J.: Prentice-Hall, 1971.

FLANDERS, N. A. Teacher Effectiveness. In R. L. Ebel (Ed.), *Encyclopedia of Educational Research.* London: Macmillan, 1969.

FURST, N., and MATTLEMAN, M. S. Classroom Climate. *NEA Journal,* 1968, *57* (April), 22-24.

GALL, M. D. The Use of Questions in Teaching. *Review of Educational Research,* 1970, *40,* 707-21.

A comprehensive review of classifications as to type of question, teacher practices, student behavior, student questions, and programs designed to change the teacher's questioning behavior.

GALLAGHER, J. J., and ASCHNER, M. J. A Preliminary Report on Analyses of Classroom Interaction. *Merrill Palmer Quarterly of Behavior and Development,* 1963, *9,* 183-94.

GUSZAK, F. J. Teacher Questioning and Reading. *The Reading Teacher,* 1967, *21* (3), 227-34.

GUSZAK, F. J. *Diagnostic Reading Instruction in the Elementary School.* New York: Harper, 1972.

HUNKINS, F. P. *Questioning Strategies and Techniques.* Boston: Allyn & Bacon, 1972.

KEAN, J. Linguistic Structure of Second- and Fifth-Grade Teachers' Oral Classroom Language. *American Educational Research Journal,* 1968, *5,* 599-615.

KRATHWOHL, D. R., BLOOM, B., and MASIA, B. B. *Taxonomy of Educational Objectives, the Classification of Educational Goals, Handbook II: Affective Domain.* New York: David McKay, 1964.

MEDLEY, D. M. The Language of Teacher Behavior. In R. C. Binkhart (Ed.), *The Assessment Revolution, New Viewpoints for Teacher Evaluation.* Albany: New York State Education Department, 1969.

MORRISON, A., and MCINTYRE, D. *Teachers and Teaching.* Middlesex, England: Penguin, 1969.

A section on communication, one of the most valuable topics, ranges from verbal behavior, to organization, to influencing attitudes (in the classroom).

OLSEN, J. When Children Are Silent. *Elementary English,* 1966, *43,* 877-79.

ROSENSHINE, B. Teaching Behaviors Related to Pupil Achievement: A Review of Research. In I. Westerbury and A. A. Bellack (Eds.), *Research into Classroom Processes.* Toronto: Ontario Institute for Studies in Education, 1971.

SHAFTEL, F. R., and SHAFTEL, G. *Values in Action: Role-Playing Problem Situations for the Intermediate Grades.* New York: Holt, Rinehart and Winston, 1970.

STANFORD, G., and STANFORD, B. D. *Learning Discussion Skills Through Games.* New York: Citation Press, 1969.

Group dynamics provides the framework for a sequence of games designed to increase students' understanding of the elements of discussion and problem solving.

TABA, H., LEVINE, S., and FREEMAN, F. E. *Thinking in Elementary-School Children,* USOE Cooperative Research Project No. 1574. San Francisco State College, 1964.

WILCOX, M. A. Comparison of Elementary School Children's Interaction in Teacher-Led and Student-Led Small Groups. Unpublished doctoral dissertation, Stanford University, 1972.

# Chapter 5 Children's Literature

## Using Language to Make It Memorable

*It is through art that we learn the "grace of understanding"; for art combines knowledge with emotion, and to the fresh minds of young children it speaks with tongues of thunder, holding them bound for life to wisdom and beauty.*

Frances Clarke Sayers, *Summoned by Books*

This chapter develops the following three important thoughts about teaching and children's literature:

- The craft of teaching literature lies in helping children to respond. That is, teachers help children make distinctions and selections by encouraging them to respond to literature—through art, through dramatizing, through discussion growing out of the experiencing of literature. Then children and teachers can get at the form, images, and characterization without flatly talking about it as such.
- Children learn more when the teacher is well-informed about child development and children's literature.
- Children learn more when a teacher reads aloud daily. In fact, the quantity and quality of children's reading is affected by the literature read aloud by the teacher.

The content of this chapter is aimed at helping you to put these ideas into practice.

## WHAT IS CHILDREN'S LITERATURE AND HOW CAN TEACHERS GUIDE RESPONSES?

*"I don't care if you seen the movie; you gotta read the book!"*

With emphasis in his voice and excitement all over his face, a child tells a classmate about *Charlotte's Web,* or *My Side of the Mountain,* or any of a number of children's books that have found their way into film. Whether or not he does this depends a lot on you.

### What Is Literature?

Literature represents a spectator's powerful use of language in that it becomes more poetic rather than merely self-expressive. Language becomes more powerful because of the author's attention to organization and to language itself used imaginatively and pleasingly. Existing in all cultures and appearing in oral, written, and enacted forms, it communicates feelings, interpretations, and visions of human life. These visions are called *vicarious experience.*

Vicarious experience

Vicarious experience with literature represents a major advantage and goal of the classroom program. It is imagined, felt, or enjoyed participation in the experience of others. It brings a heightened insight and sensitivity to experience—so rewarding, so refreshing, that once children feel it they will seek it more and more. Vicarious experience has three stages: (1) *imagination* growing into a stronger (2) *empathy* developing into an even stronger (3) *identification.* That is, the person reading (or being read to) gets more and more "into the character's skin." When children are exposed to great literature they are no longer the same persons they were before. They have lived not only their own lives but many.

Communication

When exploring literature with children in the classroom, teachers may be tempted to forget that literature is first of all *communication,* and whatever else it is—is second. When literature communicates with children, it is worthwhile; when it does not (and children suffer through it) it is a wasteful activity for them. But besides being relevant communication, literature must do more. It must give the audience the same emotional intensity and clarity of experience that the artist had who wrote it.

### What Is Children's Literature?

Children's literature (like all other literature) portrays life and mind in language. However, it has special appeal and interest for youngsters. Three qualities are necessary: substance, sincerity, and memorable language. *Substance* refers to the importance of the theme and ideas in the story. (For example, the theme in Hunt's *Across Five Aprils* is the inescapable turmoil that war brings to families.) *Sincerity* refers to the author's presentation of honest feeling and not just the sweetness or

Fairy Tales
SWL

morals that he or she thinks are appropriate for children. *Memorable language* refers to the author's choice and compression of descriptive details. Such choices evoke tone, mood, and images almost as visible as scenes on a stage. (For example, in Cunningham's *Dorp Dead* Gilly reports, ". . . suddenly a thundery clatter like nightmare comes from the carpenter shop. It's as though an enormous bird with a wingspread of six feet has got trapped in that large room and is smashing itself against the walls.")[1]

I would go so far as to repeat that children's literature (and children's own composition) are the major content of the language arts program. (Texts for children are merely reference materials.) Children's literature is not supplementary entertainment or simply recreational reading. It is vitally important to the intellectual and emotional life of the child and to his development of a private identity. "It's not a toy; it's a tool for life."

In order to better understand children's literature, writers in the field have made classifications, e.g., (1) picture books, (2) prose, and (3) poetry. The classification of literature in this chapter is an adapted, suggestive listing compiled from many sources.

*A Classification of Literature*

FICTION

- Realistic
  - Historical
  - Contemporary
    - Social or dramatic
    - Fictionalized biography
- Fantasy (modern & traditional)
  - Fairy tales, science fiction
  - Mythology and folklore
    - Fable, myth, legend
    - Folktales
- Pop literature
  - Comics
  - Jokes, chants in children's games
  - Bumper stickers, graffiti
  - Posters, tombstone inscriptions
- Picture storybooks
- Drama

NONFICTION

- Biography
- Personal narrative
- Character sketch
- Some essays, letters
- Some informational books written with literary style

FORMS OF POETRY

- Haiku
- Cinquain
- Certain limericks
- Sonnet
- Mother Goose
- Lyric
- Narrative poem
- Free verse
- Ballad
- Some folk songs
- Some lyrics

[1] Julia Cunningham, *Dorp Dead* (New York: Pantheon, 1965), p. 58.

Books for children—
present golden age

The present century's wealth of books for children is a historical event. Beatrix Potter's *Tale of Peter Rabbit* (1902) was a genuine innovation—a book expressly for young American children. You now live in the golden age of children's literature. Publishers vie to produce the most skillfully written and lavishly designed books. Because of the large number available (4000 new titles each year) and their importance to children's emotional and intellectual growth, teachers need to be able to select the best for each child. Developing this ability is part of the purpose of this chapter. Before going into recognition of elements and criteria, however, I will examine ideas useful to teaching strategy.

## How Do You Teach Children's Literature?

Teaching
developmentally

Teachers need to be aware of developmental aspects of children's imagination and their responses to literature. Teachers know that as children develop, they need to (1) fantasize, (2) explore, (3) identify with animals, (4) identify with heroes, (5) have models, and (6) have vicarious experiences. Other developmental ideas available to the teacher in selecting and using children's books follow:

- When sense of humor is developing, include books with incongruous situations, slapstick, surprise endings, and play on words.[2]
- When attention spans grow longer, begin to provide uninterrupted blocks of time for independent reading (sometimes referred to as USSR—Uninterrupted Sustained Silent Reading). Even the teacher and principal many participate in order to model their valuing of this way to "gain a private identity."
- When peer-group acceptance becomes increasingly important, provide chances in class to recommend and discuss books. Provide time to share their impact on individuals and to interpret them cooperatively through group art and dramatic activity. Provide settings in which children can read favorite passages to one another.
- As interests become less egocentric, as sense of time develops, as search for models other than parents begins, then provide exciting biographies and tales of other times and places.
- As skill in classifying in many ways develops, examine literature (in connection with dramatization) for different points of view, alternatives, biases, and problems.

Response to sounds and events

Teachers need to know about developmental aspects of children's response to the *sounds* of literature and to its *events*. Young children demand conformity to a familiar pattern. ("I'll huff and I'll puff and I'll blow your house in." The reader had better not change a single word!) Later they enjoy sheer story (or narrative) movement. They may enjoy first the familiar, then the strange and adventurous. First they become interested merely in what happened, then in why it happened. First they want story lines that are repetitive (*The Gingerbread Boy*), then they want the plot to be logical to them within the limits of the characters (cause and effect). For example, children would not be satisfied to learn that the foster parent in a story was cruel *and* the boy ran away. They would be able to see that *because* the foster parent was cruel the boy ran away from him.

[2] Some examples of humorous books for beginners are Judi Barrett's *Animals Should Definitely Not Wear Clothing* (New York: Atheneum, 1970), a picture book showing funny things that can happen should animals try to wear clothes. Also see Beatrice Schenk de Regniers' *May I Bring a Friend?* (New York: Atheneum, 1964), in which a small boy wants to bring outlandish animal friends every time he gets an invitation from the King and Queen. Caldecott Medal–winning illustrations by Beni Montresor. (This list of developmental ideas is adapted from Huck, 1968.)

Response to roles and to the whole

The teacher needs to know about children's developmental response to *roles* in literature and its *whole creative arrangement.*[3] Young children respond to a role by playing dramatically according to whim. Then, they become concerned with the role's trueness to life—at least the rudiments of well-rounded characterization. Finally, the child becomes appreciative, not just of the changing tensions of plot, but also of relationships among plot, character, theme, and style. A full maturity of this sensitive response to the total develops on through high school and adult life; it is probably never finished. But the rudiments begin in the elementary-school years and teachers can help. Unless children grow beyond the level of "what happens next," they soon tire of literature and turn back to firsthand experience, or to the vicarious experience of TV. And they may never realize that they have lost the power of literature to clarify, to reduce confusion, and to extend the imaginative awareness of their lives.

Imagination

The teacher needs to help children develop their *imaginations.* All of the advantages children gain from a program in literature depend upon this power. Teachers need to encourage extension of ordinary ideas into make-believe situations. Imagination (central to creative problem-solving) helps children to summon up images, feelings, memories, sensations, and intuitions. Imaginative children rearrange the mosaics of their world to create new, delightful relationships. Imagination transforms the child's outlook so that persons and places take on a beauty and a glow.

Some books shared with children help to develop imagination more than others. Examples are Lightfoot's *The Pony Man,*[4] in which the talent of a popular song lyricist combines with the dreamy and mood creating illustrations. Another imaginative and poetic book for young children is *Gilberto and the Wind,*[5] written in both Spanish and English. The book lends itself to children's imaginative pantomime and activity with pinwheels, bubble blowing, rhythmic body motions of pretending to be bubbles, and the enjoyment of producing sound effects for the wind. It is the person who insists upon one and only one way of

[3] For example, while children are being read the novel *Roosevelt Grady* by Louisa R. Shotwell, they may distinguish this multidimensional character's need for order, his background, his social relations, and how these influence the plot development. Children may distinguish the way the dialogue carries action forward, how the author builds a mood of despondency and jealousy heightened by figurative language and symbolism. Children may see them all building on the theme of a "stay put place to live." Children may even distinguish that the theme is characteristic of an early myth motif—"the search for a secure home by a worthy child."

[4] Gordon Lightfoot, *The Pony Man* (New York: Harper, 1972). Illustrations by Etienne Delessert. For prekindergarten up.

[5] Marie Hall Ets, *Gilberto and the Wind* (New York: Viking, 1963). Paperback; for ages 4–7.

doing things who is finally responsible for the death of the imagination in children.[6]

Using poetry

One way to help develop children's imaginations is through the use of poetry in the classroom. Poetry can furnish imaginative ways to play with language and its tempos, build upon the natural rhythm in children, and give them its sensitive, fleeting intensity of experience. The teaching strategy is for children to be able to listen to a person who likes to read poetry, who revels in the chance to share the pleasure with others. (Eleanor Farjeon and Elizabeth Madox Roberts are representative modern poets who write distinguished poems for children.) The reading of free verse such as Sandburg's "Fog" (in his *Chicago Poems*) helps children to sense that something more than a flat statement is necessary in a poem. Teachers are *participants* in the classroom experience of poetry instead of "teachers" of it. In the elementary school, periods of poetry sharing and enjoyment are short—usually five minutes in length—tossed in like spices in a good meal.

Avoid selecting poems that are not genuinely expressing children's points of view, interests, and needs (i.e., ones that are sentimentally *about* them—not for them).

Poetry ladder

One analysis of the development of children's appreciation of poetry offers a five-step ladder.[7] Some need the first rung.

[6] Also try Alice Dalgliesh's *The Bears on Hemlock Mountain* (New York: Scribner, 1952). For ages 7–9. When a boy, Jonathan, returns home via Hemlock Mountain after dark, what people say about the bears and what he experiences combine to make an exciting tale. See Borton (1973) on fantasy in the classroom.

[7] Shared during a course taught by Professor David H. Russell (University of California, Berkeley). Further source unknown.

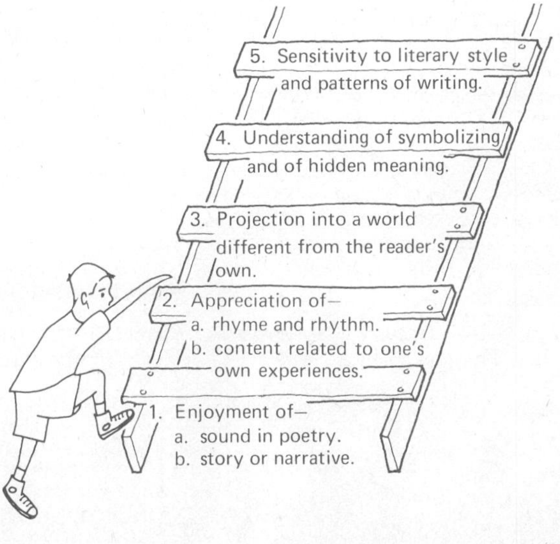

However you develop it—through prose, art, drama, or poetry—extending a child's imagination is a crucial teaching task.

*It was imagination that enabled man to extend his thumb by inventing the vise, that enabled man to strengthen his fist and arm by inventing the hammer. Step by step, man's imagination lured, led, and often pushed him to the astonishing heights of power he now occupies.*

Victor Wagner

## Why Is Oral Reading of Literature and Artistic Interpretation a Valuable Part of Teaching Children?

**Response through oral reading**

Children respond more and with greater imaginative participation when either they or the teacher can take the role of an interpretive artist in partnership with the author. When the teacher reads an enchanting or moving work aloud, he gives a great gift. The motivation to model is strong and effective. Children will want to give such a gift, too.

The oral tradition helps to make literature come alive. We live in an age with many means of preserving our literary heritage. Why think that aesthetic experience is inaccessible to children who have a (hopefully temporary) aversion to the printed page? This suggestion of oral reading does not mean that we must revert completely to the state of preliterate cultures who joined the original authors in transmitting literary traditions. But watching others enact literature on film, on videotape and on the stage represents a significant way of learning; I would say a more significant way than a diagnostic, prescriptive, individualized, and solitary way.

Fine literature needs to be heard. Children experience more fully when they can listen to portions of stories such as *Wind in the Willows,* the *Just So Stories* ("the great grey-green greasy Limpopo River"), or Marcia Brown's retelling of a folktale, *Once a Mouse*.[8] Some of the Newbery Medal books come alive best when read aloud (for example, E. L. Konigsburg's *From the Mixed-up Files of Mrs. Basil E. Frankweiler*).[9] Try reading from distinctive collections of poetry, such as Nancy Larrick's *On City Streets* (ages 10–13), Padraic Colum's *Roofs of Gold: Poems to Read Aloud* (ages 10–14), and David McCord's *Every Time I Climb a Tree* (ages 5–9).

Why does literature need to be heard? The author's artistry—intonations, structures, and uses of language—come through with oral reading. Even child interpreters can tell stories in a style suited to the story. Their artistry can range from the "swaggery" style of the tall tale to the quiet lyrical telling of a fairy tale.

**Grasping the author's indirection**

Another reason for placing a value on oral reading is its helpfulness in aiding children to grasp an author's indirect approach. One of the features of literary discourse is artistic indirection. The skilled writer has an ability to draw in readers, subtly making them imaginative participants. When the author succeeds, the experience is more vivid and memorable.

Take the example of small children hearing the ending of Grimm's tale "Henny Penny" in which Henny Penny's foolish friends go into Foxy-Loxy's den and never come out. "So what," the literal-minded child may think to himself, "maybe they liked it." But here the author's indirection (depending subtly on earlier relationships to deliver the

[8] Bold and graceful woodcuts in resplendent color tell the old Indian fable about a mouse that is changed into a cat, a dog, and then a tiger, and back again into a timid mouse (New York: Scribner, 1961). A Caldecott Medal winner. For ages 5–9.

[9] The adventures of a sister (12) and her brother (9) who run away and live undetected for a week in the Metropolitan Museum of Art. The author's attention to detail, crisp writing, and natural dialogue create believable characterizations and a humorous, suspenseful tale (New York: Atheneum, 1968). Newbery Medal winner. For ages 8–12.

From Dugald Stewart Walker, *Dream Boats and Other Stories,* Doubleday & Company, 1918.

sinister meaning) can be aided by a reader's skilled voice and facial expression (Loban, 1966).

These have been some of the reasons that oral reading of literature helps to form a valuable partnership with an author's self-expression. The oral tradition of literature makes *listening* play a vital role in development of appreciation for literature.

**Over-analysis**

Occasionally, however, there may be an attempt to push children's apprehension too far. Sometimes a teacher may demand that children orally analyze the author's text and give a thorough (slavish?) interpretation. But appreciation may be a private matter between the child and the poem or other work. Enjoyment that is best may simply come from the tune of the words stimulating the child's senses. Coleridge suggested that poetry gives much pleasure when only generally and not perfectly understood. Rather than force children to prove that they understand the meaning of an author, observe them—receptive listening and a following silence may sometimes be a more eloquent testimony of appreciation.

Apply this caution to textbooks that require children to make a detailed textual analysis of an author's work. Apply it to choral reading that becomes so involved in perfected tempos, tones, unison, chorus, parts designations, physical motions, antiphony, line-a-child, and other arrangements that communication and pleasure are lost.

This caution does not mean that a choral reading of a poem is never an enjoyable oral response. Children can discover together the physical pleasure of manipulating language with lips, teeth, throat—the total sounding board. And the sounding may become not merely added pleasure, but also part of sharing the interpretation and meaning—a productive way of participating in the author's self-expression. But perhaps simple ways of responding are more effective, such as spontaneous enactment, art, and discussion.

Next, look at some ways that teachers actually deal with literature in the classroom.

## What Are Some Specific Ways Teachers Handle the Program?

This section presents some alternatives for handling the program in literature.

1. *Traditional Subject Approach.* Some teachers set aside a daily period for a subject called literature. Their teaching methods are similar to those of their own high school and college teachers. Regarding this approach, Britton (1968) cautions that children might be taking over from their teachers an analysis of a literary work that they in turn took over from their professors, who in turn took it over from the critics—a dry dusty pitfall to be avoided passionately. Literature is about life, not just about other literature (California State Board of Education, 1974).
2. *Reliance on the Librarian.* Teachers rely on the school librarian to give guidance during the class library period.
3. *Incidental Integration.* Some teachers relate literature whenever they can as a subordinate goal to the purposes of language arts, reading, social studies, science, and human relations.
4. *Planned Program.* Other teachers use literature in a daily planned program for enjoyment of content and development of sensitive taste regarding literary structures. This program, growing out of creative activity, is built on spontaneous curiosity, imagination, and love of knowing. It employs guidance in focusing, in organizing, and in gaining insights. Many of the ideas in this chapter are relevant to this approach. (Also see Nebraska Curriculum, 1966; Wisconsin Curriculum, 1965.)

As mentioned earlier, children learn more when the teacher is well informed about literature. Part of being well informed is knowing what literature is. The next section takes a closer look at literature as communication, and at its elements.

---

## HOW DOES A COMMUNICATION TRIANGLE HELP TO DISTINGUISH LITERATURE?

Four emphases

One way that a teacher can make distinctions that provide balance and excellence is to think in terms of a communication triangle. The perspective from each of the following points reflects a certain mass of opinion as to what is a literary work.

Mirrored world (universe, nature, reality, objects and events in real life, referents)

Author (sender, composer, poet, artist, expressor)

Audience (receivers, decoders, listeners, vicarious experiencers, readers, viewers, enjoyers, lesson learners, receptors, children)

Work (structure of the artistic creation; message, signal, product; form with its organization, logic, and language style)

These points of emphasis are diagrammed in the accompanying illustration. There are various versions of this communication triangle, but basic to all users of language is a person (author in this case) who devises a message (the work) that refers to the world and is sent to and decoded by an audience. In the pages to follow, I explain each point of emphasis. I follow the explanation with a criterion for selection and an application section with activities and discussion questions to use with children.

## THE MIRRORED WORLD

**The nature of this focus**

Suppose your concept of what makes art in literature stresses a clarifying of the mirrored world. In other words you view literature as an artistic expression of alternative ways of living. It helps children to view and to live in many places. "That could have been me!" It provides them with vicarious experience to talk about and to write about. Usually children of all ages want to get to know various spheres of life. Books in this vein can bring them various periods of time, states of nature, and relationships among peoples—reality enhanced by pace and drama.

Terms for the novel have illustrated this emphasis, e.g., *realism, naturalism, regionalism,* and *local color.* By way of further illustration, more than one form of art has been popularly judged—"Great! That's telling it just like it is." But if the image does not match our experience, we condemn the work. The author asks the reader to accept a picture of the actual world, rather than a fantasy world. Sometimes a child's literary diet is surfeited with fantasy stories when he would prefer a bit more of the here-and-now. (See the cartoon on p. 195.)

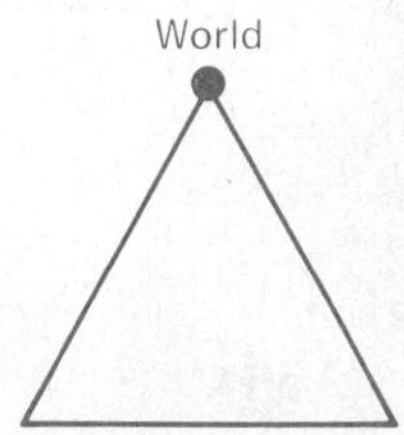


*A Communication Triangle For Literature*

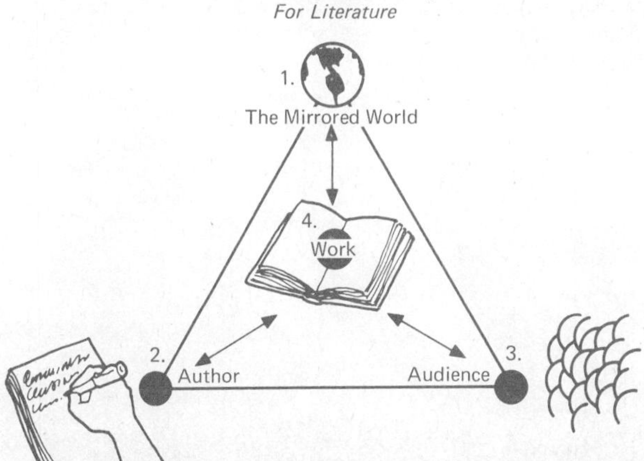


Structure based on J. L. Kinneary, *A Theory of Discourse* (Englewood Cliffs, N.J.: Prentice-Hall, 1971).

Imaginative insights

Of course, the author of realistic historical and contemporary prose fiction creates from his own imagination, but his plot and characters need to behave as they would in real life. This type of emphasis does not deny the expressive *author* and his emotions; it does not deny the power of the *language* in the *work,* nor the effect the author's convictions may have on the *audience.* But these other points of the triangle may be considered minor attributes to the author's major intent, to depict real life. Some argue that literature may offer more than imaginative insight into the mirrored world, but it cannot offer less. (Others would say it *must* offer more.)

Examples

Take a look at examples from children's literature illustrating this emphasis. Picture books with the "real world" emphasis for young children include Miles' *Nobody's Cat,* a believable portrait of a cat who knew when to run, when to fight, how to survive in city traffic, and how to scrounge for food.[10] In Schoenherr's *The Barn,* a skunk living in an old barn searches for food, almost falling prey to a hungry owl with three small owlets to feed. The struggle for survival is shown in unsentimental double-page black and white pictures.[11]

[10] Miska Miles, *Nobody's Cat* (Boston: Little, Brown, 1969). For ages 6–9.

[11] John Schoenherr, *The Barn* (Boston: Little, Brown, 1968). For ages 6–8.

ON THE EMPHASIS UPON THE MIRRORED WORLD

"Is it all right if I bring my TV set?"

Books such as these serve valuable purposes. If a teacher sees a need to help a child find an interest outside himself, books from the mirrored world may fit the purpose well. Children perhaps best approach the areas of history and geography by involving themselves in the lives of people from past ages and other countries. Judgment on political, social, economic, and educational affairs is built in large part upon the understanding derived from vicarious experience. There are, however, a number of criteria for the teacher to keep in mind—the topic of the next section.

### How Does the Teacher Make Appropriate Selections Regarding Realistic Books?

What does realism do for children? What kind or quality of vicarious experience does it give them? Does it help them not only to sense the dimensions of their world, but also to feel more in control of it? And, paradoxically, at the same time does it give them needed escape from it? In considering what realistic literature can do for children and how to select it, teachers need to take into account the child's experience background and level of concept attainment. They need to take care that the book language is not overly sophisticated, and that the character's motives are reasonably within the child's level of experience.

Assessing the child's ability to meet a book halfway

The child must be able to meet the book halfway. Chapter 3, on oral expression, presented six dimensions for language arts curriculum. Judging the child's capabilities in relation to each of these dimensions, is a good way to determine whether a particular work of literature meets this "halfway" criterion.

1. *Speech–thought dimension.* Look at the *child's* speech and thought levels, and those of the book. Can they meet at least halfway?
2. *Personal–interpersonal dimension.* Can the child let go of the egocentric, personal dimension of his being and participate in the interpersonal dimension of the characters in the book?
3. *Finished-product dimension.* How far must the child reach to be able to appreciate the author's form, style, and language in his finished product?
4. *Abstractness–concreteness dimension.* Is the concrete-thinking child able to meet the abstractness or symbolism of the author's interpretations, language, and ideas?
5. *Larger–smaller units of language.* How well developed is the child's attention span, in relation to larger, longer literary works versus very short ones? (Perhaps just the pleasing sounds of language rather than its intricate rhythms, organizations, and thought patterns are appropriate for a certain child at a certain stage.)

6. *Simple aim–complex aim.* How far along is a halfway meeting place for the child's use of language and the complex aim of literary discourse used in the book? (The range here is from simple moments of pleasant sound to a deep interweaving of themes, plots, characterizations, and symbolisms that the author aims to display.)

A balanced program

Ideally, a teacher seeks a balance of materials for the class literature program. He chooses various kinds of works reflecting life as it is or was. This variety may include the different dimensions above; different times; places; many types of people in a full range of roles and ages; different groups and their situations; various cultural, ethnic, and racial groups with different styles of living, temperaments, and values; and historical and contemporary representatives of both sexes.

Sex stereotypes

Teachers may inadvertently reinforce the unrealities of the sexual stereotypes that parents, friends, and mass culture (including some children's books) have taught children. Sexual stereotypes found in books for children are assumed differences, social conventions, learned behaviors, attitudes, and expectations. For example, boys are strong, curious, capable, and active, whereas girls are passive; boys can be doctors, but girls will be nurses; girls, who are not as smart as boys, will need to find a man to marry; the brother will be older and wiser than his timid sister. Sexism refers to attitudes and actions relegating women to an inferior status. The absence of stories about women doctors, lawyers, or professors thwarts reality.

What can the teacher do? Again, seek a balanced selection of books. Active female protagonists are appearing more and more in new, quality books for children. Select books that emphasize achievements of both men and women. Discuss the sexist elements in our language and books when they appear in the classroom. Otherwise the teacher and the material will convey to the child the impression that the demeaning of women is socially acceptable, is an unavoidable reality, rather than a form of prejudice or a lack of sensitivity.[12]

## Classroom Activities Reflecting the Mirrored World

Use enrichment activities to bring *alive* the book's situation and the characters who people it. "If it's just a story, it's likely to be just no good" (Fader, 1968). These activities involve responding with the head, the heart, and the hand.

[12] See, for example, Howe (1971), Key (1975), and a beginning reading series, supplementary, *A Woman Is . . .* (Walnut Creek, Calif.: Aardvark Media, 1974). Also see the entire October issue of *Elementary English*, 1973, *50* (7) which focuses on women and girls.

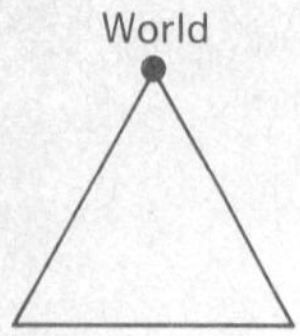


5.1. Book Show-offs. Suggest the following methods for sharing the vicarious experience gained from books: [13]

### *Manipulative and Enactive (the Hand)*

- *Talk Show.* Plan a character's guest appearance on a talk show.
- *Top Secret File.* Have children select a character and construct a top secret file about him or her.
- *Modeling and Making Mobiles.* Choose a character, object, or scene to model from clay, soap, wood, or plaster. Make a mobile employing objects mentioned in the book to serve as a visual aid for a book talk.
- *Story Dolls.* Use dolls or puppets with costumes made out of paper, cardboard, wire, or rag to represent the story characters. Tell about their roles in the story and its setting; let the dolls dramatize. Provide sound effects.
- *Graffiti Board.* Mount a large poster where children can write favorite book and poetry quotations.
- *Mapping It.* Make a map or a time-line as a device for sharing biography or historical fiction. Or construct miniature table models or dioramas. A "You Are There" newscast based on the book might use the map as a visual aid.
- *Geographical Display.* Group books according to the geographical region described in the books and run streamers to the location on a map.
- *Character Communications.* Have one character in a book write a letter or converse with another. Try to have the respondents stay in character. Or make and pretend to have found a scrapbook, a diary, or a journal that belonged to a character.
- *Character Dress-up.* Dress as one of the persons in the story and tell about the role and the setting, enact a scene.

**Objective**

*Objective:* To respond to literature *reflectively* by noting its relationship to the world; *creatively* by re-creating it through one of the aforementioned art forms; and by *sharing* and showing responses.

## What Are Some Classroom Discussion Questions Related to the Mirrored World?

The following types of general questions may be useful during class discussions concerning books that emphasize the mirrored world. Teachers and children can use these during and after activities such as

[13] The author is indebted to Dr. Julia Gottesman, Consultant, Los Angeles County Education Center, for many of these ideas.

the foregoing. The first questions are designed to encourage children's affective responses to a book (the heart). The later ones are aimed more at promoting their cognitive thinking (the head). (The enrichment methods listed within Activity 5.1 represent the hand.) For productive response, seek to involve all—the heart, the head, and the hand.

*Affective (the Heart)*

1. Is your life like the one in this book? How?
2. Have you known people like those in this book?
3. What funny part reminds you of something you've seen before?
4. How is this book more (or less) interesting than TV? Is your imagination bigger than a TV screen? How?
5. Why did you (or did you not) feel you were right alongside of this character in the book?

*Cognitive (the Head)*

1. Is the place where this story took place like a place you know?
2. Is this book a make-believe fantasy that could never really happen or is it a real-to-life story? What made up your mind?
3. Do you think it told things like they really are (or were)?

From *Obadiah the Bold* by Brinton Turkle. Copyright © 1965 by Brinton Turkle. Reprinted by permission of The Viking Press, Inc. The setting for the story about this Quaker boy is old Nantucket.

4. What kind of life do you think this author led in order to be able to write this book?

---

*Genuine emotion on the part of an author quickens the interest of children in their reading. They will sniff it out, like hounds following a scent.*

Frances Clarke Sayers, *Summoned by Books*

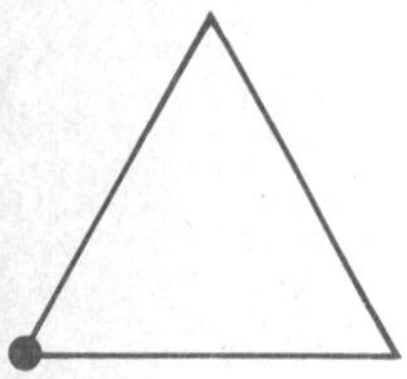


## THE AUTHOR

Suppose your concept of what makes art in literature stresses the author himself in the communication triangle. From this perspective, literary art may be viewed as self-expression by an artist who is a more emotional, sensitive, intuitive, and naturally inspired spectator than other men or women. The artist who uses an intense creative process may have a psychological viewpoint that turns within.

Consider the following idea in relation to children's inward response to literature. The mirrored-world emphasis bids the child to look *out* and *around*. This real world kind of vicarious experience sparks inquiries, investigations, expeditions, and displays of the child's re-creations and creations. But the author emphasis (especially in the case of poetry) beckons the child to look *inward*. The poetry of the self-expressive artist turns the child's thought and response inward into the poem rather than outward into the mirrored world. Whereas literature emphasizing the world may touch off whole units of study, children will tend to respond to a self-expressive poem with introspective contemplation.

Teachers understanding this withdrawal will not be disappointed if the children's response does not spread outward to drama, art, and discussion. The child's most appropriate response here may simply be silence. During this silence children need to re-create the poem with all its inner relatedness. Then they may try to relate it to their own lives. Even very young children are capable of being far more responsive to the work of poets than teachers have generally given them credit for being (Britton, 1970). Possibly the misconception "children don't like poetry" comes about because their inward responses are not readily visible.

**Examples**

The following poem by Langston Hughes illustrates some of the descriptive ideas about the self-expressive artist given in this section.

To fling my arms wide
in the face of the sun,
Dance! Whirl! Whirl!
Til the quick day is done.
Rest at pale evening . . .
A tall, slim tree . . .
Night coming tenderly
  Black like me.[14]

Not all literature with emphasis on the author's voice is poetry, of course. The following prose is a playful use of literary self-expression from Mark Twain's *Life on the Mississippi.*

> When I'm playful, I use the meridians of longitude and the parallels of latitude for a seine, and drag the Atlantic Ocean for whales. I scratch my head with the lightening and purr myself to sleep with the thunder.

### Classroom Activity Reflecting the Author

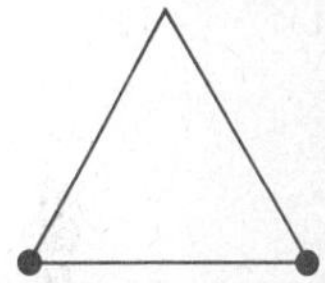


5.2. Poetry Collector's Club. (For intermediate through junior-high-school levels.) Encourage a poetry collection of each child's favorite poems (or even favorite lines) chosen for his own reasons. (No required copying.) Children may enjoy pantomiming and dramatizing their poems. For the reluctant, try the Brewtons' *Shrieks at Midnight*—with poems macabre, eerie, and humorous, and McDonald's *A Way of Knowing: A Collection of Verse for Boys*—strong, straightforward.

Four response levels

Objectives for all literary activities. If the child is going to move beyond the pure spectator role, he needs to get into highly active responding. The aforementioned activities (and the questions to follow) for the author emphasis seek to have the learner participate in the author's poetic expression in the following ways.

1. *Emotional Response.* Children move into themselves and then beyond, into more active responding. This responding may help the children to create more "literary" expression themselves.
2. *Reflective Response.* Children listen, read, witness, and respond to the author emotionally and reflectively. They understand the literature in relation to their own experiences and values.
3. *Creative Response.* Children respond imaginatively and creatively through enactive, dramatic interpretation, and re-creation. They re-

[14] From "Dream Variations." Copyright 1926 by Alfred A. Knopf, Inc. and renewed 1954 by Langston Hughes. Reprinted from *Selected Poems,* by Langston Hughes, by permission of the publisher.

spond by imitation, transformation, and adaptation using various media.

4. *Sharing Response.* The child discusses and shares feelings about the author's impact.

Remember that sometimes a child needs to respond quietly, internally.

### What Are Discussion Questions Related to the Author?

The following are questions that focus on the author corner of the communication triangle. The teacher can use them in conjunction with other types of questions. Again they move from seeking more affective responses to more cognitive responses. One deals with evaluative thinking about sincerity. Another brings to a conscious level the point of view from which the material is written, e.g., the author's omniscience (knowing all things) or self-expression through one of the characters who is speaking in the first person.

1. How do you think this book made the author feel when he or she wrote it? How did it make you feel? Why?
2. If the author were telling you the story aloud, how would he/she act?
3. Do you think the author was sincere and honest with you?
4. Does the author know everything or does he/she seem to be talking through one real person who does not know everything? Does the author talk directly to the reader? How is the story told?
5. How could you share your feelings or interest in this author's work? (This last question might lead to more activities. See, for example, Activity 5.4, storytelling.)

## THE AUDIENCE

Range of audience emphasis

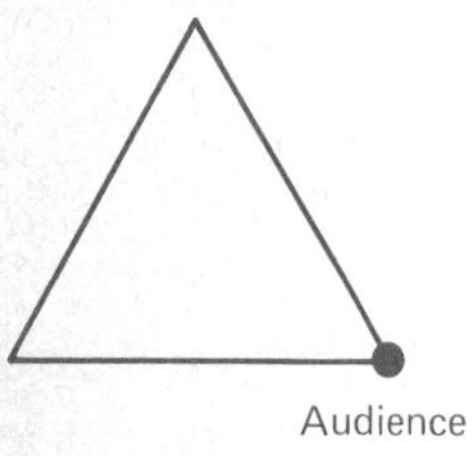


Suppose your concept of what makes art in literature emphasizes the impact on the audience. Here the focus is not on the author but on the receiver. From this point of view, if the literary work can achieve emotional conviction or intellectual persuasion in the reader, it is successful, useful, and artistic. Here there is a range of emphasis from an almost propagandistic to an ethical point of view that intrudes less on the consciousness. This section first considers the persuasive or "curative" extreme and then the more usual audience emphasis in order to arrive at a criterion.

In an extreme view, the pleasure that the audience receives from a work is merely a means to teaching. In this (teachy-preachy) communicative view, the poet may act as physician who cures the reader. An early American example aimed at a young audience was the *McGuffey Reader* which contained some of the Aesop's fables. These materials were unabashed in their intent to teach children the values of the culture. The reader of fables accepts and anticipates the moral as belonging to this form of literature. The moral at the end is an explicit statement of what was implicit in the tale. Moving to more recent books for children, note the number of volumes with the theme of brotherhood with respect to racial minorities.[15]

The extreme view

Some would argue that message hunting in literature leads to the heresy of paraphrase, and abstraction to the handy maxim—both derailing the aesthetic response. "What does this poem teach?" is a horrid question from almost any view, and especially this one. (Relevantly, Samuel Goldwyn once remarked that if there's a message to send, call Western Union.) A story written for children presenting a human value but without artistic form is no more memorable than a guidance pamphlet on "First Dates" (and other disasters).

But rather than make the child the intellectual slave of the author, reflective vicarious experiences through reading that are rich and varied can serve to synthesize within the child a new private identity. They are children's means to becoming individuals (instead of members of the peer-group pack) as they pursue their developing interests from book to book. If children "know more than they ever know they know," isn't it the richness of literature that helps them bring to the author's words the undiscovered resources within themselves? A focus on the audience can mean helping them savor and privately accept a sensitive comment on the human condition.

Private identity

The criterion for teachers in connection with this emphasis is that there be art in the work as well as impact on the audience. Naturally there are limits on a child's ability to be an audience for some kinds of literature. (Recall the "halfway criterion.") But perhaps the worst mistake is consistently giving children material that is too simple for them, or not allowing them to be an audience for a selection because of the fear that they will not understand every single part.

Criterion

[15] An example of this emphasis might be William Armstrong's powerful *Sounder,* the story of the life of a boy in a sharecropper's family 50 years ago (and his dog), and their tenacity for life against crushing opposition to the Black man (New York: Harper, 1969). For age 11 up, Newbery Medal winner. Another and a happier example is Zilpha Keatley Snyder's *Egypt Game,* which shows a modern integrated community where Black, Chinese, and Caucasian children invent games that represent ancient Egypt and play them with no forced feelings of integration. The well-drawn characters solve a murder during the story (New York: Atheneum, 1967). For ages 8–12; Newbery Medal runner-up.

## Classroom Activity Reflecting an Emphasis on the Audience

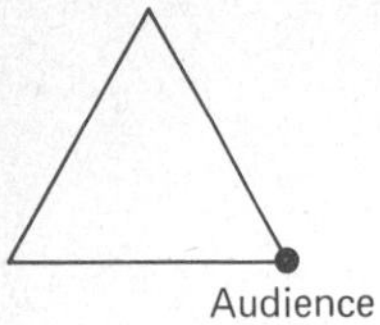


5.3. Choral–Oral Collection. Have a committee select conversational sections, descriptive passages, episodes, or poems that they feel have had a great impact on them or made them feel strongly. Have them tape these selections for an unseen audience and have them listen to themselves. (The teacher might record something for the collection, too.) The selections might be spliced with introductory material and woven into a pictorial presentation using a roller movie (long strips of butcher paper rolled on sticks across an opening cut in a box); or they might be used with a display of drawings or photographs; or they might be accompanied by a series of pantomimes or a puppet enactment. An interested group might give certain favorites a choral reading treatment.

## What Are Discussion Questions Related to the Audience?

*Affective (The Heart)*

1. Did you enjoy this tale? What kind of person would like this book? What happened that made you smile or feel happy? Mad? Scared or uneasy?
2. What did a character do that you would not do? That you would be afraid to do?

*Cognitive (The Head)*

1. What do you think this author wants his/her audience to think about? How does he/she want the audience to feel or act?
2. What experience was the author trying to tell you about? Why? Is he/she trying to tell us anything about ourselves?

Although these activities emphasize the effects on the audience, it is the qualities within the work that bring about any lasting impact. Thus the next section deals with the organization, and the language and style of the work itself, the central point of the triangle.

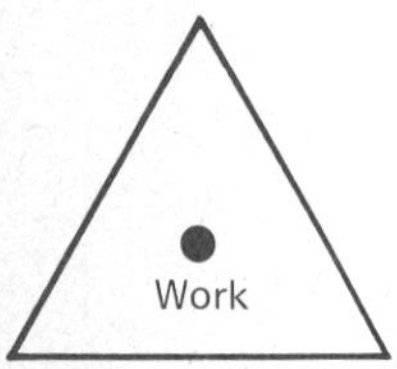


## THE WORK

This way of looking at literary art emphasizes the worth of the *work* itself and the characteristics that establish it as artistic. The emphasis is on the organization of the *work* and on its sensuous language components with their coloring and rhythm. (The term *work* may refer to a printed page, recording, film or other form.) If the *author* receives attention, it is for his craftsmanship and technical abilities that enable the production of this artistic organization with effective and memorable language. If the *audience* receives attention, it is for the sheer pleasure they derive from contemplation of the literary work of art. If the *mirrored world* receives attention, it is for the forms and structures that the work has imposed on nature, not for mere reproduction. The pleasure given, the vicarious experience, is something enjoyable, not merely useful.

Two major divisions

The work may be thought of as having two major divisions: its organization of form and its language.

## ORGANIZATION OF LITERATURE

### What Is The Organization of Form?

It is not easy to separate plot, characterization, and theme that go into the organization of a work. But when an author fashions a story, poem, or drama, artistic arrangement is a deliberate part. Most people are displeased by mess and confusion. Even children are. Singer (1969) suggests that children are logical about the literary work designed for them. They demand consistency, clarity, precision, and "other obsolete qualities."

An example of a simple but magnificently organized story is Else Minarik's *Little Bear*.[16] The four chapters resemble a "four part symphony." In the "final movement," when Little Bear asks Mother Bear to tell him stories about himself, she touches each of the three preceding "movements" or themes. The first-grade teacher does not discuss organization, plot, design, theme, logic, and closure. But he might ask, "When did you hear that story before?" "How do you like this way of ending a book?" And he might even suggest that the class members themselves try to create an oral composition in this pattern.

#### What Is the Nature of Plot and Its Use in Children's Books?

Any piece of literature has a deliberately planned structure that may be called a plot. It includes the complete action of the story (or poem), and organizes the time, place, and characters in a unified whole. How this whole begins and ends is important. An effective plot is not just a series of happenings (as it often is in stories that young children write themselves). It unfolds a strong dramatic idea, not a series of weak anecdotes. For example, in a well-plotted story, from the beginning almost anything is logically possible. In the middle things become prob-

[16] This example is from Loban (1966). A beginning reader can tackle this book, illustrated by Maurice Sendak, an award-winning illustrator (New York: Harper, 1957). For ages 5–8. See also other books in the *Little Bear* series.

able. And in the ending everything is necessary within the universe of the literary work.[17]

The plots in books for children are usually ordered more sequentially than in books for adults. Flashbacks can be confusing to children. Armstrong Sperry's *Call It Courage* illustrates a clean plot line. Chapter headings such as "Flight," "The Sea," "The Island," "Drums," and "Homeward" tend to reveal the plot development. Starting the tale as if it were told by the Polynesians and ending with the same paragraph (save one line) adds to the feeling of authentic legend. Some children are helped to appreciate and write their own tales when shown a formula such as the following:

| *Title* | *Beginning* | *Middle* | *High Point* | *Ending* |
|---|---|---|---|---|
| | Introduction<br>Where<br>Who | Problem<br>Happenings<br>(Episodes) | (Climax) | |

If a plot reveals and influences character, it naturally follows that without highly developed characters, there is less likelihood of a tightly knit combination with the plot. That idea leads to the next structural element, *character*.

## What Is Characterization and Its Use in Children's Literature?

**Flat characters**

Children's storybook characters have two general classifications: *flat* and *round. Flat* means that the characters have no family, no past, no inner-selves. They are impersonal abstractions, not dressed in elaborate descriptions. They are either all evil or all good, either totally ugly or beautiful. They have a fixed image and a definitive role to play.

Such characters appear especially in fables and in folktales where they serve a useful purpose. Because of the consistent tradition, they are useful archetypes: the prince, the mean stepmother, the reliable and kindly cobbler or hunter, the industrious ant, the clever fox, the threatening wolf or tiger. These types of flat characters require little description.

**Round characters**

Characters in children's books who are well rounded are a somewhat recent development. Although there are exceptions, books for children of the 1900s rarely depicted well-rounded characters. If an author develops a character, this story figure is not the same at the end as he or she was at the beginning of the story. He or she has undergone some change or acquired some insight. Today, books for children usually have at least one character who is fully rounded. Skilled authors can make their characters unique ones to whom children relate.

[17] In the magnificently plotted stories of Steinbeck or Hemingway the ending is implicit in and consistent with the first few paragraphs.

Harriet Welsh in Louise Fitzhugh's *Harriet the Spy* is an example of a rounded and changing character.[18] The author gives us ample description about Harriet's subway rides, what she likes to eat, what her father says to her. She is drawn from the real world as we know it. She is precocious, brash, self-centered, ingenious, uninhibited, and she wants to be a spy. Through interaction with other characters and events in the plot, Harriet puts aside the substitute role of spy and becomes a participant in life.

Although children's book characters are usually less complex than those found in books for adults, characterizations include the usual revealment by (1) flatly telling about the character; (2) describing the character in his or her surroundings; (3) showing the character's actions, conversations, dialect, thoughts; (4) revealing what others say to and about the character.

### What Is Theme and Its Use in Children's Literature?

Next examine the organizational component of theme. Growing out of the interaction of plot and character, it is the central topic or proposition of the work. Theme may be related to archetype plots and characters, for example, the theme of the hero or heroine who journeys into the unknown, encounters a problem, overcomes it, and returns wiser than before, or the rags to riches theme (in *Cinderella*).[19]

Some school programs in literature carry the *heroic* theme from earliest to highest levels. Throughout the grades these programs put various kinds of literary heroes and heroines side by side, e.g., *fictional* (Hans Christian Andersen's *The Steadfast Tin Soldier* and Tolkien's fantasy *The Hobbit*) alongside the legendary (*Pecos Bill*).[20]

The proposition type of theme is found in young children's picture books such as these: Beatrice Schenk de Regniers' *A Little House of*

[18] *Harriet the Spy* (New York: Harper and Row, 1964). For ages 10–12. Comical at times, grim at times, a realistic study of cliques and cruelty provoking feeling and identification in child audiences (in paper, Dell).

[19] Marcia Brown has made illustrations for this tale with dash and flair. A Caldecott Medal winner. (New York: Scribner, 1952). For ages 5–9.

[20] Hans Christian Andersen, *The Steadfast Tin Soldier* (New York: Atheneum, 1971). Modern brightly colored, action-filled illustrations in an oversized picture book depict this tragic, classic tale of the duty-bound soldier and the lovely dancer. Illustrated by Monika Laimgruber. For ages 4–9. In J. R. R. Tolkien's *The Hobbit* (New York: Houghton, 1938; in paperback, Ballantine) there can be no turning back for the dwarfs until the dragon is slain. For age 9 up. Harold W. Felton's *Pecos Bill and the Mustang* (Englewood Cliffs, N.J.: Prentice-Hall, 1965) tells how the hero of all the cowboys from the Mississippi to the Pacific Ocean got his horse. For ages 6–10.

From the book *Pecos Bill and the Mustang* by Harold W. Felton, illustrated by Leonard Shortall. © 1965 by Prentice-Hall, Inc., Englewood Cliffs, N.J.

*Your Own* (theme: everyone needs privacy) and Becky Reyher's *My Mother Is the Most Beautiful Woman in the World* (theme: we do not love people because they are beautiful, but they seem beautiful because we love them).

---

*Language is the clothing of life and no child should go naked into the world.*

Dan Fader

## LANGUAGE OF LITERATURE

The next section deals with the language that clothes the organization—sound, figurative language, symbolism. All these language elements combine to make up a writer's style.

### What Are Sounds of Literature and Their Use with Children?

Sounds of words

A primary part of the language of literature is the writer's use of *sound*. How much more memorable is Paul Revere's story cast in verse by Longfellow to the rhythm of hoofbeats, than it would be in expository description! ("Listen my children and you shall hear/ of the midnight ride of Paul Revere . . .") Similarly, children respond to the rhythm and repetition of sound in verse such as the following from "To My Cat": You've been rolling in the dust;/ I can smell your dusty fur./ You've been soaking up the sun;/ I can feel your warm soft purr./ Purr, purr, purr, pur-r-r.

Sounds of sentences

Besides the sounds of words, sounds of *sentences* of various kinds and lengths are also used for literary effect. Short staccato sentences may build feelings of tenseness; longer, more rambling ones may build an ethereal mood. In Armstrong's *Sounder* there is a scene in which the boy has taken a cake to his father in jail only to have the sheriff wantonly plunge his hand into it while looking for a hacksaw. The varying pattern of sentence rhythms adds vividly to the picture of tension and restraint in the boy. It is an example of the author's craft of presenting choice words in a choice order to produce a memorable pattern of sounds (Cullinan, 1971).

### What Is Figurative Language in Children's Literature?

Besides responding to language that evokes auditory images, children also respond to visual images.

Examples are the *metaphor* of a "thunderous voice," the *simile* of Virginia Sorenson's snow-covered bushes that look "like popcorn balls," and icy trees "like a wilderness of shining threads." [21]

The fragment from the following song-poem illustrates the use of sound, figurative language, and rhyme.

> Black is the sky of a jungle night,
> Leopard spot and zebra stripe,
> Black is the color of a storm at sea,
> Eye of a lover, belly of a bee,
> And you are beautiful, too, my son.
> And you are beautiful, too! [22]

[21] *Miracles on Maple Hill* (New York: Harcourt, 1956). A story of changing family relationships as a father recovers from being a prisoner of war. Newbery Medal winner. For ages 9–12.

[22] From Helen Chetin, *Tales of an African Drum* (New York: Harcourt Brace Jovanovich, 1970). In connection with this book of tales children might enjoy the making of masks. See the article by Maya Sharpe, "An African Mask in Your Kitchen," in *Ebony Jr.*, 1973 *1* (2 and 3), 32-33. The address of this magazine (directed especially toward Black children) is 820 S. Michigan Ave., Chicago, Ill. 60605.

From the book *The Music of Africa: An Introduction* by Dr. Fred Warren and Lee Warren, illustrated by Penelope Naylor. © 1970 by Dr. Fred Warren and Lee Warren. Illustrations © 1970 by Prentice-Hall, Inc., Englewood Cliffs, N.J.

### What Is Symbolism in Children's Literature?

*Symbols,* visible signs that stand for abstract ideas, are found in children's literature. Children may realize that *Charlotte's Web* is much more than a fantastic story about a spider and a pig. They can intuitively sense deeper symbolic meaning when the artist signals them indirectly. The character of Hunter in *Dorp Dead* is reported to be a symbol of any person who passes through one's life to give it strength and meaning, or represents the archetype of the quest or the hunt (in this case the quest is for the boy's reunion with humanity). The dog in this story might be the symbol of devotion and companionship, and the tower the symbol of refuge and hope. Symbols tend to resist total explanation by suggesting and concealing at the same time.

> . . . In the mansion called literature
> I would have the eaves deep and the walls dark,
> I would push back into the shadows
> the things that come forward too clearly,
> I would strip away the useless decoration [23]

### How Is Irony Used in Children's Literature?

The child's response to irony grows out of the skills of *abstracting,* which are necessary to grasp symbolism. Irony intentionally uses incongruous comparisons in order to create some feeling of conflict, or opposite occurrence.

For example, few young children miss the irony (though they would not call it that) in Ruth Carroll's picture book *What Whiskers Did.* In the story, Whiskers (a dog who chases a rabbit) is chased in his turn by a fox. Forced to crawl into the hole of the rabbit he chased, Whiskers is saved and entertained by his formerly intended victim, the rabbit. Even kindergarten children recognize the discrepancy between what might have been expected and what actually happened.

Older children even show appreciation of irony in their own writings. Take these examples from a collection on "What Christmas Is":

Christmas is having lost something and then finding it in your present from your brother.
Christmas is giving something that the person already got (on Christmas).[24]

[23] From Tanizaki Junichiro, "In Praise of Shadows," Edward Seidensticker's adaptation in "Perspective of Japan," *Atlantic Monthly Supplement,* January 1955.

[24] Thanks to the teacher, Judith Mitchell, for sharing these.

## What Is Style and Its Use in Children's Literature?

All the language elements just presented (sound, imagery, symbolism, irony) go to make up the *style* of the work, to distinguish its expression. Style separates the great, imaginative writer who can make language serve well and the poor, pedestrian writer who cannot. The key is to be unique without being too extreme, to be unpredictable and compel attention but not to go too far and become merely sensational or create a monstrosity. The balance is delicate. The raw material for the author's style comes from many sources and is combined in unique ways.

Style in books for young children

Authors of books for children keep an eye on the needs and interests of children in regard to their style of writing. That is, in order to capture their interests children's literature needs to attain an appropriate blending of the novel with the known. This combination is enhanced by the whole range of tongue-tickling sound-play that children love so well. Besides belonging to an author individually, style is related to the different types of children's literature. For example, the style of the folktale and fable is brief, simple, terse, and sometimes ironic. The sophisticated and humorous style of Ogden Nash's poetry appeals to almost everyone.

*The Panther* [25]

The Panther is like a leopard
Except it hasn't been peppered.
Should you behold a panther crouch
Prepare to say OUCH!
Better yet, if called by a panther
Don't anther.

## Classroom Activity Reflecting the Organization and Language of the Work

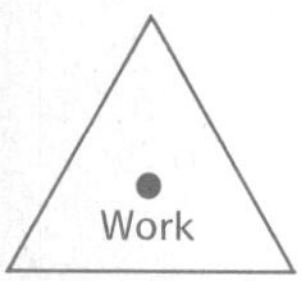


The following activity not only serves as an illustration of the elements in the work, its organization and language, but also reviews the other points of emphasis in the model of literature as communication.

5.4. Storytelling. A child cries, "Tell it again! Tell it with just your face!" (meaning without the book). Children's storytelling grows out of an appreciation of an author's powerfully heightened and poetic work.

Storytelling for everyone, anytime

Storytelling is an interesting way to start almost any lesson, as many great teachers throughout the ages have known and shown. But storytelling is not so great an art that it is not also for young shy children, and their teachers, too. The teacher tells and the children listen, and then they tell and the teacher listens—a delightful way of learning through sharing vicarious ex-

[25] From *The Moon Is Shining Bright as Day* by Ogden Nash, by permission of Little, Brown and Co. and the Estate of Ogden Nash. Copyright 1940 by The Curtis Publishing Company.

perience. Storytelling makes language and literature come alive in the classroom. Enjoy the experience of creating in this art form; it does not matter whether it is artful or not.

How to get started

How do you get started with storytelling in the classroom? After having read aloud a number of simple tales, the teacher might simply ask, "Now who would like to tell a story of their own?" It might be about a weaker person winning out, or about a trickster, or a person who had a big scare (a threatened person), or about a search, or a journey someplace and back, or about getting lost (any archetype plot).

If a completely original story is too much, the teacher might ask, "Who wants to retell another old tale?" Then the teacher might offer to tell part and the child tells what happens next. Or the teacher might say, "Who will invent a story about what his pet does?" (or the classroom pet). Or children might tell a story by using just the pictures in a filmstrip and not using the tape that goes with it.[26]

Then children can engage in a brief discussion of what they enjoyed. There is no negative criticism allowed (that might discourage children) in light of the rule that the story belongs to the teller.

Use of folktales

Folktales are excellent for stimulating children's response through storytelling. All extraneous words have been disciplined away in these works because they have been told and retold until they are like a cut stone with every facet left clean and reflecting directly to its target. In these tales something has to be resolved (plot) and the teller and his audience enter into the story together to find out what the resolution is going to be.

A story format

Having a simple format for storytelling may help some teachers and children. An example follows with a "1, 2, 3, and back to 1" type of organization. (See Slobodkina's *Caps for Sale,* Young Scott Books.)

1. The story starts with an introduction of the characters and the situation.
   For example: "There once was a pedlar who sold caps and went about calling, 'Caps for sale! Caps for sale!' "
2. The plot thickens and the problem or conflict emerges.

   There may be accumulations and repetitions of certain refrains:

   > "You monkeys give me my caps back!" and he stamped his feet, but the monkeys just stamped *their* feet high, high up in the tree. "You monkeys give me my caps back!" and he clapped his hands, but the monkeys just clapped *their* hands high, high up in the tree.

3. Then the story winds up; the plot is resolved.
1. The story is finished by returning to some motif, idea, or words that began the story in the first place:
   ". . . and the pedlar who sold caps again went about calling, 'Caps for sale! Caps for sale!' " (Note language repetition and rhythm.)

Thus the story has a 1,2,3,1 kind of pattern.

[26] See, for example, *The Children's Literature Series* (designed by Ciancioli for McGraw-Hill), a sound–filmstrip program for primary grades, six sets with teachers' guides to help get the most out of the vicarious experience and to encourage creative expression.

Examples

A story that a child tells in class could be modeled after this pattern. You could also use the form of Titus' *The Two Stonecutters,*[27] a Japanese tale similar in theme to the Grimms' tale "The Fisherman and His Wife," in which the fish grants the wife more and more wishes for power until in the end she is returned to the same status she had in the beginning. An excellent and simple book to stimulate children's storytelling about everyday happenings is Ezra Jack Keats' picture book, *The Snowy Day,* an account of a Black child's glorious day in deep, new snow. Older children can prepare stories to tell children in younger grades.

## A FEW SELECTED DISCUSSION QUESTIONS ON THE ORGANIZATION AND LANGUAGE OF A WORK

### Enjoying the Organization of Literature

*Plot*

1. Did the book seem to go fast or slowly? What made it exciting? How did one thing lead to another? Who or what was against the main character?
2. In what part did the author let us know what the book was to be about? What kind of story did you think it would be from the opening?
3. Can you describe the beginning, the middle (or turning point), and the end? What clues did you have for the ending?
4. How might you have changed this story?

*Character*

1. How did we come to know this character? (By what the author said? What the character said or did? What others said or did? The pictures?) What words could we use to describe this character? What can we guess about this character that is not actually told? (Indirection)
2. Did the character change any as the story went on? Do you know anyone whose character has changed? The reasons? Who was responsible for the way the story worked out?
3. From whose point of view is this story being told? Could you retell this story (or part of this story) from another point of view?

*Theme*

1. Was the book about something you think is important?

[27] After two brothers assist an old crone (actually goddess of the forest), she offers them seven wishes. The older brother through his grasp for power would have wound up a stone if his unselfish younger brother had not rescued him with his wishes. Illustrated in Japanese style; for ages 5–9 (New York: Doubleday, 1967).

2. Do you know another book about that same idea?
3. What does the title mean to you now? What purpose might the author have had besides telling a good story?

### Enjoying the Language of Literature

A full exposure and active response to these artistic devices of indirection (sound play, imagery, symbolism, and irony) helps them to find their way into two desirable places: children's repertory of appreciations and their own craft for construction.

1. How did you feel about that language? Did it make you hear (see, smell, feel, etc.)? How did the authors describe the weather to make you feel the cold and the heat? For example, use "Softly, gently in the secret night down from the North came the soft white," [28] from the picture book *White Snow Bright Snow,* and "If I spit on the sidewalk, it will sizzle," [29] from *Emilio's Summer Day.*
2. Did the author use interesting words? Which ones would you like to collect and share? What are some of the sentences you would like to record?
3. What are some of the words hinting that this character was an unusual person? What do you think this character might stand for?
4. What does it mean "the little car was like a raisin in the snow"? (Does it really mean that the car was a raisin?) Why did the author say it that way?
5. What do the sounds of these words remind you of? (Select some that help to create the mood or style.)

This concludes the brief presentation of elements in the organization and language that contribute to an artistic work. For selection purposes teachers need to know more than they ever plan to teach.

I would not feel right, however, about leaving the area of children's literature without mentioning two more topics—the use of bibliotherapy (or values clarification), which grows out of the audience emphasis, and the place of such teaching in relation to the total language arts curriculum. (When a book is intentionally used to improve the attitudes of a reader toward himself and the problems of others, it provides a therapy.)

---

[28] Alvin Tresselt, *White Snow Bright Snow* (New York: Lothrop, 1947), p. 19.

[29] Miriam Anne Bourne, *Emilio's Summer Day* (New York: Harper, 1966), p. 23. (Illustrated by Ben Shecter.)

### Its Aim and Resources

Aim—values clarification

Once teachers become somewhat familiar with the children's literature appropriate to the youngsters they teach, have grasped criteria of quality for the experience, and have helped children to enjoy related activity, then they are ready to move naturally into the refinement of use called *bibliotherapy*. Stated simply, bibliotherapy means getting the right book to the right child at the right time. The idea is to use insights into human behavior that often come from artistic literature.

The earlier section on Audience Emphasis hinted at this process regarding social action books. But the aim of bibliotherapy is more personal. "I kept saying over and over to myself, 'Be brave like Sarah Nobel; be brave like Sarah Nobel,' " reported one child in reaction to the book by that name. Bibliotherapy's aim is to modify attitudes in desirable directions and produce better adjustments than before. Bibliotherapy helps a child to "try on life for size."

A resource

The major resource for teachers in this area is called *Reading Ladders for Human Relations* (Reid, 1972). Divided into four parts, (1) Positive Self-Image, (2) Living with Others, (3) Different Cultures, and (4) Coping with Change, this work contains annotations of books arranged according to earlier and later ages (hence, *ladders*).[30]

### Its Context

A framework

Once teachers have seen some dramatic results from the bibliotherapeutic use of books, they might conceivably get carried away and try to treat each book as guidance material. For that reason, and in order to set the idea of bibliotherapy into the broad context of a language arts program focused on the creative-problem-solving process, the next section presents a clarifying diagram. This framework has six boxes: (1) subskills, (2) creative-problem-solving process, (3) English field, (4) child response, (5) transfer, (6) other curriculum areas. The reasons for this bird's-eye view are to summarize, gain perspective, and look for relationships. (See p. 217.)

Box 1. Communication subskills. The phrase *needed subskills* simply refers to the chain-of-learning-idea (what the child needs to be able to do before he is able to do something else, and so on). In this box you can see subskills necessary to skill in creative problem-solving (which is part of a child's productive use of bibliotherapy). For example, the child needs the sub-abilities of receiving information openly, responding fluently enough, reading, writing, thinking, and inquiring.

[30] This is a "must have" item for the teacher's professional library. See Lundsteen (1972) for more detail on bibliotherapy.

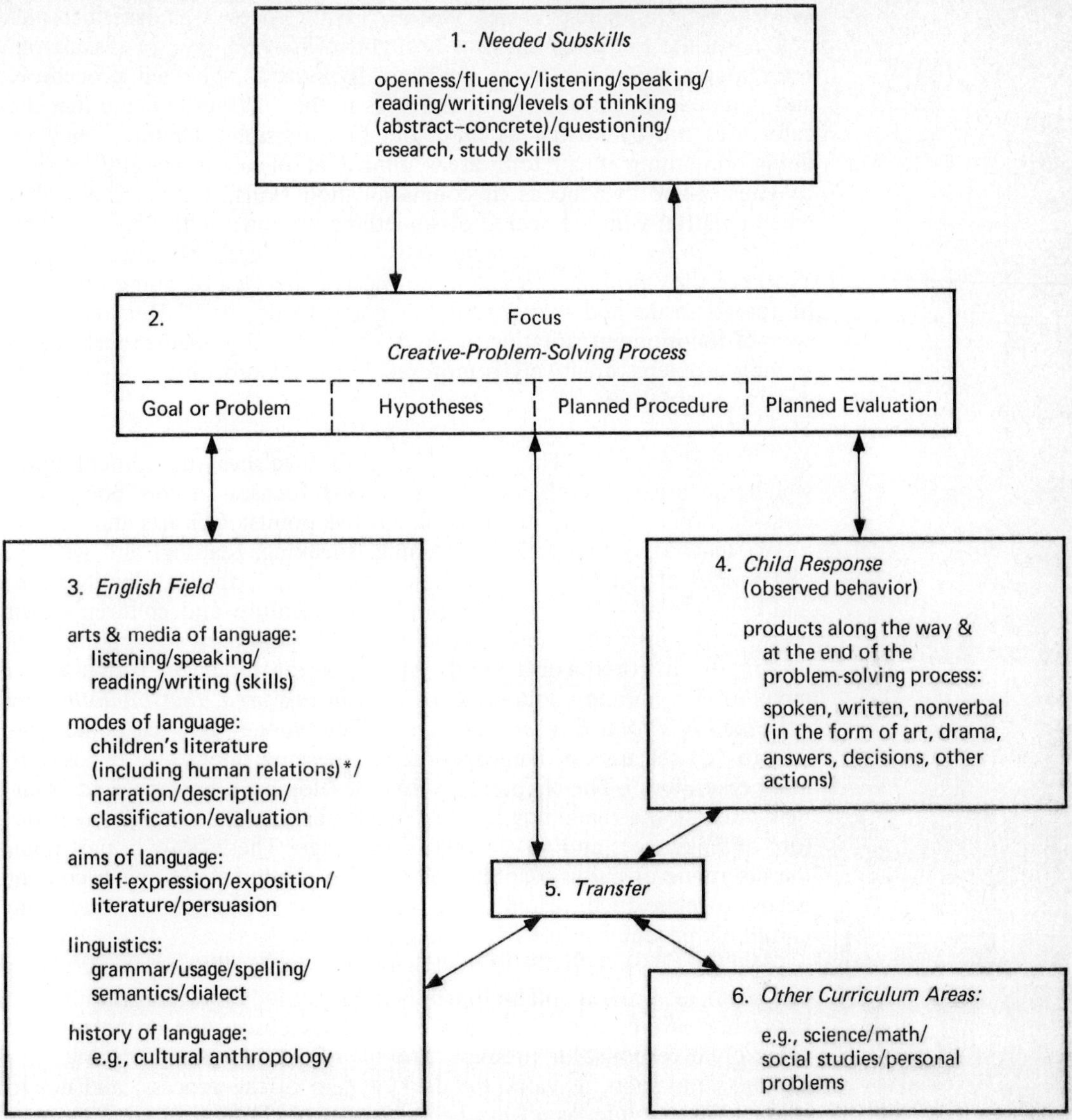


– – – Dotted lines indicate flexible categorization, that no hard, rigid division or order exists.

⟶ Arrows denote interation.

* Here is the place of bibliotherapy in a total English curriculum.

HOW DOES A PROBLEM-SOLVING FOCUS AFFECT RELATIONSHIPS IN THE CURRICULUM FOR THE CHILD?

Box 2. Creative-problem-solving process. This process was described and defined in the Prologue and was brought to life as a type of discussion. Four major areas are these: problem, hypotheses, planned procedure, and planned evaluation. The dotted lines in the diagram indicate that the categories are by no means hard and fast divisions. Children may be doing something in all four areas almost at once, or spirally as they diagnose their own needs in communication skills. I don't mean that when children who are scared of something sit down with Sperry's book *Call It Courage* they say to themselves "Oh, ho, here's Mafatu's problem and here's my problem . . . oh, ho, he got the idea of doing the thing he feared to do and that's what I'm going to do, too." But even in a spur-of-the-moment situation, a child who has had guided experience in solving problems creatively is more likely to call subconsciously on productive alternatives.

Box 3. English field. The field of English furnishes the content upon which the creative-problem-solving process focuses in this book. The classification of the field in this book has five points: (a) arts and various media (including the skills of listening, speaking, reading, and writing; (b) modes of language (including narration, description, classification, and evaluation—and especially children's literature and children's own literary composition). One special interest in children's literature (reflecting the mirrored world and the impact on the audience) is that which includes rich human relations. *It is here, in this area, that bibliotherapy is located in a total English curriculum.* The "mode" also has some relation to (c) the uses of language—self-expression, literature, exposition, and persuasion.[31] The chapters on child development, spelling, and grammar indicate the remaining areas: (d) linguistics (the nature and structure of language), and (e) history of language. These draw in part upon the discipline of cultural anthropology. The caution is that such content needs to relate to the child's natural curiosity and not take away from children's productive use of language.

Box 4. Child response. The fourth box simply indicates that the process operating on a content field sooner or later is observable in the form of some child response or product. The idea is not to push for children's products too soon, to value the development of the process, and not to think of the product as always being "one correct answer" (oral or written). The idea is to invite and arrange for a wide variety of creative, enactive, pictorial, and artistic responses. And even to value the child's response of silent thought.

[31] Because of space limits this book has given little attention to classroom use of language where the aim is exposition and persuasion. See Lundsteen (in press).

Box 5. Transfer. Transfer—without this, it doesn't really matter much what else goes on. Teachers need to seek and need to help children seek applications and uses in other times and places.

Box 6. Other curriculum areas. Much of what is learned in the language arts program (focused on creative problem-solving) transfers not only to other personal areas (as in the case of bibliotherapy) but also to other school content areas. Examples are social studies, science, and mathematics.

Finally, the arrows in the diagram indicate constant interaction among the six areas in the program. In sum, the diagram suggests that creative-problem-solving shapes transfer among personal concerns, behaviors, and curricular areas.

---

Using the diagram just described, how does the professional and artistic teacher put guidance through literature into practice? It is a little like being a juggler in the circus, who keeps perhaps 10 or 12 different objects going for just a few minutes, all at the same time—and the crowd cheers. The teacher, seeking to guide through relevant literature and to balance the curriculum, keeps dozens of different minds feeding on various activities and books at the same time, day after day, week after week, year after year, with each child reading according to self-interest and need—and sometimes nobody even notices. But the teacher, unlike the juggler, does not mind; he knows not to count on applause. Also unlike the juggler, he has seen some of his juggled objects (literature) speak to children "with tongues of thunder, holding them bound for life to wisdom and beauty."

## SUMMARY AND CONCLUSIONS

*Style, originality, intensity of feeling, and the great mystery of literature—these exist in unique forms in books for children.*

Frances Clarke Sayers, *Summoned by Books*

This chapter approached the challenge of teaching literature by (1) thinking developmentally about it and (2) considering it in light of a communication model. The chapter dealt with response to literature as vicarious experience. Response was categorized as activity for the hand (artistically manipulative and enactive), the head (cognitive), and the heart (affective and with value clarification).

Teaching

How do you teach children's literature? Some curriculum structures arrange the study of children's literature by type (genre), such as folktale, fairy tale, myth, legend, tall tales, and poetry. They simply try to sample most of these during the year and be done with it. A more productive program for children—(1) takes development into account; (2) provides for high quality of vicarious experience; (3) provides for enriched response through related music, art, drama, and creative composition; (4) recognizes that literature is communication; and (5) uses opportunities to develop creative problem-solving for unity and for motivation. In teaching, much is caught rather than taught. If the teacher esteems, enjoys, and knows literature well, the chances are greater that the children will, too. The aim of this chapter has been to remind, acquaint, and interest you so that you'll want to learn more.

Literature as communication

One way of organizing information about literary uses of language involves four emphases around and within a communication triangle. These are (1) the mirrored world (opening vistas otherwise never experienced); (2) the author (with his or her sincere and inspired self-expression kindling an intimate response); (3) the audience (inviting the child to become a learner); and (4) the work itself (with the child as enjoyer of craft, tone, and texture of language used remarkably well). Some great literary works offer a successful emphasis on all portions of the communication triangle.

Criteria

In presenting these four emphases, one purpose was to construct some criteria for selecting children's books. In the final analysis, an effective method for understanding how artistic literature for children is contrived need not be separated from *literature in general.* The same quality of vicarious reflection of the world, the same sincerity, the same impact on the audience, and the same splendor of organization and language apply to literature designed especially for the interests and needs of children.

---

## ADDITIONAL ACTIVITIES

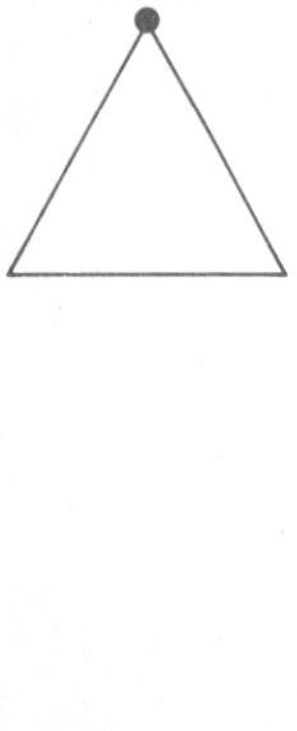


5.5. Conservation and Ecology Documentary. (For preschool through junior high.) There are a number of books that deal with topics related to conservation and ecology. Let the children experience, for example, Henry's *Mustang, Wild Spirit of the West,* Shuttlesworth's *Clean Air, Sparkling Water,* Chen's *Run Zebra Run,* Stone & Hein's *The Last Bird,* and Dr. Seuss' *The*

*Lorax.*[32] Have the children make a photographic documentary by taking colored slides of beautiful local scenes in well-preserved areas and similar scenes in polluted or spoiled areas. Children can tape background music and comments for a dramatic portrayal.

*Objective:* To promote the learner's awareness of and responsibility toward the environment, and the relationship between persons and that physical environment by means of response to literature.

Objective

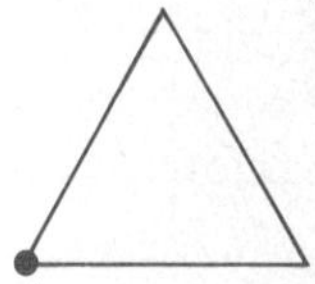

Author

5.6. Storytelling Club. (For intermediate through junior-high-school levels.) Help the children form storytelling clubs. The initiation "fee" is telling a story to the listeners. The ultimate goal is be prepared and have enough skill to be called by the school staff for telling stories to other classes.

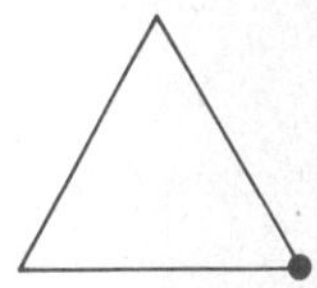

Audience

5.7. The Recommended List. (For preschool through junior-high-school levels.) Children tend to pay attention to the book recommendations of their classmates. Provide a setting for children to try to "sell" the class on reading a particular book. Book ads, posters, peep shows or dioramas illustrating scenes, book-jacket displays, and roller movies might be devised.

- Have class members respond to literature by creating a scrapbook. (See Gottesman, 1972.) Scrapbook making about literature assists in the assimilation of ideas, provides a stimulus for discussion, interests other children in the book, and provides a mini-library for browsing.
- Have the class develop an annotated list of recommendations or a large loose-leaf notebook with a page for each book.
- Use panel discussion to discuss plot, characters, illustrations, and author of a favorite; or discuss comparison of various themes in stories about bears, squirrels, or toys, for example.
- Write or tape lively reviews for the room, school, or town newspaper.
- Create a series of original illustrations for a story or poem.

[32] *Mustang, Wild Spirit of the West* (New York: Rand, 1966) relates how Wild Horse Annie Johnson led the fight first in Nevada (and then on a national level) to save the mustangs from extinction. For ages 10–14. In *Clean Air, Sparkling Water* (New York: Doubleday, 1968), the well-selected photographs may stimulate children to try to make their own to show what pollution looks like. For ages 8–10. *Run Zebra Run* (New York: Lothrop, 1972) is a lovely and important picture book with subtly warning verses in picturesque language concerning elegantly rendered animals—both familiar and exotic. For ages 5–11. *The Last Bird* (Englewood Cliffs, N.J.: Prentice-Hall, 1967), is for all ages. Accompanied by impressionistic watercolor scenes, a poignant plea is in the last bird's moving tale about the changes in the land. In *The Lorax* (New York: Random House, 1971), Dr. Seuss, in his usual ear-tickling, rhyming style, weaves a fantastic tale about the last Trufula seed and the Lorax who speaks for the trees and who guards it. But the theme on the necessity for conservation and avoidance of pollution is rooted in reality. For ages 6–10.

- Collect a tape library of brief reviews and comments about books to be used over and over by other children searching for story recommendations. Provide a quiet, inviting corner of the class partially screened.
- Group the class on the basis of literary interest. Have children report, review, or dramatize stories using the flannel board. Simple cutout figures or paper or cardboard ones can be backed by flannel or sandpaper and arranged on the board by the storyteller. Or try a magnetic board with paper cutouts attached to small magnets.

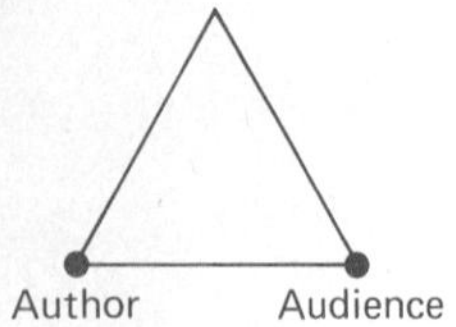


5.8. Instant Puppets. (For preschool through intermediate levels.) The quick and easy variety of puppet serves the purpose of enhancing storytelling just as well as elaborate ones. Some are made of socks or old gloves, cutouts stapled, taped, or glued to rulers or sticks, or cutout colored transparent paper forms laid on an overhead projector.

Children can also make puppets out of old stuffed animals with the stuffing removed (and the animals washed!). In order to make an instant stage, children can lay a table on its side, or stretch paper across the lower half of a doorway. And for shadow puppets, not only can children use the traditional backlighted sheets stretched tightly, but also the story can be told using figures to make shadows by placing cutouts on an overhead projector.

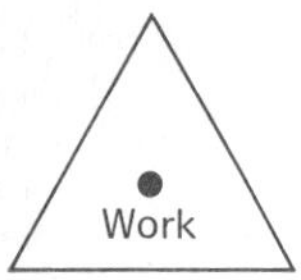


5.9. Tableau. Children in groups can pick a bookcover and get a few minutes to plan what the characters of the book are talking about and what they see as they look out of the cover. As this activity is used, it can become more elaborate, even costumed. It can improvise on the original work. The technique can be used to introduce new books to children. Or from this start the whole classroom can become the world of the book, e.g., the chocolate factory or the tollbooth. Children can start off frozen in the tableau and at a given signal step out of the tableau still in character and start improvising dramatically, talking, and interacting.

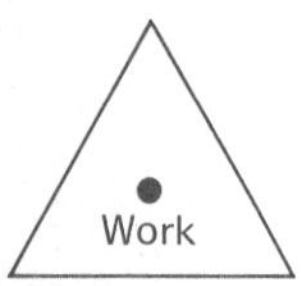


5.10. Illustration–Information. A sixth-grade class examined the Caldecott Medal–winning picture books [33] and related writings to answer questions such as Who was Caldecott? Why name an award after him? What does the picture on the medal mean? When did the award start? Who were the winners? (Reid, 1970). (Any class can formulate their own curiosities.)

Procedure ran this way: Children chose two books to compare and contrast. They rated books from 1938 to the present on a scale. What the children learned from this inquiry included awareness of the great variety of illustrations, their enhancement of texts, and the progress made in publishing books for children.

An illustration is to a book what molasses is to a pancake. It increases the nourishment, makes it more tasty, and adds a flavor of its own. (See Cianciolo, 1970.)

[33] The Caldecott medal is awarded each year to the artist who has illustrated the most distinguished American picture book for children. The winner is selected by a committee of the Children's Service Division of the American Library Association.

# If You Want to Learn More

## Professional References

ARBUTHNOT, M. H., and SUTHERLAND, Z. *Children and Books.* (4th ed.) Glenview, Ill.: Scott, Foresman, 1972.

BORTON, T. Fantasy in the Classroom. *Learning,* 1973 (January), 21-25.

BRITTON, J. Response to Literature. In J. Squire (Ed.), *Response to Literature.* Urbana, Ill.: NCTE, 1968.

BRITTON, J. *Language and Learning.* Coral Gables, Fla.: University of Miami Press, 1970.

BUCKLEY, I. Mariana Prieto: She Has Something to Say. *Elementary English,* 1967, *44* (1), 7-11.

Emphasis on "the author" (in the communication triangle).

California State Board of Education. *English Language Framework for California Public Schools.* (Proposed Revision). Sacramento, Calif., 1974.

CARLSON, R. K. *Literature for Children: Enrichment Ideas.* Dubuque, Iowa: Brown, 1970.

CARLSON, R. K. *Emerging Humanity: Multi-Ethnic Literature for Children and Adolescents.* Dubuque, Iowa: Brown, 1972.

CIANCIOLO, P. *Literature for Children: Illustrations in Children's Books.* Dubuque, Iowa: Brown, 1970.

CULLINAN, B. E. *Literature for Children: Its Discipline, and Content.* Dubuque, Iowa: Brown, 1971.

FADER, D. N., and MCNEIL, E. B. *Hooked on Books: Program & Proof.* New York: Berkeley Publishing, 1968. (Paperback)

GOTTESMAN, J. M. Making and Evaluating Literary Scrapbooks. In *Classroom Practices in the Teaching of English, NCTE, 1972-1973.* Urbana, Ill.: NCTE, 1973.

HOWE, F. Sexual Stereotypes Start Early. *Saturday Review,* October 1971, 76-82.

HUCK, C. S., and KUHN, D. Y. *Children's Literature in the Elementary School.* (2nd ed.) New York: Holt, Rinehart and Winston, 1968.

KEY, M. R. *Male/Female Language: With a Comprehensive Bibliography.* Metuchen, N.J.: Scarecrow Press, 1975.

Concerns culturally induced and falsely alleged innate differences in vocabulary, sentence structure, diction, emotional expression, forms of address, and speaking posture of men and women, both in English-speaking countries and worldwide. Highly readable. Scholarly bibliography appended.

Lidstone, J., and McIntosh, D. *Children as Film Makers.* New York: Van Nostrand Reinhold, 1970.

Loban, W. Balancing the Literature Program. *Elementary English,* 1966, *43,* 746-751.

Lundsteen, S. W. *On Exposition; On Persuasion.* In press.

Merla, P. "What Is Real?" Asked the Rabbit One Day. *Saturday Review,* 1972, *55* (45), 43-49.

Nebraska Curriculum Development Center. *A Curriculum for English.* Lincoln: University of Nebraska Press, 1966.

Odland, N. Discovering What Children Have Learned About Literature. *Elementary English,* 1970, *47,* 1072.

Reid, V. Children and Literature. In R. Ruddell (Ed.), *The Dynamics of Reading.* Waltham, Mass.: Ginn-Blaisdell, 1970.

Sebesta, S. L., and Iverson, W. J. *Literature for Thursday's Child.* Chicago: Science Research Associates, 1975.

Besides the usual features of excellent children's literature texts, has children's stories and full pages from children's books. The authors communicate with love, joy, and celebration. Has an excellent section on selected lists and reviews.

Singer, I. B. I see the Child as a Last Refuge. *The New York Times Book Review,* November 9, 1969, p. 66.

Wisconsin English Language Arts Curriculum Project. *Teaching Literature in Wisconsin.* Madison: State of Wisconsin Department of Public Instruction, 1965.

## Professional References on Bibliotherapy

Lundsteen, S. W. A Thinking Improvement Program Through Literature. *Elementary English,* 1972, *49,* 505-13.

Reid, V. M. (Ed.) *Reading Ladders for Human Relations.* (5th ed.) Washington, D.C.: American Council on Education (in cooperation with NCTE), 1972.

Divides each of the four thematic ladders into subcategories and cross-lists annotated books both by theme and age group.

## References About Poetry and Children

Arnstein, F. J. *Poetry and the Child.* New York: Dover, 1971. (A reissue of NCTE/Appleton-Century-Crofts edition dated 1962 titled *Poetry in the Elementary School.*)

HANSSON, GUNNAR. *Poetry in Profile (Dikt i Profil).* Gothenberg, Sweden: Scandinavian University Books (Akademiforlaget-Gumperts), 1964.

Constructed and used an interesting series of bipolar 7-point scales so as to cover meaning dimensions and qualities such as "tragic-happy," "still-moving," "quiet-unquiet" in student's response to poetry.

WALTER, N. W. (Ed.) Let Them Write Poetry. New York: Holt, Rinehart, & Winston, 1962.

## Some Book Lists

*A Basic Book Collection for Elementary Grades.* American Library Association, 50 E. Huron St., Chicago, Ill. 60611.

*Best Books for Children: A Catalogue.* New York: Bowker.

CIANCIOLO, P. J., and LEPERE, J. *The Literary Time Line in American History.* Garden City, N.Y.: Doubleday, 1969.

Helps locate both fiction and nonfiction in order to add to a knowledge of a period or event. Annotations sequenced according to a time-line of historic events.

Fanfare: Horn Book Honor List of Children's Books. *Horn Book Magazine,* October issue.

ROOT, S. and Committee. *Adventuring with Books.* NCTE Book List, 1973 edition. New York: Citation Press, 1973.

*Stories.* New York Public Library, 1968.

## Some Sources of Reviews

*Books for Children.* American Library Association, 50 E. Huron St., Chicago, Ill. 60611.

*The Horn Book Magazine.* Horn Book, Inc., 585 Boylston St., Boston, Mass. 02116.

Published every other month, has a long tradition.

*Bulletin of the Center for Children's Books.* The University of Chicago Press, 5801 Ellis Ave., Chicago, Ill. 60637.

Designates each title as Recommended, Marginal, or Not Recommended. (Reprinted reviews of recommended books 1966–1972 are found in Zena Sutherland's *The Best in Children's Books,* University of Chicago Press, 1973.)

*Elementary English.* National Council of Teachers of English, 1111 Kenyon Road, Urbana, Ill. 61801.

"Books in the Classroom" section eight times a year.

# Into Print

# Part 3

# Chapter 6 Developing into Composition

With this chapter begins the third and last part of this book. It deals with development and teaching of written composition. "Into Print" refers not only to the manuscript writing taught in the beginning grades, but also to children's publication of their written work in school. This publication, a natural childlike event, includes bulletin board display, work that the child takes home, and compositions duplicated and put in class or school library booklets.

This chapter suggests to you how what is known about child development applies to children's composition in the classroom. You will see examples of what some children can do at various grade levels, and what their strengths (or potential strengths) are. While the chapter gives you some procedures on beginning instructional activities, it deals with questions such as these:

- What is the nature of the young learners in this educational task, developmentally speaking?
- Why is writing so difficult for children? And how can they be motivated?
- Is there a "best" age at which to learn to compose in writing?
- What does a developmentally based curriculum take into account?
- What are first steps in teaching written composition? And how does the teacher help children to build bridges from oral to written language?
- Are there any typical developmental features from grade to grade that a teacher needs to know about? And what kinds of writing activity are a good match for them?

If part of the teacher's claim to legitimate authority hinges on knowledge of child development, the next steps had better be to examine what we think we know.[1] But first consider those children who have developed to a rather high point regarding composition.

## Children Who Write

Children truly caught up in writing are some of the world's most fortunate and most unfortunate human beings. How do we explain this paradox? They are unfortunate because their work never ceases. While their main task is being done by their imaginations, the rest of their work must be done by their hands. That means every letter, word, comma, period. And they can never stop. Almost everything they see and every emotion they feel, they write out in their inner speech.

Many of their peers, for example, might notice a cloud formation with lightning and simply think of it as possibly spoiling their play. But these "most fortunate–most unfortunate" children are also asking themselves how they feel, and how they would write to describe it—"as a clumsy, giant cat scratching the sky with gold"? The chances are that they will whip out a stub of a pencil and a scrap of paper so they'll not lose this idea.

They are never really free from this work of writing. They'd be doing it even if they had no school assignment. They'd do it because this creating of something (where before there was nothing), this assembling of their world in writing, is a joy. It brings a keen exhilaration to them, this gathering together of ideas, words, emotions, sights, sounds, and feelings into the fabric of composition. ("I can write for you exactly what happened to me!") And so these happy, hard-working children are some of the world's most fortunate. (In large part, motivation to write is a matter of a deep-seated urge to communicate in this way.)

But this is a description of perhaps one child in fifty, one child in a hundred. What about children who don't write?

[1] See Chapter 1, on the development of language and thought, the section on developmental features of the sentence and the section on teacher assistance. Sections in Chapter 3 on the aim of self-expression in oral language are also prerequisites.

## Children Who Don't Write

Some children dread the sight of pencil and paper, and heave inaudible (or audible) sighs at the mention of composition. Historically, the best instruction in writing has been reserved for the economically and socially elite. In our culture, reading has become a central goal for the education of the masses. But the ability to *write* remains a class marker. Waiting until the last years of high school to do something about writing is too late. In order to rid ourselves of this "caste-class" marker, a definition of literacy needs to include not only reading but also writing. Much of children's distaste for writing has been emotionally colored by unfortunate school practices. This chapter offers two solutions—a developmental approach and a compatible approach that is knowledgeable about the whys and hows of motivation. With such knowledge in operation there is a better chance that there will be more and more *children who write.*

### WHAT ARE SOME REASONS THAT WRITING DEVELOPMENT IN SCHOOL SEEMS DIFFICULT?

**Apparent difficulty of written composition**

Why does composition come so hard, and so unrewardingly to some schoolchildren? At certain periods, children's writing may lag as much as six or eight years behind speaking age. Maybe it is not impossible to teach a three-year-old some of the rudiments of writing; but there are certain prerequisites, such as the following:

1. Sufficient memory ability so that a child can recognize, discriminate, and recall ideas and sequences of letters.
2. At least a minimum level of holding attention to a task.
3. Ability to grasp connections between letters and sounds.

**Early writing**

In spite of the fact that many preschool children lack these minimal skills, educators have been intrigued with the ideas of Montessori. Montessori suggested that if a child is taught to write early (at four and a half or five years of age), the child responds with an explosion of abundant and imaginative use of written speech. Moreover, this explosion does not appear to be duplicated by children a few years older.

**Difficulty of abstract thought**

But why does composing appear to be one of the hardest chores for both teacher and pupil? Here is the major developmental difficulty accounting for the tremendous lag: Written speech is a separate, differing, linguistic-thought function. And the key to the difficulty is the *high level of abstract thinking* required for even minimal practice. When children learn to compose they must separate themselves, in part, from the sensory sound and facial movements of speech, and from immediate, assisting feedback from the audience. They must go to merely imagined and symbolized images in written signs for words. And they must go this route largely alone. An analogy is the increase in difficulty in going from practical concrete arithmetic to the abstractions of algebra. It is in abstraction and in complex thinking that the writing difficulty lies.

**Autonomous responsibility**

Another part of this difficulty comes from increased requirements for self-responsibility in communicating. Children may take their first steps toward the responsibility needed for written composition during the time they are standing alone in front of the class for show and tell. They hold forth alone on some idea that they want others to know about. Their contemplated experience seeks an audience. Although their language is very much intended for an audience, it is not so much promoted by them or assisting adults. It is not so much helped by feedback. That is, the product is definitely *for* an audience. What they will say next to their audience is not based on what another person has just said, but on what they themselves have just said, on their own train of thought.

Through children's inner speech–thought (or inner voice) they begin to control and shape composition. They must analyze what they are doing while they are doing it. They do this first orally and then in writing for an audience. If children want to do more than just talk to themselves (reverting to an early monologue stage), they need to anticipate and be aware of their audience's reaction—be it understanding, appreciation, or otherwise. Activities such as show and tell are valuable here, for building bridges to written composition with sustained, internal dialogues organized for display to an audience (Moffett, 1968).

**Maturity of motivation needed**

Another difficulty is motivation. When writing is addressed to an absent or to an imaginary audience or to no one in particular (except perhaps an uncaring teacher), the situation becomes new, strange, and unreal to the child. Tangible social motivation fails to operate. "What use is writing?" the child may think.

**Completeness of expression**

In addition, the completeness of expression required in writing may seem unnatural to a child, who is used to the ease of communicating in a somewhat telegraphic fashion orally. Children may become confused when they translate from their inner speech (condensed and abbreviated) into written speech. Thinking children know the subject of their inner thought. They do most of their active inner-speech thinking about the predication or action of their sentences.

*Written* speech, however, is supposed to be *complete,* to explain the subject and the predicate fully. It has to explain more than oral speech does in order to be intelligible to a reader. Children have practiced and become competent in spontaneous, unconscious, and abbreviated oral activity. But they still lack skill in fleshing out their message during abstract, deliberate, reflective activity. Again, they *lack objective analysis of what they are doing while they are doing it.* These kinds of thought functions may be barely emerging in the child and their lack hinders message completeness. Thus, difficulty lies not only in the abstractness and complexity of the process, but in making the *product* complete (Smith, Goodman, & Meredith, 1970).

**What are some implications for the curriculum?** We can draw the following conclusions:

- *Thinking.* A curriculum in writing needs to emphasize thinking—an inner dialogue that keeps an audience in mind.
- *Audience.* A curriculum apparently needs to emphasize devices for furnishing meaningful audiences for written work in order to socially motivate children (I–you).
- *Spoken Thought.* A curriculum needs to provide for spoken thought as the basis for written thought, and for thoughtful reading. (For example, let the children talk about their writing before, during, and after composition as a way to help them build bridges.)
- *Motivation.* The curriculum needs to take motivational ideas into account, as well as questions such as this one: If communication by oral means is sufficient for a child's needs, then who needs writing? Obviously, motivation for writing requires some maturity beyond the self-centered egocentricity of the young child—in Piaget's sense of these terms.
- *Acceptance.* The teacher needs to be accepting of beginning efforts in writing when ideas tumble out as they do in talk. That is, some "incoherent language tumbling" may be part of the first step. More deliberately formed statements come as children get feedback from audiences who read their work, and as they reflect upon and interpret this feedback. As with life, writing experience unexamined and unused tends to teach little.
- *Parents.* When teachers *and* parents encourage children to ask questions and to participate in searching interactive dialogue, they develop speech–thought needed for writing. Involve parents.

For example, especially in relation to minority groups (and other groups somehow denied privileges) invite parents to go on field trips with the children. Then upon returning to the classroom, ask them to join in the discussion. This activity shows parents how to inquire and interact constructively in the school context. Then parents can begin to increase encouragement of both speech—thought and written–thought in their child outside of class. An important step in a successful program of written composition is to communicate with parents and legitimate your reasons and goals. Then child, teacher, and home can all share the child's dictated and written expression. The support of additional personal acceptance can operate. Otherwise the child's imaginativeness, which you have carefully nurtured, may not be accepted or valued. And the immaturity of the language structures might be cruelly ridiculed in homes where sophisticated language use prevails. In other words, let the parents in on your developmental ideas.

These are some of the answers to the question of why writing is so difficult for some children. They lead us to examine some details that a developmentally based curriculum takes into account, such as the first step in teaching written composition and features of language that develop as the child progresses from grade to grade.

## THE FIRST STEP IN THE DEVELOPMENTAL TEACHING OF WRITING

**Dictation**

For a child, *dictation* is the major bridge to writing. Letting a child dictate an imaginative story to his or her teacher encourages inner thought with detail, invention, originality, and organization. Through dictating children begin to sense that voice terminals match the punctuation the teacher applies as part of the "scratches on paper." By *voice terminals* I mean such vocal cues as the drop in pitch before a pause that corresponds to a period, or the rise in pitch that corresponds to a question mark. (The teacher can also use the child's dictated material in a language-experience approach to reading.)

This dictating activity makes children feel like valuable persons. They generally get a better idea of what written language looks like. Not the least of the advantages is that you will enjoy the charm of a young child's language—e.g., *I saw it beginning to rain. The dirt got holes in it.*

Try to reserve time yourself to take down the words of at least a few children every day. Keep a pad and pencil handy—in your pocket, around your neck. The following section (in the format of an activity) gives further procedures.

6.1. Dictation (Child to Scribe). Burrows (1971) suggests writing down parts of imaginative stories that children have launched into during show and tell. (See Activity 3.13.) If a child tells you about a picture she has completed, jot her words down. Make every effort to record the child's exact words so that she will recognize them and so that you will capture her personal flavor.

Sometimes a child may tell you about some strong, unique, emotional response reminiscent of poetic feeling. Burrows suggests that you might tell the child it reminds you of a poem and ask to take it down. Or the response may have such sound and rhythm that you mention that children could almost skip to it and offer to record it as poetry.

**Procedure**

A few thoughts on procedure follow: for beginners, 5 to 10 minutes is a typical attention span. It is possible to squeeze time from the daily schedule, perhaps during the portions of the day set aside for free choice of activity. For the task of taking dictation, try to get some extra help. Use parent visitors, community volunteers, older children who need this service experience, and even advanced children in your own room who would be willing to play the role of "publisher" or even to collaborate in "co-authorship." A list of the children who are waiting for their turn to dictate helps the management and eases any feelings of impatience. If you use older children to help take dictation, and if five of them come for half an hour each week, then each child who wants to dictate might have a chance about every third day (given a typical class size).

**Photo captions**

A way to get started: even the youngest beginners can dictate their "autobiographies" to accompany photographs brought from home that were taken of them at various stages of growth. From these photos, young children may even be able to show you some grasp of sequence and passage of time. For example, *Here I was a little baby. Here I was bigger. I could talk. Now I am bigger and I can go to school.* These dictated captions can be mounted below the photos.

**Dictation to help older children**

Dictation is useful even in the case of older children who have trouble getting started writing or who find themselves in a writing slump. Burrows (1971) suggests that sometimes you can agree to take down just part of a story "to be continued" when you have more time (a beginning idea about one character and one happening). Or you can offer to record just the germ of an idea for those having trouble producing.

The following are some examples of dictated compositions.

**Preschool**

### *The Cookie* [2]

by Heather (age four and one half)

> *It's about a cookie. He found glasses in the street. He tried to eat them but couldn't 'cuz they were too sharp and too big and he tried to break them but still couldn't eat them. Then he tried to crunch them up but they were too crunchy to eat. Finally he stepped on them and ate them. Then he ran home to his mommy. He was sick and told her. His mommy took him to the doctor. He got sick.*

Note the *successes.* For example, the originality of the situation, the compactness, the accurate picturesque choice of words, the attempt to engage the interest of the dictation taker, the attempt to capture the totality of an imaginative experience, the use of markers such as *then* and *finally* to express relationship between ideas, the sustaining of an idea with a clear purpose guiding the selection of supporting details, and the sense of starting somewhere and ending up somewhere showing some awareness of story structure and sequence.

[2] Appreciation to Gail Swanstrom, student at the University of California, Irvine, for collecting this example.

## *Bubbles* [3]

*Once there was a chair called Bubbles. He adopted his name because everytime someone sat on him, bubbles came out of his arms and legs.*

*Bubbles was sleeping in the afternoon when a doctor sat on him. At the sight of bubbles coming out of a chair the doctor flew to his bag, took out a medical instrument and started examining him. Everyone came to see what all the excitement was about.*

*The doctor stood up and said, "It is a failure to be able to cure him." At that moment, Bubbles said, "anything is able to be cured, no matter what it is that you say can't be cured, even if I have to look for the cure myself." Everyone was startled and some people began to laugh.*

*After everyone left, Bubbles left to look for a cure. While on his way he met a witch that said, "I can cure you, one, two, three." She snapped her fingers and said he would be cured after he counted to a million. So Bubbles counted to a million and right after that he awoke and found that he had been dreaming.*

*Someone came and sat on him and when he saw that there weren't any bubbles coming out of him he said. "Boy, what a relief!"*

Note the originality of the situation, the use of personification, the typical fairy-tale ingredient of the witch, the use of dialogue, the wit, the action, the ending with the fantasy ploy of the dream but still within the fantasy situation of Bubbles, the talking chair.

## WHAT FEATURES OF LANGUAGE ARE NOTICEABLE IN THE DEVELOPING CHILD FROM GRADE TO GRADE?

### Features in Young Children

A person who observes the oral and written composition of children over the years notices the development of certain features.

**Repetition**

Even the youngest children in school can use the rhetoric of repetition effectively. Repetition gives emphasis when the child wants it and adds to the rhythmic flow of language (Golub, 1971). One first-grade child wrote his own book about Frosty the Snowman and illustrated it on four pages. He used the words *he was* and *smaller* repeatedly.[4]

[3] From a fourth-grade class at Peace Lutheran School. Dictated to Dinah Hawkey, student at the University of California, Irvine (UCI). Unfortunately the first name of the author has been lost.

[4] The author is grateful to Mrs. Polly de Graaf (at one time first-grade teacher at Cathedral Oaks School, Goleta, Calif.) for sharing this example.

**First grade**

*And*

Along the line of repetition, the frequent use of *and* in the run-on sentence is another popular device around the age of six. The *and* signals that more is coming. It represents grammar that is easy to follow. It expresses the fast-moving activity of the child going from one event directly into another as does no other sentence form (Smith, Goodman, & Meridith, 1970). Likewise, the long *because* series often conveys meaning or support for opinion, swiftly and directly.

The following is an example of response to large, round "happy faces" that a teacher had displayed on a preschool classroom bulletin board. This story was dictated by a preschool child in response to the teacher's question, "Why are the faces happy?"

> *They are happy 'cause everyone's in love, because they're rich, because the world is beautiful and they get fresh air so they won't die. Cause they look at the flowers, cause they're nice and beautiful. The water where they swim is clear and refreshing.*[5]

Tense switching

Another feature of children's early composition is the switching of tenses of verbs quickly from past to present. This appears to occur when an event is so vivid in memory that to the child it is as if it were happening at the moment. Similarly, a child may switch from the more general third person to the egocentric *I* within the same thought–word grouping.

Matching grammar

Grammatical structure, such as a simple time clause (e.g., *When I get back, . . .*) may occur. But in the case of young children it is unusual to find complex grammatical structures that hold one idea subordinate while another related idea is being developed. The simplicity of grammatical structure is appropriate to the stage of development in thinking.

Teaching implications. Is it a mistake to try to eradicate young children's immature sentence structures? In spite of the appropriateness of simple forms for young children, some teachers make the mistake of trying to discourage them from using repetition and run-on sentences. Some teachers attempt to push children into complex sentence forms before they have fully explored the simple, effective ones in their present style. The result of such interference may be a peculiar type of composition having each sentence exactly one line long. Children need many opportunities to tell and to write in their own way, for they are building connections while they practice and rehearse their own way of relating to and symbolizing the world. At the risk of repeating, the idea is to avoid pushing adult standards on children.[6]

[5] The author is grateful to Jennifer Acosta (who was a student at the University of California, Irvine) for sharing this example.

[6] Smith, Goodman, and Meredith (1970). See Chapter 1, on development of language and thought, the section on How Can Teachers Assist Development of Grammatical Sentence Maturity. Also see Chapter 10, on grammar.

Consider the earlier mentioned importance of the acceptance of one's composition by an audience of one's peers. A child's peers seem to be indifferent about the maturity of sentences. Along this line, many children begin their careers in storytelling sessions (and of course also in dictation and independent writing) by telling only a telegraphic segment of a story. But it may stand for a whole accounting in their inner speech or imaginations (Burrows, 1971). For example, Peer acceptance

I gon bren Sum rock home

might mean

> *I'm going to bring some rocks home that my mother, father, and I collected in Arizona while visiting my grandfather but were too much to take in the car this trip.*

But the chances are that when the abbreviated composition is read to other young children, they will find it acceptable and satisfying.

The following is a dictated example that also illustrates the psychological thought process of wish-fulfillment typical in many young children's compositions.

*My Wish* Preschool

> *I wish* about *my big brother.* I wish he *took me to water ski. I want to grow up fast.*

Length and complexity will come as both composer and his peer audience grow.[7]

In the following first-grade composition, see how many successes you can find. First grade

[7] See the examples on writing at the end of the chapter in Activity 6.7. Especially see the first-grade composition about the cats written by the child herself.

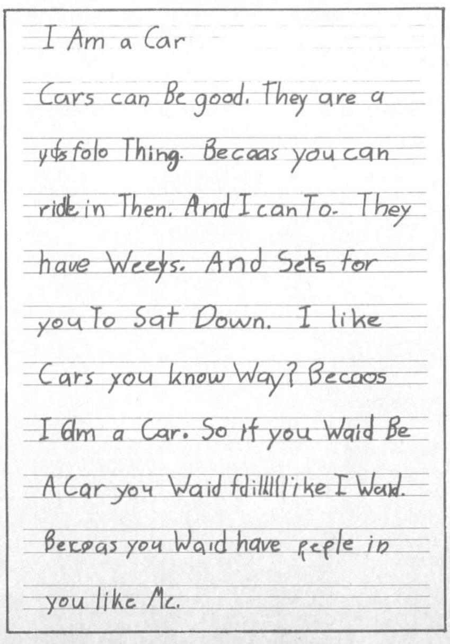
I Am a Car
Cars can Be good. They are a
ysfolo Thing. Becaas you can
ride in Then. And I can To. They
have Weeys. And Sets for
you To Sat Down. I like
Cars you know Way? Becaos
I am a Car. So if you Waid Be
A Car you Waid fdilllllike I Ward.
Becoas you Waid have peple in
you like Me.

From *The Writing of Elementary School Children: A Model for Evaluation* (Grosse Pointe, Mich.: Grosse Pointe Public School System, 1972).

Notice the unifying idea, the attempt to communicate with a reader, a character talking, cause-effect thinking. (This example was considered top-level for the first grade.)

### Features in Older Children and Teaching Implications

**Second grade**

Burrows (1971) suggests that by the second grade the teacher will notice many characters and actions coming into the composition in somewhat bewildering succession, scarcely related, and leading nowhere. But as long as something happens, it is a satisfying story to the child's peer audience. About this time the *ending* of children's stories may begin to show interesting development and become the focus, as in the earlier story of the snowman. Further, Burrows has noticed animal characters commonly used as "masks" for humans in the child's life. Children do this probably because they can make these characters behave freely and at the same time avoid a scolding from adults.

In the following second-grade composition see how many successes you can find. The composition was stimulated by three beginning sentences given by the teacher.

*Why Did It Get Dark?* [8]

by Dean

*One day I was playing outside. The sun was shining brightly. Suddenly it got very dark in the middle of the day! I looked up in the sky. I saw a gigantic bat. His wings were as big as an elephant; his head was as big as a trash can. His feet were as big as a lion. So I ran in the house because it was diving at me. It was horrible with teeth like a blade.*

[8] Thanks to Mrs. Hoyt, second-grade teacher, Nelson School, Tustin, Calif., and to her principal, Mr. Hollis F. Griffin.

Among other qualities, note the building to a climax and the use of figurative language, especially the last comparison, in getting to the essence of the imaginary experience.

**Third grade**

Third grade typically finds the child's writing reflecting his emergence from Piagetian egocentricity (Moffett, 1968). In fact, teachers may find an astounding difference in thought and language between grades two and three (Golub, 1971). The child moves definitely outside and beyond herself. Moffett notes a progressive movement from writing what he calls monologues, simple vocal dialogues, and other kinds of personal composition to narratives with more complex time and event relationships. That is, the movement is from a recording of what *is* happening to a recording of what *did* happen, in a conscious and controlled way. By this time the child is recording impressions, word pictures, and figurative and literal comparisons. These language features are inspired by models of the writing of other children and by models from children's literature.

The following are examples of compositions written independently by children in the third grade. Examine them for successes.

*Ram Rat & His Home* [9]

by Jeanette Acosta

*Once there was a rat named Ram. Ram had a very small home, a very small home indeed. He lived in a little cage right in the little corner on the floor. Then one day Ram was not in his little corner or in his little home! Ram disappeared! Ram escaped! I guessed Ram was not happy. Ram did not like sleeping or eating in his little cage or in his little corner on the floor. But one day I found Ram in a little hole! Ram went to a little female mouse and happily mated! Now Ram, the rat is happy.*

*The End*

[9] Mid-third-grade level. The author is grateful to Jennifer Acosta, sister of Jeanette, for sharing this composition with the author.

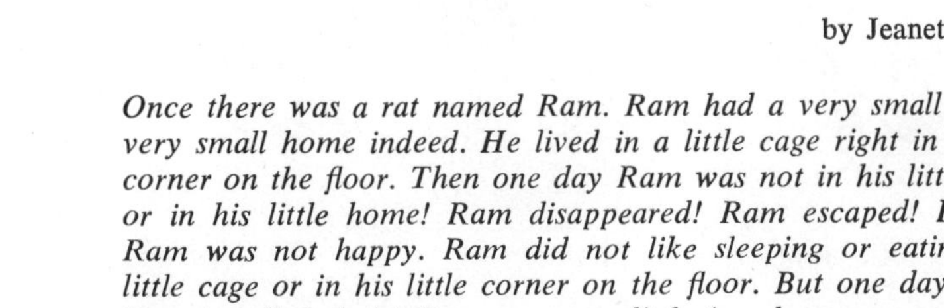


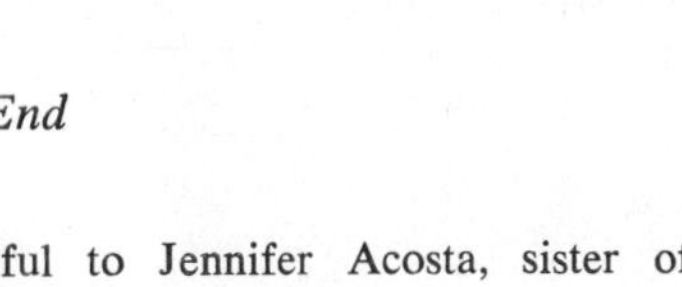

With some adroit questioning from the teacher, the child who wrote the "My Bird" composition might have been prepared to add some functional detail on just how the bird sounds, what the noise is like, how the kiss feels (though such stimulation comes better before the writing than after).

The author is grateful to Maureen Nolan, a student at the University of California, Irvine, for collecting this composition.

The following composition was stimulated by a particular kind of folk-tale, the "how it came to be" or the *pourquoi* tale. Kipling's *Just So Stories* are other examples of this type. Many teachers have found children capable of delightful and imaginative stories in this vein.

How the Rino got his horn.

One day a rinosuorvis came out
of the hills: he looked like he
wanted somthing. He wanted a horn
so he kept on walking and he
saw a man with a cow horn.
so kicked the man out of the
way and grabed the horn
and ran. he met a man
and the man siad, "hy, your
horn must of came off. i'll
go buy same glue. so he
came out of the store and
gleued the rino's horn on.
The End

A third-grade composition from the Crown Valley Elementary School. (Mrs. Wendy Stenner, teacher; Joyce Vermilyer, student-teacher)

If you try this activity, encourage the children to note vivid language, dialogue, descriptive detail, repetition, and humor that flesh out the tales in the literary examples. Once they have a setting in mind for their tale, you can ask them to brainstorm sensory words about the locale to use in their story. (Help them with any words for their list of possible material that they need help on.) For example, in Kipling's tale of "How the Whale Got His Throat," we find the whale eating "the starfish and the garfish, and the crab and the dab, and the place and the dace, and the skate, and his mate, and the mackereel and the pickereel, and the really truly twirly-whirly eel."

Growth in plot control

We can see in two of these third-grade compositions that the children are experimenting with plot. They apparently realize that some event that begins in a story needs to be resolved by the time of the ending.

Correct spelling can come later

At this time it is well to repeat a point that has been made before. Too many teachers appear to believe that children cannot express written thought until they have mastered basic literacy skills, including spelling and penmanship. A typical remark might be: "You can't let them write stories when they haven't even learned to spell!" To carry this misconception to its illogically absurd conclusion, then, children should be denied permission to talk until they have fully mastered all aspects of adult sound production, intricacies of structure, and adult vocabulary meanings (Smith, Goodman, & Meredith, 1970). This is ridiculous, of course. Children's need to express their thought is what motivates their development of oral language. The same need motivation works as the child develops written language. What is this motivation? Children want their written thoughts to be *understood,* just as they want their spoken thoughts to be understood. With this motivation, then, children do not really need formal, isolated periods of intense practice on penmanship, spelling, and writing conventions. Instead, the practice they get is relevant to their desire to make themselves understood.[10]

Intermediate grades

After third grade, what does growth in the intermediate grades look like? Gradually, the process of writing begins to take more time as fourth-, fifth-, and sixth-grade children (guided by their teachers) engage in the following sorts of activities:

1. They make decisions together concerning the purpose of a particular writing task.
2. They choose a point of view from which to write, select relevant details, and try a first draft.
3. They revise together checking the following items: attainment of purpose; clarity of thought; appropriateness, fullness (elaboration

[10] For suggested classroom activity for this age level, besides the sensory observation, memory writing and the modeling after children's literature, see Activities 6.1–6.9.

rather than flat statement); and impact of word choices and detail; adequacy of organization; and effectiveness of sentence structure.

4. They proofread together, looking at the following items: spelling, punctuation, legibility, and overall form.
5. After investing all this work, they use the composition for publication (into print).

Sometimes, something important happens between the fourth and fifth grades in the development of the child's thought and language process. A deeper sensitivity to experience may develop. A complexity of ideas in fifth-grade children's expression may become obvious in their complex sentence structure (Golub, 1971). Examine the following compositions for successes.

Fourth and fifth grade

*The Candy Man and the Witch* [11]

by Sherry (fourth grade, age nine)

*Hello, do you know who I am? Well, I am the candy man. I have any kind of candy you like right here in my store. It's the greatest candy on earth. That's why I have this terrible problem. A witch problem. There is a witch that keeps stealing my candy. Then she just will go and waste it by taking one bite out of the whole thing and throwing the rest away. And that sure makes me mad. The witch is very pretty, but she is a spoiled brat. That's why people call her a witch. Even if she is only six years old we still call her a witch. She studies witch craft all the time. She knows all sorts of magic. She is a very scary person, too. I wish it would never of happened to me. Why did she ever have to move in.*

*It all started when I saw her when she moved in next door to me. I gave her free candy every day. So now she comes over everyday and takes candy. I have to close the store early because she would eat the store out. I sure wish she would mind, but she doesn't. She won't do one thing.*

*Oh no, here she comes.*

*"Where's my candy. I want my candy. If you don't give me my candy, I will turn you into a toad."*

*"Take your candy. Take as much as you want."*

*"Goody, goody, yum, yum. Bye, bye, candy man. We're moving today."*

*"You are?"*

*"Yes, I want to because there won't be a grouchy candy man."*

*"Oh, then here is a nice big box of candy so when you are hungry you can eat it. Good-bye witch!"*

*"Goodbye candy man."*

*The End*

[11] Name of University of California student collecting this sample is unknown.

In that composition note the beginnings of rounded characterization in the imaginative situation, the revelation technique ("Even if she is only six years old . . ."), the attempts to communicate with an audience, and the attempts to make a character "talk in character."

Note successes in the following fifth-grade composition.

*All About Rover's Home and Masters* [12]

**by Lisa (fifth-grade)**

*This is Rover's home. Rover is a dog.*

*He lives in a dog house. His master goes out every day and waters the flowers.*

*There is a Father master, a mother master, a sister master, a brother master, and a baby master. Rover is not allowed in the house, because he tears it apart. When Rover tears the house apart, he gets a spanking. Rover does not like spankings.*

*Rover gets spanked with a newspaper.*

*Rover's Father master works as a T.V. seller. Rover likes to look through the window and watch T.V. Rover's Mother master does not have a job (outside the home) but she likes to grow flowers. Rover likes to smell the flowers when he walks by them. Rover's big sister master works at getting "A's" on her report card. Rover always wanted to go to school and get "A's" on his report card. Rover's brother master works as the president of his class at school. Rover always wanted to be the president. Rover's little baby sister master works at taking naps all day. Rover would like to sleep all day, but he has to keep watch for his one family.*

*One day Rover had two inches of rain in his dog house. That day Rover got to go in the house. But he came right back out because he was tearing the house apart.*

*The End*

This story was charmingly written with an audience in mind younger than the author. Notice the sustained referring to the animal's point of view after each character is introduced. Note the structure of referring to the dog's earlier mentioned character trait (tearing the house apart), bringing the story to a satisfying ending.

Sixth grade

Samples from the sixth grade may show a degree of social criticism or irony coming through as the child tests superficial social values.[13] But

[12] From Mike Di Donato, teacher, in Mariners School, Newport Beach.

[13] Many writers are telling us now that adult concerns are also the concerns of children (e.g., Golub, 1971).

there appears to be nothing like the great differences in thought and linguistic performance found between grades two and three (mentioned earlier). Again there is tremendous variation within one grade level.

Here is an autobiography written by a sixth-grade student:

David

Who Am I?

I am a boy 11 years old. I have 2 sisters but no brothers. I would like to have a brother because they are more fun. I have a pet monkey named Pete. He has a big cage in the back yard and likes to eat the leaves off our tree. I have lots of friends who like to come to my house and play with Pete. I hope after Pete dies I still have lots of friends.

The student who collected the composition made this comment: "This was written by a sixth-grade boy in response to the question, 'Who am I?' I chose this student's composition, not for its outstanding literary style, but because of the message conveyed in the last few sentences. At such a young age, David has grasped one aspect of human nature." [14]

Note the tone of the following sixth-grade descriptions to the starter, *Christmas is—*

Christmas is wearing red.
Christmas is ripping open presents.
Christmas is picking up broken ornaments and tree needles.
Christmas is decorations all over.
Christmas is the angels wings falling off and she crashes.
Christmas is when the sleigh is rusty and won't even move.
Christmas is fainting during the school program.
Christmas is Mr. Lick catching people falling off the risers.
Christmas is collapsing because you stayed up all night listening to your folks wrap presents.
Christmas is bankruptcy.

[14] Appreciation to Laura Schwalm, student at University of California, Irvine, for collecting and commenting on this composition.

Christmas is touching your head with a hot light.
Christmas is gold and red and green and silver wrapping paper.
Christmas is cookies burned and brown.
Christmas is having the lights not work.
Christmas is asking your mother if you can come down and having her say, "No, we're putting out the presents."
Christmas is when you're hoping Santa has a hole in his bag and flies over your house.
Christmas is the reindeer losing altitude.
Christmas is putting a fire in the fireplace on Christmas eve and leaving it on all night.[15]

Wit, irony, hyperbole, capsulizing of experience with vivid detail—all are present in this group composition.

The following is a character sketch and unfinished problem episode by Severin, a sixth-grade student. It shows the earlier mentioned social concern.

*Jochen*

*Jochen was about 12 years old. He had to live a hard life, because he had no friends and his parents did not accept him as their son. That's why he got in trouble and never cooperated with the teachers. He never learned anything, because he wasn't interested in the way the teachers taught the subject.*

*The subject could be interesting if the teacher would teach it in a way that he would like. All the rest of the students felt the same way, but no one dared to speak up, because it would be useless and the teacher would probably send them to the principal.*

*The teacher thought he was doing the right thing. But Jochen thought he was not. If the teacher would not act like a boss but teach in an understanding and natural way, the students would be more cooperative. But his teacher did not want to understand this.*

*Jochen was a quiet boy. He could see both sides of the school problems. He was able to sympathize with the teacher and the students. Jochen did not want to be the teacher's pet, so he teased the teacher along with the other students.*

*What could help Jochen?* [16]

---

[15] Appreciation to Judy Mitchell, presently supervisor at the University of Wisconsin, who collected these earlier when she taught in a public school.

[16] Collected by Judy Mitchell.

A developmental individualized program

Different rates of children's growth in composition depend on individual differences including chances to learn and practice. Children need a learning sequence that is developmental and yet individually tailored so that they have chances to write in a balanced way at all age levels. That means *no blanket class assignments.* Teach the individual, by conference, by the child's unique aspects as a human being. Teach as a skilled fisherman drawing out the potential subjects, experiences, and observations hidden in the child's life. *The textbook is children's own individual writing, and they find their own subject.* The program in written composition requires planning that respects the child's stage of language development. Even when it comes to practical writing that the child needs to publish in school, our demands for adherence to the conventions (e.g., punctuation) help best if they are tuned to the individual child's maturing pattern.

Learning and teaching

What does a developmental look tell us from the standpoint of learning and teaching? In general, the processes in written composition develop *longitudinally* and grow more and more *complex.* An example of longitudinal development might be a child's progress from dictating a story, to partially independent writing, to independent writing. An example of increased complexity in development might be seen in *prewriting* activities (e.g., sensory recording and memory brainstorming stimulated by actual objects, by films, by pictures, or by conversations). Increased complexity might also be seen in *composing* (e.g., a sensory recording of experience that is reworked into a mood piece, a reporting of memories that is reworked into a short story, conversations reworked into dramatic dialogue). And increased complexity might be seen in high-level *revision* (e.g., carefully selected sensory details reworked into a mood piece that reaches a climax, or into a setting for an adventure story, or into a reworking of a short story to include flashbacks, or into changes in character development with various points of view).

Elementary-school teachers can see an increase in complexity through the years in the following features (arranged in order of importance):

1. Ability to start with an idea, incident, or observation and flesh it out (or collect enough observed "flesh" in the first place).
2. Ability to choose words and details for tone.
3. Ability to move from the general through the particulars in paragraph form.
4. Ability to make choices in forming and arranging sentences, in coordination, subordination, and use of transitions.

During this growth the child's experience provides materials for his written thought. The young child's thought moves from memory of direct, sensory experience to pictured images of concrete objects held in inner speech–thought. The child's *written* thought moves from a few words to the whole incident, and finally to the complex ordering of experience through various forms of literature (such as the folktale, the fable, the myth, the fantasy). In order to match the child's developmental stage with instruction, the teacher needs to know "who" the learner is, why writing is difficult for the child, what steps might be possible in light of typical developmental features, and how to motivate each child. To summarize, examine some goals for the program. These grow out of the previous sections on development.

### *What Are Some Goals for the Developmental Program in Creative Writing?*

1. To help children grow in recognizing the worthwhileness of their own experience
2. To improve children's quality of observation
3. To amplify the range of children's experience
4. To help children select and fit language and increasingly abstract thought to the details of experience and enactment
5. To help children grow in discovering suitable forms and designs for the transfer of experience to others
6. To develop individual point of view, voice, style, character traits, and a sense of audience through opportunity for expression of feelings and ideas

## SOME GENERAL DEVELOPMENTAL ACTIVITIES

**Activities for organizing thought**

The Nebraska program is designed to guide children in grasping the structure of models of literature in order to organize their own writing. For example, in one unit the child is encouraged to write a tall tale (a special kind of folktale). Children list their favorite tall tales and incidents from them (e.g., *Pecos Bill, Paul Bunyan, Tony Beaver, Old Stormalong, John Henry*) (Nebraska Curriculum, 1966, Grade 6, p. 205). Then the teacher asks what the children see in each of these tales that makes it somewhat like the others. Some such shared characteristics follow:

- The heroes of the story are unique.
- The heroes are men of action who help build the country.
- The heroes swagger, exaggerate, play tricks, and yet solve problems or plot conflicts with good humor.
- The stories are alive with new words and sounds. There is descriptive detail as well as plot.

- Especially there is the use of exaggeration to achieve humorous effect, a very long joke, actually impossible, but told with a straight face as if really true.

Children can discuss the fact that men are the central characters in most of these folk tales and construct ones with female protagonists.

In the children's textbook series by Thomas, *The Arts and Skills of Language,*[17] there are lessons in both fifth- and sixth-grade-level books suggesting that children work together creating a "chain tale." One child starts with a few recent happenings or actual facts, which he/she proceeds to exaggerate. Then another child continues the story with other exaggerations, and so on around the group. The whole activity is taped and later replayed, transcribed, and perhaps edited for publication. At editing time children can give more attention to the plot conflicts, an effective ending, and additional "you are there" descriptive detail. Individual tall tales may be stimulated by science fiction. Thomas' texts give information on many additional resources, such as books of tall tales, recordings, and filmstrips. Other lessons in this text series give instructions for writing fantasy, myth, legend, fable, and many other forms. To help with the structure of the plot, children may need to recall the structural motifs of the many folktales they have experienced, such as:

1. The journey from home to isolation.
2. The journey from home to a confrontation with a monster—in the broadest sense of the word.
3. The rescue from a harsh home and the miraculous creation of a secure home.
4. The conflict between the wise beast and the foolish beast—again, in the broadest sense of the word (Nebraska Curriculum, 1966, Grade 3, p. 5).

The combinations and variations of these basic plot patterns serve the tall tale construction well.

**Use literature**

A caution: the best use of literature as "compost" for composition is the least obtrusive. Just as (some people say), "you are what you eat," so children are what they read; what they compose is in part what they read, and finally, they are what they compose. Children "compost" the vicarious experience, language, and forms of literature into their compositions so that the product becomes a new reality. This use of litera-

[17] O. Thomas, *The Arts and Skills of Language* (New York: Holt, Rinehart and Winston, 1972).

ture means neither limp-wristed adoration of the children's classics nor rigid phrase-by-phrase writing from literary models. Child writers are simply readers—and they have been read to a lot (Holden, 1972).

The following story dictated and illustrated by a five-year-old child shows a great deal of literature "composted" into the story—from "Hansel and Gretel," to fairy tales, to some of the language in *Alice in Wonderland,* the *Wizard of Oz* books, and other quaint characters and tales.

T'was night when all the stars fell.
Two boy and girl were there.
Frightened were they there.
Old fashioned were they.
If they went a little further into the woods, they could hear a roaring sound
of the tigers and the wolves.
So they stood by an apple tree.
The apples sweetly nodded.
Then a musical tone was heard.
Down from the moon sprang a fairy.
T'was moon fairy. She simply said to each boy and girl,
"You have no need to be afraid for morning will soon be here.
I will stay here all the night long till daybreak soon will come,
and then you shall find your lighted way. And I hope you will come back
home."
Now morning did arrive at last.
"Oh prithee, sir," we said, "the daybreak came as just we wanted."
A sunbeam flew and said, "Peekaboo. Try to catch me if you can."
The children ran and skipped in glee and it lit upon Anne's hand.
The little girl was very much surprised.
The boy ran and said, "Oh dear, how darling it is!"

---

Once responsibility is accepted for teaching children to write developmentally, the next question is, How do you motivate the very reluctant child to want to learn?

Motivation and minorities

Here special attention needs to be given to the motivation of minority [18] children, taking into consideration the following points:

- What is well-rationalized education is successful with less-privileged children as well as with the more typical.
- There are some new insights and emphases that may be particularly helpful to the teacher of the minority child.
- Service rendered to these children by the schools can use some close attention as to its actual intent for them and its amount of understanding and respect.

[18] The term *minority* replaces the unpopular term *disadvantaged* or *disprivileged.* It usually refers to what is termed *low social class* and may or may not refer to racial differences. It refers to persons outside the majority culture who have little voice, little power. Almost any one of these labels eventually becomes unsatisfactory; change is rapid. One anonymous reviewer put it this way: "These children are socially, economically, disenfranchised and denied. Because of this, they are put at a disadvantage in all areas of life. But they are not "dis" anything. Rather, they are purposely destroyed."

■ Even if you never teach a minority child, the suggestions are of value in everyday teaching. And if you do, they may be of particular value.

Teaching and motivation of the minority child is an area that is often mentioned superficially. The aim here is to give it the importance it deserves. The idea is to make teachers more aware and to give resources and materials for helping these youngsters.

## HOW DO YOU MOTIVATE CHILDREN TO WRITE?

To speak metaphorically, there are five psychological "allies" (Sheviakov, n.d.) *within* children that can help the teacher stimulate learning. These allies are especially crucial in the case of the minority child. I will first list and briefly define these aids; subsequent sections show their relationship to instruction in writing and to the sociological foundations of education. If the teacher is unable to motivate children to learn, it matters little what else the teacher of composition does.

### *What Are Five Allies for Learning and Instruction?*

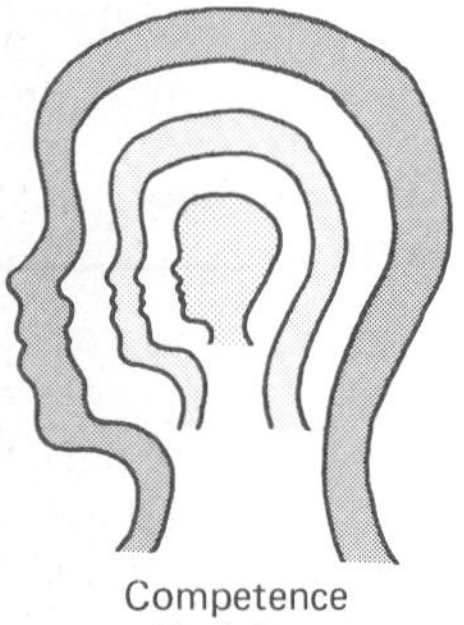


1. *Self-competence. Children want to feel competent and to respect themselves for it.* This trait is one of the reasons that a focus on autonomy and on creative problem-solving as a motivating force is effective in promoting learning.
2. *Modeling. Children want to find a strong, competent adult with whom they can identify.* Children appear to want to admire, please, and copy this adult. They want to absorb their model's useful strengths and gradually integrate his/her values into their own system and feelings.
3. *Personal acceptance. Children want to be respected, loved, forgiven, and accepted as they are at the moment.* They want this personal acceptance now, in spite of what they might be.
4. *Peer status. Children want to be liked by at least some of their classmates.* This desire to win peer approval becomes particularly typical and motivating by the time of fourth grade.
5. *Hope. Children need to have the hope that they can achieve the four preceding goals.*

Next, I will examine each of the five motivating allies to see some general implications for teaching written composition, especially with regard to minority children.

Self-competence. Children have a strong need to feel capable. In nursery school and in kindergarten there are children limited in opportunities to define themselves with appropriate confidence through language. Their sense of self may be negative. They may need redirection in relating themselves to their own small world; they may need far more redirection in relating to the wider world of the school.

Activities for self-competency

Many activities that help to lead children to a sense of their own *voices* have previously been given. Through such activities children learn how their own perceptions differ from those of others. They learn this first in oral and then in written reporting of observations. The activities in earlier chapters give children a chance to assume roles. Hearing their own voices in recorded storytelling or descriptive accounts, seeing their own words printed for them and later recording them by themselves—all of this helps to give children a sense of self and of competence in their language communication. This competence transfers to writing.

Success

It does not take children long to figure out that the ability to write is a valued skill. Once they have had the successful experience of having someone write down for them what they have composed, and once they have had it read back to them exactly as they originally said it, they are usually "hooked." It is but a short leap to the desire to write some part themselves, especially in their impatience when someone to dictate to is not readily available. The feelings of power and accomplishment that a child can get from his successfully written product can be a treasured experience. If, from the beginning, children are encouraged to feel that writing is their own creative challenge, this trait can be a powerful ally. Children can feel that they are competent creative problem-solvers all the way from the mental composition, to the motor formation of recognizable letters, to the editing for school publication, and to the final appreciation by a relatively wide audience. Such children feel that they have successfully tackled their own problems before, and they can do it again and again.

The adult who writes: a model

Modeling. If you are in the role of the adult that the child admires, it helps if you show that you value writing. It helps if your actions demonstrate that you value the child's writing in particular. And it helps if you love to write yourself. Many a preschool child has gone off happily to "write" (sometimes on the walls and floor) upon seeing a parent take pen to paper.

But a teacher's understanding and patience probably foster more children's writing than does a teacher's personal writing talent. For that reason do not be discouraged if you feel you never wrote well. You can continue to learn along with the children. It helps, especially with older children, if you know what skill in writing is all about. Then you can praise, encourage, and reinforce excellent features, a spark, a small nugget, when they occur spontaneously or after revision. Then you can set up experiences designed to bring about these excellent features.

Teacher authority as model

As a member of the majority culture, the teacher may represent an appropriate model to children of that group; however, with children who are culturally different the teacher may first have to do considerable groundwork. Keep in mind that we get our legitimate authority as teachers and as models from two sources: (1) our expertise in the subject matter, and (2) the consent of the governed.

The subject matter concerning young children in which teachers need be expert is mainly knowledge of the child's growth and development (i.e., how to introduce and continue writing instruction developmentally). Also important is knowledge of (1) ways to motivate learning, (2) thought content, and (3) principles concerning skill in composing (or the *craft*).

The consent of the governed relates in part to this question: Has the community given you the authority to be "in place of parents"? This delegation of authority is not so much a problem when teacher and parents both belong to the majority segment of society. It becomes a crucial question (affecting whether or not you are going to be thought of as an appropriate model) when the parent population represents a minority segment. Then you must work to earn this trust and to identify with the aspirations of this different culture. Otherwise the ally of modeling is not available to serve you.

Another question in relation to consent of the governed is this: Has the class had some part, some involvement, some choice in setting class standards and affairs for themselves? Have the children been invited to participate in planning routines for composition, in setting group roles for a safe and positive climate, for use of writing equipment and related aids and stimuli? That is, do the children have choices in learning about writing? Do they feel that this is "our class," "our writing experiences," rather than just the teacher's dictated assignments? To merely "do an assignment" is to hold back; to compose is to "reach out." Reaching out is what composing in a classroom for an audience is all about. How do you do this bridge building for yourself as well as for the child? The following activities show a few ways to go about it.

6.2. The Photographed Walk. You might start with a photographed walk in the spirit of the respectful anthropologist. That is, you and the class go for a walk in a "minority" neighborhood taking pictures. After the pictures are developed, you sit down with the class. The children of the neighborhood tell the story that your photos mean to them, and you say what the pictures mean to you. Then you can see through their eyes and they can see through your eyes. The two perceptions may be surprisingly different. And, if you take down their words as they talk, you have the beginnings of composing in your class right there.

6.3. Cultural Glossary. Another idea is to build a glossary of words and special meanings gotten from the minority-group child. Say to them, "I like your words; I need your words." And the chances are that they will feel the same when you tell them stories and read to them.

One more idea about models—but this time, shift from the meaning of the word *model* as a person to a second meaning. This second meaning refers to an example of written composition that furnishes the child with ideas and structure.

A program with modeling from children's literature

6.4. Models of Literature. One particularly interesting program has been developed at Northwestern University (Northwestern Curriculum, n.d.). The following section shows a lesson and the results based on using a model from literature with fourth-grade inner-city children with very low socioeconomic status in Chicago.

The specific aim of the lesson was to have the students in a group cooperatively compose a description of a place. The emphasis was to be on details suggesting a feeling.

The model selected was the description of the interior of the barn in *Charlotte's Web*.[19]

Lesson procedures

The procedure was as follows: the passage was first duplicated for distribution (better yet, display it on the overhead projector). The teacher had anticipated vocabulary difficulties, for example, with the word *loft*. After the children had read the selection silently, one of the class members read it aloud (or the teacher could do this).

Preliminary discussion concerned what the description was about, what the barn looked like, how it was different, what it smelled like and the nature of the smells, the overall nature of the place, and the author's words and details that gave this impression. In other words, the children engaged in a sensory reliving of the author's picturing.

The next step was to help the children to transfer from this vicarious literary experience to their own sensory observation, keeping the literary model in mind. The teacher asked where the children might find a place somewhat like the friendly barn, a place that was peaceful and perhaps where they could recall odors.

After a stilted first attempt the children in the project selected their own classroom as the subject of the group composition and produced the following:

*The school room was very large and old. It smelled of chalk dust and children's clothes. It often had a quiet smell—as if nothing bad could happen in school. It smelled of pencil, lead, ink paste, water-color paints, and crayons. Whenever it rained or snowed, the wet coats and boots in the dressing room smelled like a skunk. When the children walked into the room, it smelled*

[19] E. B. White, *Charlotte's Web* (New York: Dell, 1967), p. 13. This book is not particularly related to the life style of an inner-city or minority child, but it is so skillfully and powerfully written that it speaks to almost any child.

*like potato chips, candy, nuts, and pumpkin seeds. Most of the time it smelled like smoke and dust. The dust came from the windows. The smoke came from the chimneys* [*Northwestern Curriculum, n.d. p. 13*].

As a bridge, the teacher might read a composition that a child about their age had written, helping the children to point out the aspects they particularly enjoyed and the relationships to the model. The teacher might share an example that he or she had constructed.

After reading the selection from *Charlotte's Web,* for example, try first-hand observation collection, and then compose a somewhat similar paragraph yourself. Include sights, smells, and inner feelings. You might fashion your composition from sensory recordings in a journal you are keeping. The general idea is to select details that say—"I was there!" You can easily top the following product (titled "The Balcony") and share your efforts with some children.

*The balcony was large. It stretched the entire length of the apartment. It smelled of petunias and geraniums and sometimes orange blossoms. It sometimes smelled of the cool, fishy air of the ocean at the time of the red tides. It had a peaceful smell. It was as though eighteen floors up it was above all of the hurry and hate in the world. It smelled of a musty hammock and burned fat on the barbeque grill, and of marigolds. It had a pungent odor from used cat sand at one end of the balcony and pots of dried dead flowers kept in hopes of return to life. But mostly it smelled of geraniums, especially when flowers finished blooming were broken from the plants and tossed over the railing to the street far down below.*

**Literary models from the child's own cultural group**

In addition, try to find literary models of writing from the child's own ethnic and age group. Help children to feel comfortable about their literary heritage, not apologetic. That does not mean that we have to bow to separate tribes or to narrow interests and forget honest scholarship in literary tradition. But it means helping children to feel secure in their identity with their group as a comfort and as a springboard from which to move on. It means we seek balance, for we are ideally a pluralistic, not a racist society. Besides, within the ethnic minorities is a body of literature for children or adults that is of genuine literary merit and deeply satisfying.

Where do you find these models from the differing cultural group? Get the children and the community to help you look for original sources, new and emerging writers, even in the next grade, or in the closest school, and even *right in your own class*. This means you look for ideas and possible models of written composition in the following places: the jump-rope chants and other game verses and rituals the children use, the songs they like to listen to, their dictated experiences about life on their block, and the written stories and verses of other children found in some excellent published collections.[20]

Children look at compositions

Once you have found these relevant models, how can you help the children to profit from them? A great part of the technique is trusting children when you read these stories and poems aloud. You can trust them to find most of the essential elements that make for excellence in writing. The children will note features that make the work pleasing: the clarity, the action, the "right" words, the humor, the "right" details of characterization, continuity, sound, feeling, the details giving a sense of setting and rhythm.

You can add your own positive emphases to items such as those above. Remember that these commendations serve to reinforce models. These reinforced models will strengthen themselves and reappear in the writing of your children. Children tend to value in themselves the models we value in them.

Personal acceptance

Personal acceptance. Children want to be respected, loved, forgiven, and accepted as they are at the moment. What does this ally mean for the teacher planning to assist writing?

One thing it means is this: The fact that you are willing to give your time to take dictation from a child shows acceptance. Another thing it means is that when you finally get that precious bit of writing from the child (be it dictated or in his or her own scrawl), it be kept and treated appropriately, both shared warmly and filed safely. Especially if the writing is self-expression or "personal," avoid marking it up with the teacher's "red pencil," pointing out misuse of verb tense, misspelling, incorrect usage. Such marking can mean personal rejection to a child.

Looking for the positive

Furthermore, the teacher sees to it that the class avoids negative criticism about the writing when the major aim is self-expression. The idea is to foster as much pleasant feeling about writing as possible. While avoiding negative criticism, you "accentuate the positive." To children you give as immediate feedback as possible about the features of their writing that you can respond to with particular warmth, and that you want them to employ again. (Such features might be a clever reworking of their own experience; a close, honest observation; a bit of imagery; and an effective beginning or ending.) Cooperatively, the class

[20] See such books as *The World from My Window, Poems and Drawings Expressed by Minority Children,* collected by George Mendoza (New York: Hawthorne, 1969); *Here I am! An Anthology of Poems Written by Young People in Some of America's Minority Groups,* edited by Virginia Olsen Baron (New York: Dutton, 1969). See Chapter 5 on children's literature, section on appropriate selection of realistic books.

discusses and adopts the attitude that, as Burrows (1971) says, "The story belongs to the story teller."

**Sensitive composition from minority children**

The following fragments are from some writing done in the sixth grade of a ghetto school with the encouragement of one of the instructors, David Shapiro, from the Teacher's and Writer's Collaborative, an organization designed to stimulate inner-city children to write. After several unproductive trials, he had asked for a cooperative poem in which everything dances. The title was *"El Baile de la Cosa"* (or "The Dance of Things"):

This is the mystery of the dancing world . . .
Stars dance in every kind of way
The trees just swing down and swing up
The basketball players dance with their balls . . .
Willie is dancing on a football field while the football players are attacking
each other
The sun is dancing shine . . .
Books dance up in the air like little squares of puzzles
Love minus dancing equals a love scene . . .[21]

The authors of this poem were apparently thinking about and reworking their own experience. They were capitalizing on their close observations of their world. They were reporting honestly and with sense imagery that cut through to what *dance* meant to them. Organization will come.

**Peer status.** Children want to be liked by at least some of their classmates. This ally brings to mind teacher actions of providing opportunity for children to read their letters, descriptions, explanations, stories, and poems to audiences (or to have them read). This ally brings to mind the chance for children to write something that pleases their classmates, or, as in the case of expository writing, is useful to them. For example, in one child's story, on the class boat trip the captain of the boat supposedly swallowed an orange peel, accidentally, when the child threw the peel to sea gulls. Seeing the glee and sparkle on his classmates' faces when this incident happened in his story probably did something for the young writer that no amount of extrinsic rewards or correction could do. By absorbing the peer-group responses to their expression of ideas, oral and written, children learn to place themselves imaginatively in the place of their audience. Children can then learn to anticipate responses, questions, and resistances to their writing.

Of course, children do not have to share everything with their peer

[21] *Teachers and Writers' Collaborative Newsletter,* 1971, *4* (1 and 2).

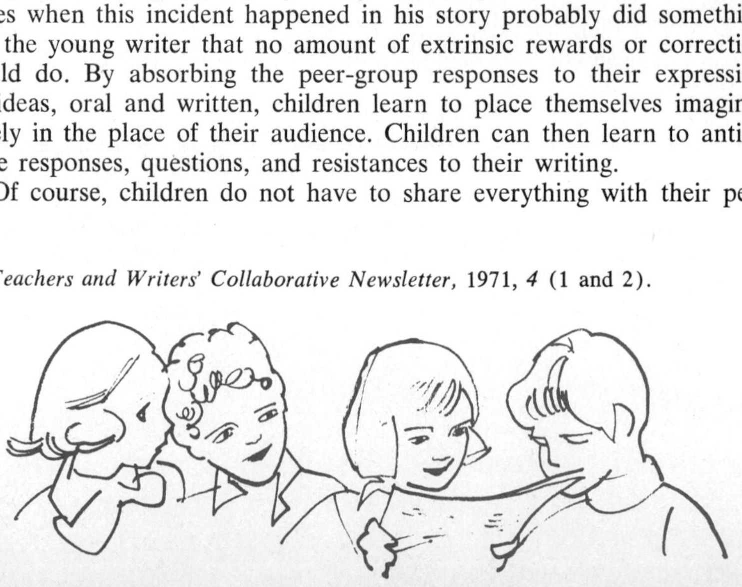

audience. Sometimes the motivation is simply private self-expression, done in isolation with intense concentration. There may be inner tension that motivates the writing, rather than outer tension to please (or to model after) an adult or peer members. This idea takes us back to the first ally, self-competence and self-respect. *Self-respect (including but going beyond the need for peer status) is perhaps the most mature of the allies.* It represents an important developmental goal.

**Various approaches needed with various social groups**

Granted, however, that you feel that you need to harness the ally of peer status, this task assumes different aspects with different groups of children: (1) the task of socializing peer groups of privileged children who have had a history of competing unmercifully with one another in the classroom means one kind of challenge for the teacher; (2) working with groups of children almost all of whom are from minorities may mean that the teacher must bring to bear all his knowledge and respect for this different culture in order to work with peer groups; (3) helping the child from outside the majority culture win peer respect when he has been supposedly integrated into a school of the privileged culture is another challenge.

Success may depend in large part on your helping minority children to respect the literature from their own heritage and your helping them to transfer this respect to their feelings of self-worth. Then maybe peer status will come. Or they can learn not to care too much if they cannot seem to win it immediately. At least they will be receptive to the fifth ally, hope.[22]

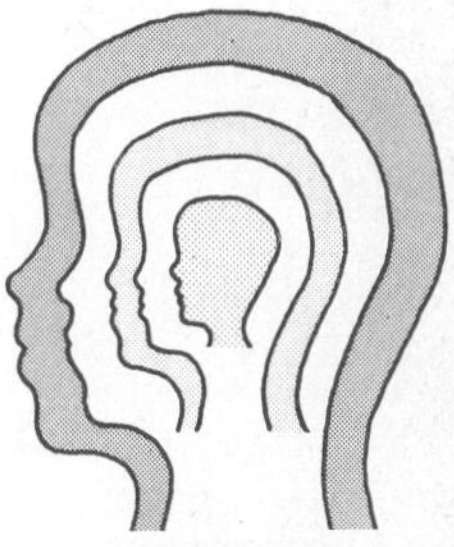


FIVE ALLIES WITHIN EACH CHILD

**Hope.** Children need to have hope that they can achieve these four preceding: self-competence, modeling, personal acceptance, and peer status. To gain hope, minority children especially need the teacher's faith, and encouragement. They need to feel that the teacher believes that even if they are apparently unable to achieve these goals now, they will. Here the teacher serves to lift and to keep the aspiration of the minority child reaching forward to writing that is both more serviceable and more creative. Almost oppositely, the teacher may have to act as a shield and protect a privileged child from unmerciful pressures and unrealistic demands of parents. Some demands are beyond the scope of reasonable child growth and reflect the goading competition of some segments of our society. (See Activity 6.9, Topics or Leading Ideas—Motivation and Organizing Assertion.)

These, then, are the five motivating allies found in children that can be used as springboards to intrinsic motivation of writing behaviors.

[22] D. Fader's book, *Hooked on Books* (New York: Berkeley Medallion, 1968), is a testimony to the peer prestige that paperback literature and even a student's poetry *can* have in prison schools and in inner-city schools.

Employ them and you can avoid using extrinsic bribes such as stars, grades, gimmicky writing ploys, nagging, commands, personal "attacks," and threats. Using psychological allies from the beginning of the child's education toward literacy will make possible the realization of the subtle joys of writing competence for almost every child.

## SUMMARY

The climax of learning to communicate is the published triumph for children when they share their written products with an appreciative audience—an ultimate act of literacy. This chapter dealt with development and motivations. The *emphasis* is on helping all children to engage increasingly in careful observation, to grow in thinking about and reworking their own experience, and then to develop in reporting it honestly with their best sense of imagery and organization. Besides experience, children's literature serves as "compost" for this composition. If you can raise children's level of composing, you have contributed to a more literate nation. You can help minority group children to find their place, too, in the literary treasures of society—a thrust forward of the common human spirit.

## ACTIVITIES FOR BEGINNING WRITING

### Introduction to Activities

Thoughtful development vs. gimmickery

The activities suggested in this chapter and the next ones are recommended mainly for their potential in extending language and thinking. They are not activity for activity's sake. There is some developmental sequence implied and some sampling of the most important aims, modes, and qualities of writing. In all the activities, reflective thinking and talking go along with doing.

Adapting activities

Since speaking and writing have much in common, many activities suggested earlier, in the chapters on oral expression for the various aims of discourse (Chapters 1 through 5) need only slight adaptation in material and method to make them suitable for writing. The ideas for most activities might be integrated into some larger plan, such as a social studies unit. They would develop from some previous learnings and evolve into further ones. The larger curriculum provides momentum.

Autonomy

In any case let the children respond in writing in their own way. Some like it private, some like it in a group. Some like titles to start them off. Others like to put their own title on after they have finished. Encourage children to use their own titles to aid them in the selection process. *One composition a child writes because he wants to is worth two dozen written to satisfy his teacher.*

No one right way

There is no one right way of using any of these activities. Three or four teachers might handle a similar writing incident in a different way and each will be successful. (And what works one time may not work another.) Each will be successful because his way is consistent with his personality interacting with the context at that time. Do not live by this textbook or by any other, but by what seems comfortable and consistent and appears to *inspire* your children. Teaching composition is your personal and creative challenge. But somewhere in this cafeteria of ideas it is likely that you will find those that are of particular use to you. If, as Burrows (1971) says, you think teaching composition is one of your most challenging problems, then you have much agreement from others. But there is little agreement about anything else.

---

Beginning observation activities

One of the first tasks of the teacher of composition is to make certain that the children's powers of observation are keen and communicable. Then children can render their experience into language. (Building skill in observation is also the first task in the teaching of science.) Consequently the activities for this part of the book start with observation, then move into activities for creative and imaginative writing that are suitable for the aims of self-expression and literature. The activities go from small units of language to larger ones such as working from enlivening details to a general idea or incident. (See the "ladder of writing suggestions" diagram at the end of Chapter 7.)

### Beginning Instruction in Imaginative Writing—Observation

Direct sensory experience promotes lively observation and precise, vivid expression. Observation has been referred to as the romance of discovery and the precision of reporting and recording. Observation fits into that teaching category of helping the child with something to write about. It is an introduction to subject matter and is an essential prewriting activity for all aims of discourse. It gives children a sense of their writing *voice* as they learn how their perceptions differ from those of others.

Definition

**What do we mean by observation?** Well, imagine an object, something important to you. (Got it in mind?) If you wanted to acquire some information about it, the first thing you might do is to look at it. That kind of observation tells you one thing. But there are many ways you can get information about an object, event, or condition other than looking at it.

You can feel it, poke it, squeeze it, rub it, listen to it, smell it—all these observational behaviors give you more and more information. Put them all together and you have a broad definition of observation. It is the employing of all senses to gain as much information as possible. In this way you identify the attributes—the obvious ones and the less obvious ones, and the ones that are distinguishing and that are unique. You need knowledge and analysis, and it helps if you have some frameworks in mind of what you might possibly observe.

Another facet of the process of observation is in examining something besides *single* objects. That is, you examine *things together* rather than separately. They may interact in such a fashion that all change. Let the object you thought of a moment ago interact with something else. Maybe it is completely changed. Or, think of fire interacting with sugar, or with a house. (Or think of your cold fingers interacting with warm laundry you are folding.) Then observation gets into the *abstracting of relationships*. (Think of characters changing one another.)

How do you teach observation? In a first lesson each child can be given a bag filled with such items as a card, a plastic spoon, a wooden fork, a thumbtack, a marble, a rubber band. Each child gets to dump the contents out onto a paper towel and is given time to observe. The teacher stands back and watches the children as they work the objects over, stretching the band, testing the tack, trading. You can observe what observation by a child means and how he/she goes about it. (This is a suitable activity for children in the preschool and primary stages.)

Relating language arts and science

What do the children learn? They learn that observation means more than looking. They learn that you really want them to observe. They learn these: description, reporting, procedure, retelling, and summarizing. Children are not always sure. They learn how to compare, classify and categorize, order, and put their objects in an array.

TEACHER: *Can you put them into two groups?*

CHILD: *Yes.*

TEACHER: *How?*

CHILD: *These are paper and these ain't.*

(You accept the classification.)

They learn abstract relationships, about cause and effect, and the support of hypotheses. They learn an important basic concept, "Property" or attribute. They need it in writing; they need it in science; they need it in mathematics.

**What do the children do?** The next teaching step is probably to get the children involved, e.g., out of doors. The following activities suggest how. A leaf walk

6.5. Leaf Walk. (For preschool through primary grades.) Take your class on a walk to observe and collect leaves. Children can collect different "greens" on their leaf walk and compare shades. They can break leaves of eucalyptus, wintergreen, spruce, and bayberry for aroma. They can feel the edges of leaves and the surface areas. They can make an "Only in Autumn" book. For example, one child wrote: *"Drifting, floating, fluttering down/ Down from the bare, empty tree/the leaf finds its rest."*

Have young children dictate a group story when they return from a walk. You duplicate it. Then each child can add a line of his own (and a picture), his own special observation.[23]

The following composition was stimulated by a leaf walk and the outline of a leaf with the story starter—"I am a pretty autumn leaf. Would you like to write a story about me?" (Note the sensory details of the first sentences and the apparent emotional involvement.)

> *I am a pretty autumn leaf. Would you like to write a story about me? Yes. I'm yellow and orange and also red too. I'm floating I'm drifting I'm swirling too. the ground is soft for me to lay. someone is coming it's collecting leaf day. All the beautiful golden and brown leaves are falling. It is autumn. Now the people are coming to rake us and burn us to ashes. what will I do. should I hide under a bundle of leaves. no no I won't do that. Should I climb up the tree and hang myself on a branch again and wait till next summer no I won't do that. I know what I'll do I'll float away and float south with the birds. There I will live happily ever after. I pretended that I was a bird. It took three years for me to go there. I was very very tired but I didn't stop. finally I got there. It was very comfortable; nobody was here to rake me and burn me up. I will live here the rest of my life until the Birds go back. I will go with them.*
>
> *THE END*

Written by Vivian Perez, third grade, El Moro School, Laguna Beach, California (Mrs. Anderson, third-grade teacher)

[23] The film, *Making Word Pictures* (Coronet, 65 E. Southwater St., Chicago, Ill. 60601), can be used to help children write paragraphs that are vivid and picturesque. Two books are especially helpful: Ann Kirn's *Full of Wonder* (New York: World, n.d.), which sensitizes the child to textural qualities and suggests ways to make rubbings, and V. Scheffer, *The Seeing Eye* (New York: Scribner, 1971), in which a biologist explores the world of nature.

On the walk children can note an object in two different situations or two different objects in the "same" situation; the children could also partially block out one sense, e.g., close eyes and be led a little way by a partner so they can observe with their ears, noses, or touch. They can pretend that today is the last day they will have a given sense. They can look at the familiar and make it new. Later they can describe the sight, sound, feeling, taste, or scent they would most like to remember. In order to really "see," they can bend over and look at the landscape through their legs, their own point of view.

6.6. Observing Construction and Other Events Outside the Classroom. (For preschool through junior high.) Another interesting thing to observe out of doors is nearby building construction. Record keeping of observation, sensation, or progress, and records about the aspects of equipment, design, color, landscaping, materials, sizes, and shapes make suitable writing material.

**Trying for metaphor**

Children can observe and describe the motion of a builder's crane lifting a heavy object. Ask if it looks like something other than it is, in order to try for metaphor. Maybe you will hear or see a jet plane. Ask for description and then ask if it looks like something else (a frightened silver fish darting in a sea-sky?).

Museums are often suitable for observation—especially historical, natural, and industrial museums. Among other things, children can watch the people walking there with various gaits. Or ask the children to examine carefully two square feet of the playground.

While out of doors they can feel the sensation of the warm sun on their skin, or the cold wind. They could go for an observational wind walk.

**In the classroom**

6.7. Observing the Classroom. Back in the classroom children can observe mealworms, (the larvae of a beetle). After children have engaged in some exploration the teacher might ask: Does the mealworm have eyes? Why do you think so? What evidence? Look at him with a magnifying glass. (Try to have a microscope, telescope, and magnifying glass on hand.) How does he use his feelers? In recording their individual observations, the children might write, for example, "He moved backwards. This is the kind of marks he makes in the sand." Children can compare their observations with those of other children, go back and check again. Or children could establish "a blue day" for which all of the children wear or bring something blue to school and note the various shades. One preschool child dictated the following words while finger painting:

*Candy on Fingerpainting* [24]

*Look at the blue water. The blue green water. It's dreamable.*

[24] Collected by Miriam Du Bois, student at the University of California, Irvine.

Or children can conduct tests of tasting using fresh, frozen, and canned foods and then record their sensations in language.

*Child autonomy*

Above all, the observation belongs to the children. If the teacher says, "This is what you should have noticed," in essence the teacher is saying to the child, "What you observe is unimportant. You are not competent. It is my authority that counts."

*Animal observation*

You might prefer having children observe gerbils instead of mealworms. They are active during the day, and are clean and tame. The writing about the observation might be a group endeavor at first. Results might be categorized and mounted on the bulletin board. Observations might be on how gerbils move, how they smell, how they drink, how they drink compared to other animals, how they feel, or how they give birth. "I held the gerbil and I think it grumbled." "I held the kitten and it purred." The next step (after writing descriptions "mirroring the world") might be to use the gerbil or the mealworm then in imaginative stories (perhaps based on literature). Or the children might observe and write about a mother cat and her kittens as did the first-grade child in this independently written composition below.

*Providing a broad range of observations, analogies*

Place before the children other objects, such as gnarled and twisted driftwood or sculpture. Have them observe, and first describe accurately, such properties as the texture, shapes, and thermal qualities. They could then compare observations. Finally, have them react comparatively, imaginatively, in new ways. Suggest they think of themselves as *being* the object, feeling like it. Then suggest they compare the object to others and then change it. (For preschool through intermediate grades.)

*"Feely boxes"*

Or give each group a covered box they can stick their hand into and feel around in without looking. Have in it such things as these: a lump of sugar, a piece of fur, an artichoke, salt, a chunk of plastic, styrofoam, fruit, a eucalyptus leaf, lemon rind, a cricket toy that clicks, shells, and rocks. Have the children guess what it is they're touching, using words that describe shape, color, and quality, e.g., "It's a round, red, crisp apple." Each child

dictates or writes his personal story about an object. *"I think I touched a baby porcupine. I think he lives under a bush."* Besides giving sensory descriptions of the objects, children can find ways to classify them. (For preschool through primary grades.)[25]

Homework: sensory recording

6.8. Observing at Home. For homework, you can ask each child to try to see, smell, hear and listen to, touch, and taste one new thing that he/she has never noticed before. Ask them to jot down notes on it, if they can. You might ask "What does milk really taste like?" "What does the water in the fountain really taste like?" The general title of the composition might be "What I Found One Day." (For preschool through intermediate grades.)

Into a paragraph or story

A direct stimulus for a composition based on this collected material might be a drawing of a child peeking over something (a wall?) and saying "WOW!" Children can write a story and create a picture about what the child saw that made him say that. Perhaps they will create their pictures first. (For intermediate through junior-high-school levels.)

---

In sum, observation prepares children for perceptive choices ("What exactly did you see?"), and for giving voice to their attitude and mood while composing ("Describe it to show you are happy"), their position and role ("How would you describe it if you were this kind of person?"), and their aim or use of language while composing ("How would you say it if you were trying to persuade someone? Entertain some one?").

## ACTIVITIES FOR MOTIVATION

Cautions

6.9. Topics or Leading Ideas. (Motivation and Organizing Assertion). (All topics are suitable for intermediate through junior-high-school grades.) Consider several cautions first about using topics to stimulate children's writing:

1. See that prewriting experience has been adequate.[26]
2. See that the topic is broad or open-ended enough so that the child has many avenues and levels for exploration. Then each child's choice and form can remain individual.
3. Let there be choices of topics that encourage *individual* reaction, that are not limiting models or frameworks just to be filled in. Writing tasks are supposed to be thinking tasks.

[25] See Mary O'Niel's *Fingers Are Always Bringing Me News* (New York: Doubleday, 1969).

[26] For an explanation of "prewriting experience" see the first stage in the next chapter, 7.

4. Sensory stimulation is more productive than the mere assignment of a topic. The idea is to encourage children to write about their experiences instead of choosing topics for them. We can educate children to observe, understand, think, and write about what they experience firsthand.

However, given that you keep these cautions in mind, one way to handle progressive selection of problems in writing (that your diagnosis leads you to believe would be profitable for a child) is by the phrasing of certain topics. Also, certain topics will usually tell you a great deal about a child's *motivational structure*—valuable information. All are enhanced by prewriting sensation, oral consultation, and choice. Teachers recognize that sometimes children need help in seeing what their interests are and how they can write about them. Written expression becomes a way to identify and develop interests.

In the following section you will find the following: (1) a topic or title, (2) the kind of motivation it refers to, (3) the kind of motivational information about the child you can get from its use, (4) the organizational assertion or kind of thinking it might provoke, and (5) how the writing might develop the assertion. Also provided is a list of a few extra topics that have been popular in the past.

Organizing thought in composition

- *What I Like; What I Don't Like—Motivation:* This topic could refer to *personal reinforcers. Assertion* and *organization:* Development by contrast and comparison are possible here. *Content:* Could refer to teachers, other children, school, physical activity, stories, color, motion, and a variety of senses.
- *Promises Kept and Promises Broken*—Refers to the same motivation and assertion as the preceding topic.
- *Kinds of Things I Can Do Right (or My Kinds of Successes)—Motivation:* This one refers to competence motivation or feedback, where probability of being correct is high. *Assertion:* Categorization is possible with the topic phrased in this way. This kind of topic teaches children to indicate for themselves the progress they are making. It is a form of self-motivating reinforcement that can be applied to their writing or to any other area.
- *Reasons Other Children Like Me (and Don't Like Me)—Motivation: Competence* or *feedback. Assertion:* Supporting a judgment with facts or cause–effect thinking are possible here.
- *About Something I Just Don't Understand (or I Wonder About . . . What Have You Touched This Week That Made You Wonder?)—Motivation:* This sort of title follows the rationale that an incentive to children is to confront them with *paradoxes* or dissonance. Educating children to frame questions is a road to logical, scientific thinking. *Assertion:* Adding the word *kinds* (some kinds of things I wonder about) could lead to categorization. Asking for times, conditions, qualities, and other observations could lead to development by relations. The addition of the word *hunches* to the beginning of the title could lead to hypothesis making (some hunches on something I wonder about).

- *How I Got Surprised—Motivation: Surprise* is usually a motivating force. *Assertion:* This title implies narrative, or development by sequence of events, what happened: first, second, then what happened to surprise the writer—then the climax.

- *Something That Made Me Laugh (or What Have You Heard Today That Made You Laugh? or Why Is a Smile?—Motivation:* Whatever makes us *laugh* can be energizing. *Assertion:* This title could be developed by sequence, or, with the addition of "and Why," could be developed by cause–effect, or judgment and reasons.

- *A Discovery (That Thrilled Me)—Motivation:* One motivational power is that of *discovery*. It is well to see if this sheer satisfaction of curiosity is an incentive and is reinforcing for the child. See if the child "appreciates" such an event, in what areas, and if it extends to language and to writing. *Assertion:* Probably narrative sequence will be a reasonable mode of development. But the composition might also get into some definition, the showing of relationships, categorization, cause–effect thinking, and judgment.

- *The Treasure Hunt* (or *The Mystery* or *Where Is Treasure?*)*—Motivation: Mystery* is motivating. *Assertion:* The sequence of events in solving a problem would probably be the basic structure in this kind of composition. These are all possible: definition, relational thinking, hypothesis making, search strategy, and evaluative and cause–effect thinking (as separate functions or within the integrative effect of problem solving).

- *These Are a Few of My Favorite Things* (or *What I Like Best to See, Touch, Taste, Hear and Listen to, Smell*)*—Motivation: Exciting stimuli* are incentives and reinforcers. It is well for the teacher to know what these are for each child. *Assertion:* Relationships of accompanying characteristics or properties (describing words) could be one way of development. Another is comparison, "What else does it remind you of? Does it look like something else?" Getting into metaphor might develop here. After hearing the song by that first title, from *The Sound of Music,* children can discuss and actually sense some items on the spot before writing. Ask what they like best and what feelings it gives them.

- *Things I Can Do Better Now (Than Before)—Motivation:* The incentive and reinforcer here is use of *self-competition.* This is the most constructive of the uses of competition to motivate. Other forms of competition apparently have little lasting and positive effect on children's performance and retention. *Assertion:* Sequence and contrast are probably major ways of developing this topic.

- *My Favorite Game(s)—Motivation: Games* of skill and of chance with competition and cooperation can be highly energizing. It's a good idea to know what favorites are. *Assertion:* This topic might develop by descriptive sequence. Or, with the addition of "Why This Is" at the front, the child could develop using support of an opinion or the support of a judgment with reasons.

- *These Are So Beautiful to Me (And These Are So Ugly, Why Is Beauty, Where and When Have You Felt Beauty in Silence? or Beauty Is . . .)—Motivation: Aesthetic elements* can be energizing and reinforcing. *Assertion:* If the last part of the title is included, the development would probably be by contrast. If not, the writing might deal with sensory descriptions.

  Stimulators could be large pictures or films of beautiful landscapes, sunrises, sunsets, real flowers, pieces of brightly colored velvet, silk, or satin, pictures of animals, people, and beautiful music (e.g., Ferde Grofe's *Grand Canyon Suite*.[27] Ask children to bring items or photographs of things that are the most beautiful to them, e.g., a most beautiful book, selections from beautiful language, words, and poetry.

  A general definition of beauty is unity in "manyness." The disorganization of a garbage can or a littered street probably represents what is ugliness to most of us. But "Beauty is in the eye of the beholder," to quote Margaret Hungerford (1878). Webster's *Second New International Dictionary* speaks of charming the senses, perfection of sensuous and spiritual order which excites admiration or delight in and of itself. Ugliness is also probably in the eye of the beholder. It may have to do with deformity, offensiveness to sight or to a more attitudinal or moral aspect. What is beauty and what is ugliness to me, to you, to both of us? This is a question that can appeal to students' interest in paradox, in discovery, mystery, wonder, and love of variety of stimuli. The topic has possibilities for a large unit of study.

- *My (Most Intriguing) Problem (What I Plan to Do About It; What Reward I'm Going to Promise Myself When I've Solved It; My Decision)—Motivation:* This topic or series of topics would bring into play *self-motivating* techniques or self-management. In the middle part of the trilogy of compositions, children pose incentives for themselves, or promise to give them-

?

[27] Columbia Records, No. ML6018. After playing the *Grand Canyon Suite* and inviting fifth-grade, low socioeconomic level children (accustomed to observing carefully) to respond in writing, one teacher obtained these nuggets: *As the music crept up on me, the picture came to me . . . sitting on my rock throne. I feel it through my whole body. I see a bird on the branches, birds flying through the air, singing everywhere. Dew trickles from the leaves of trees. Trees glisten from the light of the sun. Drops of sun shine. A bear walking strongly; worms gliding. A thousand creatures staring at someone or somewhere. A place where animals are free. I hear the sound of an eagle eating. I see a field of flowers swaying in the soft breeze like it was the ocean. I see beauty everywhere in the world. Music surrounds the world. You have love all over you. . . . Now I see slowly moving dark clouds of many shapes and sizes. Raindrops fall on the squirrels' noses. The flowers are blowing, twirling hard winds, the river goes very fast. Thunder! The animals start to yell. They start to run for they do not want to die. . . . Everything is quiet again. Everything is now soft and golden. With the coming of day it starts again—with the niceness and cruelness of the Grand Canyon with all its splendor and beauty.* (Thanks to Sharon Scheinblum, student at Pepperdine University, and teacher at Pomona School, Newport-Mesa School District, Calif., who collected this sample.)

selves rewards for their efforts. The middle part also suggests that children will indicate for themselves the progress they have made—a form of reinforcement. This activity represents the guiding or orienting function of motivation rather than just the energizing or activity–effort function of motivation. *Assertion:* The first part of the composition would involve development by definition or categorization. The second part could involve any or all of the thought processes related to creative problem-solving.

---

**Motivation: incentives & reinforcers**

From this array you can select two kinds of events. Two major ways to motivate are implicit in the topics for composition and in the information you will get from them.

1. Incentives—a "promise" of something exciting which arouses effort and activity.
2. Reinforcers—an event following behavior which increases the likelihood that such activity will occur again in these instances.

Some of the suggestions for composition combine both. Depending on the child, once you have your information about him or her and your incentives, you may need to begin with a high proportion of reinforcement so that the writing activity keeps going. But then you can gradually drop this reinforcement to a low, irregularly occurring proportion, to make it more like itself. This gives the competency of self-motivation and self-management more of a chance to operate. The development possible with this kind of compositional activity is that you can help the children to broaden their value systems and learn to appreciate a greater variety of energizing events.[28]

Of course, there are also those children with a strong predisposition toward writing. With these children, all you have to do is stand aside and give them time to write.

[28] See the highly motivating writing activities in *Ideas into Practice,* the companion guide to this text. Note the composition footnoted on p. 269.

## If You Want to Learn More

BURROWS, A. *Involving the Child in Language Arts.* Listener In-Service Cassette Library. Hollywood, Calif.: Listener Corporation, 1971.

BURROWS, A. T., JACKSON, D. C., and SAUNDERS, D. O. *They All Want to Write.* New York: Holt, Rinehart and Winston, 1964.

GOLUB, L. S. Stimulating and Receiving Children's Writing: Implications for an Elementary Writing Curriculum. *Elementary English,* 1971, *48* (January), 33-49.

GRAVES, D. Children's Writing: Research Directions and Hypotheses Based upon an Examination of the Writing Processes of Seven-Year-Old Children. Unpublished doctoral dissertation, State University of New York at Buffalo, 1973.

An exhaustive study of composing processes, including intensive, six-month-long case-study approaches. A winner of the 1974 NCTE dissertation awards.

HALL, M. *The Language Experience Approach for the Culturally Disadvantaged.* Newark, Del.: International Reading Association, 1972.

HOLDEN, W. *NCTE Convention Concerns.* Urbana, Ill.: NCTE, 1972.

KINNICK, B. J. Basic Annotated Bibliography on Creative Writing. Urbana, Ill.: NCTE/ERIC Clearinghouse on the Teaching of English, 1970. (Mimeo; copy available free)

LANDRUM, R., and Children from PS 1 and PS 42 in New York City. *A Day Dream I Had at Night and Other Stories: Teaching Children How to Make Their Own Readers.* (Teachers' and Writers' Collaborative) Urbana, Ill.: NCTE, 1971. Order No. 30157.

A record of an oral literature project with Chinese, Latin, and Black grade-school children. Tells (1) how class reading material was made out of the children's compositions and (2) of the capitalization on their native imagery and language abilities reflecting their various cultures. The reading materials were also recorded in a tape library and accompanied by a set of language exercises based on the materials and needs of each dialect. Includes both a description of the project and examples of the children's work.

MCPHAIL, A. Children's Language Development, Its Relation to Creative Writing. *Elementary English,* 1972, *49* (February), 242-44.

MOFFETT, J. *A Student-Centered Language Arts Curriculum, Grades K–13. A Handbook for Teachers.* Boston: Houghton Mifflin, 1968.

Nebraska Curriculum Development Center. *A Curriculum for English.* Lincoln: University of Nebraska Press, 1966.

Northwestern University Curriculum Center in English. *Basic Lessons, 2.* A Teacher's Experience with Composition, Lesson No. 3. Evanston, Ill.: Northwestern University Press, n.d.

Gives rationale and transcription of pupils–teacher dialogue.

SHEVIAKOV, GEORGE V. *Teaching the Disadvantaged.* Listener In-Service Cassette Library. Album No. 5. Los Angeles, Calif.: Listener Corporation, n.d.

SMITH, E. B., GOODMAN, K. S., and MEREDITH, R. *Language and Thinking in the Elementary School.* New York: Holt, Rinehart and Winston, 1970.

STEGALL, C. *The Adventures of Brown Sugar: Adventures in Creative Writing.* Urbana, Ill.: NCTE, 1967.

Tells how a teacher developed a book with her total fourth-grade class of 40 pupils. It was about a brown Pekinese. Children devised their own English text for rules of editing.

STROH, N. K. How a Diary Encouraged Creative Writing. *Elementary English,* 1969, *46* (October), 769-71. (ERIC Document Reproduction Service No. EJ 009 520)

TINGLE, M. J. Teaching Composition in the Elementary School. *Elementary English,* 1970, *47* (January), 70-73. (ERIC Document Reproduction Service No. EJ 014 250)

Presents developmental sequence in children's composing from primary through upper grades and stresses the need for oral experience.

# Chapter 7 How to Teach Composition

"But how do I teach composition?" This chapter suggests a seven-point strategy in answer to that common question. It also offers a number of classroom activities to illustrate this strategy, and a way to classify them. Does the strategy guarantee success in teaching composition? Investigate it; and then try it to see. Instructional ideas and goals in this chapter are synthesized from many sources, from Plato to the present.[1] In a practical vein, I have outlined a schedule and suggested a particular environment for a "Writing Day."

[1] Foremost among them are Burrows, Jackson, and Saunders (1964); Carlson (1970); and the unpublished words of Professor Helen Lodge (California State University, San Fernando Valley) on the importance of using the young writer's experience.

## WHY IS PROVIDING FOR COMPOSITION SO ESSENTIAL?

There are at least four major advantages that accumulate for children who write: (1) heightened power of observation, or sensitivity, to their own experience, (2) improved comprehension processes relevant to speaking and reading, (3) enhancement of self-image, and (4) increase in the teacher's understanding of them as individuals through their writing.

**Heightened sensitivity to experience**

First, consider heightened sensitivity to experience. Children who write well use their keen observation to find ways to fuse their experience with the reader's experience of their work so that it becomes shared.

*All of a sudden the deer burst out of the underbush like a top from a shaken-up bottle of Coke. A rifle bullet whined by my ear so close that it almost nicked it.*[2]

*Butterflies have beautiful wings.*
*Wings that are like colorful skies.*[3]

They may display this interpreted sensitivity to experience from the time of the first dictation in kindergarten on throughout the rest of their lives.

**Advantages—speaking and reading**

This heightened observation contributes to growth in speaking and reading. When children have practiced saying exactly what they mean through written language, the clarity of their spoken words improves. Writing aids the child's understanding of what is read to him and what he reads. It helps him comprehend ideas that may have previously been

[2] By Arthur, grade six, Irving, Texas, from his "book," *My Time to Howl.* (Cover shows a prairie scene in moonlight, howling wolf.)

[3] By Linda, grade five, Newport-Mesa school district, Calif. Thanks to her teacher, Mrs. Sharon Scheinblum, for collecting it.

incomplete or confused. Children's reading comprehension is strengthened as their writing power grows. They learn what it takes to affect an audience and how an author gets effects.

**Clarification from peers**

*Reading* comprehension difficulties have light shed upon them when several pupils discuss one another's compositions. During this sharing children see (1) how explicit the writer needs to be about ideas, and (2) how much the writer can trust readers to fill in between the lines. Communicating adequately by means of just the written word is no easy matter for any author—young or old. Children can better understand why comprehension difficulties in reading occur when they are aware of how difficult it is to write clearly. Children's understanding of writer and reader responsibilities is strengthened. For example, from a group that is discussing the members' writing you might overhear this: "I don't understand what you said; say it another way." In this kind of feedback situation, both writers and audience learn about reading comprehension.

**Development of mental processes**

Besides understanding the communication process in reading and in writing, children develop other mental processes useful in reading. Storytelling is a child's method of thinking about otherwise nameless concepts. Through stories children seek to know their world by classifying, categorizing, and using other processes of logic. Children explore their own thinking as they struggle to compose by discriminating among the various feelings and ideas swirling around in their minds.

As an example of developing mental process, the following composition written and illustrated by a first-grade child illustrates an abstract proposition followed by data and supporting evidence.

It is very easy to get killed in war.

Next followed his drawings, labeled Bomber, Paratrooper Jumping into the Woods, Tank, Dagger & Swords, Soldier Sleeping in a Tent, and Cannons Shooting.[4] All pages were stapled together to form his "book."

**Self-esteem**

Another advantage is the development of self-esteem brought about by having one's own experiences permanently recorded. This can happen even to very young children as they dictate their observations to someone who writes them down (a teacher, an aide, or an older student). This composition can then be heard, exactly as given, again and again by the child composer, and as many people who wish to hear or read it.

[4] First-grade child's "book" shared by R. V. Allen, University of Arizona, Tucson, in an address entitled "The Impact of Language on the Reading of Individuals," at the annual meeting of the International Reading Association, May 1973.

Individuals who are excited about their own ideas develop a positive self-picture, which is transferred to other skills and understandings. This satisfaction with one's achievement, this feeling of self-competence is an "ally" that has helped many a child out of the morass of destructive behavior.

**Insights about children**

Teachers also benefit from children's activity in composition. They gain otherwise unattainable insights into their pupils. Children's stories, and especially their poetry (often intense and emotionally powerful) can tell the teacher much about what is happening inside a child. In their writing children play out problems in human relations and assume various roles. The following composition, written by a child in a foster home, is an illustration:

*My Uncle*

> *My uncle said he's going to take me to Tennessee with him next summer. He tells me that every time he comes to see me. I know he isn't going to take me by now. Why does he say it?*

This projecting helps children to achieve emotional release and self-knowledge, as well as insights into other human experiences. Analysis of the subject matter of children's composition indicates such insight-seeking trends, e.g., a tendency to vindicate the young and the weak. In essence, children's compositions give the observant teacher information about children.

Thus, the process of composing in writing is one way of "coming to know." It is one of the significant means to education. The development in thinking achieved through written composition occurs in the entire curriculum.

**The problem-solving process**

It may be an overstatement to say that the composing process is creative problem-solving. But certainly the child selects. And without this selecting–solving process all instructional devices go for nothing. That is, use of models of literature, encouragement of observation,

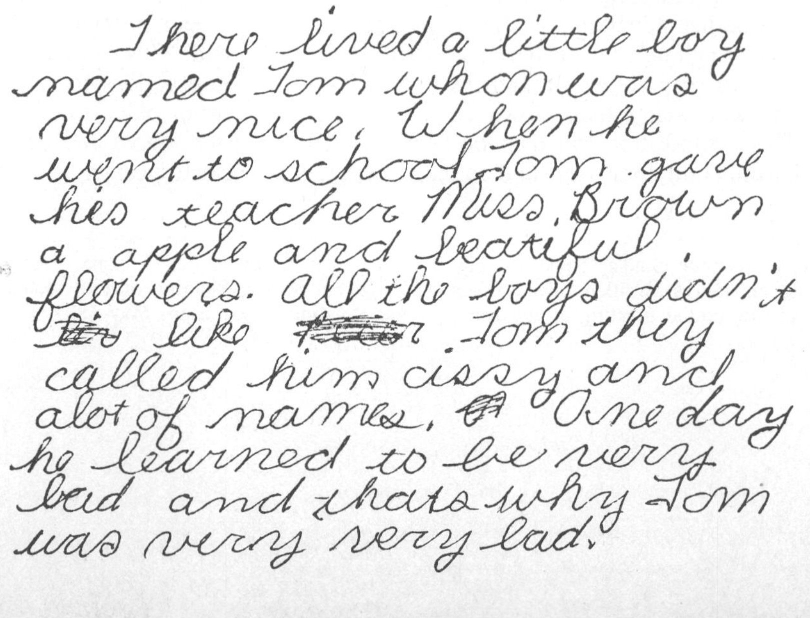
There lived a little boy named Tom whon was very nice. When he went to school Tom gave hes teacher Miss. Brown a apple and beatiful flowers. all the boys didn't like Tom they called him cissy and alot of names. One day he learned to be very bad and thats why Tom was very very bad.

recall of details of sensory experience, and various organizational ploys—all go for little or nothing without the child's process of creative problem-solving.

It is this basic creative process that makes the difference between pale thin copies and the writer the child might become. Problem solving is the force that blends compositional elements in the creation. This view is the major position in the chapters in this Part and a variation on the theme of this book.

What are problems a child processes in composition? They are the challenges of choice points along the way of the creative process. Examples are these:

Selecting the elements of experience to relate.
Selecting details to characterize, to set the mood or tone.
Deciding on a sequence of events.
Making choices among word alternatives, and as to structures within sentences.

The creativeness in the process arises from the unknowns in these problems and from the many alternatives. If children are to solve creatively, they need to be able to use self-direction in making their choices about conveying the impact of the experience and its meaning to the audience. From alternatives children create unique products—at least they are new to them. For example, a child suddenly puts the recollection of a zipper together with her viewing of two lines of children converging together, all joining hands as they come. She then writes, *Two lines of kids can make a zipper!*

One previously mentioned aspect of creative problem-solving is its fluency of associations (e.g., an *unusual* use for a tin can—a paperweight, bowling ball, doorstop, cat hat, a cookie sheet when cut and flattened). Such divergent response in thinking while writing needs to be nourished in children who show it, and developed in children who do not.

Along this line of thought Miguel Ortiz of the Teachers' and Writers' Collaborative says,

> How did I learn to write? Still learning. If you express your feelings in writing enough, you'll run into the problems. If you read enough, you'll run into the solutions. Perhaps my job is to instill the habit of reading and writing. Art will come.[5]

Thus, it seems that written composition is made up of creative problems to solve.

[5] *Teachers' and Writers' Collaborative Newsletter,* 1971, *4* (1 and 2), inside of cover.

*Mermaid* [6]

I would like to be a mermaid
I would live for 300 years
A princess mermaid
The king would let me have a garden
And let me plant anything I want in it
When I'm fifteen I can go out
And see what's in the sea
It would be winter
I would be sinking on the icebergs
And I would have a statue of a prince
In the middle of the garden
I would have a beautiful voice
My eyes would be sea-green
I could get prettier than anyone else
After 300 years I would turn into foam

Sioban
Grade two
Twin Pines Day School
Oakland, California

[6] *Teachers' and Writers' Collaborative Newsletter,* 1970, *3* (3), inside of cover.

## WHAT ARE SOME TYPES OF COMPOSITION IN THE SCHOOL?

A distinction may be made between creative writing and practical or expository writing. But there is probably an element of creativity in writing *anything* other than merely copying the creation of someone else. *Writing involves the total being in a process of translating experience into language.* An accompaniment of this process is the learning of skills that develop in greater and greater complexity.[7]

**Aims of discourse**

I find the framework of uses of language helpful when considering a program for nourishing children's writing. For example, the "hands off, teacher, don't mark it, don't correct it" point of view applies appropriately to the aim of self-expression. If the child simply wants to express and is the only audience, then the work belongs to him or to her. If children want other people to read and understand, then their writing eventually carries with it responsibilities for communication.

We emphasize use of exposition, reporting, or scientific discourse when we speak of children's practical, public writing. We think of the aim of persuasion in terms of explicit or implicit directives that the child needs in order to write to others. Such uses of language call for clear writing that follows the appropriate conventions of spelling, usage, legibility, and punctuation. In the case of the imaginative use of writing to be "published" and read by others (the literary aim), appropriate writing conventions again will need attention before final display. Written composition represents an act of self-definition in response to an audience.

**Exposition, definition and use**

If children have first had a chance to put together their sensory experience in pleasant, imaginative composition, they are more likely to take kindly to instruction in the craft of mechanics and conventions of written language. The terms *mechanics,* or *conventions* refer to spelling, handwriting, punctuation, capitalization, acceptable usage, and sentence structure. *Craft* also refers to patterns of organizing consistent, logical thought that are typical of exposition. Since someone will not always be around to dictate to, the child can lose ideas unless he has some command of these practical elements. The most appropriate kind of writing to apply this craft to is expository writing meant for a needful reader. (And these elements of craft need to be taught in the context of meaningful, useful composition.)

[7] A caution about skills and conventions of writing. We have many sacred, school-born conceptions about skills that limit the kind of creativity the child can engage in without unwarranted penalty (e.g., there must be a separate paragraph indented a half-inch for each idea; events must be stated in a certain logical sequence; the sentences must be complete and of approximately 9–12 words in length and in five different sentence patterns; margins must appear top and bottom, right and left). These conceptions become like an unseen prison limiting the thought of both the teacher and child.

What is practical, expository writing? It tends toward convergent thinking, that is, thought that retains the known, and deals with facts. It tends toward the predetermined, conserving what is. It exposes something and explains a certain point of view. A classroom example would be a child's written directions for his parents on how to get to the school carnival, what to bring, and other informative details about the carnival. Other examples would be social studies or science reports, captions, mes-

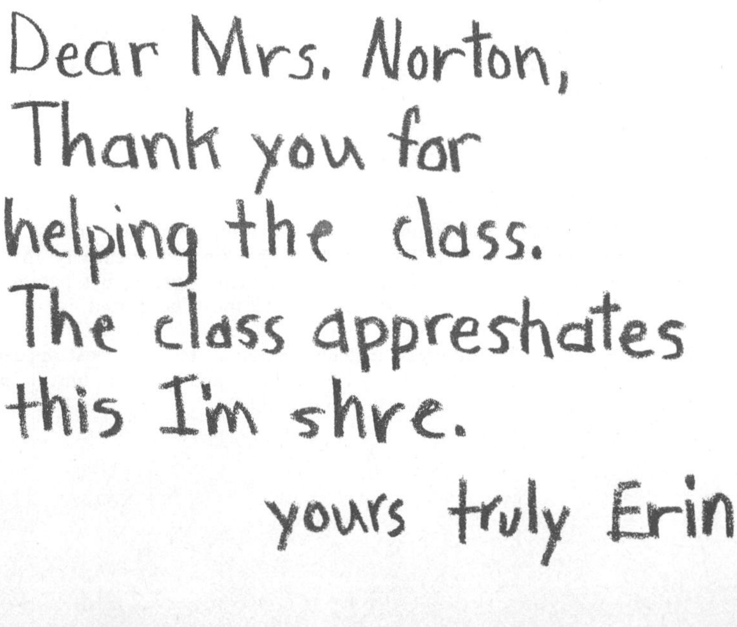
Dear Mrs. Norton,
Thank you for helping the class. The class appreshates this I'm shre.
yours truly Erin

Appreciation to Carolyn Norton, student at the University of California, Irvine, who collected this first-grade example.

sages to other classes and schools, letters, reviews, reaction papers, arguments for and against certain choices of field trips, reports of trips, bulletins, greeting cards, highlights of the history of the community, stories of newsworthy events for the class newspaper, and petitions.

The following sample of expository writing is a social studies report made by a fourth-grade child who became intrigued with the Sphinx of Egypt.[8]

[8] Thanks to Edvins Betiks, student at the University of California, Irvine, who collected this example. The personal touch (or voice) toward the end adds vitality to the report.

Arthur

In ancient times they made many smaller statues of sphinxes. They used them to guard the Egyptian tombs. And the great sphinx has a head of a woman and body of a lion and the wing of a great bird. And his eyes glow. And it is still there today. It lives in Egypt. The sphinx apears to have been a symbol of death. And it looks to me as if he wants you to go away. And it comes from the desert.

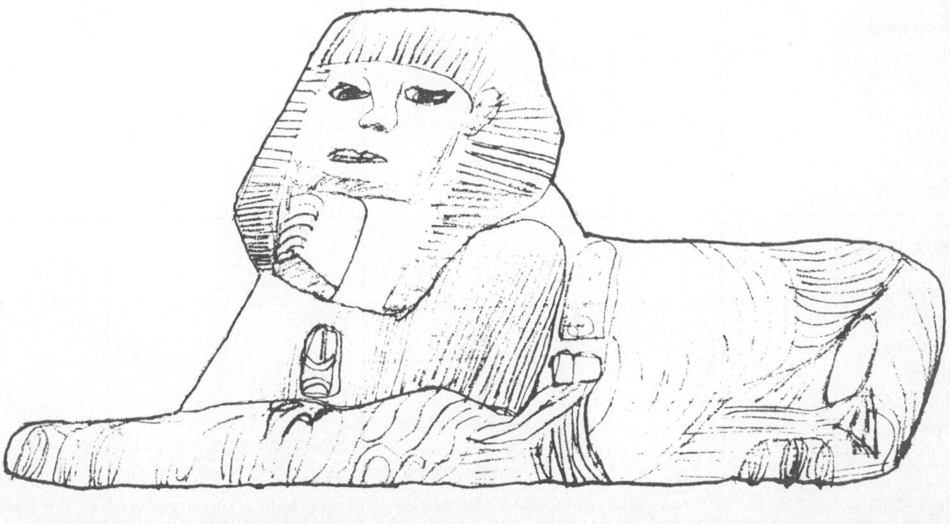

Need for reality *and* fantasy

If teachers confine the writing program solely to imaginative self-expression and literature, they restrict experience and neglect expository and persuasive forms needed for human success. Nonfiction writing has a place in the curriculum just as fantasy does. The utilitarian and artistic phases of writing are not necessarily opposed to each other. The teacher's balancing act is to guard the reality of the utilitarian writing and the personal freedom of the artistic composition (Burrows et al., 1964).

A WAY OF CLASSIFYING WRITTEN COMPOSITION ACTIVITIES (For a Balanced Program)

| MODES OF COMPOSING | CONTEXT OF COMPOSITION | | | | | | |
|---|---|---|---|---|---|---|---|
| | CHILD'S EXPERIENCE (close real-life, sensory experience) | | CHILD'S MEMORIES AND IMAGINATION | | CHILDREN'S LITERATURE | | MULTI-MEDIA |
| | Teacher structured | Self-selected | Teacher structured | Self-selected | Outside (e.g., as models) | Inside (e.g., empathy, "You were there") | (e.g., picture, film, tape, TV) |
| RECORDING<br>Observation<br>Self-expressive aim<br>Description<br>details<br>"What is happening<br>For self<br>For other<br>(Dictation included) | | | | | | | Example: ("Paired for Pictures") |
| REPORTING<br>"What happened<br>"What *was* experienced some time ago and has been reworked (e.g., as imagery) | | | | | | | |
| INTELLECTUALIZING<br>Problem-solving (Speculating, on relationships, hypothesizing, philosophizing, evaluating) | | | | | | | |

Based on ideas from Gage (1973), *Languaging: A Composition Curriculum*. This document is, in turn, based on the work of Christensen (Specificity and Additives); Gibson (Writer's Self or Persona, Audience, Tone, and Attitude); Farrell (Inside and Outside Literature); Macrorie (Sensory and Diary Writing); and Moffett (Writing Out, Down, and Up). Ideas from these writers are described in the Mt. Diablo guide. "Paired for Pictures," refers to a sample activity given.

## Using A Classificational Scheme for Balanced Activity

In order to help teachers further to provide a balanced program in composition, the preceding classificational scheme may be of some help when confronting a multitude of possible composition activities. The classificational scheme is made up of two major categories called *Modes of Composing* (down the left side of the diagram) and *Context of Composition* (across the top). Modes of Composing includes recording, reporting, and intellectualizing. Contexts of Composing include the Child's Experiences, Memories and Imagination, Children's Literature, and Multimedia contexts. These contexts may be teacher-structured or student-structured. See the diagram entitled A Way Of Classifying Written Composition Activities (p. 282).

You may have noticed in the top far right box the words "example: Paired for Pictures." This is the name of an activity I will use to demonstrate this classificational scheme. Any intriguing pictures (including slides of some dramatic paintings from museums) can be used. Start a collection.

## Paired for Pictures (Multi-media)

This activity illustrates the classificational scheme. Have students in pairs (or in small groups) generate compositions for others serving as audiences in the following way. Arrange chairs so that students face one another. But arrange the display of the media so that only one of the communicants can see the picture (say, over the partner's shoulder). Make sure that the other member of the team cannot see. After some moments of study, the partner who can see must tell the nonseeing partner what the picture is all about. The unseeing partner then acts as scribe and writes down the words of the seeing partner. (Classification: *Student Experience—Teacher Structured*)

Some alternatives for this activity involve levels of thought, for example, the student who sees and talks simply describes while the partner simply *records* this sensory description. Or, on a higher level the student who records may be more creative. He/she may imagine a series of events that led up to the frozen moment captured in the picture described. Or, on a yet higher level, students who record might use their minds to think problematically, evaluatively, or to generalize attitudinally or philosophically, say, about conditions implied in a partner's description. As a further example, they might assume a character's role or point of view and write a letter. (Classification: *Reporting, Student Memory* and *Imagination*)

Still another alternative—the partners who see and describe might do this in the form of riddles. That is, they would not actually name the scene or objects they were describing. Then the scribes would have to record and think about the details in their efforts to settle on a noun that the image implies. Or (still unseeing) they may produce a title or caption for the picture. (Classification: *Intellectualizing*) Such activity encourages dialogue and feedback. For example—

*You say you see a girl in the picture.*
*But what kind of a girl?*
*A funny girl? A freckled-faced one? One with hair like a mop?*

After a 10 or 15 minute session (depending on interest span) the students reverse position and use a new picture. (The social dimension of such activity helps children to gain the important sense of audience in composition.) But classifying systems are not nearly as important as teaching-learning strategies—the next topic.

## WHAT ARE SOME MAJOR AREAS OF A TEACHING–LEARNING STRATEGY FOR WRITTEN COMPOSITION?

In the last chapter much was said indirectly about how to teach composition (the use of the child's experience and observation, the use of literature as "compost," the use of internal "allies" for motivation, and certain developmental attitudes on the part of teachers, such as looking for successes in composition rather than errors in spelling and punctuation).

But it is possible to carry the "how to" still further and outline an optional checklist of specific steps in the process of teaching written composition. The framework suggested in this chapter (and based in part on recent research) differs from the usual "write it–correct it–rewrite it" model. The framework is the same for production of both "imaginative" and "practical" writing.

The instructor is not so much teaching separate products (a poetry form, a business letter form), but *a process*. This process is designed to produce whatever the child's subject and audience demands. The question to ask is, What portions of a process have the best chances of leading to favorable student attitudes and productivity in the classroom? Examine the following seven related parts of this process in a framework of teaching–learning techniques: [9]

[9] This framework is inspired by the writing of Golub (1969), Carlson (1970), and Murray (1968).

*Prewriting (almost 85% of the activity of composition)*

1. Stimulation of impressions
2. Re-creation
3. Creative problem
4. Oral consultation

*Writing and Rewriting*

5. Writing consultation

*Display to Appreciative Audiences*

6. Oral composition for public display
7. Written composition for public display

**The strategy in brief**

The first and second steps suggest that teachers need to arrange for a variety of stimuli. The teacher is to provide for a full awareness of that part of the world that the child's subject comes from. For example, if the child's subject is coal miners, bring one in; see a film, bring in some coal and hammer it apart, dig a hole, listen to coal miners' folk music. The teacher encourages the child to observe, research, daydream, manipulate, make notes, rearrange, and outline. The third step of this teaching–learning strategy refers to creative selection, organization by a formulated task, a focus, a chosen form that leads to a creative problem. Steps four through seven are based on the following fact: although oral and written discourse are different, they serve to reinforce one another. The diagram on the following page shows some relationships between teacher and child techniques and strategies about composition applicable to any grade level.

### 1. Stimulation of Impressions

It has been said that writing resembles the pulling of the trigger of a gun; if you are not loaded, nothing happens. Although we do not have conclusive experimental evidence that prewriting activities make a difference in written composition, such preparation makes common sense.

**Sensory stimulation**

*Prewriting activity* here refers to the stimulation that comes from—sensory experience; natural objects; vicarious (or indirect) experiences from pictures, photos, movies, from the talk of other children, or from children's literature. Or the stimulus may be a felt need, dissatisfaction, disturbance, dissonance, or paradox.

For example, the stimulus may come from the desire to write about an unfriendly relationship between two characters concerning some social issue—for example, a child sees one person confront another with, "My little brother says you beat him up!" (Perhaps the little one actually started the fight.) And from contemplation an urge to write a composition about the scene may be born.

### TEACHING-LEARNING TECHNIQUES FOR COMPOSITION

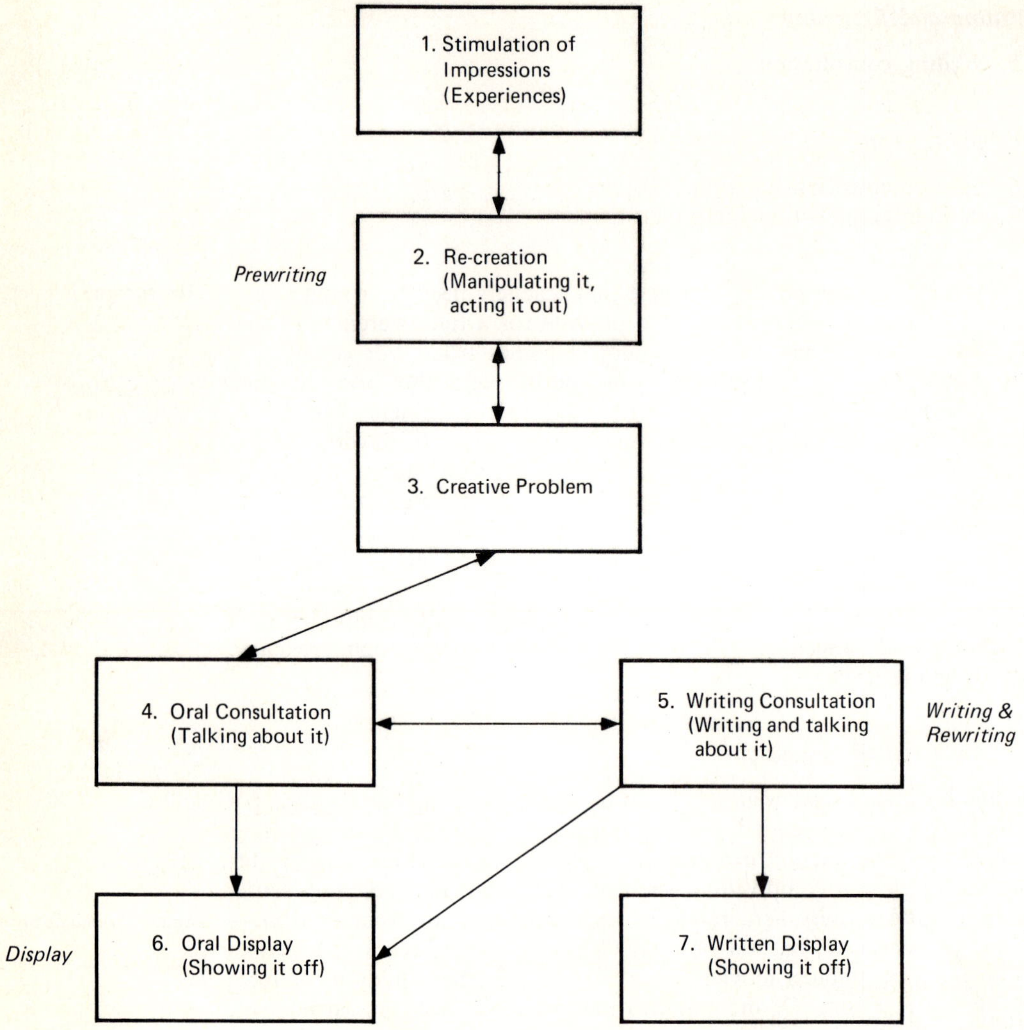


Question: What is the place of experience, re-creation, focus on a relevant problem, oral discussion, and oral composition for display?

Prewriting activity also includes the necessary steps to bring about readiness. For example, if children are going to try stories with surprise endings, the prewriting stage is the time to be sure they are well acquainted with this idea. If the task deals with Halloween, the Grand Canyon, or coal miners, this is the stage to be sure they have the vocabulary needed. Prewriting activities may include simply time to think. Or there may be small- or large-group discussions and warm-ups, group composing, and keeping of personal journals filled with raw material.

Readiness for task specifics

One question that teachers ask during this step is whether or not direct experience is a better stimulus than indirect (or media) experience when it comes to stimulating ideas in creative writing. Common sense says to weigh the developmental stage that the child is in against the richness, variety, and breadth of his previous home–community environment. Then see that both kinds of experiences become available. (There are some children who don't need any help with this step—or with any of the others.)

Experience, direct vs. media

### 2. Re-creation

Closely related to the first experiential area, stimulation of impressions, is a second—*re-creation*. Here the child recalls and sorts raw perceptions according to felt needs, skills, and earlier experience. Children need time to discover what they have to say about the stimuli. They have to acquire a motive and an aim for saying something. They need to define an audience they recognize and understand. Children must shape their own ideas—whether they get their impressions from firsthand experience or from reading, discussing, listening, or viewing. They must abstract what the experience has meant to them. Perhaps they will even find a controlling idea, theme, or an overall mood they want to convey. Children will benefit if they have time to discuss their ideas before they face that blank piece of paper. This verbalizing will help them to locate themselves in the most productive relation to their subjects—whether elephants, ants, or Vikings. This sort of ruminating of a personal nature may lead the child autonomously to the next step, the creative problem. Or the teacher may need to present some alternatives.

Reworking of impressions

What does this re-creation step mean in the case of the young child? Recall from Chapter 1 on child development that young children are usually in a stage of needing to represent their world by acting it out. In this case the teacher's best method is to get children up and about, perhaps by having them participate in creative dramatics about the idea for a bit, before expecting any writing (Hennings & Grant, 1972). Recall that young children are egocentric, that they see their world in relation to their own bodies. Then the inclusion of this physical prewriting activity seems to make sense. It places the child within the incident he

Young children need to act

or she will write about. In fact, some of this physical involvement, this nonverbal motion, may even be just what older children need. But the form for older ones may be more complex pantomime and more sophisticated creative dramatics than is enjoyed by the younger child. (See Activity 7.1, Pantomime Time.) In any case, the motto is, "Get 'em up and doing before writing!" This motto means that some teachers need to broaden their ideas about instructional techniques for written composition.

### 3. Creative Problem

Selection

About this time a writing problem suitable for creative solving appears. Ideally, the problem will come from within the child. Teachers need to help children conceive writing problems as well as solve them, that is, to help children direct their efforts at their own problems, not someone else's. In any case, there is some sort of challenge, decision, or selection needed. If not, then creative problem-solving will fail to appear. If the problem does not come from the child's own assimilations, it may be carefully selected by the teacher. The teacher, selecting in light of the child's known needs and interests, would then work to transfer the problem to the child's own valuing.

The problem might well be related to one of the aims of discourse, to some other language feature, or to certain skills needed for composition. Almost any of the suggested activities in this chapter, or from the other chapters, can be posed as writing problems.

Examples

Here are some more examples. Many teachers of intermediate grades keep story-starter file boxes. In the boxes are cards having about four words printed on each. Each word may be illustrated. Questions on the card might ask what the objects (or pictures, scenes, or settings) remind the child of. Then questions invite him to take on the problem of weaving all four words into an oral or written story. Examples of words might be *wolf, king, picnic basket,* and *full moon.* Or words might be selected from noun baskets and action or verb baskets. There might also be a sensory or "describing phrase" basket.

Composition problems

A problem for writing growing out of one of the aims of discourse might be to (1) compose something simply to express yourself; (2) construct two sides or more to an argument (e.g., why or why not kill insects); (3) or produce creative literature to share (e.g., a poem or a folktale about how the white sea gull got his black wing-markings). The writing problem might deal with trying to get into a character's skin and steeping oneself in a certain setting. An example suitable for use in intermediate grades would be writing entries in a diary such as Laura (in Laura Ingalls Wilder's *Little House on the Prairie*) might have kept during her covered-wagon journey from Wisconsin to Kansas.

These creative writing problems are akin to a search for an idea or hypothesis. But they can include more of the steps of solving, such as, the gathering of data, the filling in of needed details, the outlining or "stepping-it-out" procedure, and the planned evaluation with peers.

Skill problems

A type of problem dealing with a language subskill might be the child's felt need to learn more about and practice correspondence between voice intonation patterns and punctuation. Or the skill problem may be children's need to reinforce correspondences between sounds and spelling. (Then they can at least write the first letter of a word they need in a hurry.) Or the problem might deal with how to find or be a suitable scribe.

Finally the problem might deal with how to (1) get the composition into "publishable" form for public exposure, (2) help one another in proofreading, (3) find help for revision and profit from it, (4) find an audience, (5) add to pupil files of accumulating compositions, (6) evaluate one's own progress, and (7) get ideas as to what to tackle next.

Summary

Children can identify creative composition problems if they have sufficient autonomy. Everything that children have learned about problem solving they can apply. In order to help the child, the teacher attends to the following reminders:

- The child is not to be overwhelmed by the teacher's continual examples of professional writing that are too mature and difficult to emulate. Let the child see writing that other children have done.
- The child has a choice in the problem. He or she is not always simply handed a writing task.
- The problem is not simply an imposed drill activity where the child has no motivation. There are at least some unknowns in the problem. (But not too many.)
- The teacher can provide frameworks for writing problems, but the substance of the response needs to come from the child's own observation and imagination.[10]

Relating earlier areas of the framework of seven steps to the creative problem area

Finally, it helps if the child can see clearly how the earlier stimulation of impressions is related to the problem he or she is about to tackle. To illustrate, consider a "made-up" situation. Think how you would feel if you were asked to write an essay in "morphotactic-nexus" style on the validity of the rather "hypnopompic motivation" of character in

[10] For example, Kohl (1966) found that the composition ideas, "On Playing Around" and "Walls" did not prejudge how a child must respond, while "How Nice the Summer Is" did.

Katherine Klinkmueller's plays. With no explanation of "morphotactic-nexus" style, definite uncertainty about "hypnopompic motivation," and never having read a Klinkmueller play, you would probably be stumped. You would be just as stumped as the Chicano children Carlson (1970) tells about with the little "gold miners'" helmets on and the unfathomable task of writing about how it feels to be down in a cave digging for gold.

You and the children may need to ask some highly specific questions about the problem in order to get it clearly in mind. For example, if a child has set herself the problem of writing about a monster and is floundering, she may need to ask herself: "What does it look like? Is it large, a baby, friendly? What color is it? Where does it sleep? Who is its master? Does it have a home? Where is it now? Will I tell what it did in 5 minutes, in a week, over the years? Who is confronting my monster? Who will win?"

Small group interaction

Or it may be time for pair, trio, or group consultation—the next area of this framework. Why limit the child to his or her ideas only (or to your ideas) when the resources of the entire class are available? [11] It has been an opinion that creative teachers are not born, they are made with the help of the teachers next door from whom they have borrowed ideas. The case of children is generally the same when it comes to creative writing for the majority. They need to build upon the ideas of others. They can use small group interplay for the stimulation of creative writing problems. This idea is the essence of the next area in this framework, oral consultation.

---

### 4. Oral Consultation

Peer-group feedback and brainstorming orally

The next area in the framework, oral consultation, is unlikely to be found in the traditional model of the "write–correct–rewrite" type. But children's writing improvement depends in large part on feedback acquired in peer-group discussion and in teacher conference. Teachers need a technique designed to promote an interchange among peer groups, i.e., plain old "talk" and lots of it. One kind of peer group consultation helps to clarify the match between the first area, stimulation of impressions, and the third area, creative problem. While small-group discussion is in process, the teacher goes from group to group interacting with the children. The teacher questions the children; the children question the

[11] For example, if I give you a dollar and you give me a dollar, then we each still only have one dollar. But (miracle!) if I give you an idea and you give me an idea, then we each have two ideas. That is the wonderful thing about having children share their ideas about composition in groups.

teacher; and the children question one another.[12] During part of the oral consultation, teachers might see to it that these kinds of questions get asked:

> "How does it feel to hear thunder? Close your eyes. Pretend you are there."
>
> "How does it feel to eat an apple? Really try to tell us more."
>
> "How does it feel to be a turkey?"
>
> "What is it like to move all of the time from crop to crop as Roosevelt Grady [from Louisa R. Shotwell's book *Roosevelt Grady*] did? Can you tell us how you would put your feelings in a letter to a friend about this and in a letter to an enemy?"

The teacher's task is to help children get beyond the one-word answer and into sensory reexperiencing (or re-creating). Such discussion is still part of the prewriting activity. The point of such consultation is to bring out vocabulary of the senses, setting, tone of expression, ideas of appropriate dialect, and typical conversation. This discussion may actually take the form of dramatic play before writing, as in Activity 7.1. Peer-group explanations and suggestions during oral consultation can be invaluable communication to a child floundering in the problem of what he is to do.

**Learning about audience**

Finally, during oral consultation with classmates the child has an opportunity to learn to recognize the importance of the audience. A child feels concern for the reader when the teaching method wisely provides experiences to highlight this attitude. There is much back and forth movement between this component of the framework and the next one labeled *writing consultation*. There the child actually has some sort of rough draft to bring to the audience consultation. At times you may prefer an audience consisting of the entire class for the oral consultation segments of instruction.

### 5. Writing Consultation

**Taking the draft into consultation**

This step (also unlikely to be found in traditional models of instruction) provides for the child's initial attempts to write after the (1) stimulation of impressions, (2) re-creation, (3) focus on a problem, and (4) oral consultation. This fifth area (more than an isolated writing and re-writing) might deal with these: the first flow of ideas, a list of a few key

[12] Hoetker's research (1968) suggested that a lot of rapid-fire teacher-questions with little or no discussion or pupil interaction did *not* seem to produce much learning.

words or notes, "broken recording" type of writing,[13] portions plucked from a daily journal, or a *first draft*. The child consults with himself or herself, looking at these scribbles. And this self-expression on paper may be as far as the child wishes to take the product. *Not all stimuli should be taken to the stage of publicly exposed writing.*

**Self-consultation about one's writing**

The key aspect of writing consultation is self-consultation. "I don't know what I think until I've written it and thought about it!" The act of writing modifies the inner speech–thought. It may require almost immediate reorganization of what was scarcely put down on paper. After the first draft of inner speech has become outer written speech, children may feel dissatisfied (Golub, 1971). They may feel that they failed to express their inner speech or that it has changed. Then and only then, children may see that they really have something personal to say about the stimulus. It is the process of seeing again what one truly wants to say. A unique way of expression may come later, rather than as an immediate result of the stimulus and the first draft. This rethinking represents the primary purpose of rewriting. *The function of rewriting is not necessarily the cleaning up of spelling and punctuation errors.* The major function is self-consultation about one's ideas.

**Consultation with others**

During this learning stage children may submit their writing to consultation with others. They may move back into the oral consultation group with their first drafts in hand. Rethinking during group discussion may help to uncover and to smooth out fuzziness of thought in a written draft. The child may talk with peers or to the teacher with an eye to eventual public display either oral or written. In that case children may make some revisions in light of the consultation. Then they ask and answer these questions:

- Are the ideas organized the way I want them?
- Is this the effect I want?
- Do I need to expand, illustrate, emphasize this idea?
- Did I get it all in?
- Did I get too much in? Do I need to limit?
- Do you understand me?
- Can I make it more interesting?
- Is it worth my trouble to get it "published," or had I just as well leave it and find a new writing problem?

[13] See Activity 7.4, Scribble-Time Warm-up.

During both the oral and writing consultations children in small work groups are involved in a responsible way with the work of classmates.

More precisely, what else happens during this writing consultation when questions are asked of the would-be author? McCullough (1972) suggests questions to be asked when reading to comprehend a book. These could just as well be adapted to this writing consultation. They relate to imaginative, self-expressive, and literary writing; and to expository writing as well.

*Some Mental Spades for Digging into Writing*

Writing consultation

- What are some things we like best about the writing? What experience did it make us feel? What details or images stood out?
- What direction is the writer taking? What pattern of ideas is he/she making? [14] (E.g., Fable, folktale, tall tale, fantasy, a repetitive pattern, "framing" with ending growing out of the beginning?)
- What questions can we ask that the writer answers? Or does not answer? What idea do we get? Did he/she have an idea to tell?
- What does he/she expect us to know that we don't know?
- What is he/she leaving unsaid that we wonder about? Did we get lost any place? What does he/she mean by that? Can he/she give us some details and instances? Is the writing clear? Does it come alive?
- How can we tell if the subject or pattern is changing or not changing?
- What seems to be most important or most emphasized here? Did the writing surprise us? Hold us in suspense?
- How would it sound if he/she said it this way instead?
- What was the writer's aim? Did we get there?
- What else do we like about it? Was it funny? How?

Notice, in the phrasing of these questions, the sandwich technique of

[14] For example Bill Martin's *A Ghost Story* (New York: Holt, Rinehart and Winston, 1970) takes off from the first sentence in a repetitive pattern, "In a dark, dark woods, there's a dark, dark, house," and continues the "In a ———, ———, ———, there's a ———, ———, ———," pattern. Then the author switches to a "Out of the ———, ———, ———, through the ———, ———, ———" pattern. See the teacher's editions of Nila Banton Smith's series, *Be a Better Reader* (Englewood Cliffs, N.J.: Prentice-Hall) for more on patterns in discourse for older children in various subject areas. Also see Activity 6.9, Topics or Leading Ideas.

constructive suggestion. Any alternatives are sandwiched between the strong features that are complimented.

Usually when children discuss, even though they do not know or use the formal terms, they are talking about three basic concepts in writing:

*Unity*
*Coherence*
*Emphasis*

Criterion: unity, coherence, emphasis

Pupils are talking about *unity* when they discuss whether or not they thought they stuck to the idea they asserted. Later, they may feel the lack of unity when someone tries to tell about "everything," rather than selecting. To encourage selection and unity a teacher may ask the children, "Suppose your house is burning and you can carry away only three things. What will you select? Now think, you can carry away only one thing; what will it be?" Then the teacher may draw the analogy to the fact that a writer has to select, too, rather than trying to "carry everything."

Next, pupils are talking about *coherence* when they discuss whether or not they feel any abrupt leaps and confusing gaps. "But you never told us how he got out of the pit!"

Pupils are talking about *emphasis* when they discuss the outstanding feature, or mood, and the details that tend to support or illustrate the main feature. For example, recall the sensory touches in the barn scene from *Charlotte's Web,* the smell of the hay, the cows chewing their cud —those details that contributed to the peaceful, nothing-bad-could-ever-happen-here mood of the description. Unity, coherence, and emphasis are major principles in composition at any level.[15]

Assertion making

What else can happen during the writing consultation process? When children have expressed several suitable ideas, the teacher can help them to translate their ideas into *assertions.* These are statements that express a point of view and give some control to the rest of the writing. While ideas take form as the children write them, assertions and their relationships "hold up or fold up." (See Activity 6.9, Topics or Leading Ideas.)

Forms of assertions

When teachers guide pupils to make assertions about their material, suggestions might take one of the following forms: categorization or definition, contrast, judgment or opinion, cause, and sequence. Suppose that the children have gathered much material about astronauts. (1) *Categorization* (or definition) is seen when the child asserts that he can

[15] One thing we have learned from Piaget (see Chapter 1) is how slowly concepts develop in children. Some of us are still developing our related concepts of unity, coherence, and emphasis in writing. But the beginning is in the elementary school.

group our astronauts together with past explorers like Eric the Red, Columbus, and Amelia Earhart, or with medical explorers such as Madame Curie. (2) *Contrast* is seen when the child asserts that astronauts are different from explorers of the past. (3) *Judgment* is seen when the child asserts that being an astronaut is hard work. The development of this assertion consists in revealing what made the child think so. (4) *Cause and effect* is seen when the child asserts that every time we learn something about outer space, that learning makes us ask other questions. (5) *Relations* or sequence is seen when the child asserts that if you were going to take a trip to the moon, here are the things, in order, that you might need to do. Or, if you are going to build yourself a rocket out of scrap wood, here are some steps to follow.

Assertions are not only important when the aim of disclosure is exposition; they are also important energizers for unity, coherence, and emphasis when any of the aims of discourse are brought into play. The struggle during the periods of oral and writing consultation is to spark ideas, make assertions, and seize them in patterns that give unity, coherence, and emphasis. Such activity is a "raid on the inarticulate," to quote T. S. Eliot. (For further illustrations of assertions, see Activity 6.9, Topics or Leading Ideas.)

Rereading activity

During the period for writing consultation, pupils may need time to reread what they have written. They can read to themselves in a soft voice, or dictate into a tape recorder. (Then they can follow along by reading their writing while they listen to the tape.) They can reread what they have written in pairs or in groups of about five. Oral reading of a child's writing is a highly productive way to cause the child to notice that something does not sound right or make sense. (Particularly, he/she may catch omitted words, incomplete statements, and lack of or misplacement of punctuation.) Children need the ear as well as the eye.

Impact on reading comprehension

While they are improving their writing, they are also improving their reading comprehension skills. Every writing session can become a reading session. The two processes reinforce one another. Here is where comprehension skills in reading receive the most significant practice.

Audience qualities

Finally, for this writing consultation children need an audience that takes them and their ideas seriously—not always one that lets them say whatever they want with no responsibility toward their receivers. That audience needs to be made up of people other than the teacher. It is clear that the revision that takes place during writing consultation means having in mind the expectations of one's audience. During evaluation in writing consultation children need to know about or have had some choice in determining specific focus for each piece of writing that they take to consultation. When the teacher helps, it is by request of the young author. The teacher's function is to act as a resource: to assist the child in solving his/her own problems as independently as possible.

In summary, writing consultation entails producing a first draft. The older a child becomes, the faster this part of the process becomes. When children complete their first drafts, they *and their peer audience* begin to get an idea of how much or how little the writer has observed or experienced. *Rewriting* means a reconsidering of the idea content, the form, and the audience. Again, children grow in the use of this step, making relatively little use of it as beginners. When the goal becomes public, written display, then children need line by line editing and proofing. (See Chapters 8, 9, 10 for more about conventions.) This idea leads to the next step, an intermediate goal of *oral display*. This alternative does not require spending all the time that is needed for final polishing and editing for mechanics when the goal is *written display*.

### 6. Sharing Compositions Orally for Public Display

**To publish or not to publish**

About this time children make a decision concerning whether or not they want to publish their oral or written product, that is, display it as a finished product before an audience. When young authors want to, or need to, make their work public, they can get help in proofreading from other children, a simple class-constructed proofreading manual, and the teacher. A balanced program in composition includes activities in which that final responsibility for polish and power before publication is intrinsic to the aim of the writing. Unless you provide time for this scrutiny in class, children will probably fail to undertake this ultimately important and necessary function.

**Cautions about the push to publish**

However, in the past the balance has been too much in the other direction. When you try to say something you feel deeply, the chances are that you will say it using your best words. You will attempt structures that might otherwise intimidate you. Compare writing to gardening. Placing too much emphasis on spelling, punctuation, and perfunctory juggling of parts of sentences is like too much pruning in the garden. But working with creative imagination, disciplined reasons, concepts, and relations in language is like placing vigorous roots in fertile soil. Consequently, unless there is a valid reason for making children's writing public, it may be wiser for the teacher to merely note the kinds of difficulties, and then try to help the children to find better solutions to the problems before their next writing. Their "garden" of compositions is likely to grow better.

This point of view about publishing in the elementary school does not mean that "anything goes." But many compositions (in the elementary school especially) are shared best through a more or less polished *oral* presentation. It may consist of reading a dictated work aloud, acting it out, reading your own aloud yourself, or having it read by a skillful reader. This mode of display takes the place of the strenuous work of correcting all the mechanical errors of spelling and punctuation needed for public display of imaginative or expository work meant to be read by others.

Again, this strategy breaks with the traditional write it–correct everything–rewrite it model. This activity demonstrates that composition is *oral* as well as written.

### 7. Written Composition for Public Display

Finally, we come to written composition for public display.[16] Publishable writings come carefully selected from the child's aims of exposition, literature, and persuasion. Carefully edited, proofed, and recopied composition perhaps comes best from practical writing that *must* be read by an audience.

Examples of published work

Examples are notes sent home concerning home–school relations: *I need to bring an old shirt to school to wear while painting.* Or, *The school Book Fair is changed to Tuesday at 2:00.* This sort of communication can be revised if necessary after the children have dictated it. Then it is copied, proofed and read carefully by children, group, and teacher before they make it public.

Further examples are stories placed in the school or class library, social studies reports (passed to another class or displayed on the hall or cafeteria bulletin board), and those compositions duplicated in booklets to be sent home or to other schools.

Proofreading procedure

At proofreading time the class may have devised a system such as this:

1. Read your own.
2. Get a friend to look at it and react.
3. Get group suggestions if you want.

In the meantime the teacher, having reminded the class of what to look for, goes around ready to help. The teacher decides what needs to be taught and to whom. The same revision and proofing applies to all types of published works. Besides the questions suggested earlier for revising content the child needs to ask questions about the conventions of capitalization, punctuation, and spelling. A bulletin board displaying work labeled "Before Proofreading" and "After Proofreading" may help. (See Chapter 8 for more about *proofreading.*)

To honor energetic, toiling writers, some teachers place their creations along with their pictures or photographs in the school showcase. Some

[16] There is probably a need for a cooling-off period from the time of the first draft, to the revision and preparation of the final display—be it oral or written.

television stations invite young children to write various weather reports, giving picturesque descriptions, accompanied by illustrations using various media. An appropriate report is then selected, displayed, and read in connection with the daily weather report.

**Cautions**

A caution: if everything the child writes must be revised, proofed, and rewritten in another final copy, the child writes less and less. Writing becomes drudgery. Sometimes it is better to start over than to rewrite. However, if nothing is every polished when it basically has merit or use (if always "anything goes"), then the result is that readers get lost and writers fail to gain control over language conventions. Worst of all, the child learns nothing of the sense of pride that comes from turning out a piece of public writing. In any case, after the labor of making writing ready for display, make much of these final words, spread them out, contemplate them, admire them, and celebrate them.

Nevertheless, whenever developmentally oriented teachers measure the value of another creative experience against the value of a final, copying over of the child's "masterpiece," they may come out *in favor of another creative experience*. They may believe that growth will result more surely from creation than from an overdose of polishing a "green apple." There you are—varying facets of opinion; input to encourage you to weigh and consider individual cases concerning written composition for public display.

---

Examine some classroom activity that illustrates many of the steps and ideas in those seven major areas for a teaching-learning strategy for written composition.

### A Teacher Relates Her Procedure: Activities

7.1. Pantomime Time, Problem Solving, and Play Writing. (For preschool through junior-high-school levels.) I decided to use pantomime as prewriting activity —as stimulation, recreation, and a starter for a composition task. The first time I tried using pantomime, I began this way: I pretended to pinch my

finger in a desk, making appropriate motions and using facial expressions. The children were worried for a moment. Then I smiled; they were relieved and I asked them what had just happened. Explaining to them that this kind of acting without words was called *pantomime,* I wrote the word on the chalkboard. When I suggested a couple of situations, such as "You're coming indoors after being out in a rainstorm," several children volunteered to do this in pantomime.

I had selected committees on the basis of who would work well together, being sure that there was at least one responsible leader in each group. Then I suggested the challenge of creating a pantomime. Each group went to a corner of the room to think up a situation and present it in pantomime—with about ten minutes of preparation time. I had prepared a few situations on slips of paper in case anyone was "stuck." [17] No group was, and they never knew about the slips of paper. Some groups said they wanted to "display." (Most of the children in this class are not at all self-conscious.)

When each group finished its pantomime, the class tried to guess what the various actions in the pantomime were, and the group up front would answer. They told what they had been doing, if it wasn't guessed. For some "rumor" pantomimes the group had to guess what the original action or thing seen was and then how it got finally changed in the end.

I remember one group pantomimed someone catching a rather small fish; then as the story was told the fish got bigger and bigger, until at the end they all pantomimed it filling the whole front of the room. We also had Tom Sawyer whitewashing and his cat taking medicine, and all sorts of hearing and listening, tasting, smelling, seeing, and feeling being pantomimed. The children, even the shy ones, became excited about expressing themselves this way.

*Problem Solving.* This class is used to taking and giving feedback to one another in a constructive spirit. We talked about what the problem might be when no one could guess the pantomime. I drew a "problem rock" and we labeled it, tentatively, "Challenge: To make a pantomime that communicates." This was our tentative, main problem. Then we thought of some parts that stuck out and kept our rock from rolling (subproblems). For example:

People doing it went too fast.
Did too many things at once.
Person doing it had never really watched carefully enough what he wanted to show.

[17] Examples were these: trying to open an umbrella in a wind-and-rain storm; eating a meal you loved (or hated); seeing something thrown to you from a window fall down to you very slowly in a circular pattern; putting back something you "borrowed" and shouldn't have and you are caught; or any simple familiar tale. Others were: a child pretending to be sick so he wouldn't have to go to school; a child who overslept and must scramble to get off on time; a child at night in bed trying to fight off mosquitos; three sea gulls resting in the ocean and watching an oil slick move toward them; children in pairs pretending that one is a puppet with strings and the other moves parts of his body by pulling the strings.

Needed more practice—maybe with a mirror.
Didn't keep to the group plan; the rest got confused.
Audience didn't tune in at the beginning.
Audience jumped to a conclusion and got stuck.

Many had seen Marcel Marceau, the famous French pantomimist, on TV. Someone recalled Marceau's advice on showing resistance to supposed weight in his rope-pulling pantomime.

I thought about having the class group the pantomimes we had given and try to give them labels as to types or kinds. But I made sure to stop while the children were still interested. I thought some of my brighter students might like to do this grouping and labeling and share it with the class for possible use next pantomime time. (My aim here was to help students move from concrete to abstract levels of thought.)

Oh, yes, we also had talked about how the use of *senses* helped us to make the most believable and easily grasped pantomime, and one that could make the other kids "feel." I don't know how many in the whole group grasped that idea, but three of the five I interviewed afterward in individual conference seemed to have applied it.

7.2. Script Making. (For preschool through junior-high-school levels.) As I said, I really planned to use this pantomime as a *prewriting* activity. So the next step was to go to the *oral consultation* to get a start on furnishing possible dialogue (what *is* happening) and to get a start on the description and narration (what *has* happened, or stage directions). First came the creative talking of children, in the same small groups. Then a scribe took down a few introductory ideas in the small-group dictation. (I helped where I was needed.)

Not letting the oral consultation before writing run too long

*But,* I was careful to keep the groups from running on until they had used up all of their ideas, or until everyone agreed. Otherwise, what would they still need to write about? The writing would have been just a mechanical exercise. The whole idea is that each child is busy thinking creative thoughts during the writing. I couldn't let them wrap it all up.

So they paired off to do the writing, some going off alone. Some children need a little oral language while they are writing. For that reason I made myself available to interact with their ideas. Sometimes I would draw an idea out, sometimes reflect it back, sometimes reread parts with children to make certain it was what they wanted to say. Some wanted to put a title for their drama right away. Others saved it for the very end.

In the larger *writing consultation* groups an "editor–director" put the final script together. Then those who wanted to, read their dramas or shared in some way during *oral display* time. Naturally, since the writing began with interaction during oral consultation, it went back to that again at the time of written consultation. And for those who chose *public written display,* there was again some oral interaction.

Creative listening

We talked at the time of display about creative listening and using our imagination to enter into the drama. I feel it's important to give children a chance to reflect on their solutions and the importance of what they have written. Drama calls for talk, movement, involvement, and interaction of the whole self—directed *outside*. But writing calls for more solitary and inner language. Drama helps to motivate the more solitary form, writing. As Dixon (1967) says, learning to write (and to read) can leave children alone with language in a way they are unused to. The remedy is to precede, accompany, and follow writing with talk.

Since motivation was still high, we had some follow-up activity of illustrating to music. And one group actually went to the time and trouble to rehearse on their own outside of class so they could dramatize their script for a larger audience.

Pantomime time and playwriting time was a new experience for me. When I went to school, drama was the Christmas play, or maybe a Thanksgiving pageant with all those tedious rehearsals. I would never have thought of using pantomime and drama to stimulate writing. But it does.

---

That example completes the discussion—at this time—of a framework for the teaching–learning process for composition. To recap, the elements are (1) stimulation of impressions (experience); (2) re-creation (enactment for young children); 3) focus on a creative problem; (4) oral consultation (talking about what's in mind); (5) written consultation (talking about what's been written); (6) oral display; or (7) written display (showing it off). Again, no hard and fast order to these steps is implied, and many times all of these steps are not needed; we simply need to provide the time and the encouraging climate and then get out of the way.

Inferences drawn from a negative example

However, an earlier section made brief reference to Carlson's negative classroom example (1970). This example appears to give support for the areas suggested for this framework. A student teacher working with Chicano children failed to include (1) adequate stimulation of impressions and (2) oral discussion. Also spelling deficiencies were allowed to act as impediments. The writing problem was not clearly stated, and it was not relevant—it was too foreign to the experience and background of the children to make for likelihood of success. In spite of this teacher's unique external motivation and partial stimulation of impressions (with a paper gold-miner's lamp for each child's head, and with the stimulus of lights dimmed temporarily), in spite of the arousal of energy in the children by these devices, and the motivation of desire to please a loved adult—nothing happened. Expression flickered momentarily and then stopped.

At the moment for creation, the problem of feeling and expressing that they were digging gold in 1849 in Nevada City, California, was just too unclear and irrelevant a problem for these children. In fact the situation never reached the status of a recognizable problem for the children because it never was an experience. It was not adequately perceived through their senses or in their memory. They would have needed much additional stimulation, vocabulary development (possibly brought about by enactment), and a guiding sense of where they were going. That is, they needed a concrete sense of the creative problem and how to solve it.

However, in spite of the fact that this writing problem started out with such high hopes on the part of the student teacher and ended in such dismal failure, the encounter probably had its advantages: (1) The student teacher, with guidance from Carlson, probably learned a lot about the teaching process for creative composition with these children and what to do next time. (For example, she might have learned *not to give "blanket" writing assignments.*) (2) The children could also have learned something about the composing process, if the student teacher followed up on the situation skillfully with individual and group discussion.

---

Maybe the ideas in this teaching–learning strategy make sense to you, but you still are having trouble visualizing them in the context of the total school day, or in the daily school program. The next section gives some concrete suggestions.

## A SAMPLE SCHEDULE AND ENVIRONMENT FOR A WRITING DAY

Maybe the *time* factor still worries you. Here is a sample schedule for a writing day.

*A Sample Writing Day Schedule*

| | |
|---|---|
| 9:00 to 10:30 | Hold individual writing conferences. (See Chapter 11 and Lundsteen, in press.) Other children are engaged in independent activity, such as individual reading, proofing, art work, math and reading games, or other kinds of writing that do not require your help. |
| 10:30 to 11:00 | Physical Education. |
| 11:00 to 12:00 | Small-group work, stimulation of impressions, re-creation, oral consultation, and talking–writing workshops. (Schedule yourself for observation of the children interacting during at least part of this period.) Individual writing activity, individual dictating on tape, transcribing on paper. |
| 12:00 to 1:00 | Lunch. |

| | |
|---|---|
| 1:00 to 2:00 | Writing consultation (five to a group), papers exchanged. |
| 2:00 to 2:30 | Total class sharing of "significant" works, use of opaque projector or overhead projector for display, dramatic enactment, or other sharing of work ready to be made public, any decision that needs total group cooperation. |
| 2:30 to 2:45 | Clean-up and evaluation. |

Content integrations

What goes on in this writing day can touch almost any area of the curriculum. The content of the writing might be literary and imaginative but it might also deal with science, social studies, and mathematical observations, and certainly with reading. In the suggested activities to follow, I will try to show further interrelations with the total curriculum.

Environment for stimuli of impressions

Classroom environment. The classroom environment for this writing day can be crucial. This activity does not take place in a "chalk and teacher-talk" classroom dominated by desks and by textbooks, the same book, one for every child. A stimulating environment is arranged that can promote varied impressions.

The room environment is more like a cross between a museum, a zoo, a floral nursery, a magazine shop (with books and magazines displayed face out) and a newspaper office (i.e., an office for editors and writers). There may be a writers' corner with picture files, typewriter, dictionaries and thesaurus; a listen–speaker corner with tapes (audio and video), filmstrips, music; a swivel armchair, hassock, or stool for a "talker" to perch on before his or her audience.

There may be a reading corner with a "dress-up" box, a puppet theatre, and a rocking chair. There might be a thinker's corner with a rug, a thinker's table with stuff for thinking mathematically, junk sculpture, a bubble-blowing set, and art supplies. There may be a bird, a hamster, or gerbils, and several aquariums running different controlled conditions for an experiment that follows close on the heels of the experiments with mealworms and corn plants. There might be clipboards with paper and pencil attached to these "posts," for the children's observations.

Humanity

A workable schedule and a stimulating environment of objects may be necessary, but there must also be a varied and interactive *human* environment where you, the professional in the classroom, are out there interacting with children, helping them to set their own goals, plan their own program, and evaluate their own accomplishments. We assume the following: Written composition is influenced by the classroom atmosphere and the behavior of the teacher. The atmosphere of the classroom is determined by the teacher more than by any other person. The behavior and trust level of the teacher tend to release or to restrain the pupils in the class. The warm accepting human stimulus is probably the key to effective writing in the elementary school.

Process over product

What matters most: process or product? In the elementary school it is not the product that matters so much as the process that each child goes through—what needs each child uncovers, and the way each child plans. What matters is their growth on their way to personal fulfillment. What matters is the creative-problem-solving process, including idea selection, that children can use over and over. This process grows more useful any time any part of it is used successfully. Children are comforted to know that even a great and favorite writer such as Mark Twain felt that at times he had to struggle with every word in this process, and was sometimes bitterly disappointed with his writing product. The example says, "Have courage; pursue the process. Ideas, power, and polish will come."

In Chapter 6, I presented a list of six goals of creative writing. Review them again for a moment in light of suggested classroom environment. Here is the list, elaborated slightly, with a few additional goals:

### *What Are Some Goals for Creative Writing? (Restatement)*

Goals restated

1. To help children recognize the worthwhileness of their own experience as the basis or content for their writing—to take a look at and talk about themselves and their environment.
2. To help children improve the quality of their observation, so they can clearly observe life and feeling.
3. To amplify the range of children's experience, to help them to be more aware as persons, to express feelings and ideas.
4. To help children select and fit language and its increasingly abstract thought to the details of experience and dramatic enactment. To grasp order by playing out understanding not only in drama but also in art, music, dance, and rhythms.

5. To help children discover suitable content, literary forms, and designs for the transfer of experience to others.
6. To develop—individual point of view or *voice* (what they are and what they stand for), communication with *audience* (various types of persons), *form* (shaping ideas), *style* (individual ways of communicating), and *self-evaluation*—through varied opportunity for written expression.
7. To help children become sufficiently independent and self-motivated so that they use creative writing as profitable employment of leisure time.
8. To help children enrich their composition as a result of appreciation (and "composting") of a wide variety of literature.
9. To enhance rapport and freedom of expression among increasingly competent children and teachers during small-group discussions and individual pupil-teacher writing conferences. (See pp. 412–19.)
10. To pleasurably build competencies and skills of written composition as a form of communication linked to and motivated by *creative problem-solving.*

## SUMMARY AND CONCLUSIONS

**Reworking experience**

These chapters on composition have dealt with some whys, definitional whats, and some hows. A basic idea is that *teaching composition helps children to think about their own experiences and then to rework them selectively.* Such teaching capitalizes on children's ability to closely observe their world (no matter what the culture) and their feelings and to report them honestly. When children compose, they picture their experience in language. When children translate their experience for a reader, they show ability to use sense imagery about their experiences. This figurative language is an important way people apprehend experience and store the memory of it. When children translate their experience in composition, they may use this language-that-pictures as a way of cutting through to the central importance of the event, object, or person. Finally, teaching composition helps children to think selectively about their experience as they organize while attending to matters of where to begin, how to arrange and pattern, and how to end. These ideas clarify for us what composition is—putting experience into language form. These meanings clarify composition in relation to the teacher's role and in relation to the selective, synthesizing mental processes in creative problem-solving.

**The seven area teaching-learning strategy**

This chapter presented seven areas that teachers need to take into account and provide for. These may be grouped in four major parts: prewriting, writing & rewriting, and display. Is this a guaranteed procedure? Of course—from a developmental, common-sense point of view, at this time and because this chapter is written in a prescriptive, how-to-do-it way. Admittedly, it is presumptuous to offer a prescription. There are probably many ways to accomplish the same goals mentioned. There are many ways to modify these procedures. Some children have their own procedures and don't need these. But many teachers are searching for ideas for developing a strategy for teaching, for structuring their lessons in composition, and for pegging new knowledge. The past practices have shown a reliance on the write–correct–rewrite method, but there is little or no evidence to support it. It is in light of this need and the question "But just how do I teach composition!" that this chapter was written. The activities to follow will flesh out the method even further. (See the developmental ladder of suggestions for writing activities at the end of this chapter.)

The roles of the teacher

At this point you may have some questions bothering you. For instance, in light of the peer interaction advocated, does this framework for a teaching-learning technique leave the teacher more or less out in the cold? Does this strategy mean that the teacher is a pleasant but unnecessary adjunct to the classroom? Not at all. In the first place, who gets this framework started?

Another question: Is the teacher just a clever administrator, then, who knows how to delegate authority? No, hardly. There will be times when a child at any age level wants to share, just with you, the teacher—for example, during an individual conference about his or her composition.

The teacher has vital roles, implicit in the seven steps presented in this chapter. A listing of some of these follows.[18]

*Teaching Roles*

- Accepting children's written composition as personal and encouraging each child.
- Helping children grow in new accomplishments in a planned program (and avoiding the temptation to pick at mistakes).
- Helping children acquire the language to use in talking about composition.
- Helping children evaluate their own compositions.
- Encouraging constructive peer reactions.

All the world's a school—(to paraphrase Shakespeare)—and most individuals at almost all stages of their lives are sometimes a student and

[18] Adapted from a listing of teacher behaviors compiled by Alvina Burrows from submissions of members of the National Conference on Research in English (NCRE).

sometimes a teacher. Children can teach, too. But in the case of creative composition, teaching less is more. That is, while the teacher is talking, the child is not composing. The child learns more by writing than by talking about rules.

Maybe the teacher thinks the beginning of the story is poor. But the child wants to work on the ending. Let him. Chances are children will find they have to improve the beginning in order to make the ending more interesting (Murray, 1968, 1973).

"But what do you want me to write about, what do you want," a child asks the teacher. "I want to be surprised" responds the teacher. Or "I want to know about your experiences, your feelings, what you have seen or dreamed, or wished." In other words, the teacher has to know when to be quiet and listen, when to respond as receiver respecting children and their potential voice as they search for what they think and for what they have to say. Instead of trying to teach for finished writing, teach for "unfinished" composition and be comfortable with its unfinishedness. Even the greatest works are rarely if ever "finished" by their authors. They are "abandoned" as deadlines press. Thus, teaching skill is always needed, but use of it requires judgment so that the child is the active decision maker.

In our zeal to help all children become competent writers—a caution about writing and its instruction. This reminder comes vividly from an anecdote about two boys who had been ice-skating at New York's Rockefeller Center skating rink. They were recalling the events with glee and gloat. Suddenly one said—

> "But don't tell the teacher about it. Promise!"
>
> "Why not?"
>
> "We'll have to *write* about it!" [19]

[19] Thanks to Professor Alvina Burrows, New York University, for sharing this real-life happening.

The next chapters

Children do not have to write about everything that happens to them. And all the caution in the world is necessary, as we take up the next topics of spelling, handwriting, punctuation, and grammar, to make certain that instruction in these skills does not bring about an attitude such as that expressed in the preceding dialogue.

---

## ACTIVITIES FOR SELF-EXPRESSIVE, IMAGINATIVE, FANTASTIC WRITING

### Introduction and Rationale

What does imaginative writing do for children?

Imaginative writing fostered by the following activities serves many functions besides basing itself upon and improving the quality of observation. It provides experience in freely expressing, in valuing, in enlarging, and in ordering ideas and experiences in highly personal ways. By helping children to fit words to the details of their experience, imaginative writing contributes to the child's development in writing and as a person. Henry Miller suggested in an interview on his eightieth birthday that there should be times when you write for yourself . . . no teacher, no friend. You write to find out who you are, what makes you tick, where you're going, and what it's all about. Many texts put expository writing first and imaginative writing last as sort of a dessert. This book puts it first, deliberately, because its initial emphasis is the motivating springboard that builds a bridge to exposition and to skill in mechanics without the sacrifice of spontaneity. Offer it to all children.

Avoidance of gimmickry, the merely bizarre

Consider the following cautions, however, about some programs in imaginative writing. Some instructors confuse imaginative writing or creativity with the merely bizarre. It is generally wise to avoid resorting to all sorts of gimmickry as stimuli designed to elicit unnatural written responses from children (Golub, 1971). The fanciful does not represent simply the weird. For that matter, perhaps the most appropriate criterion of creativity is the child's expression of sincerity, ability to order observations, their translation into language, empathy, and thoughtful reflection. Stories of fancy build from observation. The make-believe that children construct from experience may be psychological in source (such as wish-fulfillment, hero or heroine worship, and wonder about the unknown). Imaginative literature conveys the human situation in ways that exposition or report cannot.

Exceptions

However, some children with a persistent set toward convergent, stifled expression, need the direct "finger-exercises" of creativity that border on the way-out gimmick (e.g., suppose you had two heads). These children may swing from never letting go at all to complete fantastic abondonment for a while. But their pendulum usually then swings back to a more useful harnessing of their fantasy, especially if the focus turns to creative problem-solving. For this reason perhaps encouragement in a classroom of "diversity in the bizarre" is preferable to 35 almost identical responses. With these thoughts in mind, now examine some specific classroom activities, most of which are adaptable to any grade level.

**Sensory experience with shadows**

7.3. Observing Light and Dark. The goal of this activity is to increase sensitivity of observation by attending to the properties of light and dark. The activity can encourage a fresh way of reporting. It is based in part on explorations at the first-grade and intermediate-grade level about shadows (Educational Services, 1964).

To begin with, the teacher of a second-grade class initiated shadow-play out of doors, asking questions, such as, "What can you make your shadow do?" "How can you make it disappear?" "Can you pick it up?" "What would happen to my shadow if I used this umbrella?" "How could we have shadows inside?" Children traced their shadows and then composed a group story.

**Integrating science learnings**

The teacher asked older children more sophisticated questions, such as, how many ways they could find to hide a shadow; if they could make it bend, divide it, or put it in an unusual place. The instructor provided materials such as lamps, string, tape, tinker toys, flashlights, mirrors, candles, bulbs, extension cords, and a prism. Besides the opportunities for communicating there are many opportunities for science learning and thought processes here. For example, in the concept of property (or attribute) with regard to shadow there is opportunity to explore these: measurement of size, estimation, shape, classification, change in property by diffusion, concentration, interaction in fields of light, inferring, predicting, formulation of hypothesis and operational definition, control of variables, and interpretation of data.

The following are some directions for moving from shadow-play to dramatization, and to script writing—possibly even to publication.

*Shadow Games and Scenarios.* Hang a white sheet up at the end of the room. The "shadow makers," who could sit on low stools, get behind the sheet facing the class. Darken the room. Place one lamp behind the shadow makers so that their shadows are thrown upon the sheet. This group might try to disguise themselves so that the other children will have difficulty in guessing who the shadow makers are.

For example, if a girl with long hair lets it fall over her face, she may appear like a man with a beard. If a shadow maker bends his finger over his nose, he may be able to give himself a very weird-looking shadow, like a troll. Or he can cover up in another sheet or large shawl, extend his arms and appear like a large bat. Arms crooked and held up to the nose might represent an elephant. Hands and arms spread overhead might give the appearance of a moose; palms together, a crocodile. Children can think of other variations.

As soon as the shadow maker's identity or representation has been guessed by the rest of the class or by a class member, he or she leaves from behind the sheet. The one who guessed correctly could then get to become a shadow maker.

Children, having acquired some skill, can talk about and write scripts, subsequently performing them via the shadow theatre. (For details on how to encourage the writing of scripts, see Activities 7.1 and 7.2.)

Stimulating poetry

About this time, you might introduce the following poem, or some other poem about shadows that might stimulate poetry writing.

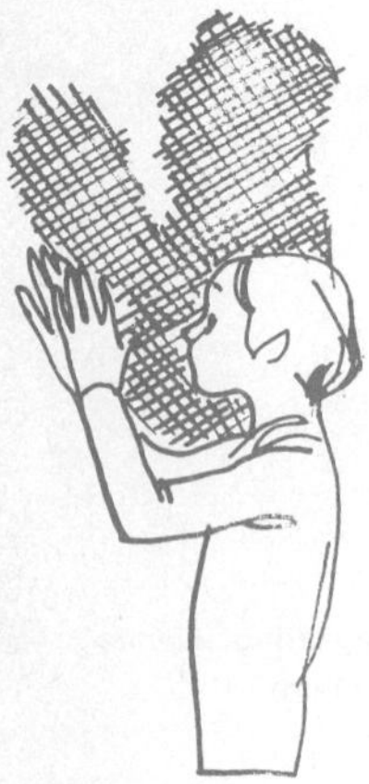

*Reflections* [20]

Shadow pictures on the wall
Shadow pictures, short or tall.
Braying donkey, ears up tight
Or a bird cast off in flight.

Shadow pictures on the wall,
Shadow pictures large or small,
Funny faces, anything,
Darkness cast on light can bring.

Ask children to furnish other thoughts or stanzas they might like to add to the poem. Also see the poem "Shadows on a Clothes Line" in Chapter 3.

Symbolism and sensory language

Shadow, frequently used in literature, is employed in figurative language and in symbolism. Shadows have been linked to death, time, man, future, evening, grief, a kiss, terror, vagueness—you name it. Robert Louis Stevenson was moved to write a famous verse, "My Shadow." Tanizaki Junichiro claimed that Orientals find beauty not only in the thing itself but in the pattern of shadows a thing produces—the light and the darkness.

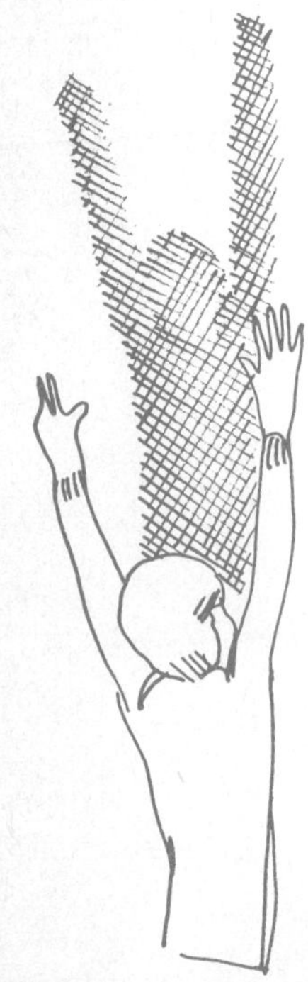

*Ask children when they report observations to pass over the obvious features and observe the play of light and shadow.* Forget the imperiousness of color for a bit. I found this request one of the best ways to get children to observe with a fresh eye. A haiku written in the seventeenth century by Kikaku illustrates:

A harvest moon!
And on the mats—
Shadows of pine boughs.[21]

[20] First two stanzas of "Reflections" by Sara Brandon Rickey. Copyright © 1969 by Sara B. Rickey. Reproduced by special permission.

[21] *Bartlett's Familiar Quotations,* 14th ed. (Boston: Little, Brown, 1968), p. 386.

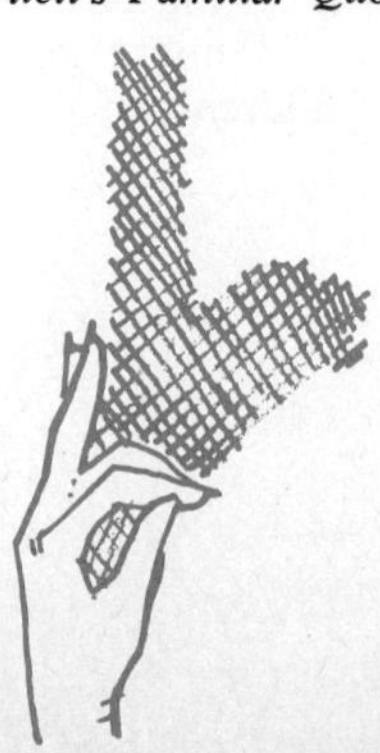

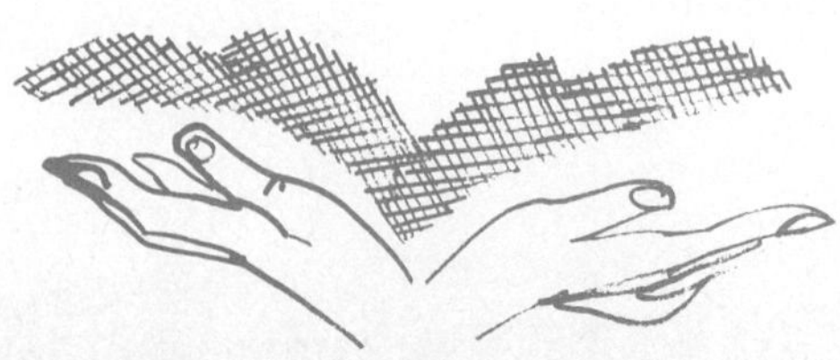

7.4. Scribble-Time Warm-up (or Broken Record). (For intermediate through junior high-school levels.) With older children this prewriting activity is related to the broken-record oral activity mentioned in Chapter 3, on the aim of self-expression. After appropriate stimuli to provoke imaginative response have been arranged in the room environment, invite pupils to free associate, to let the ideas flow as fast as they can. They write the last word or phrase over and over to keep up the motor momentum until another idea hits them. They do not have to preserve this product in their permanent file, if they do not care to. The idea is to create some stuff out of which composition may take form and to habituate the act of *daily writing.*

7.5. Hitchhike Story. (For intermediate through junior-high-school levels.) This activity starts as a prewriting experience. The goal is to work for nimbleness, fluency, and to let the less imaginative profit from interchange with more imaginative children. A child starts telling his or her story (preferably to his small group). At a signal (or when one minute has past) another child pointed to (or who volunteers) has to pick up the story and continue it. Children repeat this procedure until the end of the story or time allotment. The class can tape this activity. If the children want to preserve parts of it, scribes can transcribe the tape. Material from it can be revised and published in a Hitchhiking Book.

7.6. Some More Favorite Topics.[22] (For intermediate through junior-high-school levels.) A few favorite topics are these:

1. If you had five minutes to communicate via telestar to anyone in the world, what would you say? (Five Minutes on Telestar)
2. Who Are You?
3. The Meanest Thing I Ever Did (Kindest)
4. What Bugs You? (or Situations I Could Do Without)
5. Advantages or Disadvantages of Being a Ten-Year-Old
6. I Am Happiest When
7. A Day I Would Like to Live Over
8. A Family Argument (The Story of———, How to Avoid One, and What to Do in Case You Can't)
9. If I Could Spend Today Any Way I Wanted
10. A Baby Sitter Does More Than Sit
11. A Teacher Does More Than Teach
12. A Mother Does More Than Mother
13. Three Things You Would Carry Away if Your Home Were Burning
14. I Kissed 100 Purple Pussycats
15. Having School 12 Months out of the Year: For and Against
16. Is It Wrong to Kill Insects?

[22] See Activity 6.9, Topics or Leading Ideas, for a word on cautions about using topics. And remember that writing assignments need to be more extensive and individualized than the specification of a topic or list of topics. (These topics can be put into a fishbowl for drawing out during free writing times.)

17. Why You Should Watch This TV Program
18. A Headline I Would Like to See in Tomorrow's Paper and Why
19. If I Could Talk to Anyone Living or Dead, Who Would It Be and What Would I say? (Out of the Tomb)
20. My Imaginary Country (and What Happened to Change It)
21. Smoke
22. Street Fight
23. Left Out
24. Views on a Woman Being President
25. Autobiography: My Next 10 Years
26. Cafeteria Food
27. I Am a Beach Bag (or a Grocery Bag, or a Garbage Bag, etc.)

These topics could be filed in a freetime box or attached to an "In the Mood to Imagine?" bulletin board.

7.7. Paragraphs Based on Collages. (For preschool through intermediate grades.) The idea is to use collages to serve as a bridge and to stimulate pupils to write paragraphs containing character, setting, and problem-vignettes in points of time. Children may create collages, for example, from magazine pictures, printed labels, newspaper headlines, and objects. Since a collage features a central or controlling idea and details, it seems a natural source of impressions for stimulating a paragraph.

Themes

Ideas or themes might deal with these: motors, faces, a character from literature, buttons that talk about where they have been; "Who Am I?" "Change," "Types of People," "Landforms," "Mice Are Nice," "A Teacher Is———" "Happiness Is———" "School Is———" "Summer Is———" "Fifth-Grade Is———" "Drugs Are—."[23]

Flanigan displayed a collage of pictures—bottles containing alcoholic beverages, two toy cars that had apparently collided and two figures made from pipe cleaners lying prone by the sides of the cars ("Auto Wreck").

Some collages were three-dimensional and useful, i.e., could be used as a wastebasket. One was a collage labeled "Barrel of Laughs" (a collage of jokes). Another labeled "Please Touch," was constructed from materials such as sandpaper, glass, textured wallpaper, grass, leaves, tree bark, feathers, a piece of carpet, a bit of fur, and shells—items that invite tactile sensations. One idea was a collage representing a literary character (for example, Tom Sawyer).

A final idea, entitled "Pollution," was a collage made from discarded candy wrappers and other waste matter picked up. On the same topic, the collage might be constructed with representatives of various objects that pollute: e.g., a box of detergent, a bottle of insecticide, a model car, an airplane. Preparatory to writing about the pollution collage, children can ob-

[23] Most of these ideas were reported in a speech, "Visual and Verbal Composing, a Mixed Bag," by Dr. Michael Flanigan, Indiana University, at the annual convention of the National Council of Teachers of English, Las Vegas, 1971.

serve and take notes (reports of happenings) on the littering habits of people. They can record (even photograph) behavior from, say the vantage point of a street corner (who, what, when, conditions, obvious, less obvious, and unique and significant attributes). Or the class could take a "litter walk." They might pick up or tally the litter seen and look for other destruction. They can watch the swirls of air pollution spiral from a smokestack. Upon return, besides creating the collage, they might write some of these:

- A letter to a classmate who is absent describing the walk.
- An opinion paper.
- A letter to an editor or commissioner including possible solutions.
- A script for a pantomime, drama, puppet show, or slide show about what children can do. (Also see Activity 5.5.)

7.8. Writing Problems: To Write in the Manner of Haiku, to Make a Cinquain. The major purpose of activities with these poem forms is to help children to sharpen what their concept of observation means.

*Haiku.* As a prerequisite, children need to attain concepts of at least some of the basic qualities of haiku before writing a verse in this manner (Carlson, 1970). Otherwise writing just becomes a gadget for a stunt of counting syllables. Of course another prerequisite is that the child has attained a concept of a syllable. In classroom writing, the line and syllabic constraints of haiku are not presented as hard-and-fast rules that must be adhered to.

Five basic qualities

Besides its brevity and richness of implication, haiku has five other more important distinguishing attributes.

1. There is reference to nature in haiku. It refers to the setting and season rather indirectly.
2. Nothing is too insignificant to be worth expressing in this poetic form. E.g., "a cricket grieves near the sleeve of a scarecrow." There is a focus on individual objects.
3. The eye of the poet sees the immediacy of the moment, perhaps fleeting: "Between the branches/ patches of light blue/ with bits of bright white." Yet the poet sees the moment with contemplative spirit. And the reader is refreshed by the quiet dignity and repose as the poet shares a simple experience.
4. Haiku makes an image in the mind of the reader, a delicate painting in miniature. The audience can close its eyes and relive a compressed moment of beauty, a sensory experience, such as, "a pond listening quietly bathed in golden light."
5. A last quality, difficult to achieve, is expression of a statement that is somehow unfinished, symbolic, that each reader can interpret in his or her own way, that invites the imagination to extend beyond the poem. This quality is related to economy of statement or understatement. It

is related to the Japanese paintings that have spaces that must be filled in mentally by the beholder. Here is a sample Haiku:

Clear cascades!
Into the waves scatter
Blue pine needles.[24]

Lesson plan

The following activity (a device for capturing observations) is given in lesson-plan format.

*Objectives for Learners—Challenge to the Pupils:* Construct a creative product of language similar to a given pattern by (1) inductively uncovering the data that leads to inference of that pattern, (2) defining the pattern, (3) constructing a plan for procedure and evaluation of this writing problem, and (4) constructing an expression in the manner of haiku.

*Materials for the Teacher:*

- Books of haikus [25]
- A sprig of spring blossoms (optional)
- Japanese music (optional)
- Japanese paintings (optional)
- Haikus that other children have written
- Art materials for children

*Procedure.* After sharing a number of haiku poems and displaying several simple ones, encourage the children to discover inductively the 17-syllable structure.

## *Haiku Form*

Line 1 has 5 syllables.
Line 2 has 7 syllables.
Line 3 has 5 syllables.

[24] Matsuo Bashō (1644-1694), in *Bartlett's Familiar Quotations,* 14th ed. (Boston: Little, Brown, 1968), p. 380.

[25] Besides the well-known *Cricket Songs: Japanese Haiku,* by Harry Behn (New York: Harcourt, 1964), you might try these books of haiku. Richard Lewis (Ed.), *The Way of Silence, The Prose and Poetry of Bashō* (New York: Dial, 1970). Photographs by Helen Buttfield. James Hackett, *The Way of Haiku, An Anthology of Haiku Poems* (Tokyo: Japan Publications, Inc., 1969). Isaa, Yayu, Kikada, and other Japanese poets, *Don't Tell the Scarecrow* (New York: Four Winds, 1970). Illustrated by Talivaldes Stubis. Carl Sesar (Trans.), *Takuboku: Poems to Eat.* 2nd ed. (Palo Alto, Calif.: Kodansha International, Ltd., 1968). Tanka with woodcut illustrations by M. Keewata.

See how many of the other distinguishing attributes the children can discover (including that there is no rhyme and there are few articles or pronouns). Stress that, for children, the thought is important rather than the form; and that trying to come up with the correct number of syllables is for them a minor attribute of this problem in writing, and the *least* of their concerns.

Next, help children make a plan of attack for solving this writing problem. The plan might be cooperatively written on the board and might take a form such as the following:

*Plan*

Ideas for topics or subject: ______________________________
The season will be __________. The location will be __________.
For the first line I'll ______________________________.
For the second line I'll ______________________________.
For the third line I'll ______________________________.

(The form might be duplicated and distributed for use and "incubation," and the actual writing might take place during another period.)

Stimulating

Here the children are synthesizing, projecting a scheme or design or way of organizing. Ideas for a topic or subject might be stimulated by telling the pupils to do the following. Think descriptively of one tiny masterpiece of nature—a drop of dew, an ant, a kernel of grain, a raindrop, a snowflake, a tiny shell, a tiny cactus, a pebble, an acorn—and perhaps how they feel about the object. *It helps if you have some of these tiny masterpieces of nature for children to examine and hold in their hands.* Or ask children to close their eyes and try to recall what tells them that evening is coming, that a storm or rain is near, that a new season or change of weather is coming.

*Evaluation*

1. Concepts: Pupils constructed an operational definition of haiku woven from the distinguishing attributes they were able to uncover.

2. Pupil processes: Pupils performed inductive thinking in discovering the attributes. Pupils constructed a plan of action in attacking this writing problem. Pupils employed problem-solving steps of definition, distinguishing facts, missing data, using search strategy, testing hypotheses.

3. Product: The pupil's writing in the manner of haiku was shared and reacted to, and treated appropriately. Students read more haiku by distinguished poets and observed any changes in reaction on the part of pupils that might suggest extension of appreciation.

Children's examples

The following are some examples of writing in the manner of haiku from a fifth-grade class, Cathedral Oaks School, in Goleta, California:

*Mushrooms*

Mushrooms are tiny.
Some others are spotted or plain.
Not one is the same.

*Snake*

I saw a snake crawl,
In a field by a tunnel,
Dark, damp and scary.

*Trees*

Trees *sway arms* and *hands.*
Their *bodies* are made for climbing.
*Trees are forever.*

Illustrations

To form illustrations and bookcovers children may enjoy blowing ink with a straw, and constructing tissue-paper scenes. To give an impression of falling leaves, use a dry (or nearly wiped dry) brush technique; put one color paint on one side of the brush and another color paint on the other side of the brush and give a flicking, circular motion to your hand and brush as you descend the page.

---

Characteristics

*Cinquain.* Some teachers find the cinquain, a five-line poem, an easier form than haiku. Again try an inductive approach. A powerful influence in teaching children to think inductively is the classroom teachers who model or demonstrate inductive thinking in their classrooms. From examples, let pupils discover that a cinquain is a form of expression that can tell much in five lines.

### *Cinquain Form*

Line 1 has one word for title or subject
Line 2 has two words to describe the title.

Line 3 has three words for action about the subject.
Line 4 has four words for feeling about the subject or a short thought.
Line 5 has one word that refers back to the title.

Examples written by children in Cathedral Oaks School, Goleta, Calif.: Children's examples

| *Cranberries* | *Turkey* | *Motorcycle* [26] |
|---|---|---|
| *Dark red* | *Delicious meat* | *Racing, fast* |
| *They get smashed* | *Runs and hides* | *Hauling, ripping, whining* |
| *No life left in* | *Doesn't want to die* | *Eating the dirt* |
| *Mush.* | *Dinner.* | *Honda.* |

| *Karate* | *Basketball* |
|---|---|
| *Sweeping, deadly* | *Shooting, rebounding* |
| *Punches, blocks, kicks* | *Crowds stomping, shrieking* |
| *To throat or eyes* | *Cloud burst of baskets* |
| *Tiger-like.* | *Victory.* |

Before the children work individually have the class compose one cinquain in a cooperative effort. One way to legitimate note-passing, one writing activity children engage in willingly, is to share constructed cinquains in this fashion.

7.9. Finishing a Problem Story. After recalling a previous activity in which a problem episode was begun, in this activity children might try to complete their own composition. Or they might exchange and try to complete someone else's, either individually or through group effort.

The "people problem" might be the child's own, someone else's, partially invented, or even projected into an animal.

The idea is for the pupil to develop the problem and reveal how he would go about solving it, or having his characters solve it. As a starter, many children have been stimulated by the situation of having broken something that they borrowed. Again an outline form may help, such as the following. An outline

*Problem Story Outline*

1. What are three adjectives or traits to describe the first personality? Ask the same question if there is a second major character. (E.g., a goblin who is childish, demanding, and loquacious? A nymph who is stubborn,

[26] By Britt in Paul Reid and Ron Robbins' class, Mardan Center, Costa Mesa, Calif. From the class book of poems entitled "Take Five."

has green glass beads on a silver ring, and who has been to the moon for them?)
2. What is a goal the personality might have, or a problem? Perhaps, do the same if there is a second major character. (The goblin wants the beads? The nymph wants to keep them?)
3. What are ways the first personality might try to reach this goal or solve his or her problem? Do the same if there is a second person. (Ask for the beads? Lie in the mud and howl?)
4. What is the conflict? There might be conflict in the ways the character tries to solve his or her problem. There might be conflict about goals or problems between the first and second characters. There might be conflict of one character trait with another in the same character. (For example, two people want the same thing, or a character might like a friend a lot, but be an honest person who knows the friend is doing something wrong.)
5. What gets the conflict out into the open? (Inciting incident.) Dialogue between the characters?
6. What trait is strongest within (or between) the characters(s)? Which will win out? Stubbornness? Persistent pleading?)
7. Task: Write five or ten bits of dialogue (say, between the two characters) that—
   a. lead to the climax of the conflict,
   b. solve the problem or resolve the conflict.

This activity, for intermediate through junior-high-school grades, is designed to call upon the child's most advanced skills of thinking and composing. It calls upon highest levels of imaginative invention in a synthesis for an explanatory scheme. It represents the essence of the composing writer's use of the creative problem-solving process in the design of fiction or narrative.[27]

Alternatively, and more simply, Burrows et al. (1964) suggest the following design:

1. Begin a story with a propelling idea, suggestion, or problem.
2. Imply just enough probability of solution to start with the audience's curiosity.
3. Open several possible ways of working out a solution.
4. Hold the suspense to the very end.

They suggest that the experience of being sometimes a writer and frequently an avid listener makes children so sensitive to design that from inner necessity they naturally appropriate some elements for their own use. But a little guidance and relating to problem-solving processes in daily use can hasten the child's success and zest for contriving an engaging tale. But take great care not to become academic, deadening, and disassociated with the aim—to entertain. (This version is also suited for preschool through primary grades.)

**Example in poetic dialog**

The following poetic example reaches perhaps the ultimate of the problematic dialogue. It grows on you.

[27] You might wish to refer to the item, "Problem Solving Checklist: Teacher Diagnosis of Individual Child," given in Chapter 11, p. 414.

*Overheard on a Saltmarsh* [28]

Nymph, nymph, what are your beads?
Green glass, goblin. Why do you stare at them?
Give them me.
                    No.
Give them me. Give them me.
                                        No.
Then I will howl all night in the reeds,
Lie in the mud and howl for them.
Goblin, why do you love them so?
They are better than stars or water,
Better than voices of winds that sing,
Better than any man's fair daughter,
Your green glass beads on a silver ring.
Hush, I stole them out of the moon.
Give me your beads, I desire them.
                                                  No.
I will howl in a deep lagoon
For your green glass beads, I love them so.
Give them me. Give them.
                                    No.

[28] By Harold Monro from *Children of Love* (London: The Poetry Bookshop, 1913). To set the tone for this dialogue try music such as Maurice Ravel's "Conversation Between Beauty and the Beast," *Mother Goose Suite* (Ma Mère), Angel 36110.

## Ladder of Suggestions for Composition

A way to summarize Chapters 6 and 7 on writing is with a "ladder," a suggested conceptual hierarchy for the activities given in each one. I don't imply any hard and fast or lock-step progression. But the ideas generally follow developmental levels. Titles of illustrative activities are given in parentheses. The creative-problem-solving process pervades the whole from the beginning.

Individual writing conferences can reveal on which rung of this ladder it might be well to begin some instruction and activity in a continuous-progress curriculum. Excellent teachers of writing hook into a child's developmental stage of language, thought, and motivation; they hook into the child's content and processes of life. Then they step back and let the children take over their own learning responsibilities with plenty of time for referring to notes and journals about their actual experiences and attitudes, and with time to interact with their audience and perceive their effect.

To write clearly, with power and imagination, a child must think clearly with power and imagination. Experience→think→enact→talk→write→think→rewrite—these processes are inseparable. When children have learned to improve writing, they have learned to improve thinking. This is their creative problem.

WRITING LADDER OF SUGGESTIONS

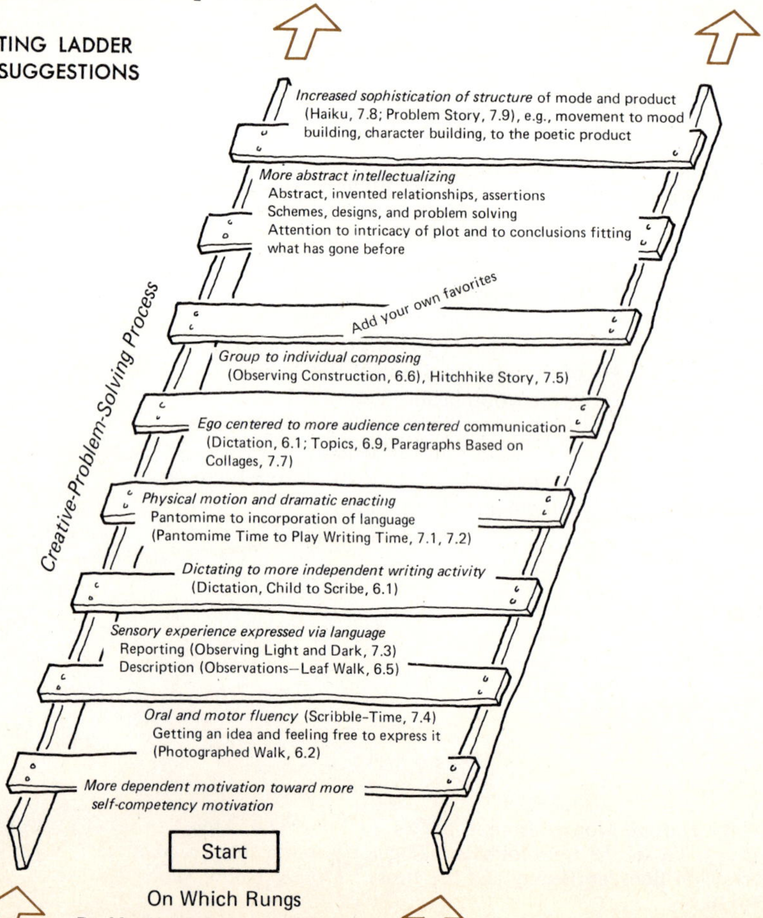


On Which Rungs
Do My Children Need to Start?

# If You Want to Learn More


Burrows, A. T. *Teaching Composition. What Research Says to the Teacher.* No. 18. Washington, D.C.: National Education Association, Department of Classroom Teachers, 1966.

Burrows, A. T., Jackson, D., and Saunders, D. *They All Want to Write.* (3rd ed.) New York: Holt, Rinehart and Winston, 1964.

Carlson, J. Six Uses of Dialog—How to Teach Them. *Grade Teacher,* 1969, *86* (April), 76-77. (ERIC Document Reproduction Service No. EJ 002 046)

Carlson, R. K. *Writing Aids Through The Grades.* New York: Columbia University Press, 1970.

Dixon, J. *Growth Through English: Guidelines for the Teaching of English from the Anglo-American Conference at Dartmouth College.* Reading, England: National Association for the Teaching of English, 1967. (NCTE Stock No. 02407, Urbana, Ill.)

Presents examples of the kind of dramatization and talk in class that intensifies meanings and vividness in writing.

Educational Services Inc. Highlights of the 1963 Elementary Science Study Summer Conference. Newton, Mass.: Author, 1964. (55 Chapel Street, Newton, Mass. 02160).

Ellis, H. M. Twenty-One Way-Out Story-Starters and How to Use Them. *Grade Teacher,* 1969, *86* (March), 95-100. (ERIC Document Reproduction Service No. EJ 002 036)

Frank, Y. H. Four Writing Assignments to Teach Observation. *Grade Teacher,* 1969, *87* (November), 78-80, 123. (ERIC Document Reproduction Service No. EJ 008 798.)

Gage, T. (Chairman) *Languaging: A Composition Curriculum.* Concord, Calif.: Mt. Diablo Unified School District, 1973.

Golub, L. S. Syntactic and Semantic Elements of Students' Oral and Written Discourse: Implications for Teaching Composition. Unpublished doctoral dissertation, Stanford University, 1967.

Golub, L. S. Linguistic Structures in Students' Oral and Written Discourse. *Research in the Teaching of English,* 1969, *3,* 70-85.

Golub, L. S. Stimulating and Receiving Children's Writing: Implications for an Elementary Writing Curriculum. *Elementary English,* 1971, *48,* 33-49.

Golub, L. S., Fredrick, W. C., and Barganz, R. A. *Present and Proposed Needs, Objectives, and Components of a Language Learning Program.* Paper No. 29. Madison: Wisconsin Research and Development Center for Cognitive Learning, September 1971.

HENNINGS, D. G. and GRANT, B. M. *Content and Craft: Written Expression in the Elementary School.* Englewood Cliffs, N.J.: Prentice-Hall, 1972.

HOETKER, J. Teacher Questioning Behavior in Nine Junior High School English Classes. *Research in the Teaching of English,* 1968, *2,* 99-106.

KOHL, H. Children Writing: The Story of an Experiment. *The New York Review, New York Times,* November 17, 1966, pp. 26, 29.

LUNDSTEEN, S. W. *On Written Composition,* in preparation.

LUNDSTEEN, SARA W. *Help for the Teacher of Composition: New Directions in Research.* NCRE/NCTE/ERIC, in preparation.

MCCULLOUGH, C. M. Package, Ritual, and Insight. *The Reading Teacher,* 1972, *25* (February), 390-95.

MURRAY, D. M. *A Writer Teaches Writing.* Boston: Houghton Mifflin, 1968.

MURRAY, D. M. What Do I Say Besides "Awk?" *California English Journal,* 1973, *9* (4), 22-28.

MYERS, R. E., and TORRANCE, E. P. *Invitations to Speaking and Writing Creatively.* Boston: Ginn, 1965.

A series of teachers' guides and workbooks designed to help the teacher help the child who needs more encouragement to be original and unique, and to give his imagination more free rein.

PALMER, W. S. What Yolly, Willy, and Harriet Learned to Do . . . the Free Modifier: A Fresh Mode of Teaching Composition. *California English Journal,* 1971, *7* (4), 17-28.

On teaching in junior high.

WEED, K., and WATSON, P. Elect Creative Writing for First Grade. *Elementary English,* 1969, *46* (March), 295-99. (ERIC Document Reproduction Service No. EJ 002 061)

# Chapter 8 Spelling: Contemporary Developments & Controversy

## What's Happened to Spelling?

Want to update your ideas on teaching spelling, reassess your teaching goals, and engage in some self-evaluation? This chapter answers some questions about the why of our spelling system, gives information about current program development and controversy, and includes some interesting bits on the history of spelling, spelling games, and teaching aids. Is it possible to make learning to spell interesting? Is there an important diagnostic role for the teacher? What do we know about patterns of letters and sounds? Each of these questions is answered.

One of the concerns in published writing in the school is spelling—it seems that almost everyone has something to say about the job that schools are doing and about "poor" spelling, which is mistakenly equated with ignorance and lack of literacy.

The cartoon illustrates how spelling can be erroneously viewed not as a means, a tool of effective communication, but as an *end* in itself. The more language changes (and the more successful that linguists become in explaining and dignifying these changes), the more the authoritarian longs for the clearly right, the permanent, and the unequivocal (Key, 1969). In a way "good" spelling appeals to this authoritarian spirit. In spite of resistance, reforms in irregular spellings are underway, such as *fantasy* for *phantasy, sulfur* for *sulphur, foto* for *photo,* and *cookie* for *cooky* (Key, 1969).

## WHAT IS SPELLING?

In general

What is this thing called spelling? Simply writing words from memory? The term *spelling system* (or *orthography*) is here defined as, and restricted to, an alphabetic writing code. According to standard usage or convention, this code represents whatever words we utter. Both sender and receiver of the code must know what each symbol stands for and in what order the symbols are arranged. A systematic spelling program for children must build an awareness of the nature of the code.

By *alphabetic* is meant that written words are made up of letters that stand for the sounds heard in spoken words. One, two, or more of these letters may function as single units called *graphemes.*[1] The alphabetic system of American English is not as consistent a code as is Spanish, Finnish, or Turkish. But it *is* made up of letters that stand for sounds. For example, we would not hesitate to pronounce such nonsense words as *brip, negland,* and *grami,* or to spell them from dictation.[2]

[1] For example, the *gh* in *laugh* is a grapheme that represents the unit of sound (or phoneme) /f/. (When we write a sound that a letter stands for we enclose it between slashes.)

[2] One way to clarify this sound-letter relationship is to contrast it with a non-alphabetic language such as the Chinese writing system, which is unrelated to sound. Each word is represented by a character, an assembly of strokes written in a particular order. The 30 strokes in the system are governed by strict rules as to disposition on paper in relation to other strokes, and size. They provide no information for distinguishing one character from another.

The writer's or reader's task is somewhat equivalent to that of a person trying to remember telephone numbers, since the strokes are arbitrary symbols. To read a Chinese newspaper appears to resemble reading several thousand words composed of these arbitrary strokes known only by memorization.

**System despite inconsistency**

However, nearly every one of the more than 40 sounds in English may be represented in writing in more than one way, some in as many as 12 different ways. To most people the spelling of English words seems erratic. For example, *heard* looks like *beard* but is pronounced like *bird. Meat, great,* and *threat* rhyme with *suite, straight,* and *debt.* And consider these:

> *hiccough, thorough, laugh, through*
> *freight, sword, guard, said*
> *come, of, choir,* and *you*

One of the related comments (that exasperate linguists) is George Bernard Shaw's statement that he could spell *fish* as *ghoti* in English (*gh* as in *cough, o* as in *women, ti* as in *nation*).[3]

[3] This spelling, *ghoti,* ignores the matter of structural pattern and position. For example, the letters *gh* represent the /f/ sound only when it comes in *final* position in a root word, and then only when the preceding vowel sound is spelled either *ou* or *au* as in *enough, tough,* or *laugh.* The letters *gh* in initial position always represent the /g/ sound as in *ghost.* The letters *ti* represent the /sh/ phoneme only when it is an *interior* one as in *nation* and *partial.* The letter *o* used to represent the short /i/ sound is admittedly a rare irregularity (see Hanna & Hanna, 1964).

ON THE PROPER PERSPECTIVE FOR ORTHOGRAPHY

"When I grow up, I'm going to be a speller!"

**Loan words**

What are the reasons for the irregularities in the spelling of words? Some words have been borrowed from other languages (e.g., *waltz* from a German word meaning "to roll"). And often accepted spellings do not shift to conform to changes in the *spoken* language (especially in the vowels and in the reduction of final syllables e.g., *rubbed*).[4]

There is enough variation from consistent one-to-one relationships between letters and sounds that the spelling of a particular word is not completely predictable from a set of simple rules. A child learning to spell must work from *options* within the language for translating a given spoken word into letters. For example, the child asks, "Will I spell it *li, ly, ligh,* or *lie*?" Children who acquire a set of phonic generalizations for spelling on their own may become phonic misspellers—e.g., *I luv u* (Smith, Goodman, & Meredith, 1970). But the child is unlikely to become this kind of misspeller if taught the options. In fact, spelling one-syllable words is rather predictable, and most words that contain consonant and short-vowel sounds are completely regular. Although our spelling system deserves its reputation for inconsistency to some extent, there *is* a system. (The argument, however, about just how regular English spelling may be has not yet ended.)

[4] Final *e,* though no longer pronounced (e.g., in *cape*), is still useful in marking the quality of the vowel preceding it. Spelling irregularities have also been caused by learned spellings (e.g., Latin words); etymological spellings (or false ones, e.g., *debt* and *reign*); French scribes changing spellings for aesthetic reasons (e.g., from *cwic* to *quick*); ignorant mistakes (e.g., *island* for *iland, could* for *coud, delight* for *delite*).

LOCATING WORD ORIGINS ON A MAP

Spelling patterns

What does the system mean for the child? Examine several ideas as an overview to a grade by grade description. Using the system means that instead of dealing with the spelling of each separate word, children can use abstractions and generalizations called *spelling patterns*.[5] By making use of these patterns, children can avoid much arbitrary, isolated memorization—the most difficult kind of learning.

---

## WHAT IS THE NATURE OF THE MODERN SPELLING PROGRAM?

### When and How Does Spelling Get Started?

What's happened to spelling?

Beginning instructional materials for spelling help children learn to form each letter at the same time they begin to make sound associations for that letter. (See the sample textbook page.) The need to spell grows with

[5] The Stanford studies (Hanna, Hanna, Hodges, & Rudorf, 1966) indicate that relationships between oral language and written spelling are between *patterns* of sounds and *patterns* of letters rather than simply between individual sounds and individual letters. It is difficult for me to see however, how so complex a set of rules could be taught to schoolchildren. But the patterns uncovered may be of use to the constructors of textbook materials. This is especially true when patterns are presented to children as options, not as rules.

## Consonant Letters Spell Consonant Sounds

Name the picture.

The consonant letter **d** spells the first sound in dog.

Write the consonant letter that spells the first sound in dog. ____og

Name the picture.

The consonant letter **f** spells the first sound in fish.

Write the consonant letter that spells the first sound in fish. ____ish the need to write. Preschool children begin to spell as they watch the visual form take shape from the teacher's hand. Young children begin their spelling instruction as they listen to, observe, and talk about what the teacher says as they write. The teacher may note beginning, middle, and end sounds and corresponding letters. Children are paced at their own rates (1) as they move from large, free letters to more controlled formations, (2) as they encounter capital and lowercase letters, (3) as they relate spoken sounds to letter sequence, and (4) as they attack complex words as well as words with simple sound–letter consistency.

### General Procedures of a Modern Program That Is Linguistically Based

First grade patterns

Examine a specific first-grade program (Monroe, Aaron, & Schiller, 1969, Book 1) that introduces children to common spelling patterns. Since the spelling of consonant sounds in English is regular, these sounds and letters are introduced first. The child learns, for example, that the /d/ sound is spelled with the letter *d* as in *dog* (see sample page). The child will also learn that the /l/ sound is spelled with the letter *l* (as in *lamp*) or the letters *ll* (as in *doll*). First-grade children are introduced to further options when they learn that they can spell the */k/* sound with the letter *c* or *k* at the beginning of a word, and with the letter *k* or the letters *ck* at the end of a word (e.g., *cap, kite; book, prick*).

Second grade

In the second grade children learn more systematic options, e.g., that the /j/ sound is not always spelled *j* but may be spelled *g* and *ge* as in *giant* and *cage*. They learn that the /s/ sound is not always spelled *s* or *ss* but may be spelled *c* or *ce* as in *city* and *prince*. It is at this level that they are shown the convention of symbols for sounds, e.g., the sound for *b* is shown as /b/.

Vowels and spelling patterns

Spellings for vowel sounds are introduced in the first grade after the child has been made familiar with some spellings for consonant sounds. With the advent of vowels, children are introduced to spelling patterns of vowels—common ways of spelling a given vowel sound. Traditionally the vowel sounds in *h***a***d, r***e***d, b***i***g, n***o***t,* and *m***u***d* are called *short* vowel sounds. Those in *b***a***ke, b***ee***t, b***i***ke, d***o***me,* and *m***u***le* are called *long* vowel sounds. At the first- and second-grade level, the following spelling patterns, in words of one syllable only, are taught:

1. A vowel letter followed by one or more consonant letters (other than *r*) as in *bat* and *bash* (vowel consonant, or *vc* or *vcc*).
2. A vowel followed by *r* as in *dark* (*vr*).
3. A vowel followed by one consonant letter and *e* as in *like* and *home* (*vce*).
4. Combinations of vowel letters, *ai* and *ee,* as in *paid* and *keep* (*vv*).

A way to use spelling patterns in the early grades is to teach a pattern, for example, the consonant–vowel–consonant (*cvc*) pattern, in one-syllable words such as *ten, ton, tin,* and *tan.* Children can use this pattern to spell many words almost as easily as they can spell one; they simply change the vowel. If a child has learned to spell *it,* he/she can soon spell such words as *bit, kit, hits, hitter,* and *lit.* A consonant–vowel–consonant–vowel (*e*) (cvce) variation of the pattern could also be used, as in *bate, make, tale.* This technique gives the child a sense of power in learning more words each week.[6]

**Using patterns in the early grades**

Linguists tell us that if we dig beneath the surface, our spelling system is full of reasons. It is more regular and more explainable than we thought it was. The first teaching task is to help children discover the patterns (e.g., *say, day, lay; fate, mate, late*). Exceptions can be learned later.

The overall goals of the aforementioned program, along with more-specific goals, objectives, and a sample page from a third-grade textbook, follow.

*Overall Goals*

- to develop the concept that correct spelling is one of the essential skills in written communication.
- to develop an ever increasing basic spelling vocabulary for immediate use in written expression from lower to higher grade levels.
- to develop ability to identify and use the spelling patterns of English.
- to develop the realization that good spelling is a mark of consideration to one's reader and a sign of intellectual and social competence.
- to develop the concept of the relationship between hand-writing and spelling, and the responsibility of the writer to master both skills. A correctly spelled word that is written illegibly does not usually communicate.
- to develop increasing competence in the use of a dictionary, glossary, and thesaurus as sources for the spellings, pronunciations, and meanings of words, thereby adding new words continuously to spelling vocabularies as well as to listening, speaking, and reading vocabularies [Monroe et al., 1969, Book 3, p. 5].

[6] Hodges & Rudorf (1965) tabulated sound–letter correspondences in terms of position and stress features, and found what they considered to be much consistency. About 88% of letter–sound relationships are determined by sound factors, 6% by stress, and 4% by word factors. The small percent of irregular words includes some of the most frequently used words in the language, which children need to learn to spell (e.g., *you*).

Third grade

At the third-grade level children are expected to develop the ability—

- to spell Basic Spelling Words related to topics of interest about which they may wish to write.
- to use and maintain a Personal Spelling List.
- to extend their knowledge of spelling patterns, including all the regular vowel patterns in mostly single-syllable words.
- to use a Reference Section of words in which the spelling patterns they are studying appear with single syllables and many syllables.
- to use the *Thorndike–Barnhart Beginning Dictionary* to look up words they need to spell and to master all major pronunciation symbols except the schwa.
- to learn the general principles of changing the spelling of certain base words when *s, es, ed, ly,* and *ing* are added.
- to use *In Other Words . . . A Beginning Thesaurus* in finding synonyms and antonyms for known words.
- to give especial attention to the spelling problems of certain homophones (e.g., *hear, here*).
- to recognize whether a word has one or two syllables.
- to recognize the accented syllable in two-syllable words (e.g., bríght-ly) [Monroe et al., 1969, Book 3, p. 5].

Intermediate grades

By the fourth grade most consonant and vowel phonemes and their written forms have been presented, if the spelling program is truly systematic. A systematic program includes a presentation of word parts (e.g., *-ing, -ment, -able*) that when added can change a word from one form to another (e.g., verb to noun, noun to adjective—*agree* to *agreement* to *agreeable*) or from one meaning to another (e.g., *understand* to *misunderstand*). Such word parts are examples of *morphemes,* the smallest parts of words having independent meaning. At this point, prefixes, suffixes, and roots are introduced as vocabulary building aids. Beginning at about fourth-grade level such homonyms as *pour/poor, mane/main,* or *sun/son* may be used in story-writing sessions to help a child understand different word meanings (Hanna, Hodges, & Hanna, 1971).

At about fifth-grade level the program might include a study of *homographs* (words alike in spelling but different in meaning and origin, such as *scale, loaf, cape,* and *toll*). Lessons might include "loan," or borrowed, words such as

chipmunk ⟶ chikmunk (Algonquin Indian)
canyon ⟶ cañon (Spanish)
chili ⟶ chili (Mexican–Aztec)

Still later the child might engage in a study of acronyms, which are words formed from initial letters or syllables, e.g., *radar,* derived from *radio directing and ranging.*

By the intermediate grades, word history begins to be of interest. The child can learn that *psyche* grows out of a Greek myth, and that the letter *k* in *knee, knock,* and *know* once had the /k/ sound pronounced. (This pronouncing was also true in the case of the *g* in *gnat,* and the *w* in *sword.*) Learning language history makes the learning of spelling more meaningful and interesting. Word history

The meanings of countless words have changed over and over again, and new words and expressions get added to our language as we need them. (Examples of new words are *astronaut, earth satellite,* and *radar.* Making collages of borrowed words from various lands (e.g., *alligator, potato,* and *barbecue* from Spanish) is a typical activity. Noting various national influences on names on a map of the United States is another.[7] Changes and borrowings

Older children, from intermediate grades on, can be helped to see that spelling regularity is based in part on a pattern of underlying root Word families: root words and patterns

[7] For word history, sources for the teacher are Hanna, Hodges, & Hanna (1971) and L. Barnett (1964). Some books for students are Sam and Beryl Epstein's *The First Book of Words* (New York: Watts, 1951); and Mario Pei's *All About Language* (Philadelphia: Lippincott, 1954).

or base-word relationships, or *word families,* e.g., *democratic, democracy; muscle, muscular; immigrate, migrate;* and *sign, signal, signature.* Such an association can be helpful to older children uncertain as to how to represent the sound indicated in the first word of each pair. A specific cultural "event" (such as language) must be patterned so that it fits into a system—if it is to survive. The system of English spelling has survived for hundreds of years with its virtues of far more regularities and regular changing patterns than irregularities (Key, 1969). In other words, the root parts (morphemes) of words have various pronunciations depending on their *position* in the words and their relationship to the *other parts* with which they combine. For example, the morpheme *flame* is pronounced /fleym/ in isolation. But when affixes (e.g., *-in, -ation, -able*) are added and the stress changes, the vowel sounds of the base word also change: *inflammable,* /inflaeməbel/; *inflammation,* /inflәmeyšәn/ (Key, 1969).

Older children can also be helped to see an advantage to this sort of spelling of English in the listing of forms in a dictionary—if the forms were spelled according to their pronunciation, they would be scattered throughout a dictionary rather than grouped together.

The teacher helps older children intermediate through junior-high-school grade level) to compare words having similar patterns, searching for a systematic reason a word is spelled the way it is. This way, the child can be helped to relate two words in a manner that will show a reason for seemingly unusual spelling.

For example older children can look at forms such as *medicine* and *medical, bomb* and *bombardier.* They can see that *medicine* and *medical* are in the same family, and can also be helped to see that the *c* in *medicine* has the /s/ sound because it is followed by *i,* whereas in the word *medical* the *c* has a /k/ sound because it is followed by *a.* When the child sees *bombardier,* the last *b* in the word *bomb* may be more easily remembered. The teacher can show how word families, letter position, and spelling patterns or generalizations can be combined to help the student understand the system.

Spelling options

Another way of using spelling patterns with older children involves noting the many various ways of spelling a sound. (An example is the phoneme /a/ in *clay, state, wait, gauge, neighbor,* and *they.*) Such knowledge entered on a chart (working from most-common to least-common options) may come in handy when children are ready for proofreading. Using such charts also helps children to find dictionary entries. (See the later section on proofreading.)

This sampling from grade to grade gives you some idea of the nature of a modern program. But there are still some personal and social values to be retained advantageously from more traditional programs.

## Personal and Social Purposes for a Spelling Program

Personal and social sides

From the *personal* point of view, learning how to spell enables one to write something today that will be understandable to the writer tomorrow. From the *social* point of view, what one writes will be understandable to any literate person tomorrow. It will not only be understandable, but also represented so that the spelling is inconspicuous, not distracting. For example, a representation such as, *He wuz gud to me,* might distract the reader and detract from the message. The goal is that at the proofreading stage of school publication children can write appropriately every word that they expect their particular audience to read by using their memories or by copying the word from a reference work or other help.

## What Words Do You Teach?

Where do the words come from that you teach to the child? First of all, they are the ones used by children in their speaking. They draw upon these words when they write. They need help in spelling words they want to write in both formal and informal situations. These are words that are likely to be familiar to most children.

In recently devised systematic programs for children, words may be chosen because they are examples of common spellings for consonant and vowel sounds. That is they are derived from generalizations about the spelling system in the language, from words that *pattern* into a generalization about sound (e.g., *home*—final *e* signals the long sound of /o/. Or words may be selected because of a word (morphological) principle such as affixation (e.g., *ex-, post-, trans-* or *-able, -ful, -ible*). A common criterion in *earlier* texts has been social utility: (1) child needs, (2) adult needs, (3) overlap between child and adult needs. Word lists may come from words commonly taught in all subject areas of a given grade level. Or words might come from the ones a child misspells in his/her work papers, reports, and letters or from commonly mispelled words. I believe the first and foremost source is the child.

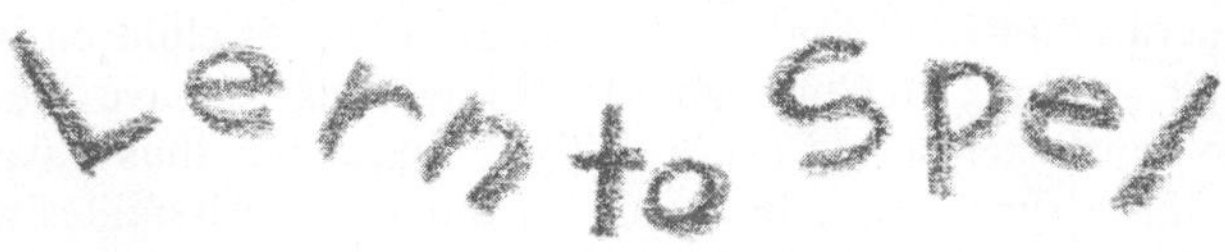

[8]

[8] The letter *l* is consistently geminated (doubled) in a single syllable word—thus *spell* instead of *spel.*

## HOW ARE CHILDREN INSTRUCTED?

Spelling is best learned the way other language skills are learned—developmentally, by use. This does not mean that spelling is to be taught merely incidentally and that there is no use for an organized spelling program utilizing concepts of patterns. But if children are motivated to communicate in writing, they will be motivated to develop increasingly complex spelling skills. An earlier section of this chapter described a modern, systematic, linguistically based program. Specific teaching techniques and components of programs ranging from the systematic to the "natural" are presented in the following sections.

### Corrected-Test Techniques

For spellers who appear to be developing normally, one of the economical classroom technique (used as early as the second grade) is simply an immediately self-corrected pretest. Pupils need to do the following: (1) clearly understand the purpose of the pretest, (2) immediately correct their errors with care, and (3) understand that alert correction contributes to the reduction of errors.

In any case it seems that a test–study procedure is superior to a study–test procedure. A pretest helps children avoid the empty ritual of studying words they already know. Some children will learn a word and make it theirs from just this one activity. They do not need to go through 5 days of ritual with it. Immediate knowledge of results is reinforcing. Ritualistic practice, merely doing something over and over, is inefficient and unproductive. Children need to know what they have spelled correctly, what they need to change, and how well they have coped with spelling patterns and options. The immediately self-corrected test can give precise, specific feedback; but a grade of A, or B, is ambiguous feedback.

**The test**

A modified sentence-recall form is an economical way to administer the test. The teacher (or child administrator) pronounces the word, uses it in a sentence, and pronounces it again. Some tests in modern spelling textbook series consist of sentences made up of words children frequently use in their writing. McCullough (1969) tells us to have the children repeat the word themselves (very softly). The child, thus having heard the word three times from his teacher, and from classmates and from his/her own mouth, is usually deterred from occupying the next 10 minutes saying, "What was the second word?" "What was the fifth word?"

After the test, children write the correct spelling above any words they missed. Having children immediately correct their own pretest may prevent errors made from becoming reinforced.

**Rationale**

Psychologically speaking, simply taking a pretest in a traditional, list-oriented program involves a child in attentive behavior. At the same time the feeling tone is not excessively threatening or unpleasant, because children are not expected to be perfect on this pretest. But they are not indifferent. Two days later they will take the test again. If they still get the word right they can assume it was not an accident. Isolated spelling lists, memorized and regurgitated in weekly spelling tests, tell little about a child's knowledge of the language, patterns applicable to spelling, and spelling consciousness.

Diagnosis of error

**Diagnosis, pronunciation, and listening.** An important part of grouping children and individualizing in the spelling program is diagnosis of error. The child can operate here as an autonomous problem solver. When children have made collections of their misspellings in their compositions, they can try to determine (with the help of the teacher) the *kind* of trouble they are having. The figure shows a system for classifying error from a modern series stressing spelling patterns.[9]

**NAME** ______________________ **DATE** ______________

**Classification of Spelling Errors**

| | | |
|---|---|---|
| (V) | Vowel Errors | Total (V) Errors ______ |
| (C) | Consonant Errors | Total (C) Errors ______ |
| (Rs) | Reversals of Letter Sequence | Total (Rs) Errors ______ |
| (AL) | Additions of Letters | Total (AL) Errors ______ |
| (OL) | Omissions of Letters | Total (OL) Errors ______ |
| (S) | Substitutions of a meaningful word in sentence context | Total (S) Errors ______ |
| (OW) | Omissions of Words | Total (OW) Errors ______ |

Reasons for error

What are some of the causes behind the seven spelling errors listed? The child may simply be lacking a knowledge of spelling patterns and options. Or, perhaps the child's spelling errors represent problems in listening skills. Children may be omitting letters because they do not hear the sound. (For example, they hear *wear* for *where, suprise* for *surprise, kep* for *kept, git* for *get, simular* for *similar,* and so on.) The spelling error usually disappears when the auditory impression is gained.

Many dialects: a source of error

Another source of difficulty is the abundance of different dialects and pronunciations of words in English. Impoverished and culturally differ-

[9] From *Spelling Our Language,* Book 2, page xi, by Marion Monroe, Ira Aaron, and Andrew Schiller. Copyright © 1969 by Scott Foresman and Company. Reprinted by permission of the publisher. This series has a section in the teacher's edition that shows how to give help with each type of error, what to review, what sentences to dictate, what words to have the pupil write (for each spelling vowel pattern missed), and so on.

ent persons are not the only ones who omit sounds in their speech. The speech of articulate and highly educated speakers of English shows much omission of phonemes and much variation (Key, 1969). (Phonic misspellers will understandably tend to misspell according to the way they speak in their own dialect, speed, and style [Smith, Goodman, & Meredith, 1970].) Even "overeducated" people often reduce consonant clusters systematically in fast speech: *windshield* becomes /winshil/, *sandwich* becomes /sanwich/, *surprise* becomes /səpriz/, and *did you* becomes /dijə/.[10]

The question is this: how do children handle words learned in isolation when they need to use them in written communication? Will they know that they know how to spell *did you* when they need to? In isolation, these "spelling words" are pronounced in ways uncommon to children. Do they need help in recoding, and gaining a mental set to reflect the more isolated words rather than their own blended sound quality? Is this need for distinction especially true for vowel sounds?

Standard spelling needed to handle various dialects

In spite of its troublesomeness, the "one-way" recording of spelling (with its emphasis on words in written English) is what makes a printed word understood in England, Australia, South Africa, India, Boston, and Mississippi. Readers who use any of the dialects associated with these places can recode and accommodate to their own sound system. (A person from Boston who says "Pahk the cah" and the Texan who says "Parrk the carer" can read the same material. In this sense, to think of spelling reform and trying to make a letter for each sound is a mistake (even if it could be accomplished!).

Our present spelling system, then, actually has a lot going for it. In spite of the fact that our language has some irregularities (you might say as many freckles, warts, and pimples as any of the rest of us), it has its regularities and advantages, too. Diagnosing the child's spelling difficulties means, in part, seeing whether or not the child understands certain patterns of this freckle-faced, warty system—English spelling.

Another aspect of helping children learn to spell has to do with the optimal use of the senses. This is stressed in the next section.

### Multichannels, Situational Choice, and Problem Solving

Speaking, seeing, and touching (or tracing) the letters of a word can all work together. (Tracing represents a way of knowing and learning useful to many children at some time, e.g., with a word such as *sulphur*.)

Internal background for spelling

Five other important contributors to accurate spelling are these: (1) a store of memorized words, generalizations, and word meanings; (2)

[10] Key (1969) mentions a phonetic transcription of four different ways she heard a speaker pronounce the word *delicious* in one single conversation. But there is generally only one accepted spelling. (We should be glad for that!)

skills of auditory discrimination; (3) awareness of accurate spelling; (4) servicable dictionary skills; and (5) personal and adaptable study skills for learning words for future use, such as auditory, visual, or touching (or kinesthetic) methods (Personke & Lee, 1971). This framework of spelling behavior in practical action includes habits, attitudes, and motivation to spell correctly. Such background is accumulated by the individual in previous spelling experiences. Here might be added abilities in the analysis of the spelling problem or challenge.

Choice of solution

When children are composing and need a word, they may do one of the following: (1) simply refer to memory with immediate solving of the problem; (2) write the word *almost* automatically; (3) decide to check with another person or check their guess with a dictionary, book, charts, or their personal card file *before* they write the word. Or (4) they may use a *proofread channel,* i.e., they write the word, but then later check with an external source for confirmation of correctness.

Breaks in the flow of thinking

Certain ways (e.g., writing immediately from memory, checking first, writing it and *then* getting proofreading help) are more suitable for one situation than for another. If words are unknown, spellers can retrieve from their memory storehouses words that seem *close* to them. Because this similarity seeking is a conscious thought process, it makes a conceptual break in the business of composing. Children are thinking of spelling rather than the message they want to communicate. The break is even *greater* if they have had to check first before writing anything at all. If children have forgotten how they intended to end a sentence or a story after laboriously spelling a word, they are not apt to do much creative writing.

TRACING AS PART OF A LEARNING MODE

Suppose that a speller writes a word using the *proofread channel* with the realization that the word may not be correct. Is there danger of reinforcing an incorrect response? Little, if they go fairly soon to external help and verification. And the break is not as it would be if they used the method of checking first.

*Conclusions*

Situational choice

- No one way is the "correct" way. Spellers must solve problems in ways suitable to the conditions and resources available.

  Situational choice not only refers to the retrieval of needed spellings but also involves a suitable way of *learning* during a practice period. That is, sometimes children may find writing the irregular word a few times fixes it for them. Or they may find that visualizing a word in a mental picture with imagery (as on a giant billboard) helps. Or sometimes children may "get it in their ears" by saying the sounds softly and accurately after a model, especially if they know they are prone to mispronounce it (e.g., *inerest* for *interest*).

- There is a need for mastery of all channels of processing, and skill in choosing the most suitable channel for the particular situation. Each kind of spelling behavior is viewed as a portion of a repertoire. Past research on and instruction in spelling has concentrated on the use of one part or one channel of processing behavior, i.e., "you have to know how to spell it immediately." This narrow perspective may account in part for such conflicts as rules versus no rules, pretest versus posttest only, auditory discrimination (or sounds) versus visual, and systematic versus incidental and individual need.

Problem solving

In other words, with help children can individualize their own approach to words. They can begin to treat them as their own creative problem. Once they have the framework of possibilities of attack, they plan the appropriate procedure and evaluation (proofreading, checking)—and away they go. The teacher's job is to show children a variety of ingenious attacks and learning–study procedures that suit various problems (e.g., a mnemonic device such as the *principal* is my *pal*). The teacher makes children aware of various diagnostic and testing devices and means of charting their *own* progress on both general and specific problems in spelling.

Practice

The teacher helps children tolerate repeated practice by helping them realize that just barely learning to spell a pattern or a word correctly is not enough. They must also need to get practice in writing the correct spellings so often that they form a muscular or kinesthetic pattern of the written word. Then the thought of the word stimulates the writing of it, and children are free to concentrate on their ideas (Monroe, 1969).

In essence, good spellers are probably ones who are well-organized, efficient, and carry patterns in their minds. By analogy, they apply these spelling patterns consistently to unfamiliar words. Exceptionally superior spellers are frequently people with superior visual perception and memory. They may be able to produce total recall in the form of a picture in the mind's eye of a whole, lengthy word (Key, 1969).

Profile of a good speller

---

### Applications from Psychological Learning-Theory

Many teachers pay attention to psychological principles along with other learning techniques as a matter of common sense. But here are a few reminders about techniques that make children's retention more probable. These thoughts offer a partial attack on the I-don't-remember problem (Hunter, 1969). These principles deal with meaning, degree of original learning, feeling tone, transfer, appropriate practice, amount of teacher guidance, and level of aspiration.

- *Meaning.* We are more apt to remember how to spell words that are meaningful to us than words that have no meaning to us at all. This idea means relate the word to the child's own experience. Use the word in a sentence containing the child's own name during a test. For example, the teacher may say, "*Valiant,* the sentence is 'Mary, you made a *valiant* attempt at proofing that story. Spell *valiant.*" Avoid trying to cover all the traditional spelling material for one grade level. Select the most important spelling patterns and concepts; make them meaningful.
- *Degree of Original Learning.* How well did the child learn the pattern or word in the first place? As implied above, with some children you have to forget the "once over lightly." If learning a spelling pattern or how to spell the word is important, see that it is well learned. Giving 20 new spelling words each week, never reviewing, and then moving on to new ones, violates this principle. Assess, redesign, and reteach if necessary.
- *Feeling Tone.* The tone of the feeling has much to do with retention in spelling or any other subject. Try to remember details of one of your worst days last month. If it is too traumatic, the chances are you repress even the memory. Now think of details of one of your best days. Now try to recall the details of an ordinary day. The chances are that you have just experienced the principle of the relation of feeling to memory. Best remembered are events associated with pleasant feeling. Next best remembered are occasions connected with un-

pleasant tone. Events least likely to be remembered are those with little or no feeling associated.

Application to spelling

What is the relation of this idea about feeling to spelling instruction? First, use all the know-how in this book on how to make learning pleasant, stimulating, and exciting. Hook into the "ally" of *self–competence;* have the children suggest several ways they would like to work at a spelling program and also at applying their know-how to proofreading. Let each child make choices from suggested alternatives. Let the children choose at least some of the words they want to learn to spell. Let committees work together on lists of words needed in social studies compositions. Let them do this for the pleasant feeling tone of *peer-group* interaction. Only the individual child can best determine what is pleasant for him, though you may have ideas if you have collected some compositions on the subjects suggested in Activity 6.9, Topics or Leading Ideas. Inject a variety of vivid means such as your sketching a cartooned smiling face over a troublesome word (e.g., *their*) handled correctly in free writing. Or, you may occasionally inject a favorite spelling game, such as the one in the following activity.

8.1. Spinner Man. (For preschool through intermediate grade levels.) The following game may be used with several spelling groups within the classroom. The material consists of an illustrated board picturing a funny man holding a circle divided into sections, with a "spinner" in the center. Each section bears one of these messages: (1) Give the meaning of the word. (2) Copy it correctly or write it on the board. (3) Use it in a sentence. (4) Find it in a dictionary. (5) Write how it is divided into syllables. (6) Tell where it came from. (7) Tell whether it is a regular or irregular spelling and what pattern (if any) it follows.

A child spins the spinner. It stops on a section. If the child can carry out the directions with regard to a selected word, then his/her group gets a point. If children play this game at the end of the week, after they have had a chance for study, it does not seem to pressure them too much and they relish it.[11] (See Activities 8.4, 8.5, and 8.6 for more games.)

Examples of positive transfer

- *Positive Transfer of Principles.* When something the child learns about spelling helps in the mastery of new words, *positive transfer* has taken place. An example is when a child grasps some information on word-families (generalizations of sound patterns) and applies this knowledge to learning how to spell a *"new"* word.

For instance, because a child knows that *prepare* is spelled with an *a* it helps her to spell the unstressed sound in *preparation*. She knows

[11] Appreciation is expressed to Mary Walstad-Lehman, student at the University of California, Irvine, for shared experience from which this activity is adapted.

that the *spelling* of the stem (or base word) remains constant while the pronunciation changes. If a child knows that more than one *dog* is spelled *dogs,* she can transfer and guess correctly that more than one *pig* is spelled *pigs.* If she knows *sowing* and *sow* and *throw,* she can probably derive *throwing.*

The positive transfer among meaningful encounters with words in reading, writing, and spelling in the method called the *language experience approach to reading* may help retention. There can also be positive transfer in study techniques, in use of dictionaries and other external aids. That is, the "old" knowledge children have about spelling can be made to assist them in acquiring and remembering new knowledge.

Reservations about transfer of spelling generalizations

While we are on the topic of transfer, let's look at the child's applications of spelling generalizations taught—a controversial area. You may have memorized at one time the rule about doubling the final consonant.[12] On the one hand, present research about the helpfulness of learning spelling generalizations about letter patterns, placement, and stress is inconclusive. Problems lie in the inductive teaching needed and in the level of abstract thinking that children must use. Some children are simply still in an early stage of thinking and need much concrete experience rather than abstract generalizations. As we get better practice in the classroom about how to teach for transfer of rules and generalizations, the knowledge about them that linguists are uncovering for us may become more useful to spellers in school.

On the other hand, the traditional spelling approach of isolated, whole-word teaching contributes little to transfer in use of sound (phonology) or word parts (morphology). The idea was that, because English spelling is so irregular, the spelling of each word must be learned as a unit. Positive transfer played little or no part. Recent research shows us, however, that English spelling is largely regular with spelling patterns representing the word patterns of the language. It shows that irregularities have been highlighted out of proportion.

- *Negative Transfer.* To avoid the memory of one learning *interfering* with another (negative transfer), a teacher needs to make certain that learnings are as different as possible.

  For example, you might avoid presenting spelling words such as *want* and *went* in the same lesson, thus separating them in time. Only if children were confusing them would you bring them together to stress the distinguishing features. For instance, certain letter sounds

[12] Monosyllables and words accented on the last syllable, when ending in a single consonant preceded by a single vowel, double the consonant before adding a termination beginning with a vowel or the suffix *y,* e.g., *infer, inferred.* (*Webster's Second New International Dictionary* then goes on to give three kinds of exceptions.)

such as /d/ and /t/, /p/ and /b/ that are highly similar are probably best introduced apart.

If we teach a spelling rule, we first group only the words that conform to the rule. That way the child has opportunity for positive transfer. After the original degree of learning is strong, we introduce exceptions. With respect to positive and negative transfer, consider the analogy of mixing paints. If you want them to mix, put them together and one will run into the other. But if you do not want them to mix, keep them separate (Hunter, 1969).

- *Practice.* Appropriate practice is essential to prevent forgetting. Questions are, How much? and How often?

  For example, how many times does the child need to—

  1. say the word and hear the sounds in it?
  2. look at it and say it or notice the letter (or letter group) that stands for each sound?
  3. think about the meaning of the word and the various associations it holds for him?
  4. note its elements such as prefix or suffix?
  5. study the unusual parts of the word?
  6. cover the word and write it from memory, if missed the first time? (Writing and comparing impress on the child the sequence of letters.)

  Probably the intensity of the practice procedures depends on the situation, the context, and the interest of the child. Some children can minimize or bypass certain sensory features in learning a word.

*How many words should a child try to learn in one week?* The answer depends upon whether you are thinking of a program with spelling patterns or a program that simply uses spelling lists. For some children one highly irregular word a week might be all they can absorb. A long, difficult word may have to be broken down into syllables. But the child might learn 20 patterned and related words easily. It is best to look for cues from the child.

*How long should the child work on his spelling at one time?* (Massed practice versus spaced practice.) Spaced practice is better in spelling. Many short practice periods are usually more effective than a few long ones. Writing an irregular but much-needed word several times during the day is probably more effective than massed practice for a lengthy period of time.

When the child is in the early stages of learning something, optimal practice periods are close together since material that is not well learned is soon forgotten. Then, if necessary, go to distributed practice. For example, after reviewing a difficult, irregular word twice the first day, review it once the second day, skip the third day, review the fourth day, skip the fifth and sixth day, review the seventh, skip a week, and then review, skip six weeks and then review. Mass at the beginning and distribute later.

- *How Much Teacher Guidance?* Under what conditions do you need to guide spelling and when do you need to draw back so that children can become autonomous in solving their own spelling problems themselves? Some children need a lot of support and reassurance, especially at the beginning of a relatively new task. Others (well aware of past competence in creative problem-solving) gladly take on a new challenge with a large degree of independence.

Simply observe each child's performance with and without your guidance to gather baseline information for learning tasks in spelling. Then put your guidance where it is needed, not where it interferes with the child's need to develop autonomy and with her need to communicate ideas. Nonetheless, at the beginning stage, having wise teacher guidance increases the rate and degree of learning.

This idea applies when introducing a new spelling pattern, a method of study, an external device (such as an aspect of the dictionary), or when moving from dictation to independent writing. As children gain proficiency, withdraw guidance gradually so that they learn to depend on themselves and can spell without guidance. Common sense tells us that if we get expert help at the beginning, we will learn faster and avoid bad habits.

- *Hope for Oneself.* Finally, psychologists tell us that how well children learn and retain depends on how well they think they will do. *Hope* is sometimes called *level of aspiration.* If children set their spelling goals too high, they can become discouraged, decide there is no hope, and avoid written communication. If level of aspiration is too low, if "anything goes," if there is little or no spelling consciousness, learning proceeds at such a snail's pace that the child need not even try.

  **Creative problem-solving**

  Here is where know-how about creative problem-solving comes in. A careful and realistic definition of the problem is vital. It helps to set appropriate time limits for spelling study with appropriate self-rewards or reinforcers for successful completing. Perhaps a child could set a 5-percent increase in the number of words systematically tackled each week or a 5-percent decrease in the number of spelling errors still made after proofreading.

### A Concerned Reflection on the Use of Psychological Know-how

All these learning principles from the field of psychological theory bring us to this question: *Is spelling really worth so much reinforcement?* Maybe we do not need psychologists to tell us how to reinforce more efficiently what we have already been emphasizing too much, what we already stress out of proportion to other aspects of communication.

The creative person and spelling

Key (1969) suggests that some spelling mistakes reflect exceptional capability or indicate creativity. Persons of extremely high intelligence are busy thinking about ideas and developing new theories. They are not concerned about how to spell out these exceptional ideas. (Shakespeare spelled his own name three different ways. Emily Dickinson, the poet, could not punctuate and could not spell.) Some editors may show consternation at "dumb scientists who don't know how to spell." There are creative persons who rebel at doing anything the same way twice. A writer does not have to be a good speller—it may even interfere with the creative process.

None of us have any idea how much creative flow of compositional energy has been cut off by constricting fears of being unable to put the ideas down on paper according to the conventions. This inhibiting climate starts in kindergarten and carries through the university. Of course spelling at exceptionally high levels of accuracy is important if the person is to be a secretary or a copy editor. But if children's ideas are worth communicating publicly, the spelling can be handled at the final editing. And if the ideas are not worth further notice, it matters little how they are spelled. Do you agree? In any case the child's first task in composition is to get thoughts down on paper, then look to logical flow, form, and lastly to mechanical details when publication is called for.

Emphasis on rich written content

These considerations lead to a developmental point of view where spelling facilitates communication of written thought rather than limiting it. Then rather than being reinforced for limiting their writing to words that they can spell correctly, children are encouraged to use their language in as rich a form as they can. It is likely that a child will learn to spell adequately the increased number of words he/she then uses and needs. *There is a danger that children will cut their writing to only those words they are sure they can spell correctly.* Classroom procedures fostering this practice involve a risky intellectual curtailment since children's concepts go far beyond what they can spell. I would rather give the child all sorts of spelling help.

### The Use of Knowledge from the Spelling Program for Proofing (Getting the Dictionary Habit)

Personke and Yee (1971) report an experimental proofreading program of 14 lessons which they developed and evaluated with experimental and control groups at sixth-grade level. Part of the rationale for this program was the realization that one of the big problems in spelling is transfer. Lack of transfer from the systematic spelling program to the planned composition program occurs when children lack any *spelling consciousness* (or motivation to correct errors). If most spelling errors are highly individual, then the added element of proofing skills is even more important.

**Needs in proofing**

Personke and Yee rationalized that children do not acquire these skills without some guidance. Many teachers have heard children say, "But how can I look it up in the dictionary, if I can't spell it?" If persons do not have some idea at least of how to spell the first syllable or the options, they do have difficulty. There are three major needs in proofreading for spelling: Children need to attain—(1) a degree of motivation toward spelling; (2) certain techniques for efficient proofing of their compositions; and (3) an understanding of the prime reference tools for such proofreading, e.g., a dictionary (or at least a speller-dictionary).

**Procedures**

In order to attend to motivation, Personke and Yee (allotting class time for the proofing) had the children write at the bottom of their paper upon completion, "Proofread for spelling," and sign their names. Children were taught the technique of underlining any word they were uncertain they could spell so that they would know to check it later.

The next technique taught was dictionary usage specifically for the correction of spelling. The major aid was a spelling chart listing the common spellings for almost every sound in the English language. The following sample from the chart (American Book, 1967) shows common spellings for ə, the *schwa*.[13]

[13] The schwa (occurring in about one-third of English syllables) plays an important part in pronunciation. It is the central, relaxed vowel (heard in the word *of*). In our borrowed Roman alphabet there is no symbol to represent this sound; instead, all five vowel letter symbols and combinations of these five letters are used (e.g., *salad, rapid, common*).

Radio announcers, English teachers, and reading teachers distort pronunciations by substituting vowel qualities suggested by spellings for the natural-sounding schwa quality. The schwa, occurring regularly in fast, natural speech in some stressed syllables and in a great many unstressed syllables, is the most frequently occurring vowel (Key, 1969). Help children to understand that pronunciation of words in ordinary rapid speech is rarely as precise as the pronunciation presented in dictionaries. Since the schwa sound is not found in many other languages of the world, children who are linguistically different may have trouble with it. See, for example, the publication by the California State Department of Education (1974).

| Dictionary symbol | Key | Most of the graphemes that represent the sound | Illustrative words for each grapheme |
|---|---|---|---|
| ə | a in across | a, ai, e, ea, eo, i, ia, o, oe, oi, oo, ou, u | banana, mountain, barrel, sergeant, surgeon, wearily, parliament, ton, does, tortoise, blood, country, but |

A chart for young children might stress more regular forms than the schwa, such as /k/ in *keg, cat, clam, crib, tack, comic,* and *choir.*

Use of a chart showing various spellings of sounds

Each child in the experimental classes Personke and Yee used had a personal copy of the complete chart of common spellings for sounds (Scott Foresman). The instructor showed the children how to use this chart in combination with their own personal copies of a dictionary to find words that they could not spell. Beginning with the first sound or syllable, the children took the best guess from among the alternate choices on the chart, checking the dictionary to see if they had estimated correctly. They kept up this process of elimination until they found the word. Then children crossed out the incorrect spelling and wrote the correct spelling above the error.

ON THE USE OF A DICTIONARY

*Wizard of Id* by permission of John Hart and Field Enterprises Inc.

Instruction included other types of lessons, e.g., the finding of guide words, alphabetical arrangement, and synonyms. One lesson provided practice in looking for errors in a prepared paragraph (presented by the teacher), that contained spelling errors designed to give practice with the chart. Another lesson gave practice in writing a dictated paragraph and proofing it for spelling errors, and the next one (the ninth in the series) was an attempt to proofread a child's personal composition. Another lesson contained lists of words supposed to be difficult for elementary-school children. The final type of lesson involved proofing a friendly letter that was actually recopied and mailed. Results were significantly higher for experimental-group students following these lessons.

**Other lessons and results**

Now that I have outlined a procedure designed to develop spelling consciousness, I want to repeat a caution. Since ideas are more important than correct spellings in children's compositions, generally *the teacher needs to give words freely as children ask for help.* Children who have to check 20 words accomplish little in a task rapidly becoming fatiguing and distasteful. Generally, by the fifth or sixth grade children might check three to five words by the dictionary at the proofreading stage. (See Activity 8.4, Dictionary Delight.)

## Grouping and Individualizing

Individualization has been touched on briefly in the earlier section about the self-corrected test. Why group and individualize? For one reason, it is unwise to expect children to spell words that are not in their speaking or reading vocabularies. Just as children read on differing levels, they will probably be more successful at spelling words on differing levels, too, depending on how the textbook series is organized. Children learn at different speeds, and their styles of learning vary also.

What about teachers who use one list for the whole class? They are assuming that all the pupils can read the words, need them, and understand the patterns—they don't. Such teachers are assuming that the next teacher will pick up the principles, patterns, and illustrative words the children do not retain—he can't. Suppose teachers abandon a systematic text approach, turn to an "anything goes" approach, and assume they are meeting each child's needs—they won't.

**Grouping for work on patterns, principles, and errors**

However, if a textbook series emphasizes spelling patterns and diagnoses typical errors instead of specific words, then major areas of difficulty for individual pupils will become apparent. A modern text will give the teacher references to earlier lessons, or extending activities appropriate for particular sound-to-letter errors. The text will refer the teacher to other skills and strategies that a child might need to review. Partner practice, committees, and individual conferences can apply to spelling, too.

What are some major teacher roles during this grouping and individualizing?

- Seeing and pointing out to the children genuine, true-to-life needs for correct spelling in writing—not just tests.
- Bringing to bear a full understanding of the writing system in the sense that rules, principles, patterns are *used* (not merely memorized).
- Developing in children habits of proofreading.

Formal tests. Besides the instructional self-corrected test mentioned earlier, and informal diagnostic measures, a published standardized test may be administered during the school year. A complete formal examination of spelling would consist of a test of all the words in the written language. In practice, standardized tests examine only a few. From the scores, teachers try to infer that a child has a certain degree of spelling skill.

Standardized tests may be designed to examine a child's ability to spell certain words representing particular difficulties in spelling patterns (such as ***night*** and *receive*). Some tests measure ability to recognize whether or not a word is spelled correctly in a multiple-choice form. Others measure the different functions of ability to recall and spell from dictation.

In any case, tests seldom control for vocabulary knowledge. Because of irregularities in our spelling system, a person who does not have a word or any variant of a word in his/her vocabulary (i.e., as if it were a nonsense word) has only a moderate chance of being able to spell it correctly.

---

## Some Advice

The literature generally warns us of several practices about teaching spelling.

1. Avoid oral spelling. Oral spelling activities of the old-fashioned "spelling bee" variety are competitive exercises in sheer recall but represent poor teaching–learning techniques in spelling. Suppose your task is to help a child hear phonemes (sounds) in a spoken word and translate them into graphemes (letters) of the written word. Nothing could be more confusing than having the child vocalize the names of letters used in spelling the word.

   This confusion occurs because there is little or *no relationship between the sound of the name of the letter and the sound represented by that letter.* To say "double-you ey el el" has little correspondence and offers little help to the child's direct response of writing the letters *w, a, l,* and *l* when he hears the sounds of the phonemes in that word *wall.*

Oral spelling is not true-to-life practice because ordinarily we are *writing* whenever we have occasion to spell. We are not mouthing names of letters aloud (Hanna & Hanna, 1964). If a child needs a word while writing a composition, *write* it rather than spelling it aloud. There are other activities for a game-like and pleasant feeling tone besides a spelling bee.

2. Avoid calling attention to hard spots in words before the *whole class*. Few words contain specific mistakes made by as many as half the children in any given class. In spite of data that indicate many words do have a particular place at which errors are made, calling total group attention to hard spots may even be a harmful practice. Instead, let children work on their own particular difficulties.
3. Avoid writing in the air as practice, making repeated writings of words without intervening attempts at recall, condemning a child for asking how to spell a word, and using the writing of words as a form of punishment. Green and Petty (1971) give reasons for each of these "commandments."
4. Avoid the empty ritual of children playing at learning to spell words they already know during textbook lessons, while other children face the same task but are overwhelmed by it week after week after week. Instead, slower learners can deal with a reasonable number of related words that facilitate transfer. The already suggested individualizing, grouping, and individual proofing techniques are alternatives.
5. Avoid having children mark out "silent" letters. It distorts the spelling pattern. Instead, have them underline patterns that form the sound, e.g., as *seat, meat, beat* (vvc), and *love, dove, glove* (vce). In the last group of examples, the final *e* is used as a marker to preserve the pattern that forbids *v* to appear in final position in our language.)

## SUMMARY AND CONCLUSIONS

A historical background helps to explain the origin of some modern spelling patterns. Linguistic research has shown that there are more regular patterns than previously thought. These patterns bear a regular correspondence to the modern pronunciation. Probably no language ever had a purely phonemic system of writing. Inevitable changes in spoken language (in the case of even a fairly phonemic alphabet) in time bring about a decrease in representing accurately all the society's current pronunciations. From a modern linguistic point of view there is no such thing as a correct pronunciation. (There may be a *standard* pronunciation, however.)

Criteria for pronunciation are intelligibility and usefulness. In time, when the spelling of a word fails to have a regular relationship to its pronunciation (or is represented with different spellings associated with different meanings) the language reverts to a prealphabetic state. But almost every word in English is at least partially alphabetic. (For example, in *slough, /slōō/* or */sluf/,* at least the *sl* is an alphabetic representation.)

Word roots and affixes have been making an appearance in spelling programs for a long time, but their significance has not been understood fully. For example, there is the tendency in our language to spell a morpheme the same way no matter what the pronunciation, as in *sign, signal, signature.* The spelling of the stem remains fixed but the pronunciation changes. Sometimes there is a combination of morphology and position of the sound working to determine the spelling. For example, the sound of /t/ is represented by the past tense suffix *-ed* only after voiceless consonants (other than *t*)—as in *popped,* and *jumped* (sounded /popt, jumpt/).

Such generalizations *may* be helpful to children, although research on this matter is inconclusive. In any case, it would seem advisable to correlate word analysis in any reading with spelling. Within the two programs it is advisable to use similar terminology and ways of representing sounds that letters stand for in order to prevent confusion.

**Spelling: a subskill to writing, not an end in itself**

Finally, if we follow what we know about development of thought and compositional ability, we realize that *spelling is a subsidiary skill in writing, not an end in itself.* We realize that *children learn to spell the words they need now,* not words for some use in the distant future, or words that happen to fall nicely into some linguistic pattern that the text propounds. They learn to spell words *if they need them and use them in their written communications.* Much time spent on isolated spelling lessons is a complete waste of children's valuable time. They could have spent that time on thoughtfully read and written material—and come up with better spelling *and* communication.

*What's happened to spelling?* Plenty. This chapter was designed to synthesize and highlight the recent literature. The task was to share a balanced perspective on the whole contemporary "elephant" called spelling. This review managed to touch on the "tusks" of linguistics, the "tip of the tail" from psychology and cultural anthropology, a "hoofprint" from language history, part of the sharp "eye" of research, and some of the thick "skin" of common sense. Next you will find some of the "ear flap" of some practical and delightful classroom activity.

Children can probably think of modifications and adaptations of the activities and games to follow. The most helpful part in some of the games may be the time interval during which mental rehearsal of the letter images, subvocalizations of the corresponding sounds, or use of muscular tracings take place. In some games the child responds by moving physically to the appropriate letters and in others the child must collect or encode letters and move them.[14]

Many of the lessons and activities suggested in Hanna, Hodges, and Hanna (1971) are fun and have game-like overtones. Examples are these: the beginners' (level 1) activity of developing a letter-for-sounds chart, the level 2 activity of helping a class invent an alphabet (p. 150), and the level 8 activity of assessing pupil's knowledge of syllabication by using Mary Poppin's word *supercalifragilistic-expialidocious* (su per cal i frag i lis tic ex pi al i do cious).

8.2. Charts, Boxes of Powerful Words, and Other Self-help Devices. Even beginners can use a simple chart of spelling options once they learn some sound–letter(s) correspondences, and gain some competence in recognizing words and in making letters match sounds that they hear and say. This chart (in full view, or possessed individually) can aid recall of these accomplishments and be of some help to beginning writers.

Children can collect and alphabetically arrange the words written for them (that they have traced and used) in a small index box. A recipe box, a cheese box, or a cracker box will do. Children can refer to these slips of paper again and again when writing compositions. Or the file might be a personal notebook with a page for irregular words beginning with the same letter. (It is well to use any help you can get to verify the words children have added themselves. It is easy to copy a word incorrectly.) As children search for words they need for their stories, they may find help from having seen it in a book, around the room, on another child's list, and (later) in a picture dictionary.

One group of older children engaged in this activity needed the word *pencil*. Having a feeling that it was *not* spelled *pensil,* they decided they could get help from the map indicating the state of Pennsylvania. They were very pleased with themselves until a group member verified it in a dictionary. That made one member curious enough about the word *Pennsylvania* that she managed to uncover its etymology and report it to her group. More important, one of the group discovered for them in the reference section of the spelling book that *c* has the /s/ sound when followed by *i* or *e*.

One second grade boy engaged in writing a tale about an army headquarters became stumped over the portion "quarter," but triumphantly solved his problem when he pulled a quarter out of his pocket.

[14] One additional source of games is Cratty (1971).

As a device to keep the composition going, children can be encouraged to write as much of the word as they can sound out and then leave a blank space. This way they will have written just enough of the word so that they can retrieve the idea.

Word aids

8.3. Writer's Aids. (For intermediate grades.) Set aside some time to introduce various children's dictionaries, a children's thesaurus, books on homonyms, spelling aids, sound–letter aids, sections of language texts that children can use as references, and other helps.

More ideas: encourage children to make their own picture dictionaries. Children can also be directed to glossaries in the back of reading series, and to simple social studies and science books. Children can form categories of useful spelling words (especially irregular ones) such as seasons, animals, words about human beings, various social studies and science areas, the sense of sight (color, size, condition, texture, pattern, motion), the sense of feel, and the sense of hearing (amplitude, timber, pitch, rhythm, duration, distortion).

Also see the filmstrip *Dictionary Skills,* and related materials, produced by International Film Bureau, Chicago (for grades three and four) which covers alphabetical order, dividing the dictionary into letter sections, guide words, syllables, accents, sound symbols, correct spellings, and the like.

8.4. Dictionary Delight.[15] (For intermediate through junior-high-school levels.) The idea of a dictionary is not new, dating back 2600 years ago when the Assyrians had one. There is quite a gap between the Assyrian dictionary and the controversial *Webster's Third* edition (considered to be so because it contains words believed to be substandard or slangy). There is one designed for the elementary grades, *Webster's New Elementary Dictionary.*

Given explanation, and some fun in making their own picture dictionaries, children may appreciate the tremendous amount of effort that has gone into the production of the published dictionaries in the classroom and library. The idea that *Webster's Third International Dictionary* was "born" in 1961 might be a focal or starting point. First of all, the scholars sorted out all the words in *Webster's Second* into 109 categories so specialized definition writers could work on certain categories. Five women spent two and a half years on this task. From this work, 350,000 entries were produced for *Webster's Third,* but the lexicographers had to write new definitions for some of these entries. Scholars selected and wrote 100,000 new entries, collected 4.5 million quotations to illustrate variants in word usage, and distributed them among the definition writers. In the subject of chemistry alone, the lexicographers gathered 250,000 quotations and took six and a half years to write the definitions.

We might add that the tome weighs 13.5 pounds and contains 450,000 entries on 2662 pages, and cost $3.5 million to produce!

Basic dictionary skills are as follows:

[15] Adapted from material distributed in the Tustin Elementary School District, Education Center, Tustin, Calif.

1. To locate words
2. To guide pronunciation
3. To see what words often do mean when used in various ways
4. To use the dictionary for acceptable spelling (at a particular time and place)
5. To comprehend derivations and to see how words may have changed their meanings

Here are two games that teachers can use to stimulate learning of some of the dictionary skills or for "dictionary readiness" (a term used by Downing & Sceats, 1974). The first, *Secret Message,* is a limbering-up exercise that provides practice in alphabetic sequencing in order to speed location skills. The *preceding* letter is used to decode the message. You may make up your own message. But in order to illustrate the procedure, the following is an example:

Xf xjmm hp up Nztufsz Dbwf cz pvstfmwft ofyu Tbuvsebz.
We will go to Mystery Cave by ourselves next Saturday.
Ep opu ufmm bozcpez. Nbsl.

Pupils may write their own secret messages.

The purpose of the second game, *Animal Trainer,* is to give children practice in using dictionary guide words. Ask the children to imagine that the guide-word boxes are animal cages. They need to figure out which of the three animal names to choose from would fit between the two guide words given. Have individual pupils come to the board and put the right animal in the right cage by printing its name inside the cage on the bottom line. You may vary the game by using groups of words other than animals. After you have had pupils demonstrate, then have them work in groups. For feedback, use cards and have pupils illustrate on the back with the correct animal. A question and answer might be added about the spelling pattern illustrated. Children can make a permanent game collection for a game table. They can add acetate protectors so that the user can trace over the words.

*allied* — *aloes*
antelope, alligator, armadillo

*courtly* — *crack*
coyote, crocodile, chimpanzee

*lived* — *locate*
lobster, louse, lamb

*dizzy* — *dolphin*
deer, dove, dog

*moonbeam* — *more*
mountain goat, moose, musk ox

*egg* — *elevation*
ermine, elk, elephant

8.5. Live Letters. (For preschool through intermediate grades.) In this active game, the teacher gives competing groups of children cards with a letter of the alphabet on each card. Five chairs (or more) are positioned to accommodate a five-letter word. When a leader calls a word, the vowel letters in that word rush out and try to arrange themselves with the help of another leader. The person who calls out the word writes it on the board and decides who the winning group was.

If a vowel appears more times than the group has cards for it, the child can appear first in the beginning part of the word and then in the last part. The consonants can be used in this game, too. (A child can handle more than one consonant by standing it up in a chair.) Words can be the children's own Powerful Words (words best liked or most feared). Or words might be seasonal or related to a content area, or used because of a spelling generalization, or other source.

Enactive way of knowing

8.6. Jump on It. (Hopscotch). (For preschool through intermediate grades.) Cratty (1971) relates a series of enactive games all basically using a large grid of letters that is placed on the floor. Young children can respond to the stimulus to spell certain words by physically jumping on the letter much in the way one plays hopscotch, or by throwing a bean bag on the letters. Thus, the basic equipment is a large grid of letters placed on the floor to hop upon and a board for writing and erasing words to be "jumped out."

Games can progress by—(1) simply writing one consonant on the board, erasing it, having the child say a word beginning with that sound, and then jumping on the letter that corresponds to that sound; (2) spelling out a word by jumping on the letters in it in sequence;[16] (3) making directions more subtle, e.g., jumping out words in a sentence, building a sentence, jumping out a word that means almost the same, or the opposite; (4) playing a variation of musical chairs. (5) Older children might be given a word and be invited to jump out its homonym. Such pairs as the following might be used:

*pane, pain*
*fare, fair*
*lane, lain*
*tale, tail*
*wait, weight*

[16] The chart would need to include vowels. Competition can be injected by having two or more grids and by children trying to see who can jump out the word first. Or have children use a stopwatch and try to beat their own time.

## If You Want to Learn More


AMERICAN BOOK COMPANY. *What's Happening to Our Language Today? A Handbook for Parents.* New York: Author, 1967. (Pamphlet.)

AMMON, R. I. A Practical Way to Teach Spelling. *Elementary English,* 1969, *46* (December), 1033–35. (ERIC Document Reproduction Service No. EJ 01 3 628)

Elaborates the idea of the child's own personal spelling box, that a child does not need to learn to spell every word on a predetermined list. Suggests children's words be taken from misspellings in their own writing. In other words, functional spelling is best taught in conjunction with a program of writing.

BARNETT, L. *The Treasure of Our Tongue.* New York: Knopf, 1964.

BLAKE, H. E., and EMANS, R. Some Spelling Facts. *Elementary English,* 1970, *47,* 241-49.

Contains a useful glossary.

CALIFORNIA STATE DEPARTMENT OF EDUCATION. *Bilingual–Bicultural Education and English as a Second-Language Education.* Sacramento, Calif.: Author, 1974.

CRATTY, B. J. *Active Learning: Games to Enhance Academic Abilities.* Englewood Cliffs, N.J.; Prentice-Hall, 1971.

Provides a variety of spelling games intended to aid children to translate letter shapes and combinations into the variety of sounds that they are likely to represent in the English language.

DOWNING, J., and SCEATS, J. Should School Dictionaries Be Banned? *Elementary English,* 1974, *51,* 601-3.

DUCKWORTH, E. The Language and Thought of Piaget and Some Comments on Learning to Spell. In M. L. King, R. Emans, and P. J. Cianciolo (Eds.), *The Language Arts in the Elementary School: A Forum for Focus.* Urbana, Ill.: NCTE, 1973.

Suggests that children learn to spell not by avoiding wrong spellings in a panic, but by actively seeking out every possible wrong spelling. When the children read, they *notice* the spellings of new words, "So that's the way they spell that!"

GREENE, H. A. *Developing Language Skills in the Elementary Schools.* Boston: Allyn & Bacon, 1971.

HANNA, P. R., and HANNA, J. S. *The Teaching of Spelling.* Boston: Houghton Mifflin, 1964.

HANNA, P. R.; HANNA, J. S.; HODGES, R. E.; and RUDORF, E. H. *Phoneme-Grapheme Correspondences as Cues to Spelling Improvement.* USOE Cooperative Research Project No. 1991. Washington, D.C.: U.S. Government Printing Office, 1966.

HANNA, P. R., HANNA, J. S., HODGES, R. E., and RUDORF, E. H. *Power to Spell, Teacher's Guide and Annotated Edition.* Boston: Houghton Mifflin, 1967.

HANNA, P. R., HODGES, R. E., and HANNA, J. S. *Spelling: Structure and Strategies.* Boston: Houghton Mifflin, 1971.

HODGES, R. E., and RUDORF, E. H. Searching Linguistics for Clues for the Teaching of Spelling. *Elementary English,* 1965, *42* (May), 527-33.

HUNTER, M. *Teach More Faster!* El Segundo, Calif.: TIP Publications, 1969.

JACKSON, G. L., and GUBER, A. M. The Way Out of the Spelling Labyrinth. *Elementary English,* 1972, *49* (1), 90-100.

Describes two schools of thought concerning spelling—the sight-minded method, and the phonic approach (where the child learns the "spelling of sounds" so that he can unlock new words). Advocates the spelling of sounds.

JOHNSON, H. W. Flow Chart for Spelling a Word Correctly. *Elementary English,* 1972, *49,* 416.

KEY, M. The English Spelling System and the Initial Teaching Alphabet. *Elementary School Journal,* 1969, *69,* 313-25.

LEFCOURT, A. Spelling and the Dictionary. *Elementary English,* 1972, *49* (8), 1228-32.

A large portion of this whole issue of *Elementary English* is focused on spelling, with articles on spelling consciousness, use of nonsense words to test generalization ability, relations to Black English pronunciation, and relations to reading.

MCCULLOUGH, C. M. *Handbook for Teaching the Language Arts.* Scranton, Pa.: Intext, 1969.

MONROE, M. Spelling—A Tool of Written Expression. In M. Monroe, I. Aaron, and A. Schiller (Eds.), *Spelling Our Language,* Book 1. Teacher's Edition. Glenview, Ill.: Scott, Foresman, 1969.

MONROE, M., AARON, I., SCHILLER, A. *Spelling Our Language.* Teacher's Edition. Glenview, Ill.: Scott, Foresman, 1969.

NEBRASKA CURRICULUM DEVELOPMENT CENTER. *A Curriculum for English.* Grade 7, Language and Its Written Uses. Units 77-79: Form Classes, The Dictionary, Phonology and Spelling. Lincoln: University of Nebraska Press, 1967.

PERSONKE, C., and YEE, A. H. *Comprehensive Spelling Instruction (Theory, Research, and Application).* Scranton, Pa.: Intext, 1971.

SMITH, E. B., GOODMAN, K. S., and MEREDITH, R. *Language and Thinking in the Elementary School.* New York: Holt, Rinehart and Winston, 1970.

Chapter 9

# New Approaches to Handwriting, Punctuation, & Other Conventions of Written Composition

This chapter contains information about the teaching of handwriting, punctuation, and other mechanics of composition. (These areas are often neglected in teacher education programs.) Some trends in teaching are new, growing out of educational research. Since some teachers find that discipline becomes their biggest problem during the teaching of these skills, I again offer suggestions from the field of educational psychology. Some how-to examples applied in the classroom enable you to tie in ideas you've learned elsewhere. Is one of the major factors of apparent misspelling actually illegible handwriting? Can punctuation be related as a system to pitch and intonation in speaking—rather than being treated entirely as a set of unrelated rules? How important is punctuation and a flawless formation of characters in a child's writing experience? These are some of the questions probed in this chapter.

## HOW IS HANDWRITING RELATED TO PROBLEM SOLVING?

**First steps**

Suppose you know that one of your challenges is to teach handwriting. Where do you go when it is time to learn about teaching it? The first thing to do is to find out what practices are expected in the district where you teach. The second step is to examine the handwriting textbook selected for pupils, its rationale and procedures. Third, actually work through one of the books yourself so that your own writing can serve as a consistent model. Fourth, examine specific teaching steps and practical advice, such as how to place the children at the board at "fight-proof" intervals (McCullough, 1969). Fifth, go beyond what is to what might be and examine the latest research on handwriting. Such an article is one by Furner (1970),[1] describing her study in detail.

[1] Other sources are W. Otto & D. W. Anderson (1969), and Freeman (1954). If you are interested in the history of writing, a delightful source is UNESCO (1965), *The Art of Writing.* If your problem is teaching left-handed writers, see W. Otto & R. A. McMenemy (1966) and W. N. Williams (1964). (There is no justification for demanding that left-handed writing look like right-handed writing as long as it is legible.)

ON DEVELOPMENTAL APPROACHES TO HANDWRITING

"Does neatness count?"

**A modern method**

First, Furner defined handwriting as a perceptual-motor learning. The child spends time developing accurate perceptions of the distinguishing aspects of letters while concept attainment serves as the basis for practice. In her work, Furner used multisensory techniques: observational, auditory, and kinesthetic: (1) Children looked at the teacher-model observing her movement, the formational act, and the finished product. (2) Children learned the vocabulary and described the process (hearing themselves say it). They used this speaking to help them to see likenesses and differences and to guide their motor practice. This specification gave children a definite way of planning and executing self-evaluation and self-correction.

**Problem solving**

Problem solving came into the experience even for first-grade beginners, who helped to identify a writing problem. New problems grew out of the ones just solved. An analogy was drawn to the act of learning to bat a ball: First, it is necessary to learn what to do and how to do it. The next step is practice with care so as not to get into any poor batting habits. Learning handwriting proceeds in a similar way. Showing efficient ways of placing paper and holding pencil, and illustrating seating posture and letter formation help avoid poor writing habits.

During each lesson the children actively participated in development of the problem task and in its solution. Handwriting became a definite intellectual method, rather than merely repetitive practice toward muscular control. The first problems concerned how to make lowercase circle letters, e.g. o, a; then lowercase straight-line letters, e.g. i, l; next, lowercase slant-line letters, e.g., w; lowercase tail letters, e.g., g, y; and finally lowercase hump letters, e.g., n, m.

**Language of instruction**

Auditory stimulation was a precise verbal description of the act. The teacher asked leading questions in order to get the children to observe sequential aspects of the task of forming a letter: the stroke, where to begin the stroke, the direction, size, and stopping point for the stroke. Take the example of lowercase manuscript a . First-grade children who showed readiness observed the number, order, direction, and size of strokes in this way:

The teacher asked, "How many strokes does it have? What kind of strokes are they?"

Upon watching the teacher form the letter, the children said, "There are two strokes. You made the circle first and then a straight line."

Next, the teacher asked the children to watch the formation of the circle to see where the stroke began. After discussion, the children decided:

"The circle begins a bit below the middle line, the light middle line. See where the top will be. It begins a bit to the right of that."

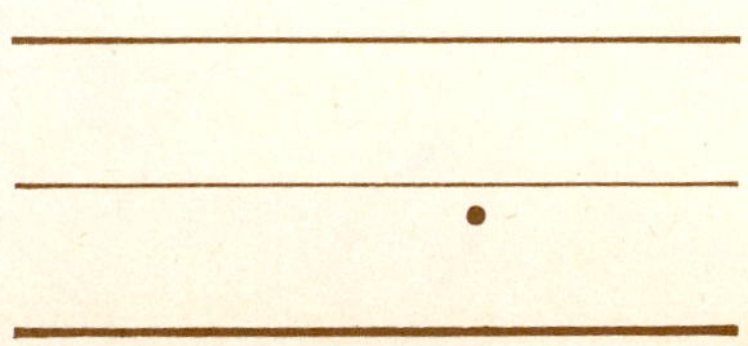

The teacher then asked the children to observe the formation of the circle again to see in what direction the stroke moved.

"It curves left." The instructor then introduced the term *counterclockwise*. "You make a complete circle in a counterclockwise direction."

Next followed the problem of size. To introduce this problem the teacher made a very large circle and then asked: "Is this correct?"

"No, make it smaller." Then the teacher, pretending to follow their directions, made the circle very small. At that moment the children realized the need to fully describe the size of the circle by where it touched. "Touch the center line and the baseline." When the teacher made the circle stopping on the baseline, the children saw the need to tell where to stop. "Keep going; stop where you started."

After the straight line was described in the same way, a child described the entire letter as the other children made it. This oral directing brought about the use of the description as a guide for motor practice. "Would you like to try it by yourself?" They would.

Children then wrote the letter independently, thinking (aloud if they liked) of the description, trying to improve each time. As the teacher and children described other letters in the circle group, the children noted any similarities and differences as compared with the letter a (in an attempt to seek transfer, e.g., a ).

At the end of a letter group, children verbalized any generalizations about form that were common to all the letters in the group. They did this in order to strengthen concept attainment for the class of letters. As soon as children attained concepts, they practiced with meaningful words, such as their names, colors for a book they made, signs, and ads.[2]

**Meaningful and unpressured tasks**

I have a couple of general suggestions: *begin* with meaningful words—something the child wants to say immediately so that there is a purpose of communication in the first lesson. Then children can go back and practice individual letters as they need them. Avoid any pressure at the beginning of writing to keep the letters in straight lines or to space them evenly. To refer to the cartoon at the beginning, does neatness count in this respect? No.

[2] Children may associate a pleasant feeling tone with writing if it is practiced to the accompaniment of music with a strong rhythm that they enjoy.

**9.1. I'm Thinking of a Letter.** (For preschool through primary grades.) The children in the Furner study played this game. One child described the sequence of formation of an unidentified letter while the others made the letter and attempted to tell which letter it was. This game encourages precise description during verbalization. In order to identify the letter, children had to rely on their perceptual image by either writing or thinking the movements described. Variations could include the common characteristics of, say, the round letters, or some other class of letter formation.

## SOME ADVICE

There are many "commandments" about handwriting. Some of them are conflicting. Each school district seems to have its own gospel. Here are some guidelines for which there is broad general agreement.

1. *Consistency.* Whenever children view the written form, attempt to have the features (letter formation, line width, style, size, spacing) consistent with instruction so that sight reinforces rather than interferes (negative transfer). This idea means that spelling books, handwriting texts, and basal readers need to display the same system.
2. *Fatigue level.* Avoid asking children to write functionally in class more than is appropriate for their motor development. Help individual children to finish stories or notes when handwriting begins to get burdensome. Avoid the use of copywork to keep them busy. This kind of writing, which encourages children to "get finished," easily deteriorates. The practice defeats the perceptual and motor training discussed earlier. Consider how long and how much a child can write comfortably without reaching the point of diminishing return.
3. *Surface.* Avoid writing in the air; the most effective kinesthetic experience is on a surface. (Save skywriting for pilots.)
4. *Relaxation.* Avoid hurry at the beginning; handwriting takes time and absence of tension.
5. *Reality.* Avoid drill on abstract forms (e.g., push-pulls, ovals). Children learn to write by writing.
6. *Purpose.* Remember that handwriting, like spelling, has a personal purpose and a social purpose. Instruction is concerned with the social purpose of communicating publicly.
7. *Readiness.* Watch for readiness levels of children by noting the large drawing and painting of beginners, and the degree of assurance or readiness of third-grade children whom you think are ready to switch

to cursive writing.[3] Readiness for either manuscript or cursive writing is dependent on neuromuscular development, eye–hand coordination, visual discrimination, and recognition of the usefulness of writing.

File keeping

8. *Evaluation.* Keep a file for each child as a motivational (competence) technique. Have each child compare several papers, collected over a period of time, with a present sample. Legibility is the most important quality. This can be the same file in which the child keeps imaginative and expositional writing. Again children can be enlisted as creative problem-solvers to work on their own challenges.

Self-diagnosis of error

Once children have mastered the basic letter forms, time is most efficiently used by helping children to diagnose and remedy their own errors (individualize). There are mainly eight letters often written illegibly that account for apparent spelling mistakes in cursive writing; these are: *r, n, e, a, d, o, t,* and capital *I*.[4] Messy papers can be readable and may reflect progress toward legibility. That is, awkward erasures may result from the child's initial attempts to make a letter come closer to his perceptual model. Teachers need to examine what effort toward legibility may lie behind a messy paper. (Recall the cartoon at the beginning of this chapter.) Many publishing companies have charts for diagnosing strengths or faults in handwriting.[5] Goals for skills include these:

[3] The idea of starting with manuscript is that the forms are simpler for the child to make, being based on the circle and the straight line. Moreover, the similarity to print in books supports beginning reading. Research shows no advantage for cursive writing from a utilitarian and efficiency standpoint (Otto & Anderson, 1969). Maybe one day the community will be sufficiently educated in attitude to that it is willing to forgo the aesthetic embellishment of having children switch to cursive, or at least willing to offer them the option.

[4] See Quant (1946) for cursive difficulties.

[5] For a book for children on self-instructed typing see Fry (1971).

USING A TRANSPARENT OVERLAY WITH MODELS OF LETTERS TO CHECK ONE'S OWN

- Correct letter formation
- Appropriate spacing between letters and words
- Uniform slant
- Satisfactory alignment
- Appropriate size of letters

Goals

A transparent overlay showing the correct formation of letters is a self-evaluative device a child can use as he compares his letters with a model.

The following are some sample learner objectives:

Sample learner objectives

- Given a pattern of the alphabet, the child demonstrates ability to form each letter by copying the pattern. (Tracing letters)
- The child can distinguish between the capital and lowercase form for a letter. (Discriminating capital and lowercase letters)

---

## PUNCTUATION AND MECHANICS OF WRITTEN COMPOSITION

Although there is general agreement among dictionary guides, there has rarely if ever been total agreement among authorities or among the public on any single element of the various conventions of written composition. These conventions include punctuation and capitalization, business letter form, and appearance of margins and headings. The reason for these surface features is that they facilitate communication. Getting this idea across to children is not easy.

Watching the teacher

The conventions first become apparent to children when they watch while you are taking dictation from them. Upon looking over your shoulder, the children see you putting in periods, commas, question marks, exclamation points, and making capital letters. Children may inquire about their meaning or may begin to model their own first written efforts on your example. Thus the "ally" of modeling helps in getting the child to understand what conventions are and why they are used.

Intonation and juncture

Also of help in teaching concepts about punctuation are intonation and juncture (or pause—the absence of sound) in oral communication. So much meaning can be conveyed by manipulating tone, pitch, and pause that children are cheated if they don't get a chance to see the relationship of these aspects of language to punctuation. See the following activity for ways to develop these concepts.

**9.2. Punctuation Traffic Signals.** As children listen to contrasting readings of a paragraph, the teacher can draw an analogy about punctuation marks. He can refer to them as traffic signals along the way designed to show readers how the author wishes them to proceed when a voice is not there to guide. Or, with older children you might use the term *sounds of silence* (Cecil, 1972). You could explain the signals as follows:

- Capital letters signal the beginning of a sentence or thought with subject and predicate.
- Periods, question marks, or exclamation points signal the ends of sentences. Sentences can be spotted by intonation patterns—drops for periods, raises for question marks (yes–no questions), and intensity for exclamation points. We pause briefly between the last word of one sentence and the first word of the next.
- Commas are partial stops, suggestions that the reader slow his pace slightly.

You might use the following sample paragraph:

> What do you think about this? Within a billion years human beings may be able to change life itself and make themselves immortal. They will take on the task of repairing planet Earth from the ravages of earlier mortals—us. They will make the killer whale their partner in tending the life forms in a civilization beneath the ocean waves. This whale already has rudimentary fingers which will be further developed by genetic modification.

The paragraph could be read one way with awe and interest and another way with scorn and disbelief. Periods, question marks, and accompanying pauses could also be moved around, e.g., "What do you think about this within a billion years?" "The life forms in a civilization beneath the ocean waves this whale already has." "Which will be further developed by genetic modification?"

## Intonation

**A scheme for intonation**

Intonation describes the changes in pitch, stress, and juncture. Our patterns are unique to English; other languages have their own. *Pitch,* the highness or lowness of sound, is usually thought of by linguists in four levels:

4 Very high
3 High

[6] Based on an article by Jacques Cousteau in *PSA Magazine,* February 1974, pp. 57-59.

2 Normal
1 Low

One of the most common patterns is the 2–3–1 pattern of the declarative sentence followed by a period.

```
     3
2
          1
Jim is an astronaut.
```

One common kind of question also has the 2–3–1 pattern. This kind usually begins with a question marker, such as *what, who, where,* or *how.*

```
    3
2
         1
Where are you?
```

Questions anticipating a yes or no answer usually end with a rising pitch.

```
          3
2
Are you sure?
```

Suggested activity

Secure a sample of a few foreign languages on tape. After playing them for older children, the chances are that they will be able to recognize Spanish, German, or Japanese (without knowing a word of the language) simply by their unique patterns of pitch and stress. Contrast with the robot talk one hears on science fiction TV programs with its absence of pitch, stress, and intonation. Then the students can generalize about what is there, in the earlier case, and lacking in the case of the robot talk.

Role playing can enter at this point to help children discover the 2–3–1 falling pattern of information questions (*Where are you going?*) and the rising pattern of yes/no questions (*Are you sure?*). As children roleplay various slang expressions, the intonation contours are particularly apparent.

Oh, yeah? (to express surprise)
Oh, yeah! (to express approval)
Oh, yeah. (to express doubt)

### Juncture

Pause (or juncture) describes the stops or breaks between sounds, words, and word groups. Comedians are masters at using this aspect of language.

Suggested activity

Tape some comic examples and suggest that children listen for others. (A spliced tape of examples could be made.) In an earlier chapter the old example was mentioned: *What's that in the road ahead?* versus *What's that in the road, a head?*

After such experiences the teacher is ready to ask the children the following questions: "If the letters of our alphabet stand for the sounds of English, how are these long pauses, medium pauses, and short pauses shown in our written language?" and "How are our intonation patterns shown?" (Such questions search for a generalization about parallels in symbolism.)

Show sentences such as these:

Who is calling me, Jane?
Who is calling me Jane?

I smell something burning, John.
I smell something burning John.

In each case, the writer would insert a comma where his/her voice would normally pause on a level 2 pitch. If the voice goes down to a level 2 pitch before the pause, either a period or a question mark would be the appropriate symbol. If the sentence begins with a *wh* question or with *how,* the punctuation at the end is a question mark. After more examples, the teacher can help the children see that a statement with a high, level-4 pitch somewhere in its intonation pattern usually ends with an exclamation point. (See examples in Activity 9.7, What Does It Mean.)

For practice, tape a selection in your natural voice and let the students (with dittoed copy of the selection in hand) insert the punctuation marks that they think your voice has expressed. Then replay the tape and discuss why the children think certain punctuation fitted your vocal rendition, and differences of opinion. You can replay parts where there is disagreement. The activity can then be carried out in partner pairs (or in small groups). Each child has a copy of a composition (ideally, one the students have written themselves). One student reads aloud while the other(s) inserts punctuation in a copy that has no punctuation. Then the writers can see if the punctuation corresponds to what they wanted to say and how they wanted to say it. Such a controlled inductive teaching strategy can be used to help children attain language concepts and may help them with punctuation. (See American Book [1967] for more information on juncture.)

## Other Suggested Activities

9.3. Punctuation with Cards and Rhythm Instruments. You can use rhythm instruments to punctuate oral language. Or give each child a set of punctuation cards and play a game of "show me" for oral and written punctuating. You may recall Victor Borge's act where he "speaks" punctuation, making sounds for commas, periods, and so on as he read a poem.

Certain conventions of punctuation, however, are apparently unrelated to intonation and simply require memorization and practice to reinforce patterns. You can simply say it is like a game with invented rules. Whoever heard of a game without rules? But people make them and people can change them. In fact, what people did in the beginning was to draw lines to segment their language. (See Activity 9.4.)

9.4. Punctuating Greek Monuments. (For intermediate through junior-high-school levels.) You might then give older children a humorous selection or a poem typed in all capital letters (instead of all small letters) and with slashes to separate the lines of poetry, or to indicate where periods would be. Leave no spaces between the words. Tell them this is how it might look if the selection were printed on a Greek pillar or monument of the first century BC. Invite them to fix it as we would today, e.g., rewrite separating the words, inserting punctuation, and using capitals only when needed. For example:

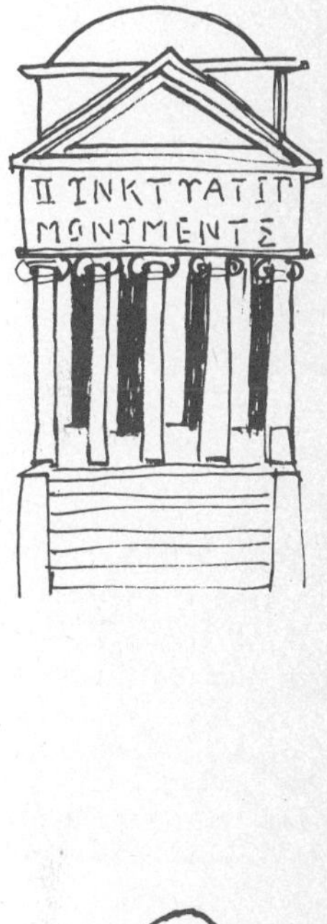

ITSUREISAPRETTYNIGHTSAIDTHEMOUSE/BUTNOONE

ANSWEREDHER/THEGRASSWHISPEREDTOITSELF/THETREES

TALKEDBEHINDHERBACKANDTHEMOONGAVEALLITS

ATTENTIONTOAWISPYCLOUDPASSINGBY

Using the grammatical or structural pattern of the example, children can create their own monument sentences to punctuate. (Idea adapted from Hanna, Hanna, Hodges and Rudorf, 1967, p. 107.)

9.5. Nonstop Reading. (For preschool through intermediate grades.) Read a paragraph without stopping for any punctuation (if you can hold your breath that long). This will also help demonstrate to children that putting in punctuation marks is the way to better understanding.

9.6. Hopping on Punctuation. (For preschool through primary grades.) If children are in the enactive stage, get them to act out punctuation, i.e., to *be* punctuation. Put the punctuation marks on a grid on the floor in hopscotch fashion and have the children jump on them at appropriate stimulus points, for example, "Are you here?" would signal that the question-mark square is to be jumped on.

9.7. What Does It Mean? (For intermediate grades.) Older children will appreciate how confusion is avoided by correct punctuation. (Have children try to find newspaper headlines that are *ambiguous,* because they show no punctuation.) For example,

Wow, great lakes!
Wow, Great Lakes!

Dont! Stop!
Don't stop.

He left us happily.
He left us, happily(!)

See the earlier section on Juncture for other examples.

9.8. Business Letter Collections. (For intermediate grades.) Asking children to bring in a collection of business letters and then inductively comparing the forms in class is one way to begin to get across the conventions of business letter writing. See together what changes are emerging and agree upon conventions. Allow the children to participate in decisions about conventions used in the class. Is there an inside address? How is the person addressed and what comes after the greeting? Are paragraphs indented? How many find a comma after the complimentary close? Pupils infer their own rules for the conventions.

9.9. Punctuating Your Own Dictation. (For preschool through intermediate grades.) Invite the child to compose for himself by speaking into a tape recorder (or use conversation or class discussion). Then ask him to replay a small bit at a time and write it down as he listens. Aides, partners, and the teacher can help the child segment and punctuate his own speech. In light of any communication troubles, children can next make revisions.

9.10. Class Proofreader's Manual. (For junior high.) Older children might participate in making their own writer's guide or proofreader's manual with rules they need and a few symbols.

1. ∧ means something is to be inserted.
2. lc means lower case.
3. ℊ means omit (or simply use a line drawn through the word)
4. ¶ means begin a new paragraph.
5. ≡ means Capital letter.
6. ⊙ means insert period.

One chapter of this class book can be on punctuation.

**9.11. Historical Approach to Punctuation.** Historical interest may be stimulated in some classes when it is time to think about the apostrophe in possessives. Children might ask, "Why is there an apostrophe in belonging-words, like in 'the dog's ear'? You just taught us to use apostrophes when letters are left out. But there're no letters left out in 'the dog's ear.' "

And you might answer: "But some scholars think that there *used* to be a letter there when people spoke Old English. The apostrophe was put in as the letter came to be left out. *Dog's ear* used to be pronounced something like *dogges ear,* with a nonsignificant /e/ sound where we now have an apostrophe" (Seymour, 1968).[7]

These little historical bits, especially when presented in the mode and with the magic of the storyteller, are motivating to children and help them to remember seemingly arbitrary conventions. They are not given as additional content of English to be mastered.

## Some Sample Learner Objectives

The following are some sample learner objectives for the area of punctuation.

- Given the reading of a story printed on the board with no punctuation or capitalization, the child will follow along and indicate places where pauses are needed and punctuation and capitalization should be inserted. (Proofreading for punctuation and capitalization)
- Given the class's cooperative development and publishing of their own manual for proofreading, a child completes a proofreading assignment uncovering most of the errors of special focus. (Proofreading)
- Given a kindergarten or first-grade child as a partner, the older child transcribes and punctuates a narrative dictated by the partner, and then reads it back. He/she discusses what the author wanted to say and adds the partner's name as author, his or her own name as transcriber. Then the author rereads the story. (Socialized transcribing)

## Conclusions

Perhaps the best learning comes during the group writing conference (mentioned in Chapter 7, on imaginative writing). Or the most transferable learning may come when pupils read their compositions aloud or others try to read them. Then they can see how punctuation helps.

[7] According to Hanna et al. (1966) the history of our language indicates that years ago people showed possession by adding in the word *his.* For instance, the phrase *Tom's brother* would have been stated as *Tom his brother.*

But often punctuation is taught in drills that are isolated from the expression of thought that such skills are supposed to promote. Some children may be able to learn specific skills in isolation (e.g., how to form a manuscript a, how to spell *dog's,* and how to indicate a paragraph). But too frequently the gap between isolated skills and written thought is left unbridged. The assumption is that transfer somehow occurs automatically; it doesn't.

### Psychological Approaches to Teaching Mechanics

Teaching methods

What I am going to illustrate next is applicable in the teaching of a group composed of either majority or minority culture members. But perhaps the ideas are especially useful for the impoverished and the less motivated groups. Here is an illustrative drama.

TEACHER: But, you didn't put a period at the end. And where is the capital? You've got three sentences here run together!

CHILD: But I have to finish my picture and I put all the other periods in.

TEACHER: You'll put them *all* in. I'm tired of the sloppy work you always try to turn in. If you don't put them in, I'll let someone else lead the lunch line tomorrow. You should be ashamed of this messy paper!

Muttering, the child takes back the paper and gets out a pencil. After the child leaves for home, the teacher discovers that the uncapitalized letters remain. The teacher sighs, exhausted, thinking that most of the children resist writing correctly, and never do anything unless they are reminded again and again, no matter how much complaint and threat there is.

Not a unique drama. Many children forget, and many resist the mechanics of writing. They begin to find compelling reasons why they cannot do the most simple of writing tasks.

Objectivity and cause-effect

Balanced against this scene is the classroom of the teacher down the hall who used to nag and predict dire consequences. But now, this teacher simply tells the result of the desired action, e.g., "When your proofreading is complete, your work will be in line for display; and that is the time you get to *paint* the illustration for it." Reasonable facts of life, short statements of expectations, substituted for threats and commands reduce resentment and gain children's cooperation.

This teacher avoids three common mistakes found in some teaching behavior:

1. Reciting past errors or misdeeds: "I'm tired of the sloppy work you always turn in."
2. Listing future threats: "I'll let someone else lead the lunch line tomorrow."
3. Blaming and shaming: "You ought to be ashamed of this messy paper!"

Shame, threats, and angry commands undermine the pupil's self-esteem (self-competence). The child feels personally attacked and even more obliged to resist.

Besides stating the factual result of the desired action, the successful teacher uses other techniques, too. He gives the children some choice or autonomy. Children do not have to display and correct every paper. They can choose the ones that are most motivating for them. Or they have a choice, at least in the order and duration of the proofreading. "Which will you concentrate on today—capitals and periods, or spelling?"

This more successful teacher also tries a little of those precious ingredients—humor and playful fantasy for pleasant feeling tone. For example, at the start of the period children might notice this sign displayed:

Use of pleasant feeling tone

WANTED!

Neat, correct papers for bulletin board.
Writers must have:

- The persistence of an archaeologist to ferret out mistakes.
- The patience of a great lion trainer in making a neat copy.
- The responsibility of an astronaut to get it done on time.

Applicants please place their completed papers in the treasure chest on the counter.

Putting such requests in writing and asking for cooperation in solution tends to make requests clearer and arouses less resentment.

Here is another example:

GOOD MORNING!

Today you do *not* have to do the following things to your written papers:

1. You do not have to manufacture the paper (only the spelling needs to be checked).
2. You do not have to manufacture the ink (only reread softly to yourself to see if you left any words out).

3. You do not have to chop down a tree and make the pencil (just check the punctuation).

Love,
Mr. Williams, teacher, class 4B

Respect for the child

The common denominator is the teacher's respect for and acceptance of the child as a person. Cooperation in working with conventions of writing is largely a matter of willingness teachers can nurture into an attitude and value. The child has to feel right about these responsibilities before there is much genuine, lasting cooperation and sense of responsibility. This illustration goes back to those "allies" of self-competence and personal acceptance. If we use these approaches, children will resist less. That is about what we can expect—less resistance, not full conformity.[8]

The following list from Golub et al. (1971) is made up of rules accounting for an average of 80 percent of the punctuation needs in elementary school.

*Survey of Rules of Punctuation Taught in Elementary School*

1. A period is used to mark the end of a complete sentence which is neither mandatory, interrogatory, nor exclamatory.
2. The colon is used after several words used as the salutation of a business letter.
3. A comma should be used after the complimentary close of a business letter.
4. The apostrophe is used in forming the possessive case of singular nouns.
5. The apostrophe is used to indicate the omission of a letter from the interior of a contraction.
6. The comma is always used before the abbreviation "etc." when the latter is in the interior of a sentence.
7. A comma is used to separate independent clauses joined by "and" if there is a change of subject.
8. The interrogation point is used at the end of a whole sentence used as a question.
9. The comma is used to set off a dependent "if" clause preceding the main clause.
10. The comma is used to separate nouns in series when they are not connected by a conjunction.

[8] Applegate (1963) found that the more original the writer, the more fierce the resistance to working with conventions.

11. A direct quotation at the end of a sentence may be separated from its preceding introductory material by a comma.
12. Quotation marks are used before and after a direct quotation at the end of the sentence.
13. The period is placed inside the quotation marks at the end of directly quoted discourse.
14. A period is used to separate dollars and cents.
15. A comma should be used after the salutation of an informal letter.
16. A comma is used after the last word of a series of words, phrases, or clauses, or letters not connected by a conjunction.
17. The semicolon may be used between two coordinate clauses which are not connected by a conjunction.
18. A colon is placed after a single word used as the salutation of a business letter.
19. Quotation marks may be used to enclose the titles of books.
20. A period should be placed inside quotation marks. (This variant covers situations not involving quoted conversation.)
21. A period is used after the abbreviations "Mr." and "Mrs."
22. A comma should be used after the complimentary close of an informal letter.
23. Parentheses may be used to enclose sums of money in business letters.
24. The comma is used to separate prepositional phrases in series when they are not connected by a conjunction.
25. A comma may be used to separate any other elements which might otherwise be improperly joined in reading.
26. Commas are used to set off a noun in apposition in the interior of a sentence.
27. A comma is used to set off a noun in apposition at the end of a sentence, title, or quotation.
28. The colon may be used before enumerations.
29. A comma is used to separate independent clauses joined by "but" or "only" if there is a change of subject.
30. The comma is used to set off certain introductory phrases [Golub et al., 1971, pp. 16–73]

**The need for grouping and systematizing**

The point made by this long, formidable list is that content needs to be grouped, systematized, and redirected so that *less is taught better*. In other words, avoid attempting to introduce the thousands of available isolated facts about usage, terminology, and mechanics (Golub et al., 1971). More emphasis is to be placed on the production and use of discourse and less upon its correctness. Successful writers range from almost complete disuse of punctuation to the use of so much that their sentences are broken into many little fragments. Research indicates that the successful adult writer worries about organization, about having something to say, about clarity, purpose, or directness, and about being to the point. The writer rated as poor worries about none of these. Instead he may worry about spelling, vocabulary, handwriting, and other mechanical features. Usually he is less able to recognize effective writing in others (Barch & Wright, 1957).

If children have something to say, let them say it. The best way to master the skills is to be given many opportunities to use them in writing that fulfills the desire to communicate.

## SUMMARY AND CONCLUSIONS

Emphasis on beautiful handwriting and perfect punctuation in the first draft is being lessened in schools today. The concern is more with letting the child express thoughts through written language. The emphasis is on "Write it now; correct it for mechanics later."

A drama of conventions

Think of writing as being like a blind person putting on a play for an unseen audience. But props and assistance are available. For example, *punctuation* represents the play's director. This director takes care of the timing and moves the words, word parts, and their surface features in the sentences around like actors—that is, a slight pause for a hyphen, a longer one for a comma, and yet a longer one for a period or semicolon, and occasionally a capital letter. This director does all this manipulation in order to prevent audience misinterpretation.

Then there is all the scenery of polite convention and arbitrary decision. Style of *handwriting,* or style of printer's type, and usage might be represented by the decision to play the work in the formal manner of the Elizabethan theatre or in the elaborate manner of the 19th century (cursive writing), the regional theatre manner (colloquial usage), or to employ the *bare-bones* stripping of the set as in some modern theatre representations (similar to the appearance of manuscript writing and telegrams).

And *grammar* might represent the whole underlying nature of what theatre was and is all about—a description of it from its history to its present function in our lives. The basic parts of sentences and word classes as we have known them can be taken into account in this analogy. Subjects and nouns can represent the actors. Predicates and verbs can represent their action. Adverbs can elaborate this action and gesture. Adjectives can describe the actor's appearance, dress, and scenery. Pronouns can wait as stand-ins ready to substitute for overworked nouns. And function words can glue the various phrases of the play action together.

In any case, all these surface features of composition need to be included in the language arts program with selective care. Then, just those items are stressed that seem to advance understanding, effectiveness, and appropriateness in the drama of your classroom program in composition.

The following are some expository writing activities that call for publication. Therefore children will have a natural need to attend to the mechanics of spelling, handwriting, and punctuation in order to communicate.

## ADDITIONAL ACTIVITIES FOR EXPOSITORY WRITING

9.12. Greeting Cards. (For preschool through intermediate grades.) Have groups in the classroom assigned to compose cards to be given to each child in the class on his or her birthday or in the event of illness.

9.13. Reports of Happenings. (For preschool through intermediate grades.) When children are writing reports of happenings for a class newsletter or newspaper they can consider these specifics: (1) who was involved, (2) what happened, (3) when it happened, (4) the conditions under which it happened, (5) where it happened.

9.14. Pen Pal. (For intermediate grades.) Have the children write a letter describing themselves and the clothing they will wear so that there will be no chance they will be unrecognized should their pen pals meet them at the airport. This assumes that the pen pal has never seen this correspondent before. Or the two might want to exchange letters about their burning interests, such as a collection of stamps or rocks.

Note the following example, a letter written by a child in the fourth grade.[9]

[9] Thanks to David Hill, a student at the University of California, Irvine, who collected this example from a neighbor.

Dear Pen Pall,
I have a Tool and engine-part collection.
I have collected Them For eight years.
My Favorite Thing in my collection
are Parts From airplanes given To Me by My
Friend who owns an airporT.
For seaplanes.

Sincerely,
Paul

THE END

The following sources supply names of children who wish to exchange letters:

Executive Secretary
International Friendship League
40 Mount Vernon Street
Boston, Massachusetts
(Letter exchange entirely in English)

Swedish Central Committee for International Exchange Between Schools
Skolgränd 2
Stockholm SV, Sweden

School Affiliation Service
American Friends Service Committee
160 North Fifteenth Street
Philadelphia, Pennsylvania

The Canadian Education Association
151 Bloor Street West
Toronto 5, Ontario, Canada

9.15. Adopting Forgotten Mental Patients. (For intermediate grades.) The Forgotten Patient Project, a well-organized program of the Indiana Mental Health Association, began with one woman's small act of thoughtfulness. Programs have been started in some other states. For information on these programs and on where children may send letters to patients, contact the association, 1433 North Meridian Street, Indianapolis, Indiana 46202.

9.16. Historical Perspective. If resources are available, take older children to a library. Look at original drafts of manuscripts written by famous people. Note the repeated revisions. For example, the beginning paragraph to *Gone With the Wind* was rewritten over 50 times. Franklin Roosevelt is reported to have rewritten one fireside chat over 20 times. (How realistic is it to expect a child to turn in a perfect paper the first time?)

## If You Want to Learn More

AMERICAN BOOK COMPANY. *What's Happening to Our Language Today? A Handbook for Parents.* New York: Author, 1967.

Linguists usually refer to four kinds of juncture divided into two categories: internal juncture and terminal or end juncture. Internal juncture (+) refers to that very slight slowing of pace between words and between parts of words. For example, it shows the difference between: *it* + *sins* and *its* + *in*. The second major category, terminal juncture, is closely related to the pitch pattern in a sentence. The "stops" increase and are represented with a single bar |, double bar ||, and with two lines that cross #. In a broad sense, single-bar juncture is a slightly longer stop than plus juncture between words and corresponds to a comma. Double-cross juncture corresponds to a period or a semicolon. For example:

No, | you cannot go to the moon #

Double-cross juncture also occurs after a question with the 2-3-1 pitch pattern:

Where is my oxygen mask #

But, in discourse, questions with a rising pitch usually only show double-bar juncture:

Don't you know ||

APPLEGATE, M. *Easy in English.* New York: Harper & Row, 1963. (Out of print)

ASKEV, E., OTTO, W., and ASKEV, W. A Decade of Research in Handwriting. *The Education Digest,* 1971, *36,* 43-46.

Conclusions: (1) simplification of letter forms would encourage more legible writing from adults and more effective learning; (2) tracing was the easiest task for children, but was third preference of teachers (who first of all preferred copying); (3) it is more important for the child to have a clear concept of his or her own handwriting than to drill on letter formation; (4) posture was the most important factor affecting slant of letters; (5) improvement was shown by using diagnostic tests as an individual approach. The authors concluded that progress in improved instruction (neither rapid nor dramatic) was being made.

BARCH, A. M., and WRIGHT, R. L. The Background and Self-picture of Good and Poor Writers. *Journal of Communication,* 1957, *7,* 192-93.

CECIL, L. Students Learn Punctuation as Symbols of the Sounds of Silence in Tape-Recorded Language Study. *California English Journal,* 1972, *8* (3), 39-43.

ENSTROM, E. A. The Left-Handed Child. In H. D. Funk & DeWayne Triplett (Eds.), *Language Arts in the Elementary School.* Philadelphia: Lippincott, 1972.

FREEMAN, F. N. *Teaching Handwriting: What Research Says to the Teacher.* Washington, D.C.: NEA, 1954.

FRY, E. *Typing Course for Children.* Highland Park, N.J.: Dreier Educational Systems, 1971. (For grades 3-6)

FURNER, B. A. An Analysis of the Effectiveness of a Program of Instruction Emphasizing the Perceptual-Motor Nature of Learning in Handwriting. *Elementary English,* 1970, *47* (January), 61-69. (ERIC Document Reproduction Source No. EJ 015 233)

GOLUB, L. S., et al. *Present and Proposed Needs, Objectives, and Components of a Language Learning Program.* Madison: Wisconsin Research and Development Center for Cognitive Learning, 1971.

GREENE, H. A., and PETTY, W. T. *Developing Language Skills in the Elementary Schools.* Boston: Allyn & Bacon, 1971.

HANNA, P. R., HANNA, J. S., HODGES, R. E., and RUDORF, E. H. *Phoneme–Grapheme Correspondences as Cues to Spelling Improvement.* USOE Cooperative Research Project No. 1991, OE-32008: Washington, D.C.: U.S. Government Printing Office, 1966.

HANNA, P. R., HANNA, J. S., HODGES, R. E., and RUDORF, E. H. *Power to Spell,* Book 6. Boston: Houghton Mifflin, 1967.

HORN, T. D. *Research on Handwriting and Spelling.* A Research Bulletin Prepared by a Committee of the National Conference on Research in English (NCRE). Urbana, Ill.: NCTE, 1966.

LEWIS, H. P., and LEWIS, E. R. Written Language Performance of Sixth Grade Children of Low Socio-economic Status from Bilingual and Monolingual Backgrounds. *Journal of Experimental Education,* 1965, *3,* 327-42.

McCULLOUGH, C. M. *Handbook for Teaching the Language Arts.* Scranton, Pa.: Intext, 1969.

OTTO, W., and ANDERSON, D. W. Handwriting. In R. L. Ebel (Ed.), *Encyclopedia of Educational Research.* (4th ed.) London: Macmillan, 1969.

OTTO, W., and MCMENEMY, R. A. *Corrective and Remedial Teaching.* Boston: Houghton Mifflin, 1966.

QUANT, L. Factors Affecting the Legibility of Handwriting. *Journal of Experimental Education,* 1946, *14,* 297-316.

SEYMOUR, D. Z. Make Your Language Lessons Interesting. *Elementary English,* 1968, *45,* 41-43.

UNESCO (United Nations Educational, Scientific, and Cultural Organization). *The Art of Writing.* Paris, France: Author, 1965.

WIESE, K. *You Can Write Chinese.* New York: Viking, 1973. (Paperback)

A book for children. Bold brushstrokes show some simple Chinese characters while drawings show their origins—an association of ideas and pictures. (Caldecott Honor Book) (Ages 7 and up)

WILLIAMS, W. N. What Do You Know About "Lefties"? *Grade Teacher,* 1964, *81,* 44-45.

# Chapter 10 Grammar & Usage

## Contemporary Developments & Controversy

This chapter gives you a window to new trends and controversy about grammar and usage—two different concepts. The intent is to help you work toward a point of view. I will share some of my opinions with you and how I arrived at them. The sections present recent attitudes and contributions from linguistics and how to apply them in the classroom. What are the most currently referred to English grammars? What is usage? Should instructors "hammer in the grammar"? These are some of the questions treated.

## WHAT IS GRAMMAR? (THREE KINDS)

*This the of rest of life your day first is the*

If you find that each word above has a meaning, but that the words as they stand fail to give you an idea, try changing them around.

*This is the first day of the rest of your life.*

Now you not only have meaningful words, but you also have meaningful relationships. *Grammar* is that part of the study of language dealing not only with forms and structures of words (morphology), but also with their customary arrangement in phrases and sentences. The relationships among words in a language are called its grammar (Lodge & Trett, 1968). Grammar is a theory of how language works.

**Three ways of looking at grammar**

There are three generally used ways of looking at grammar. Although not completely antagonistic (some of the elements and terms are similar), they vary greatly. The emphasis of each is different. These grammars are *traditional* (old school or formal), *structural linguistic* (a product of descriptive linguistics), and *transformational-generative* (a more-recent product of linguistics). All have made contributions to our understanding of how language works. And the discoveries through linguistics are by no means finished. A continuing problem for English teachers has been a confusion of these major theories.

**What traditional grammar was supposed to do**

But whether or not any grammar can help elementary-school children (in regard to the usual goals set for it) is another matter. This is a question that has been researched in this country, with apparent repeated failure, for over 70 years. For example, traditional grammar was believed to do the following:

- Help children become more effective language users. (It won't.)
- Influence children to reduce errors in usage and speak in socially preferred ways. (It usually doesn't.)
- Provide children with knowledge and terminology so that they will understand how language works on how to revise a composition. (There is little research to date, but the question is this: How much of that knowledge has a functional use in the elementary school?)

ON GRAMMATICAL TERMINOLOGY AND USAGE

Although children have learned to write effectively while being taught grammar, they have probably learned in spite of it rather than because of it. Since grammars are abstract constructs designed to explain how language works, students below high school age (and many high school students) have difficulty understanding these abstractions.

If grammar is taught in school, attention is better placed on concrete, manipulative experiences rather than on labels. For example, completing a sentence—"Wild elephants . . ." is more helpful for concept attainment than is naming the part to be added a *verb phrase* or a *predicate*. Children will attain the concept of "nounness" more quickly by finding and listing words that they can use after "The ________ . . ." than they will by trying to memorize labels and abstract definitions. Concept attainment comes faster when children hunt for slot substitutes such as *rocker* or *throne* for the stimulus word, *chair* (rather than identifying these as *nouns*). Next, examine three types of grammar in more detail.

### Traditional School Grammar

Traditional School Grammar prescribes rules for how language is to be used. It classifies words into eight parts of speech. It emphasizes the subject-predicate relationship. The prescriptive rules of this grammar derived from Latin fail to describe adequately how English is used.

Inappropriate frameworks for English

What are some more specific reasons that traditional school grammar has been of so little use in helping children use language more effectively? One reason lies in its ignoring of the significant English language feature—word order. Of the most widely used modern languages, only English and Chinese are characterized by word-order (or distributive) grammar. Other languages possess grammars that show relationships through changes in the spelling of word-endings (inflection) to a great extent. These (including classical Greek and Latin) are called inflected grammars. Take these sentences as an illustration.

> The man killed the tigress.
> The tigress killed the man.

In the first sentence we grasp the subject and the object (who did what to whom) by means of *position* in the sentence. In *our* language, if you put the tigress in the man's place in the sentence, you have another story! In English language, word order shows meaning and word meaning frequently depends on word order. Word order is the strongest signal system in English. For example, it almost forces us to supply an appropriate missing word in the sentence—*Cats meow and dogs ________*.

A mistake that traditional school grammar made was the attempt to borrow inflected Latin grammar and to try to fit English to its mold.

(This is something like a six-year-old child trying to get into old baby shoes.) One of the main difficulties is that the intended model, Latin, depends heavily on word endings for sense in relationships. Modern English, however, is no longer primarily a word-ending language, but is now positional. Any word ending forms still used are remnants. In a language like Latin or Anglo Saxon you could put the man and the tigress almost anywhere in a sentence and the inflected endings on the words would help you grasp the sense. To repeat, we see the essential relationships in the English sentence (who does what) by means of the position of the words—the order. Other words in our grammar must also be positioned, e.g., *a fierce tigress* rather than *a tigress fierce.* Finally, take these examples:

> The *pack* of cards is new.
> I want you to *pack* your trunk.
> He rode the *pack*-horse.
> *Pack* the ice around the bottle.

The dictionary (or lexical) meaning of *pack* is clear only if you know the grammatical meaning, only if you know its *position* in a particular sentence.

Vestiges of inflection

Vestiges of word endings in English left from a grammatical system we no longer have are exemplified by changes in the forms of these nouns—*tiger, tigers;* verbs—*kill, kills, killed, killing* (addition of suffixes); pronouns—*he, his, him;* and adjectives and adverbs—*good, better, best;* and *bad, worse, worst* (internal change). Formal word endings in English are few. English language is becoming even more tied to word order, for example, *who* is slowly replacing the use of *whom.* Language rather resembles a person, changing, growing—dependent on mankind.

Usage

What is usage? But this idea of change takes us into *usage* and there is a distinction between usage and grammar. Whereas grammar is concerned with theoretical description and analysis of the workings of language, usage is concerned with the conventions of language. Usage is concerned with choices appropriate to a particular context and a particular situation. Usage is suited to (1) the speaker or writer, (2) the subject, and (3) the audience. But the rule consciousness of traditional grammar forces awkward sentences such as this one:

> That's the motorcycle on which I came.

in place of the more natural

> That's the motorcycle I came on.

A school program growing out of more modern descriptive linguistics (structural grammar) accepts change in usage. What was acceptable in the past may be unacceptable today. What is acceptable today may have been inappropriate in the past. *People* make these changes. If a language is not flexible enough to change, it dies. The spoken language, however, tends to change more swiftly than the written language. **Change in usage**

A right-or-wrong attitude toward usage in the classroom creates many problems. Effective English is not simply correct or incorrect, but is found in language that creates genuine communication with the audience.

The diagram to follow is based on the various situations in which language is used—(1) formal, (2) general, and (3) nonstandard (Lodge & Trett, 1968). These groupings, called *circles of usage*, represent occasions that most people encounter at some time during their lives. Vocabulary, sentence structure, and word forms (e.g., verbs and pronouns) of each area overlap into the other areas. For the general picture of *written* language the circles are pushed further apart and there is much less overlap when compared with circles for *spoken* language. Whether you say *To whom do you wish to speak?* (formal) or *Who do you want to talk to?* (general); *I am finished,* or *I am done; I teach English,* or *Me teach English!; It did well for them,* or *It done 'em some good* (nonstandard)—whether you say one or the other depends on your *situational map.* **Circles of usage**

That is what usage is all about. It is influenced by the idea from descriptive linguistics that the *use of the majority of the speakers determines the standard*. It is also influenced by the ideas of flexibility, of *language to suit the occasion and the rights of minorities to use their own dialects in speech and in writing*. And keep in mind that the language uses of children today will result in some changes in our language tomorrow. Many people, influenced by traditional school grammar, still believe that the dictionary is the Emily Post, the end-all in correctness of language. But modern dictionary makers have stopped subscribing to this valuational attitude because a dictionary is a record book of how people use a word. As for the traditional practice of diagramming sentences, all that did was produce a few good diagrammers, not writers or "correct speakers. **Conclusion**

A SITUATIONAL MAP OF ENGLISH

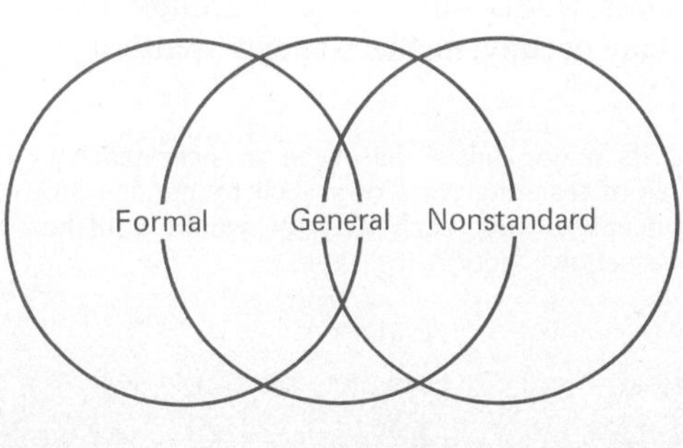

## What Is Structural Linguistic Grammar?

Contributions of descriptive linguistics

Structural Linguistic Grammar emphasizes several concepts. Among them are the importance of word order, word forms, the actual spoken English language working to convey meaning, and a few basic sentence patterns. Although descriptive linguistics (the discipline responsible for this grammar popularized by Fries [1952]) has contributed to many areas, it is best known for helpful explanations about sentence patterns and the simplification of word classes and their functions.[1]

According to structural linguistic theory, English words fall into two major groups: an almost infinite number of meaning-carrying words (called form-class or open-class words) and a small class of perhaps 300 words that connect and show relationships (called closed-class or structure words). Form-class words (so labeled because they change form) are referred to traditionally as nouns, verbs, adjectives, and adverbs. The 300 closed-class words connect in a variety of ways (e.g., a traditional label for one would be a *preposition*).

Basic sentence patterns

**What are basic sentence patterns?** Basic patterns are the foundation for any sentence we write or speak. The language user can achieve variety with the few basic sentence patterns by compounding, modifying, and subordinating these sentences. There is some disagreement among descriptive linguists about how many basic patterns there are, but the number is small. Here are five, all primarily noun–verb patterns:

1. Noun–verb — *The ghost floated.*
2. Noun–verb–noun — *The ghost scared the wizard.*
3. Noun–verb–noun–noun — *The ghost brought the wizard a hat.*
4. Noun–linking verb–noun — *The ghost is a spirit.*
5. Noun–linking verb–adjective — *The ghost is ghoulish.*

Attempts at application to children's texts

A number of children's elementary textbook series were then supposedly designed to do something for children by teaching them these patterns and how to expand them by loading them with adjectives and other words. There is apparently no conclusive research evidence to date that such activity does anything for improvement of children's composition, beyond some surface variation.

Word classes

**What are word classes and function?** From the view of the descriptive linguist, form-class words fall into four groups, defined mainly by the positions they can occupy in the sentence patterns.

[1] Perhaps one of its major "gifts" has been to steer teachers away from the unproductive practice of teaching parts of speech by handed-down, abstract definition under the misconception that such activity would somehow improve student's writing or was somehow "good" for them.

For example, a *noun* (or class 1 word) fits into the slots or frame represented by the blanks in the following pattern: *The* ________ *scared the* ________. Many substitutions can be made here. (And this is another new ritual that elementary children are often put through.) Nouns can be inflected to show plural number and to form possessive case, or nouns may have a suffix (such as *-ion*); and they "pattern after" *the,* or after a preposition. (*The* ________ *floated to the* ________. Words to fit in both blanks would be nouns.)

As another example, *verbs* (or class 2 words) fit into slots such as these: *The ghost* ________ *the wizard.* Or, *The ghost* ________ *white.* Besides position in the sentence, other distinguishing features of verbs are their inflections. To the base form of verbs you can add *-ing,* or *-s* (if the subject is singular), and *-ed* to form the past tense of most verbs. For example, since you could not say, *Yesterday I candlesticked, candlestick* must not be a verb.

The descriptive linguist is not as concerned as the traditional school grammarian is with definitions of parts of speech, but is instead concerned with the functions of four classes corresponding to nouns, verbs, adjectives, and adverbs.

Structure words

Besides the initially mentioned features of word order, and form-class words with their functions and word endings, there is the system of closed-class or *structure words.* Example:

> ________ ghost floated ________ scared ________ wizard ________ broom.

What must you add into the preceding sentence to make it understandable? Try *the, and,* and *on. The* ________ ________ *and* ________ *the* ________ *on the* ________. Thus, a descriptive grammar also includes a set of words with little lexical meaning that serve as signals, that glue the discourse together. These structure words provide *grammatical* meaning by indicating how the other words are related in the sentence. Native speakers of a language have little trouble with them. Their labels are fairly self-explanatory, e.g., noun marker (*the*), verb marker, negative, intensifier (*very*), conjunction, phrase marker (*into*), question marker, and clause marker (*after*).

## What Is Transformational–Generative Grammar?

Emphasis on process

Just as some schoolteachers thought they were becoming able to cope with the new descriptive or structural linguistic grammar, another new grammar loomed on the horizon—*generative grammar* as presented by Chomsky (1965). Whereas the descriptive linguists emphasize describing the product (recording data, sorting it, classifying their findings), the transformational linguists are chiefly interested in the *process* by which the product comes to be (Braddock, 1969). Chapter 1, on development of language and thought, mentioned how children can generate an almost infinite number of sentences in their language that they have never heard before. This school of thought believes that the speaker masters a number of rules for transforming the basic sentence patterns (kernels) by substituting, reordering, deleting, embedding, and combining of parts. Meaning, introspection, and inference are added to the tools of the transformational-generative linguist, who is concerned with competence, not just with performance.

Briefly, transformational grammar consists of a set of rules for building sentences. It is not a procedure for cutting up already-formed sentences and labeling their parts and surface features (as in both traditional and descriptive grammar). The transformational linguist sees all possible sentences as either kernel sentences or transforms of kernels.

Kernel sentence

What is a kernel sentence or source sentence? It is a simple, affirmative, active, declarative sentence with no compound elements or elaboration. A kernel sentence may have a direct object or a subjective complement, but no noun modifiers other than determiners and no adverbs other than place or time words (or prepositional phrases) in the predicate. All the "ghostly" illustrations of the basic sentence patterns in the examples on p. 384 are kernel sentences.

Deep and surface structures

*Deep structure* as opposed to *surface structure* are two important concepts in transformational grammar (Smith, Goodman, & Meredith, 1970). Each utterance is said to have a deep or underlying structure. From this you can derive a surface structure (through a series of transformations by means of rules). Deep structure contains those rules that relate directly to the meaningful content of a sentence. Surface structure contains those rules that relate to the sound, letter, or other forms of the sentence. For example, here are two sentences that differ in surface structure, but have the same deep structure:

> The broomstock hit the wizard.
> The wizard was hit by the broomstick.

In the second sentence a passive transformational rule was applied to the deep structure shown in the first sentence, *The broomstick hit the wizard.* The transformation resulted in several changes in the passive surface structure. For example, the *wizard* moved to the front position of the subject of the sentence; the verb *hit* took on the structure word or auxiliary *was,* and *the broomstick* became the agent that *by* introduced.

A further transformation could produce the simpler surface structure, *The wizard was hit.* An agent (or doer of the hitting) is absent in this surface structure; a deletion transformation has removed the agent.

But the agent is still present in the deep structure: *(Something) hit the wizard*. This deep structure becomes *The wizard was hit by something.* Then (by deletion transformation) the sentence becomes *The wizard was hit.*

A question transformation could produce another surface structure, *Was the wizard hit?* This transformation still has the same deep structure: *(Something) hit the wizard.*

Thus a transformational grammar seeks to show the *connections* between related sentences rather than to describe one separately.

---

**Attempts at application in the classroom.** The advantage teachers hope for from transformational grammar is that it will give practical steps for them to follow in order to help students put series of simple kernel sentences together by means of transformations. Teachers hope such activity will assist students to create more complex, concise sentences. (In other words, they hope for compact surface structures transformed from *multiple* deep structures.)

For example, *The ghost saw the goblin who hit the wizard* is a surface structure that combines two deep structure sentences: *The ghost saw the goblin,* and *The goblin hit the wizard.* A relative clause transformation transforms the last sentence, *The goblin hit the wizard,* into a relative clause and embeds it in the surface structure noun phrase *The goblin who hit the wizard.*

Making complex, embedded sentences

Thus, the first sentence (to be converted into a relative clause) is called the insert sentence. Example:

> *Insert sentence:* The goblin hit the wizard.
> *Relative clause:* who hit the wizard.

The main sentence or *matrix* sentence is the next sentence—the one into which the relative clause is to be inserted.

> *Matrix sentence:* The ghost saw the goblin.

The relative clause is inserted into the matrix sentence.

> who
> The ghost saw the goblin. ~~The goblin~~ hit the wizard.

The resulting sentence (which contains all the meaning of the two original sentences) is called a transform:

*Transform:* The ghost saw the goblin who hit the wizard.

Take another example, this time concerning adjectives which are regarded by transformational linguists as derived from deep structure sentences. In the deep structure sentence, *The little goblin hit the wizard,* the sentence *The goblin is little* is embedded in the noun phrase *The little goblin.*

We could go on to other deletions and transformations, but you have probably had enough of ghostly creatures in this violent phantasy. See the sample page from a sixth-grade text.

### SPECIAL ADJECTIVE WAY OF COMBINING SENTENCES

Here are the four steps again. Try to explain what happens in each step. (Don't look back unless you need to.)

1. The man broke the balloon.
2. The man (S) broke the balloon.
3. The man (the man is tall) broke the balloon.

3a. The man (~~the man~~ is (tall)) broke the balloon.
4. The tall man broke the balloon.

Try to use the special adjective way to combine these sentences about the boy who ran away:

The boy ran away.
The boy is lazy.

■ Now try to think of some good insert sentences to add to these matrix sentences. Remember that each insert sentence must have a "be" word and an adjective. Then use the special adjective way to combine the sentences. (The first one is done for you. The second one is almost done.)

1. The horse ate the sugar.
   The horse (*S*) ate the sugar.

   The horse (*~~the horse~~ is (brown)*) ate the sugar.
   *The brown horse ate the sugar.*
2. The pencil fell on the floor.
   The pencil (*S*) fell on the floor.

   The pencil (*~~the pencil~~ is* (____)) fell on the floor.
3. The giraffe munched on some leaves.
4. The girl walked in the rain.
5. The lion escaped from his cage.
6. The boy surfed in the ocean.
7. The man swallowed a sword.

From Owen Thomas and William C. Cady, *The Arts and Skills of English* (Book 6) (New York: Holt, Rinehart and Winston, 1972). Teacher's edition page 104. The (S) indicates that another sentence can be added to this main sentence.

As still further examples, John C. Mellon's (1967) sentence-combining operations (also coming from transformational grammar) may have some promise—if it is sentence-combining skill that is needed at the junior-high level and above (Cooper, 1971). In the examples to follow, the student is to embed the *indented* form in the form just above. The first line is always the main clause (or main sentence or matrix sentence).

Problem #1

> SOMETHING would be almost unbearable.
> The rocket fails. (Transformation: *infinitive* type) [2]

The student writes out:

> For the rocket to fail would be almost unbearable.

Problem #2

> SOMETHING seemed to suggest SOMETHING.
> Adam finished his term paper in less than 2 hours.
> (Transformation: *fact* type)
>
> He had received special help from another person.
> (Transformation: *fact* type)

The student writes out:

> The fact that Adam finished his term paper in less than 2 hours seemed to suggest that he had received special help from another person.

Although gains were made in compactness of sentence structure in the Mellon study (1967), overall grading of quality of the compositions showed an experienced control teacher to be better at teaching composition. However, the experimental group did show some gains in the mastery of resources of the sentence. In relation to *elementary*-school children, much that comes to us in this vein is of little or no use (Smith, Goodman, & Meredith, 1970).

Basic sentence plus free modifiers

Other attempts to improve children's sentence structure. Other studies have attempted to get children to achieve better "texture" in their threadbare sentences by adding modifier structures (e.g., *-ing* phrases)

[2] This infinitive transformation leads to the insertion of the words *for* and *to* and to the form-change from *fail*s to *fail*.

*after* the subject and predicate in the manner of Christensen (1967). That is, the teacher showed the children how to make cumulative sentences with free modifiers. The teacher presented this technique without trying to explain and label all the grammatical structures (Palmer, 1971). The changes in low-achieving students' compositions in the Palmer study did appear to show great improvement. Palmer, however, goes on to illustrate how sometimes efforts to produce expandings by embedding and extending (especially with *bound* modifiers) can result in awkward sentences such as this one:

> The little girl on the brown pony galloping across the green meadow comes from the south side of town by the cemetery next to Mr. Smith's house.

A *traditional* way of getting more sensory detail into a simple statement might be to take a sentence such as *The boy looked at the dog* and elaborate it by adding adjectives, e.g., *The little barefooted boy looked at the grubby little dog*. Then the teacher might ask the child to pick even more-vivid words as in, *The little barefooted waif gazed at the grubby little mongrel.*

The Christensen method

*But the Christensen method says first look at the scene.* The language itself through its structures provides the person who *observes carefully* with the detail necessary to verify the experience.

> The boy looked at the dog, longingly, his eyes taking in the thin flanks and droopy tail, his big toe of the right foot scratching his left leg as he thought about carrying the dog home to his mother.[3]

In the first elaborated sentence, the writer is striving for effect but is overloading the basic pattern of the sentence. This practice may render him (and his teacher) tone deaf. The Christensen way,

| (Simple sentence) | (The boy looked at the dog . . .) |
|---|---|
| | (take)ing |
| | (scratch)ing |
| | (carry)ing |

does not overload the basic sentence.

When it comes to maturity in sentences, it is not "how long you make them, but how you make them long."

A case study. Movements such as the foregoing probably prompted one study concerned with revising sentences in the fourth, fifth, and sixth

[3] Thanks to Professor Helen Lodge for manufacturing this example.

grades (Folta, n.d.). The strategies used were these: (1) elimination of those words or phrases that garble meaning or repeat unnecessarily; (2) substitution of more specific, vivid, or concrete expressions; and (3) addition of modifier structures—words, phrases, and clauses—in order to improve focus on tone and to enhance the texture of the prose. The children spent a great deal of time examining and criticizing sentences by means of an overhead projector. They revised sentences according to the three suggested strategies.

Some time was spent working over similes produced by the children that did not, in their opinion, correspond to reality. For example, comparing clouds to a dim room was considered inappropriate. Some of the activity may have helped to sharpen the children's observation, and some may have limited the expression of the children.

Here is a "before" example of uncombined language from a child of about the same age level as children in the Folta study: [4]

Child's example

> I am a California Indian. I go to the sweathouse all the time. I go there with my friends after my chores are done. I race with my friends. They call me Small Lightning. I am small. I am the smallest one in my tribe.

Here is the "combined" version:

> I am a California Indian named Small Lightning, the smallest one in my tribe. I got my name from racing with my friends. I go to the sweathouse all the time with my friends after my chores are done.

(In this case one might argue that the uncombined language of the first draft is more appropriate to the character who is supposed to be speaking, a small Indian boy of long ago.)

## GROUPING LANGUAGE CONCEPTS

The following list [5] groups some of the hundreds of language concepts found in children's textbooks today. It is offered for a summarizing perspective related to the topic of grammar.

[4] By Michael, a fifth-grade student at Harbor View Elementary School, Corona del Mar, Calif.; collected by Jill Susson, University of California, Irvine, student. Taken from a longer composition.

[5] This list is adapted from a 30-page listing by Golub et al. (1971) of concepts in current language arts textbooks.

Some language concepts in children's texts

*Language in General*

- The purpose of using language is to communicate ideas (including just for fun) and feelings; the standard is success in communicating.
- Language is an arbitrary assignment of meanings to sounds with words working together to produce meaning. Words are a part of the system of language.
- Words do not mean the same to all people. (Semantics)

*Grammar in General*

- Everyone knows a great deal intuitively about grammar. You unconsciously obey the basic rules of English grammar in putting words together and in making sentences.

*Morphology*

- A morpheme is a meaningful unit of language which cannot be divided into smaller meaningful units.
- A morpheme can have one or more syllables.
- A morpheme can be a word or a part of a word.
- Morphology is the study especially of changes of word form that affect meaning or function.
- A word part added to a word to change its meaning is an affix; prefixes come before, suffixes come after.
- Many words are members of word families, e.g., *direct, indirect, direction,* and *director.*
- Every English word has at least one vowel sound.

*Syntax*

- You can group English words according to their function in sentences. Some words may belong to more than one group.
- Word order helps to signal meaning; a different word order can give a sentence a different meaning. English is a word-order language.
- English sentences are based on distinct patterns that can be elaborated or compressed.
- A basic sentence contains a subject and a predicate.

- Most English sentences have a noun followed by a verb.
- Sentence patterns include:
  N + V; N + V + N; N + LV + N; N + LV + A; N + V + N + N.
  (N, noun; V, verb; LV, linking verb; A, adjective.)
- Words are often added to basic sentences to give more information (modified).
- You can create alternative sentences by resolving choice in these ways:
  - Transforms (passive, negative, question, imperative, etc.)
  - Modification (noun cluster, prepositional phrase, adverbial phrase, participial phrase)
  - Compounding (subject, predicate, whole sentences)
  - Apposition
  - Subordination
- A phrase is a group of words that does not contain a subject and predicate working together.

*Phonology*

- Phonology is the study of sounds of a language, of stresses, pauses, rising and falling intonations, and the melody of speech patterns.
- A phoneme is the smallest unit of sound that makes one word different from another.
- You can identify specific sounds for the English language; you can identify corresponding graphemes (letters).

*Usage*

- Usage concerns the selection of specific words to be used in a certain speech or writing situation. The standard is suitability of context.
- There are various levels of acceptable or appropriate usage.
- Every person speaks a dialect. Speech dialects differ. Even standard English allows for variety of acceptable speech. Language is not the same in all places.
- TV and radio are beginning to break down dialect differences.

*Conventions*

- Skills, mechanics, and conventions facilitate communication of ideas and feelings.

*Punctuation*

- We signal the end of one spoken sentence and the beginning of the next by the way we raise and lower our voices. We also pause between the last word of one sentence and the first word of the next.
- Juncture is the pause between words or sentences.

*Proofing*

- Self-editing attitude: try to decide at least partly what you want to say before you write, realize that the first draft is mainly just to get the ideas down.

*Uses of Discourse*

- Skill in effective communication is gained through having aims and ideas and composing them in various types of messages.

*Language History*

- Language changes as time passes—words are isolated and not used; new words are added, borrowed; pronunciation changes; meanings change.
- Word history includes these: coined words; borrowed words (e.g., *taboo* from the South Pacific); adapted words (e.g., *villain*—first meant serf—one of lowly birth—finally, scoundrel); names of persons (e.g., Nicholas Chauvin of Rochefort—*chauvinism*); imitation of sounds (e.g., *buzz*); fusions or combinations of known words (e.g., *applesauce, rock-and-roll*).

---

## SUMMARY AND CONCLUSIONS

Three types

This chapter has described three major grammars with their differing emphases. *Traditional School Grammar* prescribes rules for language use, emphasizes subject–predicate relations, and classifies words into eight parts of speech (determined by function in the sentence). This Latinate grammar fails to describe adequately how English is used.

*Structural Linguistic Grammar* emphasizes the importance of word order, word forms or classes, the actual spoken English language (how it works to convey meaning), and a few basic sentence patterns. One can achieve variety with the sentence patterns through compounding, modifying, and subordinating. Grammatically essential sentence elements (e.g., subject, predicate) generally occupy fixed positions. Grammatically less essential elements tend to be movable.

*Transformational–Generative Grammar* emphasizes process and shows relationships among sentences by guessing at (or postulating) the source sentence (or kernel sentence). Then the transformational process is to shift, delete, insert (or embed) words and phrases or combine two or more sentences. Theoretically speaking, this process is able to generate all the sentences in the English language.

**Perspective**

From the perspective of child development, rushing children into mature sentence patterns before they have fully explored their own childlike ones may be a risky business. I feel that patterned methods to achieve syntactic fluency may have some justification for children who appear to remain poor in syntactic fluency into junior high and high school. But exercises can be limiting to children and may even have a negative effect on the "I've got something to say!" aspect of composition.

*At this time of writing, there is no evidence anywhere that the study of grammar (whatever kind it is) fosters correctness and syntactic maturity in a fashion superior to far less time-consuming, more joyous, informal, creative, and naturalistic procedures.* We can be teaching a huge number of punctuation, grammar, or usage rules, sentence games, parts of speech, vocabulary and spelling drills—and still not have a composition program. Working over someone else's workbook or worksheet sentences has been of limited usefulness, and most students have always known it (Cooper, 1971). Teaching terminology and abstractions are secondary (if not unnecessary) to helping children discover inductively how language functions. (Recall the cartoon at the beginning of this chapter.)

Have pupils spend the time they have learning how to form their *own* sentences in extended compositions, not merely analyzing the grammar of the sentences of others (Braddock, 1969). If the purpose of language instruction is to help children to use language more and more effectively, then time is *not* well spent on the content of any one abstract grammar. But time is well spent on the content of the child's own oral and written composition and on children's literature. The need for effective uses of oral language as a base for all learning remains undiminished throughout schooling. A major part of this oral experience is manipulative activity and discussion about children's own language.

But some influential people (feeling that what's new is good) force recent linguistic scholarship prematurely into texts for the elementary school. The practice alienates both teachers and children. Language study that crowds out the composition program is unfortunate. Should instructors "hammer in the grammar"? The answer is NO!

Usage

On the topic of usage—each person has a range of dialects to use in different situations with various types of people. No matter what socioeconomic, cultural, or linguistic background persons are from, they can enlarge their ranges of communication by learning more about the natural dignity of dialectal varieties and various usages—alternative ways of saying things. The language arts classroom is a suitable place to explore the richness, diversity, and complexity of the varieties of language and (with older children) the sensitive problems and realities of acceptance and rejection among ages, sexes, and ethnic, occupational, and status differences.

Unless older students have compelling motives to participate in the mainstream, know precisely what differences to listen for, and have appropriate chances to try out standard pronunciations, word forms, and syntax, they will fail to successfully add standard to non-standard language facility. It is unlikely that any students have ever modified their usage through absorbing a presentation of bewildering traditional grammatical rules followed by written exercises for selecting "correct" grammatical forms (English Language Framework, 1975).

## ACTIVITIES ON GRAMMAR AND USAGE

Fredrick, Golub, and Johnson (1970) reported on a multiple-choice Language Ability Test (LAT) for children. These items could be used as grammatical activities—if (and this is doubtful) a genuine need is apparent. Some adapted examples follow. The correct response is marked by an asterisk.

10.1. To Determine Pronoun Referents. (Important in reading comprehension and in clear, "published" composition.)

In the sentence, *The challenge is difficult, but it can be attacked,* the word *it* refers to *challenge*. For each item following choose the word that the underlined word refers to. Circle the letter of the word you think is correct.

A child can get a cold and be very ill unless he takes care of *it* and rests.
a. child b. cold * c. ill d. he

10.2. To Identify Prefixes, Roots, and Suffixes (Morphology). (Important to spelling and one aspect of vocabulary development.)

The word *unmindful* has three parts, *un* + *mind* + *ful*. The first part, *un*, is called a prefix; *mind* is called the root word; and *ful* is a suffix. In the following, you are to put a *P* before prefixes, *Rw* before root words, and *S* before suffixes.

| P * | S * | Rw * |
|---|---|---|
| ——— trans | ——— ness | ——— lone |

10.3. To Recognize Form Class and Function Slots in Sentences. (This is one of the basic understandings of the nature of our language. Most of us have grasped this understanding unconsciously. Analysis is probably appropriate as early as junior high school for any child who just might want to be a linguist when he or she grows up).

You are given sentences with some parts underlined. Decide which of the parts in the second sentence is used in the same way as the underlined part in the first sentence.

A police car *blocked* the alley.
*This* piece of *candy* *tastes* *good.*
a b c * d (Both words are verbs.)

10.4. To Recognize the Structures of Various Questions in Order to Produce the Appropriate Response. (Very important for taking objective tests and as an aid to getting *some* meaning from a communication in which words are unknown or unintelligible.)

Choose a response to the following question:

What did the klib hinkle?
A. The klib hinkled a snafrat. *
B. The klib hinkled in a boofram.

10.5. To Embed One Base Sentence in Another Base Sentence to Produce a Well-Transformed Sentence. (A *small* part of the craft of writing; more appropriate in junior high and high school for those few who need it.)

Choose the correct transformation (A, B, or C) of the following:

The sky was gray.
Rain fell from the sky.
The rain was frozen.
A. The sky, from which the fallen rain was frozen, was gray.
B. The frozen rain which fell from the sky was gray.
C. The frozen rain fell from the gray sky.*

10.6. The Problem-Solving or Inquiry Approach to Grammar. Try the creative problem-solving or inquiry approach to teaching grammar (learning how language works). The teacher organizes this discovery activity around key questions (problems). Children can seek to answer them through their own experimentation (in the manner of linguists). The children as learners are not just acquiring concepts. In a traditional way concepts can be memorized when the teacher simply tells them over and over or uses some other highly controlled way. But more productively the child can acquire a sense of the structure of the discipline of linguistics through *using* its methods of inquiry.

In the inquiry approach to learning about grammar, the children collect language data from themselves, and from their own groups, e.g., family, friends, and class. They compare and contrast forms heard on the playground, in the community, on trips, in the mass media, in business, and in antiquated literature. They can then begin a descriptive grammar for their own dialects (or very own idiolects).

Children's "How come" questions

The child can start with "How come?" or "Why is it that . . . ?" types of questions.

"What would happen if we wrote *every* word the way it sounds and changed the spelling of all our words now?"

"How come some of the German words my grandmother speaks are a lot like our words?"

"How come we say 'bright, blue sky,' but we don't say 'blue bright sky'?"

Children can discover what rules English language uses in class membership for ordering adjectives. Children can begin to uncover the proposition that users follow the rules of their language that they have absorbed (Smith, Goodman, & Meredith, 1970).

Oral pattern practice

10.7. Pattern Drills. Some students scarcely able to communicate may enjoy the social security and attention and may profit initially from *brief, spaced* oral pattern drills in a small group. An outline of methods of pattern practice follows. (The author would personally avoid using or recommending such activity in favor of more creative experience, e.g., "That's an interesting idea. I hadn't thought of it that way. Tell me more.")

- Repetition—Listen and repeat exactly as heard.
- Analogy—Repeat exactly with one word change.
- Inflection—Repeat but change the form of a word (e.g., *kill, killed, is killing*).
- Completion—Finish the cue statement.
- Response—Answer a question or make a rejoinder.
- Expansion—Use methods of expansion such as joining and embedding. ("The cat *and* the dog who live next door ran away.")
- Transformation—Change a sentence to negative or interrogative form. *(They did not run away. Did they run away?)*
- Restoration—Make a sentence from a group of words.
- Practice with pitch, stress, and juncture. With each change, compare any changes in meaning.

For some elaboration see Burrows (1956).

Loban, Ryan, and Squire suggest a game, a few minutes in length, in which children try to guess an object selected by a child (1969, pp. 124–26). The game is designed for practicing an alternative to *ain't,* using the Response pattern. (Also see Activity 1.7.) For example:

Question: Is it a police car?
Answer: No, it isn't a police car.
Question: Is it a surfboard?
Answer: No, it isn't a surfboard.

10.8. Create a Word and Put It in the News. First invite children to "invent" objects by bringing in materials that would otherwise be thrown away. (Furnishing paper, tape, pins, and paint.) Next ask the children to give their objects names so that they become new words in their language. The next step is to describe the inventions in sentences and put them into a class dictionary. Then use an existing school newspaper (or start one) to survey the children about their creations. Questions following the journalistic organization of the "who, what, when, where, and how" can be set up for the roving reporters.

History, development, and change of language

"Just who invented the 'whopper machine'?"
"Just what is it?"
"When was it invented?"
"Where is it kept on display?"

Such activity might lead to playing with grammar as children change their nouns to verbs, adjectives, or adverbs. For example: "Is just about anything *whoppable?*" "Is the person using it *whopping?*" "Is it whoppedly changed?" Older children might add diacritical pronounciation marks to their entries in the dictionary.

Finally, the children might pretend to be cavemen who wish to leave a message about their invention on the wall of their cave for the next cave dweller. Children could record about their invention and themselves using pictures. Later have the children exchange their "cave wall" pictures and have their partners translate into standard English. When the translations come back to the original creator, the children can discuss the difficulties in communication, including the organization of the picture language. In this way the teacher is able to help students attain some concepts about history, development, and change in language at the same time that they engage in its productive, expository use. (Activity adapted from material developed by Dr. Dan Donlan, University of California, Riverside.)

10.9. Using Dependable Grammatical Patterns in Children's Literature. Use the predictable language patterns in delightful books for children (such as the one to follow) to help the young child experience the structure and working ways of language. Using dependable patterns in literary models helps children to use the semantic environment of language for developing strategies to handle unfamiliar words and grammatical structures (important skills for reading).

First of all simply enjoy a story such as *Drummer Hoff.*[6] Children can join in on the noun—verb—noun pattern and the "But Drummer Hoff fired it off" refrain, develop a sense of sequence, explore the rich pictorial detail and the phonology of the rhymed couplets, and enjoy ending this story with a tremendous, appropriate, and sanctioned amount of noise. (The final illustration—award-winning with brilliant colors over the lines of the woodcuts—

[6] Ed Emberly and Barbara Emberly, *Drummer Hoff* (Englewood Cliffs, N.J.: Prentice-Hall, 1967).

satisfactorily shows the cannon finally nestling in flowers with birds building nests and spiders spinning webs over it.) The text follows:

General Border
gave the order,
Major Scott
brought the shot,
Captain Bammer
brought the rammer,
Sargeant Chowder
brought the powder,
Corporal Farrell
brought the barrel,
Private Parriage
brought the carriage,
but Drummer Hoff fired it off.

From the book *Drummer Hoff* by Barbara and Ed Emberley. © 1967 by Edward R. Emberley and Barbara Emberley. Published by Prentice-Hall, Inc., Englewood Cliffs, N.J.

The text is then partially repeated as some of the characters are reintroduced with a full page illustration in vivid color. After the story is read aloud, children can have fun when the reader pauses and lets the children finish a verse. Then children can look at the book and read it together. Finally, (using the story pattern and structure words) children can substitute other content words (form class or open class words). For example, maybe the theme could be making and using a birthday cake with verses such as the following:

Father Mandles
Lit the candles,

And with the following refrain:

But Betsy Stout blew them out.

The story can be finished up with everyone making the biggest blowing noise possible, and then rereading their newly written story. Chances are that the stories will be spontaneously picked up and shared again and again. This activity represents a natural, delightful way to grasp the workings of English grammar to convey meaning.

## If You Want to Learn More

AMERICAN BOOK COMPANY. *What's Happening to Our Language Today? A Handbook for Parents.* New York: Author, 1967.

BRADDOCK, R. English Composition. In R. L. Ebel (Ed.), *Encyclopedia of Educational Research.* (4th ed.) London: Macmillan, 1969.

BURROWS, M. *Good English Through Practice.* New York: Holt, Rinehart and Winston, 1956.

CHOMSKY, N. *Aspects of the Theory of Syntax.* Cambridge, Mass.: M.I.T. Press, 1965.

CHRISTENSEN, F. *Notes Toward a New Rhetoric.* New York: Harper & Row, 1967.

*College Composition and Communication,* Special Issue, Fall 1974: Students' Right to Their Own Language. Urbana, Ill.: NCTE, 1974. (Stock No. 27624)

Affirms students' right to their own patterns and varieties of language—the dialects of their nurture or whatever dialects in which they find their own identity and style. Asserts that the claim that any one dialect is unacceptable amounts to an attempt of one social group to exert its dominance over another. Includes a 129-item annotated bibliography. Explains with clarity many language concepts.

COOPER, C. R. A No-Grammar Approach to Sentence Power: John C. Mellon's Sentence-Combining Games. *California English Journal,* 1971, *7* (1), 35-40.

*English Language Framework for California Public Schools: The Student and English Language Arts (Kindergarten through Grade 12).* Sacramento: California State Department of Education, 1975.

FOLTA, B. *Three Strategies for Revising Sentences.* Terre Haute: Indiana State University, n.d.

FREDRICK, W. C., GOLUB, L. S., and JOHNSON, S. L. *Analysis of the Linguistic Ability Test, Grades 4 & 6.* Technical Report No. 121. Madison: Wisconsin Research and Development Center for Cognitive Learning, 1970.

FRIES, C. C. *The Structure of English.* New York: Harcourt, 1952.

GOLUB, L., FREDRICK, W. C., and BARGANZ, R. A. *Present and Proposed Needs, Objectives, and Components of a Language Learning Program.* Madison: Wisconsin Research and Development Center for Cognitive Learning, 1971.

LOBAN, W., RYAN, M., and SQUIRE, J. R. *Teaching Language and Literature.* New York: Harcourt, 1969.

LODGE, H. C., and TRETT, G. L. *New Ways in English.* Englewood Cliffs, N.J.: Prentice-Hall, 1968.

A secondary-school text, informative for teachers, too.

MELLON, J. C. *Transformational Sentence Combining: A Method for Enhancing the Development of Syntactic Fluency in English Composition.* Urbana, Ill.: NCTE, 1967.

PALMER, W. S. What Yolly, Willy, and Harriet Learned To Do . . . the Free Modifier: A Fresh Mode of Teaching Composition. *California English Journal,* 1971, *7,* 17-28.

SEYMOUR, D. Z. Make Your Language Lessons Interesting. *Elementary English,* 1968, *45,* 41-43.

SMITH, E. B., GOODMAN, K. S., and MEREDITH, R. *Language and Thinking in the Elementary School.* New York: Holt, Rinehart and Winston, 1970.

# Chapter 11 Evaluation & Accountability in Language Arts Instruction

This chapter is specifically about assessment, especially the evaluation of composition. However, it also gives examples for the assessment of children's listening, speaking, and response to literature. Here you will find some test items and checklists. Toward the end, this chapter examines some of the current concepts and happenings in accountability and their impact on the language arts. I have already said much about evaluation, because it is interwoven with the learning process of children. Too often, evaluation is stuck on at the end of instruction for the purpose of reporting to parents or significant others.

If you would like some measure of your growth from reading this section, I suggest that you turn to the questionnaire, The Me in Measurement, at the end of the chapter. You can answer the questionnaire now, as a "pretest." After reading the chapter, you can try it again and compare.

Whole courses could be (and sometimes are) taught on this area. This chapter touches on a few of the contours most important to language arts teachers. For those who want to learn more, there are the references at the end of the chapter.

## WHY ASSESS?

Why assess in the first place? Well, don't you think it is at least a partial waste of time to formulate goals and objectives carefully, select delightful materials and activities, develop skills necessary—and then never know whether your children learned anything? To fail to assess is like getting ready to be married and never knowing to begin with if the person chosen has ever agreed. It's not just the same, but it could be nearly as frustrating. And sometimes it is—especially to the learner.

### ON ASSESSMENT OF COMPOSITION

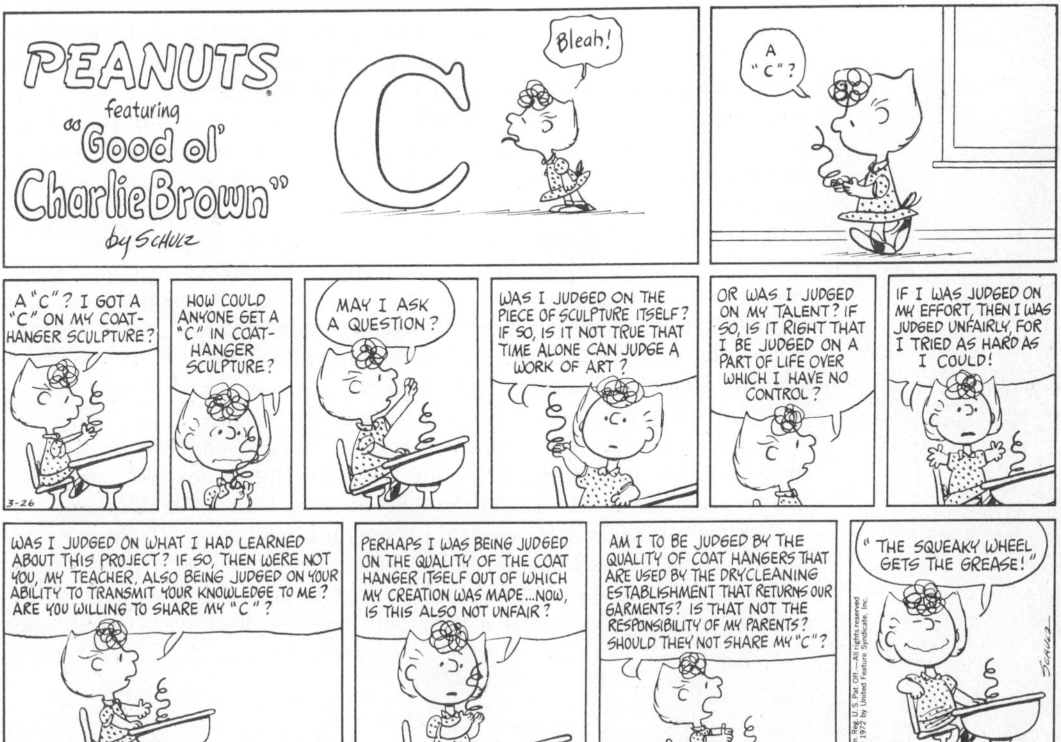

Finding out what children have learned and next steps

What is the purpose of assessment? Ideally, the purpose of measurable objectives, a prerequisite to assessment, is to be ready to determine what children have already learned and what they still need to master—to see if the decisions made, actions taken and documented, and kinds of learning activities the children have engaged in are helping them. And if not, what should be tried next. It is *not* to be educationally fashionable, not primarily to furnish a possibility of feedback to school district management for evaluating cost effectiveness and teacher performance.

A range of possibilities

What does assessment do? Whether it is objective or subjective—based on attitude scale or on teacher judgment—whether the performance observed is role playing, discussion, or writing a poem—assessment before instruction can help you and the child to find out where he/she is starting. In light of goals and objectives designed by you and the child, assessment can set reasonable levels of aspiration. When children achieve these, they strengthen feelings of success and competence. In the long run, assessment during and at the end of instruction can help to answer questions about the child, about materials, about the most effective of alternative programs at that time, and even about basic questions on the nature of teaching and learning.

Emphatically, assessment does not have to always concern "immediately observable, overt behavior," or "objective tests with low levels of thought." By *objective* tests, I mean multiple-choice, true–false, short-answer types of items for which a scoring key is devised. A look at the conception of items and at the scoring shows that such tests are not very "objective" at all.) For example, I have previously mentioned these aids to assessment: individual conferences, tapes revealing patterns of language and thought development, cumulative files of written work, quality and quantity of literature read by the children, tabulation of levels of response to media and cultural events, examination of process (not just product), and self-report. There is a wide range of possibilities.

Assessment can bring about many things. To engage in cooperative assessment can mean the basis for inspiring self-improvement in the immediate present, and can mean friendly, genuine interest in the growth of one another. It can mean that no child is allowed to fall by the wayside. It can mean that every individual pupil is considered worthy of the best that teachers can do for him or for her.

In that spirit, teachers avoid rating and labeling children as failures or as geniuses; instead, they develop them all. But no teacher can make the decisions involved without the help of some form of evaluation.

A stimulus to clarity

There are other, more personal reasons for evaluation. There is nothing like trying to set down goals and objectives and ways to assess them that exposes fuzzy-headedness and clarifies thought quite so well. Then sometimes teachers uncover a wide gap between objectives desired and what actually happens in the classrooms. Once uncovered, this gap can be closed.

For example, if one of my goals is creative problem-solving for children or critical listening, but I never give them a chance to do either one, I have a gap I need to do something about. With evaluation I clarify the relationship between what I do every day and my long-term goals.

Knowledge of success

Finally, knowledge of progress, even the smallest bit, is rewarding. It is an important part of taking heart and trying again. A question a teacher might ask is How, today, can I help a child I haven't been reaching to have a successful experience with language? Such success may depend on having clearly in mind—

1. the nature of the child's strength or difficulty.
2. how this assessment has been made.
3. what is being done to improve performance.

And that is, ideally, why we assess—to guide individual student growth.

## WHAT ARE NEEDS AND PROBLEMS IN ASSESSING WRITTEN COMPOSITION? (THE MORE NEGATIVE SIDE)

Emphasize major, not minor behaviors

Sometimes makers of objectives and those who assess become completely engrossed with inconsequential matters. One of the things we need to do while setting goals, especially in the area of written composition, is to try to find a tentative hierarchy of specific objectives that lead toward large, important goals. Then we need to concentrate on the uppermost, the more complex and high-level objectives because they tend to get neglected. We cannot accomplish everything in the world. We must select objectives carefully, on the basis of the different types of communication–thought processes and actions that children need help with most, now, and those that *prepare them to help themselves.* In the elementary school we need to avoid trivia (such as having children memorize that there are around 650,000 words in the English language, or that Middle English was spoken from about the year 1100 to about 1450). We need to concentrate on the crucial.

When I mention a *tentative hierarchy,* I realize that there is no set sequence that every child must follow for developing language arts skills. Children learn differently, have different backgrounds, come to us already knowing things, and have different interests and needs. A rigid sequence through which all students must move does not make sense and does not allow for innovative teaching.

On the other hand, teachers are bombarded with important objectives and goals such as development of children's self-assurance as communicators, proficiency in self-expression, understanding communication in a pluralistic culture, and on and on. In order to function, teachers need to set up priorities. They need to give attention first to the goal at the top of the hierarchy, and make sure major behaviors don't get lost in multiple-choice trivia.

**A caution about convergent, multiple-choice thinking**

Basically the trouble with a steady dose of right-or-wrong, multiple-choice types of questions and answers is that it may unintentionally teach the child that responses showing learning come only in the form of certain predictable conclusions. Heavy emphasis on such kinds of testing in a school accountability program could bring about a breed of totally convergent, multiple-choice, behavior-percentage oriented thinkers. For example:

"Do you love me?"
________ 10% of the time
________ 45% of the time
________ 80% of the time
"Will you be my wife (or husband)?"
________ 10% of the time
________ 45% of the time
________ 80% of the time
"Sorry, your time limit is up."

Programs and tests that only accept one answer limit children's perception, inhibiting them rather than extending their thinking. We need divergent thinking, too, and more subjective assessment.[1] Along with more subjective, divergent measurement, we need the kinds of *activities* and *program* that justify more than just objective assessment. Most of the suggested activities throughout this book have been of that nature, especially those stressing creative problem-solving.

**Inquiry difficult to measure**

Granted, open-ended inquiry activities (be it with free linguistic investigations, mealworms, or with social problems) may lead students and teachers into unsettled areas. In these areas even the most up-to-date, scholarly references may disagree, offer no aid and almost defy immediate assessment. (See Activity 10.6, the Problem-Solving or Inquiry Approach to Grammar.) There is a necessary tentativeness and openness to improvisation in a program using inquiry teaching. Much incidental learning takes place that is difficult for the teacher to measure, evaluate, and report to significant others. And it is impossible to predict

[1] In the guide, *Ideas into Practice,* I have included an open-ended task of problem solving and a task stimulated by questions but with *no* multiple alternatives. Instead there is the rating scale used and a step-by-step practice on judging the composition according to the criteria.

specific objectives and outcomes, or to quantify results in terms of pupil behavior at the completion of instruction. In fact, in *most* cases it is impossible to predict completely what children will learn and when they will learn it.

In some cases during inquiry a "Eureka" of insight occurs after a few moments of data immersion. In other cases, *years* of tackling a problem may not be adequate. With inquiry, the teacher has to forgo the role of language judge for the role of co-inquirer. But life in the classroom studying language is no longer dull. Highly (and intrinsically) motivated children and teacher live their own language. Such engagement in creative problem-solving and inquiry is the height of learning behavior. It reflects the real world of those who push back the frontiers of knowledge both for themselves and for others.

The difficulty of measurement of the complex processes of inquiry and of written composition (itself a form of inquiry in pursuit of written thought) makes us aware of dangers. The danger of accountability forcing attention on narrow, trivial, but easily measured objectives has justifiably caused concern. Many resolutions have been passed by the National Council of Teachers of English. Many position papers have been written (e.g., Cooper, 1971).

**Inadequacy and dangers of published tests**

Before we choose objectives, it makes sense to acquaint ourselves with the most advanced knowledge of assessment in the language arts field. In the past, teachers have turned in some awe to published tests. There are many standardized, published tests of grammatical knowledge and usage. But most of these fail to distinguish between linguistic competence with regard to rules of the standard or formal usage and competence in distinguishing between formal, general, and nonstandard usage (Carroll, 1971). Indeed, many of the tests fail to recognize that a number of presumably substandard usages have become standard.[2] These published tests with predetermined criteria often penalize the children who answer on the basis of usages now accepted. If such measurement is imposed, we may not only perfect the errors of our present ways but may regress and pick up a few errors we had discarded because we know they will be on "the test." The English language arts, dealing with a living language and a growing literature from changing people and amid evolving research, cannot remain static.

Perhaps even more importantly, in writing their own stories and letters children must *put everything together*. They cannot afford the luxury of being concerned solely with the isolated skills that are measured in most standardized tests of writing (Moore & Kennedy, 1971).

[2] Carroll mentions, for example, the Language Usage Test of the *Differential Aptitude Tests.*

These tests measure solely knowledge of that small area concerned with certain mechanical manipulations of language terms, facts, and convention. STEP Writing (Sequential Tests of Educational Progress, put out by the Educational Testing Service), has been criticized because the child is required to make only editorial revision and is not measured on the progress of writing itself (Carroll, 1971). STEP is a multiple-choice test of knowledge of certain writing skills rather than of actual free composition.

Even the test publishers themselves rail at the unwise misuse of the so-called grade-level-equivalent score, "a statistical monstrosity." Many educators have assumed that these tests provide a precise yardstick of each student's progress to points above or below grade level. In assuming this, such educators have allowed children, parents, and school boards to believe these scores and have even believed them themselves. Such measurement designed for groups is actually imprecise, especially for the individual. They have more of the accuracy of a "belly whopper" than of a precise dive into the ocean of skillful behavior.

So many factors can influence these grade-level scores that they become almost meaningless. Some such factors are these: a child's simply maturing a bit more, testing conditions, the timing of tests, attitude of the child, and pure chance. Such irrelevant variables can create statistical increases that would fulfill an objective used in a scheme for accountability (such as a performance contract) without the child's ever having learned anything. (See the section on the performance contract, later in this chapter.) Or they can make the results look like apparent failure when efforts for the *long range* have been mainly successful (Mecklenburger & Wilson, 1971). It is fallacious to judge performance in terms of grade level. Moreover, because children differ so widely in classrooms it is nonsense to specify what a "fourth-grade" pupil will be able to do.

It is not surprising that specialists in English fail to find published tests useful for evaluating achievement in writing. Braddock (1969) stated that a complex phenomenon such as composition quality defies careful analysis into parts. Some investigators measure pupils' products and assume that they are evaluating the intangible mental processes by which children created those products.

Thus, one of the special testing problems is measuring writing in its entirety. (I will try to give a solution for this problem in a later section.) We need diagnostic methods of evaluating written language ability that give more attention to the process underlying the teaching of written composition. There is a measurement lag; teachers can teach better than we know how to test.

## ASSESSING SOME SPECIFIC LANGUAGE ARTS AREAS (COMPOSITION, LISTENING, LITERATURE, AND PROBLEM SOLVING

A framework for skill and response mode

In Chapter 2, on relations among listening, speaking, writing, and reading, I concluded with a diagram showing the child at the center and language processes operating in pairs—receiving and expressing. When it comes to evaluation, teachers rely on observable responses that are spoken, written, and nonverbal. Keeping in mind (1) the child's language processes and skills in reading, writing, speaking, and listening and (2) the type of observable child response related to such skills (spoken, written, and nonverbal), a teacher can use a framework such as the following in planning assessment for the yearly program.

**A FRAMEWORK FOR PLANNING LANGUAGE ARTS ASSESSMENT** [a]

| The Child's Language Process or Skill | The Type of Observable Response Inferred to Relate to a Language Process or Skill | | |
|---|---|---|---|
| | Spoken | Written | Nonverbal |
| Listening | | | |
| Speaking | *X* [b] | | |
| Reading | | | |
| Writing | | *X* [b] | |

[a] Adapted from the proposed revision of the *English Language Framework for California Public Schools* (Sacramento, Calif.: State Board of Education, 1974).
[b] *X* signifies most direct match of process and observed response.

The imprecision in evaluating children's abilities in listening and reading (receiving processes) by having them write and speak (expressive processes) is another reason for regarding tests with caution.

Diagnosis, formative and summative evaluation

Evaluation using the framework just presented falls into three types, *diagnosis, formative evaluation,* and *summative evaluation. Diagnosis* usually comes prior to teaching. It helps the teacher to individualize objectives and instruction for particular children. Formative evaluation comes during the teaching process. It prompts the revision of objectives, materials, and teaching strategies. *Summative evaluation,* coming after the instruction, is designed to measure whether or not, or the degree to which, children have met the program objectives.

With the aforementioned framework in hand and the types of evaluation, the teacher is ready to formulate objectives and matching activity, first working on highest priorities. As an example let's tackle the important goal of trying to assess the entire process (rather than some isolated mechanical skill) in children's written composition. We will try to assess children's composition by actually examining what they do while and after composing, not by looking at multiple-choice scores on a grammar, spelling, or punctuation test.

### Attempting to Measure the Entire Process: The Individual Writing Conference

Looking backward

One way to evaluate the child's "entire process" in composition is through the individual writing conference. Take the following example. Perhaps you have decided to look backward to see where the child started and whether progress has been made (diagnosis). In conference with children you open their folder, look at the table of contents, and turn back to their earliest work. Teachers often hear children make such comments as, "Did I write that? I've learned a lot since then!" This is motivation for going on with more arduous tasks (competence motivation).

Record keeping

Perhaps the next part of this conference is to find out how children are coming along with their record keeping. You move from helping children with the keeping of their writing records to having them do the recording independently. One thing that the child might keep in the folder is a chart of the kinds of writing he/she is doing.

Has the child tried all of the aims: self-expression, exposition, literature, and directive language or persuasion? What are the various modes of writing tried within each aim? A tall tale? A cinquain? A character description? How is the child's diary or journal coming along? On the social studies chart for studying a South American country, would he/she like to gather information so the class can fill in the empty slot for language and climate, or the slot for how the people of the country get food, clothing, or shelter? Or would she write her group's science observation on the mealworms this time? Record keeping helps to ensure a balanced program.

Other recording

Another thing children might record is information about their quantity of writing done. "Now, with all this writing I'm a walking library!" Children might also record brief comments on particular items: Do they think that this is the best composition they have ever written? Fair to middling? Or do they wish they had not bothered? They may also have noted a challenge, problem, or difficulty with which they would like some help.

At first the child may try to conceal any problems he/she has. In a school where classes are run as a total group situation, that may be part of the name of the game. At first, most people tend to bring out their fanciest "glassware" or "best apparel." Then, as they feel more secure in a situation, they bring out their favorite old cracked mugs and comfortable old clothes. When the child says, "I don't think I do this very well yet in writing; can you help me with it?" you know you have helped to bring about positive attitude in coping with problems. Such an event is worth recording.

About this time in the conference (if you have not done this before) it is well to try to find out just what children's attitudes are toward themselves as growing writers, and record them. Is it—"I can write, but I can be a better writer," "I can write fairly well," "I'm hopeless in spelling," or perhaps "I haven't much of an idea about sounds and matching letters in spelling," or "I'm good at making characters talk."

The Teacher's record keeping. What about your record keeping? For your records you may use a notebook, a card form, or you might keep *your* record right in the child's personal folder along with *his/her* records. From time to time you may wish to check off a summary sheet of the child's writing up to that point. You might include the best features, the aims and modes of writing attempted, information on supporting skills, or conventions and mechanics apparently mastered. A note on sentence patterns, spelling, handwriting, a note on her own picture glossary, or personal word-box collection, a note on attitudes and appreciations, perhaps a note on the child's feel for form.

For example, can the child sense the assertion and development in comparing and contrasting? Can he make predictions when a story begins as the following one does?

"It looked like ________ and it looked like ________ and it looked as if it would be________. But it wasn't that. It was this."

Can the child use such a form or model and plug in her own story content? Your records might show if children seem to have ability to develop a sequence of events, or if they have basic sentence sense. Records might indicate their emotional depth, sincerity, and role-taking ability (or empathy), and whether or not their thinking style is consistently concrete or has some abstract leaps.

Child writer as a creative problem-solver

Or your records might show what kind of *problem solvers* you find the children to be: Are they persistent, free-wheeling brainstormers, systematic manipulators using successive steps? Or do they focus on necessary or most important features? Or are they trial and error kinds of processors who try out ways unsystematically? You might want to make note of any outstanding growth or jumps and any specific subsequent practice material you think you would recommend for skill development (formative evaluation). Presently I will present two items of use in examining problem-solving skill. The process of problem solving underlies progress not only in writing but also in all other learning areas.) The first item is a checklist about problem solving for the teacher to use in spotting areas he feels need attention. It could represent one in an array of instruments that the teacher has available for the conference.[3]

[3] The checklist was used in the author's Thinking Improvement Project (Lundsteen, 1970). See lessons on problem solving in the companion guide, *Ideas into Practice.*

## PROBLEM SOLVING CHECKLIST

## TEACHER DIAGNOSIS OF INDIVIDUAL CHILD

**Suggested Basis for Individual Conference and Evaluation**

Teacher ____________________

Date ____________________

Child ____________________

| GENERAL BEHAVIOR | YES | NO | NOT OBSERVED |
|---|---|---|---|
| 1. Made a contribution in the last problem-oriented discussion. (Participation) | ____ | ____ | ____ |
| 2. Has understanding of terms and phrases.[a] (Comprehension) | ____ | ____ | ____ |
| 3. Interprets accurately comments made by teachers and by other children. (Accuracy) | ____ | ____ | ____ |
| 4. Brings relevant knowledge e.g., to the discussion of compositions that children in the class have written and grasps directions for offering advice. (Relevance) | ____ | ____ | ____ |
| 5. Avoids working so rapidly that he/she fails to secure an understanding of the problem; e.g., starts on a writing problem with an apparent plan. Takes attitude that the problem-solving process is of value; e.g., does *not* think, "You either know the answer or not; you can either be quickly finished with the writing task or not." (Carefulness) | ____ | ____ | ____ |
| 6. Solves problem with much thought (brings elaboration and multiple alternatives to bear on writing problems, e.g., concerning word choice, image choice, and idea selection). (Thoughtfulness—elaboration of facts) | ____ | ____ | ____ |

[a] Such as, *problem* or *challenge, subproblem, definition, missing information* or *data, search* or *inquiry, hypothesis* or *solving ideas, planned procedure* or *steps, evaluation* or *testing it out.*

7. Constructs or selects an answer or alternative on the basis of many clues (does *not* jump to conclusions); e.g., would *not* tend to say, "I don't like the story because I don't like it. That's all." [b] (Multiplicity—elaboration of facts) ____ ____ ____

8. Constructs or selects answers on basis of impressions or feelings regarding the situation. (For example, might say, "That poem makes my ears happy!") (Empathy) ____ ____ ____

9. Is self-confident enough to attempt to reason about a problem. (Would *not* tend to say, "I don't know what I could write to end my composition—or start it. I never can think of anything.") (Self-confidence) ____ ____ ____

10. Gives time to considering the problem while keeping attention focused; not easily distracted from the writing problem. (Unlikely to say, "What was it, again, you said to think about before writing?" or "How did I say I was going to start my story?" (Focused attention) ____ ____ ____

INTO PROCEDURE AND QUALITY

1. Makes attempt to organize the problem into areas. Can break complex writing problems into workable parts recognizing subproblems and important details. (Might say, "First, I'll write about the happy home setting; then I'll have the young mouse lured away by the young owl; then I could have the mouse trick the owl—now how could I do that?") (Planning) ____ ____ ____

2. Attempts to define and clarify meanings. (Might say, "I still don't understand what a fable is." Or, "What do you mean when you wrote, 'He skulked'?") (Definition) ____ ____ ____

3. Makes use of *own* hypotheses in coming to a solution. (Might say, "I think the boy in the book *Roosevelt Grady* could solve his problem this way." (Autonomy) ____ ____ ____

4. Can justify, give reasons for, and consequences of choices of solution if and when they would be made. Can think of ways to *test* hypotheses, plan what to do next, and can transfer ideas. (Might say, "I know how the mouse could trick the owl! Since an owl's eyesight is so poor, he might put a dummy mouse in his place. That fits." (Evaluation) ____ ____ ____

5. Identifies missing data and searches. (Might say, "But you still didn't explain in your story how he got out of the nest, down that big tree and all the way home!" (Missing data) ____ ____ ____

6. Shows unusually deep understanding of a problem, especially regarding cause–effect relationship. (Might say, "I think the reason Charlotte died in the book *Charlotte's Web,* is that she unselfishly gave and gave of her web stuff, and gave too much of herself trying to save Wilber." Or, "When my pet bird dies, I hope I will still have friends." (Cause–effect) ____ ____ ____

[b] Would be able to answer some of the questions in Chapter 5 on children's literature, concerning, e.g., character, plot, and language.

TEACHER FUNCTIONS[c]

1. When it comes to responses that are unique, I would rate this child's progress in relation to initial performance as: (Originality)

| *Needs help* ☐ | *Better* ☐ | *Excellent* ☐ |
|---|---|---|
| (Might write: "The dancer dances.") | ("Stars dance in every kind of way." | ("Leaves danced in the air like pieces of a puzzle.") |

2. Can I list any particular areas where this child "shines" in the problem-solving–writing process, and where I want to compliment and reinforce him/her? Are there any areas I could use as strengths to assist weakness? ______________________________

______________________________________________

This is the behavior we hope to substitute: ____________________

______________________________________________

For example: (a) Thinking about and reworking his/her own experience in writing; (b) close observation; (c) honest reporting; (d) appreciation and use of sense imagery; (e) organization—beginning, arranging, and ending.

This will be our first step (formative evaluation): ______________

______________________________________________

The next item is a form for the use of upper-elementary-school children in checking up on their *own* progress as problem solvers. It can have other items added as children become more conscious of general problem-solving skill. (The guide is elaborated upon in *Ideas into Practice.*) Half of the items can be used one time, half another. Encourage children to enact (or dramatize) and to make pictures for each point in the guide (enactive and pictorial ways of knowing).

[c] If it is not possible to use this checklist with each child, make use of it with a random or representative sampling of, say, five children, and/or use a random sample of the items using different items with different children.

LOOKING BEHIND ME:
A PROBLEM-SOLVING GUIDE

Name ______________________

Date ______________________

Directions: These are some ideas you have met. Use this page as a guide when you are having a problem-solving discussion in your classroom or are writing a composition.

☐ 1. *Elaborate Facts* [a] *(Make us feel we're there.)*

☐ 2. *Define* [b] *(Make it really clear.)*

☐ 3. *Think of Subproblems → Main Problem*

☐ 4. *Stick to It*

---

☐ 5. *Don't Be Afraid to Be Original and Openminded*

☐ 6. *Empathize and Sympathize (Get in Another's Skin)*

☐ 7. *Think of the Whys and the Consequences*

☐ 8. *Communicate with Others.*

How many of the boxes can you check for each discussion or composition?

Use these ideas outside of class, too. Record your successes.

---

[a] See items 6 and 7 (under General Behavior) of the Problem Solving Checklist for teachers.

[b] See item 2 (under Into Procedure) of the checklist for teachers.

In any event—at the end of your record-keeping portion of the individual writing conference, you might want to jot down your decision: "This is the most important thing to work on now. . . ." Again, avoid trying to do everything at once. Instead try to teach at the child's "least best" place.

Grading

**Grading.** Rigid approaches to evaluation of children's writing that overwork the teacher and discourage the child have got to go. Grading compositions (summative evaluation) that children write with joy makes the task wearisome for you and fearful for the children. There is no need to "hemorrhage" with a red pencil all over a child's composition or to give it a grade. You may remember writing in school yourself with some degree of horror.

Evaluation does not have to be a frightening, terminal experience for children. The brief, cozy individual conference keeps you from adopting a laissez-faire attitude of just letting children's writing grow like a weed. Yet it keeps the evaluative process sensitive, humanistic, and with emphasis on constructive self-competency motivation. It is one of the best data-gathering devices, too.

After giving the individual-conference method a try, teachers will usually feel, "I didn't know what I didn't know!"

Keep in mind that not even your best writers are going to produce compositions that are sensitive, bright, and witty every time. Just as the rest of us do, children have their ups and downs in writing. And these ups and downs occur with composition perhaps more than with any other area of competence. Able pupils show more variation in quality from one written product to another than do less able pupils, as they tend to explore differing forms and styles of expression.[4]

Creative-writing scales

There are two published scales of creative writing, by Carlson (1968) and Yamamoto (1964) from which you might get some ideas (for diagnosis, formative and summative evaluation). The original Carlson Analytical Originality Scoring Scale deals with five categories: story structure, novelty, emotion, individuality, and style of stories. In the Yamamoto measure of imaginative writing there are seven categories of scores: organization, sensitivity, originality, imagination, psychological insight, and richness. Also see scales by Tway (1971).

These scales give you a lot of ideas. But avoid making your records too elaborate. Work yourself just enough to gain a picture of the continuity of the child's development, to answer the question, What kind of a "writing" child is she now? Record enough so that you give yourself a "cuing in" place for the next conference. Let the child see what you are recording so that he can agree or say, "Well, that is almost right, but I would change it so that it says . . ." It is motivating for children to feel your concern with them as writers and your acceptance.

[4] *The Students' Right to Write, NCTE Composition Opinionnaire* (Urbana, Ill.: n.d.).

You help the child take the long view—"Where have I been; where am I now; where do I want to go?"

In sum, the best way to evaluate is through observing behavior highly relevant to the goal. The best way to evaluate instruction in swimming is to see how well the learner performs in the water, not on a multiple-choice test. The best way to evaluate language arts instruction is to see how well children do the communication processes we have tried to teach them to do.

Having looked at evaluation with possibilities for examining large portions of writing processes, next let's look at fairly innovative measures of *basic,* cognitive language abilities measured in objective format. I have been highly critical of objective, formal assessment. But this is not to say that we cannot use creative imagination in order to create better formal assessment in the future. In fact some experimental measurement already shows a bit of progress.

---

## Some Efforts and Items for Possible Formal Objective Assessment of Basic Cognitive Processes Probably Needed for Composition

If composition is a deep process of the mind, we can turn to tests designed by cognitive psychologists for some insights. For example, Harris and Harris (1971), in a technical report for the University of Wisconsin Research and Development Center, have put together a battery of 56 short tests (two or three to each ability) to study the structure of concept attainment abilities. And one of the areas for basic concepts is the language arts. Of special interest are some of their basic tasks that deal with letter symbols, word forms, tasks of classifying, and excluding or naming in meaningful verbal material. There is measurement of rule naming and rule-applying behavior. They have adapted tasks involving word fluency, memory, induction, and deduction (administered to 250 fifth-grade children).

Analogy

For instance, some of the tests deal with basic abilities in making analogies. The following examples are adapted from the Harris and Harris tests:[5]

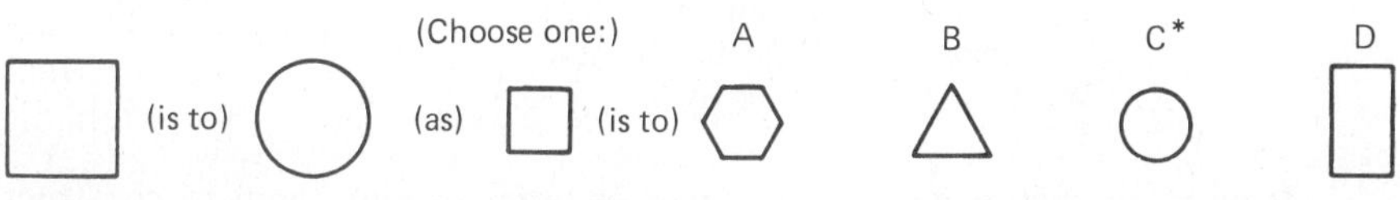


[5] Words in parentheses added by author for reader's clarification. The correct answer is marked by an asterisk.

Here is another example of a test item, this one dealing with verbal analogy:

*Hand* is to *man* as *paw* is to:
A. tail
B. dog *
C. leg
D. fur

If children cannot perform this kind of basic cognitive task, it is doubtful that they are going to be highly successful in the creative writing of similes or in developing a paragraph by comparison and contrast.

Generalizing trends

Another test related to basic ability in advanced composition (essay and exposition) is The Best Trend Name Test. The child is to infer a trend and select the name of that trend.

For example,

horse—car—propeller plane—jet
A. usefulness
B. speed *
C. shape

Sequencing

Another set of tests deals with basic abilities in sequence. These go beyond motor arrangement to the kind of comprehension of sequence necessary to composition. One test deals with sequence in pictures, another with scrambled words for a sentence, and another with scrambled sentences. Here's an example:

with begin capital names a letter

(When these words are correctly rearranged, do they make a true or false statement?)

And, in another test question, the child is given three short, simple sentences in random order, and is asked to (1) infer the proper order of events, (2) arrange the three in order, and (3) tell which should come first and which last. The items can require closer and closer discrimination which is basic to composition.

An example:

I picked up some supplies there.
The teacher sent me to the office.
We used the supplies in our class.

If children cannot put the sentences in order, asking them to construct a narrative story may be unrealistic.

So much for some basic language abilities measured in objective format. Moving to the evaluation of still broader cognitive skills of problem solving, useful in composition (but still in the multiple-choice vein) we turn to recent experimental tests in the Purdue Elementary Problem-Solving Inventory. The general form includes cartoons depicting problem situations, which are shown to the students on slides with descriptions and directions on audiotape (to get around reading problems). Children can examine the alternatives printed in a test booklet at the same time they hear them on audiotape. They respond by marking an *X* on a pictured box.

Problem solving skills

The abilities measured include the following items: (1) sensing if a problem exists—yes, no; (2) identifying the same problem precisely from three alternatives; (3) asking questions to clarify that problem ("Which of the following three questions would be best to ask so we can figure out what is going on?"); (4) guessing causes ("What is the most likely cause?"); (5) asking questions to clarify the goal in a problem situation ("What do you need to know to get there?"); (6) judging if more information is needed before a conclusion can be reached ("Do they have enough information for going ahead with planning the party?"—yes, no). There are other types of questions that can be used to check on problem-solving skills (Feldhusen et al., 1971). These skills are useful in plot construction. With the kinds of guidance I have been stressing in this book, they can transfer to any other in-school and out-of-school activity.

*The Productive Thinking Program* (Covington, Crutchfield, Davies, & Olton, 1972) includes semiobjective measurement, stimulation of multiple alternatives, and self-comparison with models of parts (examples of some possible responses) in the problem-solving process.[6]

---

Conceivably there could be objective-type tests, checklists, or scales to check on the child's wide range grasp of elements in effective writing. These, once recognized and appreciated, may find their way into the child's own writing. The following is an example of such a checklist.

Elements in successful composition: a checklist

*A Partial Checklist for Analyzing Students' Writing*

A. Ability to pick out and use writer's elements in paragraphs found in fiction, such as,
   1. Descriptive paragraphs (rendering experience into language)

[6] Also see problem-solving judgmental rating scales for oral and written composition in the companion guide, *Ideas into Practice*.

a. Dominant impression (texture)
———Selection of observed details (and emphasis given to particular ones)
———Choice of words
———Relation of details to the whole

b. Pattern
———What the observer can see
———What the observer's attitude is
———What the scene symbolizes

2. Narrative paragraphs

a. Movement in time and manipulation of time
———Amount of time covered
———Narrative time versus natural time
———Order of events

b. Proportions of action
———Selection of significant actions
———Panoramic view versus sharp focus

B. Ability to pick out and use writer's elements in expository and argumentative nonfiction, for example,

1. Expository paragraphs

a. Identification
———Introductory statements
———Definition of terms or concepts

b. Classification
———Inclusion
———Exclusion

c. Comparison and contrast
———Analogy and illustration
———New details relating to familiar principles
———Familiar details relating to *new* principles

d. Relationships
———Cause and effect
———Opinion and reason
———Question and answer
———Conclusion and proof
———Problem and solution (steps in a process)
———Hypothesis and evidence
———Least important and more important
———General to specific
———Subordinate and coordinate

2. Argumentative paragraphs

a. Proposition
———Something is true

————Something ought to be done

b. Evidence

————Fact
————Opinion
————Generalization
————Deduction

c. Persuasion

————Audience–author points of view
————Treatment, devices, and style

C. Ability to pick out and use units longer than paragraphs.

1. Pointing out and using overall design or symmetry of the plot of a story, or general plan of a report [7]
2. Recognizing and using large thought-divisions within the written work

————Topics, parts, chapters, sections, acts, scenes

3. Recognizing informal thought divisions

————Essay introduction, discussion, and conclusion
————Story introduction, build-up or complication (conflicts that give unity to the action), climax, denouement
————Series of episodes (and the emphasis given to particular ones)

4. Recognizing and using transitions

————Transition paragraphs that connect sections and episodes
————Transitional sentences that connect paragraphs and other sentences
————Words that provide transitions and connections between paragraphs and sentences

D. The ability to recognize techniques by which an author creates effects or emotional colorations

————Abstract and concrete words
————Denotative and connotative words
————Parallelisms
————Sound patterns, e.g., sound reflecting the sense (onomatopoeia, rhythm and accent patterns)

[7] Elementary-school children will ordinarily not be writing novels or textbooks, but they *might.*

———Feelings and emotions embedded by the author: disillusionment, broad comedy, dislike, idealism, interest, irony, horror, objective detachment, satire, sentimentality, tragedy, wit, and others

———Ways of representing character: direct statement, dialogue, and the like

———Completeness of character: single dominant trait (flat), stereotype, complex configuration of traits (round).

———Function of the characters: relation to the plot, relation to other characters

———Recognizing setting for what the author intends it to mean: emotional quality, shaper of events

E. Selecting an aim for a piece of writing

———Self-expression, exposition, literature, persuasion, or other more specific uses

---

*A Partial Check List for Analyzing the Classroom Writing Situation*

A. Quantitative assessment of time and resources available, amount of pupil writing and types of writing [8]

1. Time available for pupil writing

———What amount of time is available?

———What amount of this available time does the student actually spend in writing?

———How else does the student spend his/her available time?

2. Availability of resources

———Do the children have access to a physical environment conducive to writing?

———Where do the children do most of their writing?

———Do the children have access to materials, human reaction and encouragement, enactive opportunities, writer's (or editorial) aids, publishing opportunities?

[8] This assessment asks not how well the child has done, but about *what* he or she has done, and the resources available, the attitudes, and motivation.

__________Do they avail themselves of these facilities?
__________How much writing do the students produce?
__________What types of writing do they do?

B. Assessment of attitudes about writing [9]

__________Is willing to write
__________Occasionally shows a preference for writing
__________Seeks out additional writing activity

C. Assessment of motives for writing (consensus of reasons)

__________Habit, compulsion, or assigned and required automatic, ritualistic writing (such as name and heading) done without real meaning or awareness; or externally required, such as assigned in school, forms
__________Status or prestige among peers or with teacher as model
__________Diversion and escape, pleasant feedback, communication and emotion as incentive and as reinforcer
__________Self-explanation, to discover what one thinks, self competency
__________Reinforcement and reassurance to affirm one's own values, sense of right or wrong, personal acceptance, or resolution of paradoxes
__________Production of a total commitment in the search for truths or literary pleasures

Need to retain complex ideas

Afterthought. I have deliberately gone into detail in order to illustrate that there is much more to assess (and capable of being assessed) in composition than just spelling, punctuation, and usage on some objective test. And I have proposed that those objectives about conventions are far less crucial to the writing program than are other objectives. Furthermore, the higher-level items on the checklist are actually the same objectives that are needed for *reading comprehension* programs.[10]

[9] This attitudinal division and the next can furnish material for making inferences about what student writers are really like.

[10] In fact these objectives are adapted from original drafts of ideas for the National Assessment of Reading Progress.

## Activity for the Reader of this Text

**Hunting for successes in a third-grade composition**

11.1. Evaluating a Composition. Examine the following third-grade composition rated high according to a scale devised by the Grosse Pointe, Michigan public school system. See how many successes you can find. Then turn this book upside down to see the criteria that the judges felt this composition met.

[11] Composition from page 23 and criteria adapted from page 13 of the publication *The Writing of Elementary School Children, A Model for Evaluation,* Dept. of Instruction, The Grosse Pointe Public School System, 389 St. Clair, Grosse Pointe Michigan 48230.

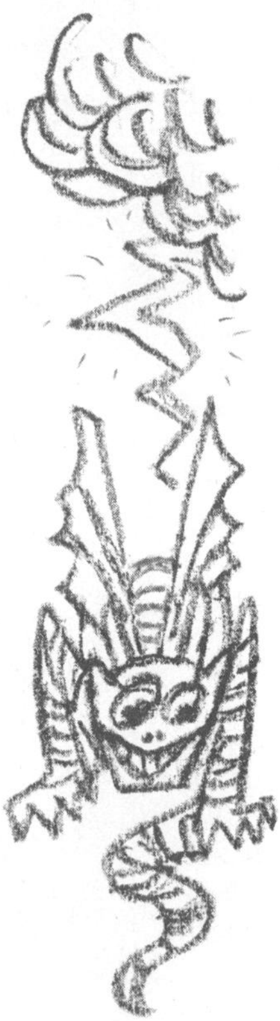

My Faverite Monster

One Day Billy said "there are many monsters in the wrold but mine is the best." I think I will take My monster for a walk! So billy went for a walk with his monster. Then when he came home it began to rain So Billy went to let his monster out To play in The lighting. When the monster came in Billy and he wached the later later later later later Show. The next morning Billy fed his monster a bowl of baterys and a glass of wires.

The End

1. Specific detail: accurate word choices
2. Most meaningful language units expressed as sentences
3. Evidence of a controlling idea and a clear purpose
4. Selection of ideas
5. Chronological or logical ordering of all or most sentences
6. Use of own ideas as the source for writing
7. Adequate information and idea loading in the writing taken as a whole
8. Spelling of basic words and high quality of spelling miscues
9. Sentences formed on patterns other than subject-verb and subject-verb-noun
10. Words show relationship between ideas

Besides these criteria, the composition also shows the following:

11. Recognizing the needs of a created character
12. Originality
13. An unexpected idea
14. Emphasis
15. Metaphor
16. Play on word sounds
17. Wit [11]

Next, look at this unpromising composition and find strengths. Then think of questions and comments you could use to draw this child out for details, feelings, letting him dictate part to make the audience feel "they were there." For example you might say "I'm dumb, I guess; I always kinda thought softball was a pretty dull game compared to. . . . See if you can't convince me I should have been there." Or, "You get me excited, but I want to know more."

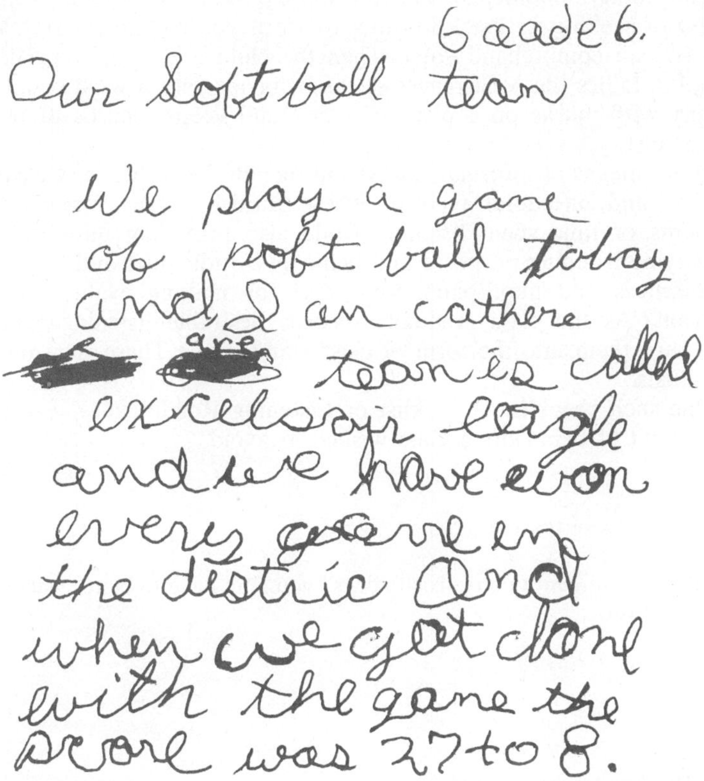

Grade 6.

Our Soft ball team

We play a game of soft ball today and I an cathere are team is called excelsoir eagle and we have won every game in the distric And when we got done with the game the score was 27 to 8.

---

Thus far I have dealt with questions about assessment rationales, types, a process and response mode framework and some specific ways to evaluate processes and higher levels of thought. I have had specific reference to composition and the individual writing conference. Next consider another important curricular area needing new, imaginative assessment—listening.

---

## Use of Informal Devices to Evaluate Listening Skills

**Teacher and pupil informal observation methods**

Both teachers and pupils can simply informally observe much diagnostic, formative, and summative information related to listening needs and growth. They can use informal devices rather than formal, standardized tests. One method is called *pinpointing and charting.*

The child pinpoints a behavior he/she wants to change (e.g., increase of seeking feedback in order to see if you comprehend or if your listener can comprehend you). Then the child selects appropriate time samples, tallies the occurrences of the behavior with a wrist counter (or simply with marks on a piece of tape) and keeps records of progress (charting).

Other means of informal assessment include individual and class logs, diaries, and anecdotal records. These furnish survey material about amounts of time spent listening while also providing information for classifying listening purposes and behaviors. Individual and small-group conferences and pupil-pairs are useful for making evaluation highly relevant. As the class gradually records desirable listening behaviors, they turn them into the form of class standards.[12] These they turn into checklists.

**Checklists**

One such checklist (Checklist of Listening Roadblocks) was written as a result of behaviors a class wished to avoid.

### CHECKLIST OF LISTENING ROADBLOCKS

See if you can identify any "roadblocks" you may have to better listening and remove them.

| HEARING: | (Check if it applies) |
|---|---|
| 1. The speaker talked too softly. | ( ) |
| 2. He spoke loudly enough, but not clearly. | ( ) |
| 3. The room was too noisy. | ( ) |
| Noise came from: a. people around me | ( ) |
| b. outside the building | ( ) |
| c. the hall | ( ) |
| d. other sources (explain) | ( ) |

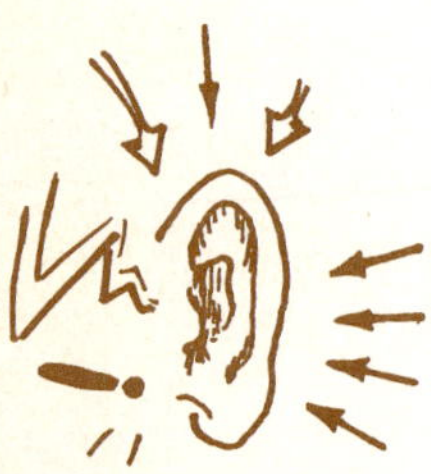

[12] For examples see Lundsteen (1966) on critical listening; Russell and Russell (1959); and the companion guide to this book, *Ideas into Practice.*

LISTENING:

1. I didn't pay attention because I wasn't interested. ( )

2. I didn't attend because I was thinking about what I was going to say. ( )

3. The speaker or sound began before I got settled. ( )

4. I missed a large bit and could not figure out what was going on. ( )

5. I was thinking about other things. Explain— ( )

______________________________________________

______________________________________________

______________________________________________

6. I got wrapped up like a cocoon in my own argument and planning. ( )

7. I couldn't understand so I quit listening. ( )

   a. I couldn't find anything I already knew about to match up with what was said. ( )

   b. I couldn't summarize in my own words. ( )

8. It was hard to keep up because I couldn't figure out what might come next. ( )

9. I listened like a sponge. I got so concerned with details I could not tell what was the main part and what was just supporting. ( )

**Coding devices**

As another useful method of informal assessment, the teacher can incorporate valued behaviors during class discussion into coding devices. Once the children have cooperatively derived these behaviors, these coding sheets can be duplicated and given to pupils. The use of such material (and the standards upon which it is based) is best built up bit by bit with children. Then they genuinely understand it while feeling it exists partly by their choice. A sample coding sheet followed by a lesson plan is provided.

### CODING RESPONSES OF LISTENERS

### (SOME SKILLS AND ELEMENTS IN LISTENING)

| CODE SYMBOL | ITEM |
|---|---|
| 1. TW | Two-way responsibility |
| 2. D | Details |
| 3. Se | Sequence |
| 4. M Id | Main Ideas |
| 5. S | Summary |

### LESSON PLAN FOR CODING A TAPED DISCUSSION[a]

**CHALLENGE TO PUPILS: (LEARNER OBJECTIVE)**

- Identify, name, and describe aspects of listening by coding parts of a taped discussion.

**MATERIALS:**

Guide(s) for each pupil, Coding Responses of Listeners; taped segment of class discussion for coding; paper, pencil for pupils

[a] There were many lessons before this one in which concepts of listening skills had been built up as children were guided to notice them. See the companion guide, *Ideas into Practice,* for earlier lessons and for explanation of a listening unit of instruction.

SUGGESTED STEPS

1. Distribute coding sheet to pupils.
2. Discuss the coding sheet and check understanding of behaviors on it.
3. Play a segment of a tape recording of a class discussion.
4. Use the coding sheet as a guide.
5. Encourage the children to be the question askers.
6. Discuss elements of listening behavior inferred from the responses (or lack of response) on the tape.
7. Replay the tape segment to verify the coding and confirm inferences by checking with the listener whose response is being examined.
8. Have children tabulate the frequency of occurrence of various items on the coding guide.
9. Encourage children to see which desirable types of response have low or no occurrence and try to plan for more practice or situations that would elicit such responses.
10. Have children (once they are familiar with the procedure) repeat these steps in small groups which they direct themselves.

**Informal listening inventory**

Teachers could also use graded children's texts and published paragraphs of various grade levels in order to form a diagnostic tool usually called an *informal reading inventory.* But instead of determining the *child's* oral reading and comprehension level (as indicated by the most difficult selection read successfully by the child), the *teacher* can read the paragraphs in the inventory aloud to the child. Then by asking questions on the content the teacher can determine the highest level at which the child can understand material when it is spoken. Such an informal device is especially helpful in getting a gross idea of the level of listening comprehension of a child who is linguistically different.

**Evaluations made by pupils**

If the listener's first task is to mentally re-create the meaning of the speaker, then an advisable assessment activity is to have the children author their own passages for listening tests. Children can then have a hand in designing the questions to be asked about their passages. In this way the child becomes the best authority on what the passage means and can settle conflicts of opinion that might arise.

## Activity for Children

11.2. Listening Center Task Cards. This activity illustrates how six levels of listening comprehension (corresponding to the Bloom Taxonomy of Educational Objectives) can be activated and informally assessed. The material (or unit of discourse) is advertising. Each of various objectives could be placed on task cards used in a file in a listening/learning center. A child might want to diagnose himself and start with the easiest and first questions (on the level of "knowledge of specifics"). Then, finding success, he/she could move on to questions requiring higher and higher levels of listening comprehension skill. Activity could be closed (with examples and answers given) or open (with the child invited to collect and analyze his/her own examples). Children using the task-card series might engage in formative evaluation and make suggestions for changing or elaborating the material. The response mode observed could be oral (with a partner or aide), written, or a nonverbal selecting, checking, cutting and pasting, and pictorial representation.

### *Creating Task Cards for Levels of Comprehension*

STRAND: LISTENING TO MEDIA—Advertising—Television

OVERALL OBJECTIVE: The child will analyze, compose, and evaluate an original TV advertisement.

SOCIAL STUDIES CONCEPT: Demand is the consumers' willingness to buy a certain product at a given price.

1. *Knowledge of specifics:* Become an ad collector. (Take these food ads, for example, or with a tape recorder "collect" or recall commercials for different brands of a product you have chosen.) Note the differences.
2. *Comprehension:* Using your own words, summarize and rewrite the commercials aiming for an audience of your own age group (or translating for another selected group).
3. *Application:* Take a survey asking (1) what the person's favorite commercial about the product is, (2) why it is appealing to him, (3) and whether or not it makes him/her buy the product. Apply what you have understood and the skills you have developed from making earlier surveys.
4. *Analysis:* What are the minimum elements that an ad must have in order to present necessary information? What parts? Make a survey to find out from a sample of "consumers" what parts affect them most and why. Try to include different types of consumers in your survey. Spot how much nutritional information is actually given. Analyze how your actions about the food (based on persuasion through child actors, lights, words, and canned laughter) might affect your health.
5. *Synthesis:* Write and produce your own 30-second commercial for a product. (Decide who your audience is that you are appealing to and how you will appeal.)
6. *Evaluation:* Plan and carry out an evaluation of your ad. Ask sample potential consumers to react to your ad according to its appeal to them. Were you successful in light of the criteria you had set? Why or why not? What do you conclude are some essential parts of this kind of composing in order to create a demand? What moral or ethical ideas (rights and wrongs) do you need to consider about your ad's impact on users (e.g., their nutrition and health).

If these questions were placed in a task file box at a learning center in a classroom, the set might represent only one of several. Other, related ones could be designed to help a child attain a certain social studies

egocentrically communicating writers and speakers. They pour forth unconcernedly over the heads of almost everyone, feeling no responsibility. It is rare that we are in communication with a person who has the same attributes, aims, vocabulary meanings, and perspective that we do. It is rare that we do not need to recode. Whether a child wants to explain a game, share a story, give a compliment, persuade, or help someone—abilities in nonegocentric communication with empathy and role-taking are important, observable skills. (Role-taking skill is, of course, essential to effective teaching at any age.) [14]

---

Leave informal ways of assessment. Consider formal, standardized, commercial tests.

*"Is there any standard a teacher can refer to so he can determine a child's progress in listening year by year?"* [15]

[14] See the work of Flavel, Botkin, Fry, Wright, and Jarvis (1968) for experimental tasks from a developmental perspective for this kind of interactive communication. (Reference annotated.)

[15] This is an actual question raised by a teacher, as are like questions occurring later in this chapter. The ideas in this section apply to more areas, of, course, than just listening.

Nonegocentric Communication

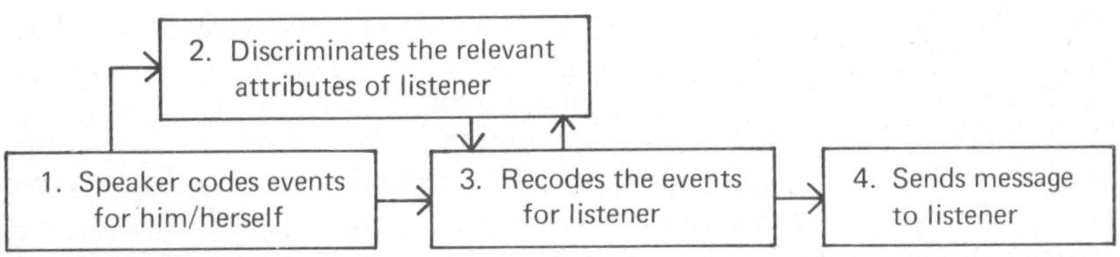

## Standardized, Norm-Referenced Tests

What does *standardized test* mean? Test producers commonly give such a test to a sample that represents the potential market population for the publisher. The information from the sample's scores are used to show the range of performances expected from those who take the test. Designers plan the procedures of standardized tests so that users may examine many persons in essentially the same, consistent way.

What does *norm-referenced test* mean? Users of such tests can see how certain groups (norms) perform. Then users supposedly have a common interpretation for scores. That is, a norm-referenced achievement test is designed to compare one group of pupils' performance to that of another group. Such tests measure performance on a few selected tasks. Reasonable time limits do not allow for complete assessment of all skills a listener (or a reader) is capable of performing.

How are standardized, norm-referenced tests used generally? Educators use standardized, norm-referenced tests if the purpose of evaluation is to compare the achievement of pupils in one program (class, school, district, or state) with another group of pupils. Percentiles or grade-level equivalent scores are the usual way results of such achievement tests appear.

Caution: validity corrupted by special preparation

What are some cautions? Test validity depends on an appropriate match between the sample of tested content or skills and the objectives of the instructional program. For example, if the test does not measure the listening skills introduced in the program, but measures skills developed later, scores fail to show the effects of teaching. But, if the sampling of tested skills is all that is taught, the test results become biased from this "teaching for the test." When teachers are under pressure to show high achievement scores for their classes, standardized tests may be used in this invalid way.

Caution: results apply to groups not to individuals

The test score of any one child reflects a sizable error of measurement. At the high and low ends of the distribution of scores one or two items guessed wrong (or right) changes the grade-level equivalent score greatly. Group tests measure achievement of groups—not individuals—particularly over a year or less. School people misuse group achievement test scores when they employ them to determine placement of individual children. Another caution is to avoid comparing groups that were not represented in the population on which the test norms were developed.

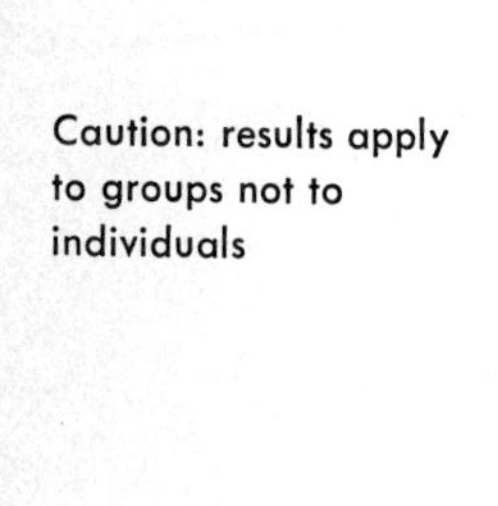

The teacher's question at this section's beginning was, "Is there any standard a teacher can refer to so he can determine a child's progress in listening year by year?" In light of the preceding discussion, *standardized, norm-referenced tests do not fill the teacher's needs.* Tests especially designed for individual administration give a closer assessment. However, an inordinate amount of testing (required by individual measurement), with the tensions that usually accompany it, may rob the child of instructional time and create an unhappy classroom atmosphere. As a final caution, standardized commercial tests can reflect only a portion of the child's total performance. And to be entirely valid, each teacher would have to teach the same content in the same way and order.

What are specific uses of standardized listening tests? Keeping these just-mentioned cautions in mind, what are some uses of standardized, norm-referenced tests of listening? [16]

1. To assess the range and distribution of listening ability in a particular group so that the teacher can adjust the difficulty of material.
2. To assess and predict very grossly the listening ability of individual children with respect to some language features measured on the test.
3. To give some direction to general placement, instruction, and improvement of instruction.
4. To see if the group has learned what it is being taught, or needs more or various kinds of instruction.
5. To measure the group's improvement of certain listening skills over a period of time.
6. To grossly estimate the group's reading potential.
7. To compare reading and listening skills in order to make the most of the mode of reception.
8. To give children some feedback on the results of their efforts and to give some evidence for advising next steps.
9. To test assumptions, proposals, and models concerned with listening.

### Criterion-Referenced Tests

*Criterion-referenced tests* have entered the classroom more recently than have standardized, norm-referenced ones. A criterion-referenced test is designed to assess whether or not a pupil can perform a defined task. For example, when listening to material of a certain length and complexity, the child is either able or not able to identify the main idea in nine out of ten items. Criterion-referenced tests are used in making short-range instructional decisions and in seeing how well the teacher's own instructional objectives are being mastered by their pupils.

[16] A critical review and description of standardized listening tests, and publishers' tests to accompany materials is given in Lundsteen (1971). Some of these publishers' tests resemble the criterion-referenced tests discussed in the next section. Lundsteen (1971) also describes some unpublished, experimental tests and tasks that may furnish interesting ideas to teachers.

A further examination of criterion-referenced tests, however, reveals that they are nothing new. Previous examples are the scores on such work-sample tests as typing, where the score is stated in terms of words per minute. But if those typing scores are compared to those made by other people (e.g., "that score places at the 80th percentile"), the test is norm-referenced.

Another example refers to the instructor of a business training program who will refuse to allow new workers to begin until they have made perfect scores on the firm's safety test. These criterion-referenced-test givers make inferences about the on-the-job behavior of those taking their tests. They hope that every person answers or performs correctly on all test items (or gets a certain set percentage correct). Thus they hope that every person receives the same score on the criterion behavior. (An example out of past history might be the requirement of a score of 100 on the weekly spelling test before trying to learn any more new words or a 90% mastery of one sound-letter correspondence before learning another.) This lack of variability is not the aim of norm-referenced tests, which are designed to discriminate among those who know and those who do not. Criterion-referenced tests best lead to useful inferences when the behavior sought is obvious and simple. This kind of observation has been with us for a long time.

**Highly specific versus general predictive assessment**

Do not let the labels *norm-referenced testing* and *criterion-referenced testing* intimidate you with respect to evaluating listening. Actually the teacher who asks a child to repeat last-minute instructions is administering an informal listening test, with results which may have predictive value for similar encounters. A teacher who adjusts his speech according to his estimate of the ability of his listener to interpret it (role-taking) is estimating ability to comprehend spoken language. A principal is testing listening when he adopts one level of speech for a child of six, and another for a child of twelve, and when he revises his estimates in light of his listener's responses (nonegocentric communication). But in each of these instances the immediate (if not the only) interest of the "tester" is *not* to find out about *general* listening ability, but to find out about grasp and retention of specific information. The need for both informal and formal means of assessment exists in today's classroom.

---

## Other Considerations

*"What about testing for affective responses in listening?"*

**Affective responses**

Affect. Terms such as *esthetic appreciation, emotion,* and *empathy* suggest areas of communicable experience. These are difficult to explore by means of quantifiable test responses. Laughter, tears, and signs of embarrassment may give better evidence of affective listening than any objective test yet designed. But such evidence is colored by the listener's control of expression, and the power and the bias of the observer. Assessing behaviors in the affective domain remains a challenge.

*"What about pupil motivation and testing?"*

Motivation through consequences. In spite of advantages of standardized, norm-referenced tests, the trouble with using many paper-and-pencil types of evaluations is the lack of intrinsic motivation. They may give little or no opportunity for children to see the genuine consequences of how they listen. Children need to see direct cause–effect relations (important to *them*) that are the product of the quality of listening they do.

Child realization of skill—key motivation for progress

For example, can children see that they are missing out on listening fun, beauty, joy, and fascination? ("I heard a jet tear a rough edge across the silent sky.") Can a child see that when he garbled the directions, the game was spoiled? Can the child see that friendships bloom during empathic listening and shrivel during one-sided (egocentric) communication? Can children see that the smooth-voiced TV announcer talked them into spending all their hard-earned allowance on a stupid, flimsy toy when a little critical listening could have saved them this disappointment? These are the real-life evaluations that the constructors of paper-and-pencil tests find it hard to simulate.

Seeing growth in listening as a creative problem-solving process. If children see their problems in listening as their *own* challenges to be overcome creatively, then much of the struggle is won. When children see the paper-and-pencil test as giving them information that helps to solve their problem, learning is enhanced. It is doubtful, however, that this autonomous, creative problem-solving emphasis can be activated by published directions in the manual. Long-term development of this crucial learning set rests with the teacher and instructional materials.

Motivation through autonomous problem-solving

Leave the listening program and its assessment (both formal and informal) now and think about another important, but difficult to measure area—literature.

---

## How Does the Teacher Evaluate the Literature Program?

How does the teacher check on the child's personal response to literature? How does he know if the pleasure was weak, average, or strong?

Collecting feedback

These are some of the ideas explored in this section. In any case the idea is to teach and assess by collecting responses as ingeniously as possible. Evaluate what you do and how the child responds in order to create a more rewarding program.[17]

Observation

Perhaps your best, most comprehensive mode of evaluation is observation. You can observe nonverbal facial expression, posture, and response to your open questions and to questions formulated by the children. You can observe the interaction of pupil discussion, the number of books checked out, the related activity of dramatic play, artwork, composition, uninterrupted and sustained silent reading (USSR). An excellent way to get information on children's response is by examining their written composition related to or based upon literature.

Goals and objectives

Means of attempting evaluation may vary. (But do try to evaluate.) First, seek to get your priority goals and objectives clearly in mind. For example, a general goal is to help children to know and enjoy our literary heritage of prose and poetry. Restated—"The child will understand literature as communication raised to the level of an art, an artistic expression of alternative ways of living," and "will appreciate literature both in the work of professional authors and in the work of peers."

Categories of objectives

Instruction to this end is generally concerned with the following categories:

1. *Affective behavior* (the development of affective behaviors such as values).
   - Looks forward to the story time and reminds the teacher if it's forgotten
   - Voluntarily takes home a book read to the class
2. *Attitudes* (the development of attitudes such as acceptance and appreciation).
3. *Active participation.* Since teachers want children to become active participants in literature, they encourage overt responses to poetry and to prose. (This emphasis on values, attitudes, and physical participation does not mean that cognitive knowing is neglected in evaluation of the literature program.)
4. *Cognitive behavior.* In fact, a teacher might use a checklist such as the following:

| | Yes | No |
|---|---|---|
| ■ Knows terms such as plot, setting, character | ☐ | ☐ |
| ■ Knows the conventions of a fable or of haiku | ☐ | ☐ |
| ■ Knows criteria for evaluating a novel | ☐ | ☐ |

[17] This section draws upon the work of Moore and Kennedy (1971).

- Can relate to a character ☐ ☐
- Exchanges information about authors, story plots, and other aspects of form and style ☐ ☐

5. *Autonomy.* Whether you are evaluating cognitive or affective objectives, one of the main ideas is that pupils need to learn to evaluate their own behaviors. They need to learn to assess their own abilities, attitudes, and knowledge on the basis of more than emotional, unconscious, or spur-of-the-moment criteria. Rather than being a separate category, autonomy may be a dimension of any of the other divisions—affective behavior, active participation, and cognitive behavior.

**Informal devices.** As already suggested, one help to the pupil and teacher seeking evaluation is the construction and use of attitude inventories, checklists, and rating scales to tap the aforementioned categories of objectives. These devices assist observation and make attitudinal and subjective evaluation more systematic and useful. Then the teacher has a more defensible statement than, "Well, I think they all like the literature we've been having."

**Formulating items**

For example, in order to informally rate interest level, try constructing a checklist of affective attitudes. (Administer it to an adult for trial and subsequently to children. Assure children that there is no right or wrong answer.)

1. *Awareness level.* You might first formulate items to see if children will be aware of and give selected attention to literature. An example of an item designed to tap awareness might be the following:

   > "Can you show where the fiction and the nonfiction and poetry books are located in this classroom?"

   An example designed to tap selected *attention* might be:

   > "When listening to poetry do you ever note the difference between 'hard' words and 'soft' words?" [18] "Have you ever heard a humorous story that rhymes?"

2. *Appreciation level.* Just as there as two aspects of the awareness level (awareness itself and then attention), there are at least two aspects of the appreciation level, *acceptance* and *appreciation.*

[18] Letters that symbolize hard sounds in words might be *d, f, k, p, t,* e.g., *cot.* Letters that symbolize soft sounds might be the long vowels and *l, m, n,* e.g., *bloom.*

An example of an item designed to see if children will *accept* literature, that is, are open and responsive to it might be the following:

> "Do you listen to stories read aloud?"

Then construct items to see if children go beyond acceptance to *appreciate* literature, that is, value it and enjoy it during their own leisure time. See if they seek it independent of an assignment. An example might be the following:

> "Do you ever want to stay in a bit from recess to finish a story, or want to take it home?" [19]

3. *Participation level. Willingness* refers to less-strong behavior; that is, it might be stimulated or mandated. *Enjoyment* refers to stronger voluntary behavior with a high level of personal involvement and emotion. This category refers to behaviors such as motor and nonverbal, as well as listening, speaking, reading, and writing.

   An example of items designed to tap *willingness* might be the following:

> "Would you be willing to discuss a story read to you in a small group?"
>
> "Would you be willing to give (orally or in writing) an evaluation of whether or not the characters in the fifth episode of *The Saturdays* are true-to-life?" (or whatever work is familiar to the child).
>
> "Would you be willing to tell a story to some younger children if I asked you to?"

Examples of items designed to tap *enjoyment* might be the following:

> "Do you enjoy reading certain parts of books aloud to others on your own?"
>
> "On your own, do you enjoy discussing the similarities and differences among stories you have read with others who have read them too?"
>
> "Do you enjoy dramatizing or playing the roles of book characters and try to get this started?"
>
> "Do you bring new books to class to share without being told?"

[19] Of course, among the categories of items and objectives suggested thus far (and the next ones) there is probably overlap. Such fine distinction of behavior and motivation is difficult to make.

**Teacher self-evaluation and checklist.** Lastly, teachers can devise rating scales to evaluate themselves. The following are some examples:

- Reads aloud stories and poems to children.
- Suggests books and poems to individuals and to groups that are appropriate to their interests and to topics under discussion.
- Sometimes uses questions that guide children's attention and enjoyment to organization and language of literature (e.g., character, plot, setting, point-of-view, style).
- Keeps large rotating classroom library readily available to children.
- When reading aloud, exposes "quality" models of author's writing and encourages children to discuss effective writing.
- Knows many authors and their works.
- Can direct a child to a specific book in light of the child's development, needs, and interests.
- Has children in class by the end of the year "well read" for their age levels.
- Has children who check out many library books.
- Employs certain books in a certain way because such use is apparently *effective with* his *children,* i.e., they like the books and get experience they otherwise would miss; they make use of the literature as a springboard to their own talking, writing, creating, feeling, and sharing. (Does *not* use books and methods just because "it's new" or "famous" or "required.")

It is worth repeating that objectives evaluated for the literature program deal with the *head,* and the *hand,* but mainly with the *heart.*

Leave assessment of specific skills and content areas of the curriculum and next, examine more specifically the nature of (and current ideas about) accountability, PPBS, and performance contracting.

---

## What Is Accountability and How Is It Relevant to the Teacher?

Trying to pinpoint responsibility

**How does accountability operate?** From a historical perspective, accountability is an abstract concept that has been and is present in any ordered society (Harsh, 1971). Society holds its members responsible and accountable for specified individual development. The important question about this concept is, Who is responsible for what? As our society grimaces from the pain of defective communication and antagonistic social values, it reacts to the discomfort by saying, "Something is responsible." The institutions of our society? Education?

Interpretation of the term *accountability* depends upon what you think this means or holds in store for *you.* And a cluster of relevant concepts is related to *systems* by which to attain accountability. Two of these systems are PPBS (Planning, Programming, Budgeting System) and performance contracting, which I will talk about later.

Harsh (1971) suggests that the understatement of the year might be that the education profession does not enthusiastically embrace accountability. Emotions run high over questions such as these: What are the schools (and the language arts teacher in particular) accountable for? Who shall be accountable? How shall accountability be established? By whom?

Aspects of accountability: legal

Dyer (1970) has added three interrelated aspects of accountability: legal, moral, and informational. The *legal* aspect, including any authority and contractual relationships, deals with means for ensuring that all the people in the educational system will act in accord with the goals of that system. That means voters, policy makers, administrators, teachers, specialists, parents, and pupils. All the parties have a responsibility to some or to several other parties. The National Council of Teachers of English (NCTE) has been explicit about presenting their side of this issue on responsibility, as we shall see later.

Moral and informational

The *moral* aspect of accountability refers to caring about and being concerned for others, especially students. The *informational* aspect refers to having accurate and comprehensive data about the context, input, content, process, and outcome of the educational program. People in the system are accountable for supplying, receiving, and using information for decision making.

The legal, moral, and informational aspects all are related. For example, legal directives based on information are not likely to be accurately and effectively implemented unless supported by a mutual moral commitment to the importance of meeting needs of the children served by the educational system.

Most English teachers have been accountable as they formulated their goals and objectives into daily lesson plans for their pupils while keeping one eye on the context spreading out from the local to the world scene. They have given willingly of information about their aims and outcomes. Libraries are full of journal articles giving testimony of this accountability.

Mutual accountability

The NCTE, in its yearly resolutions (1971 to date) has dealt with the question, Who is accountable to whom? The NCTE resolved that just as the language arts teacher is accountable to his students, to his colleagues, and to the communities that have a responsible interest in his activities, so each of these groups is accountable to the teacher. Students are responsible for being active participants in the learning process. Parents are responsible for supplying a nurturing environment and for helping to develop appropriate learning programs. Administrators and others are responsible for fostering and protecting the school climate for the teaching process. The wider communities are responsible for providing financial, cultural, and social support. All in this large social context need to participate so that the nature of the assessment program reflects those persons most affected by it.

What PPBS is

**What questions do English teachers ask about PPBS (Planning, Programming, Budgeting System)?** Next we examine PPBS, a system for implementing accountability. What is it? PPBS is a management technique first employed by the national defense effort. Originally it was designed to identify the relationships between the quantity and quality of products and the costs of alternate methods of production. There are efforts in states to design and implement such a system for education for school districts to use. The system requires an integrating of these: (1) goals and objectives (planning in light of role in the community and anticipated accomplishments), (2) program planning and measurement, and (3) budgeting.

Goals and objectives

*Goals and objectives* furnish the first problem area. The objectives that support and advance the large goals are supposed to reflect observable, measurable pupil behaviors that can furnish data to the other parts of the system. They are supposed to be desirable accomplishments that can be measured within a given time period. Writing these objectives for the language arts is fraught with difficulties that were outlined earlier in the discussion of assessment.

Conditions

Cooper (1971) suggests that language arts teachers should go ahead and try to write objectives. But he gives a list of conditions he thinks teachers should be ready to fight for. Some are these:

1. That any student assisting in curriculum planning be allowed to write his/her own objectives or add some to those the teacher has written for the class so that they are relevant and modifiable.
2. That higher-level cognitive and affective objectives in the areas of literature and composition be written so that a number of different measures can assess accomplishment. These measures need to include children's own introspective accounts of what they have learned and how they have changed.
3. That measuring be kept to a *minimum* so that it does not crowd out meaningful classroom activity.

4. That every objective be for an activity that the teacher honestly thinks is engaging and worthwhile for the child (high priority).
5. That objectives not violate any well-established research findings in the language arts, such as the findings on the lack of relation of formal grammar study to correct usage and fluency. (See Chapter 10, on grammar.)

Can-do, may-do, and will-do

Hoetker (1970) has suggested a distinction among "can-do," "may-do," and "will-do" behaviors for English. Can-do behaviors include knowledge, comprehension, and application of knowledge in familiar situations—the first three levels in the Bloom cognitive taxonomy of objectives (e.g., the pupil can pick out a fable—given a fable, a myth, and a fairy tale). May-do behaviors include the remaining levels in the cognitive taxonomy and all the levels in the affective taxonomy, except the highest (e.g., the pupil may work on and even chair a committee to discuss literature). The last, will-do category is characterized by a value shown by the choices and preferences that describe the quality of an adult's life (e.g., the pupil grows up to write a novel). The will-dos are present only fractionally during the school years. Hoetker argues that we need to write only learner objectives for may-do behaviors, stated in "yes, he does," or "no, he does not" terms, rather than in percentages.

NCTE's suggested questions for teachers

The NCTE passed a resolution on objectives: that teachers put in the position of using or developing behavioral objectives secure satisfactory answers to certain questions. Some are these:

1. Do changes of surface behavior constitute genuine changes in the language competence of learners?
2. Does the concern to control short-term, easily measured objectives work against the attainment of basic long-range goals?
3. Are behavioral objectives and their sequencing based on sound theory and research on the processes, competencies, and behaviors being developed?
4. Are behavioral objectives, the methods of their presentation, and the system of intrinsic and extrinsic reinforcement likely to cause any unintentional and undesirable learning, or emotional strain, or other unplanned outcomes detrimental to the well-being of the learners?
5. Who has the right to predetermine and control what shall or shall not be the limits of acceptable behavior of young people? In short, do we help children to grow, or shape them to a mold?

Back to the system, PPBS, and its goals and objectives. The argument for it is that without some plan for evaluation, the school district is not able to assess the accomplishment of an objective. Moreover, objectives must be feasible in the light of the political, economic, and social constraints in which a district functions. Some constraints that might be documented are these:

Constraints on goals and objectives

- Geographic. For example, the district is remote from scientific and cultural centers.
- Demographic. There may be a majority of children from families with low educational attainment.
- Financial. The tax base has just about reached the limit the citizenry will accept. (Steinberg & Nielsen, 1972).

Programming and analysis

*Programming and analysis* are key elements in PPBS. A program is a group of interdependent, closely related activities or services progressing toward a common set of objectives. They basically require the following: criteria for selection, identification, development of schedules in light of time periods specified in the objective, and assignment and scheduling of resources. Ideally, there is continuous evaluation and modification of alternative programs. Program analysis includes these: the criteria for selection; development of alternative programs; applying of cost to alternative programs; defining benefits (e.g., percentage of children who improved with respect to test scores); analyzing cost-benefit relations within constraints; and the selection of one preferred program. (Dangers are easily apparent here.)

Budgeting

*Budgeting* is related to the goals, objectives, and programs. The budget thus shows where the education emphasis is being placed and reflects the priority interests of the district. There is attempt to project several years into the future.[20]

Evaluation: danger of teaching the test

Evaluation is the most difficult step in any system designed to implement accountability, and I have already had much to say about this. Apprehension develops over the practice of trying to subtract the pretest score from the posttest score to measure the performance of personnel. PPBS participants (and especially performance-contracting people), upon seeing the necessity to show change on whatever is selected as the measure of accountability, have unfortunately sometimes adopted this position: "We'll show 'em; we'll teach the content and answers to the test items." I have said before that any test represents only a sampling of a very large content domain. When the comprehen-

[20] About this time I cannot refrain from recalling the fourth-grade child, who, along with 50,000 other children, was required to composed a letter to a New York City Council President and other council members on the subject of the Board of Education budget. He wrote: "Dear Sir, I hate school. Please cut the budget in my school. Thank you."

sive curriculum is abandoned for the limited samples of test items, the lack of enduring achievement is likely to be reflected in the next year of instruction.

The make-or-buy concept

What is performance contracting? Another system where one agent holds another formally accountable for a specified outcome is performance contracting. Strictly speaking, it is a variety of legal contract. Again the motivation is to attain for education some of the advantages of practice from large private and public enterprise. The idea comes from "make or buy" planning criteria. Can we buy what we need from someone else more conveniently than we can make it ourselves? The newness, if any, comes from the extension of make or buy to all aspects of education, including instruction (Schutz, 1971).

In performance contracting a school system specifies desired outcomes with a certain pupil population and enters into a contract with an agency for the provision of educational experiences. These are supposed to produce the desired outcomes in the pupil population. Guaranteed performance contracts specify that the contractor will not be paid if the specified outcomes are not achieved. Paying according to how much children learn was new to public schools. Contracting for a study skills package with prespecified outcomes is feasible; eliminating dropouts is about as complex as eliminating illness. If one were to seek to contract for *happiness,* there would undoubtedly be willing vendors (or quacks).

There are many different varieties of this performance-contracting practice. The first instructional performance contracts followed steps of—request for proposal, bid evaluation, contract negotiation, and contract agreement. Because of the potential restructuring of the public education system, most educators have an opinion on this subject—usually a vehement one. Performance contracting as a vehicle for accountability will probably be here today and gone tomorrow, only to emerge later with some variation and, of course, a new label.

## CONCLUSIONS ON ACCOUNTABILITY AND EVALUATION IN THE LANGUAGE ARTS

Evaluation can occur before, during, and after instruction (diagnostic, formative, and summative evaluation). It can be formal (standardized) or informal, norm-referenced or criterion-referenced. It can be useful to children or cause them boredom and pain. The test of the program is in the classroom and in later life. Grade level competency is an inaccurate abstraction. A teacher's commitment to oral language and its use in creative problem-solving will give many children a chance to communicate effectively, while helping and respecting themselves and others. Since language arts is a complex, subtly integrated curriculum, evaluation devices are crude, and are to be viewed with caution.

Perhaps the greatest danger from the fast-moving events in accountability and evaluation is within ourselves. An inanimate system is rarely bad or good inherently. But there may be something in language arts teachers (or in any teacher) that is irresistibly drawn to authority and to conformity. On the one hand there may be something that causes us to take authority freely to our hearts, and then to take some pleasure as the agent to hand down its convergent influence. Maybe not. On the other hand, most teachers realize that *education is not an industrial process with the child as a rigorously specified "identical product unit." Education is a social process.* In it humans interact with other humans in ways that are imperfectly measurable, unpredictable, and never finished. In humility we realize that, like an iceberg, much human behavior fails to be externally visible.

Some honored antagonists to the whole accountability movement express themselves in all the overstated rhetoric, generalizations, clichés, appeal to emotions, logical inconsistencies, and name calling of some unfortunate persuasive discourse (or "double speak"). And they do this to an embarrassing degree! Yet their angry, free spirit needs to be attended to and opportunities for its expression guarded. For it is this unconforming, creative spark (that hopefully moves into informed disagreement with well thought-out alternatives and consequences) that distinguishes us as humans, not animals or automated robots. This thoughtful creativeness not only gives us promise of survival in a world of intricate problems yet undefined, but also gives us warm gentle grace of spirit that glories in the unpredictable. This spirit is as valuable to science and our governmental institutions as it is to the humanities. Basically we agree on our hopes for the welfare of children and need to keep communication open.

---

The final thoughts in this book are presented next in the form of an Epilogue, a companion to the Prologue. It is designed as a "send-off" statement.

## AN ACTIVITY FOR THE READER OF THIS CHAPTER

Self-evaluation

11.4 The Me in Measurement. (Number a separate piece of paper and write your answers so that you can use this form as both a pre- and posttest.) (Check one)

Pretest Posttest

1. Evaluation tools that I now use with my class (or that are used in the class I observe) are ________________________________.

2. To me, now, the purpose of assessment is ________________.
   The advantages of assessment are ________________.
   The disadvantages of assessment can be ________________.

3. I know these things about tests in the language arts ________________________________.

4. This is the way I have learned to handle daily evaluation of my pupils for language arts ________________.

5. For individual conferences I use (or would use) ________________.

6. My children are (or would be) independently involved in assessment in these ways: ________________.

7. This is the way I feel about assessment of myself ________________.
   These are instances in which I have sought self-evaluation and to be accountable for my skill ________________.

8. These are some references or other sources on measurement, evaluation, and accountability which I have found helpful with respect to my language arts program ________________.

## If You Want to Learn More


BOURQUIN, C. F. Behavioral Objectives, Program Budgets, and the Teaching of English. *California English Journal,* 1970, *6,* 28-32.

BRADDOCK, R. English Composition. In R. L. Ebel (Ed.), *Encyclopedia of Educational Research.* (4th ed.) London: Macmillan, 1969.

CARLSON, R. K. *Language Arts Sparklers for Intermediate Grades.* Berkeley, Calif.: Wagner Printing Co., 1968.

CARROLL, J. B. Development of Native Language Skills Beyond the Early Years. In C. F. Read (Ed.), *The Learning of Language.* Urbana, Ill.: NCTE, 1971.

COMBS, A. W. Educational Accountability from a Humanistic Perspective. *Educational Researcher,* 1973, *2* (9), 19-21.

COOPER, C. R. Conditions for Accountability: The English Teacher Is the Expert in the English Field. *California English Journal,* 1971, *7,* 7-13.

COVINGTON, M. V., CRUTCHFIELD, R. C., DAVIES, L., and OLTON, M. *The Productive Thinking Program: A Course in Learning to Think.* Columbus, Ohio: Charles E. Merrill, 1972.

DIETERICH, D. J. NCTE/ERIC Report: Performance Contracting: Pot of Gold or Pandora's Box? *Elementary English,* 1972, *49* (April), 612-22.

DYER, H. S. Statewide Evaluation–What Are the Priorities? *Phi Delta Kappan,* 1970, *51* (June), 558-59.

FELDHUSEN, J. F., et al. Review of Problem Solving Measurement Tasks. Paper presented at the annual meeting of the American Psychological Association, Washington, D.C., September 1971.

FLAVEL, J. H., BOTKIN, P. T., FRY, C. L., WRIGHT, J. W., and JARVIS, P. E. *The Development of Role-Taking and Communication Skills in Children.* New York: Wiley, 1968.

Gives experimental tasks for interactive communication. For example, children who saw an entire series of pictures telling a story in sequence were introduced to a listener who they knew had only seen a few of the pictures. Then each child was instructed to retell the story from the listener's point of view. Young children were less skilled than older children in role-taking while speaking.

FREDRICK, W. C., GOLUB, L. S., and JOHNSON, S. L. *Analysis of the Linguistic Ability Test, Grades 4 & 6.* Technical Report No. 121. Madison: Wisconsin Research and Development Center for Cognitive Learning, 1970.

GAGNÉ, R. M., and KNELLER, G. F. Behavioral Objectives? Yes or No? *The Education Digest,* 1972 (May), 24-27.

HARRIS, M., and HARRIS, C. *Newly Constructed Reference Tests for Cognitive Abilities,* Working Paper No. 80. Madison: Wisconsin Research and Development Center for Cognitive Learning, 1971.

Harsh, J. R. Biopsy of an Educational Growth. *Research Resume: Proceedings of the 23rd Annual State Conference on Educational Research—Accountability and the Curriculum.* Burlingame, Calif.: California Teachers Association, 1971.

Hoetker, J. Limitations and Advantages of Behavioral Objectives in the Arts and Humanities. In A. Tovatt (Ed.), *On Writing Behavioral Objectives for English.* Urbana, Ill.: NCTE, 1970.

Lundsteen, S. W. In S. Duker (Ed.), *Listening: Readings.* Metuchen, N.J.: Scarecrow Press, 1966.

Lundsteen, S. W. Manipulating Abstract Thinking as a Subability to Problem Solving in the Context of an English Curriculum. *American Educational Research Journal,* 1970, *7,* 373-96.

Lundsteen, S. W. *Listening: Its Impact on Reading and the Other Language Arts.* Urbana, Ill.: NCTE, 1971. (a)

Lundsteen, S. W. Teaching Listening Skills to Children in the Elementary School, 1966-1971: Research Review and Suggested Directions. In H. A. Robinson & A. T. Burrows, Eds., *Teacher Effectiveness in Elementary Language Arts: A Progress Report.* Urbana, Ill.: NCTE, 1971. (b)

Gives objectives and a framework for teaching (relying on modeling) dealing with the where, what, why, and how.

Maloney, H. B. (Ed.) *Accountability and the Teaching of English.* Urbana, Ill.: NCTE, 1972.

Includes the matter of teacher accountability, pros, cons, review of humanistic goals, bibliography.

Maloney, H. B. (Ed.) *Goal Making for English Teaching.* Urbana, Ill.: NCTE, 1973.

Within context of systems approaches and accountability, attempts to identify humanistic goals of English teaching. Possible alternatives for future English teachers.

Marshall, J. C., and Hales, L. W. *Classroom Test Construction.* Reading, Mass.: Addison-Wesley, 1971.

Contains an exhaustive description of test forms.

McNeil, J. D., and Wanat, S. F. Performance Tests: Assessing Teachers of Reading: A Proposal—A Response. *The Reading Teacher,* 1972, *25* (7), 622-33.

Mecklenburger, J. A., and Wilson, J. A. Learning C.O.D.: Can the Schools Buy Success? *Saturday Review,* September 18, 1971.

Moore, W. J., and Kennedy, L. D. Evaluation of Learning in the Language Arts. In B. S. Bloom et al., *Handbook on Formative and Summative Evaluation of Student Learning.* New York: McGraw-Hill, 1971.

NATIONAL COUNCIL OF TEACHERS OF ENGLISH. *Uses, Abuses, Misuses of Standardized Tests in English.* Urbana, Ill.: Author, 1974. (Stock No. 99958)

A packet of brief articles, reprints, pamphlets, and so on.

PURVES, A. C. The Nature of Achievement in Literature. Some Notes on Evaluation and Accountability. *California English Journal,* 1971, *7* (3), 8-15.

RUSSELL, D. H., and RUSSELL, E. F. *Listening Aids Through the Grades.* New York: Columbia University, Teachers College, Bureau of Publications, 1959.

SANDERS, J. R., and CUNNINGHAM, D. J. A Structure for Formative Evaluation in Product Development. *Review of Educational Research,* 1973, *43* (2), 217-36.

SCHUTZ, R. E. Measurement Aspects of Performance Contracting, NCME *Measurement in Education* (Newsletter of the National Council on Measurement in Education), 1971, *2,* 1-4.

SMITH, VERNON H. A Do-It-Yourself Test: How Do You Rate as a Judge of Children's Writing? *Elementary English,* 1970, *47,* 346-48.

STEINBERG, H. I., and NIELSEN, R. A. PPBS for a School District. *Management Adviser,* 1972 (March–April), 28-37.

*STEP Writing.* Sequential Tests of Educational Progress. Princeton, N.J.: Educational Testing Service, Cooperative Testing Division, 1957.

Form 4 is for grades 4–6 and measures skill in five categories: (1) organization, (2) conventions, (3) critical thinking, (4) effectiveness (e.g., adequacy of emphasis, development; exactness of expression; economy in combining sentences or in omitting sentences; simplicity; and variety), and (5) appropriateness (e.g., level of usage suitable to purpose and reader; appropriate diction; and tact). The student identifies an error or weakness in a passage and selects from four multiple choices a revision that most satisfactorily solves the problem in relation to the purpose of the writing. Some items are based on material actually written by students using a variety of materials.

Of the new STEP II tests (the Language Series), *English Expression* for grades 4–14 (40 minutes) contains editorial exercises—detecting errors in grammar, usage, choosing between various recastings of phrases or sentences. *Mechanics of Writing* for grades 4–12 (40 minutes) contains spelling, capitalization, and punctuation in given sentences.

Also see the new ETS Cooperative Primary Tests (grade 3), *Writing Skills* (spelling, punctuation, and usage).

TWAY, E. A Study of the Feasibility of Training Teachers to Use the Literary Rating Scale in Evaluating Children's Fiction Writing. Unpublished doctoral dissertation, Syracuse University. Ann Arbor, Michigan, 1971. No. 71-10997.

TYLER, R. W., and WOLF, R. M. (Eds.) *Crucial Issues in Testing.* Berkeley, Calif.: McCutchan, 1974.

YAMAMOTO, K. *Experimental Scoring Manuals for Minnesota Tests of Creative Thinking and Writing.* Kent, Ohio: Kent State University, Bureau of Educational Research, 1964.

# Epilogue

In the Preface I mentioned the analogy of a timepiece—the watch taken apart, its pieces thrown to a class with these words: "There! That's all you need to make a watch!" My aim throughout this book has been to give you unifying structures related to teaching, not an unstructured pile of information about the disciplines of English. If I have succeeded, you will take these structures with you as you learn how to create successful language arts classrooms.

Again looking at the "timepiece analogy," see the parts not as mere pieces but as interrelated structures of which creative problem-solving is the mainspring that makes all the parts work together.

The stages in the child's development of language and thought might be likened to the numerals on the face of a human timepiece. The successful language arts classroom is based on the teacher's developmental expertise. The language arts themselves (in constant, meaningful interrelationship) are the balance wheel of the timepiece. Listening, speaking, reading, and writing are meaningfully interwoven in daily classroom activity, not isolated and rendered into ritual.

The cogs of the timepiece (*skills* of listening, speaking, reading, and writing) all mesh through the conceptual structures given throughout the book—mainly the four aims of language and the six dimensions of the curriculum. Some of the other structures are seven types of discussion, a communication triangle for literature, five motivational allies within each child, and a teaching-learning strategy for instruction in composition.

If there is anything common to classroom success, it is probably first of all the teacher's concern and ability to listen to what the children have to say, and to respond to them as honestly as possible. If children are afraid to talk, or know that the teacher will not listen, they will fail to write, read, or communicate in any but the most minimal way. Sometimes the successful teacher just listens; always, he or she is learning from the children.

If there is anything else common to teaching success, it is probably the help-the-child-to-think approach, the development of the child's self-competence. Here teaching is built on helping children attack the challenge of their own individual problems in a creative way. Such an approach stresses both children's own composition and literature as the major content areas of student-centered classrooms.

Implicit in the structures given in this book is the realization that we cannot teach any of the language arts at any one division of schooling once and for all. The language arts grow and develop for as long as they are nurtured. Recall the statement in the Prologue, "The limits of my language mean the limits of my world." Consider the meanings that you now have for that idea.

Successful classroom sequences take into account the social, cultural, physical, emotional, and intellectual aspects of each child. Only through an understanding of and communication with social forces can we make our authority as teachers legitimate in a pluralistic culture.

Above all, the successful curriculum sequence appears to be one where there are overtones of joy, excitement, creative discovery, and problem solving. Whatever the specific classroom topic or activity, it is these overtones of gleeful, self-directed inquiry that make a successful classroom.

If such ideas become practice, early instruction of children will affect the content and process of secondary programs. And the relationship between early and late education will become better understood as programs become based, more and more, on creative problem-solving and interdisciplinary approaches. I must against stress the integrating effectiveness of a focus on thought processes for both child and teacher.

In essence—behind the skills of communication are the skills of thinking. Behind the meaningful use of skills of thinking lies the process of creative problem-solving.

Out of currently existing fragmentation, this book has tried to create organization. The hope is that you will, in turn, help your children to induce the larger structures within their communication lives. Finally, I hope that you will continually build upon this unity, because I feel its use is the easiest and most human way for children to learn to communicate.

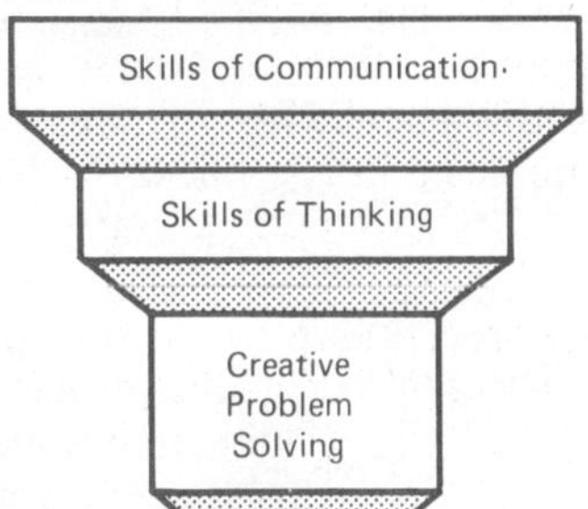

# Index


AARON, I., 328, 329, 330
Abstract thinking, writing and, 230–31
Accountability
  behavioral objectives and, 447–49
  defined, 445–46
  mutuality of, 446–47
  performance contracting and, 446, 450
  PPBS and, 446, 447–50
Activities by name
  Adopting Forgotten Mental Patients, 376
  Art and Language, 66
  Back to Back, 119–20
  Ball-Roll-Say, 124
  Book Show-offs, 198
  Bounce It, 99
  Brainstorming, 176–77
  Bull Session, 175
  Business Letter Collections, 368
  Choral-Oral Collection, 204
  Class Proofreader's Manual, 368
  Comic Strip, 101
  Concept Development Story Collections, 68
  Conservation and Ecology Documentary, 220–22
  Constructing a Word Building, 139–40
  Create a Word and Put It in the News, 399
  Cultural Glossary, 254–55
  Dictation from Junior Authors, 65
  Dictionary Delight, 352–53
  Evaluating a Composition, 426–27
  Finishing a Problem Story, 317–19
  Friends and Challenges, 119–20
  Fun with Exaggeration, 141
  Grammatical Patterns in Children's Literature, 399–401
  Graph-sems, 121–22
  Greeting Cards, 375
  Historical Approach to Punctuation, 369
  Historical Perspective, 376
  Hitchhike Story, 311
  Hopping on Punctuation, 367
  How Many Ways Can You Say It?, 123
  I-Am-Going-To, 99
  Illustration-Information, 222
  I'm Thinking of a Letter, 361
  Instant Puppets, 222
  Jump on It, 354
  Language Ability Test as, 396–97
  Last Day to Hear, 85
  Leaf Walk, 263–64
  Listening Center Task Cards, 431–32
  Listening in Order to Solve, 433–35
  Live Letters, 354
  Me in Measurement, The, 452
  Message Checkout, 82, 83
  Mirroring, 82, 83–84, 127–28
  Models of Literature, 255–56
  Mystery of the Missing Sound, 126
  Name Game, 92
  New-Word-Bird, The, 100
  Nonstop Reading, 367
  Object Sorting by Sound, 92
  Observing at Home, 266
  Observing Events Outside the Classroom, 264
  Observing Light and Dark, 309–10
  Observing the Classroom, 264–66
  Octopus Grabbing Game, 122–23
  Outer-Space Dictionary, 129
  Paired for Pictures, 283–84
  Pantomime Time, 298–99
  Pantomiming a Poem, 141–42
  Paragraphs Based on Collages, 312–13
  Partner Skip-Chant, 121
  Pattern Drills, 398
  Pen Pal, 375–76
  Photographed Walk, 254
  Poetry Collector's Club, 201
  Polly Parrot, 66–68
  Problem Compo, 66
  Problem Solving, 299–300
  Propaganda Trick, 50
  Punctuating Greek Monuments, 367
  Punctuating Your Own Dictation, 368
  Punctuation Traffic Signals, 364
  Punctuation with Cards and Rhythm Instruments, 367
  Recommended List, 221–22
  Reflecting on a Poem, 103
  Reports of Happenings, 375
  Scribble-Time-Warm-up, 311
  Script Making, 300
  Show-and-Tell, 130–33
  Some More Favorite Topics, 311–12
  Something-out-of-Almost Nothings, 128–29
  Sound-Based Compositions, 85
  Spinner Man, 340
  Storytelling, 212–14
  Storytelling Club, 221
  Tableau, 222
  Task-Group Discussion, 177
  Thinkbox Hideaway, 66
  Through the Looking Glass, 65
  Time-Machine Sound Finder, 124–25
  Twenty Questions, 101–3
  Two-Sided Mirror Game, 101
  What Does It Mean?, 368
  What-Would-Happen-Ifs, 125–26
  Word Liberties for Laughter, 140–41
  Word-Tells, 127
  Writer's Aids, 352
  Writing Cinquain, 316–17
  Writing Haiku, 313–16
Activities by subject
  for composition
    developmental, 233–35
    imaginative, 263–66, 308–20
    motivating, 248, 254–56, 266–70, 298–301
    for observation, 263–66
  for concept development, 50, 68
  for dialect, 123, 254–55
  for grammar, 396–401
  for handwriting, 361, 375–76
  to interrelate language arts, 82–84, 85, 100, 101, 103, 141

- for language development, 65–68
- for listening
  - to assess, 431–35
  - auditory discrimination in, 92–93, 99
  - auditory sequencing in, 99–100
  - composition and, 85, 100–101
  - interactive, 101–3
  - speaking and, 83–84, 100–101
- for punctuation, 364, 367–69, 375–76
- for reading, 220–22
  - on audience, 204
  - on author, 201–2
  - for eliciting response, 198–200, 201–2, 204, 215
  - on organization and language, 212–14
  - on realistic literature, 198
- for speaking
  - concrete-abstract dimension of, 124–26
  - discussion as, 175–77
  - exposition as, 130–33
  - personal-interpersonal dimension of, 122–23
  - self-expression as, 119–20, 139–42
  - small-large parts dimension of, 126–28
  - speech-thought dimension of, 121–22
  - unfinished-finished product dimension of, 128–29
- for spelling, 340, 351–54, 375–76
- for teacher assessment
  - of composition, 426–27
  - of self, 452
- for usage, 397–98, 399

Affective, defined, 11*n*

Alphabetic, defined, 324

American Book Co., 345–46, 366

*Apple* used to illustrate concept-building, 39

*Arts and Skills of Language, The,* 249

Ashley, A., 91

Aspiration, level of, in teaching spelling, 343–44

Assertions, forms of, in composition, 294–95

Assessment
- of composition
  - activity for, 426–27
  - and of classroom situation, 424–25
  - cognitive processes in, 419–21
  - elements in effective, 421–24
  - grading in, 418
  - individual writing conference in, 412–19
  - needs and problems in, 407–10
  - problem-solving skill and, 413–17, 421
  - record keeping in, 412, 413–18
- of discussion, 154–56
- framework for, 411–12
- of inquiry teaching, 408–9
- of listening
  - activities for, 431–35
  - affective, 440–41
  - checklists for, 428–29
  - by coding, 430–31
  - criterion-referenced tests for, 439–40
  - egocentric vs. nonegocentric communication and, 435–37
  - by informal listening inventory, 431
  - motivation and, 441
  - pinpointing and charting for, 428
  - standardized, norm referenced tests for, 438–39
  - by task cards, 431–33
- as motivation, 406, 407, 412–13, 418, 441
- multiple choice tests for, 408
- objectives for, 407–10
- published tests for, disadvantages of, 409–10
- purpose of, 406–7
- of reading, 411, 425, 441–45
- of speaking, 411, 435–37
- of teacher, activity for, 452

Attitude cutoff, 81

Audio equipment, use of
- to check teaching, 18, 159
- safety factor in, 77
- to teach composition, 269*n*, 295, 302, 303, 311
- to teach punctuation, 365, 366, 368
- to teach reading, 94–95, 96, 204, 221, 222
- to teach speaking, 118–19, 123, 129, 141, 168

Auditory discrimination, 88–89, 93, 94

Authority of teacher, 254

Autonomy, 9–10, 118–20, 153–54, 231, 335, 443
- defined, 9

BARCH, A. M., 374

BARTOLOME, P. I., 162

Basic sentence patterns, 384

*Basic Teaching Skills,* 163

Behavioral objectives for language arts, 447–48

Behaviorist approach to readiness, 60

Best Trend Name Test, 420

Bibliotherapy, 216–19

BINSTOCK, J., 10

Black child. *See* Cultural variation; Dialect; Minority child

BLANK, M., 24

BLOOM, B. S., 162

BRADDOCK, R., 386, 395, 410

Brainstorming discussions, 169, 173, 176–77

Brainstorming in composition, 290–91

BRITTON, J., 116, 117, 192, 200

BROWN, R. A., 75, 77

BRYANT, J. E., 77, 93

Bull sessions, 169, 172–73, 175

BURKE, C., 63

BURROWS, A., 7, 151, 233, 234, 237, 238, 261

BURROWS, M., 398

Caldecott Medal, 222

California State Board of Education, 192, 396

CARLSON, R. K., 290, 301–2, 418

Carlson Analytical Originality Scoring Scale, 418

CARROLL, J. B., 409, 410

CARVER, M. E., 97

Categorization in writing consultation, 294–95

Cause and effect in writing consultation, 295

CECIL, L., 364

Challenging, by teacher in discussion, 158, 159

Characterization in children's literature, 206–7, 214

Characterization in compositions, 238, 244, 246

Checklist of Listening Roadblocks, 428–29

Children's authors
- ADELMAN, BOB, 54*n*
- ANDERSEN, HANS CHRISTIAN, 95, 207
- ARMSTRONG, WILLIAM, 203*n*, 209
- BARRETT, JUDI, 185*n*
- BONHAM, FRANK, 135
- BOURNE, MIRIAM ANNE, 215
- BREWTON, JOHN E., 201
- BREWTON, SARA, 201
- BROWN, MARCIA, 189
- CARROLL, RUTH, 211
- CHETIN, HELEN, 210
- CLAYTON, ED., 134*n*
- COLUM, PADRAIC, 189

Cunningham, Julia, 183
Dalgliesh, Alice, 187*n*
de Regniers, Beatrice Schenck, 185*n*, 207
Ets, Marie Hall, 186
Farjeon, Eleanor, 187
Felton, Harold W., 208
Funk, Charles E., 122
Gill, Joan, 120
Gwynne, Fred, 121
Hein, Sheila, 220
Henry, Marguerite, 220
Hoberman, Mary Ann, 132
Hunt, Irene, 181
Keats, Ezra Jack, 214
Kipling, Rudyard, 141, 241, 242
Konigsburg, E. L., 189
Kuskin, Karla, 101*n*
Larrick, Nancy, 189
Lawson, R., 60
Lear, Edward, 141
Lightfoot, Gordon, 186
McCord, David, 189
McCormack, Joanne, 122
McDonald, Gerald D., 201
Martin, Bill, 94, 293*n*
Miles, Miska, 195
Minarik, Else, 205
Pope, J., 85*n*
Potter, Beatrix, 184
Reeves, James, 209
Reid, Alastair, 121
Reyher, Becky, 209
Rickey, Sara Brandon, 67, 103, 142, 310
Roberts, Elizabeth Madox, 187
Ruttan, Robert A., 194
Schoenherr, John, 195
Seuss, Dr., 141, 220
Shotwell, Louisa R., 186*n*
Shuttlesworth, Dorothy E., 220
Skorpen, Liesel Moak, 59
Snyder, Zilpha Keatley, 203*n*
Sorenson, Virginia, 210
Sperry, Armstrong, 206, 218
Stevenson, R. L., 132
Stone, A. Harris, 220
Titus, Eve, 214
Tolkien, J. R. R., 207
Tresselt, Alvin, 215
Turkle, Brinton, 199
Ward, Lynd, 185
Warren, Dr. Fred, 210
Warren, Lee, 210
Welsh, Harriet, 207
White, E. B., 94
Wilder, Laura Ingalls, 288
Wojciechowska, Maia, 135
Yashima, Taro, 18
Children's literature
abundance of, 184
audience for, 202–4
author of, 200–202
authors of, referred to in text (*see* Children's authors)
bibliotherapy and, 216–19
classified, 183
communication triangle and, 192–93, 220 (*see also* Children's literature, audience for; Children's literature, author of; Children's literature, language of; Children's literature, organization of; Children's literature, realistic)
composition and, 248–51, 255–56
defined, 181, 183
developmental approach to, 184–88
grammar and, 399–401
importance of, to language arts program, 183
language of
discussion questions on, 215
figurative, 209–10
irony in, 211
memorable, 183
sound in, 209
style in, 212
symbolism in, 211
literature in general and, 220
oral reading of, 94–95, 188–91
organization of
characterization in, 206–7, 214
discussion questions on, 214–15
plot in, 205–6, 214
theme in, 207, 209, 214–15
realistic
defined, 193, 195
discussion questions on, 198–200
selecting, 196–97
value of, 196
response to
affective, 199, 201, 202, 204, 214–15
cognitive, 199–200, 201, 202, 204, 214–15
developmental, 184–87
manipulative and enactive, 198, 201–2, 204, 212–14
realism and, 193, 196
teaching strategies for, summarized, 191–92, 220
titles of, referred to in text (*see* Children's titles)
*see also* Reading
Children's titles
*Across Five Aprils,* 181
*Adventures of Oolakuk,* 194
*Animals Should Definitely Not Wear Clothing,* 185*n*
*Any Me I Want to Be,* 101*n*
*Barn, The,* 195
*Bears on Hemlock Mountain, The,* 187*n*
*Biggest Bear, The,* 185
*Call It Courage,* 18, 206
*Charlotte's Web,* 94, 181, 211, 255, 256, 294, 415
*Clean Air, Sparkling Water,* 220, 221*n*
*Crow Boy,* 18–21
*Don't Play Dead Unless You Have To,* 135
*Dorp Dead,* 183, 211
*Egypt Game,* 203*n*
*Elephant Child, The,* 141
*Emilio's Summer Day,* 215
*Every Time I Climb a Tree,* 189
*From the Mixed-up Files of Mrs. Basil E. Frankweiler,* 189
*Ghost Story, A,* 293*n*
*Gilberto and the Wind,* 186
*Gingerbread Boy, The,* 185
*Harriet the Spy,* 207
*Heavens to Betsy,* 122
*"Hello and Good-by,"* 132
*Hobbit, The,* 207
*Horton Hatches the Egg,* 141
*"How the Whale Got His Throat,"* 242
*Hush, Jon,* 120
*If I Ran a Zoo,* 141
*In the Middle of the Night,* 187
*Just So Stories,* 189, 241
*King Who Rained, The,* 121–22
*Last Bird, The,* 220, 221*n*
*Little Bear,* 205
*Little House of Your Own, A,* 207, 209
*Little House on the Prairie,* 288
*"Little Match Girl,"* 95
*Lorax, The,* 221
*McGuffey Reader,* 203
*Martin Luther King: The Peaceful Warrior,* 134*n*
*May I Bring a Friend?,* 185*n*
*Miracles on Maple Hill,* 210
*Music of Africa, The,* 210
*Mustang, Wild Spirit of the West,* 220, 221*n*
*My Mother Is the Most Beautiful Mother in the World,* 209
*My Side of the Mountain,* 181
*Nobody's Cat,* 195
*"Noise,"* 85*n*
*Obadiah the Bold,* 199

*On and Off the Street,* 54*n*
*Once a Mouse,* 189
*On City Streets,* 189
*Ounce, Dice, Trice,* 121
*"Overheard on a Saltmarsh,"* 319
*Pecos Bill and the Mustang,* 208
*Pony Man, The,* 186
*Rabbit Hill,* 60
*Roofs of Gold,* 189
*Roosevelt Grady,* 186*n*, 415
*Run Zebra Run,* 220, 221*n*
*"Sea, The,"* 209
*"Shadows on a Clothes Line,"* 142
*Shrieks at Midnight,* 201
*Single Light, A,* 135
*Snowy Day, The,* 214
*Sounder,* 203*n*, 209
*"Steadfast Tin Soldier, The,"* 207
*Story of Our Language, The,* 122
*Street Smart,* 54*n*
*Stuart Little,* 94, 95
*"Swing, The,"* 132
*Tale of Peter Rabbit,* 184
*Tales of an African Drum,* 210
*"Talkative Parrot, The,"* 67
*Thudwich the Big Hearted Moose,* 141
*Two Stonecutters, The,* 214
*Viva Chicano,* 135
*"Water Magic,"* 103
*Way of Knowing, A,* 201
*We Were Tired of Living in a House,* 59–60
*What Whiskers Did,* 211
*Where the Wild Things Are,* 134
*White Snow Bright Snow,* 215
*Wind in the Willows,* 189
*Winnie the Pooh,* 135
*Yertle the Turtle,* 141
CHOMSKY, NOAM, 385
CHRISTENSEN, F., 390
Cinquain, writing, 316–17
Clarifying role of teacher in discussion, 158–59
Classroom environment, 76–77, 156–57, 303–4, 424–25
Cognitive, defined, 11*n*
Cognitive conceit, 53
Cognitive motivation, development of, 55, 57–58
Cognitive processes, assessing, 419–21
Coherence, defined, 294
COLERIDGE, SAMUEL TAYLOR, 191
Communication
barriers to, 4, 10–13, 14–15 (*see also* Autonomy; Cultural variation; Mass media; Parents, involving; Peer acceptance; Problem solving, simplistic)
in discussion, roles as, 148–52
basic to learning, 13–14
egocentric to nonegocentric, 435–37
intraindividual vs. interindividual, 122–23
literature as, 181
*see also* Language
Communication diagram interrelating language skills, 97–98
Communication subskills in bibliotherapy, 216, 217
Communication triangle in children's literature. *See* Children's literature, communication triangle and
Composition
activities for, 282–84 (*see also* Activities by subject, for composition)
advantages of, 274–76
assessing, 407–27 (*see also* Assessment, of composition)
audio equipment and, 269*n*, 295, 302, 303, 311
brainstorming in, 290–91
children's literature and, 248–51, 255–56
creative problem-solving in, 276, 288–90, 304, 305
developmental features of *and* and *because* as, 236
characterization as, 238, 244, 246
complexity as, 239, 243, 247
in fifth grade, 242, 243, 244
figurative language as, 239
in fourth grade, 242, 243–44
grammatical structure as, 236
plot as, 238, 239, 242
realism as, 239, 244, 245, 246
repetition as, 235
in second grade, 238–39
in sixth grade, 242, 244–45
teaching implications for, 236–37, 247–48
tense switching as, 236
in third grade, 239–42
in young child, 235–38, 247–48, 287–88
developmental requirements for curriculum determined by, 232–33 passim (*see also* Composition, teaching strategy for)
explain difficulty of, 112, 230–32
exposition in, 279–82 (*see also* Exposition)
imaginative, functions of, 308
ladder of suggestions for, 320
listening and, 84–85, 97–98
minority child and, 51, 232–33, 251–52, 254–56, 258–59
motivation for, 229, 231, 232–33, 242, 251–60, 412–13, 418
peer acceptance and, 231, 232, 237, 238, 252, 257–59
reading and, 274–75, 295
spelling secondary in, 242
teaching strategy for
classroom environment and, 303–4, 424–25
creative problem in, 285, 288–90
developmental features and, 236–37, 247–48
dictation in, 233–35
examples illustrating, 298–302
goals of, 248, 304–5
oral composition for public display in, 285, 296–97
oral consultation in, 285, 290–91
re-creation in, 285, 287–88
sample schedule for, 302–3
stimulation of impressions in, 285–87
teacher's role in, summarized, 306–8
writing consultation in, 285, 291–96
written composition for public display in, 228, 279, 285, 297–98
topics for, 266–70, 288
types of, 279–84
unity in, defined, 294
*see also* Grammar; Handwriting; Punctuation; Spelling
Concept-building, stages of, 39
Concepts
attainment of, 46–50, 68
diagnosis of child's, 43
formal, defined, 49
Concrete, defined, 35
Concrete-abstract dimension of oral language program, 124–26, 196
Concrete operations stage
defined, 35
vs. sensorimotor stage, 36–37
sentence production in, 40–42
skills characterizing, 34, 35–36
sound production in, 37
teacher assistance during
abstractness and, 43

adult-child dialogue as, 44–46
cognitive motivation and, 55, 57–58
for concept attainment, 46–48, 50
for concept diagnosis, 43
cultural differences and, 50–52
gradualness of growth and, 55–56
listening, child, to develop, 55, 59–60
listening, teacher, as, 55, 58–59
modes of thought and, 55, 56–57
readiness and, 55, 60–61
reading and, 55, 61–63
social dimensions of language and, 52–55
vocabulary in, 37–40
Contrast in writing consultation, 295
Conventions of writing, 279, 393. *See also* Grammar; Handwriting; Punctuation; Spelling; Usage
Convergent thinking, defined, 23
COOPER, C. R., 389, 395, 409, 447
COOPER, R. L., 84
COVINGTON, M. V., 421
Craft, of writing, defined, 279
CRATTY, B. J., 354
Creative dramatics, 133–38
defined, 133
Creative problem in composition, 285, 288–90
Creative problem-solving. *See* Problem solving, creative
Creative writing scales, 418
Creativity and spelling, 344
Critical thinking in listening and reading, situational variants, 95, 97
Crucial attributes of concept, to distinguish, 46, 47
CRUTCHFIELD, R. C., 421
Cultural variation, 50–52. *See also* Dialect; Minority child
CUNNINGHAM, R. T., 163

DAVIES, L., 421
Deaf children, writing skills of, 84
Deafness, noise causes, 76–77
Decoding, defined, 87*n*, 98*n*
Degree of original learning in teaching spelling, 339
DELILE, 97
DESTEFANO, J. S., 55
Developmental tasks related to language, 53–54
Development of language and thought
activities for, 50, 65–68
common ground between, 64–65
composition and (*see* Composition, developmental features of)
creative problem-solving and, 64–65
linguists on, 63–65
Piagetian theory of, 33–37 passim
reading and, 55, 61–63, 184–88
spelling and, 327–33
*see also* Concrete operations stage
Diagnosis in assessment, 411
Dialect
activities for, 123, 254–55
listening and, 88–89, 91
reading and, 88–90
social implications of, 52, 54–55, 64, 91, 124, 396
spelling and, 335–36
*see also* Cultural variation; Minority child; Usage
Dialogue, adult-child, 44–46
Dictation in teaching composition, 233–35
Dictionary in teaching spelling, 345–46, 352–53
Disagreements, handling, 54, 149–50
Discourse
aims or uses of, 116–18, 279, 394
defined, 42, 110–12
a dimension of oral language program, 129, 197
*see also* Exposition; Persuasion; Literature; Self-expression
defined, 111
exploratory, discussion as, 147
Discussion
activities for, 175–77
classroom environment of, 156–57
creative problem-solving, 169–75
disorder in, 153–54
evaluating, 154–56
functions and objectives of, 147
motivation of, 150–51, 159, 166–69
reading and, 169
role of teacher in, 154, 157–66
roles of participants in, 148–54, 171–72
time factors in, 157
types of, compared, 169, 172–74
*see also* Oral language program; Speaking
DITTMAN, A. T., 59
Divergent thinking, defined, 23
DIXON, J., 301
DOWNING, J., 353
Dramatic play, defined, 133
DUKER, S., 77
DUPREE, D., 119
DYER, H. S., 446

EDFELDT, A. W., 86
Educational Testing Services, 409
Egocentrism and self-expression, 116
ELIOT, T. S., 295
ELKIND, D., 52, 53, 56, 58
Emotional reactions in listening and reading, situational variants, 95, 97
Empathy in communication, 435–37
Emphasis, defined, 294
Encoding, defined, 87*n*, 98*n*
English field and place of bibliotherapy, 216, 218
English Language Framework for California Public Schools, 396
Equilibrium seeking and cognitive motivation, 57–58
ERIKSON, E. H., 53
Ethnic factors in teaching. *See* Cultural variation; Dialect; Minority child
Evaluation. *See* Assessment
Evaluation, formative vs. summative, 411
Evaluation, planned, in creative problem-solving, 22, 24, 170
Exposition
activities for, 130–33
child uses, 130–38
in composition, 279–82
defined, 111, 129, 130
self-expression and, 117–18
*see also* Discussion
Extending in discussion, 162, 163

Fact giving, failure of, 12–13
Facts, eliciting, in creative problem-solving, 18–19, 24
FADER, DAN, 197, 209
Feeling tone in teaching spelling, 339
FELDHUSEN, J. F., 421
Fishbowl game, 155
FLANNAGAN, J., 4
Focusing in discussion, 162, 163

FOLTA, B., 391
Foreign students, guidelines for teaching, 90
Formal operations stage, 33, 34, 55
FREDRICK, W. C., 396
FRIES, C. C., 113, 384
FURNER, B. A., 358–60

GAGNÉ, R. M., 60
GALL, M. D., 163
GERWICK, J. A., 89, 90
GETZELS, J. W., 23
GILLIGAN, C., 61
GILSON, J. W., 91
GLASSER, W., 10
GOLUB, L. S., 235, 239, 243, 292, 308, 372–73, 396
GOODMAN, K. S., 232, 236, 242, 326, 336, 386, 389, 398
GOODMAN, Y., 63
Grading, of composition, 418
Grammar
  activities for, 396–401
  concepts of, in children's texts, 391–94
  defined, 380
  developmental aspects of, 40–42, 236
  structural linguistic, 380, 384–85, 394–95
  teaching strategies for, 381, 387–91, 395
  traditional school of, 380–83, 394
  transformational-generative, 380, 385–91, 395
  usage and, 382–83
  value of questionable, to child, 380–81, 384, 395
GRANT, B. M., 287
Grapheme, defined, 324
GRIFFIN, W. J., 41
Grouping in teaching spelling, 347–48
GUILFORD, J. P., 23
GUSZAK, F. J., 162

Haiku, writing, 313–16
*Handbook for Teaching the Language Arts,* 89–90
Handwriting
  activities for, 361, 375–76
  errors in, self-diagnosis of, 362–63
  goals for, 362–63
  problem solving and, 358–61
  teaching strategy for, 361–62
HANNA, J. S., 330, 351, 367
HANNA, P. R., 330, 351, 367
HARRIS, C., 419
HARRIS, M., 419
HARSH, J. R., 445, 446
HAVINGHURST, R. J., 54
HAYAKAWA, S. I., 6
HEATHCOTE, D., 134
HELSEY, M. J., 52
HENNINGS, D. G., 287
HODGES, R. E., 330, 351, 367
HOETKER, J., 448
HOLDEN, W., 250
Hope motivates learning, 252, 259, 343–44
HORN, T. D., 91
HUGHES, LANGSTON, 200–201
HUNTER, M., 339
Hypothesis testing, process of, in development, 64–65
Hypothesis vs. reality in concrete operations stage, 52–53

*Ideas into Practice,* 22, 25, 47, 99, 119, 141, 151, 167, 203
Identity, literature develops, 203
Imagination, composition and, 308. *See also* Activities by subject, for composition, imaginative
Imagination, literature and, 184, 186–88
IMHOOF, M. I., 89, 91
Indirection in children's literature, 189, 191
Individualizing in teaching spelling, 334–35, 338, 347, 348
Informal listening inventory, 431
Information, collecting, for discussion topics, 167
Inquiry teaching, assessing, 408–9
Inquiry-training discussions, 169, 173
Instant Reader Program, 94–95
Internal listening, 84
Interpersonal teaching in Piagetian theory, 58–59
Intonation in teaching punctuation, 363, 364–65

JOHNSON, K. R. A., 91
JOHNSON, S. L., 396
Judgment in writing consultation, 295
Juncture in teaching punctuation, 363, 366
JUNICHIRO, TANIZAKI, 211

KENNEDY, L. D., 409
Kernel sentence, defined, 386
KEY, M., 324, 336, 339, 344
KLEE, L. E., 77

LABOV, W., 51
Language
  of children's literature, 183, 209–14, 215 (*see also* Children's literature, language of)
  development of (*see* Concrete operations stage; Development of language and thought)
  history of, 331, 367, 369, 376, 399
  restricted vs. elaborated, 42
  social dimensions of, 52–55
  uses of, 116–18, 279, 394
    defined, 42, 110–12
    *see also* Exposition; Literature; Persuasion; Self-expression
  *see also* Dialect
Language arts
  basic to learning, 13–14
  behavioral objectives for, 447–48
  classroom environment for, 76–77, 156–57, 303–4, 424–25
  defined, 3
  interrelationships among, 75, 80–98, 112, 169, 188–91, 248–51, 255–56, 274
    activities for, 82–84, 85, 100, 101, 103, 141
  *see also* Communication; Composition; Listening; Reading; Speaking
Language concepts in children's texts, 391–94
Language difference vs. language deficiency, 64
Learning theory in teaching spelling, 339–44
*Let's Communicate, A Guide for Teachers with Foreign Speaking Students,* 89, 90
Lifting in discussion, 162, 163
Linguistically different child. *See* Cultural variation; Dialect; Minority child
Linguists on language development, 63–65
Listening
  accurate, techniques for, 87
  active, techniques for, 78–80
  activities for (*see* Activities by subject, for listening)
  assessing, 428–45 (*see also* Assessment, of listening)
  child, to develop, 55, 59–60
  coding devices to assess, 430–31
  composition and, 84–85, 97–98
  dialect and, 88–89, 91
  instruction in, needed, 75–77
  interactiveness of, 98–99

literature and, 188–91
minority child and, 51, 88–91
noise pollution and, 76–77
primacy of, 75–78
problem solving and, 78–80, 433–35, 441
reading and, 86–97, 98
speaking and, 80–84, 97–98
teacher, 55, 58–59
uncritical, 77
Literature
children's (*see* Children's literature)
defined, 111, 129, 181
Loan words in English, 326
LOBAN, W., 191, 398
LODGE, H. C., 380, 383
LONGFELLOW, HENRY WADSWORTH, 209
LUNDSTEEN, S. W., 11, 41, 46, 55, 63
Lysophobia, defined, 170

MCCULLOUGH, C. M., 89–90, 293, 334, 358
MALMSTROM, J., 91
MARCKWARDT, A. H., 110
MARKLE, S. M., 49
Mass media, 6–9
Materials, concrete, 34
Meaning
development of, 41
in listening and reading, 93–94, 96
in teaching spelling, 339
Mechanics, defined, 279
Mechanics and punctuation, 363–76. *See also* Punctuation
MECKLENBURGER, J. A., 410
MELLON, JOHN C., 389
MEREDITH, R., 232, 236, 242, 326, 336, 386, 389, 398
MILLER, HENRY, 308
Minority child
defined, 251*n*
developmental approach to teaching, 50–52
motivation of
to listen, 91
to punctuate, 370–72
to write, 232–33, 251–52, 254–56, 258, 259
parents of, 232–33
reading-listening problems of, 88–91
social dimensions of language and, 52, 54–55
*see also* Dialect
Misconception, symptoms for, 49
Modeling as motivation, 252, 253–57
Modeling in problem solving, 13
MOFFETT, J., 231, 239
Monopolizer, role of, 148–50, 151, 152
MONRO, HAROLD, 319
MONROE, M., 328, 329, 330
MONTESSORI, BENI, 230
MOORE, W. J., 409
Moral development and readiness, 61
Morpheme, defined, 330, 392
Morphology, concepts of, in children's texts, 392
Motivation
assessment as, 406, 407, 412–13, 418, 441
for composition, 229, 231, 242, 251–60, 412–13, 418
for discussion, 150–51, 159, 166–69
hope as, 252, 259, 343–44
for listening, 91, 441
for mechanics and punctuation, 370–72
of minority child (*see* Minority child, motivation of)
modeling as, 252, 253–57
peer status and, 91, 252, 258–59
personal acceptance as, 252, 257–58
for reading, 94–95, 188
self-competence as, 252–53, 259
for speaking, 118–20
Motive attributing in listening, 81
Motor, defined, 11*n*
Motor learning, defined, 11*n*
Multichannels in teaching spelling, 337, 338
MURRAY, D. M., 307
Music to motivate discussion, 168–69

NASH, OGDEN, 212
National Council of Teachers of English (NCTE), 14, 95, 409, 446–47, 448
Nebraska Curriculum, 192, 248–49
NIELSEN, R. A., 449
Noise pollution, 76–77
Nonparticipant, role of, 148, 150–51, 152, 154–55
NORRIS, R. C., 41

Observation, 261–66, 274
defined, 261–62
Observers in evaluating discussion, 155
O'DONNELL, R. C., 41
Off-the-tracker, role of, 148, 151–52
OLSEN, J., 151
OLTON, M., 421
Operations, defined, 35
Oracy, defined, 112
Oral composition for public display, 285, 296–97
Oral consultation in composition, 285, 290–91
Oral language program
creative dramatics in, 133–38
dimensions of
aims of discourse as, 129, 197
concrete-abstract, 124–26, 196
personal-interpersonal, 122–24, 196
small-large parts of language, 126–28, 196
speech-thought, 120–22, 196
unfinished-finished product, 128–29, 196
used to select realistic books, 196–97
need for, 112–13
teacher responsible for, 113–15
*see also* Discussion; Speaking
Oral reading, 94–95, 188–91
Oral spelling, 348–49
Organizational mixup in listening, 81
ORTIZ, MIGUEL, 277
Overgeneralization, symptoms for, 49

Pacing in questioning, 162–63
PACKARD, V. O., 7
PALMER, W. S., 390
Pantomime, 135, 141–42, 298–300
defined, 133
Parents, involving, 232–33
Parts of language, small-large, dimension of oral language program, 126–28, 196
PAST, R., 91
Peer acceptance, 231, 232, 237, 238, 252, 257–59
Performance contracting, 446, 450
Personal acceptance motivates learning, 252, 257–58
Personal-interpersonal dimension of oral language program, 122–24, 196
PERSONKE, C., 337, 345–46
Persuasion, 111, 129, 279
Phoneme, defined, 93, 393
Phonics, 88–89, 93, 94
Phonology, concepts of, in children's texts, 393
PIAGET, JEAN, 12, 33–36 passim

Piagetian developmental theory
chart of stages in, 33
concrete operations stage in (*see* Concrete operations stage)
formal operations stage in, 33, 34, 55
sensorimotor stage in, 33, 36
Pinpointing and charting, 428
Pitch, 364–65
Planning, Programming, Budgeting System (PPBS), 446, 447–50
Plot in children's literature, 205–6, 214
Plot in compositions, 238, 239, 242
Poetry ladder, 187
Postponement to control disorder, 153–54
Practice, appropriate, in teaching spelling, 339, 342–43
Prejudice, causes of, 52, 77
Prewriting activity, 285–91
defined, 285
Problem solving
simplistic, 4, 6, 8
state of, in classroom, 10–13
Problem-solving, creative
assessing, 413–17, 421
bibliotherapy and, 216–19
composition and, 276, 288–90, 304, 305
defined, 22–24
development of, 64–65
discussion and, 169–75
discussion illustrating, 18–22
examples illustrating, 15–17
grammar and, 397–98
handwriting and, 358–61
individual in, 17 (*see also* Autonomy)
listening and, 78–80, 433–35, 441
procedure for, 20–24, 169–71
self-expression and, 118–19
spelling and, 338
teachers as models of, 13
for young children, 24–25
Process maps, 163–66
*Productive Thinking Program, The,* 421
Program, defined, 449
Proofreading
concepts of, in children's texts, 394
procedure for, 297
for punctuation, 368, 369
for spelling, 333, 337, 338, 345–47
Pronunciation, criteria for, 350
Propaganda concepts, 46–48, 50
Publication of composition, 228, 279, 285, 296–98
Punctuation
activities for, 364, 367–69, 375–76
audio equipment and, 365, 366, 368
concepts of, in children's texts, 394
intonation and, 363, 364–65
juncture and, 363, 366
learner objectives for, 369
motivation for, 370–72
rules of, 372–73
Purdue Elementary Problem-Solving Inventory, 421

Questioning
in adult-child dialogue, 44
to elicit problem solving, 18, 19, 20, 21, 23, 24
to guide discussion, 157–63, 168

Readiness, 55, 60–61, 95–96
Reading
activities for (*see* Activities by subject, for reading)
assessing, 411, 425, 441–45
audio equipment and, 94–95, 96, 204, 221, 222
beginning, 55, 61–63, 112
composition and, 274–75, 295
dialect and, 88–90
discussion and, 169
listening and, 86–97, 98
minority child and, 51, 88–91
motivation for, 94–95, 188
*see also* Children's literature
*Reading Ladders for Human Relations,* 216
Recoding, defined, 87*n*
Recorder, role of, in discussion, 149, 158
Record keeping to assess composition, 412, 413–18
Re-creation in composition, 285, 287–88
REID, V., 216
Reinforcing role of teacher in discussion, 158
Relations in writing consultation, 295
Relaxed social situation in reading-listening instruction, 95, 96
Rewriting, 279, 292–95, 296, 297–98. *See also* Proofreading
Role-taking in communication, 435–37
ROOT, S. L., 135
RUDORF, E. H., 367
RUSSELL, D. H., 51, 77
RYAN, M., 398

SANDBERG, CARL, 187
SAYERS, FRANCES CLARKE, 200, 219
Scapegoat, role of, 148, 152
SCEATS, J., 353
SCHILLER, A., 328, 329, 330
SCHUTZ, R. E., 450
*Schwa,* defined, 345*n*
Science Research Associates, 163
Self-competence motivates learning, 252–53, 259
Self-evaluation in discussion, 156
Self-expression
activities for, 119–20, 139–42
creative dramatics and, 133–38
defined, 111, 116
exposition and, 117–18
motivation of, 118–20
precedes other uses of language, 116–18
teacher encourages, 42, 118–20
uses of, 116–20
Self-image, composition and, 274, 275–76
Self-image, language, 52–54
Self-preoccupation in listening, 81, 82
Semantics. *See* Meaning
Sensorimotor stage, 33, 36
Sentence maturity, 40–42
Sequential Tests of Educational Progress (STEP), 409
SEYMOUR, D. Z., 369
SHAFTEL, F. R., 162, 168, 172
SHAFTEL, G., 162, 168, 172
SHAPIRO, DAVID, 258
SHEVIAKOV, GEORGE V., 252
Shocker, role of, 148, 152
SHUY, R., 64
Signals, common, in listening and reading, 95, 96–97
Silent classroom, 114
SIMONS, H. D., 91
Sincerity in children's literature, 181, 183
SINGER, I. B., 205
Situational choice in teaching spelling, 338
SMITH, E. B., 232, 236, 242, 326, 336, 386, 389, 398
SMITH, F., 63
Social "registers" of language, 54–55
Socratic discussions, 169, 173
Soliciting, a teaching function, 6*n*
Sound production, developmental features of, 37

Sounds, spelling chart for, 345–46
Speaking
- activities for (*see* Activities by subject, for speaking)
- assessing, 411, 435–37
- audio equipment and, 118–19, 123, 129, 141, 168
- importance of, 112–13, 115
- listening and, 80–84, 97–98
- teacher inhibits, 113–14
- *see also* Discourse; Discussion; Exposition; Oral language program; Persuasion; Self-expression

Speech-thought dimension of oral language program, 120–22, 196
Spelling
- activities for, 340, 351–54, 375–76
- composition and, 242
- creativity and, 344
- defined, 324
- developmental program for, 327–33
- developmental teaching of, 334–50 (*see also* Spelling, teaching techniques for)
- dialect and, 335–36
- an end in itself, 324, 350
- errors in, reasons for, 335–36
- inconsistency of, 325–26
- internal background for, 336–37, 339
- teaching techniques for
  - corrected test, 334–36
  - dictionary, 345–46, 352–53
  - faulty, to avoid, 348–49
  - formal test, 348
  - grouping and individualizing, 334–35, 338, 347–48
  - multichannels, 337, 338
  - problem-solving, 338
  - proofreading, 333, 337, 338, 345–47
  - psychological learning theory, 339–44
  - situational choice, 338
  - spelling chart, 345–46, 351

Spelling patterns, defined, 327
Squire, J. R., 398
Steinberg, H. I., 449
Stereotypes, sex, in books, 197
Stevenson, Adlai, 7
Stimulation of impressions in composition, 285–87
Structural linguistic grammar, 380, 384–85, 394–95
Structure, deep vs. surface, 386–87
Substance in children's literature, 181
Sullivan, H. S., 54
Syntax, concepts of, in children's texts, 392–93. *See also* Grammar

Taba, H., 165, 166
Task cards for listening comprehension, 431–33
Task group discussions, 169, 173, 177
*Taxonomy of Educational Objectives,* 162–63
Teacher's and Writer's Collaborative, 258, 277
Templin, M. C., 37
Testing. *See* Assessment
Tests
- of cognitive processes, 419–21
- criterion-referenced, for listening, 439–40
- multiple choice, 408
- published, disadvantages of, 409–10
- spelling, 334–36, 348
- standardized, norm-referenced, for listening, 438–39

Theme in children's literature, 207, 209, 214–15
Thinking space, leftover, 78–80
Thomas, O., 64, 249
Thought
- development of (*see* Development of language and thought)
- language arts a tool for, 3
- modes of, development of, 55, 56–57
- processes of vs. materials of, 51
- *see also* Problem solving; Problem-solving, creative

Tiemann, P. W., 49
Traditional school of grammar, 380–83, 394
Transfer
- in bibliotherapy, 216, 219
- defined, 22*n*
- positive and negative, in teaching spelling, 339, 340–42

Transformational-generative grammar, 380, 385–91, 395
Trett, G. L., 380, 383
Tutorial discussions, 169, 172
TV, 6–9
Twain, Mark, 201, 304
Tway, E., 418

Undergeneralization, symptoms for, 49
Unfinished-finished product dimension of oral language program, 128–29, 196
Units of comprehension in listening and reading, 95, 96
Unknowns, use of, in creative problem-solving, 23
Usage
- activities for, 397–98, 399
- concepts of, in children's texts, 393
- vs. grammar, 382–83
- teaching strategies for, 396
- *see also* Dialect

Values, cultural, affect listening and reading, 91
Vicarious experience
- defined, 181
- *see also* Children's literature, response to

Violence, causes of, 6, 8, 10
Vocabulary
- developmental features of, 37–40
- interrelated in language arts, 80–81, 86–87

Voice terminals, defined, 233
Vygotsky, L., 128

Wagner, Victor, 188
Wilcox, M. A., 11, 172
Wilkinson, A., 112
Wilson, J. A., 410
Wisconsin Curriculum, 192
Word classes, 384–85
Word order in English grammar, 381–82
Wright, R. L., 374
Writing. *See* Composition; Grammar; Handwriting; Punctuation; Spelling
Writing conference, individual, assessment by, 412–19
Writing consultation in composition, 285, 291–96
*Writing of Elementary School Children, The: A Model for Evaluation,* 237
Written composition for public display, 285, 297–98

Yamamoto, K., 418
Yee, A. H., 337, 345–46